ELDER LAW:
CASES AND MATERIALS

ELDER LAW: CASES AND MATERIALS

Fifth Edition

Lawrence A. Frolik
Professor of Law, Distinguished Faculty Scholar
University of Pittsburgh
School of Law

Alison McChrystal Barnes
Professor of Law
Marquette University Law School

ISBN: 978-1-4224-9038-9

LCCN: 2011933317

This publication is designed to provide accurate and authoritative information in regard to the subject matter covered. It is sold with the understanding that the publisher is not engaged in rendering legal, accounting, or other professional services. If legal advice or other expert assistance is required, the services of a competent professional should be sought.

> **NOTE TO USERS**
>
> To ensure that you are using the latest materials available in this area, please be sure to periodically check the LexisNexis Law School web site for downloadable updates and supplements at www.lexisnexis.com/lawschool.

Editorial Offices
121 Chanlon Rd., New Providence, NJ 07974 (908) 464-6800
201 Mission St., San Francisco, CA 94105-1831 (415) 908-3200
www.lexisnexis.com

MATTHEW◆BENDER

(2011–Pub.3039)

Dedications

To
Winnefred and Cornelius
— L.A.F.

To
Walter O. Weyrauch, 1919–2008
Mentor and Friend
Professor Emeritus, University of Florida College of Law
— A.M.B.

Preface

ELDER LAW CASES AND MATERIALS, Fifth Edition, integrates new developments in law and policy into the familiar framework of past editions. We have selected new cases and excerpts from expert commentators with care and have weaved them together with narratives that develop the issues in the reader's mind and raise the questions that remain to be resolved. With this fifth edition, we have the privilege to introduce to law students the legal issues of aging at the time when the baby boomer cohort comes to retirement age.

We recognize that a casebook of this length and scope of issues will seldom be covered in its entirety in a single course. The chapters generally are intended to be freestanding to accommodate any number of different approaches. We recommend, however, that certain related chapters be read in the sequence in which they are presented. For example, Chapter 5, Health Care, should be covered before Chapter 6, Long-Term Care: Payments Sources, since the second is a latter-day development that extends the concepts and quirks of the first. Other chapters can be reordered to better fit the approach of the user. Some users of the book may prefer to cover Chapter 9, Property Management, after Chapter 4, Income Maintenance. Others may find it best to cover Chapter 10, Health Care Decision Making, before Chapter 8, Guardianship.

Chapters 1 and 2 warrant special treatment because they introduce issues ripe for analysis in many areas within the field of elder law. The first invites the reader to grapple with the question: Why is aging a subject for the law? The possible justifications are demographic, economic, technological, sociological, and psychological. The first part of Chapter 2 helps the student clarify his or her possible role as a private practitioner, legal services specialist, legislative advocate, or as an aging member of an aging family in an aging world. The last half of Chapter 2 examines the ethical issues that arise when working with older persons, particularly those of impaired mental capacity.

We believe the issues presented in Chapters 1 and 2 cannot be fully developed unless they are raised during the substantive discussions of the other chapters. For example, Chapter 1 describes issues relating to income, natural aging processes, and the incidence of chronic disability in the elderly. The complexity of public policy issues, however, is revealed only with an examination of the history, eligibility criteria, and benefits of the Social Security, Supplemental Security Income, and private pension programs discussed in Chapter 4, and issues in health and long-term care and housing in Chapters 5 through 8. Similarly, the questions raised in Chapter 2 about conflicts of interests among the elderly, their family members, and professionals in law, medicine, or finance assume their real significance in cases on guardianship and alternatives in Chapters 9 and 10, and health care decision making in Chapter 11. We therefore recommend that students read Chapters 1 and 2 at the beginning of the course as a basis for later discussions as more specific issues arise throughout the course.

Changing public policy in the beginning of the 21st century brings to the field important discussion and some major changes. The Social Security debate, for example, to date has raised much awareness without radical change. Medicare has a new dimension with different payments for equal benefits depending on beneficiary income. The long-term care payment issues continue to be a source of public policy debate. Older workers

Preface

may now be favored by employers without risk of violating the ADEA.

Thanks to many are due from the authors for the existence of this book. Special thanks go to four of our colleagues who were present at the very birth of the field of elder law, who joined us at a lunch table where we first conceived the possibility of this book. We were gathered in 1988 at Wingspread, the Frank Lloyd Wright-designed home located near Racine, Wisconsin, for a conference on guardianship convened by the American Bar Association Commission on Law and Aging. A snapshot (intended to capture the architecture) shows the authors and Marshall Kapp, now at Florida State University College of Law; Allan Bogutz, of Bogutz and Gordon in Tucson and the first president of the National Academy of Elderlaw Attorneys; Penelope Hommel, of the Center for Social Gerontology in Ann Arbor; and Charlie Sabatino, of the ABA Commission on Law and Aging and past president of NAELA. All were important actors in the evolution of elder law and policy, all had experience teaching Elder Law, and all were convinced of the need for a casebook to use in law school courses.

The authors also thank those who made this book possible by providing their valuable time, their priceless criticism, and their invaluable moral support. Important researchers include (at the University of Pittsburgh) Julia M. Tedjeske, Maryann Bozich-DiLuigi, Pamela J. Waggoner, Rayni Moutsos, Susan L. Herilla, and Stephanie Gallo, upon whom fell the otherwise thankless task of basic research and making case citation precise. At Marquette, all the members of the Elder's Advisor, whose judgment and diligence helped to develop the topics in these chapters.

Professor Frolik also gives a special note of thanks for notable efforts of the Document Technology Center: LuAnn Driscoll, Karen Knochel, Darleen Mocello, Valerie Pompe, and Barbara Salopek. Professor Barnes specially thanks Catherine Pfeffer, whose stalwart support and computing skill made preparation of this work possible.

We welcome your comments, questions, and reactions to this latest version of ELDER LAW: CASES AND MATERIALS.

Lawrence A. Frolik
frolik@pitt.edu
Alison Barnes
alison.barnes@mu.edu

TABLE OF CONTENTS

TABLE OF CONTENTS

TABLE OF CONTENTS

TABLE OF CONTENTS

TABLE OF CONTENTS

TABLE OF CONTENTS

TABLE OF CONTENTS

TABLE OF CONTENTS

TABLE OF CONTENTS

TABLE OF CONTENTS

TABLE OF CONTENTS

TABLE OF CONTENTS

TABLE OF CONTENTS

TABLE OF CONTENTS

TABLE OF CONTENTS

TABLE OF CONTENTS

Chapter 1

AN AGING POPULATION: THE CHALLENGE TO THE LAW

Youth, large, lusty, loving — Youth, full of grace, force, fascination. Do you know that Old Age may come after you, with equal grace, force, fascination?

— Walt Whitman

A. INTRODUCTION

The world's elderly population, those age 65 or older, is expected to double between 2000 and 2025, a rate far greater than general population growth. The extraordinary growth in the number of old people is attributable to improvements in medicine and nutrition beginning more than 60 years ago that greatly increased life expectancy, particularly for those age 65 or older. The developed countries of North America and Europe, Japan, and Australia have already experienced rapid growth in their elderly populations with the result that the elderly comprise between one-sixth and one-fifth of their populations. The developing countries are now experiencing similar rapid increases.

America has more elderly people than ever before. Whether measured by an increase in percentage or in absolute numbers, more Americans are age 65 and over than in any past era. In 1990, 31 million Americans were age 65 or older and represented 12.6 percent of the population. In the year 2010, there were over 40 million or 13 percent of the population. By 2020, the number is expected to reach 54 million and represent over 16 percent of the population. By 2030, the elderly will represent 20 percent.

The aging of our society presents significant challenges for individuals, families, and policymakers, which are reflected in changes in education, business, and media, and our everyday lives. Articles and talk shows, for example, examine such topics as retirement lifestyles, health, self-sufficiency in later life, and post-retirement careers. Books and movies explore emotional and existential aspects of growing old. Professional conferences convene to analyze practical and ethical responses to "problems" of aging while a growing number of academic programs offer degrees in gerontology (the social science of aging) and geriatrics (medicine for elderly patients). Web sites on topics about old age increase in number. More elderly individuals appear everywhere: on the job and in university classes; at spas and vacation resorts, political and business gatherings; in supermarket lines; and even at day care centers.

At the outset of our discussion of the elderly and the law, note that any generalized profile of the aging of the population obscures the differences among various subpopulations of older people, which include African-Americans; Latino groups with very different characteristics such as Mexican-Americans, Puerto Ricans, and Cuban-Americans; and native Americans. Another significant subpopulation is Asian-Americans, including native Hawaiians and persons of Chinese, Japanese, Korean, Philippine, and subcontinental Indian descent. Individuals in these subpopulations present differing economic circumstances, lifestyles, and values. Moreover, women and men have distinct characteristics and needs, as do the elderly who live in rural areas. The rate of increase in numbers within these population groups varies; the number of Latino-American elderly, for example, is increasing faster than other populations. The needs of the various subpopulations in regard to health care, income support, and other formal assistance must be distinguished from those of the general population.

B.   WHO IS ELDERLY?

Statistics number who is old merely as a function of chronological age. But it is more accurate, and a reflection of how most of us think, to define the elderly by more than just one criterion. Typically, before we think of someone as old we look to a combination of factors such as chronological age, functional capacity, social involvement, and physical and mental health.

Chronological age merely measures the passage of time. Yet it also denotes certain rites of passage or the granting of legal rights such the right to drive or the right to vote. Individuals typically choose significant friends early in life when chronological age is especially significant in determining the young person's appropriate activities. With young adulthood, a person is permitted to drive and drink alcohol. Many live by themselves for the first time, and may choose — and perhaps marry — a sexual partner. Later in life, chronological age determines other legal rights, such as the right to receive income for retirement rather than work. But unlike the right to vote or the right to retire with a pension, there is no absolute age at which someone is "old." At age 21, many consider anyone over age 50 to be old, although those who are age 50 seldom believe themselves to be old.

Yet at some point age alone is enough for any of us to label an individual as "old" or "elderly." Everyone, for example, would concur that an 85-year-old is elderly. For purposes of this book we shall generally use age 65 as the entry age for those referred to as elderly or old. Although this is an arbitrary age, it is the traditional age of retirement and the age most commentators use to delineate older persons.

Before we simply say that all who are age 65 or older are elderly, however, we ought to ask, "Why do we care?," for if we classify people we should do so for some reason. We group and count individuals by race, for example, because we consider race relevant in many respects, if only to ensure that race is not used as an irrelevant criterion. Conversely, we do not officially classify people by eye color because the resulting categories would be irrelevant for almost any conceivable purpose.

Why, then, do we so frequently group individuals by age, whether for official ends, such as eligibility for Social Security benefits, or in informal discussions? We seemingly do so because the elderly have something in common that they do not share (or share to a much lesser extent) with the rest of the population. Just as we group babies or teenagers together because of their respective shared characteristics (dependency for the former, adolescence for the latter), so do we also group together the old.

What are the common characteristics of the old that differ from the rest of the population? Some might say that the qualities of senescence distinguish the elderly from the young. Typically, we identify the elderly with loss of physical capacity and, to a lesser extent, loss of mental capacity. Though certainly not always true, the elderly often experience a loss of mental alertness and agility. Even more common, if not universal, is the loss of physical strength, flexibility, endurance, and acuity of the senses. Although many who are not elderly suffer the loss of physical or mental capacity, it is the inevitable, age-related loss of physical vigor and the increasing possibility of mental impairment that makes it sensible to label those age 65 and older as elderly and consider them as a group with similar wants and needs.

Of course, being old in years does not signify that one has lost physical or mental capacity. The correlation of age and incapacity is a false and particularly pernicious generalization since labeling the entire group with the infirmities of some of its members inevitably leads to the perception that all in the group suffer from diminished physical and mental capacity, thereby tainting all with the problems of a minority.

Nevertheless, we do group together the chronologically old and label them as "elderly." We do so because the term serves as a shorthand means of identifying common characteristics. Do not forget, however, that the term "elderly" is only a generalization that draws together people of vastly different characteristics.

Admitting the falsity of generalizations, and so concentrating on the individual, it is difficult to say with certainty who is old and who is not. We have no definition that crisply cleaves the old from the non-old. One cannot say, "Today I became old." At some point we will admit that we are old, but just when a person "became old" is unknown even to the individual.

Though the age for Social Security retirement eligibility is rising to age 67, the age of 65 will undoubtedly continue to have special significance. In our culture age 65 is commonly used to demarcate the onset of old age. The reliance on age 65 is attributed to Germany's Chancellor Otto von Bismarck, who in 1889 created the German social welfare system. Among the welfare programs was a forced retirement age and public pension program. Originally the retirement age was set at age 70, but in 1916 it was reduced to 65. At that time Germany was fighting in World War I, so it seems probable that the reduction was intended to elicit public support of the government. This was certainly not the last time that the onset of public benefits for the elderly was changed for political gain rather than as a result of new insight into when people become old.

The use of a precise chronological age arises out of practical necessity. Governments, employers, and other institutions prefer bright line tests over subjective determinations. For example, the government has offered full Social Security retirement payments to all individuals at age 65, rather than upon a showing of financial need. Employers likewise usually prefer to retire employees at a fixed age, rather than upon determination of an individual employee's work ability.

The use of chronological age as an indicator is so common that it reinforces the general cultural sense that the 65th birthday marks the onset of old age. We, too, shall use the chronological age 65 as a shorthand indicator of "oldness," while remembering that it is only a rough indicator. In reality being old is neither limited nor universal to those age 65 and older.

QUESTIONS

1. At what age do you consider someone to be "old"? Why? At what age will you consider yourself to be old?

2. Is it helpful or harmful to label someone as old? Does it depend upon who is doing the labeling?

3. If you were age 70, what label would you prefer: elderly, old, senior citizen, aged, or some other term? No label?

4. If you were age 21, would it bother you to be labeled "young"? Why or why not? If you were age 81, would it bother you to be labeled "old"? Why or why not?

C. STATISTICAL PROFILE OF THE ELDERLY

Current and projected demographics in the United States reveal that the absolute number of elderly is increasing and that the percentage of the total population that is elderly also is increasing.

Number of Elderly Age 65 and Over in the American Population

Year	Population Millions	65 and Over Percent
Actual		
1980	25.6	11.3
1990	31.2	12.6
2000	35.0	12.4
Projected		
2010	40.1	13.3
2020	53.4	16.4
2030	71.5	20.0
2040	80.0	20.0
2050	86.7	20.0

Source: Bureau of the Census, 65 Plus in America 2005: Current Population Reports. Based on the 2000 U.S. Census.

Growth in the number of Americans age 65 or older increases every year chiefly because of higher birth rates 65 years ago. (Immigration is also a source of rising numbers of individuals turning age 65.) Because of low birth rates in the depressed economic years of the 1930s, little growth occurred in the number of individuals turning age 65 in the early 2000s. The annual increase in the number of individuals turning 65 begins again in the year 2010, reflecting the aging of the baby boomers, those born between 1946 and 1964. Both the absolute and proportional increase in the number of the elderly is likely to have significant political and economic consequences.

Because the average age of people in most minorities is lower than that of the general population, the "boom" in minority elderly will trail that of the white population. The differences arise from higher birth rates, shorter average life spans, and immigration patterns. (Typically, immigrants are younger statistically than the population into which they immigrate.) The average ages of these subpopulations are expected to rise rapidly, however, because of lower birthrates, improved health care, and reduced rates of immigration. And as they age, the proportional growth in the elderly sub-populations will be greater than in the white population.

A few other countries such as Japan are "ahead" of the U.S. in aging demographics, having a greater percentage of the population age 65 and older. Developing countries, such as India and China and much of South America, present yet a different picture. While the numbers of elderly people there are growing faster than in developed countries due to the effectiveness of modern healthcare, change in the proportions of young and old in those populations is less spectacular because birthrates remain high.

Increased life expectancy is the other major contributor to the increase in the number of elderly. Life expectancy in the United States has gradually increased, with the consequence that more individuals survive until age 65 and those who reach age 65 live longer.

Life Expectancy at Birth by Race and Sex in 2000
(in thousands)

White

Men —	75.0
Women —	80.2

Black

Men —	68.6
Women —	75.5

Source: National Vital Statistics Reports 2004, Table 12.

By virtue of the unprecedented rise in average life expectancy, the 65 and older age group has grown more than twice as fast as the population as a whole. The population distribution reflects the "graying" of America. By the year 2030, the number of those age 80 and older is projected to more than double, while the number of individuals age 20 to 29 will remain static or even decline from 1980 levels.

Life expectancy charts can be deceiving, however, because they merely predict the average age of death for all those born in the same year, known as an age cohort. To say that American women born in 1990 have a life expectancy of "x" years means only that if death rates do not change, "x" years is the average number of years that this specific age/sex cohort is expected to live. Life expectancy tables, however, have only modest predictive value because the death rate in the U.S. has always fallen from that projected. That is, to date, because of improved medical care and healthier lifestyles, the average life span of American age cohorts has always increased.

Projected life expectancy statistics also can be misleading because well over half of the individuals of an age/sex cohort will live past the projected life expectancy age. If we say that life expectancy is "x" years, we predict only an average age of death for a cohort. Since some members of the cohort die soon after birth, thereby greatly lowering the average age, many must live past the average age.

More relevant than life expectancy at birth is how long a person can expect to live from the present. If you are age 65, for example, how much longer can you expect to live? Life expectancy at any given age is a function of the average date of death for all persons of that age. That projection will be higher than at birth since it will not include those who died before reaching age 65.

The following chart shows the average number of years of life remaining to individuals who reached the age of 65.

		At age 65
All —		
	Men	17.2
	Women	19.9
White —	Men	17.3
	Women	19.9
Black —	Men	15.2
	Women	18.7

Source: Table 24. Life expectancy at birth, at 65 years of age, according to race and sex: United States, selected years 1900–2007.

Clearly, those who live until the ages of 65 on average have a number of years to live.

A common misperception regarding the elderly is that they are trapped in a cycle of poverty and despair, isolated from the community, abandoned by family and friends, and incapable of self-sufficiency. On the contrary, the majority of the elderly are married, in good health, and do not live in poverty. Although 1.5 million elderly individuals live in nursing homes, only about five percent of the elderly are nursing home residents on any given day. The 2000 census showed that 27.8 percent of those age 65 or older live alone. However, by age 75 and older, four times more women live alone than do men.

The distribution of the elderly is not uniform across the nation. Not surprisingly as of 2005 (interpreting 2000 census numbers), Florida, with 17.6 percent of its population age 65 or older had the greatest concentration of the elderly. Pennsylvania with 15.6 percent was second. West Virginia was third with 15.3 percent and Iowa, 14.9 percent and North Dakota, 14.8 percent. The states with the lowest percentage of elderly are Alaska with 5.7 percent, Utah with 8.5 percent, and Colorado, 9.7 percent, and Georgia, 9.6 percent. In terms of absolute numbers of elderly, California had the largest number, nearly 3.6 million, then Florida, with 2.8 million and 2.4 million, respectively. Pennsylvania had the fifth largest number — 1.9 million age 65 or older.

D. GROWTH IN THE POPULATION OVER AGE EIGHTY-FIVE

The elderly are by no means a homogeneous group. We would not think of lumping together any other age group that ranges more than 35 years (ages 65 to 100). In recognition of the wide age span, many observers now subcategorize the elderly into three groups: the young old, ages 65 to 75; the old, ages 75 to 85; and the old-old, ages 85 and over. The utility of subcategorizing by age is debatable. It may be more sensible to group the elderly by physical and mental capability; for example, the well elderly, the frail elderly, and so on.

Still, few would deny that those age 85 or older are "elderly" and create special social and political concerns such as the provision of adequate and affordable long-term care. As stated by one commentator,

> The extreme elderly seldom work, and most have chronic disabilities that limit their life style to some degree and may affect their living arrangements. Partial losses of health, mobility, hearing, and sight, plus the death of spouse, friends and neighbors have a powerful impact on living arrangements and life style.

I. ROSENWAIKE, THE EXTREME AGED IN AMERICA 93–94 (1985).

If the very old in the future are extremely impaired, there may be reason for concern. The population age 85 or older by percentage is currently the fastest growing segment of the population. In 2000, about two percent of the population were age 85 or older. By 2050, the percentage in this age group is projected to increase to almost five percent of the U.S. population. Yet our current laws and governmental programs were created when the number of individuals in this age group was far lower. Whether those laws and programs will meet the needs and the problems of future elders is problematical. The anticipated growth of this group alone gives good cause to examine the relationship between the elderly and the law.

Whether the growth of the very old will pose a significant burden to society will depend on the extent to which they are functionally capable. Today's healthier lifestyles and technologically sophisticated medical care might result in more independence and self-sufficiency for those past age 85. Rates of disability and institutionalization already are declining as more older people remain active and benefit from more effective healthcare. In 1995, almost 20 percent of those age 85 or older lived in a nursing home. By 2004, the percentage had declined to 14 percent. It may be possible to extend a human being's vigor and virtually eliminate the need for long-term care. Most theories of aging, however, propose either a largely unavoidable process of "wear and tear" on the human body over time or the existence of a genetically programmed "clock" that dictates the manner and rate of physical decline and death. The ideal of long, vigorous old age and swift decline to death might not be a realistic expectation.

E. AGING PATTERNS BY GENDER

Women outlive men. The following chart shows just how much the aging of America is a female phenomenon.

	2009 (estimate)	
	Age 65 and over	Age 80 and over
Men	16,900,000	3,300,000
Women	22,600,000	6,100,000

The overwhelming preponderance of elderly women to elderly men cannot be overemphasized. At every year, past age 65 women outnumber men, and the ratio of women to men increases as the cohort ages. When we refer to elderly people we should visualize women. If the term "elderly individual" conjures up a picture of a man, bear in mind that he is a minority representative.

For society and its policymakers the predominance of elderly women has profound significance. How society allocates its resources to assist the elderly should (but does not always) take into account that the elderly are mostly women. For example, before we assume that the elderly have sufficient financial resources we must ask whether elderly women, many of whom were not in the wage force when younger, have adequate independent income. Social Security benefits represent a larger portion of the income of elderly women than of men, as nearly half of older men receive income from a private sector pension compared to less than a quarter of older women. On average women who do have a private pension receive only half of the amount received by male pensioners.

When considering health care support, planners should be aware that women and men do not share the same health problems. Heart disease, for example, is more often diagnosed in males, while breast cancer is more often a female malady, though deadly to males. Women are disproportionate users of nursing homes, in part because wives can more often provide long-term care at home to their older husbands reflecting the fact that 75 percent of older men are married, but only 43 percent of older women. That in turn is in part a result of there being four times as many widows as there are widowers.

F. AGING PATTERNS BY RACE

The current elderly population is predominantly white, but we can expect to see more racial diversity and more persons of Hispanic/Latino origin within America's elderly population in the coming years. Although the life expectancy of most minorities is increasing (as are the numbers of African-American and Latino elderly), the gap between whites and minorities remains. For some subpopulations the gap is particularly dramatic. Native Hawaiians, for example, have a life expectancy a decade shorter than other minorities who share their location and circumstances.

Of those age 65 and older in 2008, 80.4 percent were white; 8.3 percent were African-American; 6.8 percent were Hispanic; 3.4 percent were Asian and Pacific Islander; and 0.4 percent were American Indian and Alaska Native. The elderly population will become even more racially and ethnically diverse in the future.

Hispanic elderly, for example, are expected to increase to 16 percent of all elderly by the middle of the century. The percentage of African-American elderly in the total elderly population will increase to 10 percent, and Asians and Pacific Islanders to seven percent. The white elderly are expected to decline to about 67 percent of all elderly by the year 2050.

For social policy planners the shorter life expectancies of non-white minorities means that benefit programs for the elderly disproportionately favor the white elderly. For example, although all employees, regardless of their race or gender, pay Social Security taxes, many minority employees, because of their higher death rates, will not live long enough to collect retirement benefits. When the minimum age for collecting Social Security benefits is raised, all employees are disadvantaged, but minorities suffer greater harm because on average they will collect benefits for fewer years than will white retirees.

QUESTIONS

1. Should social policy towards the elderly take cognizance of different life expectancies on account of gender? On account of ethnicity?

2. Would you favor lowering the age of eligibility for retirement benefits for minorities with lower life expectancies? In lieu of a lower retirement eligibility age, would you favor greater monthly benefits for those with shorter life expectancies?

3. Should men and women be treated the same, or should retirement benefits be adjusted for the shorter life expectancy of men?

G. DEPENDENCY RATIO

Rapid growth in the number of elderly people has sparked fears of an increasing financial burden on the rest of the population. Most over age 65 are retired and receive Social Security retirement benefits paid for by the tax on younger workers' wages. This statistical ratio in the population of workers (age 18 to 64) to elderly (age 65 and older) is commonly referred to as the "dependency ratio." In 1970, there were about 18 persons age 65 or older for every 100 persons age 18 to 64. By 2000, the ratio was about 20:100. In 2020, the ratio is projected to be about 27:100. With fewer young to support so many more elderly, the question arises whether the younger population will be able to afford to continue providing the same level of benefits, including Medicare and Social Security.

Yet dependency is not a function of age. It is a function of physical or mental well-being, wealth, and cultural attitudes. Does the ratio serve any function? Should it be retitled? "Dependency ratio" assumes that everyone over age 65 is a dependent and that everyone from age 18 to 64 is a producer. Since both assumptions are false, the usefulness of the ratio is significantly undermined. Moreover, the term dependent is ambiguous. Just because a person is not a wage earner (the most probable meaning of the term) does not mean that he or she is not productive or that he or she is dependent upon others.

To be sure, many of the elderly rely upon Social Security benefits as their only source of income. To the extent that they do they can be considered dependent upon the younger, working population because Social Security retirement benefits are financed by taxes paid by current workers. Such benefits do not represent a return of prior Social Security taxes. Indeed, it is estimated that in four or five years the average retiree receives in retirement benefits an amount equal to all he or she contributed to the Social Security trust fund during a lifetime of employment. Receipt of those benefits does not mean complete dependency, however. The majority of the elderly have other sources of income such as work-related pensions and many enjoy income from their savings. Conversely, many over age 65 help support younger relatives, either by cash gifts or in-kind assistance such as free childcare. As a result, just who is dependent is not always a function of age or retirement status. The use of concepts, such as dependency ratio, that obscure the financial relationships between the old and the young confuse rather than clarify complex policy issues.

QUESTION

The nature and existence of dependency for some groups, including women, has been subject to debate, in part because the typical work of individuals in the group — child bearing and rearing for women, unskilled labor for some disadvantaged by race or ethnicity — is undervalued by society. Do some elderly by the characteristics of their "group" contribute to the support of society?

H.   THE PHYSICAL EFFECTS OF AGING

Generalizations about the elderly are fraught with falsehoods, because individuals vary greatly. Generalizations can be true, however, in a statistical sense. The following generalizations, while they may be false as to any particular individual, are true as to the elderly as a group and therefore have significance for public policy.

Inevitable decline in physical vigor is the most salient feature of aging. With advancing age, bones gradually lose calcium, become weakened, and fracture more easily. The bones in the hips widen, shoulders narrow, joints become stiff and painful, and walking becomes more difficult.

Almost all of the elderly suffer some loss of vision, including loss of ability to see close objects, sensitivity to glare, loss of peripheral vision, and difficulty adjusting from light to dark. An elderly person's eyes are particularly weak in dim light, less able to focus on moving objects, and less capable of perceiving color.

Hearing also declines with age. Beginning around age 50, there is a gradual loss of perception of higher and lower frequencies. This permanent loss of hearing, called presbycusis, is the result of a gradual physical deterioration of structures in the inner ear.

While severe memory loss is a sign of illness, some mild short-term memory loss is common among those in their seventies or eighties. Such loss is confined to very specific brain regions and most people "compensate" by using some other part of the brain. The loss is not due to deterioration of brain function per se. Loss of function is attributable to changes in the way information is transmitted from one part of the brain to the other; actual reduction in activity is confined to specific regions. As a result some older people experience loss in the capacity to retrieve some kinds of information and to recall recently acquired knowledge. By the same mechanisms more distant memories may become more vivid. This does not imply that the older brain is less capable overall or that healthy older people cannot think or learn new things. Certainly, many people continue to learn and develop abilities throughout their lives.

QUESTIONS

1. Do people tend to associate the physical changes of the elderly with mental changes? If so, is the association valid?

2. Do the physical changes of the elderly make the young reluctant to be around them?

3. It is said that old age is more difficult for women than men because of the perceived loss of beauty. Do you agree?

4. Does the loss of physical vigor mean that the elderly are less capable of managing their affairs?

In addition to predictable physical changes, the elderly tend to suffer more from chronic conditions. A condition, which may be acute or chronic, is any departure from physical or mental well-being. An acute condition is a temporary condition, whether as serious as pneumonia or as nonthreatening as a head cold. A chronic condition is a permanent or long-term condition, such as diabetes, heart disease, arthritis, or deafness. Acute conditions (short-term injuries or illness) actually decline with age, with those age 65 and over experiencing fewer than other age groups. (The number of days of restricted activity resulting from each acute condition, however, is greater for the elderly.) Conversely, the incidence of chronic conditions rises with age. Those age 65 and over have the highest incidence of chronic conditions as well as the greatest limitation on activity as a result of such conditions.

Fortunately, chronic disability among older Americans has sharply declined in the last 20 years. The National Long-Term Care Survey published in 2006 found that the prevalence of chronic disability among individuals 65 or older fell from 26.5 percent in 1982 to 19 percent in 2005. The report also noted that the rate of decline has been accelerating. The decline was the greatest in those age 85 or older.

The general decline in physical vigor coupled with a greater incidence of chronic illness can affect the outlook of elderly individuals. Some experience a loss of self-esteem and may feel less in control of their lives or environment. Because of chronic conditions, some elderly are less able to participate in formerly valued activities; they can become isolated, and may lose hope in the future. Clinical depression, which may accompany these changes, is the most common chronic psychological condition diagnosed among the elderly with the rate of prevalence much higher among women. Interestingly, however, older men are much more likely than older women to commit suicide.

QUESTIONS

1. How should society respond to the higher incidence of chronic conditions among the elderly? More research into the causes of chronic conditions? More long-term care benefits, or more cash assistance? More programs to encourage independent living? More assistance to families of the elderly?

2. Since an individual can estimate anticipated health care costs and plan accordingly, how much of the cost of chronic care should be the responsibility of the elderly individual, and how much should be society's responsibility?

3. Should helping the elderly pay the costs of chronic care be a national priority? Why?

I.   THE CHALLENGE TO THE LAW: THE UNIQUE CIRCUMSTANCES OF THE ELDERLY

An aged man is but a paltry thing,
A tattered coat upon a stick, unless
Soul clap its hands and sing, and louder sing . . .

— W.B. Yeats

Law orders and reorders society by altering social arrangements to meet changing realities and newly recognized needs. New legal rights evolve as custom, case law, and statutes create new expectations and entitlements. Legal protections recede as political and legal standards commit responsibilities for order and quality to the private sector of business, religious or charitable entities, or individuals as consumers or litigants. Either change translates into new rules and regulations, new official attitudes, and new expectations in the elderly population. Making these changes for the good of society as a whole, the disparate segments of population, and for the individual in need of protection from exploitation is the challenge to the law.

[1]   MORTALITY: THE NEED FOR HASTE

Although the numbers of elderly are increasing, the life expectancy of any particular individual is decreasing. Social planners may have time to research and ponder solutions, but the lawyer and an individual client have no such luxury. The lawyer who does not solve the client's problem soon may find that death makes it moot. Even if death does not intervene, changes in the client's circumstances — health, income, or social support — may radically limit the range of choices. The elderly client who seeks legal assistance needs help now, not in the distant future or when it is convenient for the lawyer.

QUESTIONS

1. Lawyers owe clients duties of diligence and competence. Does the mere fact that the client is older alter the attorney's ethical responsibility? If so, how?

2. In cases involving an older plaintiff or defendant, does the judicial system have an obligation to hasten a conclusion?

3. Is it ethical for an attorney whose client is young or an institution, and whose opponent is older, to delay resolution on the assumption that "time is on our side"?

Social planners, including scholars and policymakers, also need swift decisions if elders are to be served. In ELDERS ON TRIAL: AGE AND AGEISM IN THE AMERICAN LEGAL SYSTEM (University Press of Florida 2004), Howard Eglit raises repeatedly the utmost urgency since "there is little time left . . . to resolve the issues generated by the burgeoning population of older Americans intersecting with the pervasive American legal enterprise." Deferred solutions, which may be politically expedient, may arrive too late to help today's elderly. While the elderly are always with us, the individual is not. Promises of improvements in nursing home conditions five years from now, for example, offer no comfort to abused and neglected nursing home residents now. Though precipitous action is to be avoided, we must be aware of the passage of time and its inevitable consequences for the elderly population.

[2] COMPLICATIONS OF DECLINING PHYSICAL AND MENTAL CAPACITY

The elderly as a group present special challenges to the legal system because some suffer serious losses of physical and mental capacity that cause them to become dependent on others and less capable of defending their rights and interests. How the law should respond is a central theme of any study of the elderly and the law. Of course, the elderly are not alone in suffering from these problems; younger persons also lose physical or mental capacity.

Why identify the elderly for special legal consideration? The question is central to the definition of elder law. Three aspects unique in the aging population, at least in proportion to the larger population, call for special legal recognition. They are the greater frequency of the loss of physical capabilities, the decline in mental capacity, and greater economic vulnerability.

[a] Alzheimer's Disease and Related Disorders

The elderly suffer more often from a loss of mental capacity than any other age group because they are susceptible to dementia, a generic term for the decline in memory and cognitive function sufficient to affect daily life. While there are over 50 causes of dementia, at least two-thirds of all cases with aged patients are caused by Alzheimer's disease. The disease affects an estimated 4.5 million Americans. According to some researchers, about one in four of those age 85 or older have Alzheimer's disease-like symptoms. In the past it was difficult to distinguish Alzheimer's from dementia arising from other causes. However, improved clinical techniques allow more alternative causes to be excluded with the result that the rate of accurate identification has risen to 90 percent.

An individual with Alzheimer's disease typically undergoes progressive decline in cognitive and emotional integrity over the course of eight to ten years. The progress of decline varies widely and may last as much as 20 years. The earliest stages include memory impairment, with patients having trouble learning new information and retaining it for more than a few minutes. Typical experiences are difficulty planning meals, managing finances or medications, using a telephone, or driving without getting lost. Many skills remain intact for some time, so Alzheimer's patients can provide their own personal care. Social skills may remain intact even longer. However, patients may develop mood changes, delusions, and depression. Motor skills inevitably decline and eventually the ability to speak is lost. Finally the patient falls into a terminal coma, though most Alzheimer's patients die of other causes developed over the course of the disease.

The debilitating symptoms of Alzheimer's disease, including depression, confusion, and deterioration of motor skills can now be controlled somewhat by the use of several targeted medications. But to date there is no cure for Alzheimer's disease.

Alzheimer's disease presents society with a host of problems, in particular the provision of appropriate medical and long-term care services. The cost of such care at home and in institutions, plus the lost productivity of informal caregivers, approaches one billion dollars annually.

The traditional legal response to the individual's loss of competency due to Alzheimer's or other mental disorders has been court-ordered guardianship. That system, however, was not created with a vision of the sheer numbers of aged incompetent persons, nor was it designed to effectively handle varying degrees of capability or myriad financial and health care issues that may now attend old age. The law has responded with new solutions such as durable powers of attorney for financial management and advance directives for health care that permit individuals to prepare for possible mental incapacity.

QUESTIONS

1. Have you ever known anyone who experienced Alzheimer's disease or other dementia? What were the symptoms of the illness and the effects on that individual's daily activities? How did you respond?

2. How did the illness affect the victim's spouse or family?

3. Should Alzheimer's disease be considered primarily a personal or family problem, or is it a social problem? How much of the burden of caring for someone with Alzheimer's disease should fall upon the spouse or family? How much upon society?

4. How much of the government funding allocated for research and social services for Alzheimer's disease patients should be spent for the alleviation of the problems of the spouse and family?

[b]   Chronic Illness

Chronic illnesses, which are disproportionately experienced by the elderly, include atherosclerosis, cancer, emphysema, diabetes, cirrhosis, and osteoarthritis. The severity of chronic symptoms is contingent upon the individual patient's genetic predispositions, previous lifestyle, and willingness to follow medical advice.

Treatment of chronic illness is, in the aggregate, very expensive. People with chronic conditions require health care costing approximately four times the amount used by the average healthy person. However, the more significant pattern involves the costs of acute illnesses that may arise from chronic conditions.

Consider the following scenario:

> Ben develops pneumonia at age 30 because he has smoked two packs of cigarettes daily for 15 years. In 1900, he might have lingered for three days and died. He would have enjoyed a vigorous life and incurred few medical expenses. Now, Ben survives pneumonia. Continuing to smoke or exposed to environmental toxins, Ben suffers a heart attack at age 55. In the past he would have died, but quick intervention saves his life and ongoing medications can now control his heart arrhythmia. Ben develops circulation and blood clotting problems and, at age 65, has a stroke. Quick (and costly) intervention saves his life. He spends days in intensive care and weeks in a rehabilitation facility. Ben contracts lung cancer at age 70, a disease that has not been limited in most cases by medical technology. He spends additional days with tests and treatment to determine whether anything further might be effective to prolong his life, but finally the disease is fatal.

The above hypothetical is just an example, and is not intended to suggest that the responsibility for Ben's death, whether sooner or later, lies solely with his lifestyle choices, his environment, or even his genetics. In an era of increasing confusion (both professional and consumer) about the great promise of medical interventions and the inevitable disappointments of patient deterioration and death, there is an unfortunate inclination to "blame" someone for a bad result. Realistically, complex problems do not lend themselves to simple solutions.

QUESTIONS

    1.   Many people can, in part by good diet and exercise, maintain physical and mental capability throughout their lives and reduce the incidence and severity of chronic illness. If individuals choose to live an unhealthy lifestyle, should society assist them less if they become chronically ill? Or would that be confusing morality with physical health?

    2.   Does the incidence of chronic illness suggest that more prevention is needed? Studies indicate that a change to a healthier lifestyle at any age leads to fewer chronic conditions. Should the government emphasize healthier lifestyles for the elderly? If so, how? Free nutritional meals? Free exercise classes? Free smoking cessation clinics?

3. Who should be responsible for paying for the cost of chronic care? The individual? His or her family? The government?

[c] Economic Vulnerability

Most elderly have modest incomes, but that obscures great disparities in income as revealed in comparing median versus mean incomes, as well as comparing incomes among sub-populations of those age 65 and older in 2009.

	Median	Mean
All	$19,157	$29,497
White	$20,357	$31,185
Black	$14,357	$22,694
Hispanic	$11,957	$19,818
Other	$14,595	$26,224

Approximately 10 percent of those age 65 and older have incomes below the poverty index, which is about the same as the percentage below age 65.

The causes of elderly poverty and the solutions to it are quite different from poverty among the young. Elderly poverty often can be traced to low wages and lack of pension plans when they were employed, age discrimination in hiring, mandatory retirement, disability, poor health, and widowhood for the non-wage earner in a couple.

Elderly people also are economically vulnerable when the extra cost of care and assistance exceeds their incomes. Chronic illnesses increase living costs permanently and sometimes unexpectedly. Hearing impairments may limit the ability to use the telephone and require individuals to conduct their affairs in person. Declining eyesight may prevent driving, shopping independently, or even reading the mail. Recreational opportunities and pastimes may become difficult or even impossible. Housecleaning, walking inside and outside the home, bathing and dressing may be precarious or impossible, further limiting an individual's choices and self-sufficiency.

Impairments caused by chronic illness and the need for long-term care increase with age. According to the National Center for Health Statistics, almost half of those over the age of 65 report a limitation of an activity due to chronic diseases. Relatively few Americans require assistance in performing basic daily activities before age 65, but after age 65 chronic impairment unfortunately becomes more common.

The following chart provides percentages of the population by age who receive help with various activities.

	65 to 74 years	75 to 84 years	85 years and older
Eating	.5%	1.4%	5.5%
Bathing/Showering	2.3%	5.3%	15.2%
Dressing	2.0%	4.0%	10.7%
Getting Around Inside Home	1.3%	3.1%	9.2%

Source: Centers for Disease Control and Prevention, National Center for Health Statistics, National Health Interview Survey, family core questionnaire, Table 58 (2004).

How the law should respond to the need for long-term care for the elderly remains to be resolved. The cost of community-based care and nursing home care has risen sharply over the last decade, following a pattern similar to the increases in other health care costs.

[3] THE OLD DEPEND ON THE PROMISES OF THE YOUNG

The elderly are vulnerable because they are often economically dependent on the nonelderly. The elderly may be directly dependent; a son or daughter, for example, may provide regular financial assistance, such as paying for rent or for an expensive item such as a new car. Most of the elderly are not so explicitly dependent, but almost all are indirectly dependent by virtue of their receipt of various government benefits.

[a] Formal Assistance

The elderly find support in both formal and informal networks. The need for a formal network is great when an elderly individual is functionally impaired or in poor health with limited informal network resources. Formal support and resources are provided by institutions, agencies, and their representatives. For example, state or county Area Agencies on Aging provide formal social services support systems for many elderly.

Federal and state benefit programs provide a crucial margin of income and healthcare access for many elderly persons, yet the continuation of these programs depends greatly on the willingness of the nonelderly to continue to assist the elderly. For example, Social Security retirement benefits represent almost 40 percent of the income of those age 65 and older. For over half of those over age 65, Social Security provides more than 90 percent of their income. Medicare, which is financed partly from general tax revenues, pays over half of the enrollees' health care expenses, while Medicaid pays all of the basic health care costs of the poor and about half of the nation's total nursing home bill.

Popular support for federal income and health benefits for the aged remains strong. Yet despite the opposition to direct reductions in benefits, many fear for the future solvency of Social Security and Medicare. To avert shortages in the Social Security Trust Fund the current retirement age will gradually rise until it reaches age 67 in the year 2022. Medicare has been amended to include managed care to contain costs, and payments to physicians, hospitals, and other health care providers have been limited to fee scales set by the government. If these reforms prove insufficient, more drastic changes may be necessary.

[b] Family and Social Networks

Most elderly who live in the community are linked into social support networks that enable them to cope psychologically, emotionally, and physically with the vagaries of life. Such support can range from help with household chores to intervention on account of a health crisis. Support may come from relatives, a church, volunteers, neighbors, and friends. As individuals age, they generally rely mostly on their spouses for both practical and psychological support. Women are far less likely to have such support in advanced age since they tend to outlive their husbands. Wives are four years younger on average than husbands and, because women outlive men an average of seven years, married women can expect an average widowhood of 11 years.

Minority elderly populations present a somewhat different picture. The majority of Asian-Americans, often presumed to have their needs met within a traditional family structure, in fact more often live alone. Past immigration patterns that excluded women and inhibited the formation of families resulted in many isolated elderly Asian-Americans. Some immigrants, such as Cuban-Americans, have been cut off from their extended families. Other minority elderly have lost traditional cultural family support patterns as the younger generations have adopted the values of the "American" nuclear family with its lack of intergenerational support. Some African-American women experience isolation, with one-fifth of their number living alone in rented public housing. Conversely, many older African-American women are central to intergenerational households. Three-fourths of elder African-American heads of households, most of whom are women, own their own homes. A substantial number live with their children and young grandchildren.

If an elderly spouse becomes frail or disabled or dies, the survivor must rely on other family members for assistance. The first choice is usually an adult child, although the proclivity to rely upon a child depends upon the child's proximity, the family's cultural background, and the socioeconomic status of the elderly individual: poorer elderly individuals are more likely to rely upon children.

The elderly most commonly turn to a female for help. Neither the increased participation of women in the work force nor the demographic trend of the smaller-sized families has eliminated the traditional female dominance of the caregiver role. However, male participation is increasing. One survey of caregivers for adults (Nat'l Alliance for Caregiving and AARP, Caregiving in the U.S. (2004)) reported that 61 percent of caregivers were women, while 39 percent were men. *See* Peggie R. Smith, *Elder Care, Gender, and Work: The Work-Family Issue of the 21st Century*, 25 Berkeley J. Emp. & Lab. L. 351 (2004). Why women are so often the primary caregivers is a combination of complex cultural and economic factors. For one, caregiving falls within the purview of the domestic realm that traditionally has been considered as work more appropriate for women. To the extent that women in the wage force on the average earn less than men, caregiving represents less of an opportunity cost to them than it does to men.

QUESTIONS

1. Do you know of any elderly individuals who have relied upon family members as caregivers? Was the caregiver male or female?

2. If your parents needed a caregiver, who would they choose? Why?

3. Should the government provide support to caregivers? If so, in what form? An hourly wage? In-kind assistance? Tax credits? Credit towards Social Security retirement benefits?

4. Should employers be required to accommodate their employees who act as caregivers for their parents or other relatives? If so, how?

The longer older individuals live in the same neighborhood, the more likely they are to rely for help from friends and neighbors. The use of informal, nonfamilial support systems also depends upon the individual's attitude toward self-reliance, an attitude that is often culturally as well as individually based. Older Asian-Americans, for example, are more likely to seek help from friends than from governmental support systems. Hispanic elderly who lack available relatives are more likely than any other ethnic group to seek government assistance in times of need.

Many older individuals seek support and assistance from social or religious organizations. Participation in organizations, clubs, or religious groups is strongly related to gender (women use such organizations more than men), social class (reliance declines as wealth increases), and the degree to which the individual was involved with the organization earlier in life. For the minority of elders who belong to such groups, participation and involvement decreases with age.

Only when their informal support systems prove insufficient do older persons turn to more formal support institutions such as church programs and senior citizen centers. When faced with more intensive needs, some refuse or do not know how to seek help and so gradually become more isolated and put their physical and mental health at risk.

[c]　Family Support Statutes

Some adult children voluntarily provide financial support for their aging parents. An estimated 10 percent of the elderly receive regular or significant financial assistance from children or grandchildren. More often, adult children provide in-kind assistance such as rent-free housing, assistance with household chores and repairs, errand running and transportation.

Some contend that voluntary assistance is not enough, and that adult children, who have the resources, have an obligation to support their impoverished parents. An estimated 30 states have so-called filial responsibility laws. Two models dominate, the first being the requirement that an adult child with the financial means support a parent because of the existence of the relationship between them. That is, the statute assumes that the status of being an adult child creates a duty to assist. The second type of statute allows the adult child, upon suit for support of a needy parent, to offer evidence that the parent failed in fulfilling the duties of parenthood and thus is not worthy of support by the child.

In 2005, Pennsylvania enacted a filial responsibility statute, replacing one repealed years ago. The current statute reads, in pertinent part:

(a) LIABILITY. — (1) Except as set forth in paragraph (2), all of the following individuals have the responsibility to care for and maintain or financially assist an indigent person, regardless of whether the indigent person is a public charge:

(i) The spouse of the indigent person.

(ii) A child of the indigent person.

(iii) A parent of the indigent person.

(2) Paragraph (1) does not apply in any of the following cases:

(i) If an individual does not have sufficient financial ability to support the indigent person.

(ii) A child shall not be liable for the support of a parent who abandoned the child and persisted in the abandonment for a period of ten years during the child's minority.

(b) AMOUNT. — (1) Except as set forth in paragraph (2), the amount of liability shall be set by the court in the judicial district in which the indigent person resides.

(2) For medical assistance for the aged other than public nursing home care, as provided in section 401 of the act of June 13, 1967 (P.L. 31, No. 21), known as the Public Welfare Code, the following apply:

(i) Except as set forth in subparagraph (ii), the amount of liability shall, during any 12-month period, be the lesser of:

(A) six times the excess of the liable individual's average monthly income over the amount required for the reasonable support of the liable individual and other persons dependent upon the liable individual; or

(B) the cost of the medical assistance for the aged.

(ii) The department may, by reasonable regulations, adjust the liability under subparagraph (i), including complete elimination of the liability, at a cost to the Commonwealth not exceeding those funds certified by the Secretary of the Budget as available for this purpose.

(c) PROCEDURE. — A court has jurisdiction in a case under this section upon petition of:

(1) an indigent person; or

(2) any other person or public body or public agency having any interest in the care, maintenance or assistance of such indigent person.

(d) CONTEMPT. — (1) If an individual liable for support under this section fails to comply with an order under this section, the court shall schedule a contempt hearing. At the hearing, if the court determines that the individual liable for support has intentionally failed to comply with the order, the court may hold the individual in contempt of court and may sentence the individual to up to six months' imprisonment.

(2) This subsection applies regardless of whether the indigent person is confined in a public institution.

23 PA. CONS. STAT. ANN. § 4603.

Enforcement of filial statutes is infrequent. *See* Seymour Moskowitz, *Adult Children nd Indigent Parents: Intergenerational Responsibilities in International Perspective*, 86 MARQ. L. REV. 401 (2001).

QUESTIONS

1. Assume that you live in a state that is considering adopting a filial support law. What issues or potential problems should the legislation address?

2. What is the apparent intent or purpose of the Pennsylvania statute?

J. CONFLICTING VALUES: AUTONOMY VERSUS PROTECTION

The legal problems of the elderly are enmeshed in the crosscurrents of uncertain needs and conflicting values. Some needs are easy to identify and may even apply to all older people. In the simplest of problems, someone who is hungry needs food. Surely, a lonely elderly individual wants companionship, but this is more complicated because not just any companionship meets the need. A disoriented elderly person requires assistance with his or her affairs, but what is enough and how should the need be filled? Even if the most important basic needs are apparent, no unanimity exists as to the appropriate means of meeting them. Even the simplest example, providing food for the hungry elderly, might be met by general income assistance, by vouchers usable only for food (i.e. "food stamps") or the availability of pre-planned meals at meal sites or delivered to homes of those deemed to be homebound. The preference for one solution over another is based in part upon what other values an advocate believes are worth promoting when solving the immediate problem of hunger.

QUESTIONS

1. Your community includes elderly individuals who are ill nourished. Would you favor giving them income to be spent to meet their need? Food vouchers? A prepared meal at a designated time and site? Are there any other possible solutions?

2. What are the values or assumptions underlying your choice of solution to Question #1? Who decides which value is paramount, and on what basis?

3. If you want to promote personal autonomy for the elderly, is providing them with more income the best solution?

Particular solutions to meet the needs of the elderly often depend on the relative importance given to the conflicting values of personal autonomy and protection of individual from risk and harm. Personal autonomy is the right of an individual to act independently for purposes that need to satisfy only the actor. Autonomy elevates the rights of the individual over the wishes, opinions, or needs of others.

Autonomy, however, is not synonymous with selfishness or disinterest in the needs or concerns of others. An autonomous individual may well act in an altruistic manner if that is what the individual believes is best. An autonomous and altruistic person may feel responsible for others and as a result act in the interests of others even at a cost to that individual. Because the individual made the choice, however, he or she remains autonomous. What autonomous individuals do not do is allow others to decide for them.

Autonomous individuals are characterized by the lack of dependency, and, therefore, as dependency increases, autonomy declines. All of us are dependent to some extent upon others or upon institutions, but for the autonomous individual that commonplace dependency intrudes only minimally. The more that individuals are dependent upon others or institutions not under their control the less they are autonomous. If, for example, an individual's right to food depends upon the independent or arbitrary decision of another, that individual has lost a great deal of autonomy. Dependency, however, can be counteracted by the granting of rights. For example, food stamp recipients are, to be sure, dependent upon the largess of the government for their food, but they are able to act autonomously because the food stamps are theirs as a right that cannot be taken away so long as they meet the eligibility requirements.

Autonomy and personal rights reduce dependency. To diminish elderly people's dependency we must recognize and expand their rights. Autonomy means freedom, in some sense, and freedom depends upon the individual having rights rather than being subject to the whims of others. The granting of rights, however, creates correlative duties: an elderly individual's right to food stamps creates the government's duty to provide them. The creation of a duty diminishes the autonomy of the party burdened with that duty. If the government, through its administrator of the food stamp program, must supply a particular elderly person with food stamps regardless of whether it seems prudent or desirable to do so, the autonomy of the government administrator to act has been severely circumscribed.

If we define autonomy to mean not only the ability to control our own behavior but also the ability to control the behavior of those with whom we interact, then to some degree autonomy is a zero-sum game. As an elderly individual's autonomy expands, the autonomy of the other actor contracts. The more the elderly control their own destiny the less others can, because elderly freedom expands only with the contraction of the power of others. While such competition for advantages is not always at issue, it is more likely to be so when resources are in short supply and an individual needs specific, personal benefits or assistance.

Personal autonomy translates into personal power. Autonomy for the elderly means increasing their personal power at the expense of the power of institutions and individuals who would otherwise control or direct their lives.

QUESTIONS

1.   Do you believe autonomy is the highest value? If not, what is?

2.   Could all the problems of the elderly be solved if they only had more money? Or, are there problems that even a well-to-do elder cannot solve? If so, what are they?

3.   Does the solution for an individual necessarily create an optimum solution when applied across society?

4.   Does it make any sense to speak of societal needs versus individual desires, since society is comprised of individuals? Are there "elderly" problems or do individual elderly persons have problems?

For many elderly autonomy has a very high value, and so it is very frustrating for them to become dependent. Autonomy is strongly associated with adulthood, and signs of dependency may cause a person a sense of shame or stigma. Nevertheless, the aging process often means an unavoidable loss of independence.

Even a healthy aging individual experiences a decline in physical capabilities that results in diminished autonomy. At a minimum, the elderly tire more easily, lacking the energy to do all they would like or that they used to do. One who must nap every afternoon has less time to engage in hobbies, work, or travel. Impaired vision or hearing loss cause dependence on devices or other people, or simply result in a more constricted scope of activities. If you cannot see well, you may hesitate to drive at night. If your hearing has declined, going to a play may be more frustrating than fulfilling.

Critical losses of independence, however small, can undermine the self-worth and dignity of the individual. To avoid being reminded of the limitations, some individuals withdraw from activities and interactions with others. Autonomy, freedom, and personal power for the elderly are concepts almost everyone endorses. They are ritually invoked and applauded but their true import is all too easily overlooked. Too many who invoke the value of autonomy for the elderly are either unaware of or choose to ignore the consequences of autonomy, namely an increase in risk.

As an initial reaction many would endorse the general idea that the elderly should be protected from the unkind vicissitudes of life, like economic want, poor health, abuse and neglect, and social isolation. While no one would write a blank check for protection from all of life's trials, almost everyone would endorse the goal of protecting the elderly from the worst of life's hazards, commensurate with fiscal reality.

Yet the hasty endorsement of protection for the elderly may overlook the fact that protection often is antithetical to autonomy. To protect individuals means limiting their freedom to act. Protecting the elderly diabetic from loss of a limb means intrusive measures including restricting that person's diet and compelling a non-sedentary lifestyle. Protecting the potential victims of financial abuse means monitoring and excluding some relationships, and perhaps even appointing guardians to take charge of their financial affairs.

What often is lacking in these "solutions" is sufficient appreciation of the cost of protection to the individual's autonomy. The value of protection must be balanced against the need for autonomy and independence. Because of the perceived vulnerability of the elderly, it is too easy to see only the need for protection and overlook the equally compelling need for autonomy. Lawyers, who should by training be sensitive to the balancing of competing values, have a major role to play in the sorting out of the proper mix of protection and autonomy.

Tension between the competing goals of autonomy and protection often arises. For example, policy makers must choose between sending a check to pay for in-home assistance and sending a homemaker with a plan to provide services deemed appropriate by a "case manager." Should we provide vouchers for housing the elderly poor throughout the community or to build dedicated housing for the elderly? With the first, the elderly theoretically can choose their neighborhood and living unit, wisely or not. The trade-off is the likely loss of the concentration of services that are efficiently provided in subsidized "elderly housing." Promoting autonomy requires permitting the elderly to live as they will, even if that results in their exposing themselves to risks that society considers unwise. Emphasizing protection means guarding the elderly from unnecessary risks, even if that requires overruling their wishes and diminishing their autonomy.

The competing values of autonomy and protection must be thought through each time they come into conflict. There is no magic sword to cut through the conundrum. While some observers will reflexively favor one goal or the other, most will vacillate between the two and never satisfactorily resolve the conflict. At times autonomy will be favored, while in other situations protection will prevail. While there is no one "solution," it is critical that the conflict in values be acknowledged and given due consideration in devising public policy and programs for the elderly.

QUESTIONS

1. Are the values of autonomy and protection always in conflict? Or protection a necessary precursor to autonomy?

2. Is protection the issue or is it who selects the degree and kind of protection?

3. Who decides which value is more important, the elderly or society?

4. If society subsidizes the elderly, does that give it the right to determine the proper balance between autonomy and protection?

5. Think of an elderly person whom you know well. How would you go about increasing that person's autonomy? His or her protection from harm? Are the two goals in conflict? Do the solutions work at cross purposes?

K. GENERATIONAL JUSTICE

Economic security for the elderly retiree is not controversial; everyone is for it. Debate centers not on the goal but on the means. Because the retiree's economic security rests on a proverbial three-legged stool of private savings, employer-provided retirement benefits, and Social Security, the debate focuses on how much of the retiree's income should come from each of the three sources. Typical questions include: Should the retiree be expected to save more? Should employee retirement benefits be expanded? Should Social Security benefits be increased or privatized? Underlying these questions are policy debates over individual responsibility, employer obligations, and economic justice.

Many view these issues as "generational justice." They ask, "How much do the young owe the old?" While the elderly rely to some degree upon their own savings or upon employer-provided retirement benefits (a form of deferred compensation), they also rely on the government for assistance. Whether in the form of federal income benefits, such as Social Security, or additional assistance from state and local governments, such as property tax relief or subsidized housing, the elderly reap a notable share of benefits that are largely paid for by taxes on younger people.

Public perception of the worthiness of the elderly to receive public benefits has evolved over decades. In 1965, elderly health care benefits in the form of Medicare and Medicaid were enacted. The new programs recognized the marginal financial status of many elderly and the rising costs of their medical care. In the same year, the Older Americans Act established federal funds to states for senior centers, transportation, and other community-based services. Eligibility was based solely on age, so more affluent elders could participate on the same basis as others.

So long as the size of the economic pie increased, few complained that the elderly were benefiting too much. The questions were whether the elderly needed assistance, whether it was right to help them, and whether society could afford to aid them. The debate was between the elderly and the taxpayers. The answers to these questions were translated into policy in the form of cost-of-living increases for Social Security recipients, funding for social support programs, and subsidized housing.

As the cost for these and other programs for the elderly outstripped inflation, however, the debate became three-cornered: among the elderly, the taxpayers, and advocates of other social programs. In the 1980s, the public's acquiescent tone began to change as all levels of government felt budget constraints, and taxpayers demanded lower taxes and more fiscal discipline. Federal social programs suffered cutbacks, and federal funding for state and local elderly programs failed to keep pace with demand. It became clear that the desire for federal assistance far outdistanced the available supply, and that the budget had become a zero-sum game. Every dollar given to group X was one less dollar for group Y. If the elderly programs expanded, they necessarily did so at the cost of other social programs.

Critics of aid to the elderly assert that younger taxpayers are asked to sacrifice unduly, as they pay taxes in order to benefit relatively well-off elderly. Social justice, such advocates argue, demands that the elderly lose their preferential spot so that others more needy, such as children living in poverty, can be served.

Have the needs of "the elderly" changed? While some of the benefits enjoyed by the elderly came as a result of the concern of the young for the well-being of the elderly, some are due to the elderly's vigorous political activity. Not only are the elderly more likely to vote than younger persons, but they are politically very well organized. Over a thousand organizations advocate for the elderly. The largest, AARP, which allows membership at age 50, has over 40 million members and is a significant lobbyist for programs that aid the elderly.

Much of the impetus for the generational justice argument comes from a belief that many of the elderly are reasonably financially secure and do not deserve the degree of assistance that they receive. The elderly poverty rate is somewhat below the national average. Moreover, much of the aid to the elderly is not reported as income because it is provided in-kind or in the form of reduced prices. Benefits to the elderly include free public transportation, property tax rebates, reduced prices for prescription drugs, subsidized medical care, lower fees for public recreation, and publicly financed senior citizen support centers. The cumulative effect of such benefits has been to remove the majority of elderly from poverty to an extent not measured by an examination of income alone.

Median income declines with age due in part to the disproportionate number of nonmarried women in older age groups. In every age group, nonmarried women have a lower median income than nonmarried men or married couples. The poverty rate for men is about 7.3 percent while for women over age 65 the rate is close to 12.5 percent. For all groups the rate of poverty rises with age, with those age 75 or older having a poverty rate of about 11.6 percent.

Yet income statistics do not capture the full extent of elderly poverty. Although only about 10 percent of the elderly have incomes below the poverty line, many have incomes barely above it. Also, lifelong lower-income elderly, who were never affluent, have no savings to cushion them from the extra costs of declining health and capabilities. In elderly households with incomes in the lowest quintile, nearly 80 percent of income derives from Social Security and an additional 10 percent comes from other public assistance. Moreover, elderly poverty among minorities is much higher: for Blacks it is almost 24 percent and for Hispanics nearly 20 percent.

Still the basic challenge cannot be ignored: are the elderly receiving a disproportionate amount of society's assistance, considering the need for national defense, research, for good roads, and other infrastructure? The question is not simply what do the young owe the old, but rather, what constitutes a strong, healthy society? And, finally, what is a just society — not just for all collectively, but also for individuals in their special circumstances.

With regard to fairness to the elderly, some claim that there is also *intra* generational injustice. Social Security and Medicare are available without regard to need. On the one hand one might ask, what is the fairness of assisting elderly who are not needy, while allowing other elderly individuals to remain below the poverty line?

Many who are concerned with intergenerational issues assert that *intra* generation justice is merely a symptom of a larger problem that current governmental programs are too favorable to the elderly at the expense of the young. Yet all seem to agree, whatever the reasons, that the young owe some level of care to the elderly. Consider the following instances of intergenerational responsibility:

Lawrence B. Solum,
To Our Children's Children: The Problems of Intergenerational Ethics
35 Loy. L.A. L. Rev. 163, 167 (2001)[*]

Case One: Care and Feeding. The most familiar context in which questions of duty between one generation and another arise is that of parents' duties to care for their children. Almost everyone agrees that such a duty exists as a matter of morality or ethics, and the law recognizes such a duty. Although exceptional circumstances can create special problems, care and feeding is for the most part an easy case.

Case Two: Nursing the Elderly. The first example, care and feeding, involves the moral duties of parents to their children. The obvious corollary is the duty that children may have to care for their elderly parents. Although there is general agreement that children should care for their elderly parents, there is considerable disagreement about the extent and form of that duty. Do children have a duty to take elderly parents into the children's home? How great a share of the child's resources ought to be devoted to care for the elderly? Should this be a social responsibility rather than an individual one? These are all questions of intergenerational ethics.

Case Three: Social Security. Suppose that the "Baby Boomer" generation is numerically substantially larger than two succeeding generations called "Generation X" and "Generation Y." If Social Security is financed by having each generation that is currently working pay for the social security benefits of the generation that has retired, then members of Generation X and Generation Y will be required to pay a substantially greater share of current income for the social security benefits of the Baby Boomers than the Baby Boomers paid for the social security benefits of their parents and grandparents. Such a situation would raise questions of distributive justice: is it fair for one generation to bear a larger burden than another?

Case Four: Legacies and Bequests. Another familiar context is that of intergenerational wealth transfers. Do parents have a duty to save during their lifetimes and transfer some of this wealth to their children or other descendants? Again there may be special cases, but the ordinary understanding is that bequests and legacies are gifts, and that parents do not have a duty to save for such bequests or to leave money to their children. In the usual case, parents may wish to leave such a bequest and we count such a wish as virtuous. As a matter of distributive justice, however, it might be argued that intergenerational wealth transfers are unjust, insofar as they operate to perpetuate inequalities of wealth and income.

QUESTION

Do you expect to receive a substantial inheritance from your parents or grandparents? Did your parents' generation receive such an inheritance? Has anything changed in the nature of wealth transfer from generation to generation?

L.   AGE DISCRIMINATION

Discrimination. The word conjures up images of prejudice, hate, misunderstanding, and ill-feeling. Discrimination of all kinds, whether racial, sexual, or age-related, is publicly scorned and limited by law. Yet the first dictionary definition of the word "discriminate" is to make or perceive differences, which is a neutral and possibly useful act. The pejorative implication of the word has obscured its fuller meaning to such an extent that now it is used almost exclusively to describe objectionable behavior. However, if age discrimination were always bad, Social Security retirement benefits that are limited to those age 62 or older should not be tolerated. The answer, of course, is that age discrimination is desirable when distributing government benefits. In the larger sense, we approve of discrimination that favors the elderly (positive discrimination) but condemn it if it disadvantages them (negative discrimination).

While it seems unnecessary to state why society should frown upon negative age discrimination, it is less apparent why it should condone positive age discrimination. Why, for example, should Medicare be available only for those age 65 or older? Similarly, why shouldn't individuals who retire before age 62 be allowed an actuarially adjusted Social Security pension? The answer to these and similar questions that could be asked about other special programs for the elderly is that cost considerations make it impossible for the programs to be universally offered. The elderly are selected as the favored group because old age has historically been associated with economic need.

The use of old age as a surrogate for identifying those who should be favored, however, goes beyond a crude identification of age with need. The elderly are favored because of our collective perception that they are a sympathetic group who deserve our assistance. Possibly, because we do not want to be old and fear old age, we try to ameliorate its effects, to somehow make it better. Collectively we believe we should do something for the elderly, so we support publicly sponsored social programs and attack discrimination against the elderly by legislation such as the federal Age Discrimination in Employment Act. Perhaps we support such legislation because we anticipate a need for protection in our old age.

The challenge for the law is to reconcile the tension between policies that attack age discrimination and those that promote it. To do so requires an understanding that it is not paradoxical to outlaw discrimination while simultaneously using age as a basis for governmental assistance. Negative age discrimination is wrong because it allows individuals to be judged by a largely irrelevant criterion over which they have no control. Conversely, positive age discrimination as a basis for governmental assistance is sensible because it is the least demeaning, most efficient method of identifying aid recipients. Yet merely to state the argument for positive age discrimination is not to prove it. The policy remains at risk, susceptible of being dismissed as no more justifiable than negative age discrimination.

[1] FINANCIAL JUSTIFICATIONS FOR POSITIVE AGE DISCRIMINATION

Traditionally the economic needs of the elderly have justified their special treatment. Although Americans are not particularly charitable to the poor as a whole, they are sympathetic to the elderly poor, many of whom seem "deserving." Most Americans believe that the elderly are poor not because they are lazy or will not work but because they can no longer earn their living. Moreover, the young of today realize that someday they too will be old. By helping the elderly they may protect their own futures from need. Many also protect their present interests. Public assistance to the elderly relieves many younger people from the burden of directly assisting their parents or other older relatives. The combination of the belief that it is right and proper to help the elderly, the desire to protect one's own old age, and the relief from having to directly assist older relatives provides a strong impetus for public assistance for the elderly.

The countervailing attitude, however, is that the elderly could and should have saved for their old age. After all, old age is not an unexpected event. If the elderly want to be financially secure, one can argue, they should plan ahead, save more when they are young, defer retirement. The economic problems of old age are largely the result of a personal failure to adequately plan. In short, the argument goes, elderly poverty is less a social problem than an example of individual irresponsibility.

The belief or suspicion that the elderly poor do not deserve society's help (or deserve only modest assistance) has been reinforced by the abolition of mandatory retirement. If a worker cannot be retired because of age alone, skeptics begin to ask why society should support someone who is capable of working but instead chooses to retire. In the future, retired elderly poor may be viewed less sympathetically and be seen to resemble younger welfare recipients.

Social Security benefits have always enjoyed wide support because the public thinks of them as something earned in the form of insurance rather than a welfare payment. Increasingly, however, members of the public are aware that their current taxes pay the retiree benefits. Medicare benefits supported by current taxes are also politically vulnerable. Taxpayers ask why working class taxpayers should sacrifice for middle or upper class retirees. The challenge to the law is to reconcile the conflicting images of the elderly. Are they a group who deserve special support or are they more like those active, affluent individuals so frequently portrayed in advertisements? The two views likely will never be completely harmonized but will continue to be the yin and yang of the debate over what is the proper public policy towards the elderly.

[2] HEALTH JUSTIFICATIONS FOR POSITIVE AGE DISCRIMINATION

The elderly are not as healthy as the rest of the population. The aged on average visit the doctor nearly twice as often as younger, healthy individuals. An older person is nearly twice as likely to enter a hospital in the course of a year and is likely to remain there longer once admitted. The greater health needs of the elderly translate into significant costs. For example, in 2009 Medicare served 40 million elderly at a cost of $480 billion or about one-sixth of all health care expenditures.

Arguments in favor of elderly health care benefits are compelling, though the precise mix of personal responsibility to pay and public obligation are always up for debate. Americans have long pursued a goal of securing optimal health care both to strengthen individuals' abilities to function and care for themselves and to enhance the quality of their lives. Given the modest retirement incomes of the elderly with their need of costly medical care, Medicare also represents an attempt to safeguard the old from financial ruin in their later years. The question is why the elderly are favored over the younger poor.

Concurrently, commentators have debated the limits of granting the elderly access to costly medical interventions that have high risks of failure and limited likelihood for success. A partial response of the law has been authorization for advance directives to enable the patient to refuse treatment. The responsibility of the law is to assure such directives do not establish a standard for withholding potentially effective treatments from the elderly.

As the number of very elderly individuals grows, so does the need for long-term care. Long-term care is a catchall category for services in homes, assisted living facilities, and nursing homes that support people with chronic illnesses. The cost of long-term care costs impoverish the great majority of those who require it. The ongoing question is what portion of the cost of long-term care should be subsidized from public funds and what responsibility the individual should bear.

The need for long-term care and other assistance for many elderly is clear. The appropriate role of public programs is not. As the total cost of services increases, implementing new benefits of any scope is becoming less feasible. The Medicare drug benefit implemented in 2005, with its complex benefit structure is an example of positive political will without the conviction of fiscal supports. How to pay for long-term care — a mix of health care and living expenses — is a difficult question even for individuals to answer for themselves. For a diverse society to arrive at a common understanding and agreement may be impossible. Broadly applicable answers elude articulation. Instead, policies evolve and programs are implemented. Over time the values implicit in the programs are discerned and the contradictions revealed. With the underlying values exposed, the debate over their relative merits is renewed.

At present the debate is in its infancy. For the most part the issues are at the level of "I need" and "I can't afford." Though the country has enacted massive medical aid programs for the elderly, it has not debated the values upon which these programs rest. Increasingly, we cannot debate Medicare without enlarging the talk to include basic health care access for all, a massive undertaking. As a result, complaints about the cost of Medicare are trivialized into questions about the amount of physician and hospital charges rather than about what is an appropriate share of our national wealth to devote to medical care for the elderly.

The challenge to the law, and to lawyers, is to move the arguments beyond program details and immediate financial concerns to a meaningful examination of policy choices. We cannot answer the question of how much medical assistance to give to the elderly until we can answer why we should give them any at all. Only when we appreciate why our concept of a just society demands subsidized health care to the elderly who cannot afford it, will we be able to conceive a consistent policy and create programs that translate those deeper values into reality.

M.   THE RIGHT OF THE ELDERLY TO BENEFITS

The elderly are worthy of the interest of lawyers if for no other reason than because this age group is favored by so many public and private benefit programs. From Social Security to employer-provided pensions, from Medicare to discounts at movie theaters, the elderly receive many preferences in our society. Whether they should is a compelling question, but not one here addressed. Instead, our interest is in how the existence of these programs has created a rapidly expanding need for legal assistance. It is true, to the point of being a cliché, that benefit programs whether public or private are bonanzas for lawyers. Benefit programs create entitlements, which in turn create rights. When those rights are withheld or disputed the beneficiary needs a lawyer. Medicaid, for example, has spawned a legal cottage industry as the elderly dispute governmental bureaucracies over their eligibility and levels of benefits.

Areas of concern to the aging population are distributed across the law school curriculum in courses such as estate planning, health law, pension rights, administrative law, and disability law. A substantial number of law schools and lawyers now see the legal problems of the elderly transcending such doctrinal categories. A health law course may examine Medicare and Medicaid but will seldom analyze issues of fairness in light of pension rights generally available to part of the same population. Similarly, pension rights and retiree benefits cannot be fully understood without reference to the Age Discrimination in Employment Act since without a job there are no benefits to dispute. Studying one room of the house, so to speak, does not provide an understanding of the nature of the shelter.

Practicing lawyers have begun to reach similar conclusions. In the past the area of legal specialization most closely associated with the elderly was estate planning. That practice, however, focused on the preservation and passage of private wealth. Lawyers increasingly have come to appreciate that for many elderly the largest share of their "wealth" lies in their entitlements. The value of Medicare or of a private pension often dwarfs the value of the client's other property. The ability of the client to draw upon public and private benefits might be his or her most valuable "asset" or might be the way to protect more traditional assets.

As a result of their expanded knowledge of laws that affect the elderly, many lawyers call themselves elder law attorneys. Just as academics organize courses around the legal needs of the elderly, elder law attorneys have emerged to advertise their ability and willingness to serve an elderly clientele. The practice of elder law encompasses estate planning, Medicare and Medicaid, nursing home placement and patient rights, planning for possible incompetency, health care decision making and right-to-die issues, pension rights, and employment discrimination. While the number of full-time elder law specialists is small, the number of lawyers who devote at least part of their practice to elder law is large, particularly if we count traditional estate planners who have expanded their practices to include such areas as health care decision making and guardianships.

N. AGEISM AND SELF-DETERMINATION

The quality of life for the elderly is greatly dependent upon the extent to which they are guaranteed and retain their right to self-determination. Will the elderly be permitted to act in ways that they desire, or will they be channeled into behavior deemed appropriate and safe? The matched ideals of individual responsibility and individual autonomy are the bedrock of Western jurisprudence. Individuals are presumed to be accountable for what they do or fail to do. In turn individuals generally are allowed to choose the way in which they live even if that means being irresponsible or self-destructive.

The elderly, however, are not necessarily accorded the proper respect for their individual autonomy. Too often they are treated as if they were aged children who need only protection and guidance, for whom the young should paternalistically do what is "good," with little regard for their desires. Rather than possessing the wisdom of their years, the aged have been thought to regress into irresponsibility as Shakespeare expressed in *As You Like It*: "second childishness, and mere oblivion, — Sans teeth, sans eyes, sans taste, sans everything." Act II, scene vii, lines 139 *et seq*.

In less lofty sentiments we hear it expressed in sayings such as "There is no fool like an old fool." Spunky, but immature and irresponsible, old folks have long been stock characters in movies and television. Ageist attitudes pervade our depictions of older persons.

Some views of the old are still more negative, even hostile. In 1968, esteemed gerontologist Robert Butler coined a term: "There is an extreme and unremitting bias against older adults in America, a bias so prevalent that it has been given the name 'ageism'." Psychologically, ageism can be regarded as an attitude — a negative evaluation that serves to orient individuals toward old people as a group. In particular, it frequently predisposes individuals to discriminate, that is, to avoid contact, victimize, or otherwise do injury to old people based on their age status alone. At the least ageism is a tendency to stereotype old people as rigid, meddlesome, sexless, conservative, unhealthy, inactive, lonely, forgetful, and not very bright. While the belief that the elderly might be less competent than their younger counterparts has some basis of truth on an individual basis, only a small minority of the elderly are afflicted by dementia. There is no truth to the view that, in general, the elderly lack judgment or a sense of their own best interests. Certainly there is no justification for ascribing impairment to all.

Elder law attorneys, regardless of their specific areas of concentration, have a primary role in attacking the myth that older people are not competent and inevitably in need of guidance from others. That view has been the basis for such outdated policies as mandatory retirement; it is still used to justify the refusal to hire older people. Benefits programs also are infected with the paternalistic "best interests" concept. The legal battlefield in large part is defined by the conflicting themes of autonomy and paternalism. Elder lawyers must work to promote appropriate autonomy. Sooner or later the elderly will be us. How we as a society treat the elderly not only reveals much about our collective values, but also has important implications for our individual futures.

Chapter 2

LEGAL PRACTICE AND ETHICAL ISSUES

The practices of elder law attorneys are as varied in their nature and purposes as the clients they serve. Some attorneys remain close to their traditional roots in estate planning, concentrating on wills and will substitutes and financial planning for a secure retirement. Other elder law practitioners focus their energies on Medicaid planning and the preservation of assets when the client is faced with very expensive long-term care. Others have practices that include many clients with diminished mental capacity. Many elder law attorneys actively advocate for the elderly by lobbying at the local, state, and federal levels of government.

A. THE LEGAL NEEDS OF THE ELDERLY

Elderly individuals often need an attorney. Their legal problems include: age discrimination in employment; obtaining federal benefits such as Supplemental Security Income; appeals from denial of Medicare benefits; establishing Medicaid eligibility; housing problems including landlord and property tax exemptions and assessments; mental incapacity and guardianship; substandard nursing home care; and abuse and neglect by caregivers. The elderly poor have similar legal needs, though they have more problems with public benefits and often need legal protection from high interest credit purchase arrangements and consumer loans. They also may have a greater need for protective services to guard them from physical, financial, or emotional abuse or neglect. On the other hand, various consumer scams are more likely to target the elderly with more resources. The legal needs of the elderly have resulted in every state bar having an elder law group or section, as well as the National Academy of Elder Law Attorneys with nearly 4,000 members.

B. ELDER LAW PRACTICE

Attorneys who serve a predominantly older clientele have termed their specialty "elder law," which encompasses estate planning, property management, health care planning, and public benefits. An elder law practice typically goes beyond traditional legal issues and by advice, referral, or direct assistance attempts to address problems in securing health and social services. Elder law practitioners often work closely with other professionals such as social workers and health care providers.

For the practitioner, representing an elderly client often requires recognizing situations the client has not appreciated as legal problems, including appeals of eligibility for public benefits, health care planning, and questions of housing rights. Even legal areas more traditionally associated with the elderly, such as estate planning, pension and employment issues, insurance, taxes, trusts, and powers of attorney, are affected by the special circumstances of growing older. Assisting elderly clients requires time, knowledge, sensitivity to their age-related needs and difficulties, and a particular concern for the ethical issues of loyalty and confidentiality.

ALISON BARNES, A. FRANK JOHNS & NATHALIE MARTIN,
COUNSELING OLDER CLIENTS
(ALI-ABA 2005)*

§ 1.02 DEVELOPING EXPERTISE

Before entering private practice, many attorneys develop expertise in substantive areas related to elder law by working in legal aid, or serving clients of other government-related programs by working *pro bono* through service providers such as elder senior centers, Area Agencies on Aging, food banks, government advisory boards, public interest law firms, nursing homes, and hospitals. A substantial proportion of elder law attorneys gain their expertise by working in traditional estate planning practices or bank trust departments. State bar committees provide an opportunity to share expertise with other practitioners.

The type of firm a practitioner selects or develops depends on personal experience and preferred areas of specialization as well as the needs of the community. A practitioner who has a background in Legal Services, for example, may wish to focus on such matters as government benefits and family law. A former trust officer or estate planner may wish to address retirement financial management or planning for disability.

§ 1.02(a) Entering Elder Law Practice

Before embarking on a practice, an attorney should consider the availability and the accessibility of various social services in the community, including private sector as well as subsidized or government providers, in order to tailor the firm's services to unmet needs.

Expertise in more traditional areas rarely covers the broad expanse of elder client needs. The new elder lawyer must be prepared to assess, evaluate and counsel elder clients and family members throughout the elder's later life.

§ 1.02(b) Elder Law Practice Management

Few attorneys are prepared initially to deal with the business of the practice of law. When a lawyer opens a practice, solo or otherwise, the details of management, marketing and finance infringe on the time available to serve clients. They may impede the attorney's ability to keep abreast of the many areas of law that impact on the practice. Vigilance and networking is necessary to assure sound practice,

---

and great assistance is provided by other elder law attorneys, particularly by means of Internet communications.

§ 1.02(c) Elder Law Practice Management

Few attorneys are prepared initially to deal with the business of the practice of law. When a lawyer opens a practice, solo or otherwise, the details of management, marketing and finance infringe on the time available to serve clients. They may impede the attorney's ability to keep abreast of the many areas of law that impact on the practice. Vigilance and networking is necessary to assure sound practice, and great assistance is provided by other elder law attorneys, particularly by means of Internet communications.

§ 1.03 FIRM STRUCTURE

Law firms that specialize in meeting the needs of elderly clients have developed along three basic models: The traditional firm, the clearinghouse referral source, and the comprehensive "umbrella" firm.

The traditional firm, which usually approaches elder law from its background in trusts and estates, emphasizes financial and property management.

The clearinghouse firm offers expertise on community and social-service resources, in addition to traditional legal assistance. It includes at least one staff member, often a social worker or specially trained paralegal, whose function is to refer clients to service providers in the community.

The umbrella firm also provides services beyond traditional legal counsel and financial management. In addition to these services, it furnishes direct, non-legal services performed by members of the firm's staff and refers clients to community social-service providers. An umbrella firm is more likely than the clearinghouse firm to monitor service delivery. It may also serve as fiduciary for a client. The broader the range of services the firm provides, the more likely it will include professionals like social workers and community health care providers.

Umbrella firms are particularly suited to meeting the multiple needs of elderly clients. Although traditional and clearinghouse firms can address the sufficiency or fairness of a contract for new housing, for example, they generally are not prepared to advise the client about the different types of housing available and assess whether the levels of care in each are appropriate for the client's needs. Not only can umbrella firms provide elderly clients with individualized counseling, but some will also even drive the client around to introduce housing staff.

[1] MULTIDISCIPLINARY PRACTICE

Controversy within the legal and professional community about multidisciplinary practice generally contemplates fields quite removed from elder law, which generally is practiced in small- to mid-size firms. Consider the following discussion of the role of multidisciplinary practice for lawyers generally, in its historical context.

George Steven Swan,
Legal Education and Financial Planning: Preparation for the Multidisciplinary Practice Future
23 Campbell L. Rev. 1 (2000)[*]

The Emerging Idea of MDP

During the previous century, Congress erected regulatory walls segregating banks and insurance companies, investment banks, stock brokerage firms, and securities firms. However, two years ago President Clinton executed the Financial Services Modernization Act which served to erode these barriers. This statute repealed portions of the Glass-Steagall Act of 1933, which restricted the affiliation of banks and insurance companies. This 1999 enactment likewise amended the Bank Holding Company Act of 1956, which also contained restrictions against the affiliation of banks and insurance companies. At present, a pressing, widespread threat to the legal profession arises ominously from banks, which now offer a variety of fresh planning products and services. The deregulation of major sectors of the nation's financial services economy, hitherto mutually isolated, has led to the blurring of the lines between the banking, law, and insurance sectors as a result of the financial industry's efforts to offer consumers one-stop shopping.

Multidisciplinary practice for lawyers may be defined as a partnership or entity encompassing attorneys and non-attorneys with one (yet not all) of its purposes being that of delivering legal services to a client (other than itself), or holding itself out to the public as a provider of non-legal, in addition to legal, services. Often, MDPs are styled as, but not exclusively described as, large accounting firms including a law department to serve the accountants' clients.

Such an enterprise affords multiple professional services. The more fully integrated versions of MDPs present services such as accounting, auditing, consulting, and legal assistance. In such a fully integrated MDP, these services are usually offered by captive law firms, or through attorneys serving as employees who provide legal services subject to the supervision of non-attorneys. As early as the eighteenth century, major investors routinely conferred with their attorneys prior to major undertakings. Today, such consultations are probably done through a committee that supplements lawyers with lobbyists, political consultants, and public relations advisors. Much speculation has surrounded the possibility of lawyers partnering and sharing fees relative to divorce with psychologists and financial planners. There certainly is a department store type of attraction to visiting an office where clients can enjoy financial advice, or accounting services, in addition to legal counsel. Under the MDP model, a client could discuss estate planning with an attorney, consult a financial advisor within the same on investments, and then hire an in-house accountant to prepare a tax return.

---

[*] Copyright © 2000 Campbell Law Review. Reprinted with permission.

The Problematical Application of MDP

Exclusion of non-attorneys from the provision of law-related services is a twentieth-century phenomenon. This is largely a result of the development and growth of the organized bar associations during the third and fourth decades of the past century. Since its 1878 inception, the American Bar Association has resisted any steps in the direction of allowing non-attorneys (except under specific and limited circumstances) to deliver routine legal services to the public. Overall, the ABA has proved to be successful in curtailing potential competition. Alone among common law nations in this regard, America proscribes non-attorneys from handling certain extra-courtroom representation. (In Ontario, Canada, for example, non-lawyers routinely afford representation in traffic courts and before workers' compensation boards.)

QUESTIONS

1.   What are the common traits in elder law practice and "big firm" alliances?

2.   Does your state allow lawyers to associate professionally with non-lawyers, as does the District of Columbia? Consider the requirements of Model Rules 5.4 and 5.5, and Model Code Canon 3 and DR 5-107 and EC 5-24. Why have state bars traditionally prohibited association and fee sharing with non-lawyers? Do you believe associations among, say, lawyers and social workers, or lawyers and doctors, will become widespread?

The elder law firm must structure relationships in accordance with professional rules of ethics.

Alison Barnes, A. Frank Johns & Nathalie Martin, Counseling Older Clients (ALI-ABA 2005)*

§ 1.06 STAFFING AND EXPANSION

The necessary skills for hiring new staff members vary according to the type of caseload the firm develops.

§ 1.06(a) Staffing with Non-legal Professionals

Staffing with non-lawyer personnel must fall within the rules of the state bar.

§ 1.06(a)(1) Compliance with State Bar Rules

Hiring non-legal professionals on staff as employees must comply with the state bar rules of professional responsibility. Many state bars have added some form of ABA Model Rule 5.7 -Responsibilities Regarding Law-related Services. However, when law-related services are provided by non-legal professional employees of the lawyer or law firm, the lawyer or firm in providing the law-related services must adhere to the requirements of the Rules of Professional Conduct as provided in Rule 5.7 (a) (1). When the law-related services are provided by non-legal professional employees in non-legal entities, the lawyer in providing the law-related services must take "reasonable measures" to assure that people who receive such services know that the services are not legal services, and that the "Rules of Professional Conduct that relate to the client-lawyer relationship do not apply." This is an area in which the legal profession continues to struggle. The struggle is spawned by the pressures continually building against the boundaries that define who lawyers are and what they do.

§ 1.06(a)(1) *Applying the Rules to the Hire of a Social Worker*

Usually, the first addition to the core staff of attorney, secretary, and paralegal is a social worker or case manager who can develop complex service plans and refer clients for services. The number of clients a case manager can effectively handle depends on the complexity of services and the number of clients who, at any given time, have a housing or health care crisis. If the case manager maintains ongoing contact with clients in the community, the caseload usually ranges from 40 to 70. Institutionalized clients require few services, so a manager can handle more cases.

In time, the case manager will develop cases with complex or intensive financial management needs. When client demands exceed the case manager's time and expertise, financial management is the service most likely to be delegated to another staffer with a minimum of additional effort. For all the client activity in which the social worker employee of the elder law attorney or firm is involved, there must be adherence to the state bar rules of professional conduct by the social worker. This could become difficult if the social worker only has education and experience with the ethics of the National Social Work Association. Even with knowledge and training in legal ethics, the social worker may be faced with conflicts between social work ethics and legal ethics that would impair the ability of the social worker to effectively serve clients of the lawyer or firm.

§ 1.06(a)(2) *Applying the Rules to the Hire of a Securities Analyst, Financial Planner or Certified Public Accountant*

If a client's assets are very substantial, financial management can be referred to a bank trust department or other corporate fiduciary. However, many elder law attorneys and firms find it more efficient and profitable to engage a financial manager to perform such duties as maintaining individual client accounts, making recommendations to the attorney concerning periodic investments, drafting checks, processing insurance claims, developing insurance portfolios and providing accounting and tax analysis and preparation. Initially, the most economical way to purchase these services is through a consulting contract or part-time department officer or financial planner. A caseload of affluent clients requires more sophisticated expertise that can best be provided by an attorney or other professional experienced in managing fiduciary estates.

When the financial services are provided in a separate entity other than the law firm, then the clients must be informed of the lack of legal ethics protection through measures considered to be reasonable. Like the social workers, certified public accountants have a code of ethics that should be examined against the ethics of lawyers.

§ 1.07 BONDING AND INSURANCE

Elder law firm workers who provide in-home services should be bonded by the firm in case of allegations of loss or theft. In most jurisdictions court-appointed fiduciaries are required by law to post a surety bond, although in some circumstances (generally family guardians) that requirement may be waived. Companies issuing such security bonds generally prefer to bond the fiduciary as an individual rather than the professional corporation. Even if the bond issues for the corporation, the company usually requires a personal guarantee from the attorney. This means that the attorney either must be appointed as fiduciary or must personally guarantee the actions of the firm as fiduciary. The advantages to having the corporation appointed include the flexibility of having any number of workers available to act for the client in time of need. However, the attorney's exposure for the action of other workers requires the firm to use generally accepted accounting principles in client financial management and to establish and rigorously follow protocols for client decision making. Every worker must understand the need for accurate, up-to-date records as the basis for decisions or services provision.

The elder law firm must also obtain insurance coverage, typically in the form of a policy for professional errors and omissions. The policy must provide coverage for the attorney or staff member acting in any of the variety of fiduciary capacities, including trustee, guardian, or conservator. The policy should also cover other staff members who provide direct services, such as help in the home or in transportation.

––––––––

In *"Elder-Comp, L.L.C." A Multi-Disciplinary Prototype for Tomorrow's Elder Law Practice*, 45 S.D. L. Rev. 540 (1999/2000), Professor Michael Myers proposes the natural development of successful multi-disciplinary elder law practice — a franchise or model that applies universally replicated standards and associations among professionals. After all, if it works, they (professionals and clients) will come. Evaluate the feasibility of the following proposal and its impact on the legal profession.

> "Elder-Comp, L.L.C.," the "McDonald's of Senior Services," a recognizable, one-stop firm providing comprehensive, integrated legal, financial and support services to seniors and caregivers. Elder-Comp ("Comp" is an abbreviated form of "comprehensive") offices could be adapted to towns and cities of all sizes, each responding to the demographic imperative of an aging society. They would be the "H & R Blocks" of elder law. Elder-Comp would contain professionals with knowledge of pensions, Social Security, Medicare and Medicaid, guardianships, trusts and estates, investments, income, estate and inheritance taxes, health, life and long-term care insurance, probate, nursing homes, assisted living and adult living commu-

nities. The multi-site Elder-Comp structure is designed to foster overlapping networks among its professionals. Traditionally such services have been characterized by fragmentation.

QUESTION

Absent changes to the ethical rules of most states, how can an elder law attorney structure ongoing, collaborative relationships with other professionals to meet client needs without running afoul of the ethical standards of the legal profession? Some have suggested that law schools should offer course work that would allow students to graduate with dual credentials as certified financial planners. Is there a down side to that proposal? How else could the goal be accomplished?

[2] LIMITED PURPOSE, DISCRETE TASK REPRESENTATION

Lawyers may be asked to participate in a less than comprehensive form of legal services delivery for the client who wants to save money or be active in his or her own representation. To fill the gap for seniors who cannot afford private attorney fees on a traditional, full professional service basis, but who are not eligible for government subsidized legal assistance, attorneys and advocates have devised approaches to bring together older clients and attorneys.

The concept of "unbundling" or discrete task legal representation seeks to make access to legal services affordable by explicitly providing the client with the option of choosing a single legal service. Advocates of unbundling assert that the private bar has failed to limit costs and offer adequate options to limited income clients, who should be given a voice in choosing which among the tasks the client will choose to perform independently. An often-discussed example is the client who engages a lawyer for advice and document preparation for a cause the client will argue *pro se*. Unbundling has received significant attention from legal organizations and commentators. The American Bar Association advocates unbundling as a way to stretch the limited resources of middle-class clients, including the elderly.

The concept of discrete task representation raises issues to make any lawyer or client wary no matter how attractive the prospect of affordable representation. Mary Helen McNeal, in *Redefining Attorney-Client Roles: Unbundling and Moderate-Income Elderly Clients*, 32 WAKE FOREST L. REV. 295 (1997), lists attorney-centered concerns about unbundling as including the absence of an ongoing attorney-client relationship, fear of ethical violations, court censure if the judge is critical of a client's self-representation, and malpractice liability; and worry about the client's success as a *pro se* litigant. Some lawyers, according to McNeal, believe that the client should be assisted by a paralegal, which might be appropriate except for representation in court. The client concerns, McNeal observes, are fewer:

> (1) whether the client can solve the problem better with discrete task representation than independently;

(2) whether the service will actually result in a solution to the problem; and

(3) what to do if the discrete task representation does not solve the problem. It is still unknown how discrete-task *pro se* litigants will fare in court, although judicial demands are often substantially reduced for pure *pro se* litigants.

The rules of ethics for every bar call for competent, diligent, and zealous representation (*see, e.g.*, Model Rules of Professional Conduct 1.1, 1.3). In departing from the full-service, lawyer-controlled, traditional model of representation, the evaluation of adequate representation requires new interpretation. Model Rule 1.1 states that competent representation, for example, requires the legal knowledge, skill, thoroughness, and preparation reasonably necessary for the representation. The Comments evaluate competence with reference to the skill of the general practitioner (Comment 1); the skill and knowledge, training and experience in the field in question . . . preparation and study (Comment 2); and (Comment 5) "inquiry into and analysis of the factual and legal elements of the problem, and use of methods and procedures meeting the standards of competent practitioners." While commentators have elaborated on the general requirements, the demands of discrete task representation are not well addressed.

The standards of diligence and zeal are no less problematic. The principal issue is likely to be when the duty of diligence, and the attorney-client relationship, ends. If the legal matter is ongoing, the point at which the client ceased to be a client is open to debate. The requirement of zeal is apparently more malleable, in that Comment 1 to Model Rule 1.3 instructs that the lawyer "is not bound to press for every advantage that might be realized for a client." The lawyer has "professional discretion in determining the means by which a matter should be pursued."

Malpractice liability depends on the terms of the contract between attorney and client, either expressed or implied, and which might consist solely of the client's detrimental reliance on the lawyer. There is no prohibition on representation for limited purposes. Model Rule 1.2(c) provides that a "lawyer may limit the objectives of the representation and shall consult with the client as to the means by which they are to be pursued." The Rule provides that the client must consent after consultation. In the uncharted territory of discrete task representation there is ample room for disagreement about the hazards of self-representation.

QUESTIONS

Consider the following questions in light of two different scenarios: Would this discrete task representation be acceptable to you? Would you feel obliged to acquiesce to discrete task representation if the client cannot afford full representation and would go without legal advice? If your response to each scenario differs, why?

1. Mrs. Jones, age 82, homemaker, widow of a factory worker, is engaged in a property tax dispute which she has adamantly ignored for years, asserting the city had no right to change the assessment of her home and small adjoining store. Mrs. Jones comes to you for advice as to her legal arguments and rights as a final administrative hearing approaches, immediately after which the property might be

put up for sale at foreclosure. Mrs. Jones wants to argue her own case.

2. Mr. Yafin, age 67, who immigrated to the U.S. over a decade ago, is engaged in a growing dispute with his condominium residential association about plantings he has added that are arguably contrary to association rules. He and his wife refuse to remove them, and the association president (a volunteer position held by another resident) threatens to have them removed at Mr. Yafin's expense in five days. The option for intervention is to request a temporary injunction against that action. Mr. Yafin wants to argue his own case.

[3] PARALEGAL ASSISTANCE

The use of trained, supervised paralegal assistance is very common among elder law attorneys. What activities associated with legal work can be undertaken by a paralegal or social worker?

ALISON BARNES, A. FRANK JOHNS & NATHALIE MARTIN,
COUNSELING OLDER CLIENTS
(ALI-ABA 2005)*

§ 1.05 THE USE OF PARALEGALS

Many attorneys use paralegal personnel to assist in the varied functions of an elder law office. Paralegal personnel can conduct initial interviews, discuss general options, gather facts, and obtain signatures. Clients will nearly always agree to consult with the paralegal when they understand the financial benefit of the reduced hourly fee. The initial fee agreement should include an explanation of the paralegal's role under supervision of the attorney and the hourly rate.

Paralegals in elder law usually bring to their work training either in social work or in law. Some are former hospital or social service case managers. A paralegal experienced in other areas of the law still requires training in the special needs of the elderly. There are various ways of acquiring the necessary skills: articles in gerontology and social work publications, social service training sessions in community agencies, and formal or informal consultations with other staff members. Once hired, a paralegal must be trained in unfamiliar areas at firm expense.

Paralegals with a background in social services are particularly valuable in law offices because their expertise complements, rather than duplicates, the attorney's legal skills. They are familiar with community resources like home-health agencies and transportation networks and, on instruction from the attorney, can assess the need for particular services and identify providers.

Four tasks are routinely carried out by paralegal assistants: identifying client needs by determining from the client's story the issues which require legal or other advocacy assistance; providing assistance through informal advocacy (a telephone call or letter to a public agency); serving as an intermediary by informing clients of

---

the issues raised by their claims, identifying the type of legal assistance needed, and making referral to an attorney or legal services program, when necessary; acting as a group or community spokesperson by speaking out on behalf of the elderly at public hearings or by contacting a public agency concerning a systematic or administrative problem which causes difficulties for many clients.

[4] PRO BONO ASSISTANCE

The private bar has responded to the needs of the low-income elderly. Most state bars maintain referral panels of attorneys who volunteer to provide free and discounted legal assistance to poor older clients. In Florida, for example, panels are available for low-income and elderly individuals who receive an initial consultation for little or no fee. If more complex legal assistance is needed, the attorney and client can negotiate a reduced fee. Many state bars have elder law committees, which typically provide public information through pamphlets and talks to civic groups and perform other public service activities.

Attorney *pro bono* services cannot reliably fill any community's need for legal assistance, however. There are never enough volunteers, and those who do volunteer may be caught in a bind between the time demands of paying clients and the needs of the pro bono client. The obligation to a paying client will usually be met first, perhaps to the detriment of the client receiving pro bono services. Indeed this is one of the reasons for creating the American system of full-time legal services attorneys, rather than a program like the British "judicare" system in which the government pays a private attorney a flat fee to represent an indigent client. The legal services attorney has no other clients to divert his or her attention.

Pro bono and discount assistance also raise questions about the quality of service. Volunteer and reduced fee attorneys are often those who are still building a practice. Even experienced attorneys may be inexperienced in the particular needs of the elderly and the poor. Unless experienced advisors are available to assist volunteer attorneys the result may be errors, delay, and less than optimum solutions for the client.

QUESTIONS

1. The use of pro bono legal assistance in which each private practitioner devotes a percentage of time to handling legal assistance cases is often frustrating because of lack of substantive knowledge, scheduling conflicts, and communications problems. Would it be preferable for lawyers just to make cash contributions to local legal assistance programs?

2. Would the "judicare" model, described above, be better for clients? For lawyers?

C. COUNSELING THE ELDERLY CLIENT

Common-law practice issues of time management and client communications often are more difficult with elderly clients.

ALISON BARNES, A. FRANK JOHNS & NATHALIE MARTIN,
COUNSELING OLDER CLIENTS
(ALI-ABA 2005)*

§ 1.04 RELATIONSHIP BETWEEN ATTORNEY AND ELDERLY CLIENT

Establishing an elder law practice requires an ability and willingness to accept personal responsibility for the care and well being of others; an ability to recruit, train, and retain high-quality, dedicated staff; and an ability to delegate responsibility effectively. When a client is referred for services from a specific outside provider, the firm assumes responsibility for making certain these services are provided safely, economically, and efficiently.

An attorney who specializes in the problems of the elderly is aware of their special needs and issues and can, at a minimum, counsel the client to seek specified, non-legal assistance from identified sources. The client can reasonably expect the lawyer to assist in arranging services, and the lawyer should expect the client to return for further assistance as circumstances change. The client with multiple, ongoing problems is the mainstay of the elder law firm.

Perhaps the single greatest impediment to a sole practitioner's assuming broad responsibility for elderly clients with complex service needs is the necessity of a 24-hour-a-day, on-call system for the firm. Emergencies, particularly medical emergencies, are not restricted to a nine-to-five schedule and can sometimes require a staff member to respond in person. (Fortunately, many apparent emergencies can be dealt with simply and expeditiously.)

Even the most conscientious attorney cannot ensure that community services will be delivered flawlessly or will be effective in meeting the client's needs. The limits of the attorney's responsibility should be included in a written fee agreement executed by the client at the outset.

———————

A thorough initial interview is fundamental to the development of a plan for effective counsel. These practical aspects of elder law practice, which can be summarized in a paragraph or two, require planning and consistent use until they become habits for the elder law attorney. They are the basis without which the most brilliant legal pyrotechnics are likely to be misdirected and ineffective.

For example, the information gleaned from a thorough interview allows the attorney to assess any financial or housing choices in terms of that client's likely future. Medical information may be important. Before making a commitment to a life care facility which entails an initial endowment of up to $450,000, for example, the client should have an expectation of surviving and need long-term care. Clients with smaller estates are sometimes tempted to give away their assets in order to qualify for Medicaid, although such action, when discovered by state authorities, may cause the client to be ineligible for benefits. In fact, such a client is giving away

———————

the option to pay for home care and thereby risks being institutionalized all the sooner. An attorney should be well prepared to advise clients of the realities, knowing that the motivation to avoid spending on nursing home care, a very unwanted commodity, is not entirely rational.

An elder law attorney must adapt to the special needs of elderly clients, some of whom have physical or mental impairments. A face-to-face interview is always desirable, but some elderly cannot travel to the attorney's office, so most elder law attorneys make house calls. Conducting interviews in the client's home allows the client to sit where he or she usually prefers and presumably can see well, in addition to reducing the stress of unfamiliar office surroundings.

To adequately serve clients who do come to the attorney's office, the interview room should have good, indirect lighting to reduce the effects of glare. Sitting in front of a bright window, for example, makes the attorney's face almost invisible to many persons with deteriorated vision. Background noise and music should be kept to a minimum, particularly for clients with hearing aids that amplify all sounds.

An initial interview with an elderly client may take longer than a similar interview with a younger person even if there are no particular impediments to communication. Some elderly individuals are suspicious of attorneys, having had few legal transactions over a lifetime. Building trust requires taking time to establish a common frame of reference: the facts of the problems, the choices available, and the reasons for recommendations. In addition the elderly person may have legal needs beyond the stated need, which will be identified only in a thorough interview.

Attorneys must be very sensitive to the effect of medication on their older clients. For example, an elderly woman who is the subject of a guardianship proceeding at the time of the legal interview may be alert and rational. When seen after emergency admission to the geriatric ward of a psychiatric hospital, however, she may be confused and paranoid, a condition which may be the direct result of medication. The attorney should be alert to abrupt changes in a client's personality, be aware of medications the client is taking, and use a Physician's Desk Reference book on prescription drugs and expert advice to understand the effects of medications.

A key to successful counseling is the attorney's insight into his or her personal preconceptions, attitudes, and responses to the client. Lawyers must be cognizant of the stress of working with elderly clients who, perhaps more than others, may fear their own mortality or feel anger, guilt, or regret at their experiences and behavior. Interpersonal dynamics however need cause no more difficulties in elder law than in other types of legal practice as long as the attorney is sensitive that his or her values and aspirations may not be the same as the client's.

QUESTIONS

1.   Written correspondence to an elderly client reinforces the oral advice given at the legal interview by restating it in the clearest terms for the client to reread later. How would you draft and print your letter to assure that your client understands it?

2. How can you tell if your client can hear or understand you? If the client cannot hear, but will not freely say so, how would you handle the problem?

D. ETHICAL ISSUES

In many ways the ethical issues regarding older clients differ little from those involved in representation of younger persons. The lawyer must fulfill for each client the duties of diligent representation, zealous advocacy, and communication to enable the client to make informed choices. Any differences because the client is age 85 instead of 35 are not subject to stereotypical generalizations except possibly for the press of passing time. The "need for haste" discussed in Chapter 1, the need to conduct the matter with an eye on the calendar, is a consideration the lawyer should not lightly ignore.

[1] SOURCES OF THE ETHICAL STANDARDS

The ethics of the legal profession are governed by standards adopted by each state bar. State ethics codes are based on two sets of ethical rules promulgated by the American Bar Association: The Model Code of Professional Responsibility (the Code) and the Model Rules of Professional Conduct (the Model Rules). The Code, adopted by the ABA in 1959, consists of three related parts, or levels, of instruction to the lawyer: the Canons, which state the standards of conduct normally expected; the Ethical Considerations, based on the Canons, which provide guidance toward ideal conduct or goals the attorney should strive for; and the Disciplinary Rules, which state the conduct necessary to avoid disciplinary action.

The Model Rules of Professional Conduct, adopted in 1983, have superseded the Code in many states. The Model Rules consist of mandatory statements (the Rules) that the attorney must abide by or be subject to disciplinary action. In most instances the Model Rules are followed by Comments which provide guidance for complying with the Rules. The Comments do not, however, create ethical obligations and deviation from them does not expose the attorney to official censure.

Because the state bars debate and amend the language of the ABA rules, ethical requirements vary somewhat from state to state. In addition each state bar has developed a body of standards through the opinions of its disciplinary committee. As a result some states permit the attorney to make decisions or engage in behavior which would be subject to censure in another state. State variations are reported in HAZARD & HODES, THE LAW OF LAWYERING, A HANDBOOK ON THE MODEL RULES OF PROFESSIONAL CONDUCT.

[2] WHO IS THE CLIENT?

Usually when an individual contacts a lawyer the possibility of confusion as to who is the client is limited. Frequently, however, an elderly person's family is involved in advising, assisting, and even directing financial and practical arrangements for care and property management, particularly during extreme old age or disability. A typical scenario for the elder law attorney includes an office visit, perhaps during the holiday season, when the out-of-state adult children are visiting Mom or Dad. The elderly individual arrives accompanied by at least one child (or niece or grandchild), who may have made the appointment and might provide much of the information the attorney receives about the client, the client's property, and the proposed plan to sell the house or distribute the stock and securities in order to avoid long-term care costs or a costly probate. The elderly individual who is the subject of the plan (and property owner) may say very little, apparently acquiescing to the arrangements proposed by the others, though the plan may leave that individual little control and few future options.

The attorney must first identify the client, who may be the elderly individual, or other family members (one or more of them), or all. The attorney who undertakes to represent only the elderly person must explain fully to other family members the limitations this will impose on interactions with them, including the confidentiality of the attorney-client relationship (Model Code Canon 4; Model Rule 1.6, discussed in more detail below).

The attorney might doubt that there is real agreement between the generations. To complicate matters, other adult children or family members may later contact the attorney by telephone or in person to question or challenge some aspect of the plan or the involvement of the adult child or other relative who accompanied the elder to the office.

The attorney may represent several members of a family if there is no apparent conflict of interest. There must, however, be true unity of interests for the attorney to fulfill the duties of the client-lawyer relationship with regard to all and the attorney must explain those requirements to the client family. The attorney's ability to represent various family members depends upon whether the attorney can fulfill his or her obligations to each individual, which include loyalty (i.e., avoiding conflicts of interest — Model Code Canon 5, Model Rule 1.7); competency and diligence (Model Code Canon 6, Model Rule 1.1) (the newer standard of diligence is somewhat different from the older standard of neglect); zealous advocacy (Model Code Canon 7, Model Rules 1.1, 1.2); and communication sufficient to enable the client (i.e., the designated representative of the family) to make informed decisions about the representation (Model Code EC 7-8, Model Rule 1.4).

Avoidance of conflicts of interest is particularly important. The Model Code, DR 5-105, and Model Rule 1.7(b), require that the attorney avoid direct conflicts between clients when helping one client will cause harm to another client. Model Rule 1.7(b) also prohibits indirect conflicts in which the interest of others, or the lawyer's own personal interest (*see also* Model Code DR 5-101), biases the advice given or diminishes zealous advocacy for the client. EC 5-15 says:

> If a lawyer is requested to undertake or to continue representation of multiple clients having potentially differing interests, he must weigh carefully the possibility that his judgment may be impaired or his loyalty divided if he accepts or continues the employment. He should resolve all doubts against the propriety of the representation. . . . A lawyer may properly serve multiple clients having potentially differing interests in matters not involving litigation. If the interests vary only slightly, it is

generally likely that the lawyer will not be subjected to an adverse influence and that he can retain his independent judgment on behalf of each client; and, if the interests become differing, withdrawal is less likely to have a disruptive effect upon the causes of his clients [than would withdrawal during litigation].

Generally, if there is any conflict of interest between the elderly person and any other family member, the attorney may represent one or the other but not both. The attorney who initially fails to discern a conflict of interest and forms a relationship with several members of a family must consider DR 2-110 or Rule 1.16 on withdrawal when a conflict becomes apparent. Generally the attorney may withdraw if continued representation is likely to result in a breach of another ethical provision (such as the requirements of confidentiality). However, the Rule requires that the lawyer assure that the withdrawal "can be accomplished without material adverse effect on the interests of the client" and the Code similarly requires "reasonable steps to avoid foreseeable prejudice to the rights of [the] client." DR 2-100(A)(2).

Rule 1.7,* Conflict of Interest: Current Clients (as amended by the Ethics 2000 Commission), provides:

(a) Except as provided in paragraph (b), a lawyer shall not represent a client if the representation involves a concurrent conflict of interest. A concurrent conflict of interest exists if:

(1) the representation of one client will be directly adverse to another client; or

(2) there is a significant risk that the representation of one or more clients will be materially limited by the lawyer's responsibilities to another client, a former client or a third person or by a personal interest of the lawyer.

(b) Notwithstanding the existence of a concurrent conflict of interest under paragraph (a), a lawyer may represent a client if:

(1) the lawyer reasonably believes that the lawyer will be able to provide competent and diligent representation of each affected client;

(2) the representation is not prohibited by law;

(3) the representation does not involve the assertion of a claim by one client against another client represented by the lawyer in the same litigation or other proceeding before a tribunal; and

(4) each affected client gives informed consent, confirmed in writing.

The ethical issues that arise from intergeneration representation are central to the attorneys' dilemmas in the following case:

IN RE GUARDIANSHIP OF LILLIAN P.
617 N.W.2d 849 (Wis. Ct. App. 2000)

Vincent J. Guerrero, guardian ad litem for Lillian P., the subject of a guardianship and protective placement, appeals the circuit court's denial of his motion to disqualify attorney Patricia M. Cavey from the dual representation of Lillian P. and her son, Lester P. Guerrero contends Cavey has a conflict of interest that Lillian was incapable of waiving. The circuit court noted a conflict, but it did not disqualify Cavey because attorney Jack Longert agreed to act as co-counsel to Cavey during her representation of Lillian. Because we conclude that a conflict of interest existed, that Lillian was not competent to waive that conflict, and that Longert's appearance as co-counsel to Cavey did not negate Cavey' conflict of interest, we reverse the circuit court's order, which permitted Cavey"s continued representation of Lillian.

BACKGROUND

On July 28, 1998, Lillian P., a woman who was then almost ninety years old, was found to be incompetent due to a form of dementia. The circuit court appointed a guardian of her property and of her person, and she was protectively placed. Initially, the court appointed Mely Arndt, who had a long-standing relationship with Lillian, as her guardian, and Lillian was protectively placed in her own house, with services provided by Jefferson County Human Services Department. Lester P., one of Lillian's sons, and Lester's son, Jeremy, lived with Lillian. In October of 1998, notice was given to the court and interested persons, including Lester through the attorney who was then representing him, that Lillian's placement had been changed to a community-based residential facility (CBRF) because she required more care than she was able to receive at home. The notice stated: "If anyone wishes to contest this change in placement, they may do so by sending a written request to the Jefferson County Register in Probate, Jefferson County Courthouse, 320 South Main Street, Jefferson, Wisconsin, 53549." Lester did not object to the removal of Lillian from her house. In January of 1999, Cavey filed a notice of appearance as counsel for Lester and a petition that he be permitted to purchase Lillian's house for $70,000. Also in January, Arndt, as guardian of Lillian's estate, filed a petition to sell Lillian's house. She submitted an appraisal, which valued the property at $90,000. Lillian's other two sons, Robert and Dean, both notified the court that they believed it was in Lillian's best interest to sell the house, but at a market-based price. The circuit court then appointed Guerrero as guardian ad litem for Lillian to assist in the determination of whether selling her house was in her best interests. On March 12, 1999, the circuit court denied Lester's petition to purchase Lillian's house for $70,000 and granted Arndt's petition to put the house on the market, subject to confirmation of sale by the court. Apparently, prior to March 12th, the court had directed that Lester pay rent for his occupancy of the house. Arndt requested that he pay $650 per month, which rent included electricity and heat for the house. According to the record before this court, Lester did not do so. On March 30, 1999, Arndt filed a petition to confirm the sale of Lillian's house to a third party for $115,000. Also on March 30th, Cavey, acting on Lester's behalf, objected to confirmation and moved for a Watts review of Lillian's placement.

On April 7, 1999, Arndt, who is an adult foster child of Lillian, filed her annual report as guardian of Lillian's person. In it she noted that she had visited Lillian weekly, as well as contacting her by telephone, and that "her son [is] trying [to] manipulate her well being." Shortly thereafter she wrote the court, resigning as guardian due to conflicts she had with Lester and Cavey. The court appointed Lutheran Social Services as successor guardian. On April 16, 1999 pretrial was held on Lester's motions objecting to the confirmation of the sale of Lillian's house and review of her placement. There, Cavey told the court for the first time that she represented both Lester and Lillian in objecting to the sale and in requesting a Watts review of Lillian's placement. Cavey stated that Lillian had signed a retainer agreement, a release of confidential information and a statement which outlined the "risks and benefits" of her dual representation of Lillian and Lester. She submitted none of these documents to the court. Cavey argued that Lillian told her that she wanted to go home and therefore objected to the sale. Guerrero, whom the circuit court then appointed to act as Lillian's guardian ad litem in regard to any Watts review as well as the proposed sale of her house, raised the ethical implications of Cavey's dual representation, calling it "a classic conflict of interest with her representation of [Lillian] and [Lester]. . . ."

After Guerrero moved to disqualify Cavey from representing Lillian, the court scheduled another hearing to address that issue. At that hearing, Cavey said that she recognized a potential conflict of interest but saw no actual conflict. She said that Lillian had signed a written waiver, thereby permitting her dual representation. Attorney Jack Longert of Legal Action of Wisconsin, Inc. also appeared for Lillian at that hearing. Longert said that if a conflict developed between Lillian and Lester, he would represent Lillian. The circuit court was concerned about having Lillian's estate pay for legal services that Cavey would have provided to benefit Lester. Cavey opined that she could be paid only if the court determined her services were "necessaries" under the law. Longert said no fees would be charged for his services, as Lillian qualified for free legal services under Legal Action's standards. Based on these representations, the circuit court denied Guerrero's motion to disqualify Cavey. Guerrero appeals. Cavey then moved this court to conclude that Guerrero's appeal is frivolous.

DISCUSSION

Conflict of Interest

An attorney is prohibited from representing multiple clients with adverse interests unless certain conditions are met. *See* SCR 20:1.7. A lawyer's duty to promote his or her client's interests exists in civil and in criminal law. If the representation of two or more clients by the same counsel is serial (i.e., involving a past and a current client) and an objection is made to such representation in the circuit court, we apply a two-part test to determine whether an attorney should be disqualified. "In order to prevail on a motion to disqualify an attorney, the moving party must establish: (1) that an attorney-client relationship existed between the attorney and the former client; and (2) that there is a substantial relationship between the two representations." *Burkes v. Hales*, 478 N.W.2d 37, 40 (Ct. App. 1991) (citation omitted).

If the representation is dual (i.e., one attorney is representing two parties in the same action) the circuit court will not be faced with the two-part test of Burkes. Rather, it will need to answer two questions: (1) whether the attorney "has undertaken representation which is adverse to the interests of a present client or the interests of a third party with whom the attorney has a substantial relationship," *La Crosse County Dep't of Soc. Servs. v. Rose K.*, 537 N.W.2d 142, 145 (Ct. App.1995), and (2) whether the client has made a knowing, voluntary, written waiver of actual and potential conflicts inherent in the representation. and to 'avoid . . . even the appearance of professional impropriety.' " *Berg*, 416 N.W.2d at 647 (citation omitted). The circuit court is not required to make a finding that a breach of ethical standards or client confidentiality has occurred, but only to conclude that the attorney has undertaken representation that is adverse to the interests of a client. There need not be an actual conflict of interest; a serious potential conflict of interest is enough for a circuit court in the exercise of its discretion, to disqualify an attorney.

The rule that an attorney should generally be disqualified if a conflict or serious potential for conflict exists was established to " 'preserve the confidences and secrets of a client.' "

In the case at hand, Cavey has represented to the circuit court and to this court that she is providing dual representation to Lester and Lillian in regard to objecting to the confirmation of the sale of Lillian's house and also in regard to the Watts review of Lillian's placement. Because Guerrero has objected to Cavey's representation of Lillian, we must determine whether Cavey has undertaken a representation which is adverse to Lillian's interests. We begin by noting that " '[d]oubts as to the existence of an asserted conflict of interest should be resolved in favor of disqualification.' " *Berg*, 416 N.W.2d at 648 (citation omitted). We find guidance in *Rose K.*, where we considered whether an attorney who prosecuted a father in a paternity action and represented the county in child support enforcement actions could also act as the guardian ad litem for those same children in a CHIPS proceeding. In doing so, we examined the practical effects of dual representation. In our analysis, we asked: Should [the attorney] commence a support action and satisfy her client, the state, and a person with whom she has a contractual relationship, [the county]? Or should she not do so because her other clients, [the] children, could use the extra money for an item not provided through AFDC payments? If [the father] fails to pay what is ordered, should [the attorney] attempt to incarcerate him, thus depriving the children of a father? These conflicts are real, and they place [the attorney] in a position that no attorney should face: deciding which of two clients she will serve."

The conflicts of interest here are as real as they were in *Rose K.*, and they have similar practical effects on the two potential clients. First, Lester is seeking to purchase Lillian's house at a below-market price. He is objecting to Lillian's guardian's petition to confirm a sale for $40,000 more than he has offered. Second,

Lester is living in Lillian's house without paying rent. Lillian's guardian has requested $650 per month. Third, it is in Lester's interest to persuade Lillian to seek a change in her protective placement from the CBRF to her house, so his wishes in regard to purchasing the house have a better opportunity for realization.

Lester argues that his interests are not inconsistent with Lillian's because she wants to return home. However, all the medical reports in the record and the representations of the guardian ad litem show that returning to her house may not be in Lillian's best interests. Furthermore, the house has expenses for its maintenance which Lester's rental payments would help to defray, whether Lillian returns home or not. Further, if Lillian is unable to return home, it may be in her best interest to sell the house at the highest price available. Lillian has two other sons who are in agreement to sell the house, but not at less than fair market value. However, if Cavey is to vigorously represent Lester, she must try to find ways to block the sale to the buyer secured by Arndt, she must advocate for Lester to live rent-free, and she must try to establish that Lillian should have the opportunity to return to her house, even if to do so would be contrary to Lillian's well being. Furthermore, in her efforts to help Lester, Cavey's actions have been noted by Arndt as the reason she could not continue as Lillian's guardian. Lillian's guardian ad litem has noted similar concerns about Cavey's aggressiveness on behalf of Lester. Therefore, based on the record before us, we conclude that Lillian's and Lester's interests are adverse, resulting in a conflict of interest in Cavey's representation of Lillian.

Waiver of Conflict

Having determined that Lester and Lillian's interests are adverse, we must next address Cavey's assertion that Lillian consented to the dual representation after full disclosure, thereby waiving any conflicts of interest. Cavey states that she disclosed to Lillian the "risks and benefits" of the dual representation and that Lillian signed a document waiving all conflicts, consistent with SCR 20:1.7(b). Therefore, Cavey claims there is no basis for her disqualification. Supreme Court Rule 20:1.7 addresses how an attorney should proceed once a conflict or potential conflict of interest has been established. It provides: Conflict of interest: general rule. (a) A lawyer shall not represent a client if the representation of that client will be directly adverse to another client, unless: (1) the lawyer reasonably believes the representation will not adversely affect the relationship with the other client; and (2) each client consents in writing after consultation. (b) A lawyer shall not represent a client if the representation of that client may be materially limited by the lawyer's responsibilities to another client or to a third person, or by the lawyer's own interests, unless: (1) the lawyer reasonably believes the representation will not be adversely affected; and (2) the client consents in writing after consultation. When representation of multiple clients in a single matter is undertaken, the consultation shall include explanation of the implications of the common representation and the advantages and risks involved. The parties dispute whether our analysis of this conflict should be taken under (a) or (b). However, both (a) and (b) require written consent by both clients before a waiver is effective. Having determined that a conflict of interest exists, we turn our attention to whether Lillian, who has been declared incompetent, can knowingly and voluntarily waive the conflict, thereby consenting to the dual representation. We conclude that she is legally incapable of doing so. Whether a person who has been adjudicated incompetent, such that a guardian of her person and property and a protective placement are required, has the capacity to waive a conflict of interest is a matter of first impression in Wisconsin. In order to resolve the question presented, we examine whether a knowing and voluntary waiver is possible in such circumstances.

"An effective waiver of a conflict or potential conflict of interest which is knowing and voluntary requires the lawyer to disclose the following: (1) the existence of all conflicts or potential conflicts in the representation; (2) the nature of the conflicts or potential conflicts, in relationship to the lawyer's representation of the client's interests; and (3) that the exercise of the lawyer's independent professional judgment could be affected by the lawyer's own interests or those of another client. On the part of the client, it also requires: (1) an understanding of the conflicts or potential conflicts and how they could affect the lawyer's representation of the client; (2) an understanding of the risks inherent in the dual representation then under consideration; and (3) the ability to choose other representation.

Here, the record contains no representation by Cavey of what she disclosed to Lillian in regard to her opinion of the conflicts or potential conflicts of interest inherent in her dual representation in this action or what effect such conflicts may have on her representation of Lillian. Indeed, Cavey represented to the court there were no conflicts. Likewise, the record contains no testimony of what Lillian might have understood about the conflicts which we have identified or her understanding of the effect they could have on Cavey's representation of her. However, we note that when a client consents to dual representation in the face of a conflict of interest, that consent puts the client on notice that the attorney's loyalty may become impaired at some juncture. Therefore, the client's understanding is a necessary component of dual representation. Here, by asserting that Lillian consented to the dual representation, Cavey in essence contends that Lillian has the ability to fully understand all that dual representation imports. However, Cavey has never contended that the circuit court erred when it found Lillian incompetent under the law. Further, the petition for guardianship and protective placement for Lillian was granted because the court determined that Lillian could not care for herself and that she was confused and not oriented to place or time. The record also reflects that Lillian's dementia has progressed to the point where she has required emergency commitments to Mendota Mental Health Institute due to increasing confusion and anxiety which have resulted in physical attacks on her caregivers and on other patients. There is nothing in the record which even suggests that Lillian has the capacity to knowingly consent to the dual representation proposed by Cavey. Therefore, because Lillian has been adjudicated incompetent such that a guardian of her person and property and a protective placement are required, we conclude that, as a matter of law, Lillian was incapable of making a knowing and voluntary waiver of the conflict of interest Cavey has. Accordingly, any waiver executed by Lillian is invalid, and Cavey was never lawfully retained by Lillian.

The circuit court recognized the existence of the conflict of interest. However, the court denied the guardian ad litem's motion for disqualification because it believed Lillian would receive adequate representation so long as Longert remained Lillian's co-counsel to ensure loyalty to her affairs. While we understand the court's rationale, having co-counsel for Lillian does not negate our conclusion that Cavey has an impermissible conflict of interest and therefore cannot represent Lillian. Longert's presence does not resolve Cavey's conflict of interest, nor does it provide a substitute for Lillian's knowing and voluntary waiver. Accordingly, we conclude that the circuit court erred in denying Guerrero's motion to disqualify Cavey from representing Lillian.

CONCLUSION

Because we conclude that a conflict of interest existed, that Lillian was not competent to waive that conflict, and that Longert's appearance as co-counsel to Cavey did not negate Cavey's conflict of interest, we reverse the circuit court's order, which permitted Cavey's continued representation of Lillian. Order reversed.

The Model Rules regarding representation of multiple clients are not drafted with families in mind.

Rule 1.7 applies specifically to common clients with the establishing of or adjusting their relationship with a non-client. Such clients might be considered as one client, with a lawyer's duty to inform and advocate for the joint client. The lawyer could — initially and throughout — act on a presumption of harmonious objectives, and withhold information adverse to the common good. All must waive confidentiality with regard to the representation. However, there could be no adequate consent to a violation of the lawyer's duty or of material adverse effect on the interests of an individual. If such a conflict arose (and the presumption of harmony failed), the lawyer could withdraw from the representation of anyone who no longer "fit" within the common client.

The Comments to MR 1.7 include the following language:

[2] Resolution of a conflict of interest problem under this Rule requires the lawyer to:

(1) clearly identify the client or clients;

(2) determine whether a conflict of interest exists;

(3) determine whether the representation may be undertaken despite the existence of a conflict (i.e., whether the conflict is consent-able; and

(4) if so, consult with the clients . . . and obtain their informed consent, confirmed in writing.

. . . .

[29] In considering whether to represent multiple clients in the same matter, a lawyer should be mindful that if the common representation fails because the potentially adverse interests cannot be reconciled, the result can be additional cost, embarrassment and recrimination. Ordinarily, the

lawyer will be forced to withdraw from representing all of the clients if the common representation fails. . . . [B]ecause the lawyer is required to be impartial between commonly represented clients, representation of multiple clients is improper when it is unlikely that impartiality can be maintained. . . .

[30] A particularly important factor in determining the appropriateness of common representation is the effect on client-lawyer confidentiality. . . .

[31] As to the duty of confidentiality, continued common representation will almost certainly be inadequate if one client asks the lawyer not to disclose to the other client information relevant to the common representation. This is so because the lawyer has an equal duty of loyalty to each client, and each client has the right to be informed of anything bearing on the representation that might affect that client's interests and the right to expect that the lawyer will use that information to that client's benefit. The lawyer should at the outset of the common representation and as part of the process of obtaining each client's informed consent, advise each client that information will be shared and that the lawyer will have to withdraw if one client decides that some matter material to the representation should be kept from the other. . . .

[32] When seeking to establish or adjust a relationship between clients, the lawyer should make clear that the lawyer's role is not that of partisanship normally expected in other circumstances and, thus, that the clients may be required to assume greater responsibility for decisions than when each client is separately represented. Any limitations on the scope of the representation made necessary as a result of the common representation should be fully explained to the clients at the outset of the representation.

With regard to waiver of a conflict, new language in the Comment to MR 1.7[18] states:

Informed consent requires that each affected client be aware of the relevant circumstances and of the material and reasonably foreseeable ways that the conflict could have adverse effects on the interests of that client. The information depends on the nature of the conflict and the nature of the risks involved.

Is it possible that a lawyer skilled in communication with very elderly people could communicate the nature of the problem to one in Lillian's circumstances? How can the problem be expressed most simply for a client of limited understanding?

QUESTION

Clearly, things are simpler in terms of legal ethics if the elderly individual is the only client. Why would an attorney choose to try common representation that includes one or more family members?

Model Rule 1.7 states: "The payment of a lawyer's fee by another is permissible, so long as payment does not compromise the loyalty of the lawyer to the client." Rule 1.8(f)(1) states: "A lawyer shall not accept compensation for representing a client from one other than the client unless . . . the client consents after consultation." The Code also requires that the lawyer obtain consent from a client before agreeing to accept payment from a third party. DR5-107(A)(1) and (B). The lawyer who is to be paid by a family member may find it difficult to collect fees if the attorney declines to act as the payer prefers.

[3] CONFIDENTIALITY AND WITHDRAWAL

The requirements of the Model Rules call for withdrawal from representation of some or all in the family when a conflict of interest, often because of a potential breach of confidentiality, renders representation of less than all members unethical.

Withdrawal is unusual, for the good reason that a client who perceives the reason the lawyer withdraws while maintaining confidentiality can find another lawyer and avoid or conceal the problem.

Consider the following about a conflict arising in representation of spouses, in which the husband asserts an intention contrary to the joint plan, and seeks to conceal it:

> In the absence of a clear rule, a balancing test has been suggested: L(awyer) should weigh the known harm from nondisclosure (at least a partial defeat of H(usband)'s testamentary intentions) against the uncertain harm flowing from disclosure — at the extreme, a possible marital rupture or divorce. The balancing test may be useful in situations where L knows his clients fairly well and may be able to gauge the possibility of marital rupture rather precisely. [Generally], however, L does not have any longstanding relationship with either H or W. Should L decide against disclosure, when deciding to withdraw L will also need to consider whether his inability to serve H loyally outweighs the possibility of disclosure inherent in an unexplained withdrawal.

Burnele Powell & Ronald C. Link, *The Sense of a Client: Confidentiality Issues in Representing the Elderly*, 62 FORDHAM L. REV. 1196, 1206 (1994).

The ethics rules do not distinguish husband and wife from other family relationships, but an attorney often more readily assumes a unity of interest between spouses (perhaps especially in estate planning). One survey noted that 75 percent of estate planners surveyed did not comply with the formal ethics rules. *See* Malcolm A. Moore & Jeffrey N. Pennell, *Practicing What We Preach: Esoteric or Essential?*, 27 U. MIAMI PHILIP E. HECKERLING INST. ON EST. PLANNING § 12-10 (1993). A justification offered is that the ethics rules reflect the "radical individualism" of the 19th century, while a more realistic, holistic view would emphasize accord within the family and particularly between spouses.

The Real Property Section of the American Bar Association endorsed a substantial departure from the ethical rules in the form of two recommendations: First, that the lawyer may assume that each spouse will fulfill the ethical obligations of the marriage commitment and, second, that the ethics rules should be construed to "provide appropriate delivery of legal services without excessive cost or duplication of services, and fulfillment of client expectations about the lawyer's role whenever possible." Certainly, spouses nearly always share such goals as providing for the survivor and for their children still in need of support and education, and minimizing costs and taxes. Once assets are substantial, however, significant differences may arise. One spouse may doubt that her partner or children are appropriate recipients of an outright gift and prefer management by a trustee. Even if spouses favor a trust, they may differ on when it should end and give the younger generation full control. Successive marriages create more complex interests, particularly if stepchildren are part of the estate plan. Notably, the most frequent and bitter conflicts arise between the stepparent and children of a prior marriage or relationship.

On occasion a couple will have entered into a prenuptial agreement. About the significance of such a document in estate planning, attorney Barbara Freedman Wand writes:

> When an estate planner is asked to represent both a husband and wife who have already executed a prenuptial agreement, the existence of the agreement should alert the estate planner that there are contractual obligations between the parties that may raise a potential conflict of interest. The spouses may disagree about the interpretation of and the mode of fulfilling the obligations undertaken in the agreement. In addition, the factors that are often catalysts for the execution of a prenuptial agreement — such as significant gifted or inherited wealth, or a second marriage — may suggest possible conflicting interests between the spouses.

While there is no prohibition on representing husband and wife in these circumstances, the lawyer must be sure to fulfill ethical obligations of loyalty and confidentiality to the clients. The assumption should be that the clients authorize the attorney to make full disclosure to each of them. If, after giving that consent, one of the spouses confides in the attorney and requires confidentiality on any matter touching on the representation, the attorney is obliged to withdraw from the representation of both without divulging the "secret."

E.   MEDIATION AND OLDER CLIENTS

Alternative forms of dispute resolution, particularly mediation, have been suggested as economical, speedy methods to resolve problems which often trouble elderly clients, such as consumer complaints, landlord-tenant disputes, and residential association disagreements. Mediation is increasingly required by contracts in health care and employment. In the health care field, for example, insurers and managed care providers routinely require mediation when patients seek services that may not be covered.

Mediation may also be a way to create unity and participation by family members to help meet the needs of an elderly client. A typical example is an elderly client who needs continuing and increasing support to remain in the community. The individual has the legal right to make the choice as to how to live, but may be unable to appreciate that the choice to be left alone will result in isolation and possible physical or mental deterioration that may lead to institutionalization. On the emotional front, neither the elderly individual nor family may appreciate the rift of resentment that would attend a non-negotiated decision to move the individual into a nursing home. A mediated solution may be a much better approach.

Though mediation can lead to a satisfactory agreement, there is much skepticism about the appropriateness of mediation for elderly clients. Many elderly individuals fear and avoid litigation and lawyers, usually because of the perceived cost. The individual's most powerful "card" may be his or her legal rights. Mediation therefore must not undervalue those rights even while seeking an amicable resolution.

Kevin Gibson,

***Promises and Problems in Alternative Dispute
Resolution for the Elderly***

ELDER'S ADVISOR, Vol. 2, No. 3, at 82, 86 (Winter 2001)*

Mediation as guided problem solving is not appropriate for every dispute. For success, both the negotiating parties must at least make a commitment to the process of interest-based bargaining. They must be willing to accept the mediator's techniques, which are likely to include open disclosure and treating the situation as a problem to be overcome rather than a contest to be won. Mediation presumes that people recognize what they want, that they are capable of autonomous choices, and that they will be able to articulate their desired outcomes.

Gibson cites an example of mediation in the context of guardianship, observing that family members who differ on the appropriate services and living circumstances of an incapacitated elder. He suggests that the mediator's neutrality and expertise can "reframe" the questions of who among the children has to invest the time in providing care and assistance in the community versus how the family will choose and pay for assisted living, by providing alternatives for all to consider and, potentially, agree upon.

QUESTIONS

1. What personalities are unlikely to contribute positively to a mediated solution problem? Who is most likely to compromise?

2. Does mediation lead to a sound, fair conclusion? Or is that an invalid question for mediation, that should be set aside in a search for the solution that everyone involved can accept or at least tolerate?

F. THE CLIENT OF QUESTIONABLE MENTAL CAPACITY

An attorney has a very difficult task when attempting to fulfill the ethical requirements of the attorney-client relationship with a client who has lost some degree of mental capacity. Both the Code and Model Rules recognize the problem.

[1] THE ETHICS RULES

The older directives in the Code include no disciplinary rules or canons governing an attorney's conduct with regard to a client of questionable competency. The ethical considerations that accompany the Code, however, provide the following:

> EC 7-11 — The responsibilities of a lawyer may vary according to the intelligence, experience, mental condition or age of a client, . . . or the nature of a particular proceeding. Examples include the representation of an illiterate or an incompetent. . . .

> EC 7-12 (in pertinent part) — Any mental or physical condition of a client that renders him incapable of making a considered judgment on his own behalf casts additional responsibilities upon his lawyer. . . . If a client under a disability has no legal representative, his lawyer may be compelled in court proceedings to make decisions on behalf of the clent. . . .

> EC 7-12 further requires that the lawyer elicit all possible client input, to the extent of the client's capacity to understand the matter and contribute to advancing his own interests. The lawyer also should always safeguard and advance the client's interest. The provision prohibits the lawyer from making decisions the law requires the client to make, such as consenting to settlement in a civil case or waiving a jury trial in a criminal case.

Altogether, the Code provides little that is useful to an attorney trying to work ethically with a mentally disabled client. The attorney has only two choices: advocate the express desires of the client, regardless of how those desires are affected by the client's disabled condition, or determine what the attorney believes are the "best interests" of the client and advocate them, regardless of the desires of the client. That is, the attorney may adhere to the requirements of an attorney-client relationship, or abandon them completely. If the attorney chooses to deviate from the normal relationship, the Code offers no guidance about who should be consulted before important decisions are made for the client and how the client's best interests should be determined.

The Model Rules are more helpful because they do include a rule addressing the relationship between the lawyer and a client of questionable mental capacity. The Rules reflect a trend since the 1970s to favor advocacy for the wishes of disabled clients rather than the paternalistic, nonadversarial role similar to a guardian ad litem. The Rule begins with a strong statement in favor of those rights:

> Model Rule (MR) 1.14(a) — When a client's ability to make adequately considered decisions in connection with the representation is impaired, whether because of minority, mental disability or for some other reason,

the lawyer shall, as far as reasonably possible, maintain a normal client-lawyer relationship.

Recognizing that maintaining a normal client-lawyer relationship "as far as reasonably possible" may be insufficient, the Rule (revised in the Ethics 2000 Commission and adopted by the ABA) continues:

> (b) When the lawyer reasonably believes that the client has diminished capacity, is at risk of substantial physical, financial or other harm unless action is taken and cannot adequately act in the client's own interest, the lawyer may take reasonably necessary protective action, including consulting with individuals or entities that have the ability to take action to protect the client and, in appropriate cases, seeking the appointment of a guardian ad litem, conservator or guardian.

> (c) Information relating to the representation of a client with diminished capacity is protected by Rule 1.6. When taking protective action pursuant to paragraph (b), the lawyer is impliedly authorized under Rule 1.6(a) to reveal information about the client, but only to the extent reasonably necessary to protect the client's interests.

Comment [6] provides: In determining the extent of the client's diminished capacity, the lawyer should consider and balance such factors as the client's ability to articulate reasoning leading to a decision, variability of state of mind and ability to appreciate consequences of a decision; the substantive fairness of a decision; and the consistence of a decision with the known long-term commitments and values of the client.

Consider how these provisions differ from the preceding version:

> MR 1.14(b) — A lawyer may seek the appointment of a guardian or take other protective action with respect to a client only when the lawyer reasonably believes that the client cannot adequately act in the client's own interest.

Since the occasions when the attorney seeks a guardian or other substitute decision maker (often through protective services, discussed in Chapter 10) are limited — only when the lawyer believes the client cannot adequately act in his or her own interest — the Rule suggests there are some circumstances, perhaps many circumstances, in which the attorney cannot maintain a normal relationship but does not seek a substitute decision maker. Indeed, since (b) uses the permissive "may" rather than the mandatory "shall," the lawyer is never required by the Rule to seek a guardian. Instead, the Rule Comment instructs: "[I]f a legal representative has not been appointed, the lawyer should see to such appointment *where it would serve the client's best interest*" (emphasis added). See the text of the new full comment in the statutory supplement.

As applied to any facts, the Rule may raise more questions than it answers. First, how can the attorney determine that the client cannot adequately act in his or her own behalf? Legal training does not qualify an individual to make a professional determination of mental impairment, and, in the final analysis, only a court can determine whether the client is legally incompetent. This must be reconciled somehow with the fact that individuals — doctors, nurses, family members, and attorneys — regularly decide whether an individual's decision or action will be accepted. The Rule accepts this practice without attempting to qualify or justify it.

[2] DETERMINING CLIENT CAPACITY

Informal evaluation of capacity to make a decision is often based, at least in part, on circular reasoning: the individual's choice is considered evidence of a condition of mental impairment, which is the basis for a prediction that the individual needs assistance to make other decisions. The process of evaluating the outcome of a decision to determine the decision maker's mental capacity is incompatible with the basic value of autonomy or self-determination because it fails to recognize that an adult is entitled to make idiosyncratic or even wrong decisions.

The following standard was proposed by the President's Commission for the Study of Ethical Problems in Medicine and Biomedical and Behavioral Research, 1 MAKING HEALTH CARE DECISIONS: THE ETHICAL AND LEGAL IMPLICATION OF INFORMED CONSENT IN THE PATIENT-PRACTITIONER RELATIONSHIP 57–62 (1982):

> Decision-making capacity requires, to a greater or lesser degree:
>
> 1. possession of a set of values and goals;
>
> 2. the ability to communicate and to understand information; and
>
> 3. the ability to reason and to deliberate about one's choices.

The decision maker must, in addition, have an emotional state consistent with the task.

This definition emphasizes the individual's thinking process rather than the outcome of a decision and, though drafted with health care decisions in mind, seems to apply equally well to legal decisions. Legal capacity varies according to the decision to be made. The capacity to make a will, for example, is different from the capacity required to vote.

Professor Jan Ellen Rein, in *Clients with Destructive and Socially Harmful Choices — What's an Attorney to Do?: Within and Beyond the Competency Construct*, 62 FORDHAM L. REV. 1101, 1165 (1994), suggests screening decisions for indications of legal incapacity by posing the questions:

> 1. Does the client's chosen course of action threaten serious bodily injury to others?
>
> 2. Will it seriously invade the rights, health, resources and welfare of others?
>
> 3. Will those whose interests will be adversely affected learn about the threat in time to take self protective action?
>
> 4. Is the harm threatened by the client's action irreparable or extremely difficult to reverse?
>
> 5. Even if the threatened harm in a given case is relatively insubstantial, will similar decisions in the aggregate place such a serious strain on the

public treasury that resources for important public needs become unavailable?

The following describes how a geriatrician goes about determining whether an individual has mental capacity.

Steve Fox,
Is It Personal Autonomy or a Personality Disorder?
ELDER'S ADVISOR, Vol. 3, No. 1, at 63–65 (Summer 2001)[*]

The foremost challenge to and responsibility of geriatricians is the preservation of a patient's cognitive and functional ability. Further, the principal of clinical practice is that a physician's diagnosis of physical and mental illness will identify the cause of cognitive and functional impairment. The physician's knowledge of the patient as a person, and the patient's decision-making capacity and prognosis will assist the attorney in preserving the autonomy of the client/patient and protect the client/patient from harm, undue influence, or exploitation. In the process of assessing a client/patient's decision-making capacity and autonomy, there are four common pitfalls:

1. Underestimating the patient's ability, that is, "age equals disability."

2. Relying solely on a diagnosis;

3. Lack of independent assessment, that is, relying only on past records or hearsay reports; and

4. Failure to consider the patient's life history-adaptive behaviors, social skills, values, beliefs, personality traits and characteristics, and past psychiatric history.

In reality, a significant number of assessments conducted as part of probate or involuntary mental health treatment proceedings have relied solely on one of these four pitfalls, thereby compromising the merit and usefulness of the subsequent reports. When the legal representation, adjudication, or surrogate decision-making is based upon such reports, there is an increased risk for adverse outcomes in the older patient. For example, ageist nihilism or paternalism often creates excess disability, depression, and social withdrawal in an older patient. Reports created with a reliance on a single examination, a mental status score, or a diagnosis of "senility" or "organic brain syndrome" should be viewed as suspect and their validity challenged. Conversely, the absence of a diagnosis of a mental illness or a dementia for a patient who otherwise scores well on a mental status examination and presents well, creates an equally strong risk for adverse outcomes such as self-neglect, exploitation, and undue influence. To avoid these problems and develop standards by which to measure the quality of a physician's report, the prudent geriatrician will incorporate the patient's life history, adaptive behaviors, social skills, values, beliefs, personality traits and characteristics, and past psychiatric history into the comprehensive assessment.

A patient's personality is the core element of any assessment. Personality is defined by the traits that are the binding characteristics of an individual, but are also shared by all individuals, for example, emotions, confidence, generosity, charisma and their opposites, anxiousness, dependence, parsimoniousness, and detachment. A benchmark in assessing personality is constancy in the person-that current decision making is consistent with the processes and abilities used in the past-that there is a life-long pattern of behavior. Personality characteristics are remarkably stable well into advanced age (eighty-five or older). If a behavior is new, it is likely due to a superimposed medical condition. Late in life changes in personality mandate a careful assessment for structural brain diseases, such as Alzheimer's and Parkinson's; systemic illnesses, such as hypothyroidism; or, an acute, reversible condition, such as delirium. One must also assess for overwhelming life-changing circumstances, such as the death of a spouse or child or a diagnosis of malignancy.

Personality disorders are distinguished from recent changes in personality by the persistence and exaggeration of those personality traits resulting in difficulties in personal relationships, impulse control, and impaired social and occupational functioning. There is a persistent lack of insight, a failure in the ability to comply with treatment and management regimes, and difficulty in establishing trust. Such individuals are resistive and blaming and generally cause great upset and distress in the people around them, but they cannot see the role their own behavior plays. At first blush, it may appear that virtually everybody fits this definition. In fact approximately twenty percent of the population may have a personality disorder — a well-established mental health disorder. Frequently there is misdiagnosis in such individuals; they produce serious debilitating behavior and emotional and social problems. Suicide, substance abuse, criminality, and self-neglect often can be traced to a personality disorder.

How should the attorney respond if the client seems to lack mental capacity? Comment [5] to MR 1.14 provides:

> If a lawyer reasonably believes that a client is at risk of substantial physical financial or other harm unless action is taken, and that a normal client-lawyer relationship cannot be maintained . . . [protective measures may include] consulting with family members, using a reconsideration period to permit clarification or improvement of circumstances, using voluntary surrogate decisionmaking tools such as durable powers of attorney or consulting with support groups, professional services, adult-protective agencies or other individuals or entities that have the ability to protect the client.

QUESTIONS

1. If the attorney concludes the client is mentally incapacitated, must that attorney also question whether there is any basis for representation? Is capacity required in order to initiate the attorney-client relationship? The RESTATEMENT (SECOND) OF AGENCY §§ 20–21 states that an incompetent principal possesses no authority to empower his agent. Comment [9] to MR 1.14 instructs about emergency legal assistance:

> [When] a person with seriously diminished capacity is threatened with imminent and irreparable harm, a lawyer may take legal action on behalf of such a person even though the person is unable to establish a client-lawyer relationship or to make or express considered judgments about the matter, when the person or another acting in good faith on that person's behalf has consulted with the lawyer. The lawyer must believe that the person has no other lawyer, agent or other representative available, and must act only to the extent reasonably necessary to maintain the status quo or otherwise avoid imminent and irreparable harm.

2. If Agnes is reasonably lucid during daylight hours, but experiences "sundowner syndrome," common with Alzheimer's patients, which renders her agitated and paranoid by twilight, does she have the necessary capacity to engage you as her attorney?

[3] CONFIDENTIALITY AND THE INCAPACITATED CLIENT

Maintaining confidentiality is difficult when the lawyer needs the advice and perhaps interpretation of others to understand the client's wishes.

Rule 1.6(a) (in pertinent part) — A lawyer shall not reveal information relating to representation of a client unless the client consents after consultation, except for disclosures that are impliedly authorized in order to carry out the representation, and Comment [8] to MR 1.14 specifically says that such protected information cannot be disclosed. Comment [3] to rule 1.14 observes that the client may wish to have family members or other persons participate in discussions with the lawyer, and the arrangement does not affect evidentiary privilege. Comment [6] instructs that an attorney with a client described by MR 1.14 can consult an appropriate diagnostician.

The lawyer's ethical difficulties as others besides the client provide input. What are the limitations on the consultation? For example, can the attorney reveal the client's identity? Can the attorney send over a recording of a client interview without informed consent from the client? Comment [8] instructs that when taking protective action the lawyer is impliedly authorized to make the necessary disclosures, even when the client directs the lawyer to the contrary! The lawyer must, however, consider whether the person or entity consulted will act adversely to the client's interests — before discussing matters related to the client. The Comment concludes: The lawyer's position in such cases is an unavoidably difficult one.

The Comment to Rule 1.14 appears to permit a lawyer to disclose client confidences (obviously without the client's express consent) in seeking appointment of a guardian, protective services, or guidance from an appropriate diagnostician.

The ABA Study Committee on Ethics and Professional Responsibility examined the conflict between Rule 1.6 and Rule 1.14 and issued an opinion in 1989 (Informal

Opinion 89.1530). According to the Committee, it must be inferred that the lawyer is allowed to make "disclosures necessary to seek expert advice when there is reason to suspect impairment threatening serious harm to the client . . . in order to carry out the representation within the meaning of Model Rule 1.6." The alternative, the Committee observes, is that no action could be taken to protect a disabled client because it must involve a disclosure of confidential information. Because irreparable harm to the client might result, such a constraint on attorneys cannot be the correct standard. The advice of an appropriate diagnostician may be the least objectionable alternative to the requirements of Rule 1.6 because the diagnostician is also under a duty of confidentiality.

The participants at the 1994 Conference on Ethical Issues in Presenting Older Clients held at Fordham Law School proposed the following:

> In certain circumstances, a lawyer may act as lawyer for a purported client even without express or limited agreement from the purported client, and may take those actions necessary to maintain the status quo or to avoid irreversible harm, if
>
> i. An emergency situation exists in which the purported client's substantial health, safety, financial, or liability interests are at stake;
>
> ii. The purported client, in the lawyer's good faith judgment, lacks the ability to make or express considered judgments about action required to be taken because of an impairment of decision-making capacity;
>
> iii. Time is of the essence; and
>
> iv. The lawyer reasonably believes, in good faith, that no other lawyer is available or willing to act on behalf of the purported client.
>
> A "purported client" is a person who has contact with a lawyer and who would be a client but for the inability to enter into an expressed agreement.

The following language should be added as Model Rule 1.14(e):

> The lawyer should not be subject to professional discipline for invoking or failing to invoke the permissive conduct authorized by 1.14(b) if the lawyer has a reasonable basis for his or her action or inaction.

The appointment of a guardian may not eliminate the attorney's obligation to communicate with the client, however EC 7-12 states, in pertinent part: "Where an incompetent is acting through a guardian or other legal representative, a lawyer must look to such representative for those decisions which are normally the prerogative of the client to make." The Comment to Rule 1.14 states that, even when a client has a guardian, the attorney "*should as far as possible accord the represented person the status of a client, particularly in maintaining communication*" (emphasis added). Even a client who lacks legal competence, observes the Comment, "often has the ability to understand, deliberate upon, and reach conclusions about matters affecting the client's own well being." Regarding the elderly client, in particular, the Comment notes: "[I]t is recognized that some persons of advanced age can be quite capable of handling routine financial matters while needing special legal protection concerning major transactions."

The Comment also recognizes that many states have adopted limited guardian-ship laws that require the court to limit the guardian's powers to the actual disabilities of the ward: "Furthermore, to an increasing extent the law recognizes intermediate degrees of competence. *The attorney is to acknowledge the client's areas of competence, avoiding actions which would completely divest the client of decisionmaking powers.*" (Emphasis added.) The Comment continues, addressing specifically the circumstances of a lawyer who sought the appointment of a guardian to cope with the difficulties of representation. "The appointment of a guardian, which breaches the usual requirements of confidentiality, does not entirely elimi-nate the attorney's problem of communicating with and respecting the choices of the client, particularly an elderly client. It may, if the guardian and ward disagree, somewhat complicate the attorney's task."

Edward D. Spurgeon & Mary Jane Ciccarello, *Lawyers Acting as Guardians: Policy and Ethical Considerations*
31 Stetson L. Rev. 791 (2002)[*]

A competent lawyer should understand the physical aspects of aging and make accommodations in communicating with clients. Such accommodations might include having easy physical access to the office and appropriate lighting, providing documents in large print, speaking clearly and slowly, and addressing the client in terms that are comprehensible. If house calls are necessary, then the lawyer should attempt them. The lawyer also should attempt to understand when the client is most lucid and attempt to interview the client at those times. These accommodations are essential for providing the client with loyalty, zealous advocacy, and a normal relationship.

. . . . If the client is not communicating effectively even after the lawyer has attempted to make these accommodations, then the lawyer may take further steps to understand what the client is communicating. . . . the lawyer needs to reach an understanding in his or her own mind of whether the client's requests are merely eccentric, or potentially detrimental to the client.

. . . . A lawyer who finds it necessary to consult with a diagnostician or other third party to help determine the decision-making capacity of the client conceivably could be acting in his or her own interest. Regarding this dilemma, Comment 4 to Model Rule 1.7 provides the following guidance:

> A possible conflict does not itself preclude the representation. The critical questions are the likelihood that a conflict will eventuate and, if it does, whether it will materially interfere with the lawyer's independent profes-sional judgment in considering alternatives or foreclose courses of action that reasonably should be pursued on behalf of the client.

Arguably, a lawyer who seeks the help of third parties is acting to maintain the lawyer's independent, professional judgment to competently represent the client. Once a lawyer has a better understanding of the client's capacity to make decisions,

---

the lawyer can then decide whether to continue with the representation, which might include taking protective actions on behalf of the client.

PROBLEM

The Center for Social Gerontology in Ann Arbor, Michigan, proposed the following hypothetical case:

> Your client, Martha, bought an over-priced, very poor quality roofing job; and the roof began leaking soon after the "repairs." Martha unknowingly signed a deed to her house to secure an $8,000 note to pay for the roof, believing that it was a contract for the roofing job. A collection company which buys all the roofer's financing notes sued Martha for the $8,000. You have looked into this scam and have prepared an Answer and Counterclaim asserting fraud and consumer protection statutory remedies.
>
> You are seeking treble damages, a judgment voiding the deed, as well as your attorney's fees. The deadline for filing the Answer is the next day. You stop by your client's house to explain it; and you find her confused and in tears. She says no one loves her and she would be better off in a nursing home. "I've always paid my bills. If they say I owe this, they must be right or they would not go to court." Martha wants the debt paid and the lawsuit ended so no one will think she cheated anyone.

Must you follow Martha's instructions? How can you determine whether they represent her personal decision or are a product of mental or physical illness? Since implementation of her decision would cause great harm, does it matter?

G.   SUBSIDIZED LEGAL SERVICES

Individuals age 65 or older can receive subsidized legal assistance from providers funded primarily by federal funds allocated by the Administration on Aging (AoA) which administers the Older Americans Act (OAA, also called Title III). The OAA Amendments of 1973 added legal assistance as a service which can be provided using "Title IIIB" funding. In 1975 amendments to the OAA identified legal services as a priority area that must receive an "adequate portion" of funding by each Area Agency on Aging administering OAA funds. Twelve years later, in response to weak state implementation efforts, Congress required state units on aging to establish a minimum percentage of funds, which must be spent to satisfy the requirement of an "adequate portion." The OAA also requires that the Area Agencies involve the private bar in the provision of legal services.

A significant purpose of the OAA funds is to provide legal assistance for elderly persons whose income levels preclude eligibility for LSC services but are insufficient to pay private attorney's fees. Like other OAA services, legal assistance can be provided regardless of income, though assistance is to be targeted to the most needy first so that most clients are poor, minority elderly persons.

Controversy regarding the provision OAA legal services has paralleled concerns about other OAA services, particularly because of the lack of information about who is served and the results of services rendered. This is not a surprise given that law prohibits inquiries about income. Since the original legislation, however, Congress has mandated the targeting of services to those with greatest financial need (defined as those with an income below poverty level) or greatest social need (defined as those with physical or mental disabilities, language barriers, and cultural, social or geographic isolation). In addition the OAA requires that service providers particularly recognize and serve low-income minorities.

Because of extreme funding shortages, legal service providers place strong emphasis on reporting in order to show both the importance of their work and the needs in the community. Reporting on legal services must be handled with particular care, however, to protect the confidentiality of the clients. The OAA recognizes the need for confidentiality by prohibiting state agencies and Area Agencies on Aging, which usually directly monitor services grants, from requiring a legal assistance provider to reveal information that is protected by attorney-client privilege. The legislative history of the amendments shows that Congress meant to include the identity of clients under this protection. This does not prevent the reporting of demographic data or needs assessment but requires additional work to report without revealing client names and addresses.

In 2000, Congress reauthorized the Older Americans Act through 2005, retaining legal assistance as one of the three categories of priority OAA services. Area Agencies on Aging, which prepare plans and administer OAA services for the state, are required to allocate an "adequate portion" of funds to each priority service, and the state administrative agency is further bound to designate a minimum of OAA funds to be devoted to for the services. States that set a percentage vary from 1 percent (Florida) to 11 percent (Washington state). The State plan must give priority to legal assistance related to income, health care, long-term care, nutrition, housing, utilities, protective services, defense of guardianship, abuse, neglect, and age discrimination. Section 307(a)(11)(E).

The definition of legal services, amended and recodified at Section 102(31),

A) means legal advice and representation provided by an attorney to older individuals with economic or social needs; and

B) includes

  i) to the extent feasible, counseling or other appropriate assistance by a paralegal or law student under the direct supervision of an attorney; and

  ii) counseling or representation by a nonlawyer where permitted by law.

Legal assistance is the only service under the OAA with an explicit targeting requirement, i.e., *older individuals with economic or social needs*. However, providers are still prohibited from using a means test to determine that need and cannot deny services on the basis of income. A new provision requires that providers offer clients an opportunity to contribute funds for their legal services, as with all other OAA services. (Section 315(b)(4).) With regard to the option to deliver services to the extent feasible by paralegals or law students, the Center for Social Gerontology asserts that any program run without participation of a lawyer would fail to comply with OAA requirements. (*Best Practice Notes on Delivery of Legal*

Assistance to Older Persons, April 2001.)

Local area agencies on aging may still request a waiver of OAA requirements from the State, and the State may seek waivers from the federal government. One basis is a showing that services are sufficient to meet the need in the area. The 2000 amendments repealed the requirement that the area agency hold a public hearing before submitting its request. A new waiver provision may allow a State to receive a federal waiver, after public notice and consultation with area agencies, to the extend necessary to permit demonstrations, in limited areas of a State, of innovative approaches to assist older individuals, provided services are not diminished. Section 316(b)(1)–(3).

QUESTIONS

1.   Does the state have an interest in limiting the legal assistance available to recipients of state-funded social services and housing assistance?

2.   Considering the variety of services needed by the elderly and the comparative market value of such services as home nursing and/or home-delivered meals, as well as legal services, what is a reasonable percentage of OAA funding for legal assistance? What kind(s) of services should be purchased? One-on-one attorney-client counseling? A telephone hotline for brief analysis and advice?

The Legal Services Corporation provides legal assistance to the elderly who meet the LSC poverty requirements.

Since LSC providers tend to define their purposes in terms of the needs created by poverty, the particular needs of the elderly poor are less likely to receive specific attention. A number of generalities about poverty services affect the style and focus of representation. For example, LSC providers are more likely to engage in strong, adversarial advocacy for their clients, and to target problems — such as consumer exploitation — experienced by a significant proportion of their clients.

Chapter 3

AGE DISCRIMINATION IN EMPLOYMENT

A. LEGISLATIVE HISTORY OF THE ACT

On January 23, 1967, President Lyndon Johnson sent a message to Congress urging passage of a law that would prohibit arbitrary and unjust discrimination in employment on account of age. With little publicity and no significant opposition, Congress enacted the Age Discrimination in Employment Act of 1967 that was signed into law by President Johnson on December 15, 1967. The goal of the Age Discrimination in Employment Act (ADEA) is to "promote employment of older persons based on their ability rather than age; to prohibit arbitrary age discrimination in employment; [and] to help employers and workers find ways of meeting problems arising from the impact of age on employment." 29 U.S.C. § 621(b).

EQUAL EMPLOYMENT OPPORTUNITY COMMISSION v. WYOMING
460 U.S. 226 (1983)

Justice Brennan.

Efforts in Congress to prohibit arbitrary age discrimination date back at least to the 1950's. During floor debate over what was to become Title VII of the Civil Rights Act of 1964, amendments were offered in both the House and the Senate to ban discrimination on the basis of age as well as race, color, religion, sex, and national origin. These amendments were opposed at least in part on the basis that Congress did not yet have enough information to make a considered judgment about the nature of age discrimination, and each was ultimately defeated. 110 Cong. Rec. 2596–2599, 9911–9913, 13490-13492 (1964); EEOC, Legislative History of the Age Discrimination in Employment Act 5-14 (1981) (hereinafter Legislative History). Title VII did, however, include a provision, § 715, 78 Stat. 265 (since superseded by § 10 of the Equal Employment Opportunity Act of 1972, 86 Stat. 111), which directed the Secretary of Labor to "make a full and complete study of the factors which might tend to result in discrimination in employment because of age and of the consequences of such discrimination on the economy and individuals affected," and to report the results of that study to Congress. That report was transmitted approximately one year later.

In 1966, Congress directed the Secretary of Labor to submit specific legislative proposals for prohibiting age discrimination. The Secretary transmitted a draft bill in early 1967, see 113 Cong. Rec. 1377 (1967), and the President, in a message to Congress on older Americans, recommended its enactment and expressed serious concern about the problem of age discrimination, see Special Message to the Congress Proposing Programs for Older Americans, 1 Public Papers of the Presidents, Lyndon B. Johnson, 1967, pp. 32, 37 (1968). Congress undertook further study of its own, and Committees in both the House and the Senate conducted detailed hearings on the proposed legislation.

The report of the Secretary of Labor, whose findings were confirmed throughout the extensive factfinding undertaken by the Executive Branch and Congress, came to the following basic conclusions: (1) Many employers adopted specific age limitations in those States that had not prohibited them by their own antidiscrimination laws, although many other employers were able to operate successfully without them. (2) In the aggregate, these age limitations had a marked effect upon the employment of older workers. (3) Although age discrimination rarely was based on the sort of animus motivating some other forms of discrimination, it was based in large part on stereotypes unsupported by objective fact, and was often defended on grounds different from its actual causes. (4) Moreover, the available empirical evidence demonstrated that arbitrary age lines were in fact generally unfounded and that, as an overall matter, the performance of older workers was at least as good as that of younger workers. (5) Finally, arbitrary age discrimination was profoundly harmful in at least two ways. First, it deprived the national economy of the productive labor of millions of individuals and imposed on the governmental treasury substantially increased costs in unemployment insurance and federal Social Security benefits. Second, it inflicted on individual workers the economic and psychological injury accompanying the loss of the opportunity to engage in productive and satisfying occupations.

The product of the process of factfinding and deliberation formally begun in 1964 was the Age Discrimination in Employment Act of 1967. The preamble to the Act emphasized both the individual and social costs of age discrimination. The provisions of the Act as relevant here prohibited various forms of age discrimination in employment, including the discharge of workers on the basis of their age. § 4(a), 29 U.S.C. § 623(a). The protection of the Act was limited, however, to workers between the ages of 40 and 65, § 12(a), 29 U.S.C. § 631, raised to age 70 in 1978, Age Discrimination in Employment Act Amendments of 1978, § 3(a), 92 Stat. 189. Moreover, in order to insure that employers were permitted to use neutral criteria not directly dependant on age, and in recognition of the fact that even criteria that are based on age are occasionally justified, the Act provided that certain otherwise prohibited employment practices would not be unlawful "where age is a bona fide occupational qualification reasonably necessary to the normal operation of the particular business, or where the differentiation is based on reasonable factors other than age." § 4(f)(1), 29 U.S.C. § 623(f)(1).

The ADEA, as originally passed in 1967, did not apply to the Federal Government, to the States or their political subdivisions, or to employers with fewer than 25 employees. In a Report issued in 1973, a Senate Committee found this gap in coverage to be serious, and commented that "[t]here is . . . evidence that, like the corporate world, government managers also create an environment where young is somehow better than old." Senate Special Committee on Aging, Improving the Age Discrimination Law, 93rd Cong., 1st Sess., 14 (Comm. Print 1973), Legislative History 231. In 1974, Congress extended the substantive prohibitions of the Act to employers having at least 20 workers, and to the Federal and State Governments.

———————

Since its passage in 1967, the ADEA has undergone periodic amendment, primarily to broaden its protective scope. 29 U.S.C. § 621 *et seq.*

— The Fair Labor Standards Act of 1974 included federal, state, and local government employees, and the coverage of the Act was expanded by making it applicable to employers with 20 or more employees. (The original Act applied only to employers with 25 or more employees.)

— The Age Discrimination in Employment Act Amendments of 1978 expanded the protected age from age 40 to 65 to age 40 to 70, outlawed all mandatory retirement for federal employees, and permitted plaintiffs to request a jury trial.

— The Older Americans Act Amendments of 1984 switched the enforcement of the Act from the Department of Labor to the Equal Employment Opportunity Commission (EEOC). It also covered Americans working overseas for American firms and narrowed the exclusion for executive policymakers.

— The Age Discrimination in Employment Amendments of 1986 removed the age 70 coverage limit and prohibited discrimination against employees past normal retirement age in health and pension rights.

— The Age Discrimination Claims Assistance Act of 1988 extended the statute of limitations on the right to sue if the employee's complaint would otherwise be barred by failure of the EEOC to act in a timely fashion.

— The Older Workers Benefit Protection Act of 1990 barred an employer's refusal to hire older workers because of the costs associated with the employee benefit plan.

— In 1996, the ADEA was amended to permit public employers to discriminate on the basis of age in the hiring and mandatory retirement of firefighters or law enforcement officers.

Under the ADEA, age discrimination in employment is prohibited in hiring, termination, compensation, and terms and conditions of employment on account of age for individuals age 40 or older. In short, the arbitrary use of chronological age is no longer allowed in the employment sphere. The ADEA allows employers to use age as a factor when hiring or firing only in carefully circumscribed situations. The most noteworthy is the bona fide occupational qualification exception discussed below in Section J.

B.   THE FAILURE OF A CONSTITUTIONAL SOLUTION

In the 1960s mandatory retirement came under increasing criticism for being unfair to older employees and costly to society. The result was the passage of the ADEA, which barred mandatory retirement based upon age and removed what was considered to be an injustice to older workers. The abolition of mandatory retirement was also an attempt to increase efficiency in the employment market by forcing employers to make individualized, rational decisions about who to hire and who to retire.

The past failure of the courts to find any federal constitutional prohibition to age discrimination strengthened congressional support for the ADEA.

MASSACHUSETTS BOARD OF RETIREMENT v. MURGIA
427 U.S. 307 (1976)

Per Curiam.

This case presents the question whether the provision of Mass. Gen. Laws Ann. c. 32, § 26 (3)(a) (1966), that a uniformed state police officer "shall be retired . . . upon his attaining age fifty," denies appellee police officer equal protection of the laws in violation of the Fourteenth Amendment.

. . .

In this case, the Massachusetts statute clearly meets the requirements of the Equal Protection Clause, for the State's classification rationally furthers the purpose identified by the State: Through mandatory retirement at age 50, the legislature seeks to protect the public by assuring physical preparedness of its uniformed police. Since physical ability generally declines with age, mandatory retirement at 50 serves to remove from police service those whose fitness for uniformed work presumptively has diminished with age. This clearly is rationally related to the State's objective. There is no indication that § 26 (3)(a) has the effect of excluding from service so few officers who are in fact unqualified as to render age 50 a criterion wholly unrelated to the objective of the statute.

That the State chooses not to determine fitness more precisely through individualized testing after age 50 is not to say that the objective of assuring physical fitness is not rationally furthered by a maximum-age limitation. It is only to say that with regard to the interest of all concerned, the State perhaps has not chosen the best means to accomplish this purpose. But where rationality is the test, a State "does not violate the Equal Protection Clause merely because the classifications made by its laws are imperfect." *Dandridge v. Williams*, 397 U.S., at 485.

We do not make light of the substantial economic and psychological effects premature and compulsory retirement can have on an individual; nor do we denigrate the ability of elderly citizens to continue to contribute to society. The problems of retirement have been well documented and are beyond serious dispute. But "[w]e do not decide today that the [Massachusetts statute] is wise, that it best fulfills the relevant social and economic objectives that [Massachusetts] might ideally espouse, or that a more just and humane system could not be devised." *Id.*, at 487. We decide only that the system enacted by the Massachusetts Legislature does not deny appellee equal protection of the laws.

The judgment is reversed.

Mandatory retirement is a relatively recent phenomenon. Well into the 19th century workers retired because they chose to or were forced to because of declining physical ability. Almost no one was forced to retire merely because of an arbitrary retirement age. The concept of mandatory retirement based upon chronological age came into practice towards the end of the 19th century. It arose in the large industrial organizations in which retirement of older workers permitted the hiring of younger, more efficient, and physically stronger replacements. When workers refused to retire voluntarily in sufficient numbers, management instituted mandatory retirement policies.

Mandatory retirement, however, did not become widespread until it was coupled with guaranteed income security for the retiree. To many employers it seemed cruel to force an employee to retire if the employer did not provide pensions for retired employees. With the passage of Social Security retirement benefits in 1934 and the growth of private pensions after World War II, lack of income for the retired employee was no longer a problem. As a result, mandatory retirement became common in the workplace.

By the early 1970s, 41 percent of workers who reached age 65 were subject to mandatory retirement. Almost one-half of that group chose to retire early; that is, they voluntarily retired. Of course, not all early retirement was truly voluntary. Some employees, knowing that they soon would be forced to retire, may have elected early retirement at a time more convenient to them. If they had not been subject to mandatory retirement, they might not have retired at such an early age.

Interestingly, the passage of the ADEA has not reversed the long-term trend toward earlier retirement. In 1930, the labor force participation rate of males age 65 and older was 53.9 percent. By 1960, the participation rate was 33.1 percent and by 1986, the participation rate was only 17.5 percent. By the late-1990s, it had declined to about 13 percent. By 2010, it had risen to about 15 percent.

A number of employers now target older people as potentially reliable, well mannered, low-wage employees. For example, one article notes that Home Depot, the home improvement retailer, advertises "snowbird specials," jobs that provide work in two locations — winter in Florida and summer in Maine. Older people as WalMart greeters are a fixture in ads and reality.

The AARP showcases 13 elder friendly employers including MetLife, Pitney Bowes, and Borders books that offer flexible hours, health benefits to coordinate with Medicare, and in some cases, training. However, the overall experience of post-retirement workers is low wages that benefit the employer. *See, e.g.*, Milt Freudenheim, *More Help Wanted: Older Workers Please Apply*, N.Y. TIMES, Mar. 23, 2005, at A1.

NOTE: "REVERSE" AGE DISCRIMINATION IN EMPLOYMENT

In 2004, the Supreme Court held in *General Dynamics Land Systems, Inc. v. Cline*, 540 U.S. 581 (2004), that discrimination in favor of workers protected by the ADEA does not create a cause of action under the Act. The decision resolved a split among the federal circuit courts and reversed the long-held position of the EEOC, which is in the process of revising its regulations and other guidance for employers. In a six to three vote, the Court explained that the relatively old could be favored over the relatively young.

The case was a class action by union members between the ages of 40 and 50 who lost future retiree health care benefits when their employer eliminated them for all employees under age 50. The plaintiffs claimed reverse age discrimination under the ADEA because employees older than 50 were favored. The Sixth Circuit, which reversed the district court, stated that the ADEA prohibited discrimination against any person because of age, a fact "so clear on its face that if Congress had meant to limit its coverage to protect only the older worker against the younger, it would have said so." Justice Souter, in the Supreme Court decision and citing the legislative history, called this "clearly wrong."

QUESTIONS

1. Workers in their fifties often have great difficulty securing new jobs, yet they do not have retirement benefits to cushion their circumstances. Should there be limits to the general principle that the older worker can be favored over the younger worker?

2. Why does the ADEA apply only to persons age 40 or older?

3. Is it laudable for employers to seek older workers previously ignored in the job market in order to hire low-wage employees?

4. Which workers do you suppose are most likely to retire before age 65? What factors encourage retirement, and which factors work against it?

5. Some have called the ADEA "the white male, middle management, employee defense act." Would you agree?

A significant motive for the passage of the ADEA was the elimination of discrimination against older applicants in hiring. *See* H.R. REP. No. 805, 90th Cong., 1st Sess. 4 (1967). It was thought that the elimination of discrimination in hiring would diminish long-term unemployment in older workers and that, in turn, would reduce elderly poverty. As it turned out only about 10 percent of ADEA cases involve discrimination in hiring; the rest deal with unlawful dismissal on the basis of age. The overwhelming majority of ADEA plaintiffs are white male professionals and managers contesting the termination of their employment.

C.   WHO IS PROTECTED?

[1]   THE TWENTY EMPLOYEE REQUIREMENT

The ADEA applies to all private sector firms with 20 or more employees and to all state and local governments. 29 U.S.C. § 630(b). All federal employees are covered under separate provisions of the act. 29 U.S.C. § 633(a).

QUESTION

What is the justification for the exclusion of employers with fewer than 20 employees?

Although the ADEA does not apply to an employer with fewer than 20 employees, many states have enacted laws that bar age discrimination. These laws generally cover employers with fewer than 20 employees, though the state law may specify that a covered employer must have a minimum number of employees. For example, the Pennsylvania anti-age discrimination law applies to employers with four or more employees. 43 PA. STAT. ANN. § 954(b).

[2]   PARTNERS

The ADEA refers to employees. Partners, directors, or owners of enterprises are not employees and are not protected. Just who is a partner, however, can be a point of contention.

CARUSO v. PEAT, MARWICK, MITCHELL & CO.
664 F. Supp. 144 (S.D.N.Y. 1987)

WALKER, DISTRICT JUDGE.

Introduction

Plaintiff Conrad S. Caruso ("Caruso") has brought the instant age discrimination action against Defendant Peat, Marwick, Mitchell & Co. ("Peat Marw-ick"), his former employer. Defendant moves to dismiss, alleging that Caruso's status as a partner bars his invocation as an "employee" of the federal Age Discrimination in Employment Act ("ADEA"), 29 U.S.C. § 621, *et seq.* For the reasons set forth below, defendant's motion to dismiss is denied.

Statement of Facts

Defendant Peat Marwick is a major American accounting and consulting firm, employing several thousand professionals and consultants in more than 100 offices. About 1,350 of these accountants and consultants are employed as partners.

Peat Marwick is controlled by a 21-member board of directors. Among its policymaking duties, the board determines those Peat Marwick employees who the firm will nominate as partners. This board's policy decisions are implemented by a six-tier management hierarchy, ranging from the Chief Executive Officer, who reports directly to the board, to Partners in Charge, who are responsible for routine administrative decisions at each Peat Marwick office. About 300 of the firm's 1,350 partners hold some form of management position. The firm's New York office, where plaintiff worked, employed 128 partners. Thirty-six of these partners held management positions. Plaintiff did not hold one of these positions.

Plaintiff Caruso's career with Peat Marwick began in May 1969, when the Management Consulting Department of defendant's New York office hired him as a senior consultant. In 1970, Peat Marwick promoted Caruso to the position of manager. Caruso was promoted to partner in 1980. Plaintiff's duties and responsibilities changed little after each promotion, including his promotion to partner. As a partner, plaintiff was allowed to make some discretionary decisions on behalf of his clients, but more typically plaintiff would ask a member of defendant's management, such as the Partner in Charge, to ratify or reject his recommendations.

During his tenure as a Peat Marwick partner, plaintiff was required to submit time sheets every two weeks, showing the number of hours he had worked for various accounts. Plaintiff received five weeks of vacation each year — one more week than he had received prior to his appointment as a partner. Each year, plaintiff was subject to a formal job performance evaluation given by the Partner in Charge of the New York office.

Plaintiff could not make any personnel decisions on his own initiative. . . .

In December 1985, the Partner in Charge of Peat Marwick's New York office asked Caruso to resign from the firm. Defendant alleges that Caruso was asked to resign because he did not bring a sufficient number of new clients to the firm. When plaintiff was asked to resign in 1985, he was 50 years old.

Plaintiff agreed to resign, and left Peat Marwick by December 31, 1985. After this date, plaintiff received occasional work as an independent consultant for the firm.

Almost immediately after his resignation from Peat Marwick, plaintiff filed an age discrimination suit with both the New York State Division of Human Rights, and with the Equal Employment Opportunity Commission. Peat Mar-wick discontinued Caruso's employment as an outside consultant on May 9, 1986.

On May 21, 1986, Caruso filed the instant amended complaint, alleging principally that defendant's decision to ask for his resignation constituted unlawful age discrimination. Plaintiff's amended complaint also alleges that Peat Marwick unlawfully discontinued plaintiff's outside consulting work in retaliation for plaintiff's age discrimination action against the firm.

Discussion

1. A "Partner's" Ability to Bring an ADEA Action

A plaintiff may bring a federal age discrimination action under the ADEA only where he is an employee suing his former or current employer. 29 U.S.C. § 623(a);. It is well settled that an individual who has acted as a central corporate decisionmaker or controlling owner does not fall within the ADEA definition of "employee," and thus cannot bring an action against the company he once managed or owned. . . . On the other hand, the mere fact that an employee holds a job carrying an impressive title does not mean that this employee loses the protection of the ADEA . . . .

Defendant argues for a *per se* rule that an individual denoted as a "partner" falls outside the ADEA definition of employee. In other words, defendant contends that since Peat Marwick employed Caruso under the title of "partner," Caruso cannot sue his former employer for age discrimination.

Recent decisions are inconsistent with defendant's argument for a *per se* rule holding that the ADEA cannot apply to individuals employed under the title of partner.

. . . . [T]he Court must determine whether plaintiff in the instant case falls within the ADEA definition of employee. As discussed above, if plaintiff acted as a central corporate decisionmaker or owner, as the term "partner" is traditionally conceived, plaintiff could not qualify as an employee under the ADEA. However, if plaintiff's duties at Peat Marwick more closely resembled those of the typical salaried worker, with little role in corporate decision making, plaintiff may bring an action under the ADEA. For the reasons set forth below, the Court finds that plaintiff falls within the latter category. . . .

However, at least two other characteristics traditionally have distinguished partners from employees. First, partners typically receive their compensation as a percentage of their firm's profits, rather than in the form of a fixed hourly wage or weekly salary. As one commentator has written: "Profit sharing is the primary attribute of partnership."

Second, a partner traditionally works as a permanent employee of his firm. The typical firm may not fire a partner or otherwise terminate his employment merely because of disappointment with the quantity or quality of his work, but may only remove the partner in extraordinary circumstances.

To summarize, the Court holds the view that a determination of an individual's status as an employee or a partner, for purposes of an ADEA action, should include at least the following three considerations:

(1) The extent of the individual's ability to control and operate his business; (2) The extent to which an individual's compensation is calculated as a percentage of business profits; and (3) The extent of the individual's employment security.

An application of this test to the instant case leaves little question that plaintiff qualifies as an employee, rather than a partner. Caruso largely lacked any control over even his own office in New York, which was operated by the Partner in Charge, much less Peat Marwick's business as a whole, which was managed by a board of directors separated from plaintiff by six levels of hierarchy. Plaintiff possessed authority to make discretionary decisions only with respect to his own relatively few clients, and even on these decisions he typically sought the approval of the Partner in Charge or another management-level partner. . . .

Neither party has presented facts showing precisely to what extent plaintiff's salary was based on Peat Marwick's profits. However, the fact that plaintiff held no more than 350 "units," a relatively low figure, suggests that plaintiff's salary would vary little with the firm's profits.

As to the third factor, the permanency of plaintiff's employment, plaintiff has shown that Peat Marwick in no way considered him a permanent member of the firm. Plaintiff received annual evaluations, during which his job performance was closely scrutinized. These evaluations clearly were not a routine administrative process, or a benevolent attempt to assist plaintiff. Indeed, it is defendant's position in this case that if Caruso's performance did not meet certain standards, Peat Marwick could ask for his resignation — and did so because of Caruso's inadequate performance.

The Court concludes that plaintiff properly qualifies as an employee, rather than a partner, and thus may invoke the ADEA. Accordingly, the motion to dismiss plaintiff's principal ADEA claim, arising out of his 1985 resignation from Peat Marwick, is denied.

In the next case, a law firm asserts that its "partners" are not protected by the ADEA.

EQUAL EMPLOYMENT OPPORTUNITY COMMISSION v. SIDLEY AUSTIN BROWN & WOOD
315 F.3d 696 (7th Cir. 2002)

POSNER, CIRCUIT JUDGE.

In 1999, Sidley & Austin (as it then was) demoted 32 of its equity partners to "counsel" or "senior counsel." The significance of these terms is unclear, but Sidley does not deny that they signify demotion and constitute adverse personnel action within the meaning of the antidiscrimination laws. The EEOC began an investigation to determine whether the demotions might have violated the Age Discrimination in Employment Act. After failing to obtain all the information it wanted without recourse to process, the Commission issued a subpoena duces tecum to the firm, seeking a variety of documentation bearing on two distinct areas of inquiry: coverage and discrimination. The reason for the inquiry about coverage is that the ADEA protects employees but not employers. . . . To be able to establish that the firm had violated the ADEA, therefore, the Commission would have to show that the 32 partners were employees before their demotion.

Sidley provided most of the information sought in the subpoena that related to coverage (but no information relating to discrimination, though Sidley claims that the demotions were due to shortcomings in performance rather than to age), but not all. It contended that it had given the Commission enough information to show that before their demotion the 32 . . . were indeed partners before their demotion. Sidley has complied with all the formalities required by Illinois law to establish and maintain a partnership; the 32 were partners within the meaning of the applicable partnership law.

Although the EEOC does not concede that the 32 are bona fide partners even under state law, it is emphatic that their classification under state law is not dispositive of their status under federal antidiscrimination law. The antidiscrimination laws do not exempt partnerships from coverage (Sidley concedes that) or deny partners, as such, the protection of the laws. Employers are not protected by discrimination laws such as Title VII and the ADEA, but are partners employers? Always? Always for purposes of Title VII or the ADEA, or the other federal laws that prohibit employment discrimination? Statutory purpose is relevant. . . .

An individual who was classified as a partner-employer under state partnership law might be classified as an employee for other purposes, including the purpose for which federal antidiscrimination law extends protection to employees but not employers. Against this conclusion it can be argued that partners should be classified as employers rather than employees for purposes of the age discrimination law because partnership law gives them effective remedies against oppression by their fellow partners, because partnership relations would be poisoned if partners could sue each other for unlawful discrimination, and because the relation among partners is so intimate that they should be allowed to discriminate, just as individuals are allowed to discriminate in their purely personal relations. This is not the occasion on which to come down on one side or the other of the issue. . . .

But we do not understand how Sidley, without addressing the purpose of the employer exemption, can be so certain that it has proved that the 32 are employers within the meaning of the ADEA. They are, or rather were, partners, but it does not follow that they were employers. A firm that under pursuit by the EEOC on suspicion of discrimination redesignated its employees "partners" without changing the preexisting employment relation an iota would not by doing this necessarily buy immunity, even if the redesignation sufficed to make them partners under state law.

This case is not as extreme; it does not involve relabeling. Yet it involves a partnership of more than 500 partners in which all power resides in a small, unelected committee (it has 36 members). The partnership does not elect the members of the executive committee; the committee elects them, like the self-perpetuating board of trustees of a private university or other charitable foundation. It is true that the partners can commit the firm, for example by writing opinion letters; but employees of a corporation, when acting within the scope of their employment, regularly commit the corporation to contractual undertakings, not to mention to tort liability. Partners who are not members of the executive committee share in the profits of the firm; but many corporations base their employees' compensation in part anyway, but sometimes in very large part, on the corporation's profits, without anyone supposing them employers. The participation of the 32 demoted partners in committees that have, so far as appears, merely administrative functions does not distinguish them from executive employees in corporations. Corporations have committees and the members of the committees are employees; this does not make them employers. Nor are the members of the committees on which the 32 served elected; they are appointed by the executive committee. The 32 owned some of the firm's capital, but executive-level employees often own stock in their corporations. . . .

Particularly unconvincing is Sidley's contention that since the executive committee exercises its absolute power by virtue of delegation by the entire partnership in the partnership agreement, we should treat the entire partnership as if it rather than the executive committee were directing the firm. That would be like saying that if the people elect a person to be dictator for life, the government is a democracy rather than a dictatorship. The partners do not even elect the members of the committee. They have no control, direct or indirect, over its composition.

Perhaps the most partneresque feature of the 32 partners' relation to the firm is their personal liability for the firm's debts: not because unlimited liability is a sine qua non of partnership (there can be limited partnerships, and there are other business entities besides partnership that have unlimited liability-a sole proprietorship, for example), but because it is the most salient practical difference between the standard partnership and a corporation. Sidley does not have limited liability, and this means, by the way, that although under the firm's rules each partner is liable for the firm's debts only in proportion to his capital, a creditor of the firm could sue any partner for the entire debt owed it. . . .

The matter of liability for partnership debts illustrates the importance of referring the question whether a partner in a particular firm is an employer or an employee to statutory purpose. If implicit in the ADEA's exemption for employers is recognition that partners ordinarily have adequate remedies under partnership law to protect themselves against oppression (including age or other forms of invidious discrimination) by the partnership, then exposure to liability can hardly be decisive. These 32 partners were not empowered by virtue of bearing large potential liabilities! The 32 were defenseless; they had no power over their fate. If other partners shirked and as a result imposed liability on the 32, the 32 could not, as partners in a conventional partnership could do, vote to expel them. They had no voting power. What could be argued but is not is that because the *other* partners are potentially liable for the pratfalls of the 32, the partnership should have greater power over their employment than if the firm were a corporation and so had limited liability. To repeat, the issue is not whether the 32 before their demotion were partners, an issue to which their liability for the firm's debts is germane; the issue is whether they were employers. The two classes, partners under state law and employers under federal antidiscrimination law, may not coincide. . . .

We are not ruling that the 32 demoted partners were in fact employees within the meaning of the age discrimination law. Such a ruling would be premature. Sidley has respectable arguments on its side, not least that the functional test of employer status toward which the EEOC is leaning is too uncertain to enable law firms and other partnerships to determine in advance their exposure to discrimination suits — that it would be better if the courts and the Commission interpreted the employer exclusion to require treating all partners as employers, with perhaps a narrow sham exception. These issues will become ripe when Sidley finishes complying with the coverage part of the subpoena. We hold only that there is enough doubt about whether the 32 demoted partners are covered by the age discrimination law to entitle the EEOC to full compliance with that part, at least, of its subpoena.

Vacated and remanded with directions.

QUESTIONS

1. Why should it be legal for partnerships to discriminate against partners because of their age?

2. Is the partnership exception a valid application of the principle of freedom of association?

3. Does the partnership exception make sense for a law firm or an accounting firm with over 100 partners?

The Supreme Court has ruled on who is a partner outside the context of an ADEA claim.

CLACKAMAS GASTROENTEROLOGY ASSOCIATES, P.C. v. WELLS
538 U.S. 440 (2003)

We are persuaded by the EEOC's focus on the common-law touchstone of control, see *Skidmore v. Swift & Co.*, 323 U.S. 134, 140 (1944), and specifically by its submission that each of the following six factors is relevant to the inquiry whether a shareholder-director is an employee:

"Whether the organization can hire or fire the individual or set the rules and regulations of the individual's work

"Whether and, if so, to what extent the organization supervises the individual's work

"Whether the individual reports to someone higher in the organization

"Whether and, if so, to what extent the individual is able to influence the organization

"Whether the parties intended that the individual be an employee, as expressed in written agreements or contracts

"Whether the individual shares in the profits, losses, and liabilities of the organization." EEOC Compliance Manual § 605:0009.

As the EEOC's standard reflects, an employer is the person, or group of persons, who owns and manages the enterprise. The employer can hire and fire employees, can assign tasks to employees and supervise their performance, and can decide how the profits and losses of the business are to be distributed. The mere fact that a person has a particular title — such as partner, director, or vice president — should not necessarily be used to determine whether he or she is an employee or a proprietor. . . .

[3] GOVERNMENT EMPLOYEES

In 1974, the ADEA definition of employer was amended to apply to state and local governments. The extension of the Act to government employees was held constitutional by the Supreme Court in *EEOC v. Wyo.*, 460 U.S. 226 (1983). The Supreme Court upheld the applicability of the ADEA to states because the Act did not "directly impair" the state's ability to carry out traditional governmental functions. However, in *Kimel v. Fla. Bd. of Regents*, 528 U.S. 62 (2000), the Supreme Court ruled that the Eleventh Amendment to the U.S. Constitution prevented Congress from applying the ADEA to states. The Court pointed out, however, that almost every state had its own version of an anti-age discrimination law, and that they were free to enforce those laws to protect older employees of state and local governments.

[4] FOREIGN EMPLOYERS AND UNITED STATES EMPLOYEES OUT OF COUNTRY

The ADEA applies to commercial activities of foreign governments while operating in the United States. In *Gazder v. Air India*, 574 F. Supp. 134 (S.D.N.Y. 1983), the term "employer" was held to include an airline which was an instrumentality of a foreign state. Since 1984, United States citizens who work for U.S. corporations outside of the United States are also protected by the ADEA. 29 U.S.C. § 630(f).

[5] UNIONS AND EMPLOYMENT AGENCIES

The ADEA applies not only to employers, but also to employment agencies and to labor unions. Neither may discriminate against employees because of their age. 29 U.S.C. § 623(b), (c). Help wanted advertisements indicating an age preference are prohibited by § 4(e) of the ADEA. A violation occurs when any preference or limitation based on age is indicated in an advertisement for employment.

EEOC interpretations state that any advertisements containing age-based "trigger words" violate the ADEA:

> When help wanted notices or advertisements contain terms and phrases such as "age 25 to 35," "young," "college student," "recent college graduate," "boy," "girl," or others of a similar nature, such a term or phrase deters the employment of older persons and is a violation of the Act, unless one of the exceptions applies. Such phrases as "age 40 to 50," "age over 65," "retired person," or "supplement your pension" discriminate against others within the protected group and, therefore, are prohibited unless one of the exceptions applies.

Unions backed the passage of the ADEA and in general have supported their members who have fought against age discrimination. Indeed, by virtue of the traditional emphasis on seniority benefits, union practices often favor the older worker. For example, union contracts customarily require that the employer lay off employees in the inverse order of seniority.

NOTE: AGING, DISABILITY, AND DISCRIMINATION

In 1990, Congress created a new antidiscrimination statute, the Americans with Disabilities Act (ADA). While the typical infirmities of aging are not a disability in terms of the ADA, many older people have disabilities and consequently may experience discrimination. The ADA may offer more protection than the ADEA.

Like the Civil Rights Act of 1964, it prohibits discrimination in public accommodations and government programs as well as employment. It also requires employers to make "reasonable accommodation" to allow people with disabilities the opportunity to participate as fully as possible in the workplace.

The ADA prohibits discrimination against people with disabilities, defined as being substantially impaired in a major life activity. A covered entity may not ask about the nature of a disability, but only ask about a person's ability to perform the tasks at issue. If the nature of the disability is known or revealed by the individual, the covered entity and person with a disability are to work together to find the reasonable accommodations that are appropriate. Reasonable accommodation can include changes such as different scheduling, testing for qualifications, extra equipment, altered environment, and other adaptations to make a "level playing field" for the person with a disability. Though the ADA does not require affirmative action for persons with disabilities, it can insist upon a significant response by an employer.

D.   EXCEPTIONS

[1]   FIRE FIGHTERS AND LAW ENFORCEMENT OFFICERS

Congress has recognized a possible rational nexus between age and job competency in regard to fire fighters and some law enforcement officials (police and prison guards). In 1996, the ADEA was amended to permit public employers to discriminate on the basis of age in the hiring and mandatory retirement of firefighters or law enforcement officers.

(j) Employment as firefighter or law enforcement officer

It shall not be unlawful for an employer which is a State, a political subdivision of a State, an agency or instrumentality of a State or a political subdivision of a State, or an interstate agency to fail or refuse to hire or to discharge any individual because of such individual's age if such action is taken —

(1) with respect to the employment of an individual as a firefighter or as a law enforcement officer, the employer has complied with section 3(d)(2) of the Age Discrimination in Employment Amendments of 1996 if the individual was discharged after the date described in such section, and the individual has attained —

(A) the age of hiring or retirement, respectively, in effect under applicable State or local law on March 3, 1983; or

(B)(i) if the individual was not hired, the age of hiring in effect on the date of such failure or refusal to hire under applicable State or local law enacted after September 30, 1996; or

(ii) if applicable State or local law was enacted after September 30, 1996, and the individual was discharged, the higher of —

(1) the age of retirement in effect on the date of such discharge under such law; and

(II) age 55; and

(2) pursuant to a bona fide hiring or retirement plan that is not a subterfuge to evade the purposes of this chapter.

29 U.S.C. § 623.

QUESTIONS

1. Should Congress exempt fire fighters and law enforcement personnel from the ADEA?

2. Can an argument be made that age is an accurate surrogate for ability to perform as a fire fighter or law enforcement official?

[2] EXECUTIVES AND POLICYMAKERS

Employers may still retire bona fide executives and high policymakers at age 65, so long as each individual so retired is entitled to an immediate, nonforfeitable annual retirement benefit of at least $44,000 or a straight-line annuity of an equivalent value. 29 U.S.C. § 631(c).

29 C.F.R. § 1625.12 provides the following concerning exemption of bona fide executives or high policymakers:

(b) Since this provision is an exemption from the non-discrimination requirements of the Act, the burden is on the one seeking to invoke the exemption to show that every element has been clearly and unmistakably met. Moreover, as with other exemptions from the Act, this exemption must be narrowly construed.

(c) An employee within the exemption can lawfully be forced to retire on account of age at age 65 or above. In addition, the employer is free to retain such employees, either in the same position or status or in a different position or status. For example, an employee who falls within the exemption may be offered a position of lesser status or a part-time position. An employee who accepts such a new status or position, however, may not be treated any less favorably, on account of age, than any similarly situated younger employee.

. . .

(d)(2) Even if an employee qualifies as an executive under the definition in § 541.1 of this chapter, the exemption from the ADEA may not be claimed unless the employee also meets the further criteria specified in the Conference Committee Report in the form of examples (see H.R. REP. No. 95-950, p. 9). The examples are intended to make clear that the exemption does not apply to middle-management employees, no matter how great their retirement income, but only to a very few top level employees who exercise substantial executive authority over a significant number of employees and a large volume of business. As stated in the Conference Report (H.R. Rep. No. 95-950, p. 9):

> Typically the head of a significant and substantial local or regional operation of a corporation [or other business organization], such as a major production facility or retail establishment, but not the head of a minor branch, warehouse or retail store, would be covered by the term "bona fide executive." Individuals at higher levels in the corporate organizational structure who possess comparable or greater levels of responsibility and authority as measured by established and recognized criteria would also be covered.

> The heads of major departments or divisions of corporations [or other business organizations] are usually located at corporate or regional headquarters. With respect to employees whose duties are associated with corporate headquarters operations, such as finance, marketing, legal, production and manufacturing (or in a corporation organized on a product line basis, the management of product lines), the definition would cover employees who head those divisions.

> In a large organization the immediate subordinates of the heads of these divisions sometimes also exercise executive authority, within the meaning of this exemption. The conferees intend the definition to cover such employees if they possess responsibility which is comparable to or greater than that possessed by the head of a significant and substantial local operation who meets the definition.

(e) The phrase "high policymaking position," according to the Conference Report (H.R. Rep. No. 95-950, p. 10), is limited to ". . . certain top level employees who are not 'bona fide executives'. . . ." Specifically, these are individuals who have little or no line authority but whose position and responsibility are such that they play a significant role in the development of corporate policy and effectively recommend the implementation thereof.

For example, the chief economist or the chief research scientist of a corporation typically has little line authority. His duties would be primarily intellectual as opposed to executive or managerial. His responsibility would be to evaluate significant economic or scientific trends and issues, to develop and recommend policy direction to the top executive officers of the corporation, and he would have a significant impact on the ultimate decision on such policies by virtue of his expertise and direct access to the decisionmakers. Such an employee would meet the definition of a "high policymaking" employee.

QUESTIONS

1.   What is the justification for the executive or high policymaker exemption?

2.   Is it sensible to have a law that will not allow a corporation to discriminate against a 65-year-old secretary, but may dismiss a 65-year-old executive solely on

account of age?

3.   In theory, would the rationale for exempting executives and high policymakers extend to any other employees?

4.   Does this exemption indicate that Congress believes that elderly employees are less capable to some extent than younger employees?

5.   If mandatory retirement on account of age was not permitted for executives or high policymakers, how would an employer justify the forced dismissal or retirement of an older executive?

E.   PROVING THE CASE OF DISCRIMINATION IN HIRING

The ADEA prohibition on age discrimination in hiring is difficult to prove, particularly if the applicant was never given a reason for the refusal to hire. Under the ADEA, the mere hiring by an employer of a younger applicant, rather than the rejected older applicant does not establish age discrimination. The rejected applicant must establish that age was a determining factor in the decision not to hire the older, protected applicant. To establish a violation, the applicant must prove that "but for" the applicant's age he or she would have been hired. In many cases the applicant will submit a résumé and simply receive no response. In such a case, proving age discrimination is almost impossible. Even if the applicant receives an interview, there may be no paper record of the reasons for the rejection. The interviewer merely mentally notes the unacceptable age and rejects the applicant. (Of course, if the employer does discriminate consistently, a pattern of discrimination may develop which might support a claim under the ADEA.) Though the applicant may strongly suspect age discrimination, proving it is another matter. As a result, most applicants merely mentally complain of the injury and move on to the next possible job.

F.   PROVING TERMINATION ON ACCOUNT OF AGE DISCRIMINATION

[1]   DIRECT EVIDENCE OF DISCRIMINATION

The great majority of complaints filed under the ADEA allege illegal termination on account of age, that is, forced retirement. The victim of age-motivated discharge has a fairly good chance of success under the ADEA.

The employer may have left a paper trail that proves the discrimination. Termination of an employee is rarely done without prior internal confirmation between the immediate supervisor and higher management. If the employee is being terminated because of age, the employer's files may contain evidence of the intent to discriminate on account of age.

NATON v. BANK OF CALIFORNIA
649 F.2d 691 (9th Cir. 1981)

Hug, Circuit Judge.

This action arises under the Age Discrimination in Employment Act of 1967 (ADEA), 29 U.S.C. §§ 621-34 (amended 1978). Plaintiff Paul Naton brought this suit against defendant Bank of California, N.A. (the "Bank") alleging that the Bank terminated his employment in 1975 because of his age.

Paul Naton was hired by the Bank in 1965 at age 51 as a trust business development officer. In January of 1975 the Bank instituted a reduction in force which affected 148 employees. On January 17, 1975, the Bank advised Naton that he was terminated pursuant to a bank-wide reduction in force. Naton performed no services at the behest of the Bank after January 17, 1975. In the Bank's separation report, a copy of which was given to Naton, the exit interviewer made the following notation:

Terminated due to staff reduction.

Employee will receive 3-1/2 months separation pay from January 20, 1975 through May 2, 1975. Last day worked, January 17, 1975.

EFFECTIVE TERMINATION DATE:

May 2, 1975.

Placed on leave of absence without pay May 5th to January 2, 1976. . . .

Proof of Age Discrimination

The Bank argues that the district court erred in denying its motion for a judgment notwithstanding the verdict. Such a motion should be granted only if "the evidence when viewed most favorably to the party against whom the motion is directed cannot support a verdict in that party's favor." *Traver v. Meshriy*, 627 F.2d 934, 939–40 (9th Cir. 1980). The precise question raised by the parties is whether the evidence supports a finding that Naton's age was a determining factor in his discharge. *See Kelly v. American Standard, Inc.*, 640 F.2d 974, 984–85 (9th Cir. 1981).

The following evidence was adduced at trial. Naton was terminated pursuant to a bank-wide reduction in force, which affected 148 individuals. Naton was employed in the Bank's Trust Department as a Trust Officer. The Trust Department was an autonomous unit within the Bank for purposes of selecting employees to be terminated. Seven Trust Officers in the Trust Department were terminated, including Naton, and all seven were within the protected age group. The Trust Department of the Bank was given no criteria for the selection of employees to be terminated other than cutting costs, and the Bank management had established no uniform criteria for the selection of employees to be terminated. One pretermination document listed the Trust Department terminees by name, age, salary and the net savings that would inure to the Bank from the employees' termination. There was no discussion or analysis in the document comparing the cost of the employee with the benefit derived from the services of the employee.

Although the Bank asserted that Naton's specific position of Trust Business Development Officer was eliminated because it was an unprofitable position, the evidence shows that the Bank continued the function that Naton performed after he was terminated.

There also was testimony concerning discriminatory comments made by Bank personnel. One of Naton's superiors, Mr. Wynne, advised Naton that the Bank had considered a wage freeze in lieu of the reduction in force, but rejected such an alternative because the Bank "would lose all [its] young people." Mr. David Jackson, Vice President of Corporate Trusts at the Bank, advised Naton that Naton had "very, very good grounds for an age discrimination suit." At an employment discrimination meeting called by Bank management for the purpose of informing supervisors about its affirmative action program, Mr. Vaughn asked the representative from the Personnel Department about the Bank's policy on age discrimination. The representative laughed and said that age discrimination was not important because "older people didn't have any organization for clout." Mrs. Hughes, Head of the Trust Personnel Office of the Trust Division, stated to Mr. Vaughn that an applicant, Mr. Healy, was "over the hill" and suggested that Mr. Vaughn "seek to hire younger people whom [he] could promote."

Based on this record, we conclude that the evidence was sufficient to support the jury's finding that Naton's age was a determining factor in his discharge. The district court did not err in denying the Bank's motion for a judgment notwithstanding the verdict.

––––––––––

Even if the employee establishes direct evidence of age discrimination, the employer can attempt to show that it had legitimate reasons to fire (or not hire) the employee.

GLANZMAN v. METROPOLITAN MANAGEMENT CORPORATION
391 F.3d 506 (3d Cir. 2004)

ALDISERT, CIRCUIT JUDGE.

Here we decide two separate, but related appeals from orders of the district court granting summary judgment in favor of Metropolitan Management ("Metropolitan") in a complaint by Julia Glanzman in Appeal No. 03-4546 under the Age Discrimination in Employment Act ("ADEA"), 29 U.S.C. §§ 621–634 (2000) and the Pennsylvania Human Relations Act ("PHRA"), 43 P.S. §§ 951–963 (1991) . . .

Glanzman's primary argument is that the district court erred in determining that she had failed to present sufficient direct evidence of age discrimination.

In reviewing the district court's grant of summary judgment we consider whether Glanzman: (1) presented direct evidence of age discrimination against

Metropolitan, thereby triggering the test presented in *Price Waterhouse v. Hopkins*, 490 U.S. 228 (1989) ("Price Waterhouse test"), shifting to it the burden of showing that they would have terminated her employment even if they had not considered her age; (2) presented sufficient evidence to negate Metropolitan's evidence in support of its contention that it would have fired her, because of legitimate stated reasons, even if it had not been for her age; and (3) was harmed by the allegedly retaliatory conduct of Metropolitan.

. . .

We conclude that the district court erred in determining that Glanzman had failed to produce direct evidence of age discrimination. We decide, however, that Metropolitan met its burden of showing that it would have terminated her employment even if it had not considered her age and that Glanzman presented insufficient evidence to negate Metropolitan's evidence. We, therefore, affirm the judgment.

. . .

I.

Glanzman alleges that she was discharged because of her age from her job as the manager of Doylestown Meadows, a 150-unit apartment complex in Bucks County, Pennsylvania. The complex is owned by Appellee Metropolitan. She had managed the complex for the previous owner and was then hired, at the age of sixty, to stay on as the manager when Metropolitan acquired the complex in 1997.

She had a history of accepting, but not reporting, personal collect telephone calls with charges totaling in excess of $900.00. She said that the calls were from a sick aunt, but in reality they were from her boyfriend who was serving time in prison. She made arrangements to reimburse Metropolitan for the expense of these calls and was allowed to keep her job. She had also allowed her granddaughter to access the internet from her office computer which resulted in charges to Metropolitan. When confronted with this wrongdoing, she apologized. She was again asked to reimburse Metropolitan for the cost and allowed to keep her job.

Testimony was presented that Glanzman was not always where she was supposed to be during working hours and that she often failed to respond in a timely manner when paged. Metropolitan had reason to believe that Glanzman, who owned rental property herself, used Metropolitan employees, Joseph W. Fries and Phil Rittenhouse, to perform work at her property during hours when they were being paid by Metropolitan to work at Doylestown Meadows.

Metropolitan had reason to believe Glanzman was attempting to steal a dishwasher to place in one of her properties. She said that a tenant in Doylestown Meadows had requested the dishwasher but the tenant stated that she did not request it and did not want it because she only used her existing dishwasher to store bread and cereal. When confronted with this information, Glanzman changed her story and said that the tenant's daughter had requested the dishwasher. This proved to be untrue as well.

On her part, Glanzman relies on three statements made by her supervisors at Metropolitan. First, some ten months before her termination, Glenn Fagan, vice president of property management for Metropolitan, asked her if she had told the son of one of the residents that she was 63 years old. Second, soon after the conversation with Glenn Fagan, Trish Kotsay, her immediate supervisor, asked if she was thinking of retiring. Third, Glenn Fagan allegedly told two of Glanzman's co-workers, Joseph Fries and Phil Rittenhouse, that he wanted to fire her and "replace her with a young chippie with big tits."

Glanzman ceased her employment during a conversation between Glenn Fagan and her. Glenn Fagan confronted her with the fact that the tenant in apartment 115 had not requested the dishwasher that had been ordered for that apartment and that the tenant had specifically said she had no need for the dishwasher. Glanzman said that the woman's daughter had ordered the dishwasher. Glenn Fagan then suggested that they call the daughter. At this point, Glanzman either voluntarily resigned or was fired. For purposes of the present case, Metropolitan has agreed that she was fired. . . .

IV.

"To prevail on an age-based termination claim, a plaintiff must show that his or her age 'actually motivated' and 'had a determinative influence on' the employer's decision to fire him or her." This showing that age motivated or had a determinative influence on the decision of the employer can be made either through the use of direct evidence or circumstantial evidence. If direct evidence is used, the proponent of the evidence must satisfy the test laid out in *Price Waterhouse*, in order to prove a violation of the ADEA. If circumstantial evidence of age discrimination is used, then the proponent of the evidence must satisfy the three-step test of *McDonnell Douglas Corp. v. Green*, 411 U.S. 792 (1973).

In this case, Glanzman relies solely on direct evidence of age discrimination, and urges this court to use the Price Waterhouse framework. We will do so. Under Price Waterhouse, once direct evidence of age discrimination is presented the "burden of persuasion on the issue of causation shifts, and the employer must prove that it would have fired the plaintiff even if it had not considered . . . [her] age."

A.

To be "direct" for purposes of the Price Waterhouse test, evidence must be sufficient to allow the jury to find that the decision makers placed a substantial negative reliance on the plaintiff's age in reaching their decision. This means that Glanzman must produce evidence of discriminatory attitudes about age that were causally related to the decision to fire her.

Metropolitan points out that "not all evidence that is probative of illegitimate motives . . . is sufficient to constitute direct evidence of discrimination." Specifically, Metropolitan mentions "stray remarks in the workplace" and "statements by non-decision makers" as the type of evidence that would not rise to the level of "direct" for purposes of the Price Waterhouse test.

Glanzman points to three pieces of "direct" evidence of discrimination on the part of her superiors at Metropolitan. First, ten months before her termination, Glenn Fagan asked her if she had told the son of one of the residents that she was sixty-three years old. The district court correctly concluded that there was nothing discriminatory in this inquiry and it certainly does not provide direct evidence of age discrimination. Second, shortly after this question from Glenn Fagan, Ms. Kotsay, Glanzman's immediate supervisor, asked Glanzman about her retirement plans. Again the district court correctly determined that this was not direct evidence of age discrimination and could just as easily be explained by a desire on Metropolitan's part to do some long-term planning.

The third piece of evidence proffered by Glanzman merits a more in depth consideration. Glanzman alleges that Glenn Fagan told two of her co-workers, Joseph Fries and Phil Rittenhouse, that he wanted to fire her and replace her with an exceptionally endowed younger woman. The district court determined that this remark was not direct evidence of discrimination because, though it was offensive, it does not show that "the reason for Ms. Glanzman's termination was to replace her with a 'young chippie with big tits.' " . . . Metropolitan adds to this explanation by contending that this statement cannot be direct evidence because "the comment was not made by Judy Goldstein or Scott Fagan, the individuals who made the decision to discharge her."

. . . Glenn Fagan is the vice president of property management for Metropolitan and was, in that capacity, Ms. Glanzman's boss. It is undisputed that Glenn Fagan frequently paged Ms. Glanzman and checked in on the property about once a month. Ms. Glanzman's employment was terminated during a conversation with Glenn Fagan. . . .

. . . If Glenn Fagan was not the decision maker in the decision to terminate Glanzman's employment he was almost certainly involved in the decision-making process. . . . On the basis of the evidence in the record, therefore, a rational jury could easily find that Glenn Fagan was a decision maker, or at least a participant in the employment decision in this case.

B.

We are troubled by the district court's determination that Glenn Fagan's remark "does not in and of itself reflect that the reason for Ms. Glanzman's termination was to replace her with a" younger woman. To be sure, Glenn Fagan's statement does not support a compellable inference that ageism was the cause of the decision to terminate Ms. Glanzman's employment. Such a statement, however, is fraught with permissible inferences that he desired to fire Ms. Glanzman at least in part because of her age. One could reasonably determine that Glenn Fagan's statement that he would replace Ms. Glanzman with a younger woman is, in effect, an admission that at least part of the actual reason for the employment decision was a desire to hire someone younger and more endowed. A rational jury could find that Metropolitan placed a substantial negative reliance on Glanzman's age in making the decision to terminate her employment. Accordingly, we conclude that Glanzman met her burden and presented direct evidence.

VI.

Because Glanzman has succeeded in presenting the necessary quantum of direct evidence of discrimination, the burden of going forward with the evidence shifts to Metropolitan to "prove that it would have fired . . . [Glanzman] even if it had not considered . . . [her] age." This is a high burden on a motion for summary judgment because Metropolitan must leave no doubt that a rational jury would find that Metropolitan would have fired Ms. Glanzman even if it had not been for the discriminatory statement.

The district court concluded that Metropolitan met even this high evidentiary standard. The opinion of the district court states that "evidence of record clearly demonstrates that the defendant-employer has shown that it would have fired the plaintiff even if it had not considered her age." The district court then went on to lay out myriad non-age-related reasons for which any rational employer would have fired Ms. Glanzman.

. . .

We conclude that the district court's assessment of the facts is accurate. Glanzman had already been warned about serious violations of Metropolitan's policies, she was then caught committing even more serious violations, and lying to cover up what Metropolitan reasonably determined to be a plan to steal a dishwasher for use on a property she owned. Glanzman does not even try to rebut most of the district court's analysis in her brief. Where she does attempt a rebuttal, she simply ignores the overwhelming weight of evidence against her. Metropolitan does not have to prove that Glanzman committed these infractions, but only that it was reasonable in its belief that she had committed them. Even if she committed only a few of them, Metropolitan would have had a surfeit of legitimate reasons to fire her. We thus conclude that no rational jury could doubt that Metropolitan would have fired Glanz-man even if it had not considered her age. We affirm on the ADEA claim because we conclude that Metropolitan has succeeded in meeting its burden under the Price Waterhouse test.

Accordingly, the judgments of the district court will be affirmed.

Not every derogatory statement about an employee's age has supported a finding of age discrimination. Consider the following examples, none of which were found to create a reasonable inference of age discrimination: *Gagne v. Northwestern Nat'l Ins. Co.*, 881 F.2d 309, 314 (1989) (supervisor stated he "needed younger blood"); *Barnes v. Southwest Forest Industries, Inc.*, 814 F.2d 607 (11th Cir. 1987) (plaintiff told "you would have to take another physical examination and at your age, I don't believe you could pass it"); *La Montagne v. American Convenience Products, Inc.*, 750 F.2d 1405 (7th Cir. 1984) (recommendation that "bright young individual" be hired to replace plaintiff and that plaintiff should not be discharged until "younger man" was available to replace him); *Carpenter v. American Excelsior Co.*, 650 F. Supp. 933, 938 (E.D. Mich. 1987) (statements by company official that he liked his salespeople "young, mean and lean" and that plaintiff was not as young as he used to be); *Williamson v. Owens-Illinois, Inc.*, 589 F. Supp. 1051, 1058 (N.D. Ohio 1984) (comment "Why should I promote an older pilot when I've got a lot of sharp young guys who want to get ahead?" held insufficient).

[2]   PRIMA FACIE CASE

As employers become more aware of the ADEA, files may be "cleansed." Either no written documents that indicate the discrimination will be created or they will have been destroyed long before the beginning of any litigation and the concomitant discovery. Because of the difficulty of producing a "smoking gun," courts permit ADEA plaintiffs to prevail if they can establish a prima facie case by circumstantial evidence. Courts in ADEA cases almost uniformly rely on the standards developed for proving a prima facie case under Title VII of the Civil Rights Act of 1964 since the language of the ADEA was derived in large measure from Title VII. In particular, in *McDonnell Douglas Corp. v. Green*, 411 U.S. 792, 802 (1973), the Supreme Court devised a four-part test for establishing a prima facie case of discrimination involving hiring. The Supreme Court test, modified to fit the situation of an ADEA complaint, is:

(1) that the individual belonged to the protected group;

(2) that the applicant applied for, or was employed in and was qualified for, a job for which the employer was looking to hire;

(3) that, despite the applicant's qualifications, he or she was rejected; and

(4) that after the rejection the position remained open, and the employer continued to seek applicants from persons of the complainant's qualifications or filled the position with another employee with comparable qualifications.

If the plaintiff establishes a prima facie case, the defendant has the burden of going forward.

> Prima facie proof of age discrimination does not necessarily entitle the plaintiff to a jury determination of his claim. Such proof simply shifts to the defendant employer the burden of producing evidence of nondiscriminatory reasons [for the discharge or termination]. . . . If the employer offers proof which raises a genuine issue of fact as to whether it terminated the plaintiff for good cause, or for some basis other than age, the presumption of discrimination engendered by plaintiff's initial evidence is dispelled.

Bohrer v. Hanes Corp., 715 F.2d 213 (5th Cir. 1983).

[3]   PRETEXTUAL REASONS FOR TERMINATION

Once the plaintiff has provided proof of discrimination, the defendant can attempt to prove that it would have taken the same action in regard to the defendant even if it had not taken the defendant's age into account. This burden on the defendant was enunciated in a sex discrimination case, *Price Waterhouse v. Hopkins*, 490 U.S. 228 (1988), but the holding also applies to age discrimination cases.

We hold that when a plaintiff in a Title VII case proves that her gender played a motivating part in an employment decision, the defendant may avoid a finding of liability only by proving by a preponderance of the evidence that it would have made the same decision even if it had not taken the plaintiff's gender into account.

Id. at 258.

Even if the defendant has articulated a legitimate, nondiscriminatory reason for the dismissal, the plaintiff can attempt to prove that the legitimate reasons offered by the employer were not its true reasons, but were a pretext for age discrimination.

Pretext exists when an employer does not honestly represent its reasons for terminating an employee. . . . And while rejection of the employer's explanation does not compel a finding of discrimination, "it is permissible for the [factfinder] to infer the ultimate fact of discrimination from the falsity of the employer's explanation." *Reeves*, 530 U.S. at 147.

Miller v. Eby Realty Group LLC, 396 F.3d 1105, 1111 (10th Cir. 2005).

––––––––––

In 1993, the Supreme Court decided *St. Mary's Honor Ctr. v. Hicks*, 509 U.S. 502 (1993). By a five to four vote (and a confusing majority opinion), the Court held that if the plaintiff claimed the defendant's explanation of its actions was pretextual, the plaintiff had to prove discriminatory actions or animus as the reason for the termination (or refusal to hire or promote) by the defendant.

The Court explicitly stated that the plaintiff *may* prevail in a discrimination case by establishing a prima facie case and by showing that the employer's proffered non-discriminatory reasons for her demotion or discharge are factually false. *Hicks* at 509. This "will permit the trier of fact to infer the ultimate fact of intentional discrimination." *Id.* "[N]o additional proof of discrimination is required." *Id.*

However, "the ultimate burden of persuading the trier of fact that the defendant intentionally discriminated against the plaintiff remains at all times with the plaintiff." *Id.* at 507 (citation omitted). As such, the plaintiff might be well advised to present additional evidence of discrimination, because the fact-finder is not *required* to find in her favor simply because she establishes prima facie case and shows that the employer's proffered reasons are false.

The Supreme Court again addressed the plaintiff's assertion of "pretext" in the following case.

REEVES v. SANDERSON PLUMBING PRODUCTS, INC.
530 U.S. 133 (2000)

I

Justice O'Connor.

In October 1995, petitioner Roger Reeves was 57 years old and had spent 40 years in the employ of respondent, Sanderson Plumbing Products, Inc., a manufacturer of toilet seats and covers. 197 F.3d 688, 690 (CA5 1999). Petitioner worked in a department known as the "Hinge Room," where he supervised the "regular line." Joe Oswalt, in his mid-thirties, supervised the Hinge Room's "special line," and Russell Caldwell, the manager of the Hinge Room and age 45, supervised both petitioner and Oswalt. Petitioner's responsibilities included recording the attendance and hours of those under his supervision, and reviewing a weekly report that listed the hours worked by each employee.

In the summer of 1995, Caldwell informed Powe Chesnut, the director of manufacturing and the husband of company president Sandra Sanderson, that "production was down" in the Hinge Room because employees were often absent and were "coming in late and leaving early." Because the monthly attendance reports did not indicate a problem, Chesnut ordered an audit of the Hinge Room's timesheets for July, August, and September of that year. According to Chesnut's testimony, that investigation revealed "numerous timekeeping errors and misrepresentations on the part of Caldwell, Reeves, and Oswalt." Following the audit, Chesnut, along with Dana Jester, vice president of human resources, and Tom Whitaker, vice president of operations, recommended to company president Sanderson that petitioner and Caldwell be fired. In October 1995, Sanderson followed the recommendation and discharged both petitioner and Caldwell.

In June 1996, petitioner filed suit in the United States District Court for the Northern District of Mississippi, contending that he had been fired because of his age in violation of the Age Discrimination in Employment Act of 1967 (ADEA), At trial, respondent contended that it had fired petitioner due to his failure to maintain accurate attendance records, while petitioner attempted to demonstrate that respondent's explanation was pretext for age discrimination. Petitioner introduced evidence that he had accurately recorded the attendance and hours of the employees under his supervision, and that Chesnut, whom Oswalt described as wielding "absolute power" within the company, had demonstrated age-based animus in his dealings with petitioner.

During the trial, the District Court twice denied oral motions by respondent for judgment as a matter of law under Rule 50 of the Federal Rules of Civil Procedure, and the case went to the jury. The court instructed the jury that "if the plaintiff fails to prove age was a determinative or motivating factor in the decision to terminate him, then your verdict shall be for the defendant." So charged, the jury returned a verdict in favor of petitioner, awarding him $35,000 in compensatory damages, and found that respondent's age discrimination had been "willful." The District Court accordingly entered judgment for petitioner in the amount of

$70,000, which included $35,000 in liquidated damages based on the jury's finding of willfulness. Respondent then renewed its motion for judgment as a matter of law and alternatively moved for a new trial, while petitioner moved for front pay. The District Court denied respondent's motions and granted petitioner's, awarding him $28,490.80 in front pay for two years' lost income. 2 *id.* Doc. Nos. 40, 41.

The Court of Appeals for the Fifth Circuit reversed, holding that petitioner had not introduced sufficient evidence to sustain the jury's finding of unlawful discrimination. After noting respondent's proffered justification for petitioner's discharge, the court acknowledged that petitioner "very well may" have offered sufficient evidence for "a reasonable jury [to] have found that [respondent's] explanation for its employment decision was pretextual." The court explained, however, that this was "not dispositive" of the ultimate issue — namely, "whether Reeves presented sufficient evidence that his age motivated [respondent's] employment decision." Addressing this question, the court weighed petitioner's additional evidence of discrimination against other circumstances surrounding his discharge. Specifically, the court noted that Chesnut's age-based comments "were not made in the direct context of Reeves's termination"; there was no allegation that the two other individuals who had recommended that petitioner be fired (Jester and Whitaker) were motivated by age; two of the decisionmakers involved in petitioner's discharge (Jester and Sanderson) were over the age of 50; all three of the Hinge Room supervisors were accused of inaccurate recordkeeping; and several of respondent's management positions were filled by persons over age 50 when petitioner was fired. On this basis, the court concluded that petitioner had not introduced sufficient evidence for a rational jury to conclude that he had been discharged because of his age. *Id.* at 694.

We granted certiorari, 528 U.S. 985 (1999), to resolve a conflict among the Courts of Appeals as to whether a plaintiff's prima facie case of discrimination (as defined in *McDonnell Douglas Corp. v. Green*, 411 U.S. 792 (1973)), combined with sufficient evidence for a reasonable factfinder to reject the employer's nondiscriminatory explanation for its decision, is adequate to sustain a finding of liability for intentional discrimination.

II

Under the ADEA, it is "unlawful for an employer . . . to fail or refuse to hire or to discharge any individual or otherwise discriminate against any individual with respect to his compensation, terms, conditions, or privileges of employment, because of such individual's age." 29 U.S.C. § 623(a)(1). When a plaintiff alleges disparate treatment, "liability depends on whether the protected trait (under the ADEA, age) actually motivated the employer's decision." *Hazen Paper Co. v. Biggins*, 507 U.S. 604 (1993). That is, the plaintiff's age must have "actually played a role in [the employer's decision-making] process and had a determinative influence on the outcome." Recognizing that "the question facing triers of fact in discrimination cases is both sensitive and difficult," and that "there will seldom be 'eyewitness' testimony as to the employer's mental processes," the Courts of Appeals, including the Fifth Circuit in this case, have employed some variant of the framework articulated in *McDonnell Douglas* to analyze ADEA claims that are based principally on circumstantial evidence. This Court has not squarely addressed whether the *McDonnell Douglas* framework, developed to assess claims brought under § 703(a)(1) of Title VII of the Civil Rights Act of 1964, 78 Stat. 255, 42 U.S.C. § 2000e-2(a)(1), also applies to ADEA actions.

McDonnell Douglas and subsequent decisions have "established an allocation of the burden of production and an order for the presentation of proof in . . . discriminatory-treatment cases." First, the plaintiff must establish a prima facie case of discrimination. . . . It is undisputed that petitioner satisfied this burden here: (i) at the time he was fired, he was a member of the class protected by the ADEA ("individuals who are at least 40 years of age," 29 U.S.C. § 631(a)), (ii) he was otherwise qualified for the position of Hinge Room supervisor, (iii) he was discharged by respondent, and (iv) respondent successively hired three persons in their thirties to fill petitioner's position. See 197 F.3d at 691–692. The burden therefore shifted to respondent to "produce evidence that the plaintiff was rejected, or someone else was preferred, for a legitimate, nondiscriminatory reason." This burden is one of production, not persuasion; it "can involve no credibility assessment." Respondent met this burden by offering admissible evidence sufficient for the trier of fact to conclude that petitioner was fired because of his failure to maintain accurate attendance records. Accordingly, "the *McDonnell Douglas* framework — with its presumptions and burdens" — disappeared, and the sole remaining issue was "discrimination *vel non*."

Although intermediate evidentiary burdens shift back and forth under this framework, "the ultimate burden of persuading the trier of fact that the defendant intentionally discriminated against the plaintiff remains at all times with the plaintiff." And in attempting to satisfy this burden, the plaintiff — once the employer produces sufficient evidence to support a nondiscrimina-tory explanation for its decision — must be afforded the "opportunity to prove by a preponderance of the evidence that the legitimate reasons offered by the defendant were not its true reasons, but were a pretext for discrimination." That is, the plaintiff may attempt to establish that he was the victim of intentional discrimination "by showing that the employer's proffered explanation is unworthy of credence." Moreover, although the presumption of discrimination "drops out of the picture" once the defendant meets its burden of production, the trier of fact may still consider the evidence establishing the plaintiff's prima facie case "and inferences properly drawn therefrom . . . on the issue of whether the defendant's explanation is pretextual."

In this case, the evidence supporting respondent's explanation for petitioner's discharge consisted primarily of testimony by Chesnut and Sanderson and documentation of petitioner's alleged "shoddy record keeping". Chesnut testified that a 1993 audit of Hinge Room operations revealed "a very lax assembly line" where employees were not adhering to general work rules. As a result of that audit, petitioner was placed on 90 days' probation for unsatisfactory performance. 197 F.3d at 690. In 1995, Chesnut ordered another investigation of the Hinge Room, which, according to his testimony, revealed that petitioner was not correctly recording the absences and hours of employees. Respondent introduced summaries of that investigation documenting several attendance violations by 12 employees under petitioner's supervision, and noting that each should have been disciplined in some manner. Chesnut testified that this failure to discipline absent and late employees is "extremely important when you are dealing with a union" because uneven enforcement across departments would keep the company "in grievance and arbitration cases, which are costly, all the time." He and Sanderson also stated that petitioner's errors, by failing to adjust for hours not worked, cost the company overpaid wages. Sanderson testified that she accepted the recommendation to discharge petitioner because he had "intentionally falsified company pay records."

Petitioner, however, made a substantial showing that respondent's explanation was false. First, petitioner offered evidence that he had properly maintained the attendance records . . . both petitioner and Oswalt testified that the company's automated timeclock often failed to scan employees' timecards, so that the timesheets would not record any time of arrival. . . . Chesnut acknowledged that the timeclock sometimes malfunctioned, and that if "people were there at their work stations" at the start of the shift, the supervisor "would write in seven o'clock." Petitioner also testified that when employees arrived before or stayed after their shifts, he would assign them additional work so they would not be overpaid.

Petitioner similarly cast doubt on whether he was responsible for any failure to discipline late and absent employees . . .

Based on this evidence, the Court of Appeals concluded that petitioner "very well may be correct" that "a reasonable jury could have found that [respondent's] explanation for its employment decision was pretextual." . . . Nonetheless, the court held that this showing, standing alone, was insufficient to sustain the jury's finding of liability: "We must, as an essential final step, determine whether Reeves presented sufficient evidence that his age motivated [respondent's] employment decision." *Ibid.* And in making this determination, the Court of Appeals ignored the evidence supporting petitioner's prima facie case and challenging respondent's explanation for its decision. The court confined its review of evidence favoring petitioner to that evidence showing that Chesnut had directed derogatory, age-based comments at petitioner, and that Chesnut had singled out petitioner for harsher treatment than younger employees. See *ibid.* It is therefore apparent that the court believed that only this additional evidence of discrimination was relevant to whether the jury's verdict should stand. That is, the Court of Appeals proceeded from the assumption that a prima facie case of discrimination, combined with sufficient evidence for the trier of fact to disbelieve the defendant's legitimate, nondiscriminatory reason for its decision, is insufficient as a matter of law to sustain a jury's finding of intentional discrimination.

In so reasoning, the Court of Appeals misconceived the evidentiary burden borne by plaintiffs who attempt to prove intentional discrimination through indirect evidence . . . The ultimate question is whether the employer intentionally discriminated, and proof that "the employer's proffered reason is unpersuasive, or even obviously contrived, does not necessarily establish that the plaintiff's proffered reason . . . is correct." In other words, "it is not enough . . . to *dis* believe the employer; the factfinder must *believe* the plaintiff's explanation of intentional discrimination."

In reaching this conclusion, however, we reasoned that it is *permissible* for the trier of fact to infer the ultimate fact of discrimination from the falsity of the employer's explanation. Specifically, we stated:

> "The factfinder's disbelief of the reasons put forward by the defendant (particularly if disbelief is accompanied by a suspicion of mendacity) may, together with the elements of the prima facie case, suffice to show intentional discrimination. Thus, rejection of the defendant's proffered reasons will permit the trier of fact to infer the ultimate fact of intentional discrimination." *Id.* at 511.

Proof that the defendant's explanation is unworthy of credence is simply one form of circumstantial evidence that is probative of intentional discrimination, and it may be quite persuasive . . . In appropriate circumstances, the trier of fact can reasonably infer from the falsity of the explanation that the employer is dissembling to cover up a discriminatory purpose. Such an inference is consistent with the general principle of evidence law that the factfinder is entitled to consider a party's dishonesty about a material fact as "affirmative evidence of guilt." Moreover, once the employer's justification has been eliminated, discrimination may well be the most likely alternative explanation, especially since the employer is in the best position to put forth the actual reason for its decision. . . . Thus, a plaintiff's prima facie case, combined with sufficient evidence to find that the employer's asserted justification is false, may permit the trier of fact to conclude that the employer unlawfully discriminated.

This is not to say that such a showing by the plaintiff will *always* be adequate to sustain a jury's finding of liability. Certainly there will be instances where, although the plaintiff has established a prima facie case and set forth sufficient evidence to reject the defendant's explanation, no rational factfinder could conclude that the action was discriminatory. For instance, an employer would be entitled to judgment as a matter of law if the record conclusively revealed some other, nondiscriminatory reason for the employer's decision, or if the plaintiff created only a weak issue of fact as to whether the employer's reason was untrue and there was abundant and uncontroverted independent evidence that no discrimination had occurred. To hold otherwise would be effectively to insulate an entire category of employment discrimination cases from review under Rule 50, and we have reiterated that trial courts should not " 'treat discrimination differently from other ultimate questions of fact.' "

Whether judgment as a matter of law is appropriate in any particular case will depend on a number of factors. Those include the strength of the plaintiff's prima facie case, the probative value of the proof that the employer's explanation is false, and any other evidence that supports the employer's case and that properly may be considered on a motion for judgment as a matter of law. See *infra*, at 15–16. For purposes of this case, we need not — and could not — resolve all of the circumstances in which such factors would entitle an employer to judgment as a matter of law. It suffices to say that, because a prima facie case and sufficient evidence to reject the employer's explanation may permit a finding of liability, the Court of Appeals erred in proceeding from the premise that a plaintiff must always introduce additional, independent evidence of discrimination.

III

A

The remaining question is whether, despite the Court of Appeals' misconception of petitioner's evidentiary burden, respondent was nonetheless entitled to judgment as a matter of law. Under Rule 50, a court should render judgment as a matter of law when "a party has been fully heard on an issue and there is no legally sufficient evidentiary basis for a reasonable jury to find for that party on that issue." Fed. Rule Civ. Proc. 50(a) . . .

. . . Thus, although the court should review the record as a whole, it must disregard all evidence favorable to the moving party that the jury is not required to believe. That is, the court should give credence to the evidence favoring the nonmovant as well as that "evidence supporting the moving party that is uncontradicted and unimpeached, at least to the extent that that evidence comes from disinterested witnesses."

B

Applying this standard here, it is apparent that respondent was not entitled to judgment as a matter of law. In this case, in addition to establishing a prima facie case of discrimination and creating a jury issue as to the falsity of the employer's explanation, petitioner introduced additional evidence that Chesnut was motivated by age-based animus and was principally responsible for petitioner's firing. Petitioner testified that Chesnut had told him that he "was so old [he] must have come over on the Mayflower" and, on one occasion when petitioner was having difficulty starting a machine, that he "was too damn old to do [his] job." According to petitioner, Chesnut would regularly "cuss at me and shake his finger in my face." Oswalt, roughly 24 years younger than petitioner, corroborated that there was an "obvious difference" in how Chesnut treated them. He stated that, although he and Chesnut "had [their] differences," "it was nothing compared to the way [Chesnut] treated Roger." *Ibid.* Oswalt explained that Chesnut "tolerated quite a bit" from him even though he "defied" Chesnut "quite often," but that Chesnut treated petitioner "in a manner, as you would . . . treat . . . a child when . . . you're angry with [him]." Petitioner also demonstrated that, according to company records, he and Oswalt had nearly identical rates of productivity in 1993. Yet respondent conducted an efficiency study of only the regular line, supervised by petitioner, and placed only petitioner on probation. Chesnut conducted that efficiency study and, after having testified to the contrary on direct examination, acknowledged on cross-examination that he had recommended that petitioner be placed on probation following the study.

Further, petitioner introduced evidence that Chesnut was the actual decision-maker behind his firing. Chesnut was married to Sanderson, who made the formal decision to discharge petitioner. Although Sanderson testified that she fired petitioner because he had "intentionally falsified company pay records," respondent only introduced evidence concerning the inaccuracy of the records, not their falsification. A 1994 letter authored by Chesnut indicated that he berated other company directors, who were supposedly his co-equals, about how to do their jobs. Moreover, Oswalt testified that all of respondent's employees feared Chesnut, and that Chesnut had exercised "absolute power" within the company for "as long as [he] can remember."

In holding that the record contained insufficient evidence to sustain the jury's verdict, the Court of Appeals misapplied the standard of review dictated by Rule 50. Again, the court disregarded critical evidence favorable to petitioner — namely, the evidence supporting petitioner's prima facie case and undermining respondent's nondiscriminatory explanation. The court also failed to draw all reasonable inferences in favor of petitioner . . .

The ultimate question in every employment discrimination case involving a claim of disparate treatment is whether the plaintiff was the victim of intentional discrimination. Given the evidence in the record supporting petitioner, we see no reason to subject the parties to an additional round of litigation before the Court of Appeals rather than to resolve the matter here. The District Court plainly informed the jury that petitioner was required to show "by a preponderance of the evidence that his age was a determining and motivating factor in the decision of [respondent] to terminate him." The court instructed the jury that, to show that respondent's explanation was a pretext for discrimination, petitioner had to demonstrate "1, that the stated reasons were not the real reasons for [petitioner's] discharge; *and* 2, that age discrimination was the real reason for [petitioner's] discharge." *Ibid.* (emphasis added). Given that petitioner established a *prima facie* case of discrimination, introduced enough evidence for the jury to reject respondent's explanation, and produced additional evidence of age-based animus, there was sufficient evidence for the jury to find that respondent had intentionally discriminated. The District Court was therefore correct to submit the case to the jury, and the Court of Appeals erred in overturning its verdict.

For these reasons, the judgment of the Court of Appeals is reversed.

The burden of proof in cases where the plaintiff alleges that the employer's stated reason for the termination was pretextual was answered by the Supreme Court in the following case.

GROSS v. FBL FINANCIAL SERVICES, INC.
129 S. Ct. 2343 (2009)

JUSTICE THOMAS.

The question presented by the petitioner in this case is whether a plaintiff must present direct evidence of age discrimination in order to obtain a mixed-motives jury instruction in a suit brought under the Age Discrimination in Employment Act of 1967 (ADEA), 29 U.S.C. § 621 *et seq.* Because we hold that such a jury instruction is never proper in an ADEA case, we vacate the decision below.

I

Petitioner Jack Gross began working for respondent FBL Financial Group, Inc. (FBL), in 1971. As of 2001, Gross held the position of claims administration director. But in 2003, when he was 54 years old, Gross was reassigned to the position of claims project coordinator. At that same time, FBL transferred many of Gross' job responsibilities to a newly created position — claims administration manager. That position was given to Lisa Kneeskern, who had previously been supervised by Gross and who was then in her early forties. Although Gross (in his new position) and Kneeskern received the same compensation, Gross considered the reassignment a demotion because of FBL's reallocation of his former job responsibilities to Kneeskern.

In April 2004, Gross filed suit in District Court, alleging that his reassignment to the position of claims project coordinator violated the ADEA, which makes it unlawful for an employer to take adverse action against an employee "because of such individual's age." 29 U.S.C. § 623(a). The case proceeded to trial, where Gross introduced evidence suggesting that his reassignment was based at least in part on his age. FBL defended its decision on the grounds that Gross' reassignment was part of a corporate restructuring and that Gross' new position was better suited to his skills.

At the close of trial, and over FBL's objections, the District Court instructed the jury that it must return a verdict for Gross if he proved, by a preponderance of the evidence, that FBL "demoted [him] to claims projec[t] coordinator" and that his "age was a motivating factor" in FBL's decision to demote him. App. 9-10. The jury was further instructed that Gross' age would qualify as a " 'motivating factor,' if [it] played a part or a role in [FBL]'s decision to demote [him]." *Id.* at 10. The jury was also instructed regarding FBL's burden of proof. According to the District Court, the "verdict must be for [FBL] . . . if it has been proved by the preponderance of the evidence that [FBL] would have demoted [Gross] regardless of his age." *Ibid.* The jury returned a verdict for Gross, awarding him $46,945 in lost compensation. *Id.* at 8.

FBL challenged the jury instructions on appeal. The United States Court of Appeals for the Eighth Circuit reversed and remanded for a new trial, holding that the jury had been incorrectly instructed under the standard established in *Price Waterhouse v. Hopkins*, 490 U.S. 228 (2008). In *Price Waterhouse*, this Court addressed the proper allocation of the burden of persuasion in cases brought under Title VII of the Civil Rights Act of 1964, when an employee alleges that he suffered an adverse employment action because of both permissible and impermissible considerations — *i.e.*, a "mixed-motives" case. The *Price Waterhouse* decision was splintered. . . . .

The parties have asked us to decide whether a plaintiff must "present direct evidence of discrimination in order to obtain a mixed-motive instruction in a non-Title VII discrimination case." Pet. for Cert. i. Before reaching this question, however, we must first determine whether the burden of persuasion ever shifts to the party defending an alleged mixed-motives discrimination claim brought under the ADEA. We hold that it does not.

A

Petitioner relies on this Court's decisions construing Title VII for his interpretation of the ADEA. Because Title VII is materially different with respect to the relevant burden of persuasion, however, these decisions do not control our construction of the ADEA.

In *Price Waterhouse*, a plurality of the Court and two Justices concurring in the judgment determined that once a "plaintiff in a Title VII case proves that [the plaintiff's membership in a protected class] played a motivating part in an employment decision, the defendant may avoid a finding of liability only by proving by a preponderance of the evidence that it would have made the same decision even if it had not taken [that factor] into account." Congress has since amended Title VII by explicitly authorizing discrimination claims in which an improper consideration was "a motivating factor" for an adverse employment decision. See 42 U.S.C. § 2000e-2(m) (providing that "an unlawful employment practice is established when the complaining party demonstrates that race, color, religion, sex, or national origin was *a motivating factor* for any employment practice, even though other factors also motivated the practice" (emphasis added)).

This Court has never held that this burden-shifting framework applies to ADEA claims. And, we decline to do so now. When conducting statutory interpretation, we "must be careful not to apply rules applicable under one statute to a different statute without careful and critical examination." *Federal Express Corp. v. Holowecki*, 552 U.S. 389, (2008). Unlike Title VII, the ADEA's text does not provide that a plaintiff may establish discrimination by showing that age was simply a motivating factor. Moreover, Congress neglected to add such a provision to the ADEA when it amended Title VII to add §§ 2000e-2(m) and 2000e-5(g)(2)(B), even though it contemporaneously amended the ADEA in several ways.

We cannot ignore Congress' decision to amend Title VII's relevant provisions but not make similar changes to the ADEA. When Congress amends one statutory provision but not another, it is presumed to have acted intentionally. . . . .

. . . The ADEA provides, in relevant part, that "[i]t shall be unlawful for an employer . . . to fail or refuse to hire or to discharge any individual or otherwise discriminate against any individual with respect to his compensation, terms, conditions, or privileges of employment, *because of* such individual's age." 29 U.S.C. § 623(a)(1) (emphasis added).

The words "because of" mean "by reason of: on account of." 1 Webster's Third New International Dictionary 194 (1966); . . . Thus, the ordinary meaning of the ADEA's requirement that an employer took adverse action "because of" age is that age was the "reason" that the employer decided to act. See *Hazen Paper Co. v. Biggins*, 507 U.S. 604, 610, (1993) (explaining that the claim "cannot succeed unless the employee's protected trait actually played a role in [the employer's decisionmaking] process *and had a determinative influence on the outcome*" (emphasis added)). To establish a disparate-treatment claim under the plain language of the ADEA, therefore, a plaintiff must prove that age was the "but-for" cause of the employer's adverse decision. . . .

It follows, then, that under § 623(a)(1), the plaintiff retains the burden of persuasion to establish that age was the "but-for" cause of the employer's adverse action. Indeed, we have previously held that the burden is allocated in this manner in ADEA cases. And nothing in the statute's text indicates that Congress has carved out an exception to that rule for a subset of ADEA cases. Where the statutory text is "silent on the allocation of the burden of persuasion," we "begin with the ordinary default rule that plaintiffs bear the risk of failing to prove their claims." We have no warrant to depart from the general rule in this setting.

Hence, the burden of persuasion necessary to establish employer liability is the same in alleged mixed-motives cases as in any other ADEA disparate-treatment action. A plaintiff must prove by a preponderance of the evidence (which may be direct or circumstantial), that age was the "but-for" cause of the challenged employer decision.

* * *

We hold that a plaintiff bringing a disparate-treatment claim pursuant to the ADEA must prove, by a preponderance of the evidence, that age was the "but-for" cause of the challenged adverse employment action. The burden of persuasion does not shift to the employer to show that it would have taken the action regardless of age, even when a plaintiff has produced some evidence that age was one motivating factor in that decision. Accordingly, we vacate the judgment of the Court of Appeals and remand the case for further proceedings consistent with this opinion. *It is so ordered.*

JUSTICE STEVENS, with whom JUSTICE SOUTER, JUSTICE GINSBURG, and JUSTICE BREYER join, dissenting. (Opinion omitted.)

In his dissent, Justice Breyer argued that to prove the plaintiff's age was the "but-for" causation created too high a burden on the plaintiff. He claimed that the employer should have to refute the presumption of age discrimination in mixed motive cases, that is, raise an affirmative defense, because the employer is "in a better position to establish how he would have acted" had the non-age based reason for the termination not been present.

[4] SUMMARY JUDGMENT

Because of the relatively high degree of success for ADEA claimants before a jury, a defendant's best hope of victory is by way of summary judgment. Under Federal Rule of Civil Procedure 56(c), summary judgment must be entered against a party who fails to make a showing sufficient to establish the existence of an element essential to that party's case. Employer defendants move for summary judgment by virtue of the claim that they produced evidence of a nondiscriminatory motive for the employee's dismissal. Sometimes the motion succeeds, and sometimes it fails.

HARTUNG v. CAE NEWNES, INC.
229 F. Supp. 2d 1093 (D. Or. 2002)

BROWN, DISTRICT JUDGE.

FACTUAL BACKGROUND

In late summer 1998, Plaintiffs were employed by Defendant at its Sherwood lumber-handling equipment manufacturing plant. An industry-wide slowdown in the fall of 1998 caused a substantial reduction in orders, and Defendant was forced to announce a general reduction in force (RIF) on November 3, 1998. The parties agree the "business necessity and ultimate goal of the RIF was to develop a versatile and efficient workforce that could keep the plant running by performing whatever tasks were necessary," and "at no point in the decision-making process was the issue of age discussed."

As part of the RIF, Plaintiffs Hartung (mechanic, age 60), John Harvey (fabricator, age 50), Richard Harvey (fabricator, age 54), and Michael Leach(welder, age 54) were laid off. All of these Plaintiffs were over the age of forty when Defendant hired them and when Defendant fired them.

The parties disagree about Defendant's reasons for dismissing Plaintiffs and the identity of the person who made those decisions. Defendant alleges Bob Atkinson, the plant manager, was the ultimate decision-maker. Atkinson allegedly made a "mental list" of employees to lay off and then "consulted" with the six team leaders in the plant to confirm his pre-conceived selections. Plaintiffs, on the other hand, contend Ken Sonners, one of the team leaders, actually made the dismissal determinations himself. Plaintiff Leach testified he stood up immediately after the list of persons to be laid off was announced on November 3, 1998, and asked Atkinson how the decisions were made. Plaintiff Leach testified Atkinson responded that he "left the choice up" to the "lead men" and, in particular, to Ken Sonners. Plaintiffs Harvey brothers also testified they heard this exchange.

Although Plaintiffs admit Atkinson did not make any age-related comments in their presence, Plaintiffs allege Sonners made numerous derogatory, age-related comments during the course of Plaintiffs' employment. Plaintiffs maintain they heard Sonners:

1. refer to one or more of the Plaintiffs as "one of the old boys," "old guys," an "old fart," or an "old bastard";

2. explain the young guys "hustle" and wonder "why you old guys can't work like these young guys do";

3. ask Plaintiff Hartung why he was sweating and tell Plaintiff Hartung, "those young kids over there, they don't sweat like that";

4. complain about a co-worker being too slow and incapable of keeping up with "the young guys" and specifically state the co-worker "shouldn't even be in the company, he's too old";

5. express his opinion that "the younger fellows have a lot of new ideas and can get the machinery done faster"; and

6. jokingly call one of the Plaintiffs "too old and obstinate."

Defendant does not specifically deny or confirm that Sonners made these comments. Defendant alleges, however, the comments were taken out of context and, in any event, they had no bearing on the employment decisions involving Plaintiffs because Atkinson made the termination decisions on his own, Atkinson did not make any derogatory comments regarding age, and Atkinson did not discuss age during the decision-making process.

In addition, Defendant contends each Plaintiff was dismissed for legitimate, nondiscriminatory reasons. Defendant states the team leaders and Atkinson reviewed several factors, including willingness and ability to perform multiple jobs, attendance, productivity, and attitude to determine which employees would be fired. In particular, Defendant alleges Plaintiff Hartung was chosen because his skills were narrow, he was unwilling to perform different tasks, and he was inflexible with regard to his work schedule. Defendant alleges Plaintiffs Harvey brothers were selected because Atkinson knew they had applied for jobs elsewhere, and he believed they each planned to leave the company in the near term. Defendant contends it laid off Plaintiff Leach because he had a negative attitude, Defendant believed he was actively seeking other employment, and his productivity was low.

All of the six employees dismissed from Plaintiffs' group of fitter/welders were in the protected class. All of the fitter/welders under age 40 were retained. The average age of workers in Plaintiffs' entire department, however, actually increased slightly from 36.02 years to approximately 38.61 years immediately after the layoffs on November 3, 1998.

The average age of workers in the department again increased to 39.83 years after the rehire was complete. In addition, the average age of workers laid off was 36.6 years, but the average age of workers rehired between December 1998 and January 2000 was only 29.5 years of age. Defendant did not rehire Plaintiffs.

. . .

DISCUSSION

ADEA makes it "unlawful for an employer . . . to discharge any individual [who is at least forty years of age] . . . because of such individual's age." 29 U.S.C. §§ 623(a), 631(a). There are two theories of recovery under ADEA: disparate treatment and disparate impact. A disparate impact claim "challenges employment practices that are facially neutral in their treatment of different groups but that in fact fall more harshly on one group than another and cannot be justified by business necessity." *Id.* at 1423. A disparate impact claim focuses on the consequences of employment practices rather than the employer's underlying intent.

On the other hand, a disparate treatment claim under ADEA focuses on the employer's motive underlying the employment decision. The plaintiff must show the employer treated the plaintiff differently than others similarly situated because of age.

The burden of production on summary judgment and at trial shifts during an ADEA case as follows:

> [A] plaintiff must first establish a *prima facie* case of discrimination. If the plaintiff establishes a *prima facie* case, the burden then shifts to the defendant to articulate a legitimate nondiscriminatory reason for its employment decision. Then, in order to prevail, the plaintiff must demonstrate that the employer's alleged reason for the adverse employment decision is a pretext for another motive which is discriminatory.

Lowe v. City of Monrovia, 775 F.2d 998, 1009 (9th Cir. 1985), amended by 784 F.2d 1407 (1986).

Plaintiffs' *Prima Facie* Case

A plaintiff may establish a *prima facie* case of disparate treatment in one of two ways. The plaintiff may offer direct evidence of the employer's discriminatory intent. Alternatively, the plaintiff may establish a *prima facie* case through a presumption arising from proof of four factors: the plaintiff was member of a protected class (i.e., age forty to seventy), the plaintiff was performing his job in a satisfactory manner, the plaintiff was discharged, and the plaintiff was replaced by a substantially younger employee with equal or inferior qualifications.

When an ADEA claim involves a RIF, the fourth factor changes slightly, and the plaintiff instead must show "through circumstantial, statistical or direct evidence that the dismissal occurred under circumstances giving rise to an inference of age discrimination." Rose, 902 F2d at 1421. That inference may arise if the employer had a "continuing need" for the discharged employee's skills. *Id.* A plaintiff can show a continuing need exists if either the discharged employee's tasks continue to be performed by other employees after the dismissal or the employer treated the plaintiff differently than others similarly situated.

The plaintiff must produce "very little" evidence to establish a *prima facie* case of disparate treatment. Plaintiff only has to offer proof sufficient to create an inference of unlawful discrimination.

Defendant concedes Plaintiffs have established the first three *McDonnell Douglas* factors. Defendant, however, challenges Plaintiffs' evidence as to the fourth factor: that Plaintiffs were dismissed under circumstances giving rise to an inference of age discrimination. Plaintiffs, however, argue they have met their burden of production to establish a *prima facie* case of discriminatory intent because there is evidence in the record from which a reasonable factfinder:

1. could conclude Sonners was the true decision-maker,

2. could infer from Sonners's previous derogatory comments regarding age that he is prejudiced against older workers and has a preference for younger workers, and

3. could infer from Sonners's comments that his prejudice against older workers was his motive for dismissing Plaintiffs.

A genuine issue of fact exists regarding who was responsible for the RIF decisions.

Defendant admits Atkinson discussed the layoffs with all of the team leaders, including Sonners. Defendant, nonetheless, asserts Atkinson alone made the termination decisions, and the team leaders' comments merely confirmed Atkinson's pre-conceived selections. Thus, Defendant admits that Sonners was involved in the RIF process to some extent and potentially could have influenced Atkinson's final decision if he recommended firing someone not on Atkinson's "mental list." Moreover, Plaintiffs have offered direct evidence that Atkinson acknowledged his delegation of the responsibility for the RIF decisions to Sonners. The Court finds a reasonable juror could conclude from this evidence that Sonners made the decision to terminate Plaintiffs.

Defendant, however, contends Plaintiffs cannot withstand summary judgment because the statements attributed to Sonners do not give rise to an inference of discriminatory motive in the RIF decisions even if Sonners participated in the decision-making process or was the ultimate decision-maker. Defendant asserts many of the statements allegedly made by Sonners are "irrelevant because-even if true-they were plainly descriptive in nature" and the remaining statements constitute nothing more than "stray remarks." Defendant further contends the statements at issue are general statements unrelated to the termination decisions or to Plaintiffs' abilities.

The Ninth Circuit has held a "stray remark" that is "uttered in an ambivalent manner and [is] not tied directly to the plaintiff's termination is insufficient to create an inference of discriminatory motive." *Merrick v. Farmers Ins. Group*, 892 F.2d 1434, 1438–39 (9th Cir. 1990).

. . .

Plaintiffs here allege Sonners made numerous statements that, when read together, show an age-related prejudice. The statements at issue were not "stray" in the sense that they were not single remarks. Some of the alleged comments, if viewed in a vacuum, might be perceived as merely descriptive in nature as opposed to derogatory. For example, standing alone the allegation that Sonners referred to one of the Plaintiffs as an "old guy" or "one of the old boys" might not support an inference that Sonners would fire Plaintiffs on the basis of their age if given the opportunity. Sonners's alleged statements that an older employee sweats more or sits down more often than the younger employees also might be seen as merely descriptive if viewed in isolation. These statements, however, must be viewed together and in conjunction with the other, more disturbing statements attributed to Sonners. In particular, Sonners's alleged statements that Plaintiffs' co-employee was "too old" to work for the company and that younger workers have new ideas and work faster than older ones are direct evidence of Sonners's preference for younger workers in the workplace. At the very least, Sonners's derogatory comments about older workers and express preference for younger workers constitute evidence from which a reasonable juror could infer a discriminatory bias and an improper motive for the RIF decisions designed to achieve a "versatile and efficient work force."

In addition, Plaintiffs offer statistical proof to bolster their contentions. The average age of workers laid off in November was 36.6 years, while the average age of workers rehired during the following fifteen months was only 29.5 years. In addition, one hundred percent of the workers laid off in Plaintiffs' job category were members of the protected class. All of the employees in the group under forty were retained. While Plaintiffs' statistical evidence may not be definitive, it is further evidence from which a reasonable juror could infer a discriminatory motive for the RIF decisions.

Based upon the record as a whole, Plaintiffs have met their very light burden and have established a *prima facie* case of discrimination.

Defendant's Rebuttal of the Presumption of Discrimination

After the employee meets his burden to establish a *prima facie* case, a presumption of discrimination is created and the burden of production shifts to the defendant employer to show a "legitimate, nondiscriminatory" reason for the decision. If the defendant meets this burden, the presumption of discrimination disappears.

Defendant also offers several alternative reasons for terminating Plaintiffs during the RIF, including Plaintiff Hartung's alleged inflexibility, Plaintiff Leach's alleged low productivity and negative attitude, and Plaintiffs Harvey brothers' alleged plan to leave the company to pursue other careers. Defendant's proffered reasons for terminating Plaintiffs constitute legitimate, nondiscriminatory reasons for choosing to lay off these Plaintiffs.

Plaintiffs' Evidence of Pretext

After a defendant employer articulates legitimate, nondiscriminatory reasons for its employment decision, the burden of production again shifts to the plaintiff to show the defendant's proffered reasons are merely pretext. *Id.* Summary judgment is improper when a plaintiff produces sufficient evidence to allow a reasonable factfinder to conclude either: the true reason for the discharge was a discriminatory one or the alleged reason for the discharge was false.

. . .

The Ninth Circuit consistently has held an ADEA plaintiff may not withstand summary judgment by relying on a *prima facie* presumption of discrimination after the defendant employer has "*merely articulated* a legitimate, nondiscriminatory reason for dismissal." Although the fact that someone other than the decision-maker articulated the reason for Defendant's conduct could be evidence at trial that Defendant's proffered reason was mere pretext, Plaintiffs are not relieved from their burden to show some evidence of pretext in order to withstand summary judgment.

Plaintiffs, however, offered "more" than a presumptive case under the *McDonnell Douglas* factors when they established their *prima facie* case and, therefore, are not required to produce any additional evidence to rebut Defendant's proffered reasons. As noted, Sonners's statements as a whole, and in particular his comment that a co-worker was "too old" to work at the company, are direct evidence of his discriminatory animus against older workers. Plaintiffs' statistical evidence also tends to show different treatment for those in the protected class. The Court finds a reasonable factfinder could conclude from the evidence in the record that Sonners's age bias was the true reason for Defendant's dismissal of Plaintiffs. Because Plaintiffs have offered "more" than a *prima facie* case relying on the *McDonnell Douglas* presumption of discrimination, Plaintiffs need not offer any additional proof of pretext to survive summary judgment.

QUESTION

What is the test of when the court should grant summary judgment for the employer?

[5] RELEVANCE OF AGE OF REPLACEMENT EMPLOYEE

If an employee age 40 or older is terminated and replaced by a younger person, the discharged employee may sue, claiming the termination violated the ADEA. In the past, some federal Courts of Appeal held that to establish a *prima facie* showing of discrimination in cases of replacement by a younger employee required that the replacement employee be age 39 or younger, meaning that he or she was not within the age category protected by the ADEA. Other Courts of Appeals held that a *prima facie* case of age discrimination only required showing of replacement by a younger person, even if that person were age 40 or older. In 1996, the Supreme Court resolved the conflict.

> The discrimination prohibited by the ADEA is discrimination "because of [an] individual's age," 29 U.S.C. § 623(a)(1), though the prohibition is "limited to individuals who are at least 40 years of age," § 631(a). This language does not ban discrimination against employees because they are aged 40 or older; it bans discrimination against employees because of their age, but limits the protected class to those who are 40 or older. The fact that one person in the protected class has lost out to another person in the protected class is thus irrelevant, so long as he has lost out *because of his age.* Or to put the point more concretely, there can be no greater inference of age discrimination (as opposed to "40 or over" discrimination) when a 40 year-old is replaced by a 39 year-old than when a 56 year-old is replaced by a 40 year-old. Because it lacks probative value, the fact that an ADEA plaintiff was replaced by someone outside the protected class is not proper element of the *McDonnell Douglas* prima facie case. Because the ADEA prohibits discrimination on the basis of age and not class membership, the fact that a replacement is substantially younger than the plaintiff is far more a reliable indicator of age discrimination than is the fact that the plaintiff was replaced by someone outside the protected class.

O'Connor v. Consolidated Coin Caterers Corp., 517 U.S. 308 (1996).

[6]   RETALIATION AS A VIOLATION OF THE ADEA

GOMEZ-PEREZ v. POTTER, POSTMASTER GENERAL
553 U.S. 474 (2008)

JUSTICE ALITO.

The question before us is whether a federal employee who is a victim of retaliation due to the filing of a complaint of age discrimination may assert a claim under the federal-sector provision of the Age Discrimination in Employment Act of 1967 (ADEA), 29 U.S.C. § 633a(a). We hold that such a claim is authorized.

I

Petitioner Myrna Gómez-Pérez was a window distribution clerk for the United States Postal Service. In October 2002, petitioner, then 45 years of age, was working full time at the Post Office in Dorado, Puerto Rico. She requested a transfer to the Post Office in Moca, Puerto Rico, in order to be closer to her mother, who was ill. The transfer was approved, and in November 2002, petitioner began working at the Moca Post Office in a part-time position. Later that month, petitioner requested a transfer back to her old job at the Dorado Post Office, but her supervisor converted the Dorado position to part-time, filled it with another employee, and denied petitioner's application.

After first filing an unsuccessful union grievance seeking a transfer back to her old job, petitioner filed a Postal Service equal employment opportunity age discrimination complaint. According to petitioner, she was then subjected to various forms of retaliation. Specifically, petitioner alleges that her supervisor called her into meetings during which groundless complaints were leveled at her, that her name was written on antisexual harassment posters, that she was falsely accused of sexual harassment, that her co-workers told her to " 'go back' " to where she " 'belong[ed],' " and that her work hours were drastically reduced.

Petitioner responded by filing this action in the United States District Court for the District of Puerto Rico, claiming, among other things, that respondent had violated the federal-sector provision of the ADEA, 29 U.S.C. § 633a(a), by retaliating against her for filing her equal employment opportunity age discrimination complaint. . . .

II

The federal-sector provision of the ADEA provides that "[a]ll personnel actions affecting employees or applicants for employment who are at least 40 years of age . . . shall be made free from any discrimination based on age." § 633a(a). The question is whether the statutory phrase "discrimination based on age" includes retaliation based on the filing of an age discrimination complaint. We hold it does.

In reaching this conclusion, we are guided by our prior decisions interpreting similar language in other antidiscrimination statutes. In *Sullivan v. Little Hunting*

Park, Inc., 396 U.S. 229,(1969), we considered whether a claim of retaliation could be brought under Rev. Stat. § 1978, 42 U.S.C. § 1982, which provides that "[a]ll citizens of the United States shall have the same right . . . as is enjoyed by white citizens . . . to inherit, purchase, lease, sell, hold, and convey real and personal property." While § 1982 does not use the phrase "discrimination based on race," that is its plain meaning. See *Tennessee v. Lane*, 541 U.S. 509, 561, (2004) (Scalia, J., dissenting).

In *Sullivan*, a white man (Sullivan) held membership shares in a nonstock corporation that operated a park and playground for residents of the area in which he owned a home. Under the bylaws of the corporation, a member who leased a home in the area could assign a membership share in the corporation. But when Sullivan rented his house and attempted to assign a membership share to an African-American (Freeman), the corporation disallowed the assignment because of Freeman's race and subsequently expelled Sullivan from the corporation for protesting that decision. Sullivan sued the corporation, and we held that his claim that he had been expelled "for the advocacy of Freeman's cause" was cognizable under § 1982. 396 U.S. at 237. A contrary holding, we reasoned, would have allowed Sullivan to be "punished for trying to vindicate the rights of minorities" and would have given "impetus to the perpetuation of racial restrictions on property." *Ibid.*

More recently, in *Jackson v. Birmingham Bd. of Ed.*, 544 U.S. 167 (2005), we relied on *Sullivan* in interpreting Title IX of the Education Amendments of 1972. Jackson, a public school teacher, sued his school board under Title IX, "alleging that the Board retaliated against him because he had complained about sex discrimination in the high school's athletic program." 544 U.S. at 171,. Title IX provides in relevant part that "[n]o person in the United States shall, *on the basis of sex*, . . . be subjected to discrimination under any education program or activity receiving Federal financial assistance." § 1681(a) (2000 ed.) (emphasis added). Holding that this provision prohibits retaliation, we wrote:

> "Retaliation against a person because that person has complained of sex discrimination is another form of intentional sex discrimination . . . . Retaliation is, by definition, an intentional act. It is a form of 'discrimination' because the complainant is being subjected to differential treatment. Moreover, retaliation is discrimination 'on the basis of sex' because it is an intentional response to the nature of the complaint: an allegation of sex discrimination. We conclude that when a funding recipient retaliates against a person *because* he complains of sex discrimination, this constitutes intentional 'discrimination' 'on the basis of sex,' in violation of Title IX." *Id.* at 173-74, (citations omitted).

This interpretation, we found, flowed naturally from *Sullivan*: "Retaliation for Jackson's advocacy of the rights of the girls' basketball team in this case is 'discrimination' 'on the basis of sex,' just as retaliation for advocacy on behalf of a black lessee in Sullivan was discrimination on the basis of race." 544 U.S. at 176-77,

Following the reasoning of *Sullivan* and *Jackson*, we interpret the ADEA federal-sector provision's prohibition of "discrimination based on age" as likewise proscribing retaliation. The statutory language at issue here ("discrimination based on age") is not materially different from the language at issue in *Jackson*

(" 'discrimination' " " 'on the basis of sex' ") and is the functional equivalent of the language at issue in *Sullivan*, see *Jackson, supra*, at 177, (describing *Sullivan* as involving "discrimination on the basis of race"). And the context in which the statutory language appears is the same in all three cases; that is, all three cases involve remedial provisions aimed at prohibiting discrimination.

G. REDUCTION IN FORCE

ADEA claims may result if the employer reduces the number of employees for economic reasons. Nothing in the ADEA, of course, bars an employer from terminating excess employees. When an employer is shrinking the work force, however, the temptation exists to terminate the older employees, who are often the highest paid. Just because it may make economic sense to the employer to eliminate the jobs of the older, more highly paid employees, does not mean that it is legal.

As stated by one court:

> Congress enacted the ADEA precisely because many employers or younger business executives act as if they believe that there are good business reasons for discriminating against older employees. Retention of senior employees who can be replaced by younger, lower-paid persons frequently competes with other values, such as profits or conceptions of economic efficiency. The ADEA represents a choice among these values. It stands for the proposition that this is a better country for its willingness to pay the costs for treating older employees fairly.

Graefenhain v. Pabst Brewing Co., 827 F.2d 13 (7th Cir. 1987).

If the employer is unionized, layoffs must follow the terms of the collective bargaining agreement. Normally in such instances no violation of the ADEA occurs. The collective bargaining agreement will often protect the older worker by insisting that any terminations be in reverse order of seniority. The ADEA specifically exempts age discrimination that occurs pursuant to a bona fide seniority system. 29 U.S.C. § 623(f)(2).

[1] PROVING THE CLAIM OF AGE DISCRIMINATION

Business considerations often cause an employer to eliminate many positions within the company, known as a reduction in force. Often those eliminated are nonunionized, management, or technical employees. Frequently, the terminated employees will claim that the employer discharged older workers in violation of the ADEA. To sustain such a claim, at a minimum, the employee must prove that he or she:

[1] Was age 40 or older when discharged;

[2] Had a satisfactory job performance;

[3] Was discharged; and

[4] Was replaced by a younger employee or that the employer sought to replace him or her with a younger employee.

Even a discharged employee who proves the above four points may still lose to a summary judgment motion.

BIALAS v. GREYHOUND LINES, INC.
59 F.3d 759 (8th Cir. 1995)

FLOYD R. GIBSON, SENIOR CIRCUIT JUDGE.

William Bialas, Edward Christensen, and Rollin Cate (collectively "the Plaintiffs") appeal from the district court's entry of summary judgment in favor of their former employer, Greyhound Lines, Inc. ("Greyhound"). The Plaintiffs contend that Greyhound terminated them because of their ages, in violation of the Age Discrimination in Employment Act ("ADEA"), 29 U.S.C. §§ 621-634 (1988), and the Iowa Civil Rights Act of 1965, Iowa Code § 216.6 (1995). We affirm.

I. BACKGROUND

Greyhound is a national company that busses passengers and packages. Beginning in 1989, Greyhound attempted to reduce its staff and increase its efficiency. In the aftermath of a nationwide union strike in 1990, Greyhound filed for bankruptcy and intensified its efforts to reorganize the company. The Plaintiffs were employed at Greyhound's Accounting Center in Des Moines, Iowa. In early 1991, Greyhound eliminated the Plaintiffs' positions and terminated them. At the time of his termination, William Bialas was forty-five years old and the manager of the charter revenue department, which audits charter services. Because of the decline in Greyhound's charter services, Bialas' department was consolidated with the statistics department, whose work load had also decreased. Bialas' supervisor, Suzanne Bubel, determined that the manager of the statistics department, Dennis Newton, who was thirty years old, was more qualified to manage the newly-formed department than Bialas. Bubel testified that Newton was already familiar with the work performed by the charter revenue department, while Bialas admitted that he was not familiar with the statistical duties performed by Newton and his staff. Furthermore, Bubel testified that Bialas had been on probation and that he had the lowest performance evaluation of all the managers in her group.

At the time of his termination, Edward Christensen was forty-four years old and the senior director of sales accounts payable. Because of the dramatic reduction in staff and resulting decreased need for supervisors, the Accounting Center's senior director, Paul Griffith, decided to eliminate one of the departmental senior director positions. Of the five senior directors, two were older than Christensen; Joe Young was forty-three; and Suzanne Bubel was thirty-nine. Christensen testified that Griffith explained to him that his position was being eliminated and that Joe Young would oversee the consolidated departments because he had better managerial skills than Christensen.

At the time of his termination, Rollin Cate was forty-one years old and the manager of the express accounting department, which processes the invoices for package deliveries. Through Greyhound's continued downsizing efforts, the staff in express accounting had been dramatically decreased and numerous positions had been eliminated.[1] Griffith advised Cate that he needed to consolidate more positions and increase his department's efficiency. In November 1990, Cate received a poor evaluation from his immediate supervisor, Joe Young. A few months later, Greyhound eliminated Cate's position and his duties were initially assumed by Joe Young, who was several years older than Cate. Eventually, Joe Young left Greyhound and Cate's former duties were assigned to a younger employee.

The Plaintiffs filed a five-count complaint against Greyhound, including claims for age discrimination. . . . Greyhound filed a motion for summary judgment. The district court concluded that the Plaintiffs' terminations occurred during definite reduction in Greyhound's work force. The court then considered and rejected the Plaintiffs' allegations of discriminatory animus based on comparisons between the Plaintiffs' and their replacements' salaries and qualifications.

II. DISCUSSION

Summary judgment is appropriate if, viewing the evidence in light most favorable to the non-moving party, there is no genuine issue of material fact.

A. Failure to Establish a Prima Facie Case

The ADEA provides that it is unlawful for an employer to discharge any person in the protected class (age forty and older) "because of such individual's age." 29 U.S.C. § 623(a)(1) (1988). Likewise, the Iowa Civil Rights Act prohibits an employer from discriminating against or discharging an employee because of his age. Iowa Code § 216.6 (1995).

In order to state a prima facie case of age discrimination under the ADEA and the Iowa Civil Rights Act, plaintiff must establish that: (1) he was within the protected age group; (2) he met applicable job qualifications; (3) he was discharged; and (4) after his termination, the position remained open or the employer hired a person not in the protected class to fill this opening. *See Bashara v. Black Hills Corp.*, 26 F.3d 820, 823 (8th Cir. 1994); *Wing v. Iowa Lutheran Hosp.*, 426 N.W.2d 175, 177 (Iowa Ct. App. 1988). During a reduction in an employer's work force, however, the fact that the plaintiff's duties were assumed by younger person is not in itself enough to establish a prima facie case. *Johnson v. Minnesota Historical Soc'y*, 931 F.2d 1239, 1243 (8th Cir. 1991). "[O]therwise every plaintiff in protected age group would be allowed a trial simply because he was discharged during reduction in force." *Id.* Therefore, in a reduction-in force case, the plaintiff is required to come forward with additional evidence that age was factor in his termination. *Id.*; *Bashara*, 26 F.3d at 823; *Wing*, 426 N.W.2d at 178.

First, although the Plaintiffs concede that Greyhound was involved in extensive reorganization, they argue that this is not a bona fide reduction-in-force case because Greyhound was not eliminating middle-management personnel. The Plaintiffs' argument is belied by their own testimony. Christen-sen, senior director, acknowledged that by the end of 1989, he had eliminated 50 to 60 positions that had

---

[1] Cate testified that prior to the strike, his department had approximately ninety-five employees. After the strike, express accounting had been reduced to approximately fifty-five employees.

previously reported to him, including many supervisors. Furthermore, it is undisputed that two of the three Plaintiffs, Bialas and Christensen, had their departments consolidated with other departments. Cate's position was eliminated, and he admitted that his duties were assumed by Joe Young, his immediate supervisor. We conclude that there is overwhelming evidence in the record to support the district court's decision that the Plaintiffs were terminated during a definite reduction in force.

Second, the Plaintiffs argue that they have established circumstantial evidence of age discrimination because they were older, higher-paid employees who were eventually replaced by younger, lower-paid employees. Accepting the Plaintiffs' allegations that they were terminated because their salaries were greater than their replacements' salaries, this does not necessarily support an inference of age discrimination. . . . We conclude that even if Greyhound terminated the Plaintiffs because of their status as higher-paid employees, this evidence does not in itself support an inference of age discrimination.

Third, the Plaintiffs argue that the statements made by Greyhound's management constitute evidence of age discrimination. For the reasons discussed above, we believe that Joe Young's comment about salary and Frank Schmieder's statement that it was unwise to remain at Greyhound more than ten years do not establish that age played role in the Plaintiffs' terminations.

The record is clear that Joe Young, who was forty-three years old, assumed Cate's duties. The fact that Young described Cate's eventual replacement as a "a young man" does not lead to an inference that Cate was discharged because of his age. Furthermore, it is undisputed that Suzanne Bubel made the decision to terminate Bialas and that Paul Griffith made the decisions to terminate Christensen and Cate. *See Frieze v. Boatmen's Bank of Belton*, 950 F.2d 538, 541 (8th Cir. 1991) (finding no inference of age discrimination where the challenged statements were made by persons not involved in the termination decision).

We are more troubled by Schmieder's memorandum in which he noted that "people over 45 years of age, including myself, generally have serious difficulty adjusting to change." In the context of the entire paragraph, however, it is apparent that Schmieder's concern was that some of the current managers, regardless of their ages, had resisted the company's attempts to reorganize to a more profit-driven and competitive, customer-oriented business. Moreover, this memorandum was dated more than six months after the last Plaintiff was terminated and, as we have noted, was written by someone who did not take part in the termination decisions. *See Beshears v. Asbill*, 930 F.2d 1348, 1354 (8th Cir. 1991) (statement that older employees have problems adapting to changes was made by person who actively participated in the personnel decisions at issue). In sum, we conclude that the Plaintiffs have failed to come forward with additional evidence that age factored into Greyhound's decision to terminate them. . . . We affirm the district court's order granting summary judgment in favor of Greyhound.

QUESTIONS

1. Explain precisely why the court ruled against the plaintiffs. Was the court correct?

2. If an employer must implement a reduction in force, how can it minimize the possibility of age discrimination suits by the terminated employees?

[2]   TERMINATION OF HIGHER PAID EMPLOYEES

Is it a violation of the ADEA to reduce the work force by terminating only the higher paid employees? *No*, said *Holt v. Gamwell Corp.*, 797 F.2d 36 (1st Cir. 1986). There was no violation of the ADEA by discharging a higher paid employee when the position was also terminated. The employer had no duty to mitigate the injury to the employee by offering a demotion and a pay cut. *Yes*, said *Metz v. Transit Mix, Inc.*, 828 F.2d 1202 (7th Cir. 1987). The court held that the ADEA was violated when the employee was fired solely because of high wage costs when the higher wages were attributable to his having received pay increases based on seniority. Rather than terminating him, the employer should have mitigated the injury by reducing his pay.

What of termination because of seniority or pension status as the reason for dismissal?

HAZEN PAPER CO. v. BIGGINS
507 U.S. 604 (1993)

JUSTICE O'CONNOR delivered the opinion of the Court.

In this case we clarify the standards for liability and liquidated damages under the Age Discrimination in Employment Act of 1967 (ADEA), 81 Stat. 602, as amended, 29 U.S.C. § 621 *et seq.*

I

Petitioner Hazen Paper Company manufactures coated, laminated, and printed paper and paperboard. The company is owned and operated by two cousins, petitioners Robert Hazen and Thomas N. Hazen. The Hazens hired respondent Walter F. Biggins as their technical director in 1977. They fired him in 1986, when he was 62 years old.

Respondent brought suit against petitioners in the United States District Court for the District of Massachusetts, alleging a violation of the ADEA. He claimed that age had been a determinative factor in petitioners' decision to fire him. Petitioners contested this claim, asserting instead that respondent had been fired for doing business with competitors of Hazen Paper. The case was tried before a jury, which rendered a verdict for respondent on his ADEA claim.

In affirming the judgments of liability, the Court of Appeals relied heavily on the evidence that petitioners had fired respondent in order to prevent his pension benefits from vesting. That evidence, as construed most favorably to respondent by the court, showed that the Hazen Paper pension plan had 10-year vesting period and that respondent would have reached the 10-year mark had he worked "a few more weeks" after being fired. *Id.* at 1411. There was also testimony that petitioners had offered to retain respondent as a consultant to Hazen Paper, in which capacity he would not have been entitled to receive pension benefits. *Id.*, at 1412. The Court of Appeals . . . stated: "Based on the foregoing evidence, the jury could reasonably have found that Thomas Hazen decided to fire [respondent] before his pension rights vested and used the confidentiality agreement [that petitioners had asked respondent to sign] as a means to that end. The jury could also have reasonably found that age was inextricably intertwined with the decision to fire [respondent]. If it were not for [respondent's] age, sixty-two, his pension rights would not have been within a hairbreadth of vesting. [Respondent] was fifty-two years old when he was hired; his pension rights vested in ten years." *Id.* at 1412.

The Courts of Appeals repeatedly have faced the question whether an employer violates the ADEA by acting on the basis of a factor, such as an employee's pension status or seniority, that is empirically correlated with age. Compare *White v. Westinghouse Electric Co.*, 862 F.2d 56, 62 (CA3 1988) (firing of older employee to prevent vesting of pension benefits violates ADEA); *Metz v. Transit Mix, Inc.*, 828 F.2d 1202 (CA7 1987) (firing of older employee to save salary costs resulting from seniority violates ADEA), with *Williams v. General Motors Corp.*, 656 F.2d 120, 130, n. 17 (CA5 1981) ("[S]eniority and age discrimination are unrelated. . . .We state without equivocation that the seniority a given plaintiff has accumulated entitles him to no better or worse treatment in an age discrimination suit"), *cert. denied*, 455 U.S. 943, 102 S. Ct. 1439, 71 L. Ed. 2d 655 (1982); *EEOC v. Clay Printing Co.*, 955 F.2d 936, 942 (CA4 1992) (emphasizing distinction between employee's age and years of service). We now clarify that there is no disparate treatment under the ADEA when the factor motivating the employer is some feature other than the employee's age.

The disparate treatment theory is of course available under the ADEA, as the language of that statute makes clear. "It shall be unlawful for an employer . . . to fail or refuse to hire or to discharge any individual or otherwise discriminate against any individual with respect to his compensation, terms, conditions, or privileges of employment, *because of such individual's age*." 29 U.S.C. § 623(a)(1) (emphasis added). . . . Respondent claims only that he received disparate treatment.

In a disparate treatment case, liability depends on whether the protected trait (under the ADEA, age) actually motivated the employer's decision. . . . Whatever the employer's decision making process, a disparate treatment claim cannot succeed unless the employee's protected trait actually played role in that process and had determinative influence on the outcome.

Disparate treatment, thus defined, captures the essence of what Congress sought to prohibit in the ADEA. It is the very essence of age discrimination for an older employee to be fired because the employer believes that productivity and competence decline with old age.

Thus the ADEA commands that "employers are to evaluate [older] employees
. . . on their merits and not their age." *Western Air Lines, Inc. v. Criswell*, 472
U.S. 400, 422, 105 S. Ct. 2743, 2756, 86 L. Ed. 2d 321 (1985). The employer cannot
rely on age as proxy for an employee's remaining characteristics, such as
productivity, but must instead focus on those factors directly.

When the employer's decision is wholly motivated by factors other than age, the
problem of inaccurate and stigmatizing stereotypes disappears. This is true even if
the motivating factor is correlated with age, as pension status typically is. Pension
plans typically provide that an employee's accrued benefits will become
nonforfeitable, or "vested," once the employee completes a certain number of years
of service with the employer. See J. Mamorsky, Employee Benefits Law § 5.03
(1992). On average, an older employee has had more years in the work force than
a younger employee, and thus may well have accumulated more years of service
with a particular employer. Yet an employee's age is analytically distinct from his
years of service. An employee who is younger than 40, and therefore outside the
class of older workers as defined by the ADEA, see 29 U.S.C. § 631(a), may have
worked for particular employer his entire career, while an older worker may have
been newly hired. Because age and years of service are analytically distinct, an
employer can take account of one while ignoring the other, and thus it is incorrect
to say that a decision based on years of service is necessarily "age based."

The instant case is illustrative. Under the Hazen Paper pension plan, as construed
by the Court of Appeals, an employee's pension benefits vest after the employee
completes 10 years of service with the company. Perhaps it is true that older
employees of Hazen Paper are more likely to be "close to vesting" than younger
employees. Yet a decision by the company to fire an older employee solely because
he has nine-plus years of service and therefore is "close to vesting" would not
constitute discriminatory treatment on the basis of age. The prohibited stereotype
("Older employees are likely to be —") would not have figured in this decision, and
the attendant stigma would not ensue. The decision would not be the result of an
inaccurate and denigrating generalization about age, but would rather represent
an *accurate* judgment about the employee — that he indeed is "close to vesting."

We do not mean to suggest that an employer lawfully could fire an employee in
order to prevent his pension benefits from vesting. Such conduct is actionable
under § 510 of ERISA, as the Court of Appeals rightly found in affirming judgment
for respondent under that statute. See *Ingersoll-Rand Co. v. McClendon*, 498 U.S.
133, 142–143, 111 S. Ct. 478, 484–485, 112 L. Ed. 2d 474 (1990). But it would not,
without more, violate the ADEA. That law requires the employer to ignore an
employee's age (absent statutory a exemption or defense); it does not specify
further characteristics that an employer must also ignore. Although some language
in our prior decisions might be read to mean that an employer violates the ADEA
whenever its reason for firing an employee is improper *in any respect*, see
McDonnell Douglas Corp. v. Green, 411 U.S. 792, 802, 93 S. Ct. 1817, 1824, 36 L.
Ed. 2d 668 (1973) (creating proof framework applicable to ADEA) (employer must
have a "legitimate, nondiscriminatory reason" for action against employee), this
reading is obviously incorrect. For example, it cannot be true that an employer who
fires an older black worker because the worker is black thereby violates the ADEA.

The employee's race is an improper reason, but it is improper under Title VII, not the ADEA.

H. DISPARATE IMPACT

Does the ADEA bar employers from using criteria for hiring or terminating that, although neutral on their face, have a disproportionate effect on employees or job seekers age 40 or older? Known as the "disparate impact" theory, it originally arose in the context of employment tests that tended disproportionately to reject minority job seekers. As stated by the Supreme Court in *Griggs v. Duke Power Co.*, 401 U.S. 424 (1971):

> In short, the Act [Title VII] does not command that any person be hired simply because he was formerly the subject of discrimination, or because he is a member of a minority group. . . . What is required by Congress is the removal of artificial, arbitrary, and unnecessary barriers to employment when the barriers operate invidiously to discriminate on the basis of racial or other impermissible classification. (p. 431)

> The Act proscribes not only overt discrimination but also practices that are fair in form but discriminatory in operation. The touchstone is business necessity. If an employment practice which operates to exclude Negroes cannot be shown to be related to job performance, the practice is prohibited. (p. 431)

> Nothing in the Act precludes the use of testing or measuring procedures; obviously they are useful. What Congress has forbidden is giving these devices and mechanisms controlling force unless they are demonstrably a reasonable measure of job performance. (p. 436)

The use of the disparate impact theory in the context of an ADEA claim was considered in the following case.

SMITH v. CITY OF JACKSON
544 U.S. 228 (2005)

JUSTICE STEVENS announced the judgment of the Court and delivered the opinion of the Court with respect to Parts I, II, and IV, and an opinion with respect to Part III, in which JUSTICE SOUTER, JUSTICE GINSBURG, and JUSTICE BREYER join.

Petitioners, police and public safety officers employed by the city of Jackson, Mississippi (hereinafter City), contend that salary increases received in 1999 violated the Age Discrimination in Employment Act of 1967 (ADEA) because they were less generous to officers over the age of 40 than to younger officers. Their suit raises the question whether the "disparate-impact" theory of recovery announced in *Griggs v. Duke Power Co.*, 401 U.S. 424 (1971), for cases brought under Title VII of the Civil Rights Act of 1964, is cognizable under the ADEA. Despite the age of the ADEA, it is a question that we have not yet addressed.

I

On October 1, 1998, the City adopted a pay plan granting raises to all City employees. The stated purpose of the plan was to "attract and retain qualified people, provide incentive for performance, maintain competitiveness with other public sector agencies and ensure equitable compensation to all employees regardless of age, sex, race and/or disability." On May 1, 1999, a revision of the plan, which was motivated, at least in part, by the City's desire to bring the starting salaries of police officers up to the regional average, granted raises to all police officers and police dispatchers. Those who had less than five years of tenure received proportionately greater raises when compared to their former pay than those with more seniority. Although some officers over the age of 40 had less than five years of service, most of the older officers had more.

Petitioners are a group of older officers who filed suit under the ADEA claiming both that the City deliberately discriminated against them because of their age (the "disparate-treatment" claim) and that they were "adversely affected" by the plan because of their age (the "disparate-impact" claim). The District Court granted summary judgment to the City on both claims. The Court of Appeals held that the ruling on the former claim was premature because petitioners were entitled to further discovery on the issue of intent, but it affirmed the dismissal of the disparate-impact claim. . . .

We granted the officers' petition for certiorari, and now hold that the ADEA does authorize recovery in "disparate-impact" cases comparable to Griggs. Because, however, we conclude that petitioners have not set forth a valid disparate-impact claim, we affirm.

III

In determining whether the ADEA authorizes disparate-impact claims, we begin with the premise that when Congress uses the same language in two statutes having similar purposes, particularly when one is enacted shortly after the other, it is appropriate to presume that Congress intended that text to have the same meaning in both statutes. . . . Our unanimous interpretation of § 703(a)(2) of the Title VII in *Griggs* is therefore a precedent of compelling importance.

In *Griggs*, a case decided four years after the enactment of the ADEA, we considered whether § 703 of Title VII prohibited an employer "from requiring a high school education or passing of a standardized general intelligence test as a condition of employment in or transfer to jobs when (a) neither standard is shown to be significantly related to successful job performance, (b) both requirements operate to disqualify Negroes at a substantially higher rate than white applicants, and (c) the jobs in question formerly had been filled only by white employees as part of a longstanding practice of giving preference to whites." 401 U.S. at 425–426. Accepting the Court of Appeals' conclusion that the employer had adopted the diploma and test requirements without any intent to discriminate, we held that good faith "does not redeem employment procedures or testing mechanisms that operate as 'built-in headwinds' for minority groups and are unrelated to measuring job capability."

We explained that Congress had "directed the thrust of the Act to the *consequences* of employment practices, not simply the motivation." . . .

While our opinion in *Griggs* relied primarily on the purposes of the Act, buttressed by the fact that the EEOC had endorsed the same view, we have subsequently noted that our holding represented the better reading of the statutory text as well. . . .

The Court of Appeals' categorical rejection of disparate-impact liability, rested primarily on the RFOA provision . . .

The RFOA provision provides that it shall not be unlawful for an employer "to take any action otherwise prohibited under subsection (a) . . . where the differentiation is based on reasonable factors other than age discrimination. . . ." 81 Stat. 603. In most disparate-treatment cases, if an employer in fact acted on a factor other than age, the action would not be prohibited under subsection (a) in the first place. . . . .

In disparate-impact cases, however, the allegedly "otherwise prohibited" activity is not based on age. (" 'Claims that stress "disparate impact" [by contrast] involve employment practices that are facially neutral in their treatment of different groups but that in fact fall more harshly on one group than another . . ." It is, accordingly, in cases involving disparate-impact claims that the RFOA provision plays its principal role by precluding liability if the adverse impact was attributable to a nonage factor that was "reasonable." Rather than support an argument that disparate impact is unavailable under the ADEA, the RFOA provision actually supports the contrary conclusion.

Finally, we note that both the Department of Labor, which initially drafted the legislation, and the EEOC, which is the agency charged by Congress with responsibility for implementing the statute, 29 U.S.C. § 628, have consistently interpreted the ADEA to authorize relief on a disparate-impact theory. . . . The text of the statute, as interpreted in *Griggs*, the RFOA provision, and the EEOC regulations all support petitioners' view. We therefore conclude that it was error for the Court of Appeals to hold that the disparate-impact theory of liability is categorically unavailable under the ADEA.

IV

. . .

Turning to the case before us, we initially note that petitioners have done little more than point out that the pay plan at issue is relatively less generous to older workers than to younger workers. They have not identified any specific test, requirement, or practice within the pay plan that has an adverse impact on older workers. As we held in *Wards Cove*, it is not enough to simply allege that there is a disparate impact on workers, or point to a generalized policy that leads to such an impact. Rather, the employee is " 'responsible for isolating and identifying the specific employment practices that are allegedly responsible for any observed statistical disparities.' " 490 U.S. at 656. Petitioners have failed to do so. Their failure to identify the specific practice being challenged is the sort of omission that could "result in employers being potentially liable for 'the myriad of innocent causes that may lead to statistical imbalances . . . .'" 490 U.S. at 657. In this case not only did petitioners thus err by failing to identify the relevant practice, but it is also clear from the record that the City's plan was based on reasonable factors other than age.

. . .

Petitioners' evidence established two principal facts: First, almost two-thirds (66.2%) of the officers under 40 received raises of more than 10% while less than half (45.3%) of those over 40 did. Second, the average percentage increase for the entire class of officers with less than five years of tenure was somewhat higher than the percentage for those with more seniority. Because older officers tended to occupy more senior positions, on average they received smaller increases when measured as a percentage of their salary. The basic explanation for the differential was the City's perceived need to raise the salaries of junior officers to make them competitive with comparable positions in the market.

Thus, the disparate impact is attributable to the City's decision to give raises based on seniority and position. Reliance on seniority and rank is unquestionably reasonable given the City's goal of raising employees' salaries to match those in surrounding communities. In sum, we hold that the City's decision to grant a larger raise to lower echelon employees for the purpose of bringing salaries in line with that of surrounding police forces was a decision based on a "reasonable factor other than age" that responded to the City's legitimate goal of retaining police officers.

While there may have been other reasonable ways for the City to achieve its goals, the one selected was not unreasonable. Unlike the business necessity test, which asks whether there are other ways for the employer to achieve its goals that do not result in a disparate impact on a protected class, the reasonableness inquiry includes no such requirement.

Accordingly, while we do not agree with the Court of Appeals' holding that that the disparate-impact theory of recovery is never available under the ADEA, we affirm its judgment.

It is so ordered.

———————

Smith v. City of Jackson is not expected to have a major effect. The Older Worker Benefit Protection Act provided that employee benefits were covered by the ADEA; employers could be liable for providing less generous benefits to older workers. But the Act also amended the ADEA to provide that an employer would not be liable if it could demonstrate that either the costs to employer or the benefits to the employee were the same for older and younger workers — known as the "equal cost/benefit rule safe harbor." The same amendment also created safe harbors for early incentive retirement plans, and subsidized early retirement benefits. Any employer plan that fits within these safe harbors need not fear the application of the *City of Jackson* disparate impact rule.

PROBLEM

The "With-It," a chain of clothing stores featuring fashions for the teenage set, wants to hire sales personnel who relate well to its customers. The stores feature bold colors, loud rock music, and trendy clothes. The head of personnel has approached you, her attorney, about legal restrictions on advertising or hiring of new sales personnel. She shows you a proposed advertisement, which reads in part, "We are looking for young, dynamic, spirited men and women." After you explain that this would probably violate the ADEA, she responds, "So what can we do that is legal? Our customers don't want to buy clothes from my grandmother." What advice would you give? Can she hire the type of salespeople that she wants without running afoul of the ADEA?

I. REASONABLE FACTOR OTHER THAN AGE (RFOA) DEFENSE

An employer can assert that age did not play a factor in the decision not to hire or to fire, but that some legally permissible cause, such as poor job performance, was the reason for the dismissal or refusal to hire. Section 4(f)(1) of the ADEA specifically states that it is not unlawful to take action otherwise prohibited "where the differentiation is based on reasonable factors other than age." 29 U.S.C. § 623(f)(1).

The courts have split as to whether the RFOA provision is an affirmative defense or merely a burden of going forward. The Ninth Circuit Court of Appeals held that the RFOA is an affirmative defense which imposes the stringent burden of persuasion. Other appellate courts (Third, Fifth, Tenth, and Eleventh) have concluded that the RFOA requires only that the defendant satisfy the burden of production, a much easier standard to meet.

The RFOA defense offers a general "out" for employers who terminate or refuse to hire older workers. Because the ADEA does not offer a special status to older workers, an employer is under no duty to accord special treatment to them. The employer, therefore, may terminate an ADEA covered employee for almost any reason other than age. Personality conflicts, insubordination, uncooperativeness, falsification of work records, quality of production, violation of work rules, low productivity, loss of creativity, and health problems may all serve as legal bases for termination or refusal to hire.

Termination decisions based on factors that may accompany advancing age are legitimate. An employee may fire for declining health, diminished vigor, reduced competence, or even health problems related to advanced age. What the employer may not do is fire *merely* because of the employee's age.

Even the use of a seemingly "neutral" factor, such as a medical examination, can run afoul of the ADEA. The employer, for example, cannot pick an arbitrary age to begin physical testing of employees. If one is tested, then all employees must be tested. And any testing must relate to the requirements of the job and not merely be a means of dismissing older employees who fail the test.

Jeff Morneau, *Too Good, Too Bad: "Overqualified" Older Workers*
22 W. New Eng. L. Rev. 45, 48 (2000)[*]

Those who are newly unemployed are confronted with the prospects of finding a new job and stabilizing their lives often after many years in the same position with the same employer. These older workers may seek re-employment, but are often forced to apply for entry-level (and therefore lower wage) jobs because they lack the training necessary for the higher paying jobs in different industries or because middle or upper-management positions are not available. Yet, older workers are even prevented from attaining lower level positions when employment recruiters reject them on the basis that they are overqualified.

"Overqualification" is a subjective quality that cannot be measured accurately through a standardized test. Thus, when supervisors reject older applicants because they are overqualified, there is a real danger that the supervisors are in fact acting with discriminatory intent, or at a minimum, are basing an employment decision on subconscious stereotypes and prejudices. Because of this danger and its potential effect on older workers, it is important to consider whether "overqualification" should be considered a legitimate reason not to hire an applicant. This Article will examine the differences in three circuit court opinions that have considered the use of "overquali-fication" by employers as a reason to reject older applicants.

The Second, Sixth, and Ninth Circuits have addressed the issue of 'over-qualification' within the context of the ADEA in the hiring process. In *Taggart v. Time, Inc.*, 924 F.2d 43 (2d Cir. 1991) the Second Circuit held that rejecting older applicants based on 'overqualification' can be a mask for age discrimination, and is therefore not a legitimate reason for rejection. Conversely, the

Sixth Circuit in *Stein v. National City Bank*, 942 F.2d. 1062 (6th Cir. 1991) and the Ninth Circuit in *EEOC v. Insurance Co. of North America*, 49 F. 3d 1418 (9th Cir.1995) held that although rejecting applicants based on "over-qualification" grounds may at times be a mask for age discrimination, it also may be a legitimate reason to reject applicants.

. . .

The question of whether "overqualification" constitutes a legitimate nondiscriminatory reason for denying employment is important to older applicants seeking work. If "overqualification" is considered a legitimate reason for an adverse employment action, employers will be free to prevent older applicants from re-entering the workforce in entry-level positions. On the other hand, if "overqualification" is considered a prohibited reason for denial of employment, older applicants will have more opportunities available to them when they seek employment.

QUESTIONS

1. Can an employer legally fire an ADEA protected worker "for no reason at all"?

2. Is there such a thing as an arbitrary firing or is there always *some* reason for the termination?

3. It is said that the ADEA does not protect an employee against unfair personnel policies. Is that true?

4. If an employer wishes to fire an older employee, what steps should it take to protect itself against an ADEA suit?

J. THE BONA FIDE OCCUPATIONAL QUALIFICATION (BFOQ) EXCEPTION

Section 4(f)(1) of the ADEA provides that it shall not be a violation of the Act for an employer to discriminate on the basis of age "where age is a bona fide occupational qualification reasonably necessary to the normal operation of the particular business." 29 U.S.C. § 623(f). (The bona fide occupational qualification (BFOQ) defense is not allowed merely because the employer's customers might prefer to deal with younger employees.) The BFOQ defense is frequently cited by the employer who admits that age was a factor in the decision not to hire or to fire, but who offers a legally justifiable excuse for the need to rely upon age.

In *Usery v. Tamiami Trail Tours, Inc.*, 531 F.2d 224 (5th Cir. 1976), the Court of Appeals for the Fifth Circuit was called upon to evaluate the merits of a BFOQ defense to a claim of age discrimination. Tamiami Trail Tours, Inc., had a policy of refusing to hire persons over age 40 as intercity bus drivers. At trial, the bus company introduced testimony supporting its theory that the hiring policy was a BFOQ based upon safety considerations — the need to employ persons who have a low risk of accidents. In finding no violation of the ADEA, the Court of Appeals concluded that two inquiries were relevant.

First, the court recognized that some job qualifications may be so peripheral to the central mission of the employer's business that *no* age discrimination can be "reasonably *necessary* to the normal operation of the particular business." 29 U.S.C. § 623(f)(1). The bus company justified the age qualification for hiring its drivers on safety considerations, but the court concluded that this claim was to be evaluated under an objective standard:

> [T]he job qualifications which the employer invokes to justify his discrimination must be *reasonably necessary* to the essence of his business — here, the *safe* transportation of bus passengers from one point to another. The greater the safety factor, measured by the likelihood of harm and the probable severity of that harm in case of an accident, the more stringent may be the job qualifications designed to insure safe driving. 531 F.2d, at 236.

In *Tamiami*, the court noted that no one had seriously challenged the bus company's safety justification for hiring drivers with a low risk of having accidents.

Second, the court recognized that the ADEA requires that age qualifications be something more than "convenient" or "reasonable"; they must be "reasonably necessary . . . to the particular business," (*Id.* at 235), and this is only so when the employer is compelled to rely on age as a proxy for the safety-related job qualifications validated in the first inquiry. This showing could be made in two ways. The employer could establish that it " 'had reasonable cause to believe, that is, a factual basis for believing, that all or substantially all [persons over the age qualifications] would be unable to perform safely and efficiently the duties of the job involved.' " *Id.* at 236. In *Tamiami*, the employer did not seek to justify its hiring qualification under this statute.

Alternatively, the employer, like the bus company, could use age as a legitimate proxy for the safety-related job qualifications by proving that it is " 'impossible or highly impractical' " to deal with the older employees on an individualized basis. One method by which the employer can carry this burden is to establish that some members of the discriminated-against class possess a trait precluding safe and efficient job performance that cannot be ascertained by tests or interviews.

Courts have often been sympathetic to BFOQ defenses when used to justify the mandatory retirement of airplane pilots.

RASBERG v. NATIONWIDE LIFE INSURANCE CO.
671 F. Supp. 494 (S.D. Ohio 1987)

GRAHAM, DISTRICT JUDGE.

The present case is one brought under the Age Discrimination in Employment Act of 1967 (ADEA), 29 U.S.C. § 621 *et seq.*, and Section 4101.17(A), Ohio Revised Code.

Nationwide Life Insurance Company, defendant herein, maintains a small fleet of jet aircraft for transporting company executives, employees and clients. Plaintiff was employed by defendant as a pilot until he reached the age of sixty-two. At that time, plaintiff was forced to retire under defendant's corporate policy of mandatory retirement for pilots upon attaining the age of sixty-two. Defendant's mandatory retirement rule falls within the ambit of 29 U.S.C. § 623(a), which prohibits discrimination "against any individual with respect to his compensation, terms, conditions, or privileges of employment, because of such individual's age." However, defendant contends that its policy is a bona fide occupational qualification under 29 U.S.C. § 623(f)(1), thus exempting defendant from the operation of § 623(a). Defendant has filed a motion for summary judgment on that issue.

The defense of a bona fide occupational qualification is set forth in 29 U.S.C. § 623(f)(1), which provides that it shall not be unlawful for an employer to take any action otherwise prohibited under § 623(a) "where age is a bona fide occupational qualification reasonably necessary to the normal operation of the particular business."

The employer must establish that age is a bona fide occupational qualification in light of the employer's particular business. The employer must also demonstrate that all or substantially all of the individuals excluded from the job are in fact disqualified, or that some excluded individuals possess a disqualifying trait that cannot be ascertained except by reference to age because it is impossible or highly impractical to deal with employees on an individualized basis.

As a general rule, the process of aging entails a slowing down of all bodily functions, including cognitive function. (Buffer deposition, p. 17). Aging may have an impact on pacing (the amount of time to complete a task), ability to receive and respond to stimuli, reaction time, memory, degree of attention, the ability of the eye to focus on objects at varying distances or to adjust to lower levels of illumination or glare, and the ability to understand speech in the presence of noise.

Dr. Buffer expressed the opinion that the field of geriatric medicine was not advanced enough to predict on an individual basis the likelihood that a pilot who has reached the age of sixty-two will become incapacitated during a flight. (Deposition, p. 33). Dr. Sterns was unaware of any tests which could predict declines in pilot performance after a certain age, and concurred that tests of psychomotor and intellectual functions are not yet validated as predictive of the level of function of a pilot. (Feb. 11, 1986 deposition, p. 82; Aug. 16, 1983 deposition, p. 187) — Dr. Sterns further indicated that the risk of death factor in a crisis situation could not be replicated in a simulator, and that decrements in performance in older people may become apparent only in such a highly stressful situation. (Feb. 11, 1986 deposition, pp. 143–144, 146–147). Pilots have suffered disabling diseases during the period they were certified by the FAA. (Mohler deposition, p. 55).

The information before the court reveals that the aging process impacts upon mental and physical functions inherent in a pilot's performance past the age of sixty. The job qualification established by defendant is reasonably necessary to the safe transportation of defendant's passengers. The evidence further reveals that it is currently impossible or highly impractical to test for all of the various potential defects in pilot performance on an individualized basis. The excerpts from Dr. Mohler's deposition fail to contradict defendant's position that effective tests to detect all the multiple effects of aging on the performance of pilots past the age of sixty are currently unavailable. The evidence is such that a reasonable jury could not return a verdict for plaintiff. *Anderson v. Liberty Lobby, Inc., supra.*

Judgment is hereby ordered for the defendant on the federal ADEA claim.

QUESTIONS

1. If safety considerations can establish a BFOQ defense, why cannot economic efficiency arguments, e.g., most workers over age 60 are less productive when working at the particular job?

2. Suppose the employer could prove that 85 percent of individuals over age 65 were unable to satisfactorily perform a particular job. Would that establish a BFOQ defense for the use of age 65 as a mandatory retirement age?

K. EMPLOYEE BENEFIT PLAN DEFENSE

In the past, the ADEA permits age discrimination in employee benefit plans provided the discrimination did not cause termination or refusal to hire because of age. Section 4(f) of the Act provides in part that it is not unlawful for an employer to have a ". . . bona fide employee benefit plan such as a retirement, pension, or insurance plan, which is not a subterfuge to evade the purposes of this Act. . . ." 29 U.S.C. § 423(f)(2). This section was added to the ADEA to encourage the hiring of older workers without the obligation to include such workers in employee benefit plans. The idea was to lower the cost of hiring older workers.

The meaning of Section 4(f) was much in doubt. In 1989 the Supreme Court, in *Public Employees Retirement Sys. v. Betts*, 492 U.S. 158 (1989), held that the section was intended to create a wide latitude of discretion for retirement benefit plans. They could legally discriminate against older employees. The phrase "not a subterfuge to evade the purposes of this Act" was read by the court to cover only specific and blatant attempts to discriminate against older workers. According to the Court, Section 4(f) placed the burden on the employee to prove that a discriminatory benefit plan provision was intended to serve the purpose of discriminating for some prohibited reason. The holding in *Betts* was overturned by the Older Workers Benefit Protection Act of 1990, which specifically held that employee benefit plans were covered by the ADEA. Therefore the employer cannot discriminate against older workers merely because they cost more under the employer's fringe benefit plan, nor can the plan call for a freeze on contributions to a plan because of the employee's age. 29 U.S.C. § 623(f)(2) & (j) (the amendment did not apply retroactively).

L. EARLY VOLUNTARY RETIREMENT PLANS

Faced with the abolition of mandatory retirement, many employers have turned to incentives to encourage voluntary retirement. Such "early" retirement plans are lawful if they are truly voluntary and do not discriminate against older employees.

SMITH v. WORLD INS. CO.
38 F.3d 1456 (8th Cir. 1994)

Hansen, Circuit Judge.

World Insurance Company (World) appeals the district court's order denying World's motion for new trial or judgment as a matter of law filed after the district court entered judgment and awarded damages to Thomas Dean Smith on a jury verdict finding that World constructively discharged him in violation of the Age Discrimination in Employment Act (ADEA), 29 U.S.C. §§ 621-634.

I

World hired Smith as a stock clerk in 1950, when Smith was 19 years old. Smith worked his way up in the company for the next 35 years. In 1976, World promoted him to Assistant Vice-President of Home Office Services, where his duties included product purchasing, supervision of mail room, filing, and warehousing, and printing all of World's policies, contracts, advertising brochures, and newsletters. In 1986, World promoted him to Assistant Vice-President for Purchasing.

In 1985, World hired a management consulting group to analyze the strengths and weaknesses of World's operations. After the consulting group finished its review, it recommended some changes in the management structure at World. After receiving those recommendations, World hired Alan Jackson as a new vice-president to oversee many areas of World's operations, including many of the areas under Smith's supervision. Smith began reporting to Jackson on July 7, 1986. Prior to July 7, 1986, Smith had reported to World's president, Tom Eilers.

Smith reported to Jackson for approximately one month during which Jackson and Smith met a few times. Jackson admitted to another employee during that time that he was building a record against Smith and other older employees in order to get rid of them. On August 8, 1986, Jackson told Smith that he had the option of staying with World and risking termination or taking early retirement. Jackson gave Smith the weekend to decide. On Monday, August 8, 1986, Smith informed World that he would take early retirement.

On August 18, 1986, Smith signed a memorandum agreement with Tom Eilers, on behalf of World, setting out the details of the early retirement package. Smith agreed to retire voluntarily on November 1, 1986. World agreed, among other things, to pay Smith a bonus based on six-weeks of his annual salary, to provide health insurance to Smith and his dependents for six weeks, to provide Smith group life insurance for a year, to provide Smith with the services of an employment agency to help him locate work, and to provide Smith with office space and telephone service until December 15, 1986. Smith was 54 years old when he agreed to early retirement. The person that filled his position was in her mid-30's. Smith found another job in the purchasing department of Mutual of Omaha and began work on December 16, 1986. Smith's new salary was approximately $11,000 year less than he was making at World.

On the day Smith left World, he filed a complaint with the Nebraska Equal Opportunity Employment Commission. On August 11, 1987, Smith filed a complaint against World in the United States District Court for the District of Nebraska alleging that World had violated the ADEA by constructively discharging him by forcing him to take early retirement because of his age. . . . .

Smith's case against World went to trial on November 4, 1991. On November 13, 1991, the jury returned a verdict for Smith finding that World constructively discharged Smith because of his age. The jury assessed $67,321 of backpay damages and found that World's conduct constituted a willful violation of the ADEA.

II

World first argues that it is entitled to judgment as a matter of law or a new trial because there was insufficient evidence for the district court to submit to the jury Smith's claim that he was constructively discharged because of his age. We disagree.

"'A constructive discharge exists when an employer deliberately renders the employee's working conditions intolerable and thus forces him to quit his job.'" . . . To make out a case of constructive discharge, a plaintiff must show that "'a reasonable person would find the conditions intolerable.'"

The plaintiff must also show that the employer created the intolerable conditions intending to force the plaintiff to quit. *Id.* The plaintiff can satisfy the intent requirement by demonstrating that he or she quit as "a reasonably foreseeable consequence of [the] employer['s] discriminatory actions." *Huk-kanen v. International Union of Operating Eng'r*, F.3d 281, 285 (8th Cir. 1993).

The mere offer of early retirement, however, does not establish a constructive discharge. . . . [M]ost courts have found that an offer of early retirement constitutes a constructive discharge only when the offer is made under terms and conditions where the employee would be worse off whether or not he or she accepted the offer. . . . More simply stated, an offer of early retirement constitutes a constructive discharge when the choice is essentially either early retirement or continuing to work under intolerable conditions, like the threat of termination without benefits.

The evidence in this case satisfies these standards. Smith testified that in the August 6, 1986, meeting, Jackson offered him the choice essentially among immediately resigning, staying on, or taking early retirement. (Tr. at 406–07.) Smith testified that Jackson told him that if he elected to stay on that Jackson "would start to turn the screws and build a file" against Smith. *Id.* Jackson made clear to him that the only way benefits would be available is if he took early retirement. (Tr. at 408.) The meeting occurred on Thursday, and Jackson gave him until the following Monday to think it over. *Id.* Smith left the meeting feeling that given Jackson's threats, no matter what happened he was going to be terminated. (Tr. at 410.) Smith concluded that Jackson's threats to build a file and turn the screws meant that Jackson would create situations to make Smith look bad and that Smith would be given projects on which he would not be able to succeed. (Tr. at 454.) He told his wife that after reviewing the options Jackson provided, he felt he had no choice other than retirement because it would be the only way to get some benefits out of the situation. (Tr. at 413.) Smith believed that in the meeting Jackson had outlined his goal of eventually seeing that Smith was dismissed and he really had no choice other than to take the benefits. *Id.*

This evidence, viewed in the light most favorable to Smith, is sufficient to demonstrate that the options Jackson outlined for Smith on August 6, 1986, which included an offer of early retirement, left Smith with the type of "Hobson's choice" that would allow a jury to consider the offer of early retirement a constructive discharge.

In this case, however, Smith's testimony about the events leading to his early retirement does not stand alone. There is additional evidence which corroborates Smith's perception of those events. Mary Schmidt, a co-worker of both Smith and Jackson at World, largely corroborated Smith's testimony that Jackson intended to see that World would get rid of Smith one way or another.

We conclude that there was more than sufficient evidence to support submission of Smith's constructive discharge claim to the jury. Drawing all inferences in favor of Smith, the evidence establishes that the offer of early retirement left Smith with two undesirable choices: retire early or face intolerable conditions if he chose to stay. The district court committed no error in denying the motion for new trial or judgment as matter of law on this issue.

VEGA v. KODAK CARIBBEAN, LTD.
3 F.3d 476 (1st Cir. 1993)

SELYA, CIRCUIT JUDGE.

William Shakespeare once wrote that "parting is such sweet sorrow." In this case, which requires us to mull the circumstances under which an employee's "early retirement" can be considered a "constructive discharge," plaintiffs' parting with their longtime employer proved more sorrowful than sweet. When plaintiffs sued, the district court added to their pain, granting the employer's motion for summary judgment. 807 F. Supp. 872. We can offer little comfort.

Background

Defendant-appellee Kodak Caribbean, Ltd. (Kodak) decided to downsize its operations in Puerto Rico. To this end, it announced the availability of a voluntary separation program (the VSP). On September 15, 1989, Kodak held a meeting to explain the VSP to its local work force. The company distributed descriptive documents to virtually all Kodak employees, save only for certain managerial and human resources personnel, regardless of age or years of service. The written materials spelled out the benefits afforded, the method of calculating severance pay, and how the program would be implemented.

Kodak encouraged workers to participate in the VSP, but did not require them to do so. Withal, the company informed all its employees that if substantially fewer than twenty-six individuals opted to enter the VSP, others would be reassigned or furloughed in order to reach the desired staffing level.

Two veteran employees, Jorge Vega and Eusebio Leon, were among those who chose to participate in the VSP. After signing an election form on October 4, 1989, Leon received lump-sum severance payment of $28,163.16 plus other benefits. Vega followed suit on October 10, 1989, executing a similar form and receiving $52,671.00 severance payment. The men retired on the dates designated in their respective election forms. At no time did either man ask to revoke his election or offer to refund his severance payment.

In 1990, Vega and Leon brought separate suits against Kodak, each alleging discrimination on the basis of age.

III

Analysis

On this record, appellants fall prey to Rule 56 at square one, for they have failed to adduce evidence sufficient to establish their prima facie case. We explain briefly.

To satisfy the third element in the prima facie case, ADEA suitors who claim to have been wrongfully ousted from their jobs must demonstrate that they were actually or constructively discharged. Here, appellants concede that they were not cashiered. They maintain, however, that Kodak's sponsorship of the VSP effected their constructive discharges by forcing them into an unpalatable (and unwarranted) choice between early retirement and dismissal.[1] The facts of record, fused with the appropriate legal standard, belie the charge.

Mere offers for early retirement, even those that include attractive incentives designed to induce employees who might otherwise stay on the job to separate from the employer's service, do not transgress the ADEA. . . . To transform an offer of early retirement into constructive discharge, a plaintiff must show that the offer was nothing more than a charade, that is, a subterfuge disguising the employer's desire to purge plaintiff from the ranks because of his age. *See Hebert*, 872 F.2d at 1111. Under this dichotomy, offers which furnish employees choice in name only are impermissible because, in the final analysis, they effectively vitiate the employees' power to choose work over retirement. Phrased another way, the law regards as the functional equivalent of discharge those offers of early retirement which, if refused, will result in work so arduous or unappealing, or working conditions so intolerable, that reasonable person would feel compelled to forsake his job rather than to submit to looming indignities. . . . In terms of this standard, plaintiff who has accepted an employer's offer to retire can be said to have been constructively discharged when the offer presented was, at rock bottom, "a choice between early retirement with benefits or discharge without benefits," or, more starkly still, an "impermissible take-it-or-leave-it choice between retirement or discharge." *Hebert*, 872 F.2d at 1113.

Kodak's promulgation of the VSP cannot be said to have presented Vega and Leon with this sort of Hobson's choice. The offer was cast as one to be accepted or rejected at an employee's will.

Finally, nothing in the record indicates that, for any particular employee, refusing early retirement meant either discharge or the imposition of working conditions so abhorrent as to justify resignation. To be sure, Kodak said that it would likely furlough a number of employees if not enough workers elected to depart voluntarily. But, three things palliate the inference that appellants seek to draw from this statement: (1) the company simultaneously announced, both orally and in writing, that if a sufficient complement participated in the VSP, the need to thin the ranks unilaterally would never arise; (2) it did not directly or indirectly

---

[1] We use the euphemism "early retirement" in its broad, nontechnical sense to include any employer-sponsored plan that provides special benefit to an employee in return for voluntary decision to withdraw from active employment at an earlier-than-anticipated time. The VSP is such a plan.

indicate which particular individuals would be tapped should layoffs prove to be necessary; and (3) it never threatened that persons ultimately selected for involuntary separation would be treated harshly.

Notwithstanding the formidable array of circumstances weighing in favor of a finding that appellants resigned voluntarily, appellants assert that they were constructively discharged because they *believed* that rejecting the VSP was tantamount to forfeiting their jobs. We discern no genuine issue of material fact; assuming that appellants' mindset was as stated, their conclusion does not follow. An employee's perceptions cannot govern a claim of constructive discharge if, and to the extent that, the perceptions are unreasonable. . . . Were the rule otherwise, any employee who quit, and thereafter thought better of it, could claim constructive discharge with impunity. The law, therefore, demands that a disgruntled ex-employee's professed belief about the likely consequences of refusing an offer for early retirement be judged by an "objective standard," the focus of which is "the reasonable state of mind of the putative discriminate." *Id.* (citations and internal quotation marks omitted). In light of the uncontroverted facts of record here, appellants' impression that the ignominy of firing comprised the only alternative to accepting the VSP was thoroughly unreasonable.

In fine, the record is barren of evidence competent to support an inference that Kodak placed appellants "between the Scylla of forced retirement [and] the Charybdis of discharge." *Hebert*, 872 F.2d at 1112. Rather, Kodak asked its employees to choose between immediate severance with its associated benefits or continued work with its inherent risks. As the alternative to separation from the employer's service was not so onerous as to compel reasonable person's resignation, appellants cannot convincingly claim to have been constructively discharged.

QUESTIONS

1. Can an employer offer the alternatives of early retirement with an incentive bonus (or higher retirement pension) or continued employment at lower wages?

2. Is the only relevant test of an early retirement plan whether it provides greater economic rewards? Are there other aspects of continued employment that are lost by retirement and thus would offset the financial retirement incentives?

M. WAIVER AND RELEASE

When an employer terminates an employee who is over age 40 (within the coverage of the ADEA), typically the employer will offer termination benefits to the employee in exchange for a waiver of rights or release of liability concerning any possible ADEA lawsuit arising from the termination. Having the employee sign such a waiver is not an admission of wrongdoing. The employer, in essence, is only being cautious and insuring itself against possible attorney's fees and settlement costs or judgment awards. A modest payment to the employee protects against much larger risks. Suppose, however, that after signing such a waiver, the employee concludes that the termination was in violation of the ADEA. Does the waiver bar a subsequent suit? Or is it enough that the waiver of rights was signed voluntarily and with an understanding of its legal consequences.

In 1990, the ADEA was amended to create a statutory standard declaring what kind of waivers are permitted and the procedure that must be followed in their execution. Section 626(f) of the Act provides that only "knowing and voluntary" waivers are valid and lists nine factors that must be met. To be valid, the waiver must:

- be written in understandable language;

- specifically refer to rights or claims under the ADEA;

- not apply to rights or claims arising after the date the waiver is signed;

- provide the employee additional consideration for signing;

- advise the employee to consult an attorney before signing;

- give the employee at least 21 days to consider the agreement or at least 45 days if the waiver is part of an exit incentive or employment termination program;

- be revocable by the employee for at least 7 days after being signed; and

- if the waiver is part of an employment termination program, the employee must be provided details as to whom the program applies. 29 U.S.C. § 626(f)(1).

In any dispute over the validity of the waiver, the party asserting the validity of the waiver has the burden of proof that it was a "knowing and voluntary" waiver. 29 U.S.C. § 626(f)(3). If the waiver does not comply with the ADEA waiver requirements, it is not binding.

The statutory command is clear: An employee "may not waive" an ADEA claim unless the waiver or release satisfies the OWBPA's requirements. The policy of the Older Workers Benefit Protection Act is likewise clear from its title: It is designed to protect the rights and benefits of older workers. The OWBPA implements Congress' policy via a strict, unqualified statutory stricture on waivers, and we are bound to take Congress at its word. Congress imposed specific duties on employers who seek releases of certain claims created by statute. Congress delineated these duties with precision and without qualification: An employee "may not waive" an ADEA claim unless the employer complies with the statute. Courts cannot with ease presume ratification of that which Congress forbids. *Oubre v. Entergy Operations*, 522 U.S. 422, 424 (1998).

QUESTIONS

1. The threshold question is whether *any* employee should be allowed to waive ADEA rights. Does society's interest in outlawing age discrimination outweigh the employee's right to "sell" his right to sue?

2. The waiver option, assured benefits versus highly uncertain litigation possibilities, presents the employee with a difficult choice. What would you do?

3. Is there any argument that *employers* are better off by the waiver standards in § 626(f)?

4. Can waivers be seen as a typical contractual situation: the mutual promises make both parties better-off? If so, why should the government interfere with the freedom of contract?

When the ADEA was enacted, the Department of Labor was responsible for its enforcement. In 1979, enforcement responsibility was shifted to the Equal Employment Opportunity Commission (EEOC), which is also responsible for enforcing (1) Title VII of the Civil Rights Act of 1964; (2) the Equal Pay Act of 1963; and (3) Sections 501 and 505 of the Rehabilitation Act of 1973. The EEOC has been criticized in recent years for its decision to move away from broad complaints against large companies and entire industries and instead to concentrate on individual claims of age discrimination. Individuals who allege violations of the ADEA must first file a claim with the EEOC. Exhaustion of administrative remedies is required before filing a lawsuit in federal court. For an example of a claim that was dismissed for failure to exhaust administrative remedies, see *Shelton v. Boeing Co.*, 399 F.3d 909 (8th Cir. 2005).

N. ENFORCEMENT PROCEDURES

An aggrieved individual cannot file suit until all administrative remedies have been pursued. First, if the state in which the individual resides has a law that prohibits age discrimination and an agency that enforces the law, the aggrieved individual must file a complaint with that state agency. 29 U.S.C. §§ 200–219. Second, the individual must file a charge with the EEOC within 300 days following the alleged discrimination. 29 U.S.C. § 626(d). If the state of residence has no law prohibiting age discrimination, the EEOC complaint must be filed within 180 days. 29 U.S.C. § 633(b).

The individual cannot file a lawsuit until 60 days after filing the required state and federal administrative complaints. 29 U.S.C. § 626(d). The intent is to grant the state agency or the EEOC time to attempt conciliation of the complaint. If the EEOC commences a lawsuit, the employee may not commence a private suit. 29 U.S.C. § 626(c)(1). If the EEOC later terminates its actions, it must notify the employee, who has 90 days in which to sue. Once the 60-day period has passed, without action by the EEOC, the employee is free to sue. Even if the EEOC should later sue, the employee's action would proceed.

The ADEA has a two-year statute of limitations for nonwillful violations and a three-year statute for willful violations. The statute of limitations runs from the time the cause of action accrued, which is the date that the employee was notified of the termination of the job, rather than the last date the employee was on the payroll. *See EEOC v. Kimberly-Clark Corp.*, 531 F. Supp. 58 (N.D. Ga. 1981).

Since 1978, the ADEA has expressly provided a right to a trial by jury. Because juries are thought to be sympathetic to plaintiffs, they are almost always requested. Of course, the plaintiff's case will go to the jury only if it can survive a motion for a directed verdict or summary judgment. Often the issue on appeal is the court's decision whether to permit the case to go to the jury.

O.   REMEDIES

The ADEA specifically permits the court, in its discretion, to order reinstatement. 29 U.S.C. § 626(c)(2). If reinstatement is inappropriate, the court can award front pay, a substitute for lost future earnings. The court can also issue injunctions to prevent future violations. Naturally, the court can award back pay to make the successful plaintiff whole again, including the value of lost employee benefits such as medical insurance and life insurance. 29 U.S.C. § 626(b) (incorporating 29 U.S.C. § 216). The amount of the award will be reduced by any severance payments made by the employer. The employee has a duty to mitigate damages, including the duty to accept reasonable offers of reinstatement from the employer. The employer carries the burden of proof on mitigation and must show that: (1) the plaintiff failed to exercise reasonable diligence to mitigate damages; and (2) there was a reasonable likelihood that by exercising reasonable diligence the plaintiff would have found work comparable to the former position.

If the jury finds the employer's violation was willful, the award of back pay is doubled but there is no right to punitive damages or for any damages for pain and suffering. Successful plaintiffs can be, and usually are, awarded attorney's fees.

P.   STATE LAW REMEDIES

Almost all states have age discrimination laws that parallel the ADEA. Employees often sue concurrently under both the ADEA and the applicable state laws. Such suits are often consolidated in the federal court. Damages under state laws may duplicate the ADEA, or they may allow for broader remedies, including compensatory or punitive damages. State law may also provide damages for traditional tort injury, such as pain and suffering and intentional infliction of emotional distress. A terminated employee may also sue for contractual rights, claiming that the termination violated the employment contract, either explicit or implicit, between the employee and the employer.

Chapter 4

INCOME MAINTENANCE

How the elderly secure an adequate income after retirement is the focus of this chapter. For many, old age means retirement and a loss of income. Traditionally, retirees relied upon their savings and financial assistance from their families. Many retirees, for example, moved in with their children or accepted a regular allowance from them. Currently, reliance by retirees on children has paled in significance when compared to primary sources of income: personal savings, employment-related pension plans, and public benefits.

Topics in Aging: Income and Poverty Among Older Americans in 2005
CRS Report for Congress, September 21, 2006

Personal savings, Social Security, and employer-sponsored pensions are sometimes referred to as the "three-legged stool" of retirement income. While this term may be useful as a metaphor, for many older Americans, at least one of the legs of the stool is missing. In 2005, 87% of the income received by elderly individuals in the lowest income quartile (those with less than $9,600 in total income) came from Social Security. For this group, less than 4% of their income came from savings and only 3% was received from pensions. Older Americans with higher incomes had more diversified sources of income. In 2005, 20% of income received by individuals in the highest quartile of the income distribution (those with $28,130 or more in income) came from Social Security. These individuals also were more likely to have wage income and to receive income from pensions and assets. They received, in the aggregate, more than three-fourths of their income from these three sources.

Earnings, Social Security, pensions, and income from assets — mainly interest and dividends — comprise the majority of income among people 65 and older. Information on pension income has been reported separately on the CPS only since the 1970s. In 1975, Social Security comprised 42% of all income received by people aged 65 and older. Earnings and income from assets each accounted for 20% of the income of the elderly, while pensions made up 14% of their income. Public assistance and other sources each contributed just 2% to the total income of Americans aged 65 and older in 1975. By 2008, Social Security comprised 39% of the income received by people aged 65 and older. Earnings had increased to 26% of the income of the elderly, while income from assets had fallen to 13% of the total. Pensions, including withdrawals from retirement accounts, comprised 20% of the income of the elderly in 2008. Public assistance provided less than 1% of the income of the elderly, and other sources accounted for just 2%.

Although 97% of persons 65 and older had income from at least one source in 2008, in most cases household income is a better measure of available resources than individual income. Median household income rose faster among elderly households than among nonelderly households from 1968 through 2008, but in 2008, the median annual income of households in which the householder or spouse was 65 or older ($30,774) was just 54% of the median income of younger households ($56,604). Patrick Purcell, *Income of Americans Aged 65 and Older*, 1968 to 2008, Cong. Research Service, 7-5700 (Nov. 4, 2009).

Almost 90% of individuals age 65 or older receive Social Security benefits and for many Social Security benefits are the primary source of income. And so it is with Social Security that we begin the examination of how America's elderly support themselves in retirement.

A. SOCIAL SECURITY: PAST AND PRESENT

The foundation for public income support for the elderly is the Old-Age, Survivors, and Disability Insurance (OASDI) program, popularly referred to as Social Security, which in 2010 provided monthly benefits to over 36 million retired workers and their spouses.

Social Security, based in part on insurance principles, provides monthly cash benefits designed partially to replace the income that is lost to the worker or the worker's family if the worker retires, becomes disabled, or dies. This section discusses retirement and survivors' benefits. Disability benefits are discussed later in this chapter.

Social Security operates on the following well-settled (though controversial) principles:

(1) Social Security benefits are an entitlement paid to those workers (and their spouses and dependents) who paid Social Security wage taxes. Based on the concept of insurance, benefits are paid to those who paid into the fund, rather than to those who need income. Someone may still be employed and receive benefits.

(2) Benefits are designed to provide a "floor of protection," and not a complete source of retirement income or a total replacement of earnings lost upon retirement.

(3) Social Security is an uneasy balance between the goals of social adequacy and individual equity, with the former gradually becoming more apparent and more accepted than the latter. Social Security is now more frequently characterized as a social welfare program, and less frequently as retirement insurance.

(4) The level of benefits is related to the amount of wage taxes paid. The higher the income of the worker, the greater the contribution of wage taxes, and the greater the benefits to be paid to that worker upon retirement or disability.

(5) Social Security is self-financing through employee and employer payroll taxes and does not rely upon general revenue appropriations.

(6) Social Security wage taxes and coverage are mandatory and nearly universal.

(7) The system of benefits is defined in great detail. Program administrators have almost no administrative discretion in the awarding of benefits.

[1]　HISTORY

Larry DeWitt, *The Development of Social Security in America*
70 Soc. Sec. Bull. 1 (2010)

The Origins of Social Insurance

Economic security is a universal human problem, encompassing the ways in which an individual or a family provides for some assurance of income when an individual is either too old or too disabled to work, when a family breadwinner dies, or when a worker faces involuntary unemployment (in more modern times).

All societies throughout human history have had to come to terms with this problem in some way. The various strategies for addressing this problem rely on a mix of individual and collective efforts. Some strategies are mostly individual (such as accruing savings and investments); others are more collective (such as relying on help from family, fraternal organizations and unions, religious groups, charities, and social welfare programs); and some strategies are a mix of both (such as the use of various forms of insurance to reduce economic risk).

. . .

Social insurance provides a method for addressing the problem of economic security in the context of modern industrial societies. The concept of social insurance is that individuals contribute to a central fund managed by governments, and this fund is then used to provide income to individuals when they become unable to support themselves through their own labors. Social insurance differs from private insurance in that governments employ elements of social policy beyond strict actuarial principles, with an emphasis on the social adequacy of benefits as well as concerns of strict equity for participants. Thus, in the U.S. Social Security system, for example, benefits are weighted such that those persons with lower past earnings receive a proportionately higher benefit than those with higher earnings; this is one way in which the system provides progressivity in its benefits. Such elements of social policy would generally not be permissible in private insurance plans. . . .

Today's Social Security program is the direct descendant of the limited program of contributory old-age benefits signed into law by President Franklin D. Roosevelt on August 14, 1935. Although the fundamentals have remained constant, the Social Security system has been modified to meet changing work patterns and public expectations.

Social Security was enacted during the Great Depression of the 1930s, a period in American history characterized by economic insecurity and confusion. In 1932, 34 percent of the nonagricultural work force was unemployed. The savings of millions of Americans were wiped out by collapse of over 5,000 banks. Corporations faced with financial ruin were unable to pay pensions promised to retirees.

Martha A. McSteen, *Fifty Years of Social Security*
48 Soc. Sec. Bull. 36, 37 (1985)

For vast numbers of aged people, and people nearing old age, the loss of their savings brought with it the prospect of living their remaining years in destitution. At the height of the Depression, many old people were literally penniless. One-third to one-half of the aged were dependent on family or friends for support. The poor houses and other relief agencies that existed at the time to assist people who had fallen on hard times were financed mainly from charity and local funds. They could not begin — either financially or conceptually — to respond adequately to the special needs of the aged brought about by the cataclysmic events of the Depression.

Although by 1934, 30 States had responded by providing pensions for the needy aged, total expenditures for State programs for the aged that year were $31 million — an average of $19.74 a month per aged person. As the Depression worsened, benefits to individuals were cut further to enable States to spread available funds among as many people as possible. Yet states lacked the financial wherewithal to adequately support the poor elderly.

David Schwartz & Herman Grundman, *Social Security Programs in the United States*
52 Soc. Sec. Bull. 2, 7 (1989)

Meanwhile, both the States and the Federal Government had begun to recognize that in such an increasingly industrialized country, workers and their dependents could be effectively protected from certain economic risks through social insurance. In the United States, as in most industrialized countries throughout the world, social insurance began with workers' compensation (in effect in all but four States by 1929). President Franklin Roosevelt's Committee on Economic Security, formed in June 1934, recommended that two new national social insurance systems be established: A Federal/State system of unemployment insurance and a Federal system of old age benefits for retired workers who had been employed in industry and commerce. The Committee's recommendations, as modified by the Congress, were embodied in the Social Security Act signed by President Roosevelt on August 14, 1935. The law also provided for Federal matching grants-in-aid to the States to help them give financial assistance to needy persons in three categories: the aged, the blind, and dependent children. In addition, the law authorized Federal grants to the States for social services, public health, and vocational rehabilitation.

Major Milestones in the Development of OASDI

Under the 1935 law, workers in commerce and industry would earn retirement benefits through work in jobs covered by the system. Benefits were to be financed by a payroll tax paid by employees and their employers on a wage and salary earnings up to $3,000 per year (the wage base). Monthly benefits would be payable at age 65 to workers with a specified minimum amount of cumulative wages in covered jobs. The amount of benefits payable also varied with the worker's cumulative earnings in covered jobs. Individuals who continued to work beyond age 65 would not be eligible for benefits until their earnings ceased. Lump-sum refunds, in amounts somewhat larger than the total taxes paid by deceased workers, were to be paid to the estates of workers who died before attaining age 65 or before receiving benefits. Collection of taxes was scheduled to begin in 1937, but monthly benefits would not be payable until 1942.

Before the old-age insurance program was actually in full operation, important changes were adopted based largely on the recommendations of the first Advisory Council on Social Security. In 1939, Congress significantly expanded the old-age insurance program by extending monthly benefits to workers' dependents and survivors. Also, the basis for computing benefits was changed from cumulative lifetime earnings after 1936 to average monthly earnings in covered work, making it possible to pay reasonably adequate benefits to many workers then approaching retirement age and to their dependents. The 1939 law also established the concept of "quarter of coverage" as the basis for measuring if an individual had sufficient covered employment to qualify for a benefit. Also, individuals who continued to work after age 65 could receive full benefits as long as their earnings did not exceed a specified amount. The 1939 amendments made monthly benefits first payable in 1940 instead of 1942 as originally planned.

No major changes were made in the program from 1939 until 1950, when benefit levels were substantially increased, the wage base was increased, and a new schedule of gradually increasing tax rates was provided in the law. Coverage was broadened to include many jobs that previously had been excluded — in some cases because experience was needed to work out procedures for reporting the earnings and collecting the taxes of persons in certain occupational groups. Among the groups covered by the 1950 amendments were regularly employed farm and household employees and self-employed persons other than farmers and professional people. Coverage was made available on a group voluntary basis to employees of State and local governments not under public employee retirement systems and to employees of nonprofit organizations.

In 1950, when coverage under the program was extended, the law was amended to allow a worker's average monthly earnings to be figured on the basis of his or her earnings after 1950. Similar consideration was given to the groups newly covered by the program in 1954 and 1956 (including members of the Armed Forces, most self-employed professional persons, and State and local employees under a retirement system under certain conditions) by providing that the 5 years of lowest earnings be dropped from the computation of average earnings.

In 1950, benefits were sharply increased to offset the inflation that occurred during World War II. Coverage also was broadened significantly to include almost all workers in the hope that the elderly could avoid poverty and the demeaning aspects of need-based relief programs. In 1935, only six out of ten employees were covered; by the mid-1950s, after a series of amendments, 90 percent of workers were covered. Today over 95 percent of workers are enrolled in the Social Security program.

Although in the 1960s Social Security provided some income for the elderly, their medical expenses threatened to outstrip their resources. After years of debate, in 1965, Congress enacted the Medicare program, which provided a payroll tax financed hospital insurance program for persons age 65 or older. Medicare is discussed in Chapter 5.

Throughout the 1950s and 1960s, particularly in election years, Congress periodically raised Social Security benefits. While some increases in benefits were designed merely to match inflation, others were attempts to raise the relative income of retirees. As it became apparent that inflation was always going to exist, and in order to avoid vote-seeking, election year benefit increases, in 1972 Congress enacted automatic cost-of-living adjustments (COLAs) for Social Security benefits based on increases in the Consumer Price Index.

In the early 1980s, because of high inflation, Social Security benefits rose at a rapid rate, while low wage growth and changing demographics caused Social Security revenues to lag behind expenditures. To remain solvent, Social Security fund revenues had to be increased or benefits reduced. The National Commission on Social Security Reform (NCSSR), appointed by President Reagan in 1983, won bipartisan approval for its proposed compromise solutions:

— Advances in the timing of tax rate increases already scheduled in the law for employees and employers, and increases in self-employment taxes.

— A gradual increase in the age of eligibility for full retirement benefits until the normal retirement age, then age 65, became age 67 by the year 2022.

— Federal income taxation of up to 85 percent of Social Security benefits for certain higher income beneficiaries. (Previously all benefits were excluded from taxable income.)

[2] THE CURRENT NEED FOR SOCIAL SECURITY

[a] Economic Security in Retirement

The goal of Social Security is to achieve economic security or a "safety net" for retirees. The program is designed to ameliorate what were described by President Franklin D. Roosevelt as the "major vicissitudes of life": retirement, death of a worker, or long-term and severe disability. By relying upon social insurance principles, Social Security spreads the risk of such losses throughout the population by means of the wage taxes paid by almost all employees. In return, almost everyone is assured of at least a minimum level of support in the event of the death, retirement, or disability of a provider. Even inflation has been removed as a source of fear by virtue of automatic cost-of-living adjustments of benefit.

The other principle in Social Security is modest income redistribution. The program provides higher benefits to those who pay higher payroll taxes, but retirees with a history of lower wages receive proportionately higher benefits. Thus, because the program is mandatory, and because higher-income workers do not fare proportionately as well as lower-income workers, there is an element of compulsory welfare or income redistribution in the program. The redistribution aspect is arguably necessary to ensure that lower wage retirees have enough income to meet their basic needs.

[b]   Amelioration of Elderly Poverty

Social Security retirement benefits have greatly reduced elderly poverty. In 1959, the share of the elderly counted as poor was 35 percent. By 1975, it was 15 percent and today it is about 10 percent, about the same percent as the under age 65 population. Many elderly, however, are considered "near-poor" because their income is below 125 percent of the poverty threshold. For example, 28 percent of elderly unmarried women were poor or near-poor in 2007, as were 33 percent of African-American and 28 percent of Latino elderly. More than 80 percent of older African-Americans and 75 percent of older Latinos rely on Social Security for more than half of their income.

[c]   Lack of Personal Savings

A lack of personal savings was one of the reasons for the adoption of Social Security. During the Depression of the 1930s, a great number of bank failures wiped out the savings of millions of older Americans. Millions of other elderly lost their jobs and were forced to live on their savings much earlier than they had expected. Today, however, bank savings, up to $250,000 per account, are insured by the federal government, and the elderly are not faced with mass unemployment due to an economic depression. Yet many elderly still retire with relatively few assets.

The current lack of savings among the elderly can be traced to three conditions. First, many of the elderly had such low incomes when they worked that they simply could not save, because they had to use all they earned in order to live. Many individuals may have earned little more than the minimum wage. Others may have earned adequate incomes during part of their work years, but lost their jobs and their savings during the severe recession of the 1980s and the Great Recession of 2007–2009. The sharp decline of the manufacturing sector particularly undercut the efforts of many to reach economic self-sufficiency. Second, many of today's elderly were spending their savings on their children during their work years. With the dramatic increases in the cost of college and graduate school education, many parents saw their savings disappear into a flood of tuition bills. As housing prices escalated, some parents helped finance their children's first homes. Other elderly persons previously provided financial support for their own parents. Third, most Americans save only a small proportion of what they earn. Compared to other industrialized societies, the American rate of savings is very low and has even declined over the last 25 years.

It is not clear why Americans fail to save more. Commentators have suggested that the lack of savings can be traced to the easy access to credit, the constant emphasis on consumption, undue optimism about future income prospects, disincentives to save in the federal income tax code, the existence of Social Security, and a deeply ingrained cultural disinclination to save. Whatever the cause, the effect is clear. Most Americans will not save enough to adequately provide for their retirement years. As a result, Social Security retirement benefits are an essential source of income for many retirees.

QUESTIONS

1.   Why do you think Americans do not save more for their retirement?

2.   Would they save more if there were no Social Security program? Do they not save because, after paying Social Security wage taxes, they cannot afford to save? Are they disinclined to save because they believe that Social Security will financially protect their old age?

3.   Do you think that you will save enough "for a comfortable old age"?

4.   Emily, age 35, expects to retire in 30 years (at age 65) at which time she wants to have saved enough so that she can have an annual income for life of $30,000 plus her Social Security benefits. To date she has no savings and no pension plan. How much would you estimate that Emily will have to save each year on the average in order to meet her income retirement goal? (Hint — at age 65 she will require about $477,000 to purchase a lifetime annuity paying $2,500 a month for her life, assuming an estimated interest rate of 6% at the time she purchases the annuity. Several web sites provide free calculations that provide information as to the rate of savings necessary to create a projected level of income.)

[3]   CURRENT STATUS

[a]   The Statute

The Social Security Act provides a complex mixture of benefits and the frequent changes in the law and supporting regulations contribute to the challenge of understanding the Act. Title III of the Social Security Act, officially entitled Old-Age, Survivors, and Disability Insurance Benefits, is codified at 42 U.S.C. §§ 401 to 433, with regulations appearing at 20 C.F.R. § 404 *et seq.* The statute should never be consulted without an examination of the accompanying regulations that explain and illustrate the law.

[b]   Program Policy Sources

The Social Security Administration (SSA) of the Department of Health and Human Services (HHS) has primary authority for administering the Act. In addition to the Statute and Regulations, the SSA issues various policy statements. Social Security Rulings is a quarterly periodical that contains federal judicial decisions, SSA statements of policy, and SSA interpretations of the Statute and Regulations. Another source of SSA policy is the Program Operations Manual

System (POMS), published by the SSA as a guide for agency employees. The SSA Office of Hearings and Appeals Handbook discusses procedural matters relevant to the appeals process. The published SSA policies are usually available for inspection and duplication at local SSA district offices or, if necessary, through Freedom of Information Act requests.

[c] Overview of Benefits

Old-Age, Survivors, and Disability Insurance (OASDI) benefits consist of:

(1) benefits payable to workers on account of retirement or disability;

(2) benefits for dependents of retired or disabled workers; and

(3) benefits for the surviving families of deceased workers.

As of August 2010, OASDI paid benefits to over 50 million individuals, 36 million of whom were retired workers. In 2010, the average monthly benefit amount was $1,070 for a retired worker. The maximum monthly payment in 2010 was $2,346. The amounts are increased each year to reflect increases in the cost of living index. Because of the lack of inflation in 2009 and 2010, benefit amounts were not increased in 2010 and 2011. For current figures, see www.ssa.gov.

[d] Coverage

Individuals qualify for OASDI benefits through employment in jobs that are "covered" by Social Security. Covered jobs are those subject to OASDI payroll taxes on the employer and employee. In addition to paying taxes, the worker must accumulate enough calendar quarters of covered employment in order to meet the eligibility requirements of the particular benefit sought.

Coverage has spread over the years until it is now nearly universal: 95 percent of all workers are included. Those workers *not* covered are almost all in the following categories:

(1) federal civilian employees hired before January 1, 1984;

(2) employees of state and local governments, unless the governments have elected coverage;

(3) employees of nonprofit organizations hired before January 1, 1984, not covered by voluntary agreements; and

(4) railroad workers covered under the Railroad Retirement Benefit System (a parallel benefit system for employees of railroads).

[e] Financing

The Social Security program is financed through payroll taxes on wages or self-employment income. Income from rents, dividends, pensions, interest, or capital gains is not subject to the tax. The Social Security tax is officially known as the Federal Insurance Contributions Act (FICA), which is applied to wages and salaries up to a statutory maximum taxable amount. The tax is withheld from employee's wages and matched by their employers. Each year the maximum taxable amount is adjusted automatically according to the increase in the national average wage. The FICA Social Security rate in 2011 was 6.20 percent on the employee's wages up to the maximum taxable amount, which in 2011 was $106,800. (For 2011 only, the employee percentage was reduced to 4.20 percent.) The maximum tax was thus $6,621 ($106,800 x 6.2%). In addition, all wages without limit are subject to the Medicare tax of 1.45 percent. The combined rate is 7.65 percent. The employee's employer matches the contribution of the employee. The employer pays 6.20 percent on the maximum taxable amount of employee wages ($106,800 in 2011), as well as the additional 1.45 percent Medicare tax on all wages paid to that employee. The rates are doubled for self-employed individuals, who, for income tax purposes, may deduct as a business expense half their self-employment tax from their net earnings.

To keep Social Security solvent, the amount of wages subject to the wage tax increased dramatically from 1970 to 1990. In 1970, the maximum amount of taxable wages was $7,800; by 1990, the maximum was $51,300. The growth in the amount of wages subject to the wage tax since 1990 is due solely to adjustments for inflation. The amount of the wage tax (7.65 percent) has not changed since 1990. Historically, the wage tax covered about 90 percent of all wages, but in the last few years the percentage has declined to about 85 percent.

If the employer and employee taxes are combined, the total FICA rate is 15.3 percent on wages up to $106,800 (in 2011). Economists believe that the employer-paid tax is actually borne by the employee. That is, if the FICA tax did not exist, employees could expect their wages to rise by 7.65 percent, the amount paid by the employer. For example, if the employer wants to hire an employee and the going wage is $30,000, the cost to the employer is $30,000 plus the 7.65 percent FICA tax, for a total cost of $32,295. Since the employer considers the employee's services to be worth $32,295, the employer would be willing to pay $32,295 to the employee.

All FICA and SECA (Self-Employed Contributions Act, which taxes self-employed individuals) taxes are deposited in the Social Security trust fund and are used to finance current benefits and the operating expenses of the Social Security Administration. Any remaining funds are invested in interest-bearing securities guaranteed by the U.S. government and managed by the Social Security funds Board of Trustees. The operation of the fund is described in Hardy, *The Future of Social Security*, 50 Soc. Sec. Bull. 5 (1987):

> Studies show that surprisingly few people really know how the Social Security system works. Perhaps one of the best ways to understand how the system operates is to recognize how it does *not* work. First of all, because of the tremendous number of current and future beneficiaries, Social Security does not, and cannot, operate like fully funded pension or insurance plans. If Social Security were to build up the trillions of dollars in reserves needed to cover all of its anticipated obligations, the system's trustees would be in control of most of the money available in our economy. In fact, the amount would be considerably larger than the present national debt. Second, Social Security is not like a bank account. A checking or savings account is *not* established for people when they get their first social security card. Consequently, current retirees do not draw money from a

Social Security account to which they contributed while working. Instead, Social Security has historically worked on a current-cost basis. In other words, the taxes current retirees paid into Social Security were used to pay checks to yesterday's beneficiaries, just as the taxes paid today's workers support current Social Security recipients.

As a result of reforms enacted in 1983, Social Security has operated under a policy of collecting more revenue than is paid in benefits with the result that each year Social Security collects more money from the wage tax than it pays out in benefits The surplus, which was over $2.5 trillion by 2009, is invested in United States government securities; that is, it is loaned to the federal government and is a major contributor to the goal of a balanced budget. (The Social Security trust fund earns interest on the amounts loaned to the federal government. In 2009 the interest credited was over $100 billion.) In 2011, because of the lingering effects of the recession and an increase in the number of retirees the benefit expenditures exceeded revenues, which caused a modest draw down of the Social Security trust fund reserve. It is estimated that the reserve will be exhausted between 2036 and 2040.

The Social Security payroll tax is regressive; that is, as a worker's wages exceed the Social Security maximum taxable earnings, the percentage of wages paid in Social Security taxes declines. If unearned income (e.g., rents, dividends, and interest), which is not subject to the Social Security wage tax, is considered along with wage income, the tax becomes even more regressive. The more unearned income the worker has, the lower the Social Security tax is as a percentage of total income. It is argued, however, that although the Social Security payroll tax is regressive, the Social Security program is progressive (those with lower incomes benefit more than those with higher incomes) when both the payroll tax and the distribution of benefits are considered. The earnings replacement in terms of benefits for the lower income worker is significantly higher than that for the upper income employee. The fact that Social Security is tax-free for lower income retirees also adds to the total progressivity of the system. The actual progressivity for a particular employee, of course, depends upon amounts paid in comparison to benefits eventually realized. For some, it is undoubtedly regressive; for others, it is progressive.

Like all social welfare programs, Social Security results in income redistribution. Most social welfare programs represent a transfer of income from the rich to the poor, but Social Security shifts income from the young to the old, and only incidentally from the rich to the poor.

Larry DeWitt, *The Development of Social Security in America*
70 Soc. Sec. Bull. 1 (2010)

The Debate over the Program's Future

The amendments of 1983 established the general policy structure of the current Social Security program and, in particular, its current financing structure. The direct and dramatic result of the financing structure in the 1983 law was a massive buildup in the size of the trust fund reserves.

Historically, the Social Security trust funds have never been either fully funded or on a strict pay-as-you-go (PAYGO) basis. Rather, the trust funds have always contained what former SSA Chief Actuary, Robert J. Myers, characterized as a "partial reserve." We can conceptualize these two extremes (a fully funded system and a PAYGO system) as the end poles of a continuum. Over the decades, major legislation has tended to move the placement of the reserve in one direction or the other. Both the 1977 and the 1983 amendments shifted program policy noticeably away from the PAYGO end and significantly toward the fully funded end of this continuum (Myers 1993, 385-392).

The design of the 1983 financing scheme produced a large buildup of the reserve in the near term so that this source of investment income might help defray future costs when the "baby boom" generation began to move into beneficiary status." The effect of this approach to program funding can clearly be seen in Chart 3.

Although the amendments of 1983 restored long-range solvency to the program, by the time the 1988 Trustees Report was released, the program showed signs of financing shortfalls, and when the next annual report became available, it was no longer in long-range close actuarial balance — a condition which persists to the present day.

Trust fund reserves: Actual and projected, selected years 1983–2037

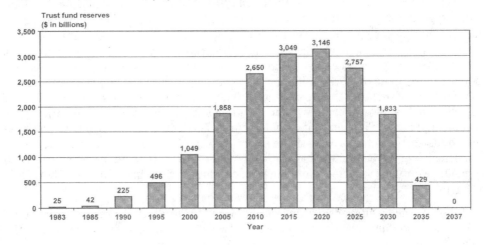

SOURCE: *Annual Trustees Report*, 2009, Table V1.A4 and Table V1.F7.

In the *2009 Trustees Report*, the projected 75-year actuarial deficit in the program was estimated at two percent of taxable payroll. In dollar terms, this means the program has a 75-year shortfall of approximately $5.3 trillion (in present value). Stated another way, after the trust funds are depleted (projected to be so in 2037), payroll tax revenues will be sufficient to pay only 76 cents of each dollar of promised benefits.

QUESTIONS

1. Social Security is said to be part insurance, part welfare. Can you explain why it should be considered, in part, insurance? Can you explain how it is a form of welfare?

2. To the extent that Social Security represents a transfer of income from one group to another, which group is the transferor and which is the transferee?

3. Are the income transfers caused by Social Security justifiable? Are they equitable? Is there a preferable arrangement?

4. Should there be any dollar limit on the amount of income subject to the Social Security tax? If the limit were raised or eliminated, the financial future of Social Security would be significantly improved. Does that justify raising the limit on the taxation of earnings?

5. Given that almost all Americans are eligible for Social Security benefits, would it make sense to eliminate the Social Security wage tax, raise the federal income tax, and pay benefits out of the regular federal budget? Who would gain or lose under such a system?

[f] Eligibility

Upon gaining insured status, workers obtain the right to benefits for themselves, their eligible spouses and children, and their survivors. The amount of Social Security benefits an individual receives depends upon that individual's earnings record.

[i] Earnings Record

All employees and self-employed individuals engaged in covered employment are required to obtain from the Social Security Administration (SSA) a Social Security account number, to which earnings and payroll tax contributions are credited. Because the worker's lifetime earnings record forms the basis for the determination of the amount of OASDI benefits, the accuracy of the record is paramount. Workers have the right to inspect their earnings and contribution records to insure their accuracy. Workers, their legal representatives, or their survivors may submit written requests to the SSA to obtain statements of their earnings records along with estimates of their retirement benefits. They can do so by submitting Form SSA-07004-SM-0P1.

The SSA will correct a mistaken earnings record, but only if the written request for correction was filed within the statutory time limit of three years, three months, and fifteen days after the calendar year in which the wages were earned. The regulations that govern requests pertaining to the earnings record are found at 20 C.F.R. § 404.810 *et seq.*

[ii]   Quarters of Coverage

Eligibility for benefits is a function of "insured status." To qualify for benefits, workers must have the requisite number of quarters of coverage (QCs). A QC is a three-month period beginning January 1, April 1, July 1, or October 1. The minimum amount of earned wages required to qualify as a QC is $1,120 in 2011. (It is adjusted annually for inflation.) Individuals, who attain age 62 in 1991 or later, are required to have 40 QCs of covered work to be entitled to retirement benefits. Earnings are measured on an annual basis and allocated to quarters. Thus, individuals who earned four times the minimum amount at any time during a year will be credited with four quarters of coverage. (The number of QCs will vary if the individual worked in agriculture or as a domestic. 20 C.F.R. § 404.141(c).) Individuals who lack enough quarters of coverage to be eligible for retirement benefits may choose to return to work or remain working until the required quarters of coverage are obtained. 20 C.F.R. § 404.1001 *et seq.*

[g]   Insured Status

By being credited with QCs, an individual qualifies for an insured status, the most important of which for old-age (retirement) and survivors benefits are "fully insured" and "currently insured." An individual who has 40 quarters of coverage is considered fully insured. (Insured status is explained in detail in the Regulations at 20 C.F.R. §§ 404.101–404.110 and 404.120.) To be eligible for most benefits, the individual must have achieved fully insured status.

A surviving spouse who was married to a retired worker who collected retirement benefits is eligible for survivor benefits, assuming the other criteria are met. If the worker died before retirement, however, the surviving spouse will be eligible for benefits only if the deceased worker was "currently insured," a status which requires having at least six quarters of coverage in the 13-quarter periods ending in the quarter of death (or entitlement to retirement benefits). 20 C.F.R. § 404.331.

[h]   Benefit Recipients

The Old-Age and Survivors Insurance program pays benefits to retired workers, their eligible family members, and the survivors of a deceased worker. About 40 percent of all Social Security benefits are paid to nonretirees and include disability, survivors, and auxiliary benefits.

[i]   Retired Workers

To be eligible for retirement benefits, an individual must:

(a) have worked enough quarters to be fully insured (discussed above);

(b) have the "full retirement age" for full retirement benefits or age 62 for reduced benefits; and

(c) not have income in the excess of the earnings test if the individual has not yet attained the "full retirement age."

Note that the "retiree" need not have ceased being employed. It is sufficient that he or she has reached the applicable "full retirement age" and have worked enough quarters to be fully insured.

[I] Retirement Ages

By virtue of the 1983 amendments to the Social Security Act, beginning in the year 2000 the "full retirement age" gradually increases to age 67 by the year 2022. The following table demonstrates how the increase is scheduled to occur:

Full Retirement Ages for Various Years of Birth (in thousands)

Year of Birth	Full Retirement Age
Before 1938	65
1938	65 and 2 months
1939	65 and 4 months
1940	65 and 6 months
1941	65 and 8 months
1942	65 and 10 months
1943–54	66
1955	66 and 2 months
1956	66 and 4 months
1957	66 and 6 months
1958	66 and 8 months
1959	66 and 10 months
1960 and after	67

Workers can claim benefits as young as age 62, but if they do, the amount of the monthly benefit is permanently reduced both for them and for their auxiliary beneficiaries such as their spouse. The reduction is 5/9 of 1 percent for each month until the worker reaches age 65 and 5/12 of 1 percent for each month after age 65. For a worker with a "full retirement age" of 66 who claims benefits at age 62, benefits are permanently reduced by 25 percent. In the future, if a worker whose "full retirement age" is 67 claims benefits at age 62, the permanent reduction in benefits will be 30 percent.

There is no requirement to request benefits at any particular age, and so workers can defer claiming retirement benefits past their normal retirement age by refraining from applying for them. Up to age 70, deferral causes a permanent increase in the benefit amount. The amount is increased for each month of deferral up to age 70. For each year of deferral, benefits are permanently raised by eight percent.

[II] Earnings Test

Social Security was created as a partial replacement for the loss of earnings upon retirement. As a result Social Security originally imposed an "earnings test" on recipients who are receiving retirement benefits and reduced benefits if the retiree earned more than the designated limit. Over the years the earnings limit penalty was reduced and finally eliminated for retirees who have attained their "full retirement age." The earnings limit penalty remains for individuals who claim benefits before they have reached full retirement age.

Individuals younger than full retirement age lose $1 of Social Security payments, for every $2 that they earn above the annual limit. For 2011, the earnings limit is $14,160. (The limit is adjusted annually for inflation.) If a 62-year-old retiree who claims Social Security benefits earns $16,160 in 2011, she will lose $1,000 in Social Security benefits. In the year that the individual reaches full retirement age, $1 in benefits is deducted for every $3 above the annual limit, but only for earnings before the month the individual reached the full retirement age. In 2011, the limit is $37,680 (adjusted annually for inflation). Beginning in the month the individual reaches full retirement age, there is no further limit on earnings.

The only income that triggers Social Security benefit reductions is earned income such as wages, salaries, commissions and earnings from self-employment. Non-earned income such as pensions, dividends, interest, rents or capital gains to not reduce Social Security benefits. To some it seems unfair that lower income retirees who claimed Social Security benefits at age 62 are limited in how much they can earn and still receive full benefits. To others, however, it seems unfair to tax the wages of younger workers to pay benefits to older retirees who are still earning adequate incomes, which may even exceed the incomes of the younger, taxed workers.

QUESTIONS

1.   One justification for the earnings test is that it reduces the benefits paid and so helps keep Social Security solvent. Is this an adequate reason for an earnings test?

2.   Can we justify taxing a 30-year-old worker who earns $30,000 per year to provide Social Security benefits to a 67-year-old who earns $50,000 per year?

3.   If we retain an earnings test for those who have not reached full retirement age, should unearned income such as pension or dividend income cause a loss of Social Security benefits?

[ii]   Spouses and Dependents of Retired Workers

Social Security is more than just a retirement pension. It also provides income for the family in the event of the worker's retirement, death, or disability. To be eligible for spousal benefits, the individual must be age 62 or older and have been married to the retired worker for at least one year. Spouses under age 62 are eligible for benefits if they are caring for a child who is under age 16 or is disabled.

Spouses of retired workers who claim benefits after reaching "full retirement age" are eligible for the greater of retirement benefits based upon their own earnings records or an amount equal to 50 percent of their spouses' retirement benefits. For example, Gary age 67 is married to Greta, age 67. By virtue of his earnings record Gary is eligible for retirement benefits of $400 a month. Instead he is automatically entitled to an amount equal to 50 percent of Greta's who receives $1,200 a month. Gary will therefore receive $600 a month.

A spouse who elects to begin benefits prior to "full retirement age" receives less than 50 percent of the worker's retirement benefits. The amount received is actuarially reduced in the same manner that a worker's benefits are reduced if commenced prior to "full retirement age." The amount of the reduction is 25/36 of 1 percent per month for the first 36 months of early receipt, with additional reductions at 5/12 of 1 percent up to the "full retirement age" of the recipient. However, the "worker's retirement benefit" is based upon what the worker would receive at "full retirement age," not what the worker actually receives. If the worker elected to take early benefits, at age 62 for example, the spousal benefit percentage would be based on the projected higher amount that the worker would have received had he or she delayed commencing benefits until having reached "full retirement age" assuming that the worker has in fact reached "full retirement age."

At the death of the retired spouse, the surviving spouse is eligible for the greater of retirement benefits based upon his or her own earnings record or an amount based equal to 100 percent of the retirement benefits paid to the deceased spouse. To be an eligible surviving spouse, the individual must have been married to the deceased worker for at least nine months prior to the worker's death, though this requirement is waived if the worker's death was accidental. For example, Max, age 68, receives $700 a month based on his earnings record, while his spouse of 20 years, Rosa, age 69, receives $1,000 a month. After Rosa's death, Max will receive $1,000 a month. Ruth and Roger have been married for 40 years. Both are age 70. Ruth had minimum earnings and receives $700 a month as amount equal to 50 percent of Roger's benefit. Roger dies. Ruth will now receive an amount equal to 100 percent of Roger's benefit, or $1,400.

If an eligible surviving spouse has reached his or her "full retirement age" he or she will receive benefits equal to 100 percent of the deceased workers benefit. If the surviving spouse has not yet reached his or her "full retirement age," his or her survivor benefits will be actuarially reduced based upon the number of months that remain until the surviving spouse would have reached "full retirement age." A surviving spouse is eligible for survivors benefits beginning at age 60 and will receive an amount equal to 71.5 percent of the deceased worker's actual benefit. The percentage gradually increases as the surviving spouse's age approaches his or her "full retirement age," which for this benefit (and only for this benefit) is calculated as if the surviving spouse's birth date was two years earlier than was actually the case. So, for example, if Arnold was actually born on July 1, 1941, to determine his "full retirement age" for purposes of calculating his survivor percentage benefits, Arnold will be deemed to have been born on July 1, 1939.

Thus if both spouses have reached his or her respective "full retirement age," they are assured of Social Security retirement benefits at least equal to 150 percent of the higher retirement benefit payable to one of them. The survivor is also certain of receiving an amount equal to 100 percent of the higher retirement benefit paid to one who dies.

For example, Julia and Jim are both age 67 and so both have reached "his or her full retirement age." Julia is a housewife and only worked outside the home for a few years. When Jim begins to claim benefits, Julia receives an amount equal to 50 percent of Jim's Social Security retirement benefit because it is greater than the amount she would have received based upon her own earnings record. Jim dies at age 70. Julia collects an amount equal to 100 percent of Jim's retirement benefit. If Julia predeceases Jim, her benefit ceases, and his benefits remain unchanged. Hence, Social Security income declines by one-third at the death of either spouse.

Next consider Dana and David, both age 67. Dana worked as an administrative assistant and David as a day laborer. Based on their respective earnings, when they retire at their respective "full retirement age," Dana is eligible for Social Security benefits of $800 a month and David, $500. Note that even if David had not worked, he could have received $400 a month based on Dana's earnings record. Some commentators note that David's contributions to Social Security, in effect, have earned him only $100 a month of benefits, not much to show for a lifetime of wage tax contributions.

[iii]   Divorced Spouses of Retired Workers

Unmarried, divorced spouses of workers can receive retirement benefits beginning at age 62 equal to 50 percent of his or her ex-spouse's full retirement benefit if the marriage lasted at least 10 years. As with a married spouse, a divorced person who applies for benefits prior to reaching full retirement will receive reduced benefit amounts. A divorced spouse can receive benefits even if the ex-spouse (the worker) has not applied for benefits, so long as the ex-spouse is at least age 62 and the divorce has been finalized for at least two years. The two-year requirement does not apply if the ex-spouse (the worker) has reached his or her full retirement age. Just as for a current spouse, the divorced spouse gets the greater benefit based either on his or her earnings record or that of the former spouse. For example, in 1975, Janet marries George. They are divorced in 2007, the same year that Janet, who never remarried, reaches her full retirement age. George has reached his full retirement age. Janet is entitled to the greater of the benefits based on her work record or an amount equal to one-half of the benefits to which George would be entitled if he were to retire that year. If George were younger than his full retirement age, but at least age 62, regardless of whether he has claimed benefits, Janet could claim reduced benefits on his earnings record if the divorce has been finalized for at least two years.

A divorced spouse who was married to a deceased worker for at least 10 years can claim benefits as young as age 60, but will receive reduced benefits similar to those of a widow if benefits are begun before the surviving divorced spouse attains his or her full retirement age. If the surviving divorced spouse is not yet age 60 or older, he or she may receive benefits if he or she cares for a child who is under age 16 or is disabled, just as a surviving spouse can.

The derivative benefit rights of a divorced spouse are terminated upon remarriage unless the divorced spouse was age 60 or older when remarried. If a divorced spouse had more than one marriage that lasted at least 10 years and had not remarried before age 60, Social Security will automatically calculate the maximum benefits by comparing what the divorced spouse would be entitled to on his or her own earnings record versus the respective earnings records of the former spouse.

Benefit amounts paid to a divorced spouse do not affect the benefit rights of the current spouse. Assume, for example, that Jane, the divorced spouse of Jerry, receives benefits based on his earning record. Meanwhile, at age sixty-seven, Jerry marries Marge. This marriage does not affect Jane's benefits that are paid to her as a former spouse of Jerry. Marge, age 67, after being married one year, has the right to the greater of an amount equal to one-half of Jerry's retirement benefits or the amount of retirement benefits based upon her own earnings record. After three years, Jerry dies. Jane will continue to receive an amount equal to 50 percent of his retirement benefits, while Marge will receive the greater of the retirement benefit based upon her earnings record or an amount equal to 100 percent of what Jerry was receiving.

QUESTIONS

1. Why should a spouse of a retired worker be paid an amount equal to 50 percent of the worker's retirement benefit without regard to need or whether the spouse paid any Social Security wage taxes?

2. Why should divorced spouses collect benefits based on the work records of their former spouses? If they should, why must they have been married for 10 years? Why not one year?

3. Why should marriage be a prerequisite for spousal benefits? What of those who live together, but who are not married? Should they be allowed to declare themselves a couple for Social Security purposes? Could this pose a problem of fraudulent declarations? Imagine that Sam, age 67, never married, is approached by Judy, age 67, single and a stranger, who suggests that they declare themselves a couple, which will give Judy a retirement benefit equal to 50 percent of Sam's, which is more than Judy would receive from her own earnings record. In return, she promises to pay Sam $10,000. Does the marriage requirement serve as a bar to such a scheme?

4. Sid and Wayne are gay and have lived together as a couple for over 30 years. When they turned age 66, each collected Social Security retirement benefits based on his own earnings record. Suppose that Sid shaped his career to the benefit of Wayne, whose job required frequent moves. As a result, Wayne qualified for the maximum Social Security retirement benefit. Sid, whose earnings were sharply reduced by the frequent moves, qualified for a much lower benefit. Wayne dies at age 67, and Sid is left to support himself solely on his Social Security. Should he be granted surviving spouse benefits?

[iv] Dependents of Disabled or Deceased Workers

Unmarried children under age 18 of a disabled or deceased worker are also eligible for benefits (up to age 19 if they are currently enrolled full-time in elementary or secondary school). Children's benefits are paid to unmarried children of covered workers regardless of age if they were disabled (defined as being unable to engage in gainful employment) before age 22. The benefits continue for as long as the child continues to be disabled. Benefits are also paid to dependent grandchildren and great-grandchildren whose parents are disabled or deceased. (The relevant Regulations are at 20 C.F.R. § 404.301 *et seq.*)

[v]   Survivor Benefits

"Mother's or father's benefits" are payable to the widowed spouse of a deceased worker regardless of the age of the surviving spouse if he or she is caring for a child who is under age 16 or disabled. Reduced benefits are also payable to surviving spouses at age 50 if they are disabled (unable to perform gainful employment). Remarriage affects the right to benefits.

Surviving unmarried dependent children are entitled to benefits up to age 18, or age 19 if they are enrolled full-time in elementary or secondary school. Under certain circumstances, survivor benefits are also payable to the deceased worker's dependent grandchildren and great grandchildren and to the deceased worker's dependent parents age 62 or older.

[i]   Benefit Computation

The amount of Social Security benefits is related to the amount of past earnings subject to the Social Security wage tax; the greater the earnings, the greater the benefits. This reflects the "insurance" aspect of Social Security and its emphasis on partial replacement of the loss of earnings due to retirement. The ratio of replaced earnings is higher, however, for the lower income worker, reflecting the redistributive aspect of Social Security and its emphasis on income adequacy. For high earners, the replacement rate is approximately 25 percent, while for lower earning workers the rate is closer to 45 percent. In 2010, the average monthly benefit for a retired worker was $1,170 while the maximum was $2,346.

Determining individual benefit amounts involves a complicated calculation, described at 20 C.F.R. §§ 404.201–404.290. A worker's monthly benefit is based upon his or her Primary Insurance Amount (PIA). Payments to auxiliary beneficiaries are based on a statutory percentage of the worker's PIA. The PIA is based on the worker's earnings for the 35 highest years adjusted or "indexed" for inflation. The PIA is based upon a formula applied to the average monthly indexed earnings during the 35 highest earning years. Based upon the Consumer's Price Index, all Social Security monthly benefits are adjusted for inflation every January.

Social Security benefits checks are made out to individuals, not couples, even if one spouse qualifies for benefits on the earnings record of the other spouse. For example, Ed and Norma are both age 67. Norma's earning record entitles her to $1,000 a month. Ed worked part-time and sporadically and so receives more by claiming benefits equal to 50 percent of Norma's benefits or $500 a month. Each month Ed and Norma will each receive a check in his or her name: Norma a check for $1,000 and Ed a check for $500. They must use direct deposit so that their benefits are deposited directly into bank accounts of their choosing.

The greater replacement of lost wages for lower-income workers is thought by many to result in income redistribution from higher to lower wage earners. The actual redistributive effects are more complicated.

Kathryn L. Moore, *Redistribution Under the Current Social Security System*
61 U. Pitt. L. Rev. 955, 960–64, 965–66 (2000)*

How the Current Social Security System Redistributes Income

Until now, Social Security has effectively redistributed income from the working generations to the retired generations. How effective it has been in redistributing income within cohorts, however, is subject to considerable debate. Advocates of the current system describe it as the country's most successful anti-poverty program. Critics, in contrast, contend that the system is more effective in redistributing income to those least in need than those most in need. This debate is due principally to the complexity of the system and the myriad most in need. This debate is due principally to the complexity of the system and the myriad of judgments and factors that must be taken into account in making such a determination. In order to help resolve this debate, this section identifies and discusses the principal elements of the current Social Security system that are relevant in determining how Social Security redistributes income. Those elements are: (1) the method by which benefits are paid out; (2) the progressive benefit formula; (3) disability benefits; and (4) auxiliary benefits. In brief, this section shows that one of these four factors, the progressive benefit formula, tends to benefit all three of the at-risk groups, women, minorities, and lower-income workers. The effect of the other three factors, in contrast, is mixed and more complex.

A. Payout of Benefits

The current Social Security system pays benefits in the form of a life annuity; that is, it pays retirees a fixed amount per month for life based on a complex benefit formula. The Social Security system, however, does not take life expectancy into account in calculating benefits (other than to make actuarial adjustments to the benefits of individuals who begin to collect their benefits before or after the normal retirement age). As a result, all workers who make identical contributions to the system (and begin to receive benefits at the same age) are entitled to identical monthly payments, but do not necessarily receive the same lifetime benefits. Rather, workers who live longer receive greater lifetime benefits than do workers who make identical contributions to the system (and begin to receive benefits at the same age) but die sooner. Thus, members of groups that tend to live longer tend to receive more benefits than do members of groups with lower life expectancies.

Women have higher life expectancies than men, individuals with lower incomes have lower life expectancies than those with higher incomes, blacks have lower life expectancies than whites, and Hispanics and Asians have higher life expectancies than whites. Because of these differentials in life expectancy, women, Hispanics, and Asians generally benefit from the way in which Social Security pays out benefits while blacks and lower-income workers are relatively disadvantaged.

Some commentators emphasize this differential and contend that the program

---

discriminates against or disfavors blacks and lower-income workers. Most analysts, however, contend that the program, in its entirety, effectively redistributes to blacks and lower-wage workers even though life expectancy differentials reduce redistribution to blacks and lower-wage workers. In any event, the method by which benefits are paid out clearly tends to favor women, Hispanics, and Asians and to disadvantage blacks and lower-income workers.

. . . .

Social Security uses a progressive benefit formula to calculate benefits; that is, as a person's average earnings increase, the formula replaces a decreasing percentage of adjusted average earnings.

This progressive benefit formula is specifically designed to redistribute income from higher-paid workers to lower-paid workers. Since women and minorities, other than Asians, tend to be lower-paid, the progressive benefit formula generally favors all three of the at-risk groups (with the exception of Asians).

Whether the progressive benefit formula is sufficient to override the adverse impact of the lower life expectancies of blacks and lower-income workers is subject to debate. Most commentators contend that Social Security's progressive benefit formula, in conjunction with its disability and survivor benefit provisions, overrides the adverse effect of life expectancy differentials and ensures that the system as a whole effectively redistributes income to minorities and lower-income workers. A few commentators, however, suggest that the progressive benefit formula is not sufficient to offset the adverse effect of lower life expectancy. Regardless of this debate, the progressive benefit formula clearly tends to favor all three of the at-risk groups, women, minorities (other than Asians), and lower-income workers.

---

[j] Application for Social Security Benefits

Individuals must apply for Social Security benefits in order to receive them. A written application can be made at the nearest Social Security Administration (SSA) office or application can be made on-line. If the individual is mentally or physically incapable of signing the application, a legal guardian, caregiver, or interested individual may complete and sign it. 20 C.F.R. §§ 404.610–404.612.

Individuals who claim or receive Social Security benefits are entitled to have an attorney or other individual assist in dealing with the SSA. This individual must apply for SSA appointment as the claimant's representative in order to establish a right of access to information or to receive notice of the SSA's actions. 20 C.F.R. §§ 404.1705–404.1707.

Claimants have the burden of establishing eligibility for Social Security benefits. They are generally required to submit evidence proving their identity and may also have to prove their age, family relationship, dependency, or the death of the worker. Original records are preferred, but properly certified copies of documents such as birth certificates, religious birth records, marriage licenses, divorce decrees, and death certificates are acceptable.

[k]   Representative Payees

Social Security benefits are paid directly to the claimant, unless he or she is incapable of managing those payments or has been declared legally incompetent. In those cases, the SSA will, upon application and submission of appropriate evidence, appoint a "representative payee" to receive the benefits and use them for the claimant's care. Normally a statement from a doctor is required, but other probative evidence, such as statements from friends and relatives or a judicial finding of incompetency, can be used to establish the need for a representative payee. The SSA prefers to appoint a spouse, close relative, or legal guardian as representative payee, but it can appoint a friend, a public or private agency, or even an institution.

A representative payee (commonly referred to as a "rep-payee") is not a legal guardian and so has no control or rights over any other assets of the claimant. The appointment of a representative payee does not mean that the individual is legally incompetent or mentally incapacitated. It merely means that the SSA believes that the claimant is incapable of safely handling a benefit check.

A representative payee has a legal obligation to use the benefits to provide for the claimant's basic support. Once those needs have been met, the payee has the liberty to use the benefits to support the dependents of the claimant or pay past debts. If the claimant is institutionalized, the benefits are used to reimburse the institution for the cost of care. The payee is required to make periodic accountings to the SSA of how the benefit check has been spent. If the benefit funds are deposited in a bank, they must be kept in a separate account for the benefit of the Social Security recipient.

If the representative payee does not use the funds properly, the SSA can dismiss the payee and appoint a new one. The claimant can sue the payee for misuse of funds in a state court, or the SSA may request that the office of the Inspector General bring civil suit or criminal prosecution against the representative payee.

[l]   Overpayments

Due to the complexity of the Social Security benefit programs, overpayments sometimes occur. If they do, the SSA may seek repayment of an overpayment by withholding future benefits or may seek a refund. Most overpayments are corrected by a reduction or suspension of benefits until the overpayment is recovered. Claimants who disagree with the SSA's determination that an overpayment has occurred can appeal the decision. The SSA cannot recover for an overpayment if the claimant was not at fault and recovery would either be "against equity and good conscience" or would "defeat the purpose of the Social Security Act." 42 U.S.C. § 404(b); 20 C.F.R. § 404.506.

[m]   Taxation of Benefits

Benefits may also be reduced by the imposition of the federal income tax. (The dollars raised by the income tax are placed into the Social Security trust fund.) Higher income Social Security recipients are subject to a two-tiered tax on Social Security benefits. (Internal Revenue Code § 86.) Essentially the tax is on higher income Social Security recipients who have income from any source, including nominally tax-exempt interest. Approximately 80 percent of Social Security recipients pay no tax on their benefits with more than one-half of the tax revenues raised by the tax being paid by families with household income in excess of $80,000.

Recipients with "income" (as defined in I.R.C. § 86(b)) in excess of $25,000 for a single person or $32,000 for a married couple who file a joint return must include one-half of the excess income over these amounts in their gross income and so may be taxed at the income tax rates (in 2011) of 10 percent, 25 percent, 28 percent, 33 percent, or 35 percent depending on their taxable income. The second tier of taxation begins at "income" levels of $34,000 for a single taxpayer and $44,000 for a married couple. Eighty-five percent of the amounts in excess of these figures are added to the taxpayer's gross income for purposes of calculating the rate of taxation.

State taxation of Social Security benefits varies. Some states have no income tax; some have an income tax but exempt all or part of the Social Security benefits; some follow the federal formula for partial taxation; and a few tax all of the benefits.

[4] ADMINISTRATIVE AND JUDICIAL REVIEW PROCESS

By law, claimants who are dissatisfied with a SSA determination regarding their right to Social Security benefits, or the amount of such benefits, may appeal the decision through an administration and judicial process. The steps in the review process are:

(1) Initial determination;

(2) Reconsideration;

(3) Hearing;

(4) Appeals council review; and

(5) Judicial review in federal district court.

The SSA conducts its administrative review process in an informal and nonadversarial manner. 20 C.F.R. § 404.900.

[a] Initial Determination

Initial determinations are the first decisions the SSA makes about a claimant's eligibility for benefits, the amount of such benefits, and the suspension, reduction, or termination of benefits. Initial determinations also include decisions concerning the obligation to repay an overpayment, the certification of payments to a representative payee, and the imposition of penalties for failure to report certain information. Such decisions are subject to administrative and judicial review, but are binding unless reconsideration is requested. A written notice of the determination is mailed to the claimant, generally in a form letter, indicating the factual and legal basis for the SSA's decision, its effect, and the right to reconsideration or a hearing. 20 C.F.R. § 404.902.

[b]   Reconsideration

Reconsideration is the first step in the review process. A written request for reconsideration must be filed with the SSA within 60 days after receipt of the initial determination notice (extension of this deadline may be granted for good cause). The standards for good cause are discussed at 20 C.F.R. § 404.911 and apply throughout this review process. The parties to a reconsideration include dissatisfied claimants and other individuals who show in writing that their rights may be adversely affected by the initial determination.

The reconsideration process consists of a case review, conducted by the same SSA office that made the initial determination, although usually by an official or claims worker who did not participate in the original decision. The review provides the opportunity for claimants to present additional evidence but does not provide for a formal adversarial hearing. Written notice of the reconsidered determination is mailed to the parties, stating the specific factual and legal reasons for the decision and the right to a hearing or, under limited circumstances, an expedited appeal to federal district court.

The expedited appeals process is available to the parties where the SSA and the claimant agree that a favorable determination is prevented by a provision of the law which the claimant believes is unconstitutional. Written request for an expedited appeal must be filed within 60 days, and all parties to the decision must agree to this process. After the parties and the SSA agree to expedite an appeal, the remaining steps in the administrative review process may be avoided, and an action in federal district court may be filed within 60 days.

[c]   Right to a Hearing

Any claimant dissatisfied with a reconsidered or revised determination may request a hearing before an administrative law judge (ALJ). 20 C.F.R. § 404.923. Other parties who show that their rights may be adversely affected by the determination may also request a hearing. A written request must be filed with the SSA within 60 days after receipt of notice of the previous decision. (An extension may be granted for good cause.) A request for a hearing may be dismissed based on the doctrines of collateral estoppel or res judicata if the SSA has previously reached a final determination of the claimant's rights on the same facts or issues.

The hearing is of great importance as it is the only opportunity in the administrative review process for a personal appearance before the decision maker. The claimant and his or her representative have the right to present new evidence, examine the evidence used in making earlier determinations, object to that evidence, request the ALJ to subpoena witnesses and documents, and cross-examine witnesses. Notice of the time and place of the hearing must be mailed to the parties at least 20 days in advance and must state the specific issues to be considered at the hearing. Claimants or their representatives must notify the ALJ in writing of any objections to the issues and must state the reasons for their objections. The ALJ will rule on these objections either in writing or at the hearing.

Under certain circumstances, the SSA may conduct a prehearing case review and provide written notice of a revised determination. Also, an ALJ may decide a case without an oral hearing. The parties will receive notice of the decision, indicating their rights to an oral hearing and to examine evidence on which the decision was based.

At the hearing, the ALJ's function is to make a complete record of the proceedings. The ALJ's role encompasses both that of a fact-finder and a neutral decision maker, but not that of an advocate for the government. After the hearing the ALJ issues a written decision, which indicates the factual and legal basis for the outcome. This decision must be based on evidence presented at the hearing or contained in the record. If appropriate, an ALJ may send the case to the Appeals Council with a recommended decision, instead of making an initial decision. The ALJ's initial decision is binding unless it is revised or unless a party makes a timely request for review by the Appeals Council or seeks an expedited appeals process.

[d]   Appeals Council Review

If the ALJ rules against the claimant, review may be sought with the SSA's Appeals Council, a centralized appellate body. This represents the final step in the administrative review process. The request for review must be filed in writing with the SSA within 60 days after receipt of the hearing decision or dismissal (extension may be granted for good cause). The request for review must be accompanied by any evidence the claimant wishes the Appeals Council to consider. 20 C.F.R. § 404.929.

The Appeals Council may grant review, deny review and issue a revised decision, issue a remand order for a new hearing, or otherwise amend the ALJ's decision. Most decisions are affirmed. The Appeals Council can also take review upon their own motion and overturn a favorable decision issued by an ALJ. The grounds for Appeals Council review are limited to where:

(1) There appears to be an abuse of discretion by the ALJ;

(2) There is an error of law;

(3) The actions, findings, or conclusions of the ALJ are not supported by substantial evidence;

(4) A broad policy or procedural issue exists that may affect the general public interest; or

(5) Submission of new material evidence, relating to the period on or before the date of the ALJ's decision, that upon review results in a finding that the decision is contrary to the weight of the evidence currently on the record.

The decision of the Appeals Council is the SSA's final determination.

[e]   Judicial Review in Federal District Court

Claimants may sue in federal district court to overturn the SSA's final determination within 60 days of the Appeals Council decision or denial (extensions may be granted by the Appeals Council upon a written showing of good cause). Claimants may submit new and material evidence, although the extent allowed varies among jurisdictions. 20 C.F.R. § 404.967.

The Secretary of the Department of Health and Human Services is the named defendant and is represented by the Department of Justice and the local U.S. Attorney. Federal magistrates may be assigned to hear Social Security claims. The scope of the judicial review is limited to questions of sufficiency of the evidence supporting the Appeals Council decision and propriety of the legal standards applied by the SSA. If the court issues a remand order and it is not appealed, the case is sent back to the Appeals Council. The Appeals Council then issues an order for a new administrative hearing. The SSA's current policy is to send the case back to the same ALJ who heard the case originally. Claimants may appropriately argue prejudice and request an order to remand to a new ALJ for a de novo proceeding.

[f] Nonacquiescence Policy

In 1976 the SSA adopted a policy of nonacquiescence in unfavorable court decisions, except those of the Supreme Court. The SSA declared that no precedential value was to be given to any unfavorable decision, and it would proceed in similar cases within the same circuit as if the unfavorable decision had never occurred. Furthermore, the SSA would refuse to appeal decisions not in its favor to the Supreme Court. The policy invited severe criticism and much controversy, as well as numerous court challenges.

In response to a congressional concern about SSA nonacquiescence, in 1985 the SSA modified its policy. Nonacquiescence was not abolished, but limited: the ALJs and the Appeals Council were to apply circuit court precedent to cases arising in that circuit. The SSA still reserved the right for the Appeals Council not to follow the circuit court decision where that decision was in conflict with SSA policy.

In January 1990 the SSA promulgated final regulations that implemented a new policy regarding the application of Federal Appeals Court decisions that are in conflict with SSA policy.

The SSA will now apply a Court of Appeals decision within the applicable circuit to claims at all levels of administrative adjudication. 20 C.F.R. §§ 404.985, 416.1485. If a decision is not appealed or if the government loses on appeal, the SSA will issue a ruling describing how it will apply the holding in future cases in the applicable circuit. If the SSA has published an Acquiescence Ruling, it may relitigate the issue only under limited conditions — for example, if Congress indicates that the court decision is inconsistent with its intent or if a subsequent Court of Appeals' decision or precedent from other circuits supports the SSA.

[5] REPRESENTATION AND ATTORNEY'S FEES

Claimants, in their dealings with the SSA, have a statutory right to representation by either an attorney or a lay person. The SSA has no duty to provide representation, but in notices of adverse determinations it must notify the claimant of the right to representation and that legal service organizations are available to provide free legal services to qualified individuals. 42 U.S.C. § 405.

Private attorneys who represent claimants before the SSA must have their fees approved by the SSA. The attorney must file a fee request with the SSA within 60 days after the notice of the determination. 20 C.F.R. § 1720. In deciding whether to approve a fee request, the SSA is required to consider the effect of the fee on the economic security of the claimant, as well as factors such as the type of services performed by the representative, the time spent, and the complexity of the case.

Almost all attorney's fees are contingent on the successful appeal for benefits. The standard contingency fee has come to be 25 percent of past due benefits because that is the amount withheld by the SSA for payment of approved fees. (Claimants and attorneys are free to agree to a different amount, which the SSA will withhold if it is less than the 25 percent amount.)

If the case proceeds to judicial review and the claimant is successful, in lieu of asking for fees under authority of the SSA, the attorney may request the court to authorize a fee under the Equal Access to Justice Act (EAJA). The purpose of the EAJA is to relieve individuals of the financial burden in contesting unreasonable government action. The court may award reasonable attorney's fees under the EAJA if the government's position was not substantially justified and if it would be inequitable not to do so. If the attorney's fee award under the EAJA would be less than it is under the SSA, the attorney can claim the balance under the SSA fee rule. 28 U.S.C. § 2412(d)(1)(B).

[6] SOCIAL SECURITY DISABILITY BENEFITS

Disabled workers under the age of 65 are eligible for monthly payments equal to the amounts payable at retirement. At age 65 they transfer to Social Security retirement benefits. Disabled spouses are eligible for benefits at age 50, as are disabled children whose disability had its onset before age 22. The disability program is explained in the following excerpt.

David Schwartz & Herman Grundmann, *Social Security Programs in the United States*
52 Soc. Sec Bull. 11, 13 (1989)

Disability Requirement

For purposes of entitlement to monthly benefits, disability is defined as the "inability to engage in any substantial gainful activity (SGA) by reason of any medically determinable physical or mental impairment which can be expected to result in death or which has lasted or can be expected to last for a continuous period of not less than 12 months." The impairment must be of a degree of severity that renders the individual unable to engage in any kind of substantial gainful work that exists in the national economy, regardless of whether such work exists in the immediate area in which he or she lives, or if a specific job vacancy exists for that person, or if he or she would be hired on application for the work. The amount of earnings that ordinarily demonstrates SGA is set forth in regulations. At present, earnings averaging more than $300 a month are presumed to represent SGA, and earnings below $190 generally indicate the absence of SGA. If the determination of disability cannot be made on the basis of the medical evidence only, consideration is given to the person's age, education, and work experience. A less strict rule is provided for blind workers aged 55 or older. Such blind workers are considered disabled if, because of their blindness, they are unable to engage in substantial gainful activity requiring skills and abilities comparable to those required in their past occupation.

Monthly benefits at a permanently reduced rate are payable to disabled widows and disabled widowers beginning at age 50. The widow or widower must have become totally disabled within 7 years after the spouse's death. The test of disability for disabled widows and widowers is more restrictive than that for disabled workers. Disability determinations for a widow or widower are made solely on the level of severity of the impairment (without regard to such factors as age, education, and work experience, which are considered in disabled-worker benefit cases). The disabling impairment must be severe enough to prevent an individual from engaging in "any gainful activity" (as distinguished from substantial gainful activity). Benefits are also payable to a worker's adult children who have been disabled since before age 22, based on the same definition of disability that applies to workers.

B.   PUBLIC ATTITUDES TOWARD SOCIAL SECURITY

Much of the support for Social Security rests on the fact that though younger workers pay for the benefits of the older, they concurrently earn entitlement to similar benefits for themselves when they retire. Unlike any private insurance scheme in which the individual only provides for himself, Social Security uniquely provides dual benefits for those currently retired and those currently employed. In this way it builds cross-generational support unparalleled in other American social programs. Even so, in recent years Social Security has come under increasing criticism. Due to the number of individuals who benefit from it, however, actual outright repeal of Social Security is improbable. Nevertheless, opponents have succeeded in chipping away at some of the benefits and the public confidence in the program. As a result, Social Security remains a bedrock of social policy, but no longer can be considered sacrosanct. In part, reform efforts reflect a lack of public confidence in the system. In particular, younger workers fear that when they retire, the Social Security program will not be able to pay them benefits comparable to those of current retirees. As a result, some advocate terminating Social Security as it is now constituted and replacing it with private savings accounts. In effect, individuals would place a small percentage of their wages into individual retirement accounts that they would manage in terms of investment. At retirement, the individual could draw down amounts in the account. Any amounts remaining the account would pass as directed by the account owner.

The following responds to private account proposals.

John Burritt McArthur, *Private Pensions and the Justification for Social Security*
48 S. Tex. L. Rev. 31–33 (2006)[*]

Social Security unquestionably needs bolstering. As President Bush never tires of mentioning, the demographics of a longer-lived baby-boom generation and a falling birth rate have reduced the worker-beneficiary ratio from 16.5:1 in 1950 to 3.4:1 today, and will drive it down to 2:1 by 2030 if current trends continue. Yet the scope of this problem is usually exaggerated. Most of the reduction in the worker-beneficiary ratio occurred between 1940 and 1965, so the recent reduction is proportionately less significant. In addition, in real economic terms the average American worker had to support more "dependent" people in 1960, in an era of larger families and lower female labor force participation. While the United States does face the same demographic challenge from an aging population and proportionately shrinking labor force as other advanced industrial nations, these factors will be offset in good part by immigration, rising productivity, and an almost inevitable extension of average retirement ages.

Some changes will be needed in benefit or payment schedules, or both, or else the trustees expect to start having to dip into the Trust Fund by 2017, and their current projections have all Trust assets exhausted by 2040. Yet the fact of having to cash in Treasury bonds beginning in 2017 should not be a crisis for the system.

The whole idea of letting the government borrow Social Security's surplus is that the government someday will have to pay the money back. The reason repayment poses a crisis in any sense is that the federal government has come to depend on the surplus to balance the budget and to pay operating expenses that have nothing to do with Social Security, all at a time when the deficit and other government obligations are increasing. A private lender would have demanded a higher return as the debtor's financial condition grew increasingly precarious. But the Social Security Administration did not have this option because Congress mandated that surplus contributions had to be invested in a special class of relatively low-return federal securities. The federal government, the debtor with this unique power to compel its own loans, should hardly be heard to complain that it has to pay its debts back.

Repayment of the securities the Treasury has posted in exchange for Social Security contributions will put pressure on the rest of the budget. In the understated language of the Social Security trustees, when the government has to start repaying its borrowings from the Trust Fund, this "change in the cash flow between the trust funds and the general fund is expected to have important public policy and economic implications that go well beyond the operation of the OASDI program itself." But that a debtor will have to work hard to repay its debt is not a reason to excuse a loan.

Moreover, even in 2040, the Fund will be nowhere near "broke." It still will be able to pay the great majority of current benefits.

---

[*] Copyright © 2006 by South Texas Law Review. Reprinted with permission.

The 2009 Annual Report issued by the Trustees of the Social Security Trust Fund noted the financial problems facing the program, but reported that Social Security could be brought back to solvency by an immediate increase of 16 percent in the wage tax from the current 12.4 percent (combined employer and employee) to 14.4 percent. Alternatively, a reduction in benefits of 13 percent would also result in actuarial solvency for the next 75 years.

Much of the criticism of Social Security arises from basic misunderstandings about how it operates. In the following material, Professor Kaplan attempts to address "The Top Ten Myths About Social Security."

Richard L. Kaplan, *Top Ten Myths of Social Security*
3 ELDER L.J. 191 (1995)*

I. There Is a Trust Fund

There is probably no single, more enduring myth among Americans than the existence of some separately constituted Social Security trust fund. In public opinion surveys and collections of anecdotes, Americans, particularly older Americans, genuinely believe that there is an accumulation of funds in some dedicated account somewhere that consists of genuine financial assets. Such a fund does not exist and was never envisioned even when Social Security was created. Quite to the contrary, Social Security collects revenues from a payroll tax on current workers. These tax revenues, however, do not get placed into some isolated fund. Instead, the program uses these revenues to pay benefits to current beneficiaries, and that has always been the program's operative design. . . .

III. Retirees Are Only Recovering Their Own Money

One of the myths that makes the Social Security program so politically untouchable is the belief that current retirees are simply recovering their own contributions. When current retirees relate their payments of Social Security taxes — both their own and their employer's share — to current benefits, a low-wage earner retiring in 1995 at age sixty-five recovers all of the Social Security taxes paid in forty months. Even a maximum-wage earner who paid tax on whatever wage cap was in effect, recovers the cumulative investment in less than seven years. In other words, after four and one-half years of receiving Social Security benefits, an average-wage-earning retiree is collecting welfare. That is, all of that worker's money has been repaid, including the employer's portion paid on the worker's behalf. Even if one includes interest earned during that interval, at some point most current retirees are receiving funds in excess of what they had put into the system.

IV. Social Security Will Not Be There When One Retires

A prevailing myth among current workers, rather than current retirees, is that the Social Security program is so doomed to insolvency that the program will not be there for them at all. In one widely quoted survey of younger Americans, only 28% believed that the Social Security system would pay benefits to them when they retire. In that same survey, fully 46% of the respondents said that they believed that unidentified flying objects (UFO's) exist. Young Americans, in other words, have nearly twice as much faith in UFO's than in the continued existence of Social Security.

In a sense, the myth of Social Security's impending collapse is related to the myth described earlier that there is a single isolated trust fund. After all, if there is a trust fund, and if that fund is depleted, then presumably no further benefits will be paid. But the obligations of Social Security are not limited to some finite trust fund. Social Security is backed by the full faith and credit of the federal government. It is precisely because there is no single segregated fund that the government's commitment to generations of future retirees continues even when the balance in that "fund" is gone. To put this matter somewhat differently, even if no balance remains in the Social Security fund, and even if benefit expenditures exceed Social Security's revenues, the government remains obligated to make those payments to retirees.

Indeed, one of the most significant differences between Social Security and other pension plans is the absolute solvency, in a cash flow sense, of the Social Security system. No matter what happens, the government cannot go bankrupt, unlike a private company. If worse comes to worst, the federal government will simply raise federal taxes generally, reduce other government spending, or borrow the funds necessary to continue Social Security's commitments. The absolute worst case scenario would have the government inflating the value of its currency by printing up enough money to meet its Social Security commitments. While this prospect is hardly reassuring, the point remains that the federal government is the single most reliable creditor. Accordingly, Social Security will be there when a person retires, and its benefits will be paid on time. . . .

VIII. One Could Do Better Investing Directly

Few myths are more violently asserted than the idea that Social Security is a rip-off to workers who could take the taxes that they pay to Social Security and obtain better benefits on their own. At a certain level, this assertion actually is true. Because of the bottom-weighted PIA benefit formula methodology described above, a person's Social Security payments could typically provide a larger benefit upon retirement, if those funds were invested privately.

But there are several major caveats to that assertion. First, one must recognize that Social Security payments are collected from the employee automatically, every year, regardless of the person's other financial needs and preferences. The payments do not depend upon the fiscal discipline of the particular person involved. Second, as indicated above, Social Security is guaranteed to make its payments on time. Unlike private pension systems, there is no realistic risk of default. Whether the government will use borrowed or newly printed funds to meet its obligations, the fact remains that private pension plans are not able to "print their way" out of any fiscal difficulties that might arise. Social Security is uniquely dependable in that regard. Third, Social Security is completely portable. With very limited exceptions, virtually every type of employment is covered by Social Security, including self-employment. No other defined benefit plan credits every year of a person's work life, regardless of that person's employer, industry, or profession.

But the benefits of Social Security go much beyond the complete portability and guaranteed liquidity of Social Security's retirement benefit program. The entire range of derivative benefits adds to a person's potential benefits far in excess of what private pension plans could ever hope to provide. For example, even in a "traditional" marriage such as Ozzie and Harriet's from the preceding section, Social Security pays the retired worker's spouse half of the worker's benefit. No private pension plan provides any spousal benefit while the worker spouse is still alive. Joint-and-survivor annuities and other survivor-oriented benefits are paid only when the worker/retiree has died. Social Security is unique in this regard. Moreover, Social Security provides benefits to a divorced spouse, or as in the case of Hank from the preceding section, to several divorced spouses. Once again, there is simply no private sector counterpart that would try to provide benefits to more than one spouse of a worker based upon that worker's work history. In addition to these spousal and former spouse benefits, Social Security pays benefits to certain children under age nineteen.

Moreover, these derivative benefits are all augmented when the retiree dies. A surviving spouse or ex-spouse receives increased benefits, as described previously. A surviving child's benefit is increased to 75% of the worker's PIA, although still subject to the "family maximum." Even a worker's parents may be eligible for Social Security benefits if they received half of their support from the deceased worker. Once again, this package of survivors' benefits simply has no counterpart in private plans.

Perhaps even more significantly, all Social Security benefits are adjusted annually, across the board, on the basis of inflation, via the mechanism of a cost-of-living allowance, or COLA. Some version of a cost-of-living allowance may characterize other public pension systems, but few are as comprehensive as Social Security's. Moreover, inflation adjustments are very uncommon in private pension plan payouts. Most private plans utilize annuities and other mechanisms that fix the payment amount when the payments begin. These private plans simply ignore inflation that occurs after payments begin. Social Security, in short, is inflation-protected to a degree that few other pension plans even attempt.

Finally, but by no means insignificantly, Social Security provides benefits beyond retirement benefits, derivative benefits, and survivors' benefits. Social Security's official name is the Old-Age, Survivors, and Disability Insurance. The focus of this article has thus far been on the old-age and survivors aspects of Social Security. But the taxes that workers pay into Social Security also provide the person with disability coverage.

The sum of these features — universal access, complete portability, guaranteed liquidity, derivative benefits, survivors' benefits, inflation adjustments to all benefits paid, and disability coverage — is a comprehensive package that would be impossible to replicate on a private basis, at any price. To be sure, some employees might prefer a less comprehensive package if they had the choice, but the fact remains that Social Security — when analyzed as an entire package — is simply better than what they could otherwise obtain.

QUESTIONS

1. Is it fair to today's workers that they pay taxes both for the retirement benefits of today's retirees and for their own retirement benefits? Would it be fairer to tax them only enough to pay for the current retirees, and tax the next generation at much higher levels to support today's workers in retirement?

2. Should Social Security benefits have priority, or should other social programs such as education be given higher priority? Should taxes be raised (or at least not lowered) to finance Social Security benefits, to pay for other social programs, or to reduce the federal debt? Or should taxes stay the same (or be lowered) and Social Security benefits be reduced?

3. If individuals have private investment accounts, some will have very low investment returns or even suffer a loss in principal. If that should occur, should the government provide aid to those individuals when they retire?

Although the age for full retirement benefits will eventually rise to age 67, some advocate an even higher age as a means of reducing benefit costs. Such proposals look to the increasing life expectancy of individuals at age 65 (almost 20 years for women and 16 for men) as justification for raising the retirement age. Age 70 is often cited as a more appropriate age to begin full retirement benefits. The Congressional Budget Office estimates that raising the retirement age to 70 for persons born after 1966 would reduce benefit costs by eight percent in 2030 and by 18 percent in 2070. Others also call for raising the earliest eligibility age, currently age 62, in tandem until it reaches age 65.

Raising the age for benefits would not only reduce benefit expenditures, but also increase labor force participation and so increase Social Security wage taxes collections and increase national productivity. The latter two claims, however, rest on the assumption that in the absence of Social Security benefits, more workers would elect to work past age 67, and that those that did continue to work would not displace younger workers from jobs. Certainly some older workers would choose to extend their working years, but studies indicate that many would not. Instead they would rely upon pensions, savings, and spousal earnings to support themselves until they reached an age at which they were eligible for Social Security benefits. Raising the earliest retirement year from age 62 to age 65 would likely have a greater effect on retirement rates, but there is little support for that possible "reform."

Even raising the full retirement benefit rate past age 67 would face strong opposition. While it is true that life expectancy past age 67 has risen, that rise does not equate with ability to work. After age 60, many workers, but particularly those in lower-income, blue collar or service jobs, find it difficult to continue to perform their jobs, which explains in part why so many workers elect to take reduced Social Security benefits at age 62. And while the health of those in their sixties has and continues to improve, a distinct minority suffer from declining health and find continued employment difficult. Those whose health prevents them from working, but who are too young to qualify for retirement benefits, would qualify for Social Security disability benefits, a program that is also facing financial deficits.

The more general criticism of raising the retirement age rests on the reality that sub-populations have different life expectancies past age 67. If the average woman has a 20-year life expectancy at age 67, raising the retirement age from 67 to 70 represents an average loss of three years of benefits or an average reduction of 15 percent. The average male at age 67 can expect to live about 15 years. Raising the retirement age from 67 to 70 would result in a loss of three years of benefits, but would represent a 20 percent reduction in average lifetime benefits. For African-American males, who have an average life expectancy of about 12 years at age 67, the percentage reduction would be 25 percent. Lower-income workers have lower life expectancies than high income workers and so would also be relatively disadvantaged by raising the retirement age. Raising the retirement age for benefits thus disproportionally impacts men, blacks, and lower-income workers. However, the counter-argument is that a rise in the retirement age is not a cut in benefits because Social Security was meant to replace lost wages. As long as the worker is employed, there are no lost wages to replace. And, of course, after the death of the retired worker, there is no longer a need to replace lost wages.

QUESTIONS

1.   What would happen if Social Security became a voluntary program?

2.   Should Social Security pay minimum basic benefits that are supplemented by voluntary savings programs?

3.   Would individuals adequately save for their retirement if Social Security did not exist?

4.   How could we privatize the disability and survivors benefits of the current Social Security program?

5.   The average age of retirement obscures great differences in individuals, and between classes and vocations. An employee who works on a production line, for example, is likely to want to retire at an earlier age than the president of the company. Should these differences affect the conditions under which Social Security is paid? How?

C.   GENDER ISSUES

On its face, the Social Security program is free of gender bias. Though it once discriminated in favor of women in the form of more favorable survivor benefits, all gender differences were eliminated in 1983. Today the statute is a model of nonsexist language. For example, the words "wife" and "husband" are eschewed in favor of the term "spouse." Yet many claim that the distribution of Social Security benefits is unfair to women. Because of discrimination in the work force against women, female work patterns, the prevalence of divorce, and the tradition of women taking primary responsibilities for child care, some claim Social Security disadvantages women. In short, the system cannot be fair to women unless it takes cognizance of how their work patterns differ from men's.

The current Social Security benefit rules favor those whose employment opportunities and work history mirror that of white males. Social Security awards greater benefits to those who have greater incomes, so women, who earn on an average less than men, are disadvantaged. Women are much more likely than men to leave the work force to care for children, or to trade-off higher wages for shorter hours. As a result, women's Social Security retirement pensions are lower on average than men's.

Social Security, it is claimed, has not kept pace with the radical changes in the American family over the past 50 years. Divorce is common, and because two-thirds of all divorces occur within 10 years of the wedding, a majority of divorcees are not entitled to retirement or disability based on their former husbands' work records. Working women claim to be disadvantaged because the system unduly favors spouses who stay at home; even though they may contribute nothing to the system, they will receive an amount equal to 50 percent of their husbands' benefits.

Women also live longer than men. The good news is that, as a result, they will receive more benefit dollars. The bad news is that they are more likely to outlive their savings and so are very dependent upon Social Security and more likely to be poor than elderly men. Even if women use their savings to purchase a lifetime annuity, because of their longer life expectancy, they will get a lower monthly payment, typically about 8 to 13 percent less. For example, if Bob and Beverly, both age 65, both purchase an annuity for $100,000, Bob will receive about $700 a month for life, while Beverly will receive about $610 a month.

The importance of Social Security to older women is demonstrated by the fact that it provides 90 percent or more of the total income for more than four in ten of the single, divorced, or widowed women age 65 or older. For more than six in ten of single, divorced, or widowed African-American and Hispanic women, Social Security represents 90 percent or more of their income.

C. Eugene Steuerle, *Social Security: The Broader Issues*
58 WASH. & LEE L. REV. 1235, 1243 (2001)[*]

. . . At least two pieces of evidence suggest that Social Security's ability to met its anti-poverty standard has hit some roadblocks.

First, the significant increase in recent decades in the number of divorced and never-married individuals indicates that a larger segment of society will not qualify for spousal and survivors' benefits in retirement. Today, single and divorced women in particular often accrue only moderate earnings in their working-age years, partly because of the amount of time many spend raising children on their own, Early in its history, primarily to ensure income adequacy for women with little or

---

no earnings, the Social Security Act was amended to include a system of spousal and survivors' benefits. This part of the system was set up as essentially a pure transfer system because no additional contributions or taxes wee required by a qualified individual and benefits were not reduced. By contrast, in the private pension system a worker must reduce his or her own benefit to pay for additional spousal benefits. While these public spousal and survivor benefits do provide old-age protection to many retirees, their size alone requires a separation of their marginal from their average effect.

The particular design of this add-on transfer system of spousal and survivors' benefits create inequities in benefits distribution. For example, add-on spousal benefits are not tied to additional contributions; instead, the system allocates benefits according to the prime beneficiary's earnings level. As a consequence, spouses of the highest-earning workers receive the greatest benefits. Meanwhile, dual-earner couples whose earnings are split fairly evenly between spouses will receive significantly fewer benefits than a one-earner couple with the same total family income and tax payments. Even more troubling in terms of anti-poverty protection, this add-on system supports the most needy retirees the least. In particular, single heads of households — again, mainly women with low incomes — do not benefit at all from spousal and survivors' benefits.

QUESTIONS

1. Can you articulate how Social Security would have to be reformed to meet the current problems cited in the above article? Should such reforms be adopted? Who is likely to object?

2. Part of the "feminization of poverty" arises from divorce. Should Social Security benefits based upon the prior spouse's earnings be more freely available? Should divorced parties have benefit rights after only five years of marriage? Should the amount of benefits increase with the length of the marriage prior to divorce?

3. Should housewives qualify for disability benefits? Retirement benefits? If so, how should the revenue for the additional benefits be raised?

4. Is it possible for the Social Security system to be fair both to women who work outside the home and to housewives? Survivor's benefits were created at a time when married women were thought to be economically dependent upon their husbands. Today, many fewer women are economically dependent, though some still are. Should there be a separate support system for spouses not in the labor force? Should Social Security support for a house spouse depending upon the existence of dependents in the house?

Some advocate so-called "homemaker credits," which would provide Social Security earnings credits based on the imputed dollar value of the unpaid homemaker services. To be consistent, spousal survivor benefits would be eliminated or greatly reduced. Such credits would protect homemakers in case of divorce before 10 years of marriage, as well as increase total benefits for couples who remained married into retirement.

The current system devalues the contributions of the lower income spouse (generally the wife) unless her earnings produce retirement benefits that exceed at least 50 percent of her husband's. That is, since she will receive at least 50 percent of the husband's benefits, the wife's earnings will not contribute anything to their Social Security benefits unless she pays enough wage taxes to be entitled to benefits that exceed 50 percent of her husband's. Earnings sharing would overcome this by giving full credit to any earnings produced by the wife (or the husband, if he were the one with the lesser income). Earnings sharing would thus strengthen the social-insurance aspect of Social Security by matching benefits more closely with contributions.

A homemaker credit, however, would have the opposite effect. To adopt it would increase the welfare aspects of Social Security since a homemaker credit is another form of a spouse's benefit that can be seen as an additional payment for the economic value of the homemaker's contributions.

D. RACIAL ISSUES

African-Americans and other minorities fare less well under Social Security than white Americans because they earn less during their working years and therefore receive smaller benefits when they retire. To the extent they are disadvantaged during their working years, they are similarly disadvantaged in retirement. That is why black elderly women, who are doubly disadvantaged by both gender and race, have the highest rate of poverty among the elderly.

African-Americans are further penalized because of their shorter life expectancies. Neither Social Security payroll taxes nor Social Security benefits are actuarially adjusted. Everyone pays at the same rate and is paid according to his or her contribution. The worker who does not survive until retirement, however, will never receive retirement benefits. Of course, the worker's spouse may, but a surviving spouse receives only 100 percent of the worker's benefits, whereas if the worker survives, the couple receives 150 percent of the worker's earned benefits. Since fewer African-Americans live to their full retirement age than whites (and black retirees die sooner thereafter), they receive fewer benefit dollars.

Changes in policy that increase the amount of the minimum benefits help minorities, while raising the retirement age only further disadvantages minority workers. Smaller benefits for more well-to-do retirees, and proportionately larger ones for retirees from lower wage employment, would help rectify the income deprivations suffered by minority workers.

E. OTHER PUBLIC PENSION PROGRAMS

Social Security is the most important, but not the only, public pension program. Railroad workers, some public employees, members of the armed forces, and veterans are eligible for similar benefits.

[1] RAILROAD RETIREMENT

The Railroad Retirement program, which was established prior to the creation of Social Security by the Railroad Retirement Act, is a retirement system covering rail industry employees. It was enacted in 1934, 1935, and 1937, and is codified at 45 U.S.C. § 231. The relevant Regulations are found at 20 C.F.R. §§ 200–266.

The Railroad Retirement Board manages the complex Railroad Retirement system, which operates in lieu of Social Security for railroad employees. Benefits and financing are coordinated with the Social Security program. *See* Regulations at 20 C.F.R. §§ 404.1401–404.1413. As with the Social Security program, the Railroad Retirement system provides monthly annuities to insured retired and disabled workers and to their eligible dependents and survivors.

[2] PUBLIC EMPLOYEE PROGRAMS

Retirement, disability, and survivors benefits are provided to public employees through programs maintained by the federal government, the 50 states, and many localities. The most prominent, and typical, of these programs are discussed briefly in this section.

[a] Federal Civilian Employee Retirement

From 1920 until 1987 the Civil Service Retirement System (CSRS) was the staff retirement program for all federal civilian employees. The 1983 Amendments to the Social Security Act mandated Social Security coverage for all federal employees and resulted in the creation of the Federal Employees Retirement System (FERS), CSRS and FERS coexist under the Office of Personnel Management, which administers the programs. (In addition to CSRS and FERS, several separate retirement systems cover certain special classes of federal employees, such as those in the Foreign Service and the Central Intelligence Agency.)

The CSRS covers all federal employees hired before January 1, 1984, who did not transfer to FERS by December 31, 1987. CSRS will no longer exist after the last covered employee dies. The FERS covers all federal employees hired on or after January 1, 1984. The CSRS is a pay-as-you-go system financed by employees' payroll taxes, the employer, and the general revenues. CSRS participants and employing agencies each contribute seven percent of the employee's salary, but no Social Security (FICA) tax. As with Social Security, CSRS benefits are adjusted to keep pace with the cost of living as measured by the Consumer Price Index.

The FERS program relies on pre-funding of benefits similar to private pension plans. Over 600,000 participants are covered under the FERS program, with benefits analogous to those provided by CSRS. The FERS provides benefits under Social Security, a defined benefit plan and a tax-deferred savings plan.

[b] State and Local Public Employee Pension Plans

Over 6,600 state and local government pension plans provide coverage to 11.4 million active and 3.1 million retired participants. About 75 percent of state and local employees are covered under OASDI, but most state and local plans are not integrated with Social Security.

The provisions of these state and local plans vary among jurisdictions, though almost all of these plans require contributions from their participants. Employee contribution rates are generally at a level of five percent to seven percent, with the state or local government contribution usually set at twice that of the employee. Most plans guarantee benefits at least equal to the amount of the employee's contributions. The benefit level under most state and local plans is usually relatively high.

[c] Military Retirement

Members of the U.S. armed forces have been covered by the Social Security program since 1957. In addition, those with at least 20 years of service, "careerists," become vested in the military retirement system.

Military retirement benefits are payable immediately upon retirement from the armed services, regardless of age or any other income, including Social Security. Benefits are fully indexed for changes in the Consumer Price Index (CPI), but retirement COLAs for service members entering the military after August 1, 1986, are held at one percent below the CPI.

[3] VETERANS' BENEFITS

Many of the elderly, as veterans of the United States Armed Forces, qualify for special veterans' benefits.

Wilmer L. Kerns, *Social Security Programs in the United States*
52 Soc. Sec. Bull. 52–53, 54 (1989)

Veterans' Benefits

A variety of programs and benefits are available to veterans of military service. Included in these programs are disability payments, educational assistance, hospitalization and medical care, survivor and dependents benefits, special loan programs, and hiring preference for certain jobs. Most of the veterans' programs are administered by the newly created Cabinet-level Department of Veterans Affairs, which replaced the Veterans' Administration in March 1989.

History

Benefit programs for military veterans had their origins in the earliest days of the Nation's history. As early as the 17th century, some of the Colonies had enacted laws to provide care for disabled veterans, and the Continental Congress provided disability pensions for veterans of the Revolutionary War.

In 1789, the first Congress of the United States enacted a pension program for veterans that was administered by the Congress. As the number of military pensioners grew, administrative responsibility for the pension program was shifted from Congress to a succession of agencies.

The initial scope of the veterans' program consisted of pensions to disabled veterans and to the widows and dependents of those who died while on active duty. Coverage was broadened early in the 19th century with the introduction of programs for domiciliary care and incidental medical and hospital care.

America's involvement in World War I triggered the establishment of several new veterans' programs. They provided disability compensation, insurance for service persons and veterans, and vocational rehabilitation for disabled veterans. In 1930, the Veterans' Administration was established to consolidate the administrative responsibility for all veterans' programs under a single agency.

Legislation in 1988 replaced the Veterans' Administration with the Cabinet-level Department of Veterans Affairs. This change reflects the importance accorded to veteran's programs and an effort to streamline their administration.

Cash Benefits

Two major cash benefit programs are available for veterans. The first program provides benefits to veterans with service-connected disabilities and, on the veteran's death, benefits are paid to the eligible spouse, parents, and children. These benefits are not means-tested — that is, they are payable regardless of other income or resources. The second program provides benefits to needy veterans who have non-service-connected disabilities. These benefits, however, are means-tested.

Compensation for Service-Connected Disabilities. — The disability compensation program pays monthly cash benefits to veterans whose disability resulted from an injury or disease incurred or aggravated by active military duty, whether in wartime or peacetime. Individuals discharged or separated from military service under dishonorable conditions are not eligible for compensation payments. The amount of monthly compensation depends on the degree of disability, rated as the percentage of normal function lost. Veterans who have at least a 30-percent service-connected disability are entitled to an additional dependents' allowance. The amount is based on the number of dependents and degree of disability.

Pensions for Non-Service-Connected Disabilities. — Monthly benefits are provided to wartime veterans with limited income and who are totally and permanently disabled (or to those aged 65 or older and not working) because of a condition not attributable to their military service. To qualify for these pensions, a veteran must have served in one or more of the following designated war periods: the Mexican Border Period, World War I, World War II, the Korean conflict, or the Vietnam era. Generally, the period of service must have lasted at least 90 days and the discharge or separation cannot have been dishonorable.

Benefits for survivors. — The dependency and indemnity compensation (DIC) program provides monthly benefits to the surviving spouse, children (younger than age 18, disabled, or students), and certain parents of service persons or veterans who die as the result of an injury or disease incurred or aggravated by active duty or training or from a disability otherwise compensa-ble under laws administered by the Department of Veterans Affairs.

Pensions for Non-Service-Connected. — Pensions are paid based on need to surviving spouses and dependent children (under age 18, students, or disabled) of deceased veterans of the wartime periods specified in the disability pension program. For a pension to be payable, the veteran generally must have met the same service requirements established for the non-service-connected disability pension program, and the surviving spouse must meet the same marriage requirements under the dependency and indemnity compensation program.

F. SUPPLEMENTAL SECURITY INCOME

Some of the elderly do not receive Social Security, while others receive the minimum amount. To ensure that all of the elderly have at least a small monthly income, Congress created the Supplemental Security Income (SSI) program, which provides cash assistance to eligible aged, blind, and disabled individuals. The program is explained in the following excerpt.

Joan Loeff, Judith Bretz & Wilmer L. Kerns, *Social Security Programs in the United States*
52 Soc. Sec. Bull. 62–65 (1989)

Supplemental Security Income

In 1972, Congress replaced the categorical Federal-State programs for the needy aged, blind, and disabled with the Federal Supplement Security Income (SSI) program, effective in January 1974. The establishment of this unified program ended the multiplicity of eligibility requirements and benefit levels that had characterized the assistance programs formerly administered at the State and local levels.

Under the SSI program, eligibility requirements were made uniform for both income and resources required to qualify for benefits and with respect to the definitional requirements such as age of eligibility and medical conditions of disability and blindness.

Federal benefit payments under SSI were also made uniform so that qualified individuals are guaranteed the same minimum amount regardless of where they live. The SSI program also established uniform amounts of income to be excluded when determining the eligibility of an individual or couple.

Factors Affecting Benefits

The basic SSI payment is reduced by the amount of other income and support available to the recipient. Recipients who live in another person's household and receive support and maintenance there receive only two-thirds of the basic SSI payment. Recipients who are in public or private institutions and who have more than one-half the cost of their care paid for by the Medicaid program receive a maximum SSI payment of $30 per month while they are in the institution. However, those in public institutions not covered by Medicaid are generally ineligible for SSI. An individual may be eligible if the institution is a publicly operated community residence with no more than 16 residents. In addition, payments may be made to persons who are residents of public emergency shelters for the homeless for a period of up to 6 months in a 9-month period.

For individuals whose expected institutional stay on admission is not likely to exceed 3 months and for whom the receipt of benefits is necessary to maintain living arrangements to which they may return, continued payment of SSI benefits for up to 3 months is permitted at the rate that was applicable in the month prior to the first full month of institutionalization. Continued payments may also be made for up to 2 months for individuals who were eligible under section 1619 of the Social Security Act (related to work incentives).

If the recipients have other income, SSI payments generally are reduced. However, the first $20 per month of most unearned income is not counted. (If the $20 exclusion is not exhausted by unearned income, the remaining exclusion amount is applied to earned income, if any.) Any additional unearned income received by recipients during the month (most often a Social Security benefit) reduces SSI payments dollar for dollar. Under SSI, recipients are required to apply for any other benefits to which they may be entitled, such as Social Security, unemployment insurance, or workers' compensation.

In order to encourage SSI recipients to work, earned income is treated differently. In addition to the initial $20 a month exclusion, $65 of earned income in any month is also excluded from countable income. Thereafter, SSI payments are reduced by $1 for every $2 earned.

Income from a number of other sources is excluded when determining payment amounts. These sources include income from scholarships, certain amounts of earnings of students, work expenses of blind persons, impairment-related work expenses of the disabled, and payments for providing foster care to an ineligible child. Income necessary for an approved plan of self-support for blind and disabled recipients is also disregarded. Irregular and infrequent income is not counted as long as it does not exceed $20 per month if unearned or $10 a month if earned.

The amount of assets a person may hold and be eligible for SSI is limited. In most cases, the limits are $2,000 for an individual and $3,000 for a couple. However, certain resources are excluded from the total. The most important of these exclusions is a house occupied by the recipient. Also excluded are personal goods and household effects with an equity value of up to $2,000.

An automobile may be excluded, regardless of its value . . .

A recipient's life insurance policies are not countable if the face values do not exceed $1,500 per insured. Finally, real property can be excluded for as long as the owner's reasonable efforts to sell it are not successful.

Special exclusions are applicable to the resources necessary for an approved plan of self-support for blind or disabled recipients. The value of burial spaces for a recipient, spouse, and immediate family member is excluded. There also is a provision for the exclusion of funds set aside for burial.

Qualifying for SSI is extremely significant because in most states the receipt of just $1 per month of SSI makes the recipient eligible for Medicaid, which in turn will pay for the recipient's medical care. See the discussion in Chapter 6.

Of the 7.2 million SSI recipients, two million are age 65 and older. All but six states provide a monthly supplement for SSI recipients.

The SSI benefit amounts are adjusted annually for inflation. As of January 2011, the maximum monthly payment was $674 for unmarried individuals and $1,011 for couples. If the SSI recipient lives with relatives, the amount of the payment is reduced by one-third. Recipients of SSI must establish their eligibility anew every year.

Couples are eligible for SSI if one or both are aged, provided they live together and meet the income and resource tests. Marriage is not required. If two members of the opposite sex hold themselves out to the community as being married, regardless of whether or not the state recognizes such common-law relationship, they are a couple for the purposes of SSI. If one spouse lives permanently in a medical care facility, he or she receives the $30 personal needs allowance each month, and the community spouse receives the individual rate. If both are institutionalized, they receive a $60 personal needs allowance. All but six states supplement SSI with additional cash grants, called Optional State Supplement (OSS), of varying amounts, based on their varying eligibility criteria.

To encourage SSI recipients to work, there is an earned income exclusion of $65, and the remaining countable earned income only reduces the SSI benefit one dollar for every two dollars earned. Unearned income, such as Social Security payments, causes a dollar for dollar reduction of the SSI payment, less a $20 per month unearned income exclusion. For example, Mary, age 67, receives $200 per month in Social Security retirement benefits, which reduce her SSI by $180. In 2007, if Mary had no other income, she would have been eligible for $443 of SSI ($623 maximum for a single individual, less the $180 of countable Social Security benefits). If the $20 unearned exclusion has not been fully used against unearned income, the remainder can be offset against earned income.

For example, Tim, age 71, receives $250 of Social Security benefits per month. He also works part-time and earns $215 per month. His countable income is:

Total unearned income	$250
Less $20 exclusion	-$20
Total countable unearned income	$230
Total earned income	$215
Less $65 exclusion	-$65
Total countable earned income	$150
Less 1/2 countable earned income	-$75
Total countable earned income	$75

Tim's combined countable income is $305 ($230 + $75). In 2011, he would be eligible for $369 ($674 – $305) of SSI.

G. EMPLOYER-PROVIDED RETIREMENT PLANS

The third leg of the proverbial three-legged stool of retirement security is employer-provided retirement plans. Over half of current retirees receive an employer-provided retirement benefit.

Employer-provided pensions existed before World War II, but were limited in number and coverage, and many failed during the Great Depression of the 1930s. Since 1950, however, under the active encouragement of federal tax and labor laws, retirement plans have proliferated and grown, until they now have assets in excess of two trillion dollars. Federal tax laws are designed to encourage employer-provided retirement benefits as part of national policy to ensure adequate income for retirees without placing undue burdens on the Social Security system.

Employer-provided retirement benefits are found more often in the public sector and manufacturing and less often in retail or service industries. The larger the firm, the more likely a pension, and unionized employees have much higher rates of coverage than nonunionized employees. Men are more frequently covered than women, and older workers more often than younger. The rates of coverage appear to be relatively static over the last decade, although they may decline if employment growth continues to be concentrated in service and retail industries.

[1] QUALIFIED AND NONQUALIFIED PLANS

The federal income tax advantages of qualified retirement plans are the key to their popularity.

Retirement plans are either "qualified or nonqualified" depending on whether the plans qualify for the federal income tax benefits provided under §§ 400–419A of the Internal Revenue Code. Qualified plans enjoy four significant tax advantages not available to nonqualified plans:

1. The employer may deduct contributions to the plan at the time they are made even though the participating employee does not include the value of the employer contribution in his or her income. I.R.C. § 404.

2. Employees do not report the pension plan benefits as income until actually received, usually after they retire and are subject to a lower marginal federal income tax. I.R.C. § 402(a)(1).

3. The employer contributes to a fund that is held by a pension trust. Earnings on the contributions held by the trust are exempt from tax until distributed to the plan participant. In the case of a 401(k) plan, the funds that are managed by the employee are also tax exempt until distributed. I.R.C. §§ 401(a), 501(a).

4. If the participant receives a lump sum distribution from the plan, the participant can elect to roll the proceeds into an individual retirement account (IRA) or another qualified plan and continue to defer taxation on the lump sum and the investment earnings until the proceeds are distributed to the individual from the new retirement plan or from the individual retirement account. I.R.C. § 402(c).

A nonqualified plan does not enjoy these tax advantages. An employer is generally not allowed to deduct contributions until the employee actually receives and reports the income. If the employer does make deductible contributions to a nonqualified plan, the employee is usually taxed upon the contribution even though the employee may not have any right to the funds until retirement. Finally, investment earnings on any contributions to nonqualified plan are taxed as earned.

[2] DEFINED BENEFIT AND DEFINED CONTRIBUTION PLANS

Qualified retirement plans are either "defined benefit" plans or "defined contribution" plans. A defined benefit plan is a promise to the employee by the employer that upon retirement the employee will be paid either a certain monthly pension or will be paid a set percentage of some formula amount, usually the employee's highest average wages for the employee's last three years of employment. The pension will continue for the life of the employee and his or her surviving spouse. The defined benefit plan uses actuarial calculations to project the amount of these promised amounts. The employer makes an annual contribution to the plan's trust fund with the amount varying according to projected employee pay and the rate of return on the trust funds investments. Many defined benefit plans are "integrated" with Social Security, meaning that the plan benefits are reduced by any Social Security benefits received by the employee. By the use of integration, the cost to the employer of a defined benefit plan is significantly reduced.

Until the 1980s most retirement plans were variants of defined benefit plans. Unions who negotiated pensions for their members were particularly insistent upon defined benefits because they offered certainty of a calculable benefit. In the last 20 years, defined contribution plans have become very popular and are now more common than defined benefit plans, which continue to decline in number. Unlike defined benefit plans, defined contribution plans do not promise any fixed retirement pension. Instead, as the name implies, the employer promises to make a set contribution each year to a retirement account in the name of the individual employee. The amount of the contribution is usually a percentage of the employee's wages. Employees are often permitted to make additional, tax deductible contributions to their accounts. Sometimes the employer and employee make matching contributions to the plan. The amount of the pension received by the employee depends upon the value of the total contributions to the employee's pension account and the investment return earned by that pension account. The risk of a poor investment return is thus borne by the employee.

Employers increasingly adopt defined contribution plans because these plans limit the employer's financial obligation. The employer need only fund the predetermined amount, usually a percentage of the employee's wages. Under a defined benefit plan, the employer's financial obligation depends in part upon the investment income earned by the pension trust. The risk of a low investment return is borne by the employer.

Defined contribution plans may be profit-sharing plans or stock bonus plans. As the name implies, under profit-sharing plans the employer has no set contribution obligation. The annual contribution can depend upon the profitability of the enterprise. Stock bonus plans are funded by the employer contributing its own stock to the employee's retirement accounts. Upon retirement the employee can either receive the employer's stock or take an equivalent value cash distribution.

Certain defined contribution plans, known as § 401(k) plans, currently the fastest growing type of retirement plans, give the employee the option to either take more current income or make a tax-exempt contribution to his or her retirement account. Many employers also match part or all of the funds contributed to the account by the employee. For example, the employee might have the right to contribute up to five percent of his or her income and the employer will match up to a three percent contribution. Educational institutions such as universities and nonprofit entities can create similar plans for their employees under I.R.C. § 403(b). All contributions by the employee in both §§ 401(k) and 403(b) plans are immediately vested and cannot be forfeited even if the employee terminates employment.

Subject to a range of investment options selected by the employer, the sponsor of the plan, the employee determines how the funds in his or her pension account are invested, which means that the value of the pension account that will be available to the employee at retirement depends significantly upon the investment success of the account during the employee's working years. Upon retirement the employee may be able to receive the account as an annuity for the life of the employee and his or her surviving spouse. More likely, the employee will "roll over" the account into an Individual Retirement Account (IRA) and withdraw the money over his or her life, subject to the complex income tax rules that govern IRAs.

Defined contribution plans transfer the investment risk of the funds set aside for retirement from the employer to the employee. The less sophisticated, less financially savvy employee must manage his or her § 401(k) account in contrast to a defined benefit plan where the employer typically hires professional advisors to manage the assets being accumulated to pay the future pension obligations. In a defined contribution plan, the employee also bears the risk of outliving the retirement account or investing poorly after retirement and so diminishing the amount of available dollars. Yet despite the possible downsides to defined contribution plans, the number of such plans continues to grow while the number of defined benefit plans continues to shrink.

QUESTIONS

1.   As an employee, would you rather receive more pay today or a pension in the future?

2.   Is it consistent for the government to allow the employer to deduct future payments to the employee from current taxable income, but not tax the employee until receipt of the pension?

3.   Do qualified plans permit tax avoidance or tax deferral?

4.   Why should pension plans not be taxed on the earnings of their investments?

5.   Many employees are very supportive of their right to direct the investments in their § 401(k) plans. Are they really capable of making wise investment decisions?

6. Defined contribution plans are much more common than defined benefit plans. Is this because of employee or employer preferences? Which would you prefer if you were an employee?

H. ERISA REQUIREMENTS

All private employer pension plans are subject to the federal Employee Retirement Income Security Act (ERISA), originally enacted in 1974 and amended several times (29 U.S.C. §§ 1001–1242). Because it was enacted to create uniform national standards, ERISA preempts state regulation of employer pension plans. The only pension plans exempt from ERISA are federal, state, or local government plans, and church employer plans which elect not to be covered. ERISA resulted from congressional concern about the fairness of pension plans to employees. It was intended to establish basic requirements that protect employee interests, including vesting of benefits, selection of the retirement age, spousal benefits, and the tax treatment of distributions.

[1] VESTING

A fundamental concern of employees is how long they must work for the employer until their pensions are guaranteed. When an employee's right to a pension is locked-in, even if the employee should quit or be fired, the employee's pension rights are said to be vested. For example, in 2000, Jane begins to work for Acme Co., whose pension plan requires five years of employment for vesting. If Jane quits before 2005, she forfeits any pension rights, whether the plan is a defined benefit or defined contribution plan. (She does not forfeit any contributions that she, rather than the employer, made to the plan.) By the year 2005 Jane is vested. If she quits work in 2007, her pension is guaranteed, though if it is a defined benefit plan, she will not collect it until she reaches the plan's specified retirement age, which is usually age 65.

To promote employee loyalty and reduce pension plan costs, employers would prefer to defer the year of vesting. In response to long service requirements before employees' rights to their pension benefits vested, Congress provided that pensions had to vest pension rights for employees with 10 years of service. Even this proved too long for many employees. Consequently, in 1986 Congress shortened the vesting schedule and gave employers two choices. Pension plans can fully vest employee defined pension benefits after five years of service, or they can provide for 20 percent vesting after three years of service and 20 percent vesting for each year thereafter, until the employee rights are fully vested after seven years. Employer contributions to defined contribution plans must either fully vest after three years or gradually vest over a two- to six-year period. Employee contributions to a § 401(k) plan vest immediately.

Under ERISA, employees must become eligible to participate in the pension plan either at age 21 or after one year of service, whichever is later. Alternatively, the plan can delay participation until the employee has completed three years of service, if the employee pension rights become 100 percent vested at the same time.

[2] RETIREMENT AGE

Defined benefit plans provide a "normal" retirement age, though many plans provide alternate retirement benefits for employees who choose to take early retirement. A plan's normal retirement age is the age at which the plan participant is eligible to receive full retirement benefits. A plan which allows early retirement benefits may actuarially reduce them to reflect the longer period over which a pension annuity is likely to be paid. Under ERISA Section 204(b), normal retirement age (NRA) is age 65 or lower if specified by the plan. Employees who elect to continue to work past the NRA must be credited with having earned additional retirement benefits.

Defined contribution plans do not have retirement ages as the employee is eligible to take distributions without tax penalties from his or her account after a separation from service from the employer or after age 59½. Any such distributions, however, represent taxable income.

[3] SPOUSAL BENEFITS

ERISA provides special rights for spouses of plan participants. Under ERISA, all plans must offer joint and survivor annuities for employees married for at least one year before retirement or death, unless the employee and the spouse specifically waive the right in writing. At the death of the employee, the benefit will continue to be paid with no diminution for the life of the surviving spouse. Similarly, the death of the spouse will not affect the continuation of the annuity to the employee. The joint annuity will have the actuarial equivalent value of a single annuity for the life of the employee. Naturally, the amount of the monthly payments will be smaller than if calculated solely a function of the plan participant's life. For example, Jason, age 65, is married to Karen, age 62. If Jason is a participant in a defined contribution plan, the monthly benefit is the amount of an annuity purchasable by the value of Jason's account that will continue until both Jason and Karen are dead. The monthly benefit will be much smaller than if the annuity were to be paid solely for Jason's life.

If a vested employee dies before the commencement of the annuity, the surviving spouse must be paid a survivor annuity based on the actuarial value of the employee's benefits.

[4] TREATMENT OF DISTRIBUTIONS

Upon retirement the participant must pay income taxes on the benefits received unless the plan permitted participants to contribute after-tax dollars to the plan. These dollars are not taxed upon distribution to the contributing employee. I.R.C. § 72. If the plan provides medical benefits to retired employees, their value is not taxable.

Most pension benefits are provided in the form of a monthly annuity. Some plans offer participants a lump sum payment of the value of their retirement benefits, which can be paid on account of an employee's death, separation from service (whether or not due to retirement), or upon reaching age 59½. Lump sum distributions are taxable in their entirety in the year received.

Participants can avoid immediate taxation of lump sum distributions by rolling them over into another qualified plan or into an individual retirement account (IRA). All rollovers must occur within 60 days after receipt of the distribution and only tax-deductible contributions can be rolled over. I.R.C. § 402(a)(5)(C). For example, after 15 years with ABC Corp., Margaret, a participant in the company's qualified defined contribution plan, quits to go to work for XYZ Co. A result of her separation from service, Margaret receives a lump sum distribution of $110,000 from her plan at ABC Corp. To avoid taxation, she rolls over the $110,000 into her IRA.

Spouses of plan participants who receive a lump sum distribution may also avoid immediate taxation by rolling over the distribution. For example, Edith, age 62, dies while in the employ of Acme, Inc. As a result, her husband, Roger, receives a lump sum distribution of $220,000 from Acme's defined benefit plan. To avoid income taxation on the distribution, Roger rolls it over into his IRA (spouses of deceased participants are allowed to roll over lump sum distributions, but only into IRAs).

The value of pension benefits that will be paid after the death of the participant are included in the participant's taxable estate, while rights that terminate at the participant's death are not. The total amount of the following benefits is included in the participant's estate, whether contributed by the employer or the employee: survivorship annuity rights, death benefits, and post-death, lump sum distributions. If these benefits are left to the surviving spouse, however, the federal estate tax marital deduction means that the benefits will not be subject to the estate tax; they are, however, subject to the federal income tax when paid to the surviving spouse.

Self-employed individuals can establish qualified pension plans, commonly known as Keogh or HR-10 plans. Contributions are tax-deductible, investment earnings accumulate tax-free, and distributions are taxable upon receipt.

Employees and self-employed persons who do not participate in a qualified pension may establish individual retirement accounts (IRAs) to which they can contribute up to $4,000 a year or $5,000 if age 50 or older. The contributions are deductible, the investment earnings accumulate tax-free, and distributions are taxable upon receipt. Distributions before age 59½ are subject to an additional 10 percent penalty tax, except in the case of death and disability. After age 59½, amounts can be withdrawn from the IRA without penalty and without regard to whether the recipient has retired. Distributions from an IRA must begin no later than age 70½. Any amounts left in the IRA at the death of its creator pass to a designated beneficiary.

Individuals may make non-deductible contributions to a Roth IRA, which accumulates tax-free income. When the Roth IRA amounts are distributed, they are not subject to the federal income tax. Individuals or couples with higher incomes are not eligible to contribute to a Roth IRA.

Employers who do not wish to operate a full-blown pension plan may elect to use a simplified employee pension plan (SEP). The employer may deduct amounts contributed, and the employee does not report the income until the amounts are distributed. The employer may contribute amounts up to 15 percent of the employee's income. Essentially, SEPs create individual, employer-funded, employee IRAs.

Chapter 5

HEALTH CARE

A. INTRODUCTION TO HEALTH CARE POLICY

Health care is a huge, increasingly complex industry in the United States and worldwide. The United States spends more of its gross domestic product (GDP) on health care than any other nation and delivers more highly skilled care than any other nation, provided the patient can pay. Questions arise on two fronts: (1) how to provide access to health care regardless of ability of pay, and (2) how to ensure efficacy and value in the delivery of health care.

The elderly need more health care than any other age group. About a third of all health care is provided to the elderly, though they represent less than 15 percent of the population. An elderly individual is nearly twice as likely to enter a hospital during the year, and is likely to need care significantly longer once admitted because of more complex health care problems and slower recovery.

For those 65 or older the United States provides universal, government subsidized health care coverage through the Medicare social insurance program. The companion program, Medicaid, provides somewhat different, broader coverage for the elderly poor. Together these programs provide hospital and outpatient coverage to 97 percent of the older population. This Chapter focuses on Medicare, which in 2009 spent $502 billion on medical benefits, making it the third largest government program after Social Security and the Department of Defense. In 2009, Medicare provided coverage to 38.7 million enrollees age 65 and older and 7.6 million disabled individuals under age 65.

Though Medicare pays more than 80 percent of the cost of care in the categories it covers, because the scope of coverage is limited, it only pays approximately half of all health-related costs for the elderly beneficiaries. The total cost of health care for Medicare beneficiaries includes premiums for insurance policies to supplement the Medicare benefits, copayments, and deductibles, and out-of-pocket payments for services Medicare does not cover. A very burdensome cost for some is nursing home care, for which Medicare covers only short-term, skilled (usually rehabilitative) care, but not long stays because of chronic impairments. Other sources of health care coverage for some retirees include employer sponsored health benefits and special Veterans' benefits programs.

NOTE: A BRIEF HISTORY OF U.S. HEALTH CARE POLICY

Health care policy in industrial nations arose from the labor movements, as organized workers began to advocate for subsidized health care. In Europe, the governmental response to workers' demands for health care coverage produced universal health care programs, which continue with some modifications today. In the United States, political energy in favor of government sponsored coverage was diverted to private rights of workers to collectively bargain for health insurance.

The Great Depression of the 1930s saw the enactment of the Social Security Act that guaranteed income to the aged and disabled, but proposals for national health insurance were rejected as too controversial. Opponents feared that federally sponsored health insurance invoked the unacceptable spirit of socialism. Physician organizations, perhaps the most vociferous opponents, maintained that a national health insurance program would create excessive governmental control of the practice of medicine.

In the face of intense political opposition, health insurance proponents sought to enact a federal health care insurance program. Legislation was introduced that proposed to cover a large share of medical expenses for all workers, retired workers, and their dependents, to be financed through payroll taxes, but the plan proved to be too sweeping for political viability. Congress filled more limited health care gaps with indirect subsidies, such as the Hill-Burton hospital construction fund that required hospitals to provide uncompensated care in return for federal assistance with building costs.

Throughout the 1950s a series of bills authorized federal grants-in-aid to the states for the provision of medical care for needy individuals. This model of federal aid, which included state administration, and direct payments to health care providers who treated poor patients, was implemented in 1965 almost unchanged as "Medicaid."

The prospects for major health legislation improved with the advent of President Lyndon Johnson's "War on Poverty." The composition of Congress had changed in the elections of 1964, with an increase in the number of legislators who supported national health insurance for the poor and aged. The components of the Medicare benefit package were the subject of lively debate among legislators and lobbyists. There was little discussion of the structure of health care delivery and fees for services, however. (Medicaid emerged very late in the debate and received little attention.)

Finally, a package of benefits that combined a number of proposals, including the AMA's, found critical support. Forces quickly gathered behind proposals that would become the Medicare and Medicaid programs, and so, in July 1965, Titles XVIII (Medicare) and XIX (Medicaid) were added to the Social Security Act. America had finally created a federally funded, subsidized health care insurance for the elderly.

QUESTIONS

1. Do health care costs grow more rapidly than the costs for other goods and services in part because of the enactment of Medicare?

2. Would the elderly have been better served with vouchers that they could use to purchase health care insurance?

B. MEDICARE

Medicare is the federal subsidized health care insurance program for those age 65 and older who are eligible for Social Security benefits. It also serves some younger, disabled individuals. Medicare pays for acute care needs, but not for chronic long-term care. It consists of four parts, Part A covers hospital care, Part B pays for physicians, Part C is optional and provides managed care, and Part D pays for some but not all prescription drug expenses. Medicare is administered by the Centers for Medicare and Medicaid (CMA) and is under the Department of Health and Human Services. The law of Medicare is found in Title XVIII of the Social Security Act found in Title 42 of the United States Code.

[1] FINANCE

Medicare Part A is financed by a mandatory payroll tax under the Federal Insurance Contributions Act (FICA). The Part A tax is equal to 1.45 percent of all wage income with a matching amount paid by employers. For example, an employee paid $100,000 would pay a Medicare wage tax of $1,450 and his or her employer would also pay $1,450 wage tax, for a total tax of $2,900.

Part B is paid for by the combination of monthly premium payments by the beneficiary and general revenues of the federal government. Premiums are collected through deductions from monthly Social Security benefit payments. By law, the Part B premium is supposed to pay for 25 percent of the costs of Part B. As a result, each year the premium for Part B is set by the Secretary of Health and Human Services. The standard Medicare Part B monthly premium for individuals who enrolled in 2011 was $115.40. Those who enrolled in prior years paid less, either $96.40 for those who enrolled in 2009 or earlier or $110.50 for those who enrolled in 2010. The different premiums reflect a law that limits increases in the Part B premium (which occur almost annually in response to increases in the cost of Part B) to no more than the cost-of-living increase in a beneficiary's monthly Social Security benefit. In 2009 and 2010, there were no increases in Social Security benefits. Therefore, there were no increases in premiums for past enrollees in Medicare Part B.

Beginning in 2007, the Part B premium was raised for enrollees with higher incomes. In 2011, the premiums were as follows:

Premium	Individual Income Tax Return	Joint Income Tax Return
$115.40	$85,000 or less	$170,000 or less
$161.50	$85,001–$107,000	$170,000–$214,000
$230.70	$107,000–$160,000	$214,001–$320,000
$299.90	$160,001–$214,000	$320,001–$428,000
$369.10	above $214,000	above $428,000

Enrollment in Part B is voluntary. Some fear, as the Part B premiums rise for those with higher incomes, many may opt out because they can purchase private insurance that covers what Part B pays for — physician's and outpatient services — at a lower cost. The loss of those who pay higher premiums would mean those remaining in Part B would have to pay somewhat higher premiums to keep the total premiums at 25 percent of the cost of Part B benefits.

The Part B premium is the same regardless of age. The use of a single rate spreads the risk of harm over the whole group of enrollees. One commentator has explained the uniform rate as follows:

A uniform premium rate for all participants was desired when the program was initiated for persons aged 65 and over. Because the program was a purely voluntary one, it would have been impossible to develop an adequate premium rate based on financing solely from the participants because of the "vicious circle of antiselection." Specifically, any uniform rate established would be too high, on an actuarial basis, for the younger and healthier participants, especially if they considered the rate only on a term-insurance basis, rather than on a lifetime basis. As a result, these individuals would tend not to join the plan (or would soon drop out of it) and the premium rate would have to be increased. This snowballing would probably go on and on, so that eventually the plan would have relatively few participants and very high per capita costs.

The solution, therefore, was to have a government contribution or subsidy, so that the plan would be financially attractive to all possible participants, not only on a lifetime basis, but also on a short-term basis. Studies indicated that, if a certain average premium rate was applicable to the entire population aged 65 and over, then a premium rate of half this amount would be somewhat less than the value of the benefit protection for the youngest members of this age group who are in reasonably good health. Accordingly, if the participants pay half the cost, all of them will be getting a good actuarial buy on a current-insurance basis.

R. MYERS, SOCIAL SECURITY ch. 8 (McCahan Foundation 1985).

Medicare Part D, the subsidy for prescription drugs, is financed through general tax revenues and by those who choose to participate in the program paying a monthly premium to an insurance company that sells the participant a prescription drug plan. The insurance company receives a subsidy from the federal government so that the monthly premium paid by the enrollee is far less than the actual cost of the insurance. Because Part D enrollees can select from a wide variety of Part D drug plans, the monthly premiums vary greatly. In 2011, the average Part D monthly premium was $30.

Part A financing poses a higher risk of actual shortfalls because the income has no relationship to the costs of care. Part B, in contrast, can adjust premiums and the matching contribution from general funds can rise annually to pay for rising costs.

The fiscal health of Medicare is the subject of intense debate. Because of ever rising costs of care, it is estimated that Part A expenditures will exceed Part A revenues by the year 2029. Prior to enactment of the Patient Protection and Affordable Care Act of 2010, expenditures were expected to exceed revenues in 2017, but the Act's attempt to rein-in costs is expected to keep Part A sustainable for the next 15 to 20 years. Yet all agree that sooner or later, Part A will not have sufficient income to meet its obligations. At present, there is no agreement whether to increase the wage tax to increase revenues, reduce the increase in expenditures by raising the age of eligibility, increase the percentage of costs paid by enrollees, reduce increases in payments to providers or to abandon the current system altogether.

Medicare Parts B and D are financed by general tax revenues, but their continual increase in costs puts a significant strain on the federal budget. Part B costs, primarily for physicians, increased by an average of 8.3 percent from 2004 through 2009 and are projected to rise at 8 percent from 2010 through 2015 unless Congress agrees to permit Medicare to reduce payments to physicians, something that Congress has repeatedly refused to do. Part D, the prescription drug subsidy program, is expected to face annual cost increases of 9.4 percent in the next few years. The continued rise in the costs of Medicare Part B and D will result either in reductions in government spending on other programs or a rise in taxes. The alternative, a sharp reduction in the increase of costs for Parts B and D, does not seem likely.

[2] ELIGIBILITY

Medicare depends on eligibility for Part A benefits, which generally derives from being eligible for Social Security retirement or disability benefits.

Individuals are eligible for Medicare Part A hospital coverage, provided they are:

   1. Over age 65, have paid FICA taxes for 40 quarters;

   2. Disabled, as determined under the Social Security Act, for at least 24 months (regardless of age);

   3. Persons with end-stage renal disease (ESRD) who require dialysis treatment or kidney transplant; or

   4. Over age 65 and ineligible for Social Security benefits because of not having worked the requisite number of quarters, but who elect to pay a monthly premium for Part A and also buy Part B.

Although Medicare eligibility requires eligibility for Social Security benefits, an individual need not be collecting Social Security benefits to enroll in Medicare. As a result, individuals routinely enroll in Part A at age 65 (there is no cost to do so and no premiums to pay) even though they are still working and do not expect to file for Social Security benefits until they turn 66. Medicare is a secondary payor of health care for those still working, so that if an individual has employment-related health care benefits enrolling in Part A will have little practical effect.

Much like Social Security, Medicare provides derivative eligibility for a spouse or surviving spouse of someone who by way of Social Security eligibility is eligible for Medicare. The spouse or surviving spouse, however, must be age 65 or older to be eligible for Medicare. A divorced spouse, who has not remarried, can qualify for Medicare based on their former spouse's eligibility for Medicare if the marriage lasted for at least 10 years. Remarriage by the former spouse will not affect a divorced spouse's derivative eligibility.

Finally, state and local government employees hired after March 31, 1986, who do not pay the Social Security wages tax and so are not eligible for Social Security but who do pay the Medicare wage tax are eligible for Medicare.

Those eligible for Part A have the option to enroll in Part B, those not eligible for Part A may enroll in Part B and pay a higher monthly premium. An individual can buy Part B coverage without buying Part A. In order to be eligible for Medicare Advantage, an individual must be eligible for Part A and enrolled in Part B.

[3] MEDICARE BENEFITS

The Medicare program does not directly provide medical care. Rather it reimburses providers. The program has four parts (codified at 42 U.S.C. § 1395 (Title XVIII of the Social Security Act) with regulations found at 42 C.F.R. Parts 405–21): Part A, Hospital Insurance (HI) that covers such institutional services as inpatient hospital and skilled nursing facility care, Part B, Supplemental Medical Insurance (SMI), pays for physicians' services, outpatient hospital, diagnostic, and therapeutic services, and durable medical supplies, Medicare Advantage, which permits Medicare enrollees to elect a managed care plan in lieu of Parts A and B, and Part D, which subsidizes prescription drugs.

[a] Parts A and B

The structure of traditional Medicare benefits derives from the original debate that considered hospital payments separately from physician payments.

Part A: Part A provides coverage for inpatient hospital services including hospital room and board, routine nursing care, diagnostic and therapeutic services, such as laboratory, radiology, and physical therapy, supplies and equipment where Part A services are provided, and prescription and non-prescription drugs.

Medicare Part A also provides limited benefits for care rendered in a skilled nursing facility (SNF). An SNF (often pronounced "sniff") is a facility which maintains a transfer agreement with a hospital and it provides skilled inpatient nursing care to those in need of medical or nursing care or rehabilitation services. Covered services under the SNF benefit are similar to those covered by the inpatient hospital benefit: room and board; nursing care; physical, speech, and occupational therapy; and drugs. In a SNF (as with hospital care), custodial care and personal convenience items, including private duty nursing, are not covered.

A beneficiary is covered only if admitted to the SNF after a hospital stay of at least 3 days, and within 30 days of hospital discharge. The admission requirements help to assure that Medicare will pay only for medically necessary acute care, not long-term nursing home care. Under these admission guidelines, Medicare nursing home patients are short-term and probably recuperating from temporarily debilitating hospital treatment. If the conditions are met, Part A will reimburse providers for SNF services up to the allowable benefit, which is determined by a prospective payment fee schedule. That is, Medicare determines what it will pay a nursing home for care to a Medicare beneficiary depending on the locality (including facility, labor, and other costs) and the intensity of the resident's needs.

Part B: Part B covers a wide range of non-institutional services not covered by Part A. Coverage is limited only by the "medical necessity" of the patient and is subject to an annual deductible. Part B pays only 80 percent of approved physician services.

Covered services include physician services, whether provided in a hospital, skilled nursing facility, or office; diagnostic studies performed in the physician's office; outpatient hospital diagnostic, therapeutic, or surgical services; dialysis services, whether provided in home or institution; rural health services; and durable medical equipment, such as walkers and wheelchairs for which Part B pays a rental fee. Part B coverage does not include prescription drugs, routine physical examinations, routine eye examinations, hearing aids, or dental services. Part B coverage supplements Part A coverage for some benefits, most notably home health care and hospice care.

The following chart shows the Parts A and B deductibles and co-pays. Note particularly the day limits of Part A hospital and nursing home benefits. The co-pays of both Parts A and B are intended to discourage excess use of medical services by Medicare enrollees.

**DEDUCTIBLE MEDICARE
CO-PAYMENTS & PREMIUM AMOUNTS
2011**

PART A

Hospital

    Deductible: $1,132.00

    Co-pay:

        Days 1–60: $0

        Days 61–90: $283/Day

        Days 91–150: $566/Day

Skilled Nursing Facility

Co-pay:

Days 1–20: $0

Days 21–100: $141.50

Home Health

No co-pay or deductible

Part A Premium (For voluntary enrollees *only*)

$248/Month

(If individual has 30–39 quarters of Social Security coverage)

$450/Month

(If individual has 29 or fewer quarters of Social Security coverage)

PART B

Deductible: $162/Year

Co-pay:

20% of approved cost of physician services

50% for most outpatient mental health services

Medicare Part B pays 80 percent of "reasonable charges" regardless of the actual amount billed by the provider. The patient pays the remaining 20 percent. Physicians who "participate" or "take assignment" in Medicare agree not to charge more than the Medicare approved amount. By taking assignment, the physician is paid directly by Medicare for its 80 percent of the fee. Some states require all physicians to take assignment. If the physician does not participate, the physician can collect an additional 15 percent of the Medicare approved amount from the patient, but the physician must collect the entire fee from the patient, who in turn is reimbursed by Medicare for its 80 percent obligation. If the Medicare approved amount, for example, is $100, the physician can charge $115 with the patient being responsible for 20 percent of the Medicare approved amount, or $20, and the added 15 percent, or $15, for a total patient liability of $35.

[b]   Spell of Illness

Medicare Part A pays for a limited number of days of inpatient hospital service under a scheme of benefit days and benefit periods, based on a "spell of illness." Generally a spell of illness begins on the first day of hospitalization and ends 60 days after discharge from the hospital or skilled nursing facility.

During a spell of illness, Part A covers up to 90 days of hospitalization. The first 60 days are covered in full, subject to a deductible ($1,132 in 2011) paid by the beneficiary. The amount is adjusted annually, and is suppose to reflect the average cost of one day of hospital care nationwide. During the next 30 days — days 61 through 90 of hospitalization — the beneficiary is responsible for a daily copayment ($283 in 2011). Days 91 through 150 are covered only once in a patient's lifetime, utilizing 60 "lifetime reserve days." That is, a patient hospitalized for 100 days in one spell of illness has used 10 lifetime reserve days, but still has 50 reserve days available for any subsequent hospitalization that exceeds 90 days. The beneficiary is responsible for a daily copayment ($566 a day in 2011) for each lifetime reserve day.

If the beneficiary is discharged and readmitted to the hospital before the spell of illness ends, a new benefit period does not begin. Medicare will pay benefits based upon the days remaining from the original spell of illness, even if the readmission to a hospital is caused by a different medical condition. The deductible, however, is charged only upon the beginning of a new spell of illness.

The following problems illustrate how the spell of illness works. Some of the answers are given, and some left to the reader. Answers are based on 2011 deductibles and co-pays.

1. Edith, age 82, is admitted to a hospital on January 1. How much does she owe the hospital?

Answer: $1,132

Why? A spell of illness has begun, and the Part A deductible is due.

2. Edith stays in the hospital from January 1 to January 31 (31 days inclusive, i.e., her charges end on February 1). How much does she owe the hospital?

Answer: $1,132

Why? A stay under 61 days requires no further payment to the hospital.

2A. Alternatively, she stays in the hospital from January 1 through March 1 (61 days). How much does she now owe the hospital?

Answer: $1,415

Why? For day 61, a copayment of $283 is due in addition to the deductible.

3. Edith had the hospital stay described in 2A. On April 1, she falls and breaks a hip. The ambulance takes her to a different hospital than before. She stays for 10 days.

How much does she owe the hospital? And why?

Has she begun a new spell of illness?

4. After her hospital stay she needs rehabilitation for her hip, and goes to Good Times Nursing Home where she receives skilled services on a daily basis. She stays for 10 days.

How much does she owe Good Times?

Are you sure she is eligible for Medicare SNF coverage? Why, or why not?

5. Edith's stay in the nursing home does not go well. She is readmitted to the hospital with symptoms of stroke, not fully conscious, and her vital signs are periodically unstable. She stays for 20 days (from May 1 to May 20).

How much does she owe the hospital for this stay? Why?

Edith's total out-of-pocket expenses for hospital care are beginning to grow rapidly as she reaches the limits of her Medicare coverage. Beyond 150 days, Medicare provides no coverage for her care. If she has used up her lifetime reserve days, her coverage will stop after 90 days of hospitalization during a spell of illness.

[c] Medically Necessary Care and Exceptions

Part A only covers care that is "reasonable and (medically) necessary." With the rapid evolution of medical technology, there is legitimate debate about what is medically necessary. For example, Medicare specifically does not cover cosmetic surgery, but does pay for reasonable reconstruction in the event of invasive and disfiguring surgery. Medicare does not pay for personal convenience items.

Medicare does not cover all medical conditions. Consider the following case.

WOOD v. THOMPSON
246 F.3d 1026 (7th Cir. 2001)

This case is almost as hard as pulling the teeth of Floyd Wood, who lost a final decision of the United States Department of Health and Human Services Secretary Tommy Thompson that the extraction of his diseased teeth was not reimbursable under Part B of the Medicare program. We now affirm the district court's decision to uphold the Secretary's ruling.

I.

Wood, an enrollee in the Medicare program, needed a heart valve replacement. At the time his physician determined the need for this procedure, Wood had severe infection in the tissue supporting his teeth. His cardiologist determined that Wood's severe periodontal disease presented a significant risk of bacterial infection to his artificial heart valve after implantation of the device. Because of his poor dental health — and the possibility of infection — Wood's doctor recommended that he undergo dental extractions prior to his surgery. On June 6, 1994, a dentist removed 14 of Wood's diseased teeth and recont-oured his upper and lower jaw (a procedure designed to prepare the tooth sockets for future denture construction). On September 13, Wood was admitted to a St. Paul, Minnesota hospital to undergo the heart valve replacement surgery. The doctor who performed the operation, Lyle Joyce, said he would not have performed the procedure if Wood had not undergone the tooth removal prior to surgery because of the risk of bacterial infection.

After removing Wood's teeth, Wood's dentist submitted a $1,156 claim for dental services to MetraHealth Companies, a Medicare carrier, which denied coverage of the services. Wood appealed this determination to a Medicare Part B hearing officer, who upheld the carrier's decision. Wood then appealed to a social security administrative law judge (ALJ), who affirmed the hearing officer's determination. The ALJ decided that Wood was not qualified for coverage because services in connection with the treatment of teeth were not covered under Part B of the Medicare Act. Congress, the ALJ concluded, specifically excluded dental care from coverage under Medicare. The ALJ did identify three exceptions to this exclusion:

dental care in preparation for radiation of the jaw; a covered medical procedure performed by the same physician doing the dental work; and inpatient dental examinations conducted in preparation for kidney transplant surgery. While the ALJ did not dispute that Wood's extractions were medically necessary, he concluded that this procedure did not fall within one of the exceptions to the blanket denial of dental coverage under Medicare. Wood requested review of the ALJ's decision by the Medicare Appeals Council, but the Council declined to review the case, stating that the ALJ's decision would stand as the final decision of the Secretary.

* * * *

IV.

Wood argues that the HCFA's interpretation of the statute is unreasonable, and attempts to show that the Secretary's proposed list of exceptions to the Part B exclusion is not exhaustive. This argument is two-pronged: first, he argues that the HCFA's current interpretation of the statute is inconsistent with prior interpretations, and second, that the rationale behind the other exceptions applies here. Wood claims the exclusion of procedures like his is inconsistent with prior interpretations because those interpretations are premised on the idea that life-saving procedures are or should be covered by Medicare. Because dental services received prior to a kidney transplant are covered under an administrative interpretation of the Act, Wood believes that coverage for dental services prior to a heart valve replacement is a "logical extension." He reasons that the rationale of the kidney transplant exception would apply in his case as well:[sic]

The [dental] examination is for the identification, prior to a complex surgical procedure, of existing medical problems where the increased possibility of infection would not only reduce the chances for successful surgery but would also expose the patient to additional risks in undergoing such surgery.

But, as the Secretary notes, the kidney transplant exception applies to *inpatient dental examinations*, a significantly worded application, considering that *inpatient hospital services* in connection with dental care are explicitly covered by the statute under Medicare Part A. Further, the Medicare Act itself singles out end-stage kidney disease for special treatment: it is the only disease that explicitly entitles an individual to Medicare coverage. While this alone may not be sufficient to justify the narrowness of the § 50-26 exception, it does provide some indication that an extension of it to include heart valve surgery is not what Congress intended. All medically necessary procedures are not covered under the Act. It is simply too long a stretch to extend this exception for an inpatient examination in connection with renal transplant surgery to outpatient treatment prior to heart valve surgery on a rationale of the comparable complexity and seriousness of the respective surgeries. In addition, the renal disease exception specifically applies to an "examination," not to treatment.

The Secretary notes that while the HCFA has outlined limited exceptions to the general exclusion, each exception is consistent with the language of the Medicare

Act and congressional intent. The only statutorily explicit coverage of services related to dental procedures does not actually cover the dental services at all; it merely reimburses providers of inpatient *hospital* services in connection with dental procedures. Also, the corollary to the "same physician rule" is for the extraction of teeth to prepare the jaw for radiation treatment of oral tumors. The Secretary argues that the ALJ reasonably limited this exception to its facts. We agree. A possibly questionable exception promulgated by the HCFA is no argument that the exception should be expanded further.

* * * *

Wood next contends that the rationale behind the exceptions to the dental exclusion for certain medically necessary services should extend to the services performed in this case. Because all the exceptions appear to be aimed at dental services that are medically necessary under the circumstances, Wood reasons, there is an implied intent to extend coverage to all medically necessary dental services. The common thread among the narrow exceptions, Wood argues, is the purpose to avoid creating "an impediment to accessing covered services." All the exceptions, he notes, involve "dental services [that] are medically necessary components of the treatment of underlying medical conditions." But the "common thread" seems actually to be that the exceptions involve dental services that are requisite to performing a procedure involving the mouth or jaw. The only exception to this logic is the coverage of an *inpatient* dental examination prior to kidney transplant surgery. But, the Secretary argues, this latter exception is only the Secretary's reasonable interpretation of the Part A coverage for *inpatient* hospital services in connection with certain dental procedures. Medicare Part A will cover inpatient hospital services in connection with dental services if the claimant has an underlying medical condition that requires hospitalization, or if the severity of the dental service itself requires hospitalization. *See* 42 U.S.C. § 1395y(a)(12). The Secretary also notes that the "underlying medical condition" exception is applicable only to claims for inpatient services — not claims such as this one, brought under Part B for outpatient dental work. We agree.

* * * *

Wood's next effort is an argument that the legislative history of the statute supports his proposed interpretation. To the contrary, the history supports the Secretary's view. Wood relies heavily on a Senate report in which the Senate Finance Committee discusses the exclusion of coverage for routine dental services. But the strongest support for Wood's argument can arguably support the Secretary's interpretation as well: "The committee bill provides a specific exclusion of routine dental care to make clear that the services of dental surgeons covered under the bill are restricted to complex surgical procedures." While Wood's procedure probably does not qualify as "routine dental care," it does not qualify as a "complex surgical procedure" either. Later in the report, the committee notes that "routine dental treatment — filling, removal or replacement of teeth or treatment of structures directly supporting teeth — would not be covered." This evidence of congressional intent arguably supports the Secretary's view, and certainly is not authority for us to fashion an additional exception out of thin air.

Wood should lobby Congress or the Secretary; the judicial branch can be of no use to him. For the foregoing reasons, we AFFIRM.

QUESTIONS

1. Is it fair that Mr. Wood's tooth extractions are not covered when others' would be?

2. Is it good public policy to create such exceptions? Why, or why not?

[d]　Medicare Advantage

Medicare Advantage provides its enrollees with health care delivery in the form of managed care. Medicare Advantage must offer basic coverage, including the services available through Parts A and B.

Individuals eligible for Part A and enrolled in Part B may elect instead to participate in Medicare Advantage, a form of managed care. Medicare Advantage consists of private provider plans that agree to accept an annual dollar amount for each enrollee. In exchange the plan will provide medical care for the enrollees according to the contract that the plan signed with Medicare. To attract enrollees, Medicare Advantage plans offer somewhat better coverage, smaller or no co-pays, provide at least partial coverage of prescription drugs, and may offer services, such as a health club membership, that are not paid for by Medicare Parts A or B. In 2011, the per person reimbursement for each enrollee was reduced after it became generally known that the annual per person cost to Medicare was over 10 percent higher for Medicare Advantage enrollees than for those enrolled in Parts A and B, known as traditional Medicare. The reduction in the annual per enrollee payment resulted in the termination of some Medicare Advantage plans that apparently did not believe they could operate profitably, or not profitably enough, at the lower rate.

Medicare Advantage plans must accept Medicare applicants who live in the plan's service area. All Plans must have provisions designed to protect the interests of Medicare enrollees. They must publish the benefits, coverage policies, and enrollment procedures in a comprehensive and accessible form; have grievance and appeal procedures for the enrollees to adjudicate; and resolve disputes that may arise.

NOTE ON MANAGED CARE

The term "managed care" denotes a system of health care payment and service utilization intended to contain costs. Typically, a health care plan, which might be created by an insurance company, a group of health care providers, or another entity designed for the purpose, offers a package of services for a set annual payment.

The goal of the plan is to enroll as many as possible to assure that its providers have an ample group of patients, and to negotiate with those providers for lower fees based on the captured market share. The managed care plan typically shifts part of the risk of high costs of care to the health care providers by paying them a predetermined amount ("capitated payment") per patient per month. If the cost of care is less than the capitated payment, the provider keeps the difference. If it is higher, the provider must pay for the care. In addition, evaluation and monitoring of utilization of services is conducted separately from direct care provider activities, to determine whether patterns of medical practice are appropriate and cost effective. The monitoring organization establishes review procedures and generally requires prior approval requirements for such costly choices as hospital admissions and specialist referrals.

The most restrictive form of managed care is an HMO (health maintenance organization). The original concept included a single location where the enrolled could receive covered care, and featured physicians employed by the HMO. Less tightly managed care with more options is the PPO (preferred provider organization), which is a network of affiliated but independent providers. Patients may be required to go to physicians who have contracts with the PPO.

QUESTIONS

1. Why might the HMO structure, with its balance between quality and cost, be more difficult for the elderly to deal with, whether they are healthy or not?

2. Employer HMOs have found that a small proportion of beneficiaries account for a large proportion of expenditures. For example, while 12 thousand employees of Sheraton Corporation spent a total of $12.2 million on health care in one year, three premature infants accounted for 10 percent of that total. Do you believe this pattern would be found in a Medicare HMO? What cost containment efforts are appropriate in response?

[e] Medicare Part D: Prescription Drugs

In 2003, Congress enacted the Medicare Modernization Act (MMA), which included a prescription drug benefit, termed Medicare Part D, effective January 1, 2006. Part D is intended to fill a need that has developed since Medicare was created in 1965, when drugs were an insignificant expense for outpatients. Today the cost of prescription drugs and their importance for maintaining health makes their coverage a priority. Part D is intended to provide that coverage at a manageable cost to beneficiaries.

Medicare Part D provides subsidies to insurance companies that offer prescription drug plans to Medicare enrollees. (Medicare Advantage plans usually include similar prescription drug coverage to their participants.) In return for the subsidy, insurance companies offer drug plans that provide at least the minimum required coverage — most offer more. The minimum coverage requirements are known as the Standard Benefit Model. Part D plans and all Medicare Advantage plans that offer drug benefits must provide coverage actuarially equivalent to a model approved by Congress. While the plans vary greatly, the model remains the touchstone. The premiums, deductibles, and copayments are adjusted annually.

In 2011, plans had to at least offer:

- a minimum deductible of $310;

- offer coverage of drugs costs up to $2,850;

- recommence coverage once the enrollee's total drug costs reach $4,550 (The gap between $2,850 and $4,550 is the "donut hole." Beginning in 2011, enrollees will receive a 50 percent discount on the total cost of brand-name prescription drugs while in the donut hole and pay a maximum of 93 percent of the cost of generic drugs. However, for both brand-name and generic drugs, the retail price of the drug will be used to determine when the enrollee has gotten out of the donut hole.); and

- each drug purchase above the donut hole limit — $4,550 — incurs the greater of a 5 percent co-pay or $2.50 for generic drugs or $6.30 for brand-name drugs.

Part D has special provisions that provide more generous subsidies for low-income elderly.

Beneficiaries who elect to enroll in a Part D, stand-alone plan pay a monthly premium, which was expected to average about $35 a month in 2011. Premiums vary greatly based on the coverage and formulary offered by the plan. Those enrolled in Medicare Advantage plans that offer prescription drug coverage do not pay an additional premium, often do not incur co-pays and do not incur the no coverage "donut hole."

Medicare Part D participation is encouraged by the imposition penalty on the monthly premium of any enrollee who fails to choose a plan whenever first eligible for Medicare. The amount is one percent for every month of delay. Since enrollment periods occur in the last two months of the calendar year, the penalty amount can accrue rapidly. The penalty is intended to assure that a maximum number of healthy Medicare beneficiaries join a plan and begin paying premiums, rather than waiting until they are ill and have high drug costs.

A beneficiary is charged no penalty for months in which he or she had coverage deemed comparable to or better than Part D coverage such as employer provided retiree health benefits coverage or drug coverage by a Medicare Advantage plan.

Medicare Part D plans are reimbursed by Medicare for approved drugs. To meet federal requirements while maintaining their high volume negotiating power with drug companies, plans use formularies, or lists of drugs, for which the plan will pay. Every formulary must include at least two drugs within each therapeutic class and category, so no beneficiary need appeal in order to receive a drug for their condition. However, plans may change drugs within categories and classes at the beginning of each plan year. As plans change formularies, some enrollees must switch plans to insure that the plan will offer the drugs that they need. Plans are required to offer appeals processes by which a beneficiary can appeal the exclusion of a drug.

Beneficiary premiums bear only 10 percent of the costs of Part D, the rest are paid for by general tax revenues.

A controversial provision prohibits the federal government from negotiating lower prices with pharmaceutical companies. It is argued that the plans with

Medicare contracts can negotiate their own deals that will be more successful than any single price negotiated by the Medicare program as a whole. Whether the negotiating power of the plans is the most effective way to obtain the lowest prices for drugs is uncertain.

Limiting drug costs depends largely on the power of volume and negotiation. States, for example, use their power as administrators for their Medicaid programs to reduce costs. In the early 1990s, states secured discounts that drug companies had extended to private sector volume buyers, such as large managed care entities, demanding similar discounts for their programs for the poor. By 2000, New York, Rhode Island, New Jersey, and Illinois expanded existing programs for the purpose of drug purchasing. California and Florida required pharmacies to sell drugs to elderly and disabled Medicare beneficiaries for the same cost as to Medicaid recipients. Missouri offers tax credits to offset higher costs. By September, 2000, twenty-two states had passed some type of pharmacy assistance law.

Notably, the state of Maine has successfully implemented a discount program that provides all Medicare beneficiaries (and, indeed, all Maine citizens) without drug coverage with a state prescription discount program worth 15 percent of the prevailing price. The discount is the same as Maine negotiated for its Medicaid program for the poor. If drug companies do not extend the discount, they will be excluded from Maine Medicaid payments. With some modifications, Maine's law withstood the industry's Constitutional challenge, which called the requirements a violation of the Commerce Clause.

QUESTIONS

1. Why is the drug benefit structured as it is, with some "front-end" coverage, a coverage gap, and more generous "back-end" coverage? Why does the donut hole exist?

2. Why does Part D subsidize drug plan providers rather than following the Parts A and B model of providing the subsidy to providers chosen by the Medicare beneficiary?

[f] Home Health Care

The Medicare home health benefit may allow individuals to avoid costly stays in a hospital or a skilled nursing facility. The cost savings from limiting hospital stays has made home health care a significant part of the health care delivery system. Home health care is far less costly than hospital care even if the same services are provided to the patient. Home health care services, however, run the risk of paying for assistance that would otherwise be provided free for a spouse or family members.

Part A provides for payment of home health care benefits for a limited amount of home health care. Part B pays for home health care for those who do not have Part A, and covers durable medical equipment and some supplies and other services for all beneficiaries.

Part A home health coverage is available only after hospitalization for not less than three consecutive days or discharge from a post-hospitalization stay in a skilled nursing facility that occurred within 14 days of a discharge from a hospital. There is no copayment. Home health care benefits provided under Part B trigger the annual deductible (if no other Part B services have been incurred in the calendar year), as well as the copayments of 20 percent. There is no prior hospitalization requirement.

In general, Medicare home health services include part-time or intermittent nursing care provided by, or under the supervision of, a registered nurse; physical, speech, or occupational therapy; medical social services under a physician's direction; and medical supplies and appliances. Medicare home health does not include transportation, housekeeping that is not directly related to patient care, or home delivered meals.

Home health care benefits are narrowly defined; they are similar to traditional nursing care and depend upon a physician's repeated authorization. The extent of home health coverage appropriate under the statute has been central to debate between advocates for non-institutional care for the aged to improve their quality of life and those seeking to limit increases in Medicare spending.

Home health care covers only "part-time or intermittent services," which are skilled nursing and home health aide's services furnished any number of days per week as long as they are furnished for a total of less than eight hours each day and 28 or fewer hours each week. Specific exceptions are provided for case-by-case review as to the need for care for less than eight hours each day (up to 35 or fewer hours per week). "Intermittent" means care that is either provided or needed on fewer than seven days each week, or less than eight hours of each day for periods of 21 days or fewer with extensions in exceptional circumstances when the need for additional care is finite and predictable.

Home health services are subject to four specific homebound conditions that can severely limit eligibility for care. The beneficiary must:

1. be confined to home and under a physician's care;

2. require intermittent skilled nursing care, or physical, speech, or occupational therapy (occupational therapy may be provided initially only in conjunction with other services, but may continue after other services have ended);

The services must be furnished:

3. under a plan of treatment established and reviewed periodically (interpreted as every two months) by a physician; and

4. by, or under arrangements made by, a Medicare participating home health agency.

The requirement that a home health services recipient be homebound is the basis for many denials and appeals. CMS at times has interpreted the requirement quite literally.

An individual shall be considered to be "confined to his home" if the individual has a condition, due to an illness or injury, that restricts the ability of the individual to leave his or her home except with the assistance of another individual or the aid of a supportive device (such as crutches, a cane, a wheelchair or a walker), or if the individual has a condition such that leaving his or her home is contraindicated. While the individual does not have to be bedridden to be considered "confined to his home," the condition of the individual should be such that there exists a considerable and taxing effort by the individual and the absences of the individual from the home are infrequent or of relatively short duration or are attributable to the need to receive medical treatment.

Medicare Home Health Agency Manual § 205.

NOTE ON MANUALS, TRANSMITTALS, AND LETTERS

The Medicare statute provides only general coverage principles. Regulations implementing and interpreting provisions of the statute are created in accord with the federal Administrative Procedures Act. Proposed changes are published in the Federal Register, and must be available for 60 days for public comment. The agency is required to consider comments. Any changes to a substantive legal standard regarding benefits, payments, eligibility, or providers must be promulgated as a regulation.

Additional information is available in the intermediary and provider manuals produced to guide Part A fiscal intermediaries, Part B carriers, home health agencies, and the states. The manuals can be downloaded at www.hcfa.gov.

Even the manuals are only an incomplete guide to current HCFA policy. Many standards appear only in the notices and bulletins providers receive from HCFA or the fiscal intermediaries. For example, a "Ruling" from HCFA may adopt the decision in particular administrative or court proceedings, and makes it the rule in other jurisdictions. Some directives are based on unpublished letters and transmittals from national HCFA officials.

[g] Hospice Care

Part A provides hospice benefits to terminally ill beneficiaries. 42 U.S.C. § 1395f(i). Most hospice care is delivered in the home, at stand-alone hospice inpatient facilities, or in hospital hospice centers. Services in support of quality of life, including pain management and household support, are generous. For purposes of hospice benefit eligibility, a terminally ill individual is one whose life expectancy is six months or less. Benefits under hospice care include home health services, outpatient drugs for pain control, physician services, counseling, and short-term inpatient care in an inpatient hospital or SNF for pain control and symptom management. The patient is responsible for the lesser of $5 or five percent of the Medicare approved cost for any inpatient respite care.

Hospice provides only palliative care. Patients who enroll in hospice care agree to give up treatment under Medicare Parts A and B. A patient who survives the initial six months of hospice can reenroll for another six months.

[h]   Mental Health Benefits

Medicare covers a variety of mental health services, but limits eligibility and caps the amount of services. For example, Medicare covers care inpatient care at specialized psychiatric hospitals for a benefit period up to 90 days, as with ordinary hospital care. The same 60 lifetime reserve days apply. However, the total psychiatric inpatient days in the patient's lifetime are capped at 190. Medicare also covers outpatient mental health services but requires a 50 percent copayment.

[i]   Level of Care

Medicare requires that services be provided in the most appropriate circumstances, i.e., the least costly that still meet the needs of the patient. The issue of level of care is a source of controversy for Medicare beneficiaries and their providers because, as described, Medicare provides services almost exclusively for acute care, and so a world of services lies outside the realm of compensated care.

Level of care is determined by the professional or technical training of the personnel required to perform or supervise the services rendered and the complexity of care needed. The three levels of care recognized under Part A are acute, skilled, and custodial care; benefits are available for acute hospital care and skilled nursing home care, but not for custodial care. Several criteria must be met for acute levels of care:

1. The care must be medically required and ordered by a physician;

2. It can only be provided in an inpatient hospital setting;

3. The beneficiary must require daily or frequent physician visits;

4. The beneficiary's condition must require the constant availability of services or equipment found in a hospital setting; and

5. Required services cannot be furnished on an outpatient basis or in a lesser care facility. Acute level care is necessary for such medical conditions or procedures as surgery, injury resulting from trauma, seizures, new onset of stroke, or myocardial infarction.

Skilled nursing care is a lower level of care than acute care. Skilled services are rehabilitative in nature or are necessary to maintain the beneficiary's condition upon discharge from a hospital. The services necessary must be sufficiently complex that they can only be performed safely or effectively by, or under the supervision of, technical or professional personnel.

Services that qualify as skilled nursing care include:

— intravenous feeding

— gastrostomy feeding

— treatment of decubitus ulcers (bed sores)

— tracheotomy aspiration

— therapeutic exercises and activities

— gait evaluation and training.

Custodial care is a level of care not covered by Medicare. Custodial services are personal care, not medical care, services. Services that are considered custodial include:

— administration of medications or ointment

— routine dressing changes

— incontinence care

— assistance in feeding, dressing, and bathing.

NOTE ON VETERANS HEALTH BENEFITS

Veterans health care programs pay for health care for many elderly. A veteran's eligibility for medical benefits depends upon a number of factors that establish a priority of recipients. No veteran is entitled to benefits, but veterans receive them on a space-available basis. Veterans with service-connected conditions, or who suffer a service-related disability and need treatment for a non-service-connected condition, receive priority. Veterans with a non-service-connected disability or who have non-service-connected condition must meet income guidelines. Those with substantial incomes must agree to pay a portion of the cost. Veterans who are eligible for or receive Veteran Administration (VA) pensions or medical assistance under Medicaid are presumed to meet the means test.

The VA maintains an extensive health care system, including over 170 hospitals that offer extensive outpatient services, and operates 117 nursing homes and a variety of community-based care programs. It has been an innovator in assessment and long-term care of the elderly.

The National Defense Authorization Act of 2001 permanently extended health insurance benefits to Medicare eligible veterans age 65 and older. The program is called TRICARE for Life (TFL). Eligible veterans are those who served in the uniformed services for at least 20 years (including National Guard and reservists), Medicare-eligible family members, widows and widowers; and certain former spouses if they were eligible for TRICARE before age 65 also are eligible. All who are eligible must be enrolled in Parts A and B, and pay the Part B premium. *See* www.tricare.osd.mil/tfl/matrix.html

TRICARE covers a range of benefits similar to Medicare. It acts as secondary payer for any benefit covered by both programs, covering all out-of-pocket expenses. TRICARE also covers benefits not covered by Medicare, including overseas care, costs for SNF care after 100 days, and costs for inpatient mental health care after 190 days. TRICARE also provides substantial prescription drug coverage.

C. MEDIGAP SUPPLEMENTAL INSURANCE

Since the enactment of Medicare, private insurance companies have offered policies with benefits that supplement and complement Medicare benefits. These policies offer coverage for out-of-pocket costs, deductibles, co-payments, and payment for hospital stays that extend beyond Medicare coverage limits.

The usefulness of such policies is not in doubt since Medicare's hospital deductible and physician copayments can quickly accumulate into a very large bill. The Medigap market was originally plagued, however, with abusive sales tactics and consumer fraud. In response, Congress in 1982 adopted requirements for Medigap policies, specifying that in order to be a "Medigap" policy an insurance policy must adhere to one of a limited number of model plans, and must

— cover Part B 20 percent copayments;

— use standardized terms defined in the law;

— have policy termination and cancellation clauses prominently displayed;

— limit the period of restricted coverage for preexisting conditions; and

— provide purchasers a "free look" period during which the policy can be cancelled for a full refund.

The model plans represent a range of coverage options from bare bones to the most desired options. Insurers must use the same format, language, and definitions. Every Medigap policy A, for example, offers the identical coverage, though premiums may vary from insurer to insurer.

Medigap Plan A is the so-called "core plan." Its coverage must be included in all Medigap policies, and all insurance companies who sell Medigap policies must offer it. Plans K and L usually have lower premiums than other plans, but they require higher out-of-pocket costs. Plan N has a copayment for each office visit.

Benefits of Medigap Plans A–N

	A	B	C	D	F*	G	K	L	M	N
Basic Benefits: All Part A hospital coinsurance	X	X	X	X	X	X	X	X	X	X
100% of additional hospital days, for a lifetime maximum of 365	X	X	X	X	X	X	X	X	X	X
Part B coinsurance, which is 20% of the Medicare-approved amount	X	X	X	X	X	X	50%	75%	X	copay for office & ER visit**
First 3 pints of blood in each calendar year	X	X	X	X	X	X	50%	75%	X	X
Hospice Cost-Share	X	X	X	X	X	X	50%	75%	X	X
Part A Hospital Deductible: First-day deductible — $1,132 in 2011 (per benefit period)		X	X	X	X	X	50%	75%	50%	X
Skilled Nursing Facility (SNF) Copayment: $141.50 per day for days 21–100 of a Medicare-covered stay in an SNF (per benefit period)			X	X	X	X	50%	75%	X	X
Part B Deductible: First $162 of Part B charges each year			X		X					
Part B Excess Charges: A percentage of the charge (either 80% or 100%). Doctors cannot charge more than 15% above the Medicare-approved amount.					100%	100%				

	A	B	C	D	F*	G	K	L	M	N
Emergency Care Outside the USA: 80% of emergency care during the first 2 months of each trip outside the USA, after a $250 deductible, for a lifetime maximum of $50,000.			X	X	X	X			X	X
Total Out-of-Pocket Limit: $4,640***/$2,320***										

*Plan F may be offered with a high-deductible option of $2,000. The benefits are the same as in the standardized plan, but the deductible must be met each year before any claims are paid.

**Patient pays up to $20 for each office visit. Plan N pays the remainder of any Part B coinsurance charges.

***After patient has paid out-of-pocket expenses for plan K ($4,640) or L ($2,320) for covered benefits during a calendar year, the plan will pay 100 percent of covered benefits for the remainder of that year.

Upon reaching age 65, and if not receiving health care insurance from an employer, an individual has a six month open enrollment period in which to choose and buy a Medigap policy, after which the insurer can delay coverage or raise rates. Insurers cannot deny or limit benefits in any policy issued to a new Medicare enrollee. Unless having been covered by employer-provided health care insurance, an individual who does not purchase a Medigap policy during the one time, six month open enrollment period must choose among Plans A, B, C, and F.

A preexisting condition cannot prevent a Medicare beneficiary from obtaining Medigap coverage who buys the policy during initial six months open enrollment period or upon certain points when new supplementary coverage is timely such as the discontinuation of employment or retiree health benefit coverage, disenrollment from a Medicare Advantage plan, or when an insurer goes bankrupt or misrepresented the nature of coverage. An insurer is prohibited from charging higher premiums because of health status, claims experience, receipt of health care, or medical condition, and may not limit coverage in future to exclude a condition as preexisting. Once sold, a policy cannot be cancelled except for nonpayment.

D.   EMPLOYER PROVIDED RETIREE HEALTH BENEFITS

Employee health benefits became widespread after World War II because they were an attractive tax-free benefit to employees and were only a modest cost for employers. Similarly, after the passage of Medicare, employers began to extend health coverage to their workers after retirement because they were a desirable part of a retirement package and not too costly. Typically, the benefits package supplemented Medicare's benefits for the retiree and spouse, with broader coverage for any dependents. Benefits usually include hospitalization, some physician fees, and some prescription drug benefits, with premiums paid entirely by the employer. Employers could offer an attractive perquisite, secure in the knowledge that Medicare would assume many of the retiree's medical costs.

Retiree health benefits are governed by the federal Employee Retirement Income Security Act of 1974 (ERISA) (29 U.S.C. § 1001 *et seq.*). Although ERISA is concerned primarily with pensions, its definition of a benefit plan extends to employer-sponsored programs for "medical, surgical, or hospital care . . . or benefits in the event of sickness, accident, disability, death." Retiree health benefit plans are subject to ERISA's reporting and disclosure requirements, but not to provisions on vesting and funding of benefits. That is, employees do not have a legally enforceable right to the benefits, and companies are not required to accumulate funds to pay for benefits.

Generally, only large companies provide retiree health care benefits. Lack of pre-funding of retiree health obligations and the rising costs per retiree has caused companies to reduce the benefits. Many seek to impose cost containment measures, like eliminating the most costly hospitals in their areas from eligibility for payment. Some retirees have questioned whether the employer can make such changes.

For individual beneficiaries, retiree health benefits must be provided on their original terms agreed upon at the time of employment or creation of the plan, unless the employer has reserved the right to modify or terminate them. The courts have determined that the employer must state in the employment contract or related representations of employee rights that the benefits are vested, i.e., nonforfeitable and nonamountable. Retiree benefits typically vest, i.e., become nonforfeitable, at the time of retirement, though by contract they might vest earlier. Many retirees have challenged the former employer's right to change the terms of their health care benefits. In *Sprague v. GMC*, 133 F.3d 388 (6th Cir. 1998), the Circuit Court reversed the lower court's decision about the rights of nonunion retirees, who had accepted the corporation's offer of benefits as part of a separate, early retirement package.

The Court noted the following representations:

> "If you retire . . . and are eligible to receive retirement benefits under the provisions of the GM Retirement Program for Salaried Employees, you may keep your basic hospital, surgical and medical expense coverages in effect . . . GM will pay the full monthly premium or subscription charge for such coverages."

> "Hospital-Medical Coverages: Your basic coverages will be provided at Corporation expense for your lifetime. . . ." Highlights of Your GM Benefits (1974).

> "Your basic health care coverages will be provided at GM's expense for your lifetime. . . ." Your Benefits in Retirement (1977).

> "General Motors pays the full cost of any basic health care coverages that are continued for most retired employees and for eligible surviving spouses and children of deceased retirees." Your Benefits in Retirement (1977).

However, most of the booklets also put plan participants on notice of GM's right to change or terminate the health care plan at any time:

> "However, GM reserves the right to modify, revoke, suspend, terminate, or change the Program, in whole or in part, at any time. . . ."

> "The Corporation reserves the right to amend, modify, suspend, or terminate its benefit Plans or Programs by action of its Board of Directors."

Based on GM's reservations, the court held that it could cut back or even eliminate health care benefits for nonunion retirees.

QUESTION

The employer promised, and the employee worked. Why does the court refuse to make the employer pay?

E.   ASSURING QUALITY HEALTH CARE

The federal legislation establishing Medicare and Medicaid accepted the premise that all licensed physicians and all accredited hospitals were providers of quality sufficient to warrant reimbursement with federal funds. Soon, however, studies raised serious concerns about the quality of care provided under these programs, which paralleled concerns with soaring costs of care. Federal legislation addressed the means of assuring quality in institutional care by designating a program to accredit hospitals to receive Medicare payments. The federal government began to gather information about physician competence to overcome the limitations inherent in state-by-state licensing. Two indications of poor quality were, and continue to be, targeted for improvement: (1) technically suboptimal services, and (2) unnecessary services. Both raise the risk of patient injury or illness and unnecessary expenditures.

[1]   INDIVIDUAL CREDENTIALS

Traditionally, the quality of medical care has been assessed in the simplest way: by controlling the qualifications of physicians and other health care providers and the resources and amenities of health care facilities. States license health care providers under their authority and responsibility for the health, safety, and welfare of citizens.

Every state has a medical practice act that defines and specifies the standards of appropriate medical conduct. These acts usually specify educational requirements for licensure and the grounds and procedures for disciplinary actions against licensees. The state requirements vary a great deal regarding the type of conduct that is subject to discipline, however. For example, one state might require an inquiry when a physician is convicted of any felony, while another may inquire only into conduct relating to practice. Some state statutes provide very limited disciplinary authority.

Rather than provide detailed guidance in the statute, state laws delegate responsibility for licensure and discipline with medical licensure boards. These boards, comprised of respected physicians appointed by the state, have for nearly 200 years established standards for good practice and monitored physician competence.

Despite attempts to promote nationwide uniformity of standards, professional boards continue to be the principal mechanism for assuring physicians' fitness to practice. Each board still controls the standards for obtaining and keeping a license to practice medicine in the state.

The ability of medical boards to identify and discipline providers of poor care, or to assure quality care, is subject to doubt. Critics argue that boards are reluctant to discipline incompetent physicians. Some boards have been shown to be self-serving, attempting to use their disciplinary powers to eliminate competition from other physicians or health-related professionals. Physicians who have been sued repeatedly, or caused multiple patient complaints, might merely be required to move out of the board's jurisdiction rather than be subjected to penalties. Such actions have been termed a "conspiracy of silence" within the profession. At the least, many state medical boards are understaffed and underfunded for a job of the volume and importance facing them today. Most rely on licensing fees that provide a limited operating budget.

[2] INSTITUTIONAL CREDENTIALS

Hospitals and other corporate health care providers, such as home health agencies, nursing homes, and hospices, must be licensed by the state. In addition, the Medicare program requires assurance of quality through a process of accreditation. The responsibility for accrediting hospitals has been delegated by the federal administrative branch (CMS) to a private organization, the Joint Commission on the Accreditation of Health Organizations (JCAHO), formerly the Joint Commission on the Accreditation of Hospitals. The JCAHO's role is to award "deemed status," in which the standards of the organization are deemed to be the equivalent of federal participation standards. A majority of states also have incorporated the JCAHO standards into their licensing processes, so there is not as much duplication as there might appear to be. JCAHO accreditation is voluntary. However, many insurers, including Blue Cross plans, require that facilities have JCAHO accreditation to receive payments. The JCAHO surveys and accredits 80 percent of all hospitals in the United States, including all with more than 25 beds.

In brief, the JCAHO survey process is based on guidelines, or standards of quality, for facilities and practices. The surveyors are doctors and nurses who, every two or three years, visit a hospital and assess compliance with the standards by reviewing "1) statements from authorized and responsible hospital personnel; 2) documentary evidence or certification of compliance provided by the hospital; 3) answers to detailed questions concerning the implementation of an item, or examples of its implementation that will enable a judgment of compliance to be made; 4) on-site observation by surveyors."

In 2003, the federal government addressed quality of Medicare HMOs by giving deemed status to a new quality monitoring entity. In the January 25 Federal Register, CMS announced that the National Committee for Quality Assurance (NCQA) has authority to "deem" that a Medicare Advantage (MA) organization is complying with Medicare requirements. MA organizations accredited by NCQA receive deemed status approval in six areas: Quality Assurance, Information on Advance Directives, Antidiscrimination, Access to Services, Provider Participation Rules, and Confidentiality and Accuracy of Enrollee Records.

QUESTIONS

1. What are the limitations of using a private organization staffed by professionals in the field to certify the quality of corporate providers? Do you see any conflict of interest?

2. What should be the limits of JCAHO's powers to sanction hospitals? Public notice of deficiencies, like nursing homes? Civil fines? Criminal findings and fines on the institution? What about criminal prosecution of administrators for egregious practices?

Medicare requires that services provided by hospitals and physicians be "reasonable and necessary" in accord with the patient's level of care. However, the statute provides no definition of the phrase. The responsibility for determining what is "reasonable and necessary" is delegated to QIC (Qualified Independent Contractor, formerly termed utilization review organizations or committees (URCs)) originally established to control the growth of Medicare costs. Limits on care raise questions about whether that care is adequate and effective. Fully effective care can be criticized as excessive or duplicative, and therefore too costly as seen by the considerable variation in the use of particular health care. One region of the country may have a significantly higher number of hospital days per 1,000 persons or do a particular surgical procedure more often. It is assumed that some portion of the procedures in high utilization regions and systems are unnecessary.

Quality assurance in Medicare relies on the Peer Review of Utilization and Quality (PRO) program (42 U.S.C. §§ 1320c to 1320c-12), subsequently redesignated Qualified Improvement Contractors or "QICs." QICs are established by contract with CMS to review physicians' Medicare hospital admissions. The QIC's staff of physicians and registered nurses reviews a random sample of discharges by examining Medicare claims as they are processed for payment. They also review 50 percent of admissions when the patient is transferred from one acute care facility to another, and readmissions occurring less than 31 days after the previous discharge.

The QIC review includes, but is not limited to, overall treatment, quality of care issues, discharge review, premature discharges, and level of care appropriateness. If a QIC finds that a facility is deficient in any of these categories, the facility is subject to sanctions, under which all Medicare admissions may be subjected to review before payment. If the problem persists, the facility's participation in the Medicare program can be terminated.

Most QIC reviews are retrospective, after the services and discharge, and so expose the provider and beneficiary to liability for the incurred costs of treatment since the care has already been delivered when the claim is denied. As a result, Medicare recipients can be left with huge, unexpected medical bills. Under "waiver of liability" provisions in 42 U.S.C. § 1395pp, Medicare can pay despite absence of liability, if both the provider and recipient of service did not know, and could not reasonably have been expected to know, that the services would not be covered. If the provider, but not the recipient, should have known, Medicare can reimburse the recipient for any charges paid and recover the amount from the provider. A facility can claim only a very small number of reimbursements under the waiver of liability clause without triggering investigation by the QIC.

If the QIC intends to deny Medicare payment for care, the recipient or provider is entitled to discuss the issues with the PRO before the initial denial. 42 U.S.C. § 1320c-3(a)(2); 42 C.F.R. § 473.20. If payment is denied, a provider or patient may seek reconsideration from the QIC within 60 days of the denial notice. A patient can submit additional evidence, such as statements from treating physicians, but is not permitted to review the record of the QIC's original determination. The PRO will re-review the patient's medical records and issue its decision within 30 days.

Prospective payment has meant shorter stays that might result in the discharge of a very ill person with multiple care needs. The problem is particularly acute since older patients take longer to recover and gain strength and may have conditions that create a high risk of need for emergency care soon after discharge.

The Medicare statute requires hospitals to take steps to assure that needed services are provided to patients when they go home. The discharge planning requirements must be in writing. The hospital must identify at an early stage of hospitalization all patients who are likely to suffer adverse health consequences upon discharge if there is no adequate discharge planning and provide a discharge planning evaluation of the patient's physical and mental condition, the likely post-hospital living situation, and the patient's ability to engage in daily living activities.

To prevent delays in an appropriate discharge, hospital personnel must complete the evaluation on a timely basis so any arrangements for post-hospital care are made in advance of the actual discharge. The hospital must include the evaluation in the patient's medical record for use in establishing an appropriate discharge plan and must discuss the results of the evaluation with the patient or person acting on the patient's behalf. If post-discharge services are needed, the hospital must develop a plan and arrange for initial implementation. Even if the hospital does not identify the need for a discharge plan, the patient's physician may request the hospital to create one.

[3] PAYMENTS AND COST CONTAINMENT

Under the original payment structure of the Medicare program, hospitals and physicians were reimbursed at a "reasonable" rate, i.e., the provider's estimate of the value of services that the same provider considered appropriate. This provided incentives to spend rather than to operate cost-efficiently, and costs soared. The revisions have the advantage of creating incentives to cut costs, but are prone to the inaccuracies and payer "gaming" found in any complex regulatory system. Hospital and physician cost containment developed first. Prospective payments systems and limits on fees for other health care services, including home health, nursing facilities, outpatient surgery, have been implemented.

[a]   The Hospital Prospective Payment System: Diagnostic-Related Groups

Hospitals are paid for services by a prospective, fixed-price-per-case system, called the Prospective Payment System (PPS). The cornerstone of the PPS is the system of diagnostic-related groups (DRGs). Payment is determined by classifying patient diagnoses into one of about 800 DRGs, each consisting of similar types of illnesses and patient characteristics for which the cost of providing service is similar.

Each DRG is assigned a fixed rate of reimbursement. The formula is based on a standard amount allocated for treatment of the condition, composed of labor and nonlabor portions, which is multiplied by a weight given for the severity of the illness. The labor cost is adjusted for the wages in the area. The resulting sum is the average cost for treating a patient in this DRG in the area.

The PPS provides hospitals an incentive to deliver services at less than the DRG rate by permitting them to keep the extra funds. On the other hand, if the cost of treatment exceeds the DRG reimbursement, even for medically necessary reasons, the hospital must pay and will lose money. The PPS allows limited extra payments, called "outlier" payments, for cases where the patient's length of stay greatly exceeds the usual length of stay for patients in the same DRG. However, approval for outlier payments apply to "atypical" cases only, not for the few extra days required by a slow recovery. A hospital that claims outliers that exceed one percent to two percent of their total cases is likely to be subjected to time consuming and costly auditing by Medicare officials.

The PPS is administered by CMS, which has responsibility for updating the DRGs annually. The Secretary of CMS has the advice and oversight of a congressional commission, the Medical Payment Advisory Commission (Med-PAC, a successor to both the Prospective Payment Assessment Commission (ProPAC), and the Physician Payment Review Commission). The implementation of DRGs at the hospital level is the responsibility of their Quality Improvement Organizations (QIOs), which monitor whether services to Medicare beneficiaries are medically necessary, reasonable, and appropriately provided on an inpatient basis (i.e., at the right level of care).

DRGs require complex calculations, and specific DRGs can be wrong through miscalculation by the federal agency. As reported in the New England Journal of Medicine, when average cost for a cochlear implant was generally acknowledged to be about $14,000, the Medicare DRG provided only $10,000. A systemic problem is that complications may result in assignment of a DRG with a higher payment rate, which inadvertently compensates hospitals that fail to prevent such developments as post-admission infections. Under law, hospitals are precluded from challenging the DRG rate, the formula used to compute the DRG, or the weighting factor for the region and hospital.

If hospitals do not receive adequate reimbursement from government programs and cannot improve their cost-efficiency, they must shift the cost elsewhere. In the current climate of managed care, however, insurers routinely negotiate to limit the amount a provider charges for a service to a beneficiary. There are fewer and fewer opportunities to cost-shift. Providers cannot sue to increase a rate of Medicare reimbursement, but have threatened to refuse to provide care to Medicare beneficiaries because the overall rates of reimbursement are too low. To date, few, if any, have actually carried out that threat.

QUESTION

What are the possible consequences if prospective payment is too low to cover provider costs?

[b] Physician Prospective Payment: The Resource-Based Relative Value Scale

In the Omnibus Budget Reconciliation Act of 1989, Congress adopted a new reimbursement methodology for physicians, developed by Harvard researchers and known as the Resource-Based Relative Value Scale (RBRVS). The RBRVS fees were phased-in over a five-year period beginning in 1992, replacing the older system of reasonable-charge reimbursement. Reimbursement is based upon the resources that go into the provision of various physician services, such as the amount of time, training, and skill applied to treating and informing a patient, overhead costs, and professional liability costs.

The government also sought to correct for perceived "overpayments" to certain specialists and "underpayments" for family practice physicians. The implementation of RBRVS had a significant impact on the distribution of Medicare income. Primary care physicians received larger payments, with family physicians receiving an initial increase of about 38 percent. Surgeons and radiologists, historically the most generously reimbursed physicians under Part B, experienced a reduction in reimbursement, with surgeons initially losing an average of 11 percent. Physicians who practice in geographic areas where health care is scarce received higher payment, intended to draw physicians to underserved areas.

The Kyl Amendment, Section 4507 of the Balanced Budget Act of 1997 (42 U.S.C. § 1395a), allows private contracting between physicians and Medicare beneficiaries for fees that exceed the Medicare approved rates. Until the passage of the Kyl Amendment, the Medicare statute and many state statutes prohibited any physician from charging Medicare beneficiaries more than an amount keyed to the Medicare reimbursement formula. No private contracts were permitted even if the patient declined to use Part B benefits to cover the costs. The Kyl Amendment imposes several conditions: (1) The contract must be in writing; (2) it must be entered into before any service is provided, and cannot be formed when the patient is "facing and emergency or urgent health care situation"; and (3) it must include specific points to alert the patient to the obligations of the contract, including the patient's agreement not to submit a Medicare claim, to accept responsibility for payment and acknowledge that Medicare will not pay, and acknowledgements that Medicare charge limits do not apply and that Medigap plans will not pay. A physician must file an affidavit with the Secretary of Health and Human Services promising not to file any claims for Medicare-covered services for two years.

In order to prevent physicians from offsetting their reductions in reimbursement by increasing the volume of services performed, Congress relies on Sustainable Growth Rates (SGR), which are yearly and cumulative spending targets. Taking into account the aging of the Medicare population and changes in medical technology, CMS sets the percentage physician fee payments will be allowed to grow. Proper application of the SGR would require a reduction in the current rates paid to physicians under Part B. Congress, however, has repeatedly intervened to block any reductions in pay to physicians with the result that the cost of Part B continues to rise more rapidly than it would if the SCR limits were implemented.

[c] Dual Eligibility: Medicare and Medicaid Interaction

Medicaid, the national health care program for the poor, cushions the impact of Medicare's shortcomings for the elderly poor. An estimated 20 percent of Medicare enrollees are also covered by Medicaid. These beneficiaries, known as "dual eligibles," are entitled to benefits from both programs. Federal mandates of the early 1990s doubled the ranks of elders eligible for some benefits of dual eligibility. The recipients of this expanded coverage are called Qualified Medicare Beneficiaries.

States must pay Medicare Part A deductibles and Part B premiums for their older Medicaid beneficiaries under a "buy-in" agreement with the federal government. For dually eligible persons, Medicare makes the primary payment for hospital bills, physician fees, and other Medicare-covered services. Medicaid supplements Medicare by paying for services that are not included in the Medicare benefit package. Theoretically, at least, dually eligible people get the greater choice of providers available to Medicare beneficiaries as well as the more comprehensive benefits of Medicaid.

Dual eligible beneficiaries have a demographic profile that differs from the general elder Medicare population. Seven out of ten have annual incomes under $10,000. Over half of dual beneficiaries (55 percent) are nursing home residents. African Americans comprise about 20 percent of dual eligibles, although they are only seven percent of those eligible for Medicare. A greater proportion are female (64 versus 55 percent). Among dual eligibles, 44 percent live alone, as compared with 18 percent of other Medicare beneficiaries. They are more likely to report poor health and limits on their activities of daily living such as eating and bathing (46 percent of dual eligibles reported poor health compared with 20 percent of other elders). In 2004, the Medicare cost for each dual eligible person was more than twice that for Medicare beneficiaries: $18,100 versus $8,400.

[d]   Medicare as Secondary Payer

If a Medicare beneficiary has other health care insurance coverage such as employee health benefits or receives covered health services due to an injury subject to a tort claim that leads to an award, Medicare can seek recovery of its payments for the cost of care. Medicare serves as the secondary payer responsible only for the covered costs no other source will pay. Note, however, that Medigap coverage is always secondary to Medicare coverage and so typically are employer provided retiree health benefits.

The Omnibus Budget Reconciliation Act of 1980 specifies:

> Payment under this subchapter may not be made with respect to any item or service to the extent that payment has been made, or can reasonably be expected to be made promptly (as determined in accordance with regulations), with respect to such item or service, under a workmen's compensation law or plan of the United States or a State or under an automobile or liability in [sic] insurance policy or plan (including a self-insured plan) or under no fault insurance.

42 U.S.C. § 1395y(b)(1). To assure that the beneficiary receives health care, Medicare may advance payment on or reimbursement from the other source of coverage.

The provision appears to be reasonable and in accord with a trend in public policy that has universally abrogated the collateral source rule that permitted recovery from both an insurer and a defendant in tort. However, under the regulations (42 C.F.R. §§ 405.322–.325), CMS seeks recovery of the full amount of Medicare payments regardless of the amount of other coverage or the structure of the settlement or award.

ZINMAN v. SHALALA
67 F.3d 841 (9th Cir. 1995)

This is a class action challenging HHS's interpretation and implementation of the Medicare Secondary Payer provisions of the Social Security Act. As first enacted, Medicare was the primary payer for medical services supplied to a beneficiary, even when such services were covered by other insurance such as an employer group health plan or liability insurance. Responding to skyrocketing Medicare costs, Congress in 1980 enacted the Medicare Secondary Payer legislation (MSP legislation), requiring Medicare to serve as the secondary payer when a beneficiary has overlapping insurance coverage.

Under the MSP legislation, when a Medicare beneficiary suffers an injury covered by a group health plan or liability, workers' compensation, automobile, or no-fault insurance, Medicare conditionally pays for the beneficiary's medical expenses. If the beneficiary receives a settlement from the primary insurer, Medicare is entitled to reimbursement from the beneficiary for its conditional outlays. HHS has interpreted the MSP legislation to allow full recovery of conditional Medicare payments even when the beneficiary's settlement is for less than her total damages (i.e., a discounted settlement). This interpretation is set forth in 42 C.F.R. § 411.24(c). This regulation provides in pertinent part that the Health Care Financing Administration [HCFA, now CMS] "may recover an amount equal to the Medicare payment or the amount payable by the third party, whichever is less."

In November 1990, several individual beneficiaries brought suit against HHS challenging the agency's interpretation of the MSP legislation. These plaintiffs were later certified as a class by the district court. They sought an injunction that would require HHS to reduce proportionately its recovery when a beneficiary received a discounted settlement from a third party.

The district court granted HHS's motion for summary judgment. This appeal followed, raising the issue whether HHS is entitled to recover up to the full amount of its conditional Medicare payments when a beneficiary receives a discounted settlement from a third party.

The following hypothetical case illustrates the issue. Assume an accident victim receives a $50,000 settlement. This is the limit of the third-party tortfeasor's liability policy. The victim alleged damages of $80,000 in medical expenses (of which Medicare paid $50,000); $20,000 in property damage; $40,000 in lost wages; and $60,000 in pain and suffering. The total claim for damages is $200,000.

In this hypothetical case, is HHS entitled to recover its entire $50,000 outlay (minus its portion of attorney fees and costs), or must it apportion its recovery, reducing it in proportion to the plaintiff's partial recovery of her total damages claim? The victim in the hypothetical example recovered only 25% of her claim. According to the beneficiaries' construction of the statute, HHS should recover no more than 25% of its $50,000 outlay ($12,500).

According to HHS's construction of the statute, HHS is entitled to recover its entire $50,000, less applicable attorney fees and costs under 42 C.F.R. § 411.37, subject only to the possibility of a full or partial hardship waiver under 42 U.S.C. § 1395gg(c).

DISCUSSION

. . . .

The beneficiaries argue that on its face the MSP legislation mandates apportioned rather than full recovery of conditional Medicare payments when a beneficiary receives a discounted settlement. The beneficiaries contend that the MSP legislation's use of the phrase "item or service" specifically limits Medicare's right to reimbursement. The beneficiaries point to 42 U.S.C. § 1395y(b)(2)(B)(i) which provides: "Any payment under this subchapter with respect to any item or service . . . shall be conditioned on reimbursement . . . when notice or other information is received that payment for such item or service has been or could be made . . . [under a workers' compensation law, liability or no fault insurance]. . . ." The beneficiaries also rely on 42 U.S.C. § 1395y(b)(2)(B)(ii) which provides: "In order to recover payment under this subchapter for such an item or service, the United States may bring an action against any entity which is required or responsible under this subsection to pay with respect to such item or service (or any portion thereof) under a primary plan . . . , or against any other entity . . . that has received payment . . . with respect to the item or service. . . ." Because Medicare's recovery is tied to payments for "item[s] and service[s]," the beneficiaries argue that Congress intended to limit Medicare's right to reimbursement to the extent that a beneficiary's settlement actually covers the "item[s] or service[s]" for which Medicare paid.

It is clear from the statute that the references to "item or service" are intended to define the payments for which Medicare has a right to reimbursement. Nothing in this language, however, compels the conclusion that Congress intended to limit the amount of recovery for a conditionally paid "item or service" to a proportionate share of a discounted settlement. The beneficiaries' reliance on 42 U.S.C. §§ 1395y(b)(2)(B)(i) and (ii) is misplaced.

The beneficiaries also rely on the subrogation provisions of the MSP legislation. Under 42 U.S.C. § 1395y(b)(1), the United States is subrogated to the rights of individuals or other entities arising under the MSP legislation. This right of subrogation gives HHS the right to be put in the legal position of the beneficiary in order to recover from third parties who are legally responsible to the beneficiary for a loss.

As the beneficiaries note, the right of subrogation is equitable in nature and generally requires application of the equitable principle of apportionment. Under this equitable principle, a subrogated right holder is limited to recovery of the proportion of its loss for which third-party reimbursement is actually received. Because HHS is a subrogee, the beneficiaries argue, its recovery must be limited to the pro rata share of an insurance settlement that includes payment for medical expenses. We disagree.

The MSP legislation does not confine the HHS's right of reimbursement to its right of subrogation. The statute grants HHS an independent right of recovery against any entity that is responsible for payment of or that has received payment for Medicare-related items or services, including the beneficiary herself. This independent right of recovery is separate and distinct from HHS's right of subrogation . . . and is not limited by the equitable principle of apportionment stemming from the subrogation right. Moreover, to define Medicare's right to recover its conditional payments solely by reference to its right of subrogation would render superfluous the alternative remedy of the independent right of recovery contained in section 1395y(b)(2)(B)(ii). We decline to construe the statute in a way that would render clear statutory language superfluous. . . .

We reject the beneficiaries' contention that HHS's recovery is limited by the equitable principle of apportionment applicable to the right of subrogation.

Finally, the beneficiaries argue that the "Coordination of Benefits" provision of the MSP legislation requires a proportionate reduction of Medicare's recovery of conditional payments when a beneficiary receives a discounted settlement. We reject this argument.

The coordination of benefits provision of the MSP legislation provides in pertinent part: "Where payment for an item or service by a primary plan is less than the amount of the charge for such item or service and is not payment in full,

payment may be made under this title . . . for the remainder of such charge. . . ."
Nothing in this language limits Medicare's right of full reimbursement. This
provision merely provides that Medicare may pay for covered medical expenses not
paid by primary insurance. With regard to the amount of reimbursement available
to Medicare, whether full or apportioned, the statute is silent.

Although the beneficiaries proffer creative constructions of the MSP legislation,
we conclude the statute does not address the issue of apportioned recovery of
conditional Medicare payments, either by its language or by its structure.

Because Congress has not "directly spoken to the precise question at issue" . . .
we turn to the second step of the Chevron analysis and consider whether HHS's
construction of the MSP statute is a permissible one. . . . If HHS's construction is
"rational and consistent with the statute," it is a permissible construction and we
will uphold it. . . .

Reading the MSP legislation to allow full reimbursement of conditional
Medicare payments even though a beneficiary receives a discounted settlement
from a third party is a rational construction of the statute. It is also consistent with
the statute's purpose. The transformation of Medicare from the primary payer to
the secondary payer with a right of reimbursement reflects the overarching
statutory purpose of reducing Medicare costs. . . . A full recovery of conditional
payments will reduce such costs.

HHS's construction also provides a practical and economical way for Medicare
to recover its conditional payments. In the hypothetical case discussed above, the
injured victim alleged a variety of damages, some capable of precise computation,
some not. Such allegations are not uncommon. HHS's ability to recover the full
amount of its conditional payments, regardless of a victim's allegations of damages,
avoids the commitment of federal resources to the task of ascertaining the dollar
amount of each element of a victim's alleged damages.

The beneficiaries argue that ascertaining the dollar amounts of a victim's
elements of damages is not a prohibitive burden. They remind us that HHS accepts
apportionment of conditional Medicare payments in workers' compensation cases
involving particularized components of damages. . . .

We reject this argument because it analogizes workers' compensation cases to
tort cases. The analogy is inept. Workers' compensation schemes generally
determine recovery on the basis of a rigid formula, often with a statutory
maximum. . . . Apportionment in workers' compensation settlements therefore
involves a relatively simple comparison of the total settlement to the measure of
damages allowed for individual components of the settlement, pursuant to a
prescribed formula. Tort cases, in contrast, involve noneconomic damages not
available in workers' compensation cases, and a victim's damages are not
determined by an established formula. Apportionment of Medicare's recovery in
tort cases would either require a fact-finding process to determine actual damages
or would place Medicare at the mercy of a victim's or personal injury attorney's
estimate of damages.

CONCLUSION

The MSP legislation is unclear as to whether HHS is entitled to full reimbursement of conditional Medicare payments when a beneficiary receives a discounted settlement from a third party. HHS has construed the legislation to permit it to recover up to the full amount of its conditional Medicare payments. This is a permissible construction of the statute. Accordingly, we uphold this construction, and affirm the district court's summary judgment in favor of HHS.

AFFIRMED.

———

The definition of a primary payer includes not just private and public insurance plans, but also any individual or entity who is found in the course of litigation to be liable for payment. When primary and secondary payers work together, they typically sort out who pays for what care, and the balance is due from Medicare within the limits of its coverage. The patient may sue to secure payments from third parties. However, the government has a right of subrogation, i.e., to step into the shoes of any party to recover amounts that were paid or should be paid.

The primary payer acquires some protection, in that if payment within the statutory 30 days constitutes a hardship, the provider is entitled to a payment period of at least six months and as much as five years. Further, the provider is presumed to have a hardship if the amount of the overpayment requested exceeds 10 percent of the amount paid by Medicare within the previous calendar year. A beneficiary may receive conditional payments from Medicare if payments by the primary payer are delayed

NOTE ON MEDICARE AND MEDICAID FRAUD

With the growing complexity and cost of health care services, providers are entering the market with an eye on profitability. Some make notable mistakes in billing government programs and must refund payments improperly claimed. Others view the benefits as an opportunity to fraudulently enrich themselves at the expense of the taxpayers.

Health care fraud ranges in its nature from elaborate schemes associated with organized crime to bill for services to people who are not in need or for services that are not rendered, to providers who routinely choose false billing codes that provide a little more service to a patient or a little more profit. The business of health care provides a different sort of opportunities. Physicians and business associates may jointly invest in entities intended to create a pool of patients in need of their facilities and services. While the basic concept is desirable and a portrait of much of the managed care industry, incentives to provide inappropriate or unnecessary care to any patient is not.

Government as a substantial payer and protector of the public purse has a special concern with fraud on public programs. Also, common law fraud is difficult to prove because it involves proving the intention in the mind of the perpetrator. In health care, the extent to which a provider believes that a treatment or test is effective is particularly problematic.

The Medicare and Medicaid Anti-Fraud Abuse and Anti-Kickback Statute, prohibits:

Any person (including an organization, agency, or other entity, but excluding a beneficiary) . . . that —

(1) presents or causes to be presented to an officer, employee, or agent of the United States, or of any department or agency thereof, or of any State agency (as defined in subsection (i)(1) of this section), a claim (as defined in subsection (i)(2) of this section) that the Secretary determines —

(A) is for a medical or other item or service that the person knows, or should know was not provided as claimed,

(B) is for a medical or other item or service and the person knows or should know the claim is false or fraudulent,

(C) is presented for a physician's service (or an item or service incident to a physician's service) by a person who knows or should know that the individual who furnished (or supervised the furnishing of) the service —

(i) was not licensed as a physician,

(ii) was licensed as a physician, but such license had been obtained through a misrepresentation of material fact (including cheating on an examination required for licensing), or

(iii) represented to the patient at the time the service was furnished that the physician was certified in a medical specialty by a medical specialty board when the individual was not so certified, 42 U.S.C. § 1320a-7a.

The statute in general prohibits the acts of anyone who knowingly solicits, receives, offers, or pays any remuneration (including any kickback, bribe, or rebate), directly or indirectly, in cash or in kind, either in return for referring an individual for the furnishing of any items of service reimbursable under Medicare or Medicaid; or in return for purchasing, leasing, or ordering any good, facility, service, or item (covered under Medicare or Medicaid). The law also prohibits kickbacks and referral fees — payments to induce a physician to prescribe more services, or continue to refer to a physician or other health services provider. 42 U.S.C. § 1320a-7b(b).

Other statutes also are used to pursue health care fraud claims. The False Claims Act makes it a fraud to present to the government any claim known to be false, or not due to be paid. More recent statutes include the Stark Physician Self-Referral statutes that prohibit referral of business between specified health care entities (such as labs, hospitals, clinics, etc.) if the physician or any designated family member has an ownership interest. The law is based on the finding that physicians are likely to refer more often if the ownership interest exists, raising the possibility that the referral is unnecessary or inappropriate. However, scienter is particularly difficult to prove in such circumstances, so the Stark laws have a strict liability standard and only civil penalties. Finally, the Health Insurance Portability and Accountability Act of 1996 (HIPAA) mandated the development of further law on health care fraud, resulting in a new crime of "health care fraud," increased penalties, and other means to more successful prosecution.

[4] ADMINISTRATION AND APPEALS

The Centers for Medicare and Medicaid Services (CMS) are responsible for resolving beneficiary claims. The agency enacts regulations to "fill in the gaps" in the law. The process, termed informal rulemaking according to the requirements of the federal Administrative Procedure Act (APA), generally requires that regulated parties receive notice of proposed interpretive rules, and have opportunity to make comments, usually in writing, for the agency to consider. The APA and the administrative rules provide process and substance for those who disagree with the agency's determinations of claims for eligibility or benefits.

Medicare appeals are held by the Department of Health and Human Services (DHHS) Medicare Appeals Council (MAC), which employs Administrative Appeals Judges (AAJs) and Appeals Officers (AOs) as decision makers. The MAC provides final administrative review of claims for entitlement to Medicare and individual claims for Medicare coverage and payment filed by beneficiaries or health care providers and suppliers.

Medicare has five stages of appeal from an initial determination, including the initial determination, the redetermination, reconsideration, and ALJ review before appeal to the federal district court. An initial determination in writing is necessary for both traditional and expedited appeals.

The beneficiary has 120 days to appeal an initial denial. The first appeal, the redetermination, goes to the same decision maker, and must be made by a person who had no part in the initial decision. The beneficiary has 180 days to appeal, and the decision maker has 60 days to issue a decision. The next level of appeal, the reconsideration, goes to the Qualified Independent Contractor (QIC). This level of decision replaces Hearing Office Review for Part B, and is entirely new for Part A. Again, the beneficiary has 180 days to appeal and the QIC has 60 days for decision. The AAJ/ALJ review follows, with 180 days for the beneficiary, and 90 days for the decision maker. The next level is the Medicare Appeals Council (MAC) (the Departmental Appeals Board, or DAB for Part B) analogous to the Appeals Council for Social Security. After 90 days for beneficiary appeal and 60 days for a decision, the next level is the federal district court.

At each level, the beneficiary provides the personal information, diagnosis, services denied, and supporting documents. The decision maker must respond with the decision supported by reasons, including any scientific bases and applicable law and regulations. The ALJ hearing is held by video or telephone, unless an in-person hearing is requested, which is cause for delay as compared with the timeline. While the administrative process generally is intended to develop the case, and therefore allows the appellant leeway to introduce omitted material and to miss deadlines for any good reason, the new standards seek greater accuracy and efficiency by excluding any new evidence at the ALJ hearing without a showing of good cause for the omission. It is unclear how rigorously this standard will be enforced, and what happens to the claim and decision if important evidence is excluded.

A beneficiary who faces termination of services from a hospital, SNF, home health agency, hospice, or other Medicare provider must receive a notice in writing of termination or discharge (Notice of Discharge and Medicare Appeals Rights — NODMAR) not later than two days or two visits before the proposed end of services. If an appeal is made, the provider must continue the services for at least two days or to the notified date of termination. The right of expedited appeal depends on the treating physician's certification that the end of services may place the patient's health at significant risk. The beneficiary can appeal the decision to the Quality Improvement Organization (QIO — formerly a PRO (peer review organization) primarily involved with hospital decisions). The appeal must issue by noon of the day prior to termination of services; it can be made by phone as well as in writing. Because of the appeal to the QIO, the provider must send the patient detailed information as to why the services are no longer reasonable and necessary or no longer covered. The QIO has 72 hours from receipt of the appeal to make a decision, which they must issue by telephone and in writing. It must include a detailed explanation, a statement of when the patient is liable to pay for the services, and information about rights of appeal.

The beneficiary then has the right to reconsideration of the QIO decision by the Qualified Independent Contractor (QIC), the entity responsible for the first outside review of traditional appeals. The request must be transmitted in writing or by phone not later than noon of the calendar day after notice of the QIO decision. The QIC must issue a decision within 72 hours after receiving the request, and may provide notice by phone followed by writing. However, the beneficiary can extend the appeals time by up to 14 days in order to gather medical documentation. In the event of a denial, the beneficiary then joins the standard appeals process at the ALJ fair hearing level.

In general, a provider, physician, or supplier of Medicare services has the same appeal rights as a beneficiary with regard to a claim. In many instances, the provider's interest in receiving Medicare payment is in accord with the beneficiary's interests. Because the provider may represent the interests of many beneficiaries, a provider and beneficiary suit for coverage can be very helpful to individual patients. A physician, with patient permission, may ask the Medicare Administrative Contractor (fiscal intermediary or carrier) for a coverage determination before the services are provided. In the event coverage is denied, the beneficiary has no right of appeal. If the health care services are provided, the beneficiary may then submit a claim. As with Medicare appeals in the past, a denial by the contractor is the basis to begin the administrative appeals process.

Chapter 6

LONG-TERM CARE: PAYMENT SOURCES

In relation to elderly individuals, long-term care refers to the provision of custodial and medical care for individuals, who because of chronic medical problems, physical frailty, or mental decline, such as dementia, need daily assistance or supervision.

Before the mid-20th century, older individuals who needed long-term care typically lived with and received care from their spouses, children or other relatives. The household provided food, shelter, companionship, and personal care for the older individual to the extent it was affordable and feasible. After the 1950s, more elderly individuals had enough income and savings to purchase long-term care and did so, as families became smaller, moved apart and so could not or would not provide care. Even families who might be willing to help found it difficult to do so with two working spouses, smaller houses, and child rearing demands. Meanwhile, as life expectancy past age 65 grew, more elderly experienced care needs, which could last for years. At the same time, the cost of care grew as labor costs rose as well as the cost of building facilities that could safely house physically and mentally incapacitated elderly individuals. Greater governmental regulation of long-term care and demands for better care also contributed to rising costs.

Over time, long-term care for the elderly became seen less as an individual problem and more as a societal concern that required governmental solutions. Unfortunately, government involvement has been piecemeal and ad hoc rather than the result of any grand plan. Essentially, government has become the payor of last resort. When individuals can no longer afford to pay for their long-term care, government will pay for their care through Medicaid, which was enacted in July of 1965, six months after the passage of Medicare. Medicaid was necessary in part because Medicare did not and still does not pay for long-term care. The federal Medicare program is an acute health care insurance program that is not designed to provide long-term care as it pays for each spell of illness for only 20 days of skilled nursing home care and an additional 100 days with a high co-payment. Medicare does pay for some home health care, but numerous restrictions prevent it from providing long-term care.

The governmental program that pays for long-term care, Medicaid, is a federal program that is operated by the states, who on average pay about half of its costs. When enacted, Medicaid only paid for nursing home care. When it became clear, however, that limiting reimbursement to care provided in nursing homes caused unnecessary expense to the program, states were allowed to seek federal permission (a "waiver" of the original Medicaid rules) to provide home and community care to a limited number of eligible elderly in need of long-term care. In 2010, the Patient Protection and Affordable Care Act expanded the right of states to use Medicaid funds to provide long-term care outside of nursing homes. Still, despite the attempt to encourage care in lower cost settings, the great majority of Medicaid dollars are paid for care provided in nursing homes.

A. LONG-TERM CARE

It is estimated of the over 40 million Americans who are age 65 and older, over nine million need long-term care. The incidence is quite low for those in their sixties, and rises to nearly half of the population above age 85. Most long-term care is provided in the community by spouses, children, relatives, and friends and is informal and unpaid. Some long-term care is provided in the home by paid providers such as visiting nurses, geriatric social workers, and paid "companions." Many elderly in need of assistance move into board-and-care homes or assisted living facilities. Some reside in nursing homes, either because they need daily assistance with medical problems or because Medicaid will only pay for care if provided in a nursing home.

It is estimated that in 2010 the annual cost of providing long-term care to the elderly was over $210 billion with Medicaid paying over $100 billion per year. In addition, billions of dollars worth of free care are provided by spouses, children, family members, and others. And while the average length of need for care among the elderly has declined over the past 30 years, the growth in the number of elderly means that the total cost will continue to rise in the years to come.

Ideally, the provision of long-term care in the future will reflect a growing understanding of how to provide necessary and effective services in a cost efficient manner. New methods of assessing individual needs and developing appropriate responses to those needs may result in better care and possible cost savings. Home and community-based long-term care promises to deliver services at a lower cost per individual, but the total cost of long-term care will continue to rise because of the increase in those needing care. Financing of long-term care is likely to include a full range of types of payments and subsidies, including tax incentives, private sector insurance coverage, public insurance programs, and direct public subsidy. By making one way to pay more convenient or less costly, policymakers can influence consumer choice of services, how and where long-term care is delivered and the extent to which individuals plan and pay for their own long-term care. Unfortunately, the current complicated financing system assures that access to long-term care services and the receipt of government payment for those services varies greatly among the elderly.

B. LONG-TERM CARE OUTSIDE THE UNITED STATES

In the aging of their populations, the United States and Canada are about 20 years "behind" Japan and Western Europe (including France, Germany, the United Kingdom, and Scandinavia), who have a greater percent of their populations age 65 and older. How these countries have responded to the need for long-term care can provide valuable insights.

While each country's system has unique aspects, there are points in common. All have the range of services normally associated with long-term care in the United States. The range of perceived problems — quality of care, funding, and targeting appropriate services — is also the same, regardless of the mix of services provided. The growth of the public long-term care package has been incremental, an expansion of services into areas of unmet need and coordination of existing services, especially between health and welfare. Each system has encouraged the development of volunteer care providers. Each calls for better assessment of the needs of the elderly.

Long-term care, unlike health care, is not usually provided as a universal entitlement without regard to income. About half of the countries provide such assistance as welfare or make a distinction among types of services provided with public funds. Home care is the type of service most likely to be targeted for government benefits to the low-income population. It is common for the medical portion of long-term care to be publicly funded, while the responsibility for room and board costs remains with the recipient who is able to pay. That is to say, health care services are covered whether the individual is acutely or chronically ill, while ordinary costs still are paid by the individual.

One difference from country to country is the rate of institutionalization. Some countries, such as Sweden, have undertaken extensive programs of group housing, while others, such as England, emphasize home care. Historically, none rely as heavily on nursing homes as the United States, although institutions are available for those who are very impaired.

The structure of long-term care finance and delivery depends on the society's perception of fairness between generations and of differently situated elders and their needs. The staffing depends on perceptions of the appropriateness of training, immigration policies, and pay scales. Consider the following on the structure of long-term care programs, and the workers who are likely to provide care:

Canada

In Canada, long-term care services are administered by the provinces rather than the federal government, which primarily provides partial funds according to the province's needs. Provinces provide varying packages of services and funds for their support. Institutional care is used frequently. Some services are covered by universal health and hospital program, but many long-term care services are funded by government only through block grants. These grants, part of the country's extended care program, include nursing home and adult residential care, health components of home care, and ambulatory services. The private sector, both for profit and voluntary, is active in all types of long-term care.

Canada has a substantial population of permanent immigrant long-term care workers, including foreign nurses because Canadian health care workers often emigrate, particularly to the United States.

Sweden

Much of long-term care in Sweden devolves to the municipalities, with support from the central government and the counties. Central government funding comes under the National Insurance Act, which provides partial reimbursement to the counties for medical care under the national health program. The Act also provides partial reimbursement to the municipalities for the organization and delivery of social services. Programs are extensive, with little private sector involvement; 96 percent of all long-term institutional beds are in regional or local public nursing homes or chronic disease hospitals.

Sweden, which along with Japan has the oldest population, supports a unique system of community-based housing and family support centers that delay institutional care. The first line of services to minimize the need for long-term care includes exercise and related companionship programs to promote good health and independence. The programs target the home environment as well as the person. Housing grants and loans, administered by local authorities, provide for renovation and adaptation.

Family members and friends can receive government payments for their work as home helpers. Most communities have access to adult day care centers where aged relatives can spend a day while family caregivers work, and sheltered housing where older people can maintain independence by simplifying their surroundings and receiving the informal help of their peers. Increasingly, day hospital care is provided as a means of delaying residence in institutions. In quest of this goal, as well, all candidates for institutions are screened by multidisciplinary assessment teams.

Sweden recognizes nursing credentials from other countries and allows such workers quite free immigration particularly from Finland and Norway. Sweden continues its emphasis on housing and assistance intended to offer an alternative to home care for a population where most women are in the workforce. The institutionalization of retirement housing and care includes the highest pay for workers with the highest educations, a standard largely absent in other countries. The effect of the recent influx of Iraqi expatriates cannot yet be assessed. In general, little data is available because Sweden considers it unethical to collect data on caregivers.

United Kingdom

In the United Kingdom, extensive programs of community-based care are administered by the social service departments of local authorities. The programs of home care and rehabilitation remain the strongest component of long-term care services despite cutbacks due to chronic national fiscal problems. Medical care, including nursing home care, is the responsibility of the National Health Service, which provides for long-stay units in general hospitals.

Non-medical residential care is provided in large part by private, voluntary organizations and, like the United States government, public-private partnerships are strongly encouraged by favorable laws and partial subsidies. As with Sweden, sheltered housing is considered key to maintaining the aged in the community and local housing authorities and associations are encouraged to offer housing projects and home improvement grants for private dwellings.

Disabled elders and their family care-givers receive government income in order to encourage independent living. In addition, attendant care allowances and transportation allowances are provided to compensate for functional impairments at home and in community activities.

Japan

In the past, Japan's compelling ethic of family care and a powerful medical profession resulted in a fragmented care for the aged population, but the picture is changing. Hospitals, typically owned by physicians, have been the site of nursing home care — a costly and thoroughly unhomelike place for older people with chronic conditions. Most elderly have traditionally relied on the unpaid care of daughters and daughters-in-law, who have been expected to be responsible for the well-being of family members regardless of their loss of career opportunities, or the compatibility of temperaments and lifestyles. Recognizing the shortcomings of private, family solutions, in 2004, Japan instituted a mandatory long-term care insurance program designed to pay for care whether provided in the home or an institution. Government employees determine the form and amount of care provided based upon an assessment of an individual's needs. Faced with a population with over 20 percent age 65 and older and a decline in the total population (due to low birth rates and severe limitations on immigration), Japan faces a shortage of caregivers in the next few years.

Austria and Italy

To fulfill its needs for long-term care workers, Austria encourages an influx of workers from Central and Eastern Europe by readily issuing temporary immigrant status and provides a substantial cash benefits program to pay for care.

In Italy, the traditional emphasis on family care has given way to recognition of women's widespread participation in the workforce. A substantial population of foreign workers constitutes a gray economy; there is no tradition supporting formal immigration and few foreign workers become citizens. Many long-term care workers come from Southeastern Europe and Africa.

QUESTIONS

1.   Why is the growth of long-term care programs and policy incremental rather than fundamental, i.e., the creation of a complete program with one set of clearly defined eligibility guidelines and qualifications for providers?

2.   In a phase-in of long-term care benefits, what components do you think are the highest priority? Do you think aged, disabled people and their families would agree?

3.   Programs in the Scandinavian countries emphasize day-care and congregate housing, and provide financial support for family caregivers. Could these strategies be readily adopted in the United States? If not, what are the cultural differences

and problems of scale which impede their adoption?

C. PAYING FOR LONG-TERM CARE

The present generation of elderly individuals may be the last that did not anticipate the possibility of need for long-term care. Individuals who grew up before the medical advances of the mid-20th century anticipated relatively brief retirements with only the expense of a short final illness. Many, who even now are reaching age 90 or more, have outlived any plans for which they could have anticipated any need. Consequently, most elderly cannot afford to pay for the extended provision of long-term care. They soon exhaust their savings and their income is far below the cost of the needed care. For example, a nursing home can cost $5,000 to $12,000 a month with the average annual cost in 2010 being over $70,000 a year. Even an assisted living facility will cost $3,000 to $6,000 a month.

[1] LONG-TERM CARE INSURANCE IN THE UNITED STATES

The need for long-term care has the characteristics of an insurable event — it is potentially very expensive, difficult to predict for a given individual, and infrequent enough that the risk, when spread over a large group, is affordable. In reality, long-term care insurance pays for less than 10 percent of the cost of such care. For a variety of reasons, long-term care insurance has not found much acceptance.

[a] Availability and Cost

Long-term care insurance is sold by private insurance companies to individuals, though some employers offer it to their employees at group rates. Some groups such as bar associations and the AARP sell long-term care insurance to their members. As with other forms of insurance, long-term care policies are governed by state insurance laws that vary in what they require. Even within a state, different companies offer policies that offer different benefits with different limitations and, of course, with different premiums. The result is that it is often difficult for a potential purchaser to compare polices.

Long-term care insurance companies insist that the insured take a physical as a condition of purchasing a policy. Companies will not insure those who are too physically sick or demented. As a result, as many as 20 percent or more who attempt to buy it are turned down with rejection percentages rising with age. Insurance companies also may not insure against a preexisting condition or at least will not pay benefits arising because of a preexisting condition until the passage of six months after the purchase of the policy.

Policies are sold to individuals and to couples. The cost of a joint policy for a couple is considerably less than two separate policies. Each spouse has an independent right to benefits, though the policy may impose a single limit on the total number of days of coverage. A few employers offer long-term care policies to their employees. Sometimes the employer subsidizes the cost of the premiums.

The average annual premium for a long-term care policy for a 65-year-old ranged from $1,500 to $3,000 per year in 2010, but premiums on policies vary a great deal even when the benefits are relatively similar. The variance reflects in part the difficulty for insurance companies to properly price the product because of the uncertain variables. For example, many who buy long-term insurance allow the policy to lapse. From the standpoint of the insurance company, a lapsed policy means that it will collect premiums but not have to pay benefits. Yet a lapsed policy also means fewer premiums collected by the insurance company, and since many policies will never pay benefits, a lapsed policy may work to the disadvantage of the company. Even more problematic is how many policy holders will eventually qualify for benefits, how soon they will qualify, and for how long must they be paid benefits. The actuarial risk presented by benefit payments is so uncertain that many companies who once sold long-term care insurance no longer do so.

Once sold, the premiums on a policy do not rise over time. If the initial annual premium is, for example, $3,000 a year, the insured will pay that amount until the policy lapses, the insured qualifies for benefits (policies usually waive premiums while benefits are being paid), or until the policy owner dies. The fixed rate of the premium is an essential selling point. Of course, the initial premium rises with the age of the insured. The same policy bought when the insured was age 60 would cost considerably more if it was purchased at age 70. The one exception to the fixed premium rule is if the insurance company is permitted by the state to raise premiums for an entire class of insurance. For example, the insurance company might request that it be allowed to raise the premiums on all of its long-term care policies by 10 percent. The state might approve the rate increase if the company can demonstrate that it is losing money on its policies because the premiums are not sufficient to pay the benefits. Over the years, most long-term insurance premiums have been raised.

[b] Benefits

Like all insurance, the terms and benefits of the policy are governed by the contract. Typically the policy will pay benefits to the insured for the cost of long-term care as defined in the policy, assuming certain triggering conditions are met. Today, almost all policies pay benefits for long-term care based on the condition of the insured without regard to where the benefits are provided. For example, a policy will pay benefits if the insured resides in an assisted living facility or a nursing home. Many policies pay benefits even if the insured lives at home so long as the insured is paying a third party to provide care.

Policies pay for skilled nursing care as well as for custodial care, which is defined as providing assistance with the activities of daily living (ADLs). The policy will typically require that the insured be unable to perform at least two ADLs. Most policies define activities of daily living as eating, bathing, dressing, toileting, mobility (getting about by foot or with an assistive device such as a wheelchair), and transferring (the ability to get out a bed or wheelchair without assistance). Policies also pay benefits if the insured has a cognitive deficit that mandates assistance, such as dementia, or require a physician certify that long-term care is medically necessary.

Policies usually require a physician's certification that the insured qualifies for benefits. Often the policy will require that the insured be examined by the insurance company's physician. Before the policy will pay for institutionalized care, the insured will have to prove that he or she resides in a facility that meets the policy definition of an "institution" and is receiving the level and kind of care required by the policy. If the policy pays for home health care, it may require that the care be provided by a licensed home health care provider. Policies pay a fixed per diem dollar benefit not to exceed the actual daily cost. For example, the policy might pay $150 per day although the actual cost to the insured is $210 per day. If the cost of care is less than the daily limit, the policy will only pay the daily limit. If the insured resides in an assisted living facility that charges $125 a day and the policy limit is $150 a day, the policy will pay only $125 a day. The daily payment benefit for home health care is often one-half the amount paid for institutionalized care. Because a policy may be in effect for years before the insured qualifies for benefits, it is common to pay a higher premium and purchase a policy that offers inflation protection by an annual fixed percentage increase in the amount of the daily benefit. Unfortunately, even an annual increase of five percent per year is unlikely to keep pace with actual annual increase in the cost of long-term care, particularly if provided in a nursing home.

Not only do policies have a daily benefit limit, but many also limit the number of days for which benefits will be paid. Policies are available that pay for an indefinite period, but their cost is naturally higher. More commonly, policies limit benefits to two, three, or five years, with a corresponding increase in the premium as the number of years increases. A policy that pays benefits for both home health care and institutionalized care may have separate daily limits for each kind of care or it may pay for set number of days regardless of whether the benefits are paid for home or institutionalized care. One well-known insurer covers twice as many days of home care as nursing home care, reflecting the relative lower cost of home care. Conversely, some policies cover only a very limited number of days of home health care.

Policies often require the beneficiary to pay for some care before the policy benefits begin. This is sometimes called the elimination or waiting period. During this time, the beneficiary must receive and pay for care of the type covered by the policy. This waiting period functions like a deductible. The longer the waiting period, the less chance there is that the beneficiary will collect benefits; consequently, the premiums are lower for longer waiting periods. Most policies offer several options, and the length of the waiting period may be capped by state law.

Waiting periods are often for 30, 60, or 90 days, but longer periods, such as six months, may be available. For some policies the waiting period need not be consecutive so long as all days occur in what is called an "accumulation period." For example, suppose the policy has an accumulation period of three years and a 60-day waiting period. The insured enters a nursing home for 40 days in 2009 and for 20 days in 2010. The waiting period has been met because the 60 days occurred in the accumulation period. Other policies have an accumulation period that restarts each time that the insured leaves the nursing home or assisted living facility.

[c] Why Many Do Not Purchase Long-Term Care Insurance

Consumer resistance to long-term care insurance arises from a number of factors. Many are in denial, preferring to ignore the potential cost of future care.

Professor Richard L. Kaplan observes in *Financing Long-Term Care in the United States: Who Should Pay for Mom and Dad?* (reprinted from AGING: CARING FOR OUR ELDERS (David N. Weisstub et al. eds., 2001)):

> . . . [L]ong term care insurance is widely regarded as a "bad investment." Better to keep the money and pray that one never needs long-term care. The extent of this denial is the key to the entire long-term financing dilemma. No one wants to imagine himself or herself as disabled and requiring full-time assistance with the basic activities of daily living. It is simply too painful. To be sure, most people do not enjoy imagining themselves dead either, but life insurance is seen as a different sort of purchase. . . . Death, of course, is a verity; it happens to everyone. Thus, the imperative to plan is obvious. Long-term care does *not* happen to everyone; hence, the imperative to plan is much, much weaker. (*Id.* at 74–75.)

The cost of the annual premium discourages many. Paying thousands of dollars per year for as long as you live and perhaps never be paid any benefits seems like a bad bargain to many. The premiums are lower the younger that the insured buys the policy, but the younger the individual, the less apparent is the need for the insurance. For example, some advocate the purchase of a policy at age 55 or 60 when the premiums are lower and the likelihood of the individual being insurable are higher. Yet the average 55-year-old is not thinking about the possible cost of long-term care that likely will not arise for 25 or 30 years. Instead, a 55-year-old is worried about how to save enough to finance a comfortable retirement. Increasing their savings for retirement seems much more compelling than buying long-term care insurance.

The more wealthy elderly do not need long-term care insurance. Someone with $4 million of savings can finance years of long-term care. Even at an annual cost of $100,000, the individual has enough assets to pay for more years of care than could ever be needed. Even an individual with $1 million of savings can pay for 8 to 10 years or more of care. In contrast, individuals with only $100,000 in savings and a modest income may not see much value in buying long-term care insurance. They know that if they exhaust their savings, the government, through Medicaid, will pay for their care.

[d] Why Some Do Buy Long-Term Care Insurance

Many purchase long-term care to protect the value of their estate. For example, individuals with $300,000 to $500,000 of savings can pay for several years of long-term care. If they reside in an assisted living facility, they can afford at least 6 years of care and likely 10 or more years. Still, these individuals may purchase insurance because they fear that paying for long-term could greatly reduce the value of their estates. The desire of many elderly to leave a financial legacy is very prevalent. For example, Ann, who has assets worth $400,000, wants to bequeath at least $150,000 to each of her two adult children. Or Bob with $300,000 wants at his death to fund a trust for his physically disabled granddaughter. As a result, both may consider buying long-term care insurance.

Protection of a spouse is often the reason that couples purchase joint long-term care policies. They fear that if one of them needs long-term care, the cost of that care will significantly diminish the income and savings available to the other spouse and so lower the quality of life. For example, Ruth and Rich, both retired, have combined pension and Social Security income of $70,000 and joint savings of $400,000 that produces additional annual income of $20,000 so that their total income is $90,000. They fear that if one of them, perhaps Rich, needs long-term care at the level that requires residence in a nursing home, the annual estimated cost of $80,000 a year would leave the other, Ruth, with only $20,000 a year income with the result that she would have to spend part of their savings. As she spends the savings, it will produce less income, requiring her to accelerate the drawdown of savings. In order to preclude this, the couple buys long-term care insurance that pays a daily benefit of $175 or $63,875 a year. If the actual cost of care is $80,000 or even $90,000 a year, they will be able to make up the difference from their income without undue financial hardship on the noninstitutionalized spouse.

Some buy long-term care insurance because they fear that Medicaid payment for care may not exist by the time they need it. While that is not likely, it may transpire that Medicaid will pay for less appropriate care or may require even greater financial sacrifice by the individual before it will pay. And some buy insurance in order that they will be able to pay for better care than that provided by Medicaid or that they could afford without insurance. For example, Medicaid will only pay for a shared room in a nursing home. The cost of an individual room is higher but to many, it is worth it. To assure that they can pay the cost of an individual room for as long as they need such care, some are willing to purchase long-term care insurance.

[e] The CLASS Act

The desirability of long-term insurance was endorsed by the adoption of the CLASS Act. The Patient Protection and Affordable Care Act of 2010 established a national voluntary insurance program known as the Community Living Assistance Services and Supports program: the CLASS Act. The Act is designed to expand options for individuals who become functionally disabled and require long-term care. The program became effective on January 1, 2011, though enrollment will not begin until the Secretary of Health and Human Service issues regulations that are due by October 2012.

The Act will permit working adults to make voluntary premium payments either by payroll deductions or by direct payments. Younger enrollees will pay lower premiums than older enrollees. The CLASS Act is not designed for elderly per se as eligibility for benefits begins if the participant has paid monthly premiums for five years and was employed for three of those five years. The cash benefits, which will be at least $50 per day, can be used to purchase care whether provided in the community or in an institution. The program is required to be actuarially sound so that the amount of the monthly premium must be sufficient to pay the anticipated future benefits, the amount of which in turn will depend on the total accumulated premium payments that will be held in a trust fund. No tax dollars may be used to support the program.

[2] TAX TREATMENT OF LONG-TERM CARE INSURANCE

The Health Insurance Portability and Accountability Act of 1996 (HIPAA) clarified the deductibility of long-term care (LTC) expenses. Payments to nursing homes and continuing care retirement communities had been deductible as health expenses, but the tax code had not kept up with the variety of ways to fund and provide LTC services. HIPAA provided uniform standards for deduction of the cost of long-term services whether provided in the home or in a facility. The cost of long-term care is deductible if the services provided are "necessary diagnostic, preventive, therapeutic, curing, treating, mitigating and rehabilitative services, and maintenance or personal care services." The services must be provided according to a plan of care by a licensed health practitioner. To qualify for the deduction, the insurance policy must meet the statutory definition of a "qualified" policy. *See* I.R.C. § 7702B(b).

To be qualified, the policy must provide benefits for specified long-term care services and meet consumer protection requirements set by the Act. Specifically, services must be those provided to a person certified to be chronically ill by a physician, professional nurse, or social worker, because the person is unable to perform at least two of six basic activities of daily living (ADLs) or can perform them only with substantial assistance from another. The ADLs include eating, toileting, transferring (e.g., from bed to chair), bathing, dressing, or continence. (The policy must take into account at least five of the six ADLs.) The coverage cannot include payments for expenses that would be reimbursed by Medicare. The policy is also required to include a variety of consumer protection provisions.

Long-term costs are deductible as a medical expenditure under Internal Revenue Code Section 213, which permits deductions for the cost of medical care to the extent that they exceed 7.5 percent of adjusted gross income. The taxpayer must elect to itemize deductions, rather than claiming the standard deduction. Premiums for a qualified long-term care insurance policy are also deductible as medical expenses up to a limit based on the age of the insured. The limits are adjusted annually. In 2010, the deduction ranged from $340 for someone age 40 or younger, to $4,240 for taxpayers age 70 or older.

Up to a dollar limit that is adjusted annually for inflation, benefits paid under a long-term policy are excluded from income. In 2010, benefits were not taxed up to a daily benefit of $290. Benefit amounts above the limit are excluded to the extent they do not exceed the actual cost of care. If the individual's employer pays for long-term care insurance, the insurance benefits are nontaxable fringe benefits up to certain limits based on the age of the taxpayer.

The National Association of Insurance Commissioners (NAIC) has adopted a model long-term care act (as a proposal for legislation and a guide to the states). Nearly all of the states have adopted some provisions of the NAIC model. The NAIC recommends, in part, that the states should:

    1. Prohibit insurers from requiring that policyholders receive a higher level of care before becoming eligible for lower levels of nursing home care, unless policies are offered without such provisions;

    2. Require coverage for Alzheimer's disease;

    3. Prohibit insurers from offering coverage for only skilled care, or substantially more coverage for skilled care than for lower levels of care; and

    4. Require that individual policies be guaranteed renewable or noncancellable.

QUESTION

Your client brings you three long-term care policies and asks you which one is the best. What would you look at in each policy? What information about your clients, the policies, or the insurance company would you want to know?

[3] LONG-TERM CARE INSURANCE PARTNERSHIP PROGRAM

Since 2006, states have been eligible to participate in the federal Long-Term Care Insurance Partnership program, which permits individuals who purchase state-certified long-term care insurance to obtain eligibility for Medicaid payment for their long-term care even though they own significant assets. For every benefit dollar paid by the long-term care insurance policy, the individual can retain one dollar of assets and still qualify for Medicaid.

To qualify for the program, the policy must meet the requirements to be "tax qualified" (see above) under Internal Revenue Code Section 7702B(b) and contain various consumer protection clauses including guaranteed renewability, avoidance of unintentional lapse, no requirement of prior hospitalization to qualify for benefits, and mandatory disclosure of a variety of policy conditions. The policies must contain inflation protection (an increase in the daily benefit) if the policy buyer is under age 76 when the policy is acquired including compound annual inflation protection if the insured is under age 61. Because partnership policies are portable among the states that participate in the program (most do), policies that qualify for the program in one state must be recognized as qualifying in another state should the policy owner move.

[4] OTHER INSURANCE OPTIONS

The life insurance industry markets policies and plans to convert the value of whole life insurance into funds available for long-term care. The basic model is a variation on whole life insurance, which acts as a savings vehicle as well as providing a payment on death. Policies that pay during life are called "accelerated benefits" or "life benefits." The option sometimes can be added by purchasing a rider for a standard life insurance policy. Such riders vary greatly in cost, often calling for 5 to 15 percent higher premiums. Some insurance issuers allow conversion of term life policies into lifetime payments.

There are two basic types of accelerated benefits policies, the so-called "lump sum distribution" type, and the "long-term care" type. With lump sum distribution the policyholder receives some percentage of the death benefit associated with the policy once he or she has met some qualifying condition. The amount might be 25 percent or more of the value of the policy. The most commonly included qualifying condition in these accelerated benefits policies is the "dread diseases" trigger. A policyholder who is diagnosed as suffering from one or more of the diseases specified in the policy will receive a lump sum distribution. The specified dread diseases usually include heart attack, stroke, cancer, and renal failure. Other diseases less frequently specified include Alzheimer's disease, blindness, organ transplants, surgery performed as a result of coronary artery disease, and Parkinson's disease. Lump sum policies may also pay the benefit if the policyholder has a diagnosis of imminent death or terminal illness. Most imminent death policies require that a physician state that death is likely to occur within a specified number of months, with one year being a fairly common limit.

Long-term care-type life insurance riders require the insurer to pay a fixed monthly sum for the expenses of a policyholder requiring nursing home or other assistance identified in the policy. Most long-term care accelerated benefits policies cover care in a skilled nursing facility. A growing number will pay if the insured requires assisted living.

A life insurance policy can be converted to long-term care funding by selling it, i.e., converting all of its value to a lender who provides income to the policyholder. The proceeds are called a viatical settlement, from the noun viaticum — provisions for a journey.

A policy suitable for conversion to a viatical settlement should have been owned for at least two years, and have a reasonably large face value. In addition, all viatical settlement companies have minimum requirements for considering offers for sale of a policy and concluding agreements. The insurance company that issued the policy must be a quality carrier with a good death claims-paying record. Applicants must release all medical records for review, and in some cases provide access to their physicians for the firms' medical consultants. Applicants must not only "irrevocably" (if allowed by the policy or state law) name the firm beneficiary — they must transfer full policy ownership to the viatical settlement firm. Finally, both written releases and consents to the transaction must be obtained from formerly named beneficiaries and potential beneficiaries, including natural heirs, and any other interested parties.

The viatical company estimates of life expectancy, based on the insured's medical records. Some firms may require the insured to engage in counseling, since the nature of the exchange involves a gamble on the person's death earlier rather than later. The sale process generally takes several months.

The tax treatment of such payouts varies according to the type of policy and terms of the policy. Qualified viatical settlement payments are excluded from taxable income if the beneficiary has a life expectancy of less than two years. Factual determination lies with the governing agencies, however, so viatical companies must file the appropriate forms to report their payments. State departments of insurance provide oversight to help insure that the company who bought the policy will be able to meet its financial commitment.

A number of companies offer calculators on the Internet to allow policy holders to estimate the amounts their policies might pay upon conversion to viatical payments.

D. MEDICAID

Medicaid is the federal health care program for the poor. Jointly financed by the federal and state governments, it is administered by the states in accord with federal guidelines. (In some states Medicaid is known as Medical Assistance (MA). In California it is called "MediCal.") Medicaid pays for the medical expenses of eligible poor persons who are elderly (age 65 and older), blind, or disabled. Around 15 percent of elderly people living in the community are eligible for Medicaid. Others become eligible for Medicaid by incurring very high health care expenses, particularly long-term care in nursing homes.

[1] FEDERAL AND STATE ADMINISTRATION AND FINANCE

The observation that there are 50 Medicaid programs, one for each state, is a fair caveat. In each state, an agency, which might be called by any of a wide variety of names, is responsible for administering the plan statewide. The state, through that agency, must submit to the federal administrative agency, the Centers for Medicare and Medicaid Services (CMS), a multi-year plan containing the state's rules for eligibility (which cannot be more restrictive than the federal requirements), the services to be provided, and fees to be paid to providers.

The federal government and the states share the cost of Medicaid services by means of a variable matching formula that is adjusted annually. The matching rate for federal to state funds ranges from 50 percent to 80 percent, calculated using a formula based on the state's per capita income. For example, a state with a very low per capita income might receive nearly 70 percent federal funding for benefits delivered under its approved Medicaid plan, to match its slightly more than 30 percent contribution of state revenues. The statutory matching formula, called the Federal Medical Assistance Percentage (FMAP), provides that a state with a per capita income around the national average would receive a federal share of 55 percent.

The federal government from time to time offers different match rates to encourage or discourage initiatives by the states. For example, the federal match rate for administrative costs is typically 50 percent or less regardless of the medical assistance share in order to encourage states to minimize their costs. Match rates up to 90 percent have been offered as incentives for the states to undertake such changes as extensive computerization of records. The rates of federal matching have been cut when states decline to undertake recommended quality assurance programs.

QUESTIONS

1. Why should Medicaid be partly financed by the states?

2. Why should it be administered by states?

3. Why should the federal government set the eligibility requirements? Why should states be permitted to create more liberal eligibility requirements?

[2] BENEFITS

All states and territories of the United States provide Medicaid benefits or a substitute benefit package approved by the federal government. Who is eligible for benefits varies, however, because each state designs and administers its own Medicaid program within the federal guidelines. Some states use the federal eligibility standards, others open the program to more individuals through more liberal eligibility requirements. Interpretation of the federal Medicaid statute, which is quite complex, also varies from state to state with the result that someone who might be eligible in one state might not be eligible in another.

While eligibility requirements vary, all states must offer basic benefits. In order to receive federal Medicaid funding, the state must provide, inter alia: skilled nursing facility (SNF) care and home health care for persons eligible for SNF services.

In the past, states could apply for waiver of federal Medicaid requirements in order to use federal Medicaid funds to provide long-term care assistance in the home or community, that is, in settings other than nursing homes. In 2010, the Patient Protection and Affordable Care Act attempted to expand the use of home and community care by replacing the waiver program with a general rule that permits a state plan to provide such care for individuals with income up to 300 percent of Supplemental Security Income (SSI) maximum benefit. In 2011, the monthly maximum SSI was $674, meaning that an elderly individual with monthly income of less than $2022 was eligible for Medicaid paid home- and community-based, long-term care services. These services may include case management, homemaker/home health aide and personal care services, adult day health care, respite care, and other similar forms of assistance. The cost of services provided to an individual must not exceed the anticipated total cost of Medicaid institutional care to that individual. The waiver program total includes the cost of physician visits, hospitalization, prescription drugs, and any other costs that might have been covered or reduced by institutionalization. The Act also creates financial incentives for states to reduce the proportion of those in nursing homes. Whether the percentage of elderly in nursing homes or the actual number will decline due to the Act remains to be seen.

Medicaid does not pay the market rate when it reimburses nursing home care. Rather, the state establishes what daily rate it will pay to each nursing home with rates typically varying across the state in recognition of different labor and other costs. For example, if a nursing home charges a private pay patient $250 a day, Medicaid might pay that nursing home $220 a day. While nursing homes would much prefer to have only higher paying private pay residents, the reality is that there are not enough private pay residents to fill the nursing homes. The great majority of nursing home residents either cannot afford the daily rate on the day they enter or else they soon exhaust their savings and their income is not enough to pay the daily rate. They therefore qualify for Medicaid, which supports them in the nursing home but at the lower daily Medicaid rate.

The nursing home industry complains that the Medicaid rate is often too low — below the actual daily care cost. As a result, a nursing home must have a proper mix of higher paying private pay residents and lower paying Medicaid residents in order to be financially viable. Absent a state law to the contrary, a nursing home may give preference in admission to private pay residents. Nursing homes routinely review financial information about prospective residents and some exclude those who will soon become Medicaid eligible.

[3] CATEGORICALLY NEEDY AND OPTIONAL CATEGORICALLY NEEDY ELIGIBILITY

Medicaid is a need-based program, whose eligibility requirements require applicants to have both low incomes and very few assets.

Those age 65 or older are eligible for Medicaid if they would be eligible for the federal Supplemental Security Program (SSI). Even the receipt of $1 per month of SSI is enough to create eligibility for Medicaid. (Thirteen states, Connecticut, Hawaii, Illinois, Indiana, Minnesota, Missouri, Nebraska, New Hampshire, North Dakota, Ohio, Oklahoma, Utah, and Virginia, do not use the SSI eligibility test. Known as Section 209(b) states, their eligibility standards are stricter than those for SSI.)

Other elderly qualify for Medicaid under the "categorically needy" eligibility standard, which states have the option of adopting. Those termed "categorically needy" are individuals who fit into a dozen or more categories, including those with income low enough to qualify for SSI but not receiving it, individuals who but for receiving state income supplements would be eligible for SSI, and institutionalized individuals who but for being institutionalized would be eligible for SSI.

[4] MEDICALLY NEEDY

Most elderly who receive Medicaid assistance that pays for the cost of their long-term care do so because they are "medically needy"; individuals with income that exceeds the SSI test but whose medical bills, including the cost of a nursing home, exceed their income.

States may elect to permit medically needy individuals to qualify for Medicaid. To qualify as medically needy, individuals must meet the SSI resource test, have income insufficient to pay for their medical care, and meet the other basic Medicaid requirements, e.g., be age 65 or older. Income is calculated in the same manner as under the SSI program. The extraordinary cost of long-term care is the usual source of medically needy eligibility. It is estimated that over 90 percent of medically needy eligible persons live in nursing homes. For example, Sam, age 77, requires long-term care and so moves into a nursing home. He has no savings and monthly income of $2,000. His nursing home charges him $6,000 a month. Sam is medically needy and so eligible for Medicaid reimbursement of the cost of his nursing home.

[a]   Income Eligibility

In determining income eligibility for a medically needy individual, states have the option to use either the "spend-down" or "income cap" tests.

[i]   Income Spend-Down Test

In states that elect the spend-down test, nursing home residents whose income exceeds the SSI eligibility limit become eligible for Medicaid by spending down all of their income, less a retained personal needs allowance of at least $30 a month. At that point, assuming they meet the resource eligibility standards, they are eligible for Medicaid. For example, Tess has no assets and monthly income of $1,240. Her state permits her to retain a personal needs allowance of $40. Tess must pay the nursing home all of her remaining income — $1,200. Medicaid will pay the remaining cost of her care, but only at the Medicaid rate. If the Medicaid rate is $5,700 a month, Medicaid will pay an additional $4,500 a month to the nursing home. The amount of an individual's income does not matter so long as it is less than their cost of care. For example, Reuben has no assets but monthly income of $5,000, but his nursing home costs $6,300 a month. In a spend-down state, Reuben would be Medicaid eligible.

Section 209(b) states must use income spend down to calculate eligibility.

[ii]   Income Cap Test

Many states do not use the spend-down test. Instead, they use the more restrictive income cap test to determine Medicaid eligibility. In income cap states, medically needy eligibility requires that the individual's income not exceed 300 percent, of the SSI monthly benefit for a single person. The SSI benefit for an individual in 2011 (adjusted annually for inflation) was $674 per month. The income cap in 2011 was therefore $2,022 a month. The cap is the same for individuals or couples. No spend-down is allowed and an individual or couple is ineligible even if their income is only $1 above the cap. In income cap states, many individuals who need nursing home care have income that exceeds the income cap limit, but who cannot afford the cost of a nursing home.

Congress addressed this problem by permitting individuals to create a qualified income trust that allows "an individual to direct excess income into a trust" (sometimes referred to as Miller trusts). 42 U.S.C. § 1396p(d)(4)(B). For example, if the individual receives $3,000 per month income, the amount in excess of 300 percent of SSI is directed to the trust where it is held until the death of the individual, at which time, the trust must use the funds in the trust to reimburse the state for all Medicaid payments made on behalf of the individual. Usually, the trust will have fewer dollars than the amount of Medicaid payments, but after paying off Medicaid, any remaining funds will be distributed according to the directions in the trust document.

[iii]   Countable and Available Income

The determination of an individual's income is usually a fairly straightforward process (unlike determining the total resources, which is described below). Income includes anything received in cash or in kind which can be used to meet needs for food or shelter. (A list of things that are or are not income is found at 42 C.F.R. § 435.811.) In the case of a married couple, only the income of the institutionalized spouse is considered to be available to pay for his or her care. The income of the other spouse, known as the community spouse, may be retained by that spouse. For example, Mae resides in a nursing home. She has Social Security income of $1,300 a month. To become eligible for Medicaid she must spend all her income less a personal needs allowance for her care. She is married to Mel who has pension income of $3,000 a month. Mel does not have to spend any of his income on Mae's care.

Only income that is legally owned by the prospective beneficiary and available for use or reachable by reasonable efforts is considered countable income. 42 U.S.C. § 1396a(a)(17).

MULDER v. SOUTH DAKOTA DEPARTMENT OF SOCIAL SERVICES
675 N.W.2d 212 (S.D. 2003)

The Department of Social Services (DSS) issued a final decision upholding its calculation of Ervin Mulder's "available" income for determining his long-term care benefits under Medicaid. The circuit court affirmed and Mulder appeals, arguing that his available income should not include the amount he pays for alimony and that the determination is an arbitrary and capricious interpretation of Medicaid. We reverse.

FACTS

Mulder entered a long-term care facility in August 2001. He applied to DSS for long-term care assistance through Medicaid. Mulder's monthly income is the $701.00 he receives in Social Security benefits. From the $701.00, $50.00 is automatically withheld by Social Security to pay his Medicare premium. Thereafter, $651.00 is direct-deposited into his account each month. Apparently, the Department reimburses Mulder for the $50 taken out to pay his premium. Pursuant to a 1995 final judgment and decree of divorce, $180.00 is simultaneously withdrawn from his account and electronically transferred to his ex-wife's account. Mulder is entitled to a deduction from his counted income of $30 per month to cover his personal needs. This leaves Mulder with $521 actually available to him each month. Taking his allowed deduction of $30 into account, Mulder has $491 actually available to him to pay to his long-term care provider. In December 2001,

DSS informed Mulder that he was eligible for assistance in the amount of $322.00 per month. This amount left Mulder responsible for paying his care facility $671.00 per month; $150 more per month than Mulder actually has available to him.

Mulder's son and daughter testified that their parents agreed that their mother would receive $180.00 per month out of his Social Security income when they divorced because their mother had qualified for less Social Security income. Mulder and his ex-wife considered the payments to be part of the marital property division. However, the amount was denominated "alimony" in the divorce decree.

The Medicaid long-term care program requires that the recipient use all of his or her "available income" to pay toward their care. The Medicaid program then covers whatever the recipient cannot pay. In determining how much a recipient must contribute, DSS considers the amount deducted or paid for alimony to be "available income." Therefore, taking all of the deductions into account, Mulder was found responsible for $671.00 per month. Because this amount is more than Mulder actually has available to him every month, his daughter, acting on his behalf, requested a fair hearing. DSS upheld its initial determination of income and Mulder appealed to the circuit court. The circuit court affirmed DSS and Mulder appeals:

It is undisputed that Mulder is eligible to receive Medicaid long-term care benefits. The only question in this case is how much Mulder is entitled to receive. The relevant portions of the federal Medicaid statute provide in part that a state plan for medical assistance must: "include reasonable standards [ ] for determining eligibility for and the extent of medical assistance under this plan which [ ] provide for taking into account only such income and resources as are [ ] available to the applicant or recipient[.]" The provisions also require that the State "provide for reasonable evaluation of any such income or resources[.]"

Since neither our state statutes nor the Department's Medicaid regulations define "available income" and since alimony is not specifically excluded from income in the regulations, the Department relied on ARSD 67:46:03:24 and turned to the federal statute and regulations to determine whether alimony was includable as income for purposes of determining the extent of benefits. ARSD 67:46:03:24 provides:

In the absence of specific regulations on income and resource requirements for long-term care assistance not otherwise defined in chapters 67:16:01 to 67:16:16, inclusive, eligibility decisions shall be based on the SSI requirements in 42 U.S.C. §§ 1382 to 1383[.]

The federal regulations indicate that alimony is considered income available to the payer under the federal SSI statute in determining eligibility. Relying on ARSD 67:46:03:24, the Department used the federal Medicaid regulations as a basis to deny benefits. However, the Department misreads ARSD 67:46:03:24. First, the regulation refers specifically to the eligibility determination and does not refer to the benefit determination. Second, the regulation is labeled, "Absence of Regulations Regarding Conditions of *Eligibility*." (Emphasis supplied.) Finally, this rule is placed under the chapter of the rules entitled, "Long-term care *Eligibility*." (Emphasis supplied.) Despite the plain language of this regulation, the

Department argues that the same determinations made for purposes of eligibility also apply in determining benefits. The regulations taken as a whole make a clear distinction between these two determinations.

. . . .

To the extent the Department insists it must use the same calculations to determine benefits as it does to determine eligibility, its interpretation is unreasonable and cannot be upheld. The Department is bound by its own rules and the State Legislature's implementing statutes for determination of recipient's benefits. Therefore, the Department acted arbitrarily and capriciously in referring to the federal statutes and regulations for its determination of the extent of Mulder's benefits.

. . . .

The federal Medicaid statute requires that the state plans take into account only "available income" and that the state provide for "reasonable evaluation of any such income[.]" 42 USCA § 1396a(a)(17) (B) and (C). . . .

These statutes and administrative rules clearly indicate that Mulder was entitled to a *reasonable* evaluation of his income. The Department is required to provide benefits to the extent Mulder cannot afford to pay. Mulder will never be able to pay the alimony and pay his share of his medical expenses. Therefore, the Department's determination that Mulder's alimony payments constitute "available income" was not reasonable.

Evidence of the unreasonableness of the Department's determination is found in the Department's own arguments. The Department points out that SSI payments are unearned income "at the earliest point when they are received or credited to the applicant's account." The Department therefore concludes that his available income is the $701 which is deposited by the SSA. The Department then reasons that since "alimony is not taken out before it is deposited into his account" it must be included in his available income. In other words, if Mulder could arrange it so that the alimony is taken out of his social security check before it hits his account, according to the Department, it would not be considered income. This distinction ignores that under either scenario, the money belongs to his ex-wife and is in no way available to him for the payment of his own support.

The results of the Department's interpretation of the statute through these rules are inconsistent with common sense and reasonable evaluation of Mulder's available income. Further, they fail to give due deference to the judgment and decree of divorce and the right of Mulder's ex-wife to effective judicial review before modification of her alimony award.

We cannot accept the Department's determination that the $180 per month Mulder pays in alimony is "available" to him. The result of the Department's decision is to make Medicaid unavailable to Mulder despite the fact that he is eligible for benefits under the program. Obviously, his long-term care facility cannot continue to room, board and care for him if it is not receiving full payment. The Department is bound by its own regulation requiring it to pay the long-term care facility for "amounts not covered by an individual's own income." Regardless of how the Department defines "income," it has failed to pay the facility for amounts not covered by Mulder.

The benefits the Department purports to grant Mulder are of little value to him if he cannot pay his share of the cost of care. By taking away with one hand what it professes to give him with the other, the Department falls short of the statutory mandate that it "provide for reasonable evaluation of [Mulder's] income." This case is distinguishable from those wherein couples attempted to protect themselves from falling into one of the "Medicaid Gaps" by divorcing and giving the vast majority of the assets to the non-institutionalized spouse. Therefore, the Department's concern for protecting Medicaid funds is less persuasive. The Department can protect Medicaid resources from those who attempt to improperly divert assets which could be used to pay for their care and still reasonably evaluate available income.

We reverse.

[b] Resource Eligibility

Medicaid recipients must have very limited resources under federal law, $2,000 for an individual and $3,000 for a couple (some states use higher dollar limits), aside from exempt items noted below. In the case of a married couple, all assets of the couple are deemed to be available for the care of the institutionalized spouse regardless of how the assets are titled. In recognition, however, of the need for the community spouse (the spouse not receiving Medicaid) to keep some of the couple's assets in order to avoid impoverishment, the Medicaid statute permits the community spouse to retain assets up to a certain value. Known as the Community Resource Allowance, it is discussed below in [5] Spousal Protection.

A state can count as resources only those assets the applicant legally owns and that can be converted to be spent for care. Before applicants can claim the resource is unsalable or unreachable, they must make reasonable efforts to sell it. If the resource is counted, its value is the fair market value. Assets most difficult to value or make liquid include limited interests such as joint ownerships.

BREWER v. SHALANSKY et al., and HELLEBUYCK et al.
102 P.3d 1145 (Kan. 2004), *cert. denied*, 125 S. Ct. 2944 (2005)

This is a Medicaid eligibility case in which the Kansas Department of Social and Rehabilitation Services (SRS) denied the application for benefits filed by Joan Seiker Wilson for her aunt, Regina Brewer (petitioner/appellee). SRS found that Brewer had nonexempt available resources in excess of regulatory limits because she held stocks worth approximately $33,000 in joint tenancy with two nieces, Joan Seiker Wilson and Regina Hellebuyck (defendants/ appellees).

Brewer inherited the stocks upon her husband's death in 1991. He had received the stock as a benefit of his employment with Southwestern Bell Telephone Company. In 1994, Brewer added her two nieces, whom she had raised, as joint tenants with rights of survivorship of the stock. In 2001, Brewer sought Merrill Lynch's assistance in tracking shares she received from stock splits and as a result of various spin-offs and mergers of telecommunications companies following the break-up of AT&T. Brewer and her nieces opened an account with Merrill Lynch as joint tenants with rights of survivorship.

At the time of the Medicaid application, the stock could not be sold or otherwise disposed of without the consent of each joint tenant. Both of Brewer's nieces refused to consent to a sale of the stock.

After SRS denied Brewer's application for Medicaid benefits, Brewer requested a fair hearing . . . and argued that the nature of the parties' ownership of the stock precluded Brewer from selling it or converting it to cash; therefore, the stock was unavailable to Brewer as a resource. The hearing officer entered an initial order upholding the denial of benefits and ruling that the stock was an available resource. The hearing officer found that Wilson, who holds Brewer's power of attorney, had not taken reasonable steps to make the stock available, including legal action to force the sale. Brewer timely petitioned for review by the State Appeals Committee, which affirmed the hearing officer's decision.

Brewer then petitioned for judicial review of the agency's action. The district court reversed SRS's decision, ruling that Brewer was not obligated to file a lawsuit seeking partition because the cost of such a lawsuit would likely exceed any benefit Brewer would receive as a result and because such a lawsuit was unlikely to succeed. The district court chose not to address Brewer's additional argument that federal law precludes SRS from considering the stock as an available resource.

SRS timely appealed, and the appeal was transferred to this court on its own motion pursuant to K.S.A. 20-3018(c).

. . . .

Federal regulations define the term "resources," in pertinent part, as

> cash or other liquid assets or any real or personal property that an individual . . . owns and could convert to cash to be used for his support and maintenance. If the individual has the right, authority or power to liquidate the property, or his share of the property, it is considered a resource. 20 C.F.R. § 416.1201.

This definition reflects two critical components: (1) ownership and (2) the power to liquidate. This case focuses upon the second aspect of the definition.

Presumption of Equal Ownership

Brewer argues that even if she retained an interest in the stock, her interest was limited to one-third of its value, or approximately $11,000. ManorCare agrees. SRS contends that Brewer's interest in the stock is its full value of approximately $33,000.

The hearing officer, and later the State Appeals Committee, found that SRS was correct in attributing the full value of the stock to Brewer because her nieces had not contributed to the equity. The administrative decisions were based upon KEESM 5200, which provides: "In situations of joint ownership of resources . . . the full equity value of jointly owned personal property shall (unless otherwise established) be considered in the determination of eligibility." Since the stock had been owned solely by Brewer before she added her nieces as owners, the hearing officer found that Brewer's equity value equaled the full value of the stock holdings, and the Appeals Committee agreed.

However, the district court found that, because joint tenants are presumed to hold property in equal ownership, the value of the stock attributable to Brewer was approximately $11,000. As stated in *Walnut Valley State Bank v. Stovall*, "there is a rebuttable presumption of equal ownership between tenants of joint tenancy property."

Although the hearing officer did not discuss the presumption of equal ownership, SRS argues the presumption of equal ownership is rebutted by any contrary evidence, including evidence that the joint tenants made unequal contributions.

However, the analysis should not focus solely upon equity contribution. . . . [T]he presumption of equal ownership "is created on the theory of donative intent." The court cited a New Jersey case, *Norcross v. 1016 Fifth Avenue Co., Inc.*, 123 N.J. Eq. 94, 196 A. 446 (1938), for its explanation of the theory of donative intent. *Norcross* explained that the opening of a joint tenancy account, with all parties agreeing that the monies deposited are to belong to the parties as joint tenants, constitutes prima facie evidence of donative intent. Under such circumstances, the parties have made a valid gift.

In this case the evidence regarding Brewer's donative intent was conflicting. As suggested by SRS, there was evidence that Brewer placed her nieces' names on the stock account to avoid probate, intended for the funds to be utilized exclusively for her own support during her lifetime, and did not intend for her nieces to access the funds until her death. Also, SRS argues that since the nieces could not sell the stock without Brewer's consent, it can be inferred that Brewer did not intend a complete gift by adding their names to the stock.

On the other hand, there was some evidence that Brewer had placed her nieces' names on the stock as compensation for the support the nieces had provided over the years. Additionally, Brewer's inability to sell the stock without the consent of her nieces can also be argued to support an inference that she gave away her rights of sole ownership.

With this factual background, we must return to the applicable standard of review which is to determine whether the agency erroneously interpreted or applied the law or whether the agency's action is based on a determination of fact that is not supported by substantial evidence when viewed in light of the record as a whole.

The district court, in reviewing the agency's action, did not state the applicable standard of review and apparently substituted its own judgment by finding that the presumption of equal ownership had not been rebutted. The weighing of the evidence against the presumption of equal ownership and a determination of Brewer's donative intent are issues of fact, and the district court could not simply substitute its judgment for that of the agency.

The agency concluded that the full value of the stock was attributable to Brewer because her nieces had not contributed to the equity. Thus, SRS rebutted the presumption of equal ownership by presenting evidence of unequal equity contribution. Further, SRS introduced evidence regarding Brewer's intent when she added her nieces as joint tenants, presenting testimony that Brewer placed the stock in joint tenancy in order to avoid probate and did not intend for her nieces to use the property until Brewer's death. Thus, the agency's conclusion was supported by substantial evidence when viewed in light of the record as a whole.

Partition

Brewer argues that the stock should not be considered an available resource because of impediments to her ability to liquidate the property. The hearing officer and State Appeals Committee recognized that there was a legal impediment preventing disposal of the stock in that Brewers' nieces refused to consent to a sale. However, Wilson, as Brewer's agent pursuant to a power of attorney, has a fiduciary duty to manage her aunt's affairs, including the pursuit of a legal action to force the sale of the stock. Because Brewer, through Wilson, had not taken reasonable steps to overcome the legal impediment, the stock was considered an available resource.

The district court, however, was persuaded that a partition action was unlikely to succeed and that the cost of such an action would likely exceed Brewer's share of the stock, $11,000. Thus, the district court reversed the decision of the State Appeals Committee.

. . . .

SRS does not dispute that there was a legal impediment to liquidation. However, at each hearing level it was determined that Wilson, as Brewer's agent through a power of attorney, could file a partition action.

However, Brewer argues that she has no right to force a partition sale of the stock because she voluntarily agreed to hold the stock in such a manner that no joint tenant could transfer the stock without the consent of the other joint tenants. In support, she cites *Hotchkin v. Hotchkin*, 105 N.J. Super. 475, 253 A.2d 184 (1969), for the premise that ownership of stock in a manner that prevents its sale without unanimous consent of the joint tenants prevents one joint tenant from seeking partition of the stock. [Facts of *Hotchkin* omitted.]

In this case, a representative of Merrill Lynch testified that the stock in question cannot be sold or otherwise disposed of without the consent of each joint tenant. Although the record on appeal does not include a copy of an executed agreement containing such a provision, the fact that such a restriction exists is not in dispute. However, what is not clear is whether the restriction was a matter of contract between the tenants or was unilaterally imposed by Merrill Lynch. If it was simply a Merrill Lynch policy that all three joint tenants consent to a sale or transfer of the stock, rather than an agreement between the joint tenants themselves, this would detract from Brewer's argument that her agreement not to sell the stock without the consent of her nieces could be raised as a defense in a partition action. The cases Brewer cited in her brief all involved some agreement, whether in a divorce settlement agreement or a real estate contract, not to partition. The fact that the stock could not be sold in this case without the consent of all three joint tenants appears less due to any agreement they made and more due to the internal policies of Merrill Lynch.

However, at the very least, Brewer has demonstrated that her nieces would have a possible defense to any partition action. Whether the manner in which the stock is held would amount to an implied waiver of the right to partition would need to be determined and would likely be hotly contested. Thus, a partition action would not necessarily be the simple procedure suggested by SRS.

. . . .

Brewer failed to meet her burden to establish that the cost of the partition action would exhaust her equitable interest in the stock value.

Reversed.

States differ on the availability of jointly held property and may deem it to be 100 percent available to the applicant, subject to equal shares or may rule it be unavailable if it can be shown there was no intent to transfer a beneficial interest.

[i]   Exempt Resources

Some resources are classified as exempt property and are not included as part of the countable resources: the home; household items and personal effects; a car; a burial plot; a burial fund up to $1,500 per person; life insurance policies with face values up to $1,500; and a home and the land pertaining to it (42 C.F.R. §§ 435.831, 435.840, 435.845).

A home consists of the actual dwelling of the applicant or recipient, in which he or she has an ownership interest. A home on a farm includes the farmland. At least theoretically, a single person's house is exempt only as long as the person has the possibility of returning to it. States vary on whether a resident of a nursing home, who does not have a spouse, will be considered to ever return to the house and thus retain it as an exempt asset. Some states count the house as being available, some permit it to be retained for a limited period, such as six months, and others permit it to be considered exempt until the death of the Medicaid recipient. The limit on the value of an excluded home is $500,000 under federal law, with a state option to allow a value up to $750,000.

[ii]   Spend Down and Valuation of Resources

An applicant for Medicaid must list and value all resources as of the first day of institutionalization, known as the snapshot date. An individual who meets the state's income eligibility test, but has too many countable assets to qualify must spend those assets on his or her care until the amount meets the state eligibility requirement. For example, Lucy resides in a nursing home that costs $7,000 a month. She has monthly income of $2,000. She has countable assets worth $62,000. The state resource eligibility limit is $2,000. Lucy will have to spend $60,000 on her nursing home or other medical care before she will be eligible for Medicaid.

The alternative to spending down is to convert excess assets to exempt property. For example, savings can be used to purchase a new car, repair an exempt house, or prepay for a funeral.

[5] SPOUSAL PROTECTION

In recognition of the need to provide adequate income for the community spouse, Medicaid eligibility requirements permit a couple to protect some assets and all the income of the community spouse. When calculating the income of the institutionalized spouse, only his or her income is counted. The community spouse is permitted to retain all of his or her income. This is referred to as the "name on the check" rule. Income is attributed according to which spouse it is payable. If the payment is jointly to both spouses, 50 percent of that income is deemed available to the institutionalized spouse and must be spent on care. All income of the community spouse is protected regardless of the amount or the source of the income. For example, if the community spouse receives Social Security retirement benefits based on the earnings of the institutionalized spouse, that benefit income belongs to the community spouse and does not have to be spent on the care of the institutionalized spouse.

For some couples, even the retention by the community spouse of his or her income will not be sufficient to live on. In response, the statute provides that some of the income of the institutionalized spouse can be diverted to the community spouse. The amount is determined by the application of the Minimum Monthly Maintenance Needs Allowance or MMMNA. The federal Medicaid statute permits the community spouse to demand income from the institutionalized spouse to raise his or her income to the MMMNA, which as of July 1, 2011, was $1,839 per month. (The amount is based on federal poverty guideline that is subject to adjustment for inflation.) For example, a community spouse with income of $1,200, in 2011 has the right to claim $639 from the income of the institutionalized spouse. The community spouse can request an excess shelter allowance, up to the cap of $2,739 in 2011. Some states use the maximum amount for all spouses. The excess shelter allowance is commuted by totaling the community spouse's cost of rent or mortgage payments, taxes, and utilities. To the extent these costs exceed 30 percent of the MMMNA (30% of $1,839 or $552 in 2011), the community spouse has right to additional income up to the cap. To the extent the institutionalized spouse contributes income to the community spouse, the institutionalized spouse pays less of the cost of his or her nursing home care.

A community spouse may also go to court for an order for additional income from the institutionalized spouse in excess of the MMMNA cap. Or the community spouse can request an administrative fair hearing and ask for additional income due to "exceptional circumstances resulting in significant financial distress." 42 U.S.C. § 1396r-5(d)(1)(B).

If diverting all of the institutionalized spouse's income to the community spouse still does not raise his or her income to the MMMNA, assets of the institutionalized spouse will be diverted to the community spouse sufficient in value to create enough income to make up for the shortfall.

Further financial protection is provided for the community spouse by the Community Spouse Resource Allowance (CSRA). (Medicaid uses the term "resources" rather than assets.) Recall that an individual is eligible for Medicaid only if his or her countable resources do not exceed $2,000 (or the state limit) and that all of the countable resources of a couple are considered available for the support of the institutionalized spouse. To avoid leaving the community spouse without any assets, he or she is permitted to retain a CSRA. Under federal law, states have the right to permit the community spouse to retain at least $21,912 (in 2011 — adjusted annually for inflation) up to a maximum of $109,560 (in 2011). A few states permit the community spouse to retain the maximum amount permitted, but most states permit the community spouse to retain the greater of the minimum amount ($21,912 in 2011) or 50 percent of the countable resources up to the maximum amount ($109,560 in 2011).

For example, Ann and Adam are married. Adam enters a nursing home and applies for Medicaid. The couple has total countable resources of $80,000. In most states, Ann would be permitted to retain $40,000. The other $40,000 would have to be spent down to $2,000 before Adam would be Medicaid eligible. Or assume the couple has only $15,000. In that case, Ann would retain the entire $15,000. If they had $250,000 worth of countable resources, Ann's CSRA would be the maximum or $109,560.

The community spouse can also keep the exempt resources such as the home (if the equity value is less than $500,000 or in some states, $750,000) and a car. If the community spouse acquires additional assets after the snapshot valuation of the couple's resources, those assets do not affect the eligibility of the institutionalized spouse or the right of the community spouse to keep the CSRA.

The availability of the CSRA, the right to a MMMNA, and the possibility of converting assets into exempt resources provides opportunity for Medicaid planning. For example, Marco and Mindy are married. Marco, age 80, must enter a nursing home on June 1. Marco has monthly pension income of $3,000 and Social Security monthly retirement benefits of $1,200 or total monthly income of $4,200. Mindy, age 77, receives $600 per month in Social Security based on her status as the spouse of Marco. The couple has $100,000 in savings, a house worth $170,000, and a car worth $5,000. The monthly cost of the nursing home where Marco will reside is $6,500.

On May 20th, the couple paid $25,000 and traded in their old car for a new car for Mindy. They paid a contractor $5,000 to repair the roof of their house and for some other minor home repairs. They also spent $5,000 for new kitchen appliances and cabinets. Marco paid $7,000 for a prepaid funeral. In total, they spent $42,000 from their savings, leaving them with $58,000.

Marco enters the nursing home on June 1. The snapshot of nonexempt assets shows the couple has $58,000. The state allows Mindy to retain 50 percent of their assets or $29,000. She is also eligible for income from Marco to bring her monthly income up to the MMMNA of $1,839. Her income is $600 per month, so she is allowed $1,239 per month out of Marco's income of $4,200, leaving him with $2,961 a month, which he uses to pay for part of his monthly nursing home bill of $6,500. Each month he also pays $3,539 from his savings of $29,000 — the remaining $29,000 is retained by Mindy as her CSRA. In a little over eight months, Marco will have exhausted his savings and, because the state is an income spend-down state, he will be eligible for Medicaid. Mindy, the community spouse, will have monthly income of $1,839 ($22,068 per year), savings of $29,000, a new car, and a house with a new roof and an upgraded kitchen. Although the new car and home repairs cost $35,000, in actuality the cost to Mindy was only half or $17,500, for if she had not spent the $35,000, it would have been applied to the cost of Marco's nursing home care. The prepaid funeral of $7,000 for Marco was an expenditure that would be made in any case and so by incurring it before the Medicaid snapshot, the state in effect paid for half of the cost. If the $7,000 had remained in their savings, Mindy would have an increase in the CSRA of $3,500 but the other $3,500 would have been spent paying for Marco's nursing home care.

[6] TRANSFERS (GIFTS) OF ASSETS

Federal law permits states to deny eligibility to individuals who dispose of their resources for less than fair market value — make a gift — in order to obtain Medicaid benefits. The restriction is intended to prevent individuals facing long-term nursing home care from transferring substantial assets in order to bring their resources below the Medicaid eligibility level.

There is no penalty, however, for transfers between spouses because all of a couple's assets without regard to ownership are considered available for the care of the institutionalized spouse. Exempt assets, such as the home, are not considered available and so couples often transfer ownership of the home to the community spouse. A couple who owns a house jointly, for example, might retitle the house solely in the name of the wife if the husband enters a nursing home and goes on Medicaid. The wife then writes a will leaving her husband the minimum that she can in light of the state's forced share statute. She leaves the house to someone other than her husband, typically the children. If the wife dies before the husband, the house will pass to the children and not have to be sold to pay for the husband's care. However, the house will have a lien on it in the amount of Medicaid paid to the husband.

Upon application for Medicaid, the applicant must disclose any gift made in the prior five years. The length of what is known as the look-back period has been increased over the years as Congress attempts to discourage individuals giving away assets in anticipation of entering a nursing home and applying for Medicaid. The five-year look-back period became effective as of February 8, 2006. Prior to that date, the look-back period was three years. Any gifts made prior to the look-back period need not be disclosed because they do not invoke any period of ineligibility.

A gift can cause a period of ineligibility, the length of which depends on the amount of the gift. The period is determined by dividing the value of the gift by the average state cost of one month's nursing home care. For example, Dana gives $36,000 to her son and then applies for Medicaid. The announced average cost of a nursing home in her state is $6,000 a month. The gift of $36,000 will result in Dana being ineligible for Medicaid for six months. The average state cost is determined by the state and in many states is a number less than the actual average cost of a nursing home, although states do periodically adjust the average cost to reflect the rise in nursing home costs.

If a gift was made after February 6, 2006, the beginning of the period of ineligibility is the first day of the month in which the individual is eligible for Medicaid and would otherwise be receiving institutional care, but for the application of the penalty period. That is, the penalty begins when the individual is out of funds and in need of a long-term care provided either in a nursing home or as home- and community-based care.

For example, Joan, age 75 and single, gives her son $50,000 on June 1, 2009. The average monthly cost of a nursing home in Joan's state is $5,000. She incurs a 10-month penalty period that begins to run only after Joan moves into a nursing home or is medically certified as requiring nursing home care *and* has spent down her assets to less than $2,000 (and is otherwise eligible for Medicaid).

State agencies detect undisclosed gifts by review of the financial documents, such as bank account statements, that must be presented along with the Medicaid application. An applicant may be required to explain unusual withdrawals from a bank account that occurred during the look-back period.

The Medicaid statute makes an exception to gifts causing a loss of eligibility if that would cause a hardship to the applicant or if the gift was not made to create eligibility for Medicaid. In practice, very few applicants have been granted relief under these provisions.

Not all transfers involve gifts. Disclaiming an inheritance in most states is considered a transfer and can cause a period of ineligibility for Medicaid. Many older people are named in the wills of friends or family members or stand to receive an inheritance by the operation of intestacy laws. If the devisee resides in a nursing home, the inheritance would make the individual ineligible for Medicaid until it is spent down on care. A disclaimer of the inheritance will have the same effect.

[7] MEDICAID PLANNING

Some individuals attempt to create Medicaid eligibility by engaging in what is known as "Medicaid planning." The goal of Medicaid planning is to preserve and pass on assets while achieving Medicaid eligibility. The practice of planning for Medicaid eligibility has been criticized by state and federal lawmakers and the public as a shirking of responsibility.

Much of the criticism arises from the evolution of Medicaid from a poverty program to one that may provide valuable benefits to people who achieved some security, however modest, by working, saving, and planning throughout their lifetimes. In that context, it is not only rational to plan to conserve assets that might be consumed by the needs of advanced old age and infirmity; it may be shirking a responsibility *not* to know the rules and engage in planning to do so.

A move to a nursing home is a difficult life event. It is a recognition of declining physical or mental health. Many see nursing homes as little more than way stations on the way to death with the last days of life spent in an institution that limits personal autonomy and choice. The move means the end of living at home, creating one's own daily life, and being surrounded by one's own possessions and memories.

Perhaps equally distressing is the extraordinary cost of a nursing home, which is so high as to soon exhaust a lifetime of savings. After spending all of their savings, and applying all of their income to their cost of care, nursing home residents on Medicaid are left with only a personal needs allowance.

The social and psychological cost of this impoverishment to the individual can be very great, knowing that after a lifetime of earning and activity, one is virtually foreclosed from activities, including giving a grandchild a birthday present, paying a restaurant meal, or buying replacement clothing. Many who receive Medicaid assistance are distressed that they will leave little or nothing to their children.

Still some commentators insist that Medicaid planning is somehow unethical. A 2003 essay published in Newsweek was particularly sharp in tone, asking "Why do so many otherwise honest citizens think it's OK to take Medicaid money they don't deserve?" The author, a middle aged daughter, discusses the impact of her mother's costs of care. She reviews her mother's reluctance to pay the current cost of assisted living, her desire to leave something for her grandchildren, and her frugal habits based in the Depression. She is offended that social workers and nursing home personnel readily ask about Medicaid eligibility. She was appalled when she was referred to an elder law attorney to assist her preserving as much of her mother's assets as possible.

In sum, she says, "we steal from the federal government . . . the state . . . and our fellow citizens." Her father says: "I never cheated on my income taxes, and I'm not going to start hiding money now." She looks to this as an example of ethical behavior "when most people are out to grab everything they can for themselves."

QUESTIONS

1. Is Medicaid planning that uses legally sanctioned planning methods ethical? If not, why is sophisticated estate planning that is designed to minimize federal estate taxes ethical? Both cost the government money. Medicaid planning results in the government spending more money, estate planning results in the government collecting less money. In both cases, the government has fewer funds.

2. Does an attorney have an ethical obligation to the client to inform the client of all possible Medicaid planning methods so that the client can decide whether to engage in such planning?

3. Is the real issue why the law is written in such a way that permits Medicaid planning or is it the planning — the artificial creation of Medicaid eligibility — that is the problem?

[8] MEDICAID APPEALS

Medicaid applications are often denied because of a dispute over the calculation of income and resources attributable to the applicant. An individual who is denied Medicaid services may seek a review of the decision. The process for review is determined by each state under the general guidelines for fair hearings (42 U.S.C. § 1396a(a)(3); 42 C.F.R. § 431.200 *et seq.*).The first step is a fair hearing before the agency which denied the eligibility or claim. The hearing must be held at a reasonable time, date, and place, before an impartial hearing officer who was not involved in the initial decision. In practice, most hearings are held by telephone or video conference. The level of formality varies, and evidence generally is accepted if "reasonable" or not unduly repetitious or clearly irrelevant. The proceedings are often electronically recorded. If the decision is adverse, most state procedures allow another administrative hearing at the state level.

The individual has the right to judicial appeal of an agency's final adverse decision in the federal district court. A notice of appeal must be filed with the agency within 30 days of the notice of decision, after which the petition for judicial review may be filed.

[9]   ESTATE RECOVERY

States must pursue estate recovery programs against the estates of individuals who received Medicaid. An "estate" is defined to include all property in which the individual had any interest, including the home or any other real or personal property in which the recipient of benefits had legal title, including nonprobate property passing by joint tenancy, survivorship, life estate, or inter vivos trust. The amount of the potential recovery is the total amount of medical assistance paid, not just the amount of nursing home expenses paid.

Generally, the most valuable asset is the home, and most states require that a lien be placed on a Medicaid recipient's home.

The state may not enforce the lien, however while the recipient is alive, unless the home is sold, as long as any of the following persons reside in the home:

1.   The recipient's spouse;

2.   The recipient's child under age 21 or disabled;

3.   A child of any age who resides in the home, had resided there for at least 24 months before the recipient entered the nursing home, and provided care to the recipient that delayed the entry of the recipient into the nursing home; or

4.   A sibling who resides in the home and resided there for at least 12 months before the recipient entered the nursing home.

A lien, which is enforced in the same manner as a mortgage foreclosure, is authorized by 42 U.S.C. § 1396p(b)(1) and is the only means by which states can recover the value of benefits paid from the recipient's estate or the estate of a surviving spouse.

IN RE THE ESTATE OF JAMES CLIFFORD SMITH
2006 Tenn. App. LEXIS 715 (Nov. 1, 2006)

The issue presented to us is whether under 42 U.S.C. § 1396p(b) the Bureau of TennCare ("State") may recover from the estate of a husband for Medicaid benefits correctly paid on behalf of his predeceased wife who left no estate. The parties have stipulated to the relevant facts. The question presented to us is a purely legal question which is subject to *de novo* review.

I. FACTS

Mr. and Mrs. Smith had been married over 60 years when Mrs. Smith suffered a series of debilitating strokes in November of 2001. In December of 2001, Mrs. Smith was admitted to a nursing facility in Madison, Tennessee. The state is attempting to recover from the estate of her husband Medicaid nursing home benefits correctly paid on behalf of Mrs. Smith. The parties stipulated to the following facts:

> The couple lived in their Hendersonville, Tennessee, home until May 1999. At that time James and Mary sold their home and moved to an independent-living apartment at Park Place Retirement Center in Hendersonville.
>
> James, 90, began having seizures that were somewhat controlled with medication. He was legally blind and extremely hearing impaired. In November 2001 Mary, 90, suffered a series of strokes that resulted in left side paralysis. . . . She received home therapy until December 10, 2001, when she was admitted to a rehabilitation facility in Gallatin, Tennessee. On December 20, 2001 she was transferred to Imperial Manor Healthcare Facility in Madison, Tennessee.
>
> In 2002, James moved to an assisted-living apartment at Park Place. Park Place assisted him in bathing, dressing, medication administration, laundry, and meals. The family provided transportation to the nursing home for Mary's visitation and James' doctor appointments.
>
> James' assisted living costs were approximately $3,000 a month. In 2002, James' monthly income was Social Security of $879 and a duPont pension of $43.10. Mary's monthly income was $406 from Social Security. At the time of Mary's institutionalization, the Smith's total assets were $217,117, in various financial instruments that were titled in the name of James Smith, Mary Smith, or James and Mary Smith (that is, as tenants by the entirety). The $217,117 included the proceeds from the sale of their Hendersonville home. However, all of these assets are marital assets.
>
> A Medicaid resource assessment was done on April 16, 2002. That three-page document, which is a part of the record of the hearing on this claim, lists the assets that the couple owned on the date of Mary's institutionalization and how the assets were titled. Ruby Bankhead, an eligibility caseworker for the Davidson County Department of Human Services, approved Mary for Medicaid nursing home benefits starting July 1, 2002. Mary had less than $2000 in her checking account, which met Medicaid regulations. James paid $376.00 in patient liability to Imperial Manor each month for Mary's care. All assets that were jointly held were transferred to James within one year after the Medicaid approval, thereby meeting Medicaid regulations.

The Medicaid benefit approval is not disputed and all parties agree that Mrs. Smith appropriately received Medicaid nursing home benefits from her eligibility date of July 1, 2002 until her death in September of 2003.

At the time Mrs. Smith was approved for Medicaid benefits, she had less than $2,000 in her account. As stipulated above, the assets that were jointly held by Mr. and Mrs. Smith were transferred to Mr. Smith after Mrs. Smith was deemed eligible in a timely fashion that met the Medicaid guidelines. The stipulation does not explain how this was accomplished other than the transfer met Medicaid guidelines. Therefore, the parties agree that this transfer to Mr. Smith was lawful and had no effect whatsoever on Mrs. Smith's continued eligibility. Therefore, Mrs. Smith had no assets at the time of death. Mr. Smith did not receive Medicaid benefits.

Three months after the death of his wife, Mr. Smith died in December of 2003. The state filed a claim in Mr. Smith's estate seeking to recover for Medicaid benefits correctly paid for his deceased wife's benefit totaling $34,262.54. The probate court allowed the state to recover from Mr. Smith's estate Medicaid nursing home benefits provided to his wife. The question presented is whether under the foregoing facts the state can be reimbursed for properly awarded Medicaid nursing home benefits awarded to Mrs. Smith from the estate of her surviving spouse, Mr. Smith.

II. ANALYSIS

The answer to this question lies in the federal statute that governs recovery of Medicaid benefits. By its plain language, 42 U.S.C. § 1396p(b) prohibits recovery of correctly paid Medicare benefits with three narrowly drawn exceptions. Unless an exception applies, the state may not recover correctly paid benefits. According to representatives of Mr. Smith's estate, none of the three exceptions apply.

It is important to note that even under the three exceptions, recovery is allowed only against the estate of the person who actually received the benefits (the recipient). The applicable federal statute, 42 U.S.C. § 1396p(b), entitled "Liens, adjustments and recoveries, and transfer of assets," provides in relevant part:

> (b)   Adjustment or recovery of medical assistance correctly paid under a State plan:
>
>   (1)   *No adjustment or recovery of any medical assistance correctly paid on behalf of an individual under the State plan may be made, except* that the State shall seek adjustment or recovery of any medical assistance correctly paid on behalf of an individual under the State plan in the case of the following individuals:
>
>   (A)   In the case of an individual described in subsection (a)(1)(B) of this section, the State shall seek adjustment or recovery from the individual's estate or upon sale of the property subject to a lien imposed on account of medical assistance paid on behalf of the individual.
>
>   (B)   In the case of an individual who was 55 years of age or older when the individual received such medical assistance, the State shall seek adjustment or recovery from the *individual's estate* . . . .

(C)   In the case of an individual who has received (or is entitled to receive) benefits under a long-term care insurance policy in connection with which assets or resources are disregarded in the manner described in clause (ii), except as provided in such clause, the State shall seek adjustment or recovery from the individual's estate on account of medical assistance paid on behalf of the individual for nursing facility and other long-term care services.

(2)   Any adjustment or recovery under paragraph (1) may be made only after the death of the individual's surviving spouse, if any, and only at a time —

(A)   when he has no surviving child who is under age 21, or . . . is blind or permanently and totally disabled . . . .

. . . .

(4)   For purposes of this subsection, the term "estate," with respect to a deceased individual —

(A)   shall include all real and personal property and other assets included within the individual's estate, as defined for purposes of State probate law; and

(B)   *may* include, at the *option* of the State . . . any other real and personal property and other assets in which the individual had any legal title or interest *at the time of death* (to the extent of such interest), including such assets conveyed to a survivor, heir, or assign of the deceased individual through joint tenancy, tenancy in common, survivorship, life estate, living trust, or *other arrangement.*

42 U.S.C. § 1396p(b) (emphasis added).

Two of the exceptions are clearly not applicable as they pertain to liens and long-term care insurance policies. The state relies on the third exception in subsection (b)(1)(B) that allows recovery from the recipient's estate only if the recipient has no surviving spouse. The state argues that the definition of "estate" in 42 U.S.C. § 1396p(b)(4) is broad enough to include the assets held in the estate of the surviving spouse that had once been held jointly with the recipient spouse. Therefore, the state maintains that 42 U.S.C. § 1396p(b)(1)(B) allows recovery from the estate of the surviving spouse when one expansively defines "estate" under 42 U.S.C. § 1396p(b)(4).

We conclude that the state cannot recover under 42 U.S.C. § 1396p(b)(1)(B) since the recipient, Mrs. Smith, never left an "estate" as that term is defined in subsection (b)(4). Subsection (b)(4) provides that a recipient's "estate" may be defined in two ways. First, "estate" is defined in accordance with applicable state probate law. The state does not try to argue that Mrs. Smith left an estate under Tennessee probate law. Therefore, the state relies on the second way to define "estate." Under the second definition, a state is given the option to also include assets in the recipient's estate that may not be included in an estate under applicable probate state law.

These "optional assets" are assets that the recipient had an interest in *at the time of death* but may not become part of the recipient's estate under state law because they passed directly to the heir or survivor at death without technically passing through the estate. Depending on applicable state law, these assets may pass to the deceased's heirs or survivors through joint tenancy, survivorship, etc. The state argues that since Mrs. Smith once had an interest in the assets comprising Mr. Smith's estate, then the state can, in effect, "follow" these assets once held by Mrs. Smith to the estate left by her spouse.

The parties stipulated that the recipient spouse, Mrs. Smith, had conveyed all of her interest in their jointly held assets to Mr. Smith *before* she died. There are no allegations that these transfers were improper or fraudulent, or intended to defeat creditors. They were made in accordance with Medicaid nursing home benefits eligibility requirements. It is clear that under the express terms of the definition of "estate" relied upon by the state, in order to be a part of Mrs. Smith's "estate" under subsection (b)(4)(B), she had to have a legal title or interest in the property "at the time of her death." Because Mrs. Smith had no interest in any property when she died, there is no estate of the benefit recipient. Recovery is not allowed under 42 U.S.C. § 1396p(b)(1)(B).

Courts are divided on whether states can follow a recipient's estate through to the surviving spouse's estate. Some courts have interpreted 42 U.S.C. § 1396p(b) to prohibit the "tracing" or following of a recipient's estate to a surviving spouse's estate. Many courts, however, have held that 42 U.S.C. § 1396p(b) allows the state to recover from the recipient's estate after that estate was inherited by a surviving spouse who has since died. In other words, courts have allowed the state to "trace" a recipient's estate through to the estate of a surviving spouse. Where recovery has been allowed, we note it appears that the recipient spouse had an interest in the property comprising the estate of the surviving spouse at the time of the recipient's death. Because we have decided that the benefit recipient, Mrs. Smith, had no estate as that term is defined under 42 U.S.C. § 1396p(b)(4), we need not resolve the question of whether the state can recover from a recipient's estate through the estate of a surviving spouse.

There is one state, however, where recovery may be allowed against a surviving spouse's estate if the surviving spouse's estate is composed of property that was at *any* time held jointly with a recipient spouse, regardless of whether the recipient spouse had an interest in the property at the time of the recipient's death. The North Dakota Supreme Court reached this conclusion in *In re Wirtz*, 2000 ND 59, 607 N.W.2d 882 (N.D. 2000). The court concluded that the language in 1396p(b)(4)(B) which defined a recipient's estate to include assets conveyed to a spouse by "other arrangement" included a recipient's "interest" in assets conveyed by a recipient prior to death. The court found that the terms "interest" and "other arrangement" are ambiguous, so the court turned to "extrinsic aids to ascertain the legislative intent." *Id.* Because Congressional committee reports revealed an intent to give states a wide latitude in recovering Medicaid benefits, the court held that "any assets conveyed by [recipient husband] to [surviving wife] before [recipient husband's] death and traceable to her estate are subject to the department's recovery claim." The court in *Wirtz* found that recoverable assets did not include all property held by either spouse during the marriage but was limited to "assets in which the deceased recipient *once* held an interest." 607 N.W.2d at 885.

We must respectfully disagree with the rationale of *Wirtz* since under 42 U.S.C. § 1396p(b)(4)(B), in order to be potentially recoverable, an asset must be one in which the recipient had a "legal title or interest at the time of death."

In our case, the parties agreed Mrs. Smith lawfully conveyed the assets that are at issue to Mr. Smith before her death. The state does not argue that Mrs. Smith had any interest whatsoever in those assets when she died. Therefore, under 42 U.S.C. § 1396p(b), there existed no recipient estate subject to recovery. The trial court is reversed.

The value of the Medicaid recipient's property interest may also be at issue at the estate recovery stage.

IN RE THE ESTATE OF FRANCIS E. BARG, A/K/A FRANCIS EDWARD BARG
722 N.W.2d 492 (Minn. App. 2006)

JUDGE LANSING.

In this appeal from an order for partial recovery of medical benefits paid to Dolores Barg, the estate of Francis Barg challenges the district court's interpretation of Minnesota's estate-recovery statute (2004). Because we conclude that the determination of the deceased recipient's interest in transferred joint-tenancy property must be based on principles of real-property law as modified by specific provisions of the estate-recovery statute, we reverse and remand for recalculation of Mille Lacs County's allowable claim against the estate.

FACTS

Dolores and Francis Barg married in 1948. In 1962 and 1967 they acquired title to real property that they held in joint tenancy. In 2001 Dolores Barg's health declined, and she eventually required out-of-home nursing care. To pay for her medical care, she applied for long-term Medicaid benefits. After participating in an asset assessment, Dolores Barg transferred her interest in the jointly held property to Francis Barg. At the time of the transfer, the assessed value of the property was $120,800.

Dolores Barg died in 2004. Between 2001 and 2004, Dolores Barg received a total of $108,413.53 in medical-assistance benefits through the Medicaid program. Five months after Delores Barg's death, Francis Barg died, and his will was admitted to probate. Mille Lacs County filed a claim against the estate to recover the medical-assistance payments made to Dolores Barg. The estate's personal representative allowed $63,880 as a claim against the estate, but disallowed $44,533.53. The county thereafter filed a claim-allowance petition.

At the hearing on the petition, the county contended that it was entitled to full recovery of its claim because the value of the real property exceeded the value of the claim and, as marital property, Dolores Barg was entitled to an undivided interest in its full value. The estate contended that the court should, instead, apply a probate-law analysis that would limit Dolores Barg's interest in the property to a life estate, with a value of $63,880.

Applying probate-law principles, the district court determined that Dolores Barg had a life-estate interest in the property and that the county could not recover the additional $44,533.53. The county appeals from this determination, and the Minnesota Department of Human Services has filed an amicus brief in support of the county's position.

ISSUE

Did the district court err by applying, for purposes of Minnesota's estate-recovery statute, a probate-law analysis to calculate a medical-assistance recipient's interest in transferred joint-tenancy property that is part of the surviving spouse's estate?

ANALYSIS

In the district court, Mille Lacs County and Francis Barg's estate jointly submitted a stipulation of facts; on appeal, both acknowledge that the claim against the estate is governed by federal and state statutes. Application of a statute to undisputed facts involves a question of law.

Under Medicaid, a person who is unable to pay the cost of long-term medical care may qualify for medical-assistance benefits. Because the "spend down" requirement has the potential to impose substantial hardship on the spouse of a medical-assistance recipient, Medicaid includes provisions to avoid spousal impoverishment. These anti-impoverishment measures preclude certain assets from being considered for eligibility purposes. Specifically, in determining eligibility for Medicaid benefits, the value of an individual's home is not considered so long as a spouse or dependent child maintains the home as a primary residence.

Because the spousal anti-impoverishment measures provide an exemption for a primary residence, this property is typically an asset that is subject to estate-recovery procedures. To reach these assets, Congress amended the Medicaid Act to expand the government's ability to recover from the estates of medical-assistance recipients and to require states to seek this recovery. Although the Medicaid Act does not generally permit the government to recover medical assistance correctly paid on behalf of an individual, the government may seek recovery if one of three exceptions applies. The exception relevant to the Bargs' circumstances applies to individuals who were older than fifty-five when they received medical assistance. Under this exception, the government may recover "from the individual's estate," but may only seek recovery after the death of the individual's surviving spouse.

For purposes of recovery, federal law defines an individual's estate as "all real and personal property and other assets included within the individual's estate, as defined for purposes of [s]tate probate law." The federal law, however, permits states to expand the definition of estate beyond the definition found within probate law. If the state chooses, it may include "any other real and personal property and other assets in which the individual had any legal title or interest at the time of death (to the extent of such interest), including such assets conveyed . . . through joint tenancy . . . or other arrangement."

Minnesota's estate-recovery statute provides that the state may assert a claim against the estate of a surviving spouse to recoup medical-assistance benefits provided to the predeceased spouse. The Minnesota statute thus reflects the legislature's exercise of the option to expand the definition of estate to allow claims against the surviving spouse's estate. But Minnesota limits a "claim against the estate of a surviving spouse . . . to the value of the assets of the estate that were marital property or jointly owned property at any time during the marriage." Thus, the state may not recover from portions of a surviving spouse's estate that are not traceable to marital or jointly owned property.

In *Gullberg*, this court determined that Minnesota's statute was partially preempted by federal law. Specifically, the court concluded that Minnesota's estate-recovery statute goes further than permitted by federal law because it permits recovery "to the value of the assets of the estate that were marital property," while the federal law only permits recovery "to the extent of" the individual's interest at the time of death. To harmonize federal and state law, *Gullberg* concluded that Minnesota's estate-recovery statute "allows claims against a surviving spouse's estate only to the extent of the value of the recipient's interest in marital or jointly owned property at the time of the recipient's death." *Id.* Recovery is thus limited to "the value of the recipient's interest in those assets at the time of the recipient's death."

Prior to *Gullberg*, the state could recover up to the full value of assets that could be traced back to marital or jointly owned property. After *Gullberg*, the state's ability to recover was limited to the recipient's interest in marital or jointly owned property at the time of the recipient's death. Thus, the state's recovery depends on a determination of the recipient's interest in the specified assets at the time of death.

The county and the estate argue that *Gullberg* restricts the definition of the value of the recipient's interest in the estate of the surviving spouse to either probate-law or marital-property-law principles. The county contends that marital-property-law principles should be applied because the estate-recovery statute specifically refers to marital property. The estate counters that a recipient's interest is more appropriately determined by reference to probate law. We conclude that both the county and the estate read too much into *Gullberg*'s passing references to marital and probate law.

Gullberg's holding was limited to the narrow issue of preemption. Rather than directly addressing the method for calculating the extent of the recipient's interest in transferred property, the court in *Gullberg* remanded the issue to the district court for determination of the recipient's interest in the assets of the surviving spouse's estate. Although the *Gullberg* decision included citations to a marital-property-law case, *Searles v. Searles*, 420 N.W.2d 581 (Minn. 1988), and to a probate statute, Minn. Stat. § 524.2-402(a), (c) (2000), these citations were included merely as support for the precept that a medical-assistance recipient may continue to have some interest in property even after the recipient has transferred the property to a spouse. Notably, *Gullberg* stated that the recipient's transfer of his joint tenancy to his spouse was a conveyance by "other arrangement" and that it would therefore fall within the broader optional state definition of estate. Thus the *Gullberg* opinion essentially applied the optional definition of estate, as allowed by federal law, and established that the medical-assistance] recipient had *some* interest in the homestead after its conveyance, but the opinion did not address the extent of this interest.

We therefore reject the parties' competing arguments that *Gullberg* must be read to require either a probate-law analysis or a marital-property-law analysis when calculating a medical-assistance recipient's interest under the estate-recovery laws. We are not persuaded that either analysis applies, particularly in this case. Analysis under marital-property law would require us to read into the estate-recovery statute a definition from Minn. Stat. § 518.54 (2004), which explicitly restricts its definitions to the context of marital dissolution, and provides that marital property "means property . . . acquired by the parties, or either of them, to a dissolution, legal separation, or annulment proceeding." We are unable to find a legal basis for incorporating this definition into the estate-recovery statute.

We are similarly unable to find a legal basis for imposing a probate-law analysis, which would require the court to apply a retrospective structuring of the medical-assistance recipient's interest in the surviving spouse's estate. This method, which was proposed by the estate and accepted by the district court, results in a life-estate interest that is based on an artificial assumption that the surviving spouse predeceased the recipient instead of the converse. In this case, Francis Barg did not include a provision for his deceased wife and left his interest in his homestead to his children. Under probate-law principles, the court would have to assume that Dolores Barg survived her husband and received a life-estate interest in his property as his surviving spouse.

This probate-law analysis would also conflict with the estate-recovery laws, which require courts to calculate the recipient's interest at the time of the recipient's death rather than on the future date of the spouse's death. The estate-recovery statute specifically provides that a recipient's joint-tenancy interests "shall not be merged into the remainder interest or the interests of the surviving joint tenants" and that the joint-tenancy interests shall be subject to the provisions of the statute. Analysis under probate-law principles is also inconsistent with the federal law's expanded definition of estate, which explicitly allows a state to broaden the definition beyond the meaning used in probate law and to include joint-tenancy interests that have been previously conveyed to a spouse.

In light of the problems with the use of either probate-law or marital-property-law principles, we conclude that the plain meaning of the estate-recovery statute requires us to apply property-law principles as specifically modified by the statute. Applying this analysis, a recipient's interest in marital property for purposes of estate recovery is limited to that person's legal interest in the property at the time of death. And, under federal law and *Gullberg*, this interest includes a conveyance of a joint tenancy to a spouse.

Applying *Gullberg*, the relevant statutes, and the principles of property law to the stipulated facts, we start from the elemental threshold that Dolores Barg had a joint-tenancy interest in the property that is now in Francis Barg's estate and that her interest was acquired during their marriage. Before receiving Medicaid benefits, she conveyed her interest in the property to Francis Barg. For purposes of the estate-recovery statute, Dolores Barg's estate retained a joint-tenancy interest in the homestead at the time of her death. The "extent of her interest" is defined by the joint tenancy. A joint tenant's interest in property is an undivided one-half interest in the property's value. Because the stipulated facts state that the joint-tenancy property was valued at $120,800 at the time of Dolores Barg's death, the extent of the value of Dolores Barg's interest at the time of her death was $60,400. We therefore reverse and remand for the district court to recalculate the allowable claim against Francis Barg's estate.

Finally, the Minnesota Department of Human Resources filed an amicus brief in this case, supporting the county's position and urging reversal of the district court's decision. The department advances two independent arguments for reversal. First it asserts that *Gullberg*'s discussion of the preemptive effect of the phrase "to the extent of such interest" is dictum and should not be applied. We disagree. The *Gullberg* court did not exceed the scope of review on the preemption issue by relying on a full-text analysis of the federal act. The language of the opinion and the stated issue in the case establish that *Gullberg* squarely addresses preemption and reaches a conclusion on this issue, which became the holding of the case.

Second, the department urges this court to reverse *Gullberg* based on the department's "more complete discussion" of the preemption issue in its amicus brief. The amicus brief provides a thoughtful and comprehensive analysis of the preemption question. But that issue was decided in *Gullberg*, and nothing in *Gullberg*'s analysis suggests that the court did not consider the full spectrum of applicable law and competing policy considerations in its determination of the preemption issue. We therefore decline to reverse *Gullberg*.

DECISION

For purposes of obtaining reimbursement under Minnesota's estate-recovery statute, Mille Lacs County is entitled to a claim against Francis Barg's estate for Dolores Barg's one-half interest in the joint-tenancy property obtained during the marriage and transferred to Francis Barg. Because the district court erred by applying a probate-law method of calculation, we reverse and remand for a recalculation of the allowance based on principles of real property as modified by specific provisions of the estate-recovery statutes.

Reversed and remanded.

QUESTION

Does the allocation of ownership for the purposes of estate recovery make sense, given the spousal impoverishment provisions discussed above? What effect will it have on the choices of a surviving spouse of a Medicaid nursing home resident?

Chapter 7

LONG-TERM CARE: QUALITY ASSURANCE

One of the most difficult undertakings in developing a long-term care system, as it evolves to encompass home and institutional care, is choosing the type of services in light of the recipient's needs and preferences. Even among very impaired people, some may choose the security of institutionalization while others may sacrifice a great deal in quality of life — social contacts, adequate nutrition, personal cleanliness, and safety — for the single goal of independent living at home. Once the appropriate services are identified, the technical quality and ongoing appropriateness for the person's needs must be monitored. Thus, both the choice of services and the quality and care with which they are provided are critical to quality assurance in long-term care.

A. INTRODUCTION: COST, CHOICE, AND QUALITY

The demand for long-term care services is strongly influenced by costs and availability. Government subsidies for nursing home and some home care may increase the demand for such care — a phenomenon known as the "woodwork effect." People with unsuspected needs come out of the woodwork and overwhelm program budgets. The Patient Protection and Affordable Health Care Act of 2010 may have that effect as a result of making it easier for states to use Medicaid funds to pay for long-term care provided in the home or community. The goal is to shift funds from expensive nursing homes and provide care more efficiently in less costly settings. Some fear that many more individuals will apply for Medicaid if they can receive reimbursement for their care without having to move into a nursing home. The result may cause Medicaid reimbursement for long-term care to rise even faster than it has — the opposite of what policies makers intended.

The goal of providing the optimum amount of quality long-term care, while being sensitive to fiscal realities, is an on-going, complex problem. In theory, quality of care and cost-efficient care are not mutually exclusive. In practice, laws, regulations, and operating requirements that seek to assure quality too often result in much more costly care. And attempts to limit the cost of care can cause a decline in quality. Still, the search and need for efficient quality long-term care continues.

This chapter is primarily concerned with nursing home care and, to a lesser extent, home care and community care for those who are similarly impaired. Chapter 9 discusses other arrangements of housing and services that meet the needs of the elderly who require less care.

Long-term care quality assurance has been slow to develop, even while other industries (including health care) undertake such initiatives as economic credentialing of providers (ongoing assessment of resource utilization as well as technical skill) and total quality management (ongoing assessment to determine whether the optimum worker is providing the most useful service in the most cost efficient way). Experts have observed that because long-term care is burdened by pessimism, little quality assurance is developed because of the expectation of inevitable decline and loss of function of the service recipients. Nevertheless, more optimistic and hopefully more realistic researchers and advocates are developing measures to help improve long-term care quality.

The public image of nursing home care in the U.S. is worthy of attention.

Eric M. Carlson,
Siege Mentality: How the Defensive Attitude of the Long-Term Care Industry Is Perpetuating Poor Care and an Even Poorer Public Image
31 McGeorge L. Rev. 739 (2000)[*]

Although each day nursing facilities care for approximately 1.5 million vulnerable elderly individuals, the nursing facility industry is bedeviled by an abysmal public image. To explain this poor public image, resident advocates point to the industry's substandard performance over the years, but the industry sees itself as a scapegoat. The divergence between these two views-with nursing facilities as either victimizers or victims-has led to schizophrenic public policy. The relationship between government and nursing facilities is based nominally on an "enforcement-first" structure but, as a practical matter, loopholes within the enforcement system have crippled enforcement for all but the most egregious and longstanding facility violations. Meanwhile, nursing facility representatives are attempting, on numerous fronts and through a variety of stratagems, to divert governmental agencies further away from enforcement and towards a less adversarial, more consultative role.

II. Bad Press and Bad Feelings: Nursing Facilities as Societal Pariahs

Nursing facilities occupy a truly unique place in American society and in the American psyche. But "unique," in this context, is hardly a compliment.

Despite the fact that each day nursing facilities provide life-sustaining nursing care for approximately 1.5 million vulnerable residents more personally, for ourselves, our spouses, and our parents-the public image of nursing facilities is hardly benevolent. . . .

The "unique" status of nursing facilities results from facilities being alternately ignored and reviled. The few newspaper stories concerning nursing facilities generally convey disturbing images: a female resident being raped by a young, mentally-ill resident, an Arizona resident burning to death after being left in the sun for seven hours, a resident dying soon after being found in a bed covered with ants, a California resident having her arm pulled out of its socket by nurses, or a

---

Michigan resident strangling to death, caught between her mattress and bed rails. . . .

Behind the horror stories is the perception that nursing facility operators are disreputable in some way. For example, when the casino owned by the greedy and malicious Mr. Burns is closed on an episode of television's The Simpsons, his casino employees-"cardsharps, bottom dealers and shills"-are transferred into managerial positions in his nursing facility chain.

III. Victimizers or Victims?

. . . . From the point of view held generally by resident advocates and governmental agencies, nursing facilities have earned their societal opprobrium by providing a consistently abysmal quality of care. The necessary response? In the vernacular, "throw the book" at the many substandard facilities. More precisely, legal requirements must be refined, and enforcement of the law must be strengthened

Nursing facilities, and especially their trade associations, have an entirely different perspective, as if facility representatives and resident advocates lived on two separate planets. Facility representatives see themselves as scapegoats for families and a society that have turned their backs on sick elders The facilities are victims, not victimizers, and feel aggrieved with an intensity that is no less than that held by those who advocate on behalf of injured residents.

Specifically, from the facilities' point of view, the "facility as a victim" is subjected to an intense and punitive level of regulation. For example, in response to a scathing General Accounting Office report finding that thirty percent of California nursing facilities had caused death or serious physical harm to residents, facility representatives claimed in an editorial that "California's nursing home industry is one of the most highly regulated, and its enforcement system is probably the most effective in the country." More generally, various facility representatives regularly claim-without attribution-that the nursing facility industry is second in regulatory oversight only to the nuclear power industry.

. . . .

Both resident advocates and facility representatives are wholly dissatisfied with the enforcement status quo, but for reasons that are consistent with the disparate perspectives discussed above. Resident advocates believe that the enforcement systems at both the federal and state levels have been made impotent by procedural roadblocks and a lack of resources. The solution at either level-state or federal-is a streamlining of enforcement processes and an increase in available resources.

The arguments made by nursing facility representatives assume a dramatically different reality: the problem is too much enforcement and not enough money. The editor of one provider magazine states: "poor-performing facilities are largely the result of flawed oversight and reimbursement systems." Similarly, the executive vice president of the American Health Care Association stated that "[e]nforcement activity alone is not the answer; in fact, a single-minded emphasis on enforcement will ultimately hurt quality." From this point of view, monetary penalties simply "take money out of the system that should be spent on patient care."

According to facility representatives, enforcement can diminish the quality of care by focusing on matters essentially unrelated to resident's well-being. In the words of a vice president of a nursing facility chain, "the survey system does not measure quality." At best, enforcement activities are only beneficial in regards to those few facilities characterized as "bad apples."

In general, facility representatives argue that the government should improve care not by regulation and enforcement, but by increasing Medicaid and Medicare rates, and providing "technical assistance" regarding the best ways to provide nursing facility care. In general, facility representatives advocate a "partnership" between facilities and government. For example, the executive vice president of the American Health Care Association recommended that government agencies "should work in cooperation with the industry and put the 'emphasis on the 90% of the people who want to do a good job.' "

The quality of long-term care is a subject of recurring government investigations. The Institute of Medicine, *Long-term Care Committee Final Report* (2002), found that there was a positive correlation between reimbursement rates and quality of care. *See also* Govt. Accounting Office, *Nursing Homes: More Can Be Done to Protect Residents from Abuse* (Mar. 2002) (GAO-02-312) (stating that most incidents of resident abuse are not reported immediately, and are sometimes ignored, putting residents in fear for their safety). For two different perspectives on the provision of quality care, see the National Commission Final Report at http://www.qualitylongtermcarecommission.org/; and http://www.theconsumervoice.org.

B. QUALITY ASSURANCE

Nursing home care presents special problems of quality assurance. Though the industry is increasingly professionalized, which helps to assure quality, it also is subject to recurring incidents of notoriously poor care tied to high profit taking. A growing number of nursing homes are owned by a few for-profit organizations with loyalties to shareholders that may dominate the interests of vulnerable residents. Family members may have little power to assure quality and good value, particularly if there are few beds available for their elderly relative. Both federal and state laws attempt to assure quality care and fairness in financial dealings with nursing homes.

The quality of home care is monitored in three ways: through Medicare/Medicaid certification, state licensure, and accreditation by provider organizations. In general, the monitoring of home health agencies certified to receive government payments parallels nursing home oversight. None of these measures, however, applies to all organizations or all of the services included in home care. Some home care agencies engage only in homemaking and do not receive government payments.

A provider must comply with the Medicare conditions of participation for home health agencies in order to qualify for federal reimbursement. The standards for home health care follow a pattern similar to the nursing home requirements for participation and have been similarly affected by the reforms of OBRA 1987. The provisions require that state surveyors make home visits to interview patients, who must be allowed to make complaints without fear of discrimination or reprisal. They also require the use of a single functional assessment tool, a plan prepared in collaboration with the patients (or the representative of an incompetent person) and other consumer- and outcome-oriented strategies. However, the requirements still rely heavily on structure and process indicators that can be examined in a paper review. Home health agencies are required to show that their employees have the proper credentials, through training or licensing, and to keep extensive records of time and activities. The services assessed are only those Medicare will pay for — skilled nursing services and limited nurse aide assistance.

The second quality control mechanism for home care is state licensing of home health agencies. Most states license home health agencies, with most licensing schemes mirroring the Medicare requirements. A 1988 study by the National Academy for State Health Policy indicated that state licensure did not necessarily correlate to higher quality home health care. At that time only New York State provided surveys which examined any care other than home health, and almost all surveys were conducted by nurses.

The third measure of home care quality is accreditation by a provider organization. The accreditation process, again, tends to concentrate heavily on the home health component of home care. Two organizations provide accreditation surveys nationwide — the National League of Nursing, through its Community Health Accreditation Program (CHAP), and the Joint Commission on the Accreditation of Healthcare Organizations (JCAHO). Both of these programs have been aggressively pursuing "deemed status," i.e., recognition of their standards as the equivalent of government survey and certification. You may recall that JCAHO has deemed status for hospital certification. Few home care agencies attempt to qualify, however, because accreditation is not required by funding sources.

Quality control methods tend to "medicalize" the concept of home care, failing to take into account that home health care is only one of the many services provided by a home care agency. Other services include all aspects of homemaking and maintenance such as cleaning, meal preparation, shopping, home repair, yard work, and so on. Many more elderly people need such services than need home health care.

The assurances of quality for the broad spectrum of home care services are very limited. Many states offer a "community care" program which provides a range of preventive, maintenance, and restorative services for functionally impaired elderly people. Florida's Community Care for the Elderly (FLA. STAT. § 410.021 *et seq.*), for example, utilizes a number of monitoring and training strategies in an effort to assure quality. The state agency on aging must define each Community Care core service (e.g., homemaking, personal care, chore work) and establish minimum standards for its delivery. Wherever feasible the direct service provider must be located in a multipurpose senior center monitored by an Area Agency on Aging.

Services are provided under a plan of care developed by the client and a case manager. Service providers and staff must receive training prior to their employment and annual in-service training thereafter.

Should the measures of quality be different when a home care worker undertakes tasks the recipient was accustomed to doing for him or herself? Process measures examine what is done to and for the patient. They are task-oriented, measured through supervisor visits, chart reviews, peer review, worker skills checklists, and patient interviews. Outcome measures, by contrast, examine the results of care in terms of measurable change or stabilization as a result of services. Both rely on abstract, rather than personal, standards to identify a high quality of services.

QUESTIONS

1. Is it appropriate and sufficient to identify quality in homemaking tasks?

2. Is client satisfaction alone an acceptable standard?

[1] LICENSING REQUIREMENTS FOR FACILITIES, OPERATORS, AND ADMINISTRATORS

A fundamental aspect of quality assurance in professional services is state licensing of persons and facilities. Doctors need state approval to practice, and hospitals have had to meet at least minimal licensing standards for decades. Such licensing requirements are justified in part by the recognition that the consumer will be unable to discern quality. Licensing provides the assurance that state mandated standards for education or building and staffing have been met.

The traditional perception of long-term care services asserts that the layperson can by observation know a good individual or institutional provider. Old-age homes were not considered to deliver professional services in a health care setting. With the medicalization of long-term nursing home care, however, a growing number of service providers must meet state licensing requirements.

In the seminal long-term care quality case *In re Estate of Smith*, 557 F. Supp. 289 (D. Col. 1983), the court described the state's responsibility for assuring quality nursing home care:

> The Colorado Department of Health is responsible for the licensing of hospitals, including nursing care facilities and intermediate care facilities. The department has the authority to adopt rules and regulations setting substantive standards for license applicants, as well as the authority to revoke or suspend a license if the institution has failed to meet statutory requirements and to comply with the rules and regulations of the department. In addition to the general provision for summary suspension of a license where the licensing agency has reason to believe that the public health or welfare is endangered there is a special receivership mechanism to be used in the revocation or suspension of licenses of nursing care facilities and intermediate care facilities, which permits patients to remain at the institution on a temporary basis, and which automatically grants the receiver a new license and certifies the receiver for Medicaid participation.

A separate state statute, with an express legislative purpose of providing "a measure of protection to the aged and handicapped residents of nursing homes in this state," regulates nursing home administrators. *Id.* tit. 12, art. 39. That article creates a board of examiners of nursing home administrators which is responsible for the licensure of those administrators and for the development and enforcement of standards "designed to insure that nursing home administrators will be individuals who are of good character and are otherwise suitable and who, by training or experience in the field of institutional administration, are qualified to serve as nursing home administrators." *Id.* § 12-39-105(1)(a). Section 12-39-105(4) grants the board of examiners of nursing home administrators the authority to make rules and otherwise to take steps to enable it to comply with 42 U.S.C. § 1396(g); that section of the Medicaid Act sets out the requirements of a state program for licensing of nursing home administrators, which is a required feature of an approved state Medicaid plan, under 42 U.S.C. § 1396a(a)(29).

557 F. Supp. at 297.

Today, all states regulate and license nursing home facilities. The requirements typically include standards for the physical plant, staffing, sanitation, nutrition, and so on, which must be fulfilled before the state will issue a license to the owner to operate a facility. These requirements closely track standards for facilities participating in Medicare and Medicaid, though they may add consumer protections absent from federal law.

All states must also license nursing home administrators in order to be eligible for participation in the federal programs. 42 C.F.R. § 483.75. The administrator must be appointed by the governing body of the facility and is responsible for management of the facility.

QUESTIONS

1. Are both licensing requirements — the facility and the administrator — necessary to assure good quality of care? Is one more important than the other?

2. "Professionalization" in the traditional sense means a prescribed pattern of mandatory education, testing of knowledge, and possibly a period of internship or supervised practice. It results in a monopoly for those who obtain the license to practice their profession, and may raise costs because services are less common than without licensing. It also implies that all licensees have learned and adopted professional ethics appropriate to their undertaking. Is nursing home administration appropriate for such professionalization? Do you think it is effective?

In 1987, Congress enacted extensive new rules on the way quality of care should be assured in the nursing home reform provisions of OBRA 1987. The final rule establishing requirements for participation in the federal programs was issued by HCFA (now CMS) on February 2, 1989. It consists of "condition level statements" — statutory requirements, violation of which can lead to termination of participation, and "standard level statements" — lesser requirements which may be subject to lesser sanctions but do not threaten federal funding.

Two broad areas addressed by the regulations define the change in approach to the assurance of quality:

Survey and Certification — The purpose of these provisions is to monitor whether homes provide care and services to residents that meet federal standards for participation in Medicare and Medicaid. The surveys (inspections) focus on how staff meet the residents' individual care needs and how the physical surroundings support residents' well-being.

Standard surveys are conducted on a nine- to fifteen-month cycle, or within two months of a change in leadership in the nursing home, including ownership, administration, or medical or nursing staff. They include reviews of residents' rights and quality of care for a sample of residents. The surveyor reviews the quality of medical care, nursing, rehabilitation, dietary services, activities and social participation, sanitation, infection control, and physical environment. A nursing home providing substandard care is subject to an extended survey within two weeks of the initial survey. The surveys are conducted by a trained, multidisciplinary team, including a registered nurse. The results of the survey must be available to the public, as must Medicare and Medicaid cost reports and notices of any citations or fines. The regulations provide a 12-task survey process, and forms, in 42 C.F.R. § 488.

Resident Assessment and Annual Resident Review — The OBRA '87 set requirements for resident assessment for appropriate care. The purpose of these provisions is to provide facility staff with information about residents' needs and capabilities, to enable them to develop and implement a plan of care that supports residents in attaining or maintaining their best possible physical, mental, and psychosocial well-being. 42 C.F.R. § 483.25. Nursing homes must treat residents "in such a manner and in such an environment as will promote maintenance or enhancement" of their quality of life. The care provided must ensure that the resident's abilities and care level do not diminish, unless circumstances of the individual's clinical condition demonstrate that diminution was unavoidable. The regulations list 13 indications whether deterioration has taken place, which must be accounted for, such as use of a catheter or feeding tube. 42 C.F.R. § 483.15.

In order to implement quality of care goals, HCFA must utilize a system of resident assessment that is comprehensive, accurate, standardized, and reproducible, and which describes the resident's significant impairments in functional capacity and ability to perform daily life functions. It must use a minimum data set of core elements and common definitions for nursing homes in assessments, and provide at least one assessment instrument to capture the data set. Each resident must be assessed within four days of admission, annually thereafter, and at any significant change in mental or physical condition by a registered nurse who signs and certifies the completion of the assessment. 42 C.F.R. § 483.20.

Assessments are used to develop, review, and revise the resident's plan of care, which describes the medical, nursing and psychosocial needs of the resident and how those needs will be met. An assessment is prepared initially with the participation, to the extent practicable, of the resident or the resident's family or legal representative, by a team which includes the resident's attending physician and a registered professional nurse with responsibility to the resident. 42 U.S.C. §§ 1395i-3(b)(2)(A)–(C), 1396r(b)(2)(A)–(C).

QUESTIONS

1. Are these methods — survey and assessment — likely to assure quality of care?

2. Should this method of survey and certification be used in board and care homes?

Nursing Home Staffing. One of the most important differences (often, the only difference) between higher and lower levels of care lies in the qualifications and numbers of staff.

OBRA 1987 requires that all nursing homes offering the new level of care have a licensed nurse (LPN of RN) in the facility 24 hours a day. A registered nurse must be on duty in the facility eight hours a day. (Both requirements contemplate a seven-day week.) It would appear that nursing facilities would, for the first time, always have a nurse present.

However, faced with staffing shortages and high costs, the states and nursing home industry prevailed on Congress to grant a broader waiver authority. OBRA 1987 permits waivers for both the registered nurse and LPN requirements if:

(1) The facility demonstrates that it has been unable to recruit appropriate personnel;

(2) The state determines that a waiver will not endanger the health or safety of individuals staying in the facility; and

(3) The state finds that, for periods when licensed services are not available, a registered nurse or physician is obligated to respond immediately to telephone calls from the facility.

QUESTIONS

1. How many nurses does it take to staff a nursing home?

2. Should the nursing home be required to have someone available at all times who can provide cardiopulmonary resuscitation (CPR), or is it sufficient to call an ambulance when a resident is in distress?

A February 2002 report by CMS indicates that it is not feasible to require nursing homes to meet minimum staffing ratios required in the OBRA 1987 regulations. The report, reviewing data first considered by government in the 1980s when the report was authorized, states that a nursing home resident requires 4.1 hours of care in order to fulfill tasks such as turning, changing linens, assistance with bathing and toileting. This calls for one nurse aide for every five or six residents. Over 90 percent of nursing homes had staffing ratios too low to provide that intensity of services. Further, more than 40 percent of nursing homes would have to increase staffing by at least half to provide minimally necessary care. CMS, *Appropriateness of Minimum Nurse Staffing Ratios in Nursing Home.* According to the National Coalition for Nursing Home Reform, the average U.S. nursing facility has provided only 3.6 hours per resident per day between 1996 and 2002, and RN staffing hours have declined by 12.5 percent since 2000.

[2] NURSE AIDE TRAINING

The education and training of nurse aides is of increasing significance as more duties are shifted to them from nurses. In 1986, the Institute of Medicine reported that the majority of states had *no training requirements* for the nurse aides who perform most of the resident care in nursing homes. OBRA 1987 established new requirements for nurse aide (and home health aide) training. For the first time, nurse aides in many states had to meet minimum education and skills requirements.

Nurse aides must receive a minimum of 75 hours of training. The regulations specify that at least 16 hours must be classroom instruction prior to hands-on care of a resident. The topics must include communication and interpersonal skills, infection control, safety/emergency procedures, promoting residents' independence; and respecting residents' rights. It must also include 16 hours of skills training to ensure, at a minimum, competency in basic nursing skills, personal care skills, mental health and social service needs (particularly for residents with Alzheimer's disease and related disorders), basic restorative services, and residents' rights. There are "grandmother clauses," however, which allow prior training or substantial experience to substitute for the new requirements. The state must establish the training program and provide a formal competency evaluation before certification, and a facility which is in compliance with federal regulation may be approved to operate a training program. However, there must be an option to establish competency by some other method than written examination and at the facility where the aide is employed. The facility must not charge the nurse aides for books or the time required for training.

In addition, each state must establish a registry of qualified nurse aides which includes any official findings of abuse, neglect, or misappropriation of property or funds. A facility must consult the registry before hiring a nurse aide.

QUESTIONS

1. Must nursing homes always have aides less skilled than other facilities? Nursing homes assert that they cannot pay the wages hospitals can afford, and indeed nurse aides in hospitals receive higher wages. Therefore, it appears that nursing homes will become constant training grounds for aides who will soon leave for hospital work.

2. In 2002, CMS ruled that nursing homes could employ "feeding assistants" in response to criticism of the heavy work load of nurse aides. No similar category of worker, i.e., employed for only a single purpose, exists in the regulations and no CMS regulations have been issued. Clearly this is an expansion of the nursing home level care into workers with minimal training. Residents who cannot eat by themselves may have dementia or be very impaired physically. Is this change in rules wise? Why, or why not?

[3] RESIDENTS' RIGHTS

The right of service recipients, in an institution or the community, to choose their own services and lifestyles is balanced by the right and responsibility of the provider to deliver appropriate care of adequate quality. The standard of care is set by statutory law, industry practice, and the courts. The Federal Nursing Home Reform Act was enacted to assure the quality of life of nursing home residents. Federal law establishes a resident's bill of rights:

Under the Act residents have rights to:

Autonomy:

    a.   To choose a personal physician

    b.   To participate in planning care and treatment, based on full information from their caregivers

    c.   To reasonable accommodation of individual needs and preferences

    d.   To voice grievances and receive a response promptly and without reprisal

    e.   To organize with other residents and family groups

Information:

    a.   To be informed of resident rights at admission and on request, and receive a written copy of rights and grievance procedures

    b.   To be informed of the latest facility inspection results and any plan of correction

    c.   To be informed in advance of changes in room or roommate

    d.   To be informed of rates and extra charges for services

    e.   To be informed regarding Medicaid benefits and applications

Privacy and communication:

    a.   To participate, or decline to participate, in social, religious and community activities

    b.   To bodily and personal privacy in medical examination and treatment

    c.   To privacy in personal visiting, written and telephone communication, and meetings of residents and family (i.e., advocacy) groups

    d.   To confidentiality in personal records

e. To give consent to ombudsman access to personal records

f. To immediate access by a personal physician, representatives of the health department, and the long-term care ombudsman

g. To immediate access by relatives, if desired

h. To access to other visitors, including organizations and individuals providing health, social, legal, or other services, subject to the resident's consent and to "reasonable restrictions"

Limitations on transfers and discharges:

a. No transfers unless: the facility cannot meet the resident's medical needs; the resident has improved so that nursing home care no longer is necessary; continued residence threatens the health or safety of others; the resident has failed, after reasonable notice, to pay for continued residence in the facility

b. Notice of transfer at least 30 days in advance, or as soon as possible if transfer is required for health reasons; including reasons for transfer, information regarding rights to appeal, and the name, address, and phone number of the long-term care ombudsman or other advocacy program

c. Notice of bedhold policies, and Medicaid bedhold coverage

Personal financial protection and access:

a. To keep funds over $50 in a separate interest-bearing account

b. To keep other funds in a separate account or petty cash

c. To a complete, individual written accounting of transactions, available for review

Freedom from Medicaid discrimination (discussed above).

Freedom from abuse and use of restraints without a physician's authorization (also discussed above).

42 C.F.R. § 483.10.

Numerous cases have held that the federal standards do not create a private right of action for nursing home residents or their families. Some states have also enacted residents' bill of rights and in some instances, the resident can sue to enforce the rights.

QUESTION

If the resident cannot sue to enforce these rights, who can?

NOTE ON THE USE OF PHYSICAL AND CHEMICAL RESTRAINTS

Nursing homes in the United States frequently use physical restraints (vests, ties, and chairs that cannot be released by the wearer) and chemical restraints (tranquilizers and related medications) in response to resident agitation, delusions, wandering, and falling out of bed. Industry practice in other countries suggests that such use has been too frequent and researchers suggest that restraints cause severe stress to the resident as well as anguish to staff members who hear their cries and watch their struggles. In response to legal mandates that no restraints be used without a doctor's authorization, the widespread practice of restraining residents has receded. Yet long-term care providers have been reluctant to reduce the use of restraints in part because of fear of liability. Family members may be most concerned that their elderly relative be safe from falling or wandering away, without understanding the harm in restraint.

SENATE SPECIAL COMMITTEE ON AGING, UNTIE THE ELDERLY: QUALITY CARE WITHOUT RESTRAINTS 197–99
(Symposium, Dec. 4, 1989, Serial No. 101-H)

Health care institutions may abandon the use of physical restraints without incurring a significant risk of being sued for malpractice. There are few precedents supporting successful malpractice claims against long-term care facilities based upon a failure to restrain. In fact, the striking conclusion from an examination of cases involving restraints both in nursing homes and hospitals is that the *use* of restraints has produced more successful law suits than nonuse. Moreover, the strong trend of Federal regulations to limit use of restraints makes it even less likely that a failure to restrain will be held actionable in the future. (See particularly new Health Care Financing Administration Rules and Regulations, 54 Fed. Reg. 5363 (1989)).

Why have there been so few cases holding that injuries resulting from falls or from wandering off premises — the two most frequently cited justifications for the use of physical restraints — could and should have been prevented by the application of restraints? A primary reason is probably the lack of economic incentive to actively pursue such law suits. The amount of damages plaintiffs may anticipate recovering based upon injuries to or even upon the death of a frail elderly person without earning capacity is modest indeed.

Another reason is the difficulty of establishing a causal connection between the failure to restrain and the injury. In the few cases decided there is a clear recognition by courts of the natural propensity of the frail elderly to fall or to wander, with the implicit suggestion that accidents are, sooner or later, inevitable.

Moreover, courts in several cases have avoided a holding based on a failure to restrain and have instead found that the facility has failed to meet a reasonable standard of care which insured the safety of the patient. Some very fine line drawing is necessary. In *Horton v. Niagara Falls Memorial Medical Center*, 380 N.Y.S.2d 116 (N.Y. App. Div., 1976), the court attempted to draw the line:

[W]hile the fact that the hospital staff followed the instructions of the patient's attending physician on the use of restraints may protect the hospital from liability on that issue (assuming the physician was fully informed and that the hospital had no reason to believe that the care was inadequate), it is not conclusive in matters in which the hospital has a separate and independent duty to the patient. The duty of the hospital to supervise the patient and prevent him from injuring himself remained, even after the physician's instructions were given, and the court's charge properly instructed the jury on this responsibility.

Id. at 120.

In *Horton*, the hospital was found negligent in its duty to provide reasonable care to a patient whose capacity to care for himself was limited, not in its failure to restrain the patient.

Two Louisiana cases address the issue of the standard of care for patients known to be confused and incapable of caring for themselves. In *Booty v. Kentwood Manor Nursing Home Inc.*, 483 So. 2d 634 (La. Ct. App., 1985) and *Fields v. Senior Citizens Center, Inc.*, 528 So. 2d 573 (La. Ct. App., 1988), nursing homes had reasonably responded to the difficulty of caring for the confused, wandering patient by installing alarm systems. In both cases, the systems were not operating at the time of the injury. Additionally, the physical layout of the buildings made it difficult to keep patients under close observation.

Although the family members in *Fields* were aware that individual supervision would not be provided, and in fact had signed a release, the facility was found negligent in its care of the decedent. The release was held inadmissible.

What becomes evident in these cases and in yet another Louisiana case, *McGillivray v. Rapides Iberia Management Enterprises*, 493 So. 2d 819 (La. Ct. App., 1986), is an unwillingness on the part of the court to hold that there was a duty to restrain. Rather, the court emphasizes the duty to supervise and provide reasonable care. If the facility could have met this standard by a properly operating alarm system or by proper supervision, then negligence lies in the improper performance of those duties, not in the failure to restrain. *McGillivray* emphasizes this distinction in italics: *"The findings below refer not to the failure of nurses to place Mr. Fox in the harness that night, but to their failure to guard against his leaving the premises."* *McGillivray*, 493 So. 2d at 823.

[4] THE LONG-TERM CARE OMBUDSMAN

Section 307 of the Older Americans Act requires that each state operate a long-term care ombudsman program which:

. . . provides an individual who will, on a full-time basis — (i) investigate and resolve complaints made by or on behalf of older individuals who are residents of long-term care facilities relating to action, inaction, or decisions of providers, or their representatives, of long-term care services, of public agencies, or of social service agencies, which may adversely affect

the health, safety, welfare, or rights of such residents. 42 U.S.C.
§ 3027(a)(12)(A)(i).

The Senate Committee on Aging's DEVELOPMENTS IN AGING 264 (1989) describes
the ombudsman's duties:

> The primary role of long-term care ombudsmen is that of consumer
> advocate, and they are not limited to responding to complaints about the
> quality of care. Problems with public entitlements, guardianships, or any
> number of issues that a nursing home resident may encounter are within
> the jurisdiction of the ombudsman. A major objective of the ombudsmen is
> to establish a regular presence in long-term care facilities, so they can
> become well-acquainted with the residents, the employees, and the work-
> ings of the facility. This presence is important as it helps the ombudsman
> establish credibility and trust.

The term "long-term care facilities" includes nursing homes and non-medical (i.e.,
assisted living or board and care) facilities.

OBRA 1987 requires that a facility notify a resident of the name, mailing
address, and telephone number of the ombudsman before transfer or discharge as
part of a notice of rights to appeal. *See* http://www.ltcombudsman.org or any state
site.

A state long-term care ombudsman typically oversees and assists local long-term
care ombudsman councils, which number more than 600 throughout the states.
Most of the councils' complaint investigations are conducted by volunteers, who
must be trained for their work. The complaint reports are compiled in a state data
bank, to be analyzed and reported to the Commissioner on Aging.

The state must assure that ombudsmen have access to long-term care facilities
and patients' records, which are confidential. The ombudsmen in turn are required
to maintain confidentiality regarding any patient information. Usually the ombudsman takes action to correct a problem in a facility — if action beyond advice and
oversight is necessary — by requesting investigation by the state agency which
conducts survey and certification activities. However, under the Older Americans
Act Amendments of 1987, the ombudsman can also represent residents in partisan
actions, such as "administrative, legal and other appropriate remedies on behalf of
residents of long-term care facilities." In a number of states, the ombudsman's role
as advocate in legal causes has prompted more accessible legal representation from
the state.

QUESTIONS

1. Federal law requires that ombudsmen have adequate counsel, but does not
define "adequate." Who should that counsel be? Often, counsel for the nursing home
monitoring agency is designated to help the ombudsman at need. Does that present
a conflict of interest?

2. When the state ombudsman challenges the action of a state agency, should
the attorney general provide counsel? According to the legislative sponsors,
adequate counsel is "attorneys who are knowledgeable about nursing home related

law and who have the resources to properly assist and represent ombudsmen when the occasion requires it." Does the attorney general qualify?

Are ombudsmen effective? Upon Congressional direction, an exhaustive program evaluation conducted by the Institute of Medicine reported:

> On the basis of all the information it reviewed, collected, and analyzed, the committee concludes that the ombudsman program serves a vital public purpose. [However,] [i]n its assessment, the committee identified considerable barriers to effective performance that the ombudsman programs encounter. Significant among these are inadequate funding, resulting staff shortages, low salary levels for paid staff, structural conflicts of interest that limit the ability to act, and uneven implementation within and across states.

This generally positive evaluation of ombudsman programs (albeit not without some reservations) is shared by others, such as social policy commentator Joel Handler:

> In general, the presence of an ombudsman program enhances the quality of life and the care of nursing home residents. Apparently the mere presence of concerned outsiders increases the staff's sense of importance and motivation. In addition, attention to the needs of the residents enhances their status in the eyes of the staff, which results in greater respect and better care. [This] [p]resence also brings home to the staff and the administrators the fact of their accountability.

INSTITUTE OF MEDICINE, REAL PEOPLE, REAL PROBLEMS: AN EVALUATION OF THE LONG-TERM CARE OMBUDSMAN PROGRAMS OF THE OLDER AMERICANS ACT 41–77 (1995).

[5] ADMINISTRATIVE SANCTIONS

In the past, the state agency responsible for survey and certification of Medicare- and Medicaid-reimbursable facilities had only one type of sanction — decertification and the cut-off of federal funding. OBRA 1987 amended Section 1919 of the Social Security Act (42 U.S.C. § 1396r) to require states to authorize use of a range of intermediate sanctions against facilities which are out of compliance with regulations in addition to the severest sanction of decertification. These sanctions include civil monetary penalties and appointment of temporary management, called receivership. Monetary penalties or fines can be assessed and collected, with interest, for each day in which the facility is out of compliance. The facility may also be temporarily denied funding by denying payment for some or all federally funded patients or declaring a moratorium on new admissions. A receiver can be appointed whenever the facility's deficiencies indicate that there is need for an orderly closing or for temporary management to make improvements. The state can also create other intermediate sanctions, such as directed plans of correction, in which the state surveyor will require implementation by the current management of a detailed plan for eliminating deficiencies. A plan of correction must conclude within six months. If the deficiencies threaten the health or safety of the residents, the state must recommend immediate action to remove the deficiencies or termination of certification to receive federal payments.

If the state finds that a facility is not in compliance, but that its deficiencies do *not* immediately jeopardize the health or safety of its residents, the state may recommend to the Secretary the use of one of the intermediate sanctions. If the facility is out of compliance for three months, the Secretary must deny payments for new admissions. If failure to comply extends to three consecutive surveys, the Secretary must deny payments for new admissions and current residents.

Administrative, or "intermediate," sanctions seldom are used, however. States generally allocate no funds to pay receivers, and there is no ready force of administrators to take over troubled facilities. The use of fines for facilities serving the poor, generally with low pay to employees, exacerbates the problems of morale and lack of supplies that are a contributing cause of poor care. Fines are most effective when used against the large corporation with many homes. Large corporations have evaded fines by using corporate structures that separate corporations for care delivery and profit holdings. In such a case, the licensed care provider has few assets and the corporation that holds the money is not a recognized provider of care.

C. CONTRACTS FOR NURSING HOME CARE

Every nursing home resident has a contract with the facility, stating the conditions under which care is provided, the type of care, and the terms of payment. Such contracts are often signed in times of physical and emotional distress for the elderly person and family members, who are reluctant to make the change of residence. The terms of the contract may receive little attention until there is a problem or complaint about the facility's services.

A number of commonly used contract provisions have been found to unfairly burden the resident's rights and impose obligations on family members which are contrary to public policy. As a result, state and federal laws have placed restrictions on a number of commonly misused provisions. A number of states have drafted and encourage the use of model contracts. See, for example, Maryland's model contract at http://www.msba.org/departments/commpubl/publications/brochures/nursing contract.htm.

[1] THIRD-PARTY GUARANTEES

It has been a very common practice for nursing homes to require that a "responsible party," someone other than the resident, sign the contract and so assume responsibility for payment. One 1986 California study found such clauses in 102 of 105 contracts examined. The nursing home reforms of OBRA 1987 prohibit the use of such clauses in any contact with a facility which participates in Medicare or Medicaid. The third party cannot be required to sign, even if the contract does not require a promise of payment. Federal regulation (42 C.F.R. § 442.312) concerning delegation of resident rights has been interpreted to preclude anyone from signing an admission contract on behalf of the resident, unless the resident has been adjudicated incompetent or a physician certifies that he or she is incapable of understanding the rights and responsibilities subject to the contract. The resident has an express right, under the federal resident's bill of rights, to participate in treatment decisions and manage his or her own financial affairs. 42 C.F.R. § 405.1121(k)(3) and (6). The prohibition on delegation of rights should (but does not) eliminate such practices as consulting a third party for treatment decisions and financial matters.

Change in the law did not solve the problems. A 1994 survey of Los Angeles County nursing homes showed that 60 percent of the surveyed facilities required a guarantee for residents ineligible for Medicaid. Typically, a facility will assert that the prohibition on third-party guarantees applies only to residents eligible for federal nursing home benefits. Alternatively, a family member might be asked to sign as a "responsible party," implying that one takes responsibility for health care and other personal decisions for the resident, and subsequently using the signature as an agreement to pay.

[2] SOLICITATION OF CONTRIBUTIONS

Though there is no prohibition on genuine voluntary contributions, it is illegal under the Medicare and Medicaid antifraud and antiabuse act for a nursing home to require a "gift, money, donation, or other contribution" as a condition for admission or continued stay. 42 U.S.C. § 1320a-7b(d). It is difficult, however, to prove that payment was made in order to secure the resident's admission, and problematic for the attorney to advise a client to withhold a payment which will in fact secure a place in a preferred facility. Charles Sabatino observes, in *Nursing Home Admission Contracts: Undermining Rights the Old-Fashioned Way*, 24 CLEARINGHOUSE REV. 553 (Oct. 1990), that the mere knowledge that the institution seeks contributions may be inherently coercive upon the family in light of bed shortages and the tremendous stress attendant to seeking nursing home admissions (citing *United States v. Downtown Jewish Home for the Aged*, No. 97-4165 (E.D. Pa. Mar. 2, 1989) (Medicare and Medicaid Guide No. 45,082), which was settled by consent decree, after which the facility filed for bankruptcy).

[3] DURATION-OF-STAY CLAUSES

Duration-of-stay clauses, formerly found in many nursing home contracts, require the prospective resident and family to assure the facility a certain number of months at the private pay rate before the resident attempts to qualify for Medicaid. Such clauses are prohibited by the nursing home reform provisions of OBRA 1987. Facilities also are prohibited from requiring any additional payment for the care of a Medicaid resident. Oral agreements, however, continue to be made in states where facilities can pressure families to pay and refuse admission on the basis of financial information. In *Glengariff Corp. v. Snook*, 122 Misc. 2d 784, 471 N.Y.S.2d 973 (Sup. Ct. 1984), the court considered the terms of a nursing home contract that called for months at the private pay rate before Medicaid payment would be accepted:

> Patient and Sponsor acknowledge and agree that the Glengariff Corporation is not obligated to accept Medicaid payments in lieu of the private payments from the Patient and Sponsor required hereunder unless and until (a) the Patient shall have been a patient in the Facility for a period of at least *18 months* and (b) the Patient and Sponsor shall have paid in full

all sums due The Glengariff Corporation hereunder from the Patient and Sponsor for all periods prior to the first actual receipt of such Medicaid payments and shall have performed in full all of the obligations under this agreement on their part to be performed during such periods. The Glengariff Corporation will credit against the sums due The Glengariff Corporation hereunder from the Patient and Sponsor any reimbursements actually received from Medicare for Facility services and items furnished by The Glengariff Corporation to the Patient.

For additional information about admission contracts and some of the issues that can arise, see Amy Delaney, *Maneuvering the Labyrinth of Long-Term Care Admissions Contracts*, 4 NAELA L.J. 35 (2008).

QUESTION

Should individuals be permitted to supplement the Medicaid payment in order to obtain a bed in a nursing home where they prefer to live?

[4] WAIVERS OF LIABILITY

Many nursing home contracts include waivers, or limitations, of liability. Most often scattered throughout the document, such provisions may waive liability for loss or damage to personal property, contrary to the federal bill of rights provisions that assure that the resident has the right to retain and use personal possessions and clothing. The contract may also attempt to waive responsibility for personal injuries, whether caused by the negligence of the facility, staff, or another resident, or may set a limit on the amount which can be recovered or the length of time in which an action can be brought. These provisions contravene state tort laws which govern the injured party's right to sue and the statute of limitations.

An additional problem is a clause which gives broad advance consent to medical treatment. The resident is deprived of the right to give informed consent to specific procedures, contrary to medical malpractice law. As long as the resident is competent, treatment should not be provided without informed consent.

[5] UNFAIR TRADE PRACTICES

Many nursing home contract provisions which are not expressly prohibited by state or federal law can be challenged as unfair trade practices under state unfair and deceptive acts and practices (UDAP) laws. Every state has such statutes, which may be called "deceptive trade practices acts" or "fair trade acts." Unfair and deceptive practices include a broader range of activities than common-law fraud, such as taking advantage of the consumer by using superior knowledge or bargaining position, or coercive or misleading sales practices. Usually prosecution is undertaken by an attorney general or district attorney, but most states also authorize private action by the consumer for at least some abuses. The plaintiff can recover actual damages from a statutory minimum, punitive damages for intentional violations, injunctive relief and other equitable relief as appropriate, court costs, and attorney's fees. Some UDAP statutes exempt practices which are regulated under other statutes or regulations, which could lead the court to exclude violations by nursing homes. The statutes cannot be used to challenge the fairness or deceptiveness of any practices which are expressly permitted under regulatory law.

In *People v. Casa Blanca Convalescent Homes, Inc.*, 159 Cal. App. 3d 509, 206 Cal. Rptr. 164 (1984), for example, the district attorney in San Diego County prosecuted a nursing home for numerous failures to provide adequate care, including failure to prevent decubitus ulcers, serve an adequate diet and keep the facility free from flies and pests, and maintain adequate records. The instances of poor care were characterized as an unlawful pattern of business practices and unfair acts under California's Business and Professions Code. The court affirmed the issuance of an injunction and $167,000 in fines.

Other unfair trade practices include the use of contract terms that are vague or misleading because it is likely the consumer will assume that any terms in the contract are enforceable and so may fail to pursue a legal right because the contract appears to waive it.

A nursing home contract may be illegal because it is difficult to read. Problems have included the use of very tiny print; printing on two sides on nearly transparent paper; confusing sentence structure and obscure legal language; and nearly illegible copying.

Under the contract of admission, the resident has an obligation to pay. If the resident's cost of care is not paid, the nursing home can evict the resident subject to the federal limitation that no eviction can occur if the resident has submitted to a third-party purveyor, such as Medicaid or Medicare, all of the paperwork necessary for the bill to be paid. Only after the Medicaid or Medicare denies the claim and the resident refuses to pay may eviction occur. 42 C.F.R. § 483.12.

SLOVIK v. PRIME HEALTHCARE CORPORATION D/B/A DADEVILLE CONVALESCENT HOME
838 So. 2d 1054 (Ala. Civ. App. 2002)

Murdock, Judge.

William Slovik ("Slovik") appeals from a purported judgment of the Tallapoosa Circuit Court awarding Prime Healthcare Corporation ("Prime Healthcare") $5,282 in damages for Slovik's alleged breach of a promise to pay his stepfather's nursing-home care from his stepfather's Social Security income.

In 1994, Slovik's stepfather entered a nursing home owned by Prime Healthcare and operated under the name "Dadeville Convalescent Home." The stepfather remained in the Dadeville Convalescent Home until his death some time after January 15, 1999, the date Slovik and his stepfather filed their complaint in this matter, but before the trial of this matter on January 29, 2001. From September 1994 through December 1998 the Alabama Medicaid Agency ("Medicaid") paid the Dadeville Convalescent Home a portion of the cost of the care it provided Slovik's stepfather. During this period, the remainder of the cost of Slovik's stepfather's care came from Social Security retirement benefits received by Slovik on behalf of the stepfather.

On January 7, 1998, Medicaid notified Slovik and his stepfather that it had allegedly overpaid by $6,482 for the stepfather's nursing-home care in 1997. Medicaid requested that the stepfather reimburse the agency for the alleged overpayment. Slovik's stepfather requested an administrative hearing regarding Medicaid's claim and a hearing was held before an administrative hearing officer.

On August 12, 1998, the administrative hearing officer rendered a decision against Slovik's stepfather, concluding that the stepfather owed Medicaid $6,482. Slovik's stepfather filed an administrative appeal of the hearing officer's decision; that appeal was not successful. On December 21, 1998, Medicaid notified Slovik's stepfather that he would be disqualified for Medicaid benefits effective December 31, 1998, for a period of at least one year and thereafter until he repaid the $6,482.

During 1998, while the stepfather's dispute with Medicaid was pending, Medicaid allegedly informed Slovik and his stepfather that the amount the stepfather was responsible for paying for his nursing-home care had increased. However, Slovik, who was the Social Security "personal representative" for his stepfather and who apparently handled the stepfather's financial matters, allegedly refused to make payments at the increased rate.

Some time during 1998, Prime Healthcare sued Slovik in the District Court of Tallapoosa County. Although the record from that district court action is not included in the record on appeal, Prime Healthcare apparently asserted that Slovik had breached an alleged agreement between Slovik and Prime Healthcare to be personally responsible for paying from his stepfather's Social Security income (over which Slovik exercised control) that portion of the cost of his stepfather's care not paid by Medicaid. In December 1998 the district court entered a judgment in favor of Prime Healthcare and against Slovik. The district court amended its judgment in January 1999.

On December 30, 1998, Prime Healthcare issued a 30-day discharge notice to Slovik and his stepfather, notifying Slovik that it planned to discharge the stepfather from the Dadeville Convalescent Home on February 1, 1999, for allegedly failing to pay $6,833 for nursing-home care. The notice also informed Slovik and his stepfather of the stepfather's right to appeal this decision to the State Department of Public Health.

On January 15, 1999, Slovik and his stepfather filed a complaint in the Tallapoosa Circuit Court against Medicaid and Prime Healthcare. In their complaint, Slovik and his stepfather appealed from the district court's judgment in favor of Prime Healthcare and requested that the circuit court review Medicaid's decision regarding that agency's $6,482 reimbursement claim. Slovik also interpleaded the sum of $6,033 and requested that the court decide who was entitled to those funds. Slovik and his stepfather also alleged that Medicaid and Prime Healthcare had conspired to evict the stepfather from the Dadeville Convalescent Home; they alleged that that eviction constituted a taking of the stepfather's property without due process of law and that it violated the stepfather's rights under the United States Constitution and under 42 U.S.C. § 1983 *et seq.*

Soon after Slovik's complaint was filed, the circuit court issued an order stating that it lacked subject-matter jurisdiction over Slovik's and his stepfather's eviction claim. On April 13, 1999, Slovik and his stepfather requested that the circuit court pay the interpleaded funds to Medicaid pursuant to a settlement agreement. On April 28, 1999, the circuit court entered an order directing that the interpleaded funds be paid to Medicaid.

After an ore tenus hearing in January 2001, the circuit court entered a judgment against Slovik on Prime Healthcare's claim that Slovik had promised to be personally responsible for making payments to Prime Healthcare from his stepfather's Social Security income. The circuit court specifically determined that Slovik "was a party to the original promise to pay [Prime Healthcare], not a promise of guarantee, and, therefore, said promise is not within the statute of frauds and does not require a written document" and entered a judgment against Slovik in the amount of $5,282. After the circuit court denied a postjudgment motion filed by Slovik, he appealed.

On appeal, Slovik argues that he did not assume any personal contractual obligation to pay his stepfather's alleged debt to Prime Healthcare and that the Statute of Frauds requires that any agreement he may have made to pay the debt of his stepfather be in writing. As to the latter argument, Slovik correctly notes that the Statute of Frauds requires, in pertinent part, that "every special promise to answer for the debt, default or miscarriage of another" must be in writing. Ala. Code 1975, § 8-9-2(3). However, Prime Healthcare did not argue at trial that Slovik was liable for the alleged debt of another and specifically asserted that it was not attempting to collect the stepfather's debt from Slovik as a guarantor. Instead, Prime Healthcare argued that Slovik had agreed to be personally responsible each month for forwarding a portion of his stepfather's Social Security income, over which Slovik had control, to Prime Healthcare to pay for part of the cost of the stepfather's nursing-home care and that Slovik had failed to forward the agreed-upon funds to Prime Healthcare. As a result, Prime Healthcare argued that Slovik was liable for damages resulting from his failure to do so. Because Prime Healthcare's theory of recovery is premised upon an alleged agreement by Slovik as a primary obligor, rather than as a guarantor of his stepfather's performance, Slovik's argument that his purported obligation to Prime Healthcare was in the nature of a guaranty agreement governed by the Statute of Frauds is without merit.

. . . .

We note that the only document Prime Healthcare introduced into evidence that might have evidenced an agreement between it and Slovik was instead introduced solely for the limited purpose of proving that Slovik had executed a document as his stepfather's "personal representative." That document, Plaintiff's Exhibit 1, appears to have been compiled from two separate documents. The first two pages of Plaintiff's Exhibit 1 are an unsigned letter from Medicaid to Slovik's stepfather (in care of Slovik) regarding the deficiency amount Medicaid claimed that Slovik's stepfather owed Medicaid. The remaining pages of Plaintiff's Exhibit 1 are apparently the last two pages of a document executed by Slovik, as the stepfather's "personal representative," and by the Dadeville Convalescent Home's nursing administrator, on October 14, 1997.

An office manager for Prime Healthcare testified regarding Plaintiff's Exhibit 1:

Q: "Do you have any contract whereby he promised to pay you money?

A: "No, I don't have a contract that specifically states that, but he did sign as sponsor.

Q: "Who with?

A: "And to be responsible.

          ". . . .

Q: "Who did he sign as sponsor with? It was with the Medicaid agency, was it not?

A: "Well, with Dadeville Convalescent Home. And I'm not sure exactly what he signed with Medicaid.

Q: "He signed with Dadeville Convalescent Home. This Exhibit Number 1, is this it?

A: "I'm not really the person that should answer that.

          ". . . .

Q: "He's the sponsor, right?

A: "Personal representative.

Q: "Personal representative. It doesn't say 'sponsor.' It says 'personal representative.' . . . And who is this with?

A: "It says 'Dadeville Convalescent Home.'

Q: "And that's in 1997; is that correct?

A: "Um-hum.

          ". . . .

Q: "I'm asking you is there any contract, any written contract to back up this complaint that you have filed suit on? . . . Is there any document that you can show me where there is an agreement by Mr. Slovik to pay Prime Healthcare anything?

A: "I assume that that is the — That is one of those kinds of documents.

Q: "Anything other than this?

A: "Not to my knowledge.

Q: "Okay. So you're relying totally on page four of Plaintiff's Exhibit 1 for the basis of him owing you money?

A: "Not to my knowledge. Ms. Jo Brand may be able to indicate that there is something else, but not to my knowledge."

The office manager was the only witness who testified on behalf of Prime

Healthcare; the record contains no testimony from a witness by the name of Jo Brand. The only other witness at the trial was Slovik, who admitted only that his signature appeared on page 4 of Plaintiff's Exhibit 1 as "personal representative."

The Alabama Supreme Court has stated that "absent an admission by the defendant of the existence, execution, and content of [a] written agreement, a written contract sued upon must be put into evidence." *Alabama Life & Disability Ins. Guar. Ass'n v. Trentham,* 543 So. 2d 195, 196 (Ala. 1989). As noted above, the contents of Plaintiff's Exhibit 1 were introduced into evidence only for the purpose of proving that Slovik had executed a document as his stepfather's "personal representative." The contents of that document were not admitted into evidence for the purpose of showing the terms of a contract. Further, Slovik did not make any "admission" regarding the contents of the document.

The circuit court, however, apparently found that there was an oral agreement between Slovik and Prime Healthcare. In so doing, the trial court based its judgment on a finding that Slovik "was a party to the original promise to pay [Prime Healthcare] . . . and . . . [that] said promise [was] not within the statute of frauds and [did] not require a written document." (Emphasis added.)

In addition to her testimony discussed above, the office manager for Prime Healthcare also testified:

Q: And tell us why it is from whatever you got from Medicaid or in your record or whatever, that [Slovik] owes that money?

        . . . .

A: Because [Slovik] had charge of [his stepfather's] Social Security check.

Q: [The stepfather's] money?

        . . . .

A: Yes.

Slovik argues on appeal that there is insufficient evidence to support the trial court's finding that he agreed to "make his own debt" to Prime Healthcare. On the record presented in this case, we must agree. Based on our review of that record, we do not find that it contains "substantial evidence" to support the trial court's finding that Slovik "was a party to the original promise to pay [Prime Healthcare]."

The circuit court's judgment against Slovik in the amount of $5,282 is reversed, and the cause is remanded for further proceedings consistent with this opinion.

REVERSED AND REMANDED.

YATES, P.J., and CRAWLEY, THOMPSON, and PITTMAN, JJ., concur.

QUESTION

Do you agree with the court that this nursing facility's claim was in the nature of "a third party guarantee of payment to the facility as a condition of admission, or expedited admission or continued stay in the facility" as found in ALA. ADMIN. CODE

r. 560-X-10-.02? If not, how would you have argued the case differently?

D. NURSING HOME QUALITY OF CARE LITIGATION

In general, nursing homes are not insurers of safety for their residents. Their obligation is to adhere to the requirements of a responsible plan of care that meets the residents' health needs. The standard of care that must be provided by paid caregivers is defined by the contract of care, by professional standards for licensed providers, and by federal and state regulations, which establish detailed standards for adequate care and require a nursing home to account for any deterioration in a resident's condition.

In the past, nursing home negligence cases were rare, in part because the cost of litigation exceeded any likely return in damages. Elements that contribute to a high damage sum include the cost of future care and lost wages, neither of which amount to much in a nursing home case. Further, it may be difficult to assess the physical damage caused by the neglect or mistreatment because the resident is in poor condition to start with. Finally, the resident may be unable to provide any information about the cause of his or her harm, so the facility might assert that it is not directly responsible and, in any case, is no guarantor.

Much changed in the late 1990s. The National Law Journal reported in 1997 that the largest personal injury verdicts, $93.37 million and $83 million, were in nursing home cases. *Verdicts and Settlements: Nursing Home Loses $83M for Wrongful Death, Fraud*, NAT'L L.J., Dec. 15, 1997. Jury Verdict Research counted 27 verdicts against nursing homes that year, compared with 11 in 1996. In 1998, the average award was $1.3 million.

In another case, jurors awarded $95.1 million against Beverly Enterprises, the largest nursing home corporation in the U.S. The plaintiff was a 69-year-old woman who broke her shoulder and hip when she was being readied to be moved from her bed. An important tool to allow damages is a complaint based in the state elder abuse statute rather than medical malpractice statutes that often have caps on non-economic damages.

Cases typically include such claims as negligence in allowing a resident to wander away, to be harmed in the highway, in lake or pond, or in inclement weather. Skin breakdown into decubiti, or pressure sores caused by inadequate turning and bathing is a frequent cause of action. Assault, including sexual assault by another resident can be the basis for a claim. Other cases present claims for choking, scalding and burns, malnutrition and dehydration, and falls. Finally, abuse by staff can be attributed to the facility under theories of respondeat superior or direct corporate negligence.

A growing body of literature for practitioners shows increasing expertise in nursing home litigation. *See, e.g.,* NURSING HOME LITIGATION: INVESTIGATION AND CASE PREPARATION (Patricia W. Iyer ed., Lawyers' and Judges' Publishing Co. 1999).

Consider the following wrongful death case in light of the material above on nursing home quality of care.

MONTGOMERY HEALTH CARE FACILITY v. BALLARD
565 So. 2d 221 (Ala. 1990)

Ella Ballard, administratrix of the estate of Edna Stovall, deceased, filed suit against Montgomery Health Care Facility, First American Health Care, Inc., and Dr. Kynard Adams, alleging that the defendants provided negligent or wanton care and that their negligence proximately caused the death of Mrs. Stovall. Mrs. Stovall was a patient at Montgomery Health Care Facility, a nursing home. First American Health Care, Inc., is the parent corporation of Montgomery Health Care, and Dr. Adams was Mrs. Stovall's treating physician at the nursing home. The plaintiff claims that as a proximate cause of the defendants' negligence or wantonness, Mrs. Stovall suffered multiple infected bedsores, from which she died.

Mrs. Stovall was admitted to the nursing home on February 8, 1985, suffering from organic brain syndrome, congestive heart failure, osteoarthritis, and hypertension. The first recordation of a bedsore on Mrs. Stovall occurred on February 14, 1985. No bedsores were noted on her admitting physical examination. Bedsores, also known as decubitus ulcers and pressure sores, are caused by the compression of body tissue between a bony structure and a supporting structure such as a bed or wheelchair. This pressure obstructs the blood supply to the tissues, resulting in a deprivation of oxygen and nutrients to the area. The early stages of pressure sores involve only superficial tissues. In later stages, fat, muscle, and even the underlying bone can be affected. Bacterial infection of the sore can lead to the patient's death.

On August 14, 1985, Mrs. Stovall was sent to St. Margaret's Hospital for surgical debridement of multiple decubitus ulcers on her left hip, left upper thigh, and left heel. Debridement is the removal of dead tissue from the sore. On February 17, 1986, she was again sent to St. Margaret's Hospital, this time for debridement of a decubitus ulcer on her right hip. The operation was performed on February 21, 1986. Decubitus ulcers were also noted on her left hip, legs, and back. Mrs. Stovall died in the hospital on March 4, 1986. Her death certificate listed the cause of death as cardiopulmonary arrest due to multiple decubitus with sepsis due to a chronic vegetative state. The evidence presented at trial was disputed as to whether she was in a chronic vegetative state.

After trial, the jury returned a verdict against Montgomery Health Care Facility and First American Health Care, Inc., for $2 million, and a verdict in favor of Dr. Adams. Montgomery Health Care and First American filed motions for judgments notwithstanding the verdict and for new trial, which were denied by the trial court.

On appeal, the defendants argue that the trial court erred in admitting into evidence survey reports by the Alabama Department of Public Health, in denying their motion for a mistrial, in denying First American's motion for a directed verdict, and in denying the defendants' request for a remittitur.

The defendants argue that the trial court incorrectly admitted into evidence survey and complaint reports regarding the nursing home. These reports, compiled by the Alabama Department of Public Health, contained information about deficiencies found in the nursing home. The defendants claim that this information is inadmissible as evidence of notice to the defendants, under *Flint City Nursing Home, Inc. v. Depreast*, 406 So. 2d 356 (Ala. 1981). However, in Flint City Nursing Home, this Court held that evidence of notice to a defendant of an alleged dangerous condition or defect can be relevant to the issue of negligence and is admissible if the alleged defect proximately caused or contributed to the injury involved. In that case, evidence relating to 4 of 16 deficiencies found in a nursing home by the Alabama Department of Public Health was held inadmissible because those deficiencies did not proximately cause or contribute to the patient's death. In this case, however, there was evidence that the deficiencies noted proximately contributed to Mrs. Stovall's death. The deficiencies admitted into evidence were inadequate documentation of treatment given for decubitus ulcers; 23 patients found with decubitus ulcers, 10 of whom developed those ulcers in the facility; dressings on the sores were not changed as ordered; nursing progress notes did not describe patients' ongoing conditions, particularly with respect to descriptions of decubitus ulcers; worsening of decubitus ulcers; ineffective policies and procedures with respect to sterile dressing supplies; lack of nursing assessments; incomplete patient care plans or lack of such plans; inadequate documentation of doctors' visits, orders, or progress notes; a.m. care not consistently documented; inadequate documentation of turning of patients; incomplete "activities of daily living" sheets; "range of motion" exercises not documented; orders for placing patient up in chair not consistently documented; patients [found wet and soiled with dried fecal matter; lack of bowel and bladder retraining programs; incomplete documentation of ordered force fluids; inaccessible water pitchers; monthly weighing of patients was not done; incomplete documentation of food consumption; tube feeders were not receiving their feedings as ordered; linen was not handled properly to prevent the spread of infection; vital signs not checked as ordered; inadequate staffing; the director of nursing was not responsible for the standards of nursing practice; charge nurses had not been responsible for the supervision of nursing activities; the governing body in its management through the administrator had not enforced rules and regulations concerning patients' health and safety due to deficiencies noted in nursing services such as bowel and bladder training, activities of daily living, ambulation, patient care planning, and infection control.

There was evidence that all of these deficiencies contribute to the development or worsening of pressure sores. Pressure should be kept off the sore. One way to accomplish this is to turn the patient regularly. Proper nutrition is needed to facilitate healing. Weighing the patient regularly is one way to insure that he is being fed properly. The wound must be kept clean and must be treated regularly. The patient should be exercised and assisted with walking, if possible, to prevent contraction of joints. The less active a patient is, the more likely he is to develop pressure sores, and the more difficult the sores are to treat. Documentation of such treatment is necessary in order to monitor progress, to know which treatments have been effective with the patient, to know which treatments the previous shift has provided, etc. Adequate staff must be maintained and properly trained and supervised in order to carry out these functions.

Further, there was evidence that the care given to Mrs. Stovall was deficient in the same ways noted in the survey and the complaint reports. Her ulcers developed within the facility. . . . Mrs. Stovall's records do not contain monthly progress notes by her treating physician. Her records do not indicate that she had been exercised or turned as ordered, and they contain gaps in the documentation of am. care. Her "activities of daily living" charts are incomplete. Her records do not contain entries to show that she was ambulated or placed up in a chair as ordered. Mrs. Stovall was incontinent as early as February 1985, but there was no bowel or bladder retraining program for her until July 1985. Her food and fluid consumption was not consistently documented. One daughter testified that at times she had to get water for her mother. Mrs. Stovall was not weighed monthly as ordered. Her vital signs were not regularly documented during her first admission to Montgomery Health Care. There was evidence of lack of training and supervision of the nurses treating Mrs. Stovall. Two nurses testified that they did not know that decubitus ulcers could be life threatening. One nurse testified that she did not know that the patient's doctor should be called if there were symptoms of infection in the sore. When her daughters complained to the staff about her lack of care, they were told that staffing was inadequate. Three of Mrs. Stovall's nurses testified that the facility was understaffed. One nurse testified that she asked her supervisor for more help but that she did not get it.

The trial court gave the jury a limiting instruction stating that the deficiencies noted in the survey and complaint reports were to be considered solely on the issue of whether the defendants had notice of the alleged conditions. As discussed above, the deficiencies cited and admitted into evidence were directly related to the development of pressure sores from which Mrs. Stovall died. The plaintiff deleted deficiencies in the reports that did not relate to the development of pressure sores. Moreover, there was evidence that the care given to Mrs. Stovall was deficient in the same ways as those noted in the survey and complaint reports. Because the jury could find that the deficiencies noted were deficiencies that proximately caused Mrs. Stovall's death, this evidence was admissible and the trial judge did not abuse his discretion in admitting it.

[The defendant nursing home argues that the evidence of prior actions against it for poor care were inadmissible, and that the parent company was not responsible for negligent care.]

Last, the defendants argue that the punitive damages award of $2 million was greater than necessary to meet society's goal of punishing them and was therefore excessive, because they are bankrupt and insurance would have to cover the award. The trial court held a hearing pursuant to *Hammond v. City of Gadsden*, 493 So. 2d 1374 (Ala. 1986), on the defendants' request for a remittitur and held that the bankrupt status of the defendants did not require a remittitur. Specifically, the trial court found that, because of the bankruptcies, the defendants would not be adversely affected by the verdict. Further, the court noted that [HN3] "Alabama public policy allows liability insurance to cover punitive damages in the wrongful death context." The trial court also found that because of the large number of nursing home residents vulnerable to the type of neglect found in Mrs. Stovall's case the verdict would further the goal of discouraging others from similar conduct in the future. The evidence in the record supports these findings. Thus, the trial court correctly denied the defendants' motion for remittitur.

AFFIRMED.

In the following case, jurors had to weigh the nursing home's responsibility against the comparative fault of the resident.

PARKER v. ILLINOIS MASONIC WARREN BARR PAVILION
701 N.E.2d 190 (Ill. App. Ct. 1998)

On January 15, 1997, a jury returned a verdict of $203,116.97 in favor of plaintiff, Meta Krueger, and against defendant, Illinois Masonic Warren Barr Pavilion, reducing it by 49% to $103,589.66 for comparative fault in a negligence action. The circuit court trebled the judgment under the Nursing Home Care Act and awarded attorney fees and costs. On appeal, defendant contends that . . . the verdict was against the manifest weight of the evidence. . . .

In October 1993, Meta Krueger (Krueger), an 83-year-old woman, was admitted into the nursing home facility of Illinois Masonic Warren Barr Pavilion (Barr Pavilion) for physical therapy following a possible compression fracture of a vertebrae. Warren Barr provided both long-and short-term care, and Krueger was assigned to the short-term care unit located on the seventh floor.

Incoming patients at Barr Pavilion were given an initial nursing evaluation to determine their current condition and to judge their progress. The nurses on the floor assessed each patient daily to determine his or her ambulation status, and physical therapists summarized care and treatment of individual patients weekly. Upon admission, Krueger needed assistance with walking; therefore, at her evaluation it was deduced that her goal was to return to independent ambulation prior to her discharge. Krueger did not have a definite discharge date, but her target date for discharge was February 9, 1994.

Krueger participated in physical therapy on six occasions before November 11, 1993, and was progressing well according to physical therapy notes. However, at approximately 3:45 a.m. on November 11, 1993, Krueger fell in the bathroom of her room. It was determined that the fall occurred because Krueger did not have on her slippers. Consequently, she lost her balance and fell. A "fall follow-up" form was completed by nurse Karen Kraker, the director of nursing and associate administrator for patient care services, to prevent future falls. The form noted that Krueger had a fear of falling and increased confusion and indicated that Krueger was at risk for additional falls. Since Krueger did not use her call button to ask the staff for assistance on this occasion, nurse Kraker instructed her to use the button for assistance in the future.

On November 17, 1993, Krueger's doctor ordered that Krueger be put on stand-by assist with bed mobility, minimum assist for transfers, and ambulation of 75 feet with a rolling walker and contact. "Stand-by assist" means someone is standing next to the patient supervising, while "minimum assist" means the therapist is doing 25% to 50% of the work. On November 24, 1993, the doctor's order noted that Krueger was still on stand-by assist; however, the physical therapist's weekly note indicated that Krueger was progressing well despite her fall and recommended discharge planning.

On November 27, 1993, Krueger fell in the hallway outside her room. She alleged that a nurse entered the room and informed her that she was to be transferred to another room. When no one came to help her, Krueger packed her belongings in plastic bags, hung them over her walker, and moved them into the hallway by herself. After putting the fourth bag of clothing down, she lost her balance and fell, injuring her hip.

Krueger's nurse, Oluwayinka Adeyooye, assisted after the fall. Krueger was transferred to Northwestern Memorial Hospital, where Dr. Proctor Anderson, an orthopedic surgeon, diagnosed Krueger with an intertrochanteric fracture of her right hip. Dr. Anderson performed surgery using a plate and screws to repair the hip fracture. He last saw Krueger on December 2, 1994.

On December 6, 1993, Krueger was discharged to the Rehabilitation Institute of Chicago for physical therapy, where she was under the care of Dr. James Sliwa. After reaching her goals of independently ambulating with a walker, Krueger was discharged on December 29, 1993. On February 14, 1994, Krueger was advised to use a cane. By May 31, 1994, Dr. Sliwa advised her that she could put her full weight on her hip.

Staff notes written after the second fall indicated that on November 28, 1993, Krueger could not independently ambulate on the day she fell. However, on December 1, 1993, a "hold" note written by Krueger's therapist noted that Krueger was able to "independently perform bed mobility and ambulate" on the day of the fall. On January 24, 1994, Catherine Zapparo (Zapparo), the supervisor of physical therapy at Warren Barr, wrote a discharge summary for Krueger indicating that all of Krueger's goals had been met prior to her transfer. Zapparo had never seen Krueger prior to the fall and relied on weekly therapy notes to write her summary.

On January 15, 1997, following a jury trial on the negligence action, the jury returned a verdict of $203,116.97 in favor of Krueger and against Barr Pavilion, reducing it by 49% to $103,589.66 for comparative fault. The circuit court trebled the judgment under the Nursing Home Care Act and awarded attorney fees of $48,825 and costs of $443.40. Defendant appeals.

. . . .

Barr Pavilion first contends that it is entitled to a new trial because the jury's verdict was against the manifest weight of the evidence in that Krueger failed to establish that Warren Barr violated the Nursing Home Care Act (Act). It is well established that a jury verdict will not be overturned unless it is against the manifest weight of the evidence . . . .

Krueger filed this case as an ordinary negligence action under the Act. The elements of a cause of action for negligence are "the existence of a duty owed by defendant to the plaintiff, a breach of that duty, and an injury proximately caused by that breach." It has long been held that negligence may be proved by either direct or circumstantial evidence, and the burden of proof is on the plaintiff. Circumstantial evidence is the proof of certain facts and circumstances from which the jury may infer other connected facts that usually and reasonably follow according to the common experience of mankind.

The Illinois Supreme Court has identified certain factors that are relevant to the existence of a duty. The reasonable foreseeability of injury is one important factor; however, foreseeability alone provides an inadequate foundation upon which to base the existence of a legal duty. Other considerations include the likelihood of the injury, the magnitude of burden of guarding against it, and the consequences of placing that burden upon the defendant. The inquiry is whether the defendant could have reasonably foreseen injury to the plaintiff.

In the case sub judice, Krueger entered Barr Pavilion for short-term rehabilitative care. Specifically, she was to undergo physical therapy so that she could independently ambulate prior to her discharge. It is undisputed that the nurses on duty were responsible for the overall care of each patient. Because the elderly are more prone to falling, Krueger was at risk for falls prior to her first fall. Since the nurses had a duty to provide for Krueger's overall care in protecting her from that risk, if they failed in their duty, Barr Pavilion would be negligent.

Our review of the record establishes that, based on the evidence adduced, a reasonable jury could draw inferences of negligence regarding Krueger's nurse, Oluwayinka Adeyooye. For instance, in this case, the doctor's order of November 24, 1993 indicated that Krueger was on stand-by assist. Nurse Adeyooye testified, however, that she did not know what "stand-by assist" meant. She stated simply that if a patient needed assistance, she would assist her. Nurse Adeyooye believed that Krueger was able to independently ambulate at the time of the second fall; however, her view conflicted with other evidence on the issue.

To establish proximate cause, a plaintiff must demonstrate with reasonable certainty that defendant's negligent acts or omissions caused the injury for which she seeks recovery; otherwise, plaintiff has not sustained her burden of setting out a *prima facie* case of negligence. In this case, no one was providing care to Krueger at the time of her fall. The Act defines "neglect" as "a failure in a facility to provide adequate medical or personal care or maintenance, which failure results in physical or mental injury to a resident or in the deterioration of a resident's physical or mental condition." Although it is undisputed that Krueger did not use her call button prior to either fall, whether this lack of assistance by Barr Pavilion constituted neglect that was a proximate cause of Krueger's resulting injury was a jury question, and the jury resolved it against Barr Pavilion.

. . . .

In this case, the jury agreed with Barr Pavilion regarding Krueger's contributory negligence and, after considering the comparative negligence of the parties, reduced her award accordingly. After considering all of the evidence in the light most favorable to Krueger, we cannot find that the verdict was against the manifest weight of the evidence.

QUESTIONS

1. The cost of liability insurance for nursing homes has risen rapidly over the last 20 years. Would you seek to limit the number of lawsuits for negligent nursing home care?

2. Would you limit the amount a plaintiff might recover for pain and suffering?

Nursing homes that participate in Medicare and Medicaid are also subject to being fined by the federal Department of Health and Human Services if they fail to provide a reasonably safe environment for their residents.

CEDAR LAKE NURSING HOME v. U.S. DEPT. OF HEALTH AND HUMAN SERVICES
619 F.3d 453 (5th Cir. 2010)

W. EUGENE DAVIS, CIRCUIT JUDGE.

In this petition for review from the Departmental Appeals Board of the United States Department of Health and Human Services ("DHHS"), Petitioner Cedar Lake Nursing Home ("Cedar Lake") challenges a $5,000 per-instance civil monetary penalty levied by the DHHS against Cedar Lake for violations of 42 C.F.R. § 483.25(h). We reject Petitioner's challenge and DISMISS the petition for review.

I.

Cedar Lake is a nursing home that participates in the Medicare program. On February 20, 2008, a resident of Cedar Lake designated in the record as "Resident # 10" — a 92 year-old woman suffering from a variety of ailments — wandered away from the facility and was later discovered walking alone along a highway. Witnesses alerted Cedar Lake staff, who returned her to the facility. Cedar Lake's alarm system, designed to prevent such "elopements" by residents, did not sound when Resident # 10 opened the door to leave the facility. Cedar Lake alleges through witness testimony that the alarm did not sound because an installation contractor responsible for installing a new alarm system disconnected the old system without informing Cedar Lake personnel.

After this incident, surveyors affiliated with the Centers for Medicare and Medicaid Division ("CMS") of the DHHS conducted a survey of Cedar Lake and determined the facility to be in violation of several Medicare-related regulations, including 42 C.F.R. § 483.25(h), which requires a nursing home to "ensure that — (1) the resident environment remains as free of accident hazards as is possible; and (2) each resident receives adequate supervision and assistance devices to prevent accidents." Specifically, the surveyors found that Cedar Lake violated 42 C.F.R. § 483.25(h) with respect to Resident # 10's elopement incident. In response to these findings, CMS imposed a $5,000 per-instance civil monetary penalty on Cedar Lake for violations of 42 C.F.R. § 483.25(h).

Cedar Lake appealed this decision to an administrative law judge ("ALJ") and requested a hearing.

The ALJ's findings of undisputed fact included the following: that Resident # 10 "had a history of wandering, was at high risk for elopement, and repeatedly attempted to leave the facility"; that Cedar Lake's care plan for Resident # 10 required staff to place the resident in an area "where constant observation is possible"; and that the facility's care plan amendments for Resident # 10 included frequent observation in addition to the use of a door alarm. On the basis of these undisputed factual findings, the ALJ determined that Cedar Lake failed to take all reasonable steps to prevent Resident # 10's elopement in violation of 42 C.F.R. § 483.25(h). The ALJ, thus, granted CMS's motion for summary judgment and upheld the $5,000 per-instance civil monetary fine.

Cedar Lake appealed the ALJ's grant of summary judgment to the Departmental Appeals Board, which affirmed the ALJ's decision. Cedar Lake now seeks review in this Court.

II.

We have jurisdiction to review imposition of the civil monetary penalty against Cedar Lake pursuant to 42 U.S.C. § 1320a-7a(e). Ordinarily, review of such an administrative decision is conducted according to the deferential standards of the Administrative Procedures Act ("APA"), which permits the setting aside of agency actions, findings, and conclusions that are "arbitrary, capricious, an abuse of discretion, or otherwise not in accordance with the law" or "unsupported by substantial evidence." 5 U.S.C. §§ 706(2)(A)-(E) (2010).

. . . .

III.

Reviewing the findings and conclusions at issue here under the deferential standards of the APA, we do not consider them to be arbitrary, capricious, not in accordance with the law, or unsupported by substantial evidence.

The ALJ determined that Cedar Lake's actions with respect to Resident # 10 were in violation of 42 C.F.R. § 483.25(h)(1)-(2), which require a nursing facility to ensure that the resident environment remains as free of accident hazards "as is possible" and that each resident receives "adequate supervision and assistance devices to prevent accidents." The standard of care imposed by these "as is possible" and "adequate supervision" regulations has been consistently interpreted by the DHHS and federal courts as a "reasonableness" standard.

Based on specific, undisputed findings of fact, the ALJ determined and the Departmental Appeals Board affirmed that Cedar Lake's actions with respect to Resident # 10 were not reasonable under the standard of 42 C.F.R. § 483.25(h), in that Cedar Lake did not take all reasonable steps to prevent her from wandering out of the facility. The ALJ's undisputed findings of fact in support of this determination include not only the February 20, 2008 incident in which Resident # 10 wandered away from the facility, but also Resident # 10's history of wandering, Cedar Lake's prior knowledge of Resident # 10's propensity to wander, and Cedar

Lake's previous development of a care plan that involved frequent observation and other measures designed to prevent Resident # 10 from wandering.

Moreover, the primary facts presented by Cedar Lake, even when taken as true by the ALJ, failed to alter these core factual findings. Indeed, the ALJ accepted as true Cedar Lake's main factual presentation — affidavits by employees testifying to the effect that the installation contractor did not inform Cedar Lake that the alarm was to be turned off — but held that such facts did not show that Resident # 10's elopement was unforeseeable nor demonstrate that Cedar Lake's actions were reasonable under 42 C.F.R. § 483.25(h).

These findings and conclusions of the ALJ and the Departmental Appeals Board with regard to the unreasonableness of Cedar Lake's safety and supervision measures under 42 C.F.R. § 483.25(h) are not arbitrary, capricious, not in accordance to the law, or unsupported by substantial evidence. Therefore, this petition for review is DISMISSED.

QUESTIONS

1. If the alarm installation contractor was at fault for disconnecting the alarm system, why is the nursing home being fined?

2. A $5,000 fine is less than the cost of one month's care in the nursing home and almost certainly less than the cost of litigating the appeal of the fine. Why did the nursing home appeal?

Nursing homes can be sued for breach of contract as well as for negligence. When a tort claim is barred by the statute of limitations, contract may be the only viable theory because its statute of limitation is often longer.

SCHENCK v. LIVING CENTERS-EAST, INC.
917 F. Supp. 432 (E.D. La. 1996)

BERRIGAN, DISTRICT JUDGE.

Ms. Thelma Caruso, mother of the plaintiff, was a nursing home resident in the Jefferson Health Care Center from May, 1988 until September, 1993. The plaintiff alleges that Ms. Caruso was hospitalized on a number of occasions for broken bones and other injuries during that time, eventually resulting in partial amputation of both her legs. After the second amputation, Ms. Caruso's family chose not to return her to the home. Ms. Caruso is now deceased, apparently for causes unrelated to this litigation. The plaintiff has now brought suit, alleging on a variety of legal grounds, that the defendant failed to provide adequate care for her mother at the nursing home.

Count One — Breach of Contract

In Count One, the plaintiff alleges that the defendant breached a contract to provide Ms. Caruso with reasonable and safe care and to treat her with dignity and respect. The petition also alleges bad faith. The particular contract at issue is an "Admissions Agreement" to the nursing home, in which the home promised "reasonable care" and also pledged to protect the basic constitutional, statutory and regulatory rights of the residents. Among the rights allegedly incorporated are those set forth in 42 U.S.C. § 1396r(b)(2) which commit the home to providing services that will "maintain the highest practicable physical, mental, and psychological well-being of each resident. . . ."

Breach of contracts under Louisiana law have a ten year liberative prescription period. La. S. Ann. Civil Code art. 3499.

The defendant argues that the allegations in the complaint exclusively sound in tort with a one year prescriptive period. The defendant moves for the contract count to be dismissed.

While no Louisiana Supreme Court decision has dealt with this precise issue in this setting, an appellate decision, *Free v. Franklin Guest Home, Inc.*, 397 So. 2d 47 (La. App. 2d Cir. 1981), is directly on point. Suit was filed against a nursing home on behalf of a resident, alleging abuse and neglect over a period of several years. The issue was whether the allegations were based exclusively on tort, hence one year's prescription, or breach of contract, hence ten years. The plaintiff argued that the incidents of abuse and neglect were tortious but also violated a written contract, specifically the "Admission Agreement" and a document entitled "Patient's Rights." In the Admission Agreement, the home agreed to exercise "reasonable care" toward the resident; the Patient's Rights document pledged that the resident would not be abused and would be treated with consideration and respect.

The Second Circuit concluded that "there was clearly a contractual relationship between the nursing home and Mr. Free. . . ." 397 So. 2d at 48, and found the ten year prescriptive period to apply. The court considered it "well settled" that the same act or omission could constitute both a tort and a breach of contract. 397 So. 2d at 49. The court also concluded that even if the language of the contract added nothing to the general obligations of a nursing home towards a resident in the absence of an express contract, the home nonetheless chose to enter the contract and was thereby bound in contract. The defendant in *Free* had relied on a series of cases that held that actions for medical malpractice against a physician or a hospital are in tort and not contract, unless the doctor promised a particular result. The Second Circuit distinguished those cases on the basis that (1) in this instance a written contract existed, with contractual obligations and (2) that those other suits involved claims against an individual physician. Finally, the court appeared to find significant that the plaintiff's allegations involved several incidents of neglect and abuse which, when viewed cumulatively, were sufficient to amount to a breach of the contract if proven.

The court finds that *Free* is still good law and that the ten year prescriptive period for breach of contract applies.

The court emphasizes however that this conclusion is limited to and based on the unique circumstances of a nursing home setting, which is also the factual basis in *Free*. Residents are in the care and custody of the home on a 24-hour basis, with all their needs necessarily supplied by the facility. Residents are almost invariably in poor physical and/or mental health; they are frequently incompetent and unable to comprehend much less protest any mistreatment or neglect; their families likewise are not in a position to readily know whether injuries are caused by genuine accidents or whether they result from neglect or abuse. . . . .

. . . .

Count Three — Breach of Fiduciary Duty

The plaintiff alleges that Living Centers-East violated a fiduciary duty in its inadequate care of Ms. Caruso. The defendant argues that as a matter of law no such fiduciary duty existed. Ironically, in light of defendant's position as to Count One, part of the defendant's argument is that this case involves a contractual relationship and Louisiana courts have consistently declined to impose a fiduciary duty in that context. The defendant also points out that no specific statute imposes a fiduciary relationship on health care providers and patients.

The defendants are correct in that the mere existence of a contractual relationship does not alone create a fiduciary duty. Nor could the court find any case discussing whether or not a fiduciary relationship necessarily exists between a nursing home and its residents. Breaches of fiduciary commitments appear to arise most frequently in financial contexts, where someone has entrusted their finances to the care and custody of another, such as a conservator, receiver or trustee in bankruptcy. See La. R.S. 9:3801(2). Nevertheless, the definition of a fiduciary is not bound to a particular type of transaction; rather it is determined by the nature of the relationship between the parties.

The dominant characteristic of a fiduciary relationship is the confidence reposed by one in the other and (a person) occupying such a relationship can not further his own interests and enjoy the fruits of an advantage taken of such relationship.

. . . .

As noted already, many if not most nursing home residents are in a vulnerable physical and/or mental state. Placing a loved one in such a facility necessarily entails trust on the part of the family as well as the resident. Since the residents reside in the home, the family has comparatively limited access and opportunity to learn if the resident is neglected or otherwise mistreated. If entrusting one's money to a receiver or conservator creates a fiduciary as well as business relationship, one would hope at least in principle that entrusting a valued family member to the care of a business entity such as a nursing home would carry similar responsibilities.

The claim requires factual development to determine if in this case such a fiduciary duty was created. For that reason, the request for summary judgment is denied.

Because nursing homes provide medical care, the question can arise whether the cause of action is for negligence or for medical malpractice. In many states it is more difficult to prevail on an action for medical malpractice for both substantive and procedural reasons.

McLEOD v. PLYMOUTH COURT NURSING HOME
957 F. Supp. 113 (E.D. Mich. 1997)

This matter is before the Court on defendant's motion to dismiss. Defendant asserts that plaintiff's complaint should be dismissed because she failed to provide defendant with written notice of her intent to file a claim 182 days before filing this action, as is required when filing a medical malpractice claim. Plaintiff argues that she has alleged an action based on ordinary negligence, not medical malpractice, and therefore was not required to provide any written notice of intent to sue.

Plaintiff filed a complaint against defendant in Wayne County Circuit Court on December 20, 1996. In her complaint, plaintiff alleged that on January 29, 1995 the defendant nursing home of which she was a resident, breached the duty of reasonable care owed to her by leaving her "wheelchair unlocked and/or unstable for sitting down and/or getting up. . . ." Plaintiff further alleges that, as a result of defendant's breach of duty of reasonable care, plaintiff fell to the floor while attempting to get into her wheelchair and fractured her left hip.

Plaintiff argues that its claim is one of common negligence, not medical malpractice. . . .

In Michigan, a claim by a patient who has fallen in a hospital or other licensed health facility may be brought against that facility as a medical malpractice claim or as a claim for ordinary negligence. The law which will be applied to the case "depends upon the theory actually pled when the same set of facts can support either of two distinct causes of action."

Medical malpractice . . . has been defined as the failure of a member of the medical profession, employed to treat a case professionally, to fulfill the duty to exercise that degree of skill, care and diligence exercised by members of the same profession, practicing in the same of similar locality, in light of the present state of medical science.

Plaintiff here alleges in her complaint that defendant breached its duty of reasonable care, the duty element required for ordinary negligence. No reference is made to any breach or violation of a duty to exercise the degree of skill, care, or diligence exercised by hospitals in the same or similar locality.

Nevertheless, a complaint cannot avoid the application of the procedural requirements of a malpractice action by couching its cause of action in terms of ordinary negligence. Where the parties dispute whether plaintiff has alleged malpractice or ordinary negligence, courts have attempted to ascertain whether the facts alleged present issues which are within the common knowledge and experience of the jury or, in the alternative, raise a question of medical judgment. The cases presenting a question of medical judgment have all been distinguished from [cases] in which patients' suits for falls were held to sound in ordinary negligence.

This Court is satisfied that plaintiff's complaint alleges a theory of ordinary negligence as the basis for recovery. Further, to the extent that the theory of recovery as presented in plaintiff's complaint is ambiguous, the Court finds that the facts alleged present issues within the common knowledge and experience of the jury rather than those of medical judgment.

Some nursing home claims now are brought under state elder abuse statutes, because many state medical malpractice statutes cap non-economic damages such as pain and suffering.

NOTE: AN ASSESSMENT OF REGULATION AND QUALITY OF CARE

What effect do the detailed regulations have on nursing home quality? Consider the following comments on quality of care, resident rights, and the use of restraints.

Marshall B. Kapp,
Quality of Care and Quality of Life in Nursing Facilities: What's Regulation Got to Do with It?
31 McGEORGE L. REV. 707, 718–28 (2000)[*]

III. The Impact of Regulation

A. General Quality of Care and Quality of Life

In terms of OBRA 87's impact on the general quality of care and quality of life within NFs, the overall verdict to date has been largely, although not unanimously, positive. Not surprisingly, past and current HCFA administrators have given the law (and, not coincidentally, themselves) a glowing endorsement, by pointing to such post-OBRA quality indicators as reduction in resident dehydration, decreased utilization of indwelling urinary catheters, lowering of the hospitalization rate, and an increase in the number of hearing impaired residents who now have hearing aids. Interviews with nursing home employees, regulators, advocates, and representatives of professional associations have yielded favorable perceptions regarding the law's impact. It has also been suggested that physicians are now more thoroughly involved in resident care and the QA process in NFs than ever before.

Much of the existing empirical research has focused on OBRA's requirement that the NF use a standardized Resident Assessment Instrument (RAI) to collect data, consistent with a mandated Minimum Data Set (MDS) and standardized Resident Assessment Protocols (RAPs), from each new resident to assist with individualized care planning for that resident. The RAI has been praised as an important tool, valuable in this endeavor and contributing to improved results by several research teams. Among the QA improvements cited in favorable evaluations of the RAI are: more accurate information in residents' medical records; greater comprehensiveness of written care plans; reduced use of indwelling urinary

---

[*] Copyright © 2005 by the McGeorge Law Review. Reprinted with permission.

catheters; higher rates of residents executing advance medical directives; more resident participation in activities; better use of toileting programs for residents with bowel incontinence; and improvements in specific health conditions (namely, dehydration, falls, decubitus, vision problems, stasis ulcers, poor teeth, and malnutrition). Additionally, advocates for the RAI argue that the information generated through the instrument can be used to evaluate a particular NF's performance according to certain quality indicators, which results in turn can inform both government and private QA initiatives in the future.

While the evidence cited in support of OBRA 87's salutary influence on resident outcomes is encouraging, some commentators sagely urge caution before embracing the regulatory strategy too wholeheartedly. According to one noted geriatrician, "[l]ike most clinical studies, there are many potential pitfalls in the interpretation and applicability of the findings." One team of authors found that while the RAI may have improved the quality of care of NF residents by reducing overall rates of decline in important areas of resident function, this innovation may have created tradeoffs in that it may have reduced improvement rates in some other areas of function. A group of NF medical directors suggests that the regulations may even be counterproductive:

Those with the most training are often forced to preoccupy themselves with administrative responsibilities such as required documentation. The documentation required for the minimum data set (MDS), resident assessment protocols (RAPs), and care planning often takes time away from staff supervision, staff education, and direct patient care activities.

B. Residents' Rights

Assuring and enhancing residents' rights has consistently been one of the primary goals of federal and state NF regulation. Among other rationales, the creation and enforcement of detailed residents' rights through regulatory mechanisms is predicated on evidence that feelings of having choice and control over important aspects of one's own life produces tangible therapeutic benefits for most individuals.

Many persons involved in the long-term care field consider OBRA 87's effect of calling greater attention to residents' rights to be its most significant accomplishment. In contrast to these general perceptions, the available empirical evidence reveals little about the effect of OBRA 87 on the actual exercise of residents' rights. For instance, very little is documented about whether OBRA 87 has had an impact on the resident's right to choose a personal attending physician, the right to receive medical care in privacy, the right to be able to contact the attending physician, the right to be informed of his or her total health status, or the right to refuse treatment.

C. Restraints

Perhaps the most important change intended by supporters of OBRA 87 and its implementing regulations concerned the permissible use of physical and chemical restraints on residents in NFs. Unlike the status quo ante, today a resident has the right to be free from any physical restraints imposed for the purpose of discipline or staff convenience, rather than imposed under a physician's order to treat the resident's medical problems after less restrictive or intrusive interventions have been considered and attempted unsuccessfully. The same statutory and regulatory restriction applies to psychotropic drugs, which have (in the not very distant past) commonly been administered to NF residents as chemical restraints rather than as a thoughtful, unavoidable piece of the particular resident's therapeutic plan. Similar provisions restricting the permissible scope of physical and chemical restraints appear in the "Resident Bill of Rights" adopted by each state. . . .

Moreover, lower rates of restraint use appear to have been achieved with no increase in serious resident injuries, economic costs, or legal liability exposure for the NF. Further, when restraints have been removed, with independence and rehabilitation encouraged as an alternative, the functional status of many residents — in terms of being capable of carrying out Activities of Daily Living (ADLs) — improves. Thus, the causal connection between improvements in the process of care and improved resident outcomes appears established.

Chapter 8

HOUSING

A. INTRODUCTION

Appropriate housing is particularly critical to the well-being of older individuals who typically spend so much of their time at home. As individuals reach very advanced age, some become frail, and their ability to walk and drive may be limited by functional impairments. Consequently, their home environment becomes a larger factor in their safety, well-being, and self-sufficiency.

Many elderly want relief from home maintenance responsibilities or may need some help with looking after themselves. Those who have sufficient assets and income can pay for services delivered in their homes or buy or rent housing that is easy to care for and near to services. Because of limited retirement incomes, however, many elderly people have difficulty affording appropriate housing and services.

The elderly are not a homogenous group, and so meeting their diverse housing needs calls for a range of solutions. Although most seek to "age in place," that is, to continue to live in the homes where they lived when they were younger, doing so is not always feasible. Some must move to housing more appropriate to their physical condition. For others, housing with individualized support services delivered to independent units is ideal, provided costs and maintenance requirements are low and the design is free of barriers. For very frail or disabled individuals, however, where they live must be rich in services and protective oversight in order to postpone, perhaps indefinitely, the need for a nursing home or other institutional setting. Known as "supportive housing" it can include in-unit assistance, preventive health care, dining room and individual meal services, common areas for activities, and transportation. As the residents age, more services can be added, so that the environment and services meet an individual's needs for care and protection.

Family members are typically the primary providers of assistance to their elderly relatives. An older person who has a very capable caregiver, or sufficiently helpful younger relatives, can live longer in housing not adapted to the needs of an older resident. However, because of changes in work patterns, family size, and less family stability, fewer family members are available to provide this supportive role. Further, a growing population of adult children are in their sixties or seventies, caring for parents in their nineties. As a result, the caregiving children may have health problems or may also be providing needed financial help to their children, making it difficult to provide the care their parents need.

Caregiving demands on sons and daughters tend to reflect traditional distinctions. Daughters have been the main source of personal, in-home services for elderly parents. With women in the work force in unprecedented numbers, however, many adult daughters lack the time to provide care that homemakers might have provided in the past. Some have to balance work, their children, and the needs of their parents. Adult sons who in the past might have helped by running errands or helping with home repairs find their own lives too busy or too filled with children from one or more marriages to offer much help. Even if the adult children wish to help, their careers may have caused them to move away from their aging parents.

B. PLANNING FOR CHOICES IN HOUSING: THE CONTINUUM OF CARE

Planning for housing for an older person requires an assessment of a client's values and wishes, likely needs, and economic possibilities. An analysis of the available housing options requires an understanding of the different kinds of housing that caters to the elderly.

Professionals in elder care refer to a "continuum of care" as appropriate lodging and services that maximize independence and minimize dependency and unnecessary costs. While not yet perfected, it is developing. Consider the following "snapshot" of housing choices.

HOUSING AND SERVICES CONTINUUM

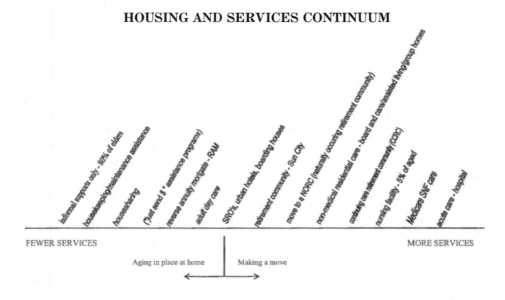

QUESTIONS

1. What would cause someone to move from the left to the right of the continuum?

2. Is life better or worse depending where someone is on the continuum? Or should the question be, are an individual's housing and care needs being adequately met?

3. If you know an older individual or couple, where would you place them on continuum? Are they satisfied with where they live? Why, or why not?

C.   AGING IN PLACE

Many elderly often want to remain where they have lived when they were younger — that is, to age in place. Their current residence represents years of memories, friendly neighbors, familiar shops and services, and membership in social and religious organizations. The decision to age in place is sensible if the individual has the ability to deal successfully with their physical, mental, and emotional needs.

The many benefits of remaining in the current home must be weighed in the balance with the possibility that the house is "too much" and in need of repairs, that services are difficult to arrange, and that family and friends may have moved from the neighborhood, leaving the elderly person isolated. The question is whether the individual has a satisfactory quality of life, access to needed help, and enough money to pay for necessary support.

Often a move seems the best option. Yet for anyone, moving can be unsettling and disruptive. For the elderly, it can be particularly painful. Loss of familiar surroundings can be disorienting and stressful. If the move is involuntary, it can be a harsh psychological blow and a cause of depression and withdrawal. The "transplanted" older individual may be unable to successfully adapt to living in a new environment with new neighbors and service people. A move may undermine or even terminate informal support networks that provide psychological and physical support.

Technology may enable many more elderly individuals to age in place. New devices make it possible for adult children to monitor their parents in their homes. (Monitoring by non-family members is possible, but unusual.) By keeping tabs on parental movements and habits, the children can know whether the parent is leading a healthy independent life or shows signs of needing assistance. Sensors, for example, can disclose whether the parent has left the house, gotten up in the night or fallen, whether a prescription drug has been taken, or even if the refrigerator has been opened — if it has not suggests the parent may not be eating properly. The parent can use health monitors in the home to test blood pressure or blood sugar and the information can be automatically sent to a physician or family member. "Spy cams" in the living room can observe the parent so that the child can see how well the parent is doing. The degree of monitoring is limited only by the parental desire for privacy and autonomy. But it appears that many elderly are willing to surrender some degree of privacy and accept monitoring technology in return for being able to live independently and age in place.

[1]   PAYMENT SOURCES FOR IN-HOME SERVICES

Some who age in place find that they need increasing amounts of assistance, either with the house or in the form of personal care. Finding the money to pay for that care often requires new financial arrangements.

[a] Reverse Mortgages

Reverse mortgages are a form of home equity conversion that permits the homeowner to borrow against the value of the home. The loan provides income to live on, but is not repaid until the sale of the house or the death of the homeowner. The homeowner can receive a lump-sum loan or the homeowner can be supplied a fixed monthly sum by the lender until the total mortgage debt reaches a predetermined dollar amount. The interest due on the loan continues to mount until the debt is repaid.

Celeste M. Hammond,
Reverse Mortgages: A Financial Planning
Device for the Elderly
1 Elder L.J. 75 (1993)[*]

Private sector reverse mortgages are available to elderly homeowners of all incomes and can be used for any purpose. Three different types of reverse mortgages are available: the uninsured loan, the lender-insured loan, and the FHA-insured reverse mortgage. Certain characteristics are common to all basic types. In its simplest form, the reverse mortgage involves an agreement between the lender and borrower to create a rising-debt loan, that is, one in which the balance increases over time because the lender periodically "advances" additional payments to the borrower. Often, the interest due on the loan also is added to the principal loan amount. Both the accumulated principal indebtedness and all the accrued interest become a lien against the house. The borrower will not be obligated to repay the loan until the occurrence of an event, including: (1) sale of the property, (2) the maturity of the loan, or (3) the death or extended absence of the borrower from the premises. Thus, the reverse mortgage is structurally similar to an open-ended mortgage, a negative amortization mortgage, and a balloon mortgage.

The reverse mortgage is very different from the common, "forward" mortgage that the purchaser of a home gives to the lender in exchange for a loan of a portion of the sale price. Although the principal amount of the conventional mortgage is the highest at the beginning and decreases (or is self-amortized) as the borrower makes payments, the reverse mortgage principal amount is highest at the end, and the interest charges will be "back loaded" because the elderly borrower is not making any payments. On the contrary, the lender typically makes monthly disbursements throughout the borrower's life. Also, the parties to the conventional mortgage limit the amount of the loan depending on the appraised value of the real estate at the start; an eighty percent loan-to-value ratio is common. The reverse mortgage, in contrast, sets the total loan amount based on current appraised value, anticipated appreciation, and the life expectancy of the borrower.

The borrower may elect a shared-appreciation option. If chosen, the borrower pays an additional amount of interest equal to a percentage (a maximum limit of 25 percent) of the net appreciated value of the house during the life of the loan. By

---

[*] Copyright © 1993 by The Board of Trustees of the University of Illinois. Reprinted with permission.

agreeing to share the value of the future appreciation of the house with the lender, the borrower presumably can borrow the loan at a lower rate of interest.

Typically under the terms of the reverse mortgage loan, the lender can require full and immediate payment when: (1) the last borrower dies, (2) the borrower conveys all of the title and no other borrower retains title or a long leasehold, (3) the property is not the borrower's principal residence, (4) a borrower fails to occupy the premises for more than 12 consecutive months because of physical or mental illness, or (5) the borrower otherwise defaults.

Because most reverse mortgages are nonrecourse, the homeowner is not personally liable for the debt should it exceed the amount netted when the house is sold. That is, the creditor is limited to the proceeds of the sale of the house to repay the debt. Neither the borrower nor the borrower's estate is liable for any deficiency.

The homeowner can usually borrow between 30 percent and 70 percent of the value of the home. The interest rate and the amount of the loan are based in part on the homeowner's age. The Internet offers access to several reverse mortgage calculators, including one by the AARP.

[b]   Family Financing: Sale and Leaseback

A sale and leaseback arrangement can make the value of the home equity available to the owner while permitting continued occupancy. The simplest form is for the owner to sell the house and simultaneously enter into a lease agreement with the buyer that guarantees the seller the right to occupy the house until his death or until he chooses to move. Only then does the buyer obtain possession of the property. Finding a buyer who is willing to postpone possession for an indefinite period is not easy. Not many are willing to enter into a lease that either lasts the life of the seller or is renewable at the seller's option.

As a practical matter, therefore, most sale and leasebacks take place between family members. The buyer, typically an adult child, does not expect to occupy the house and is willing to rent it to the parent for as long as the parent wishes to live in it. The child, as owner, usually assumes the responsibilities of maintenance. The child can buy the house with a traditional purchase money mortgage, which permits the child to pay a lump-sum dollar amount to the parent, who then draws down the sale proceeds to meet living expenses.

Alternatively, the parent can self-finance the sale, so the child is buying the property with essentially no money down by borrowing the purchase price from the parent. The child then makes monthly mortgage payments to the parent. Because the child purchases the house primarily to create income for the parent, the parent's rent is less than the child's monthly mortgage payment, so the parent has more disposable income. For example, the child's monthly mortgage payment obligation might be $600, while the parent pays rent of $350 to the child. The parties net the payments so the parent actually receives $250 a month. If the parent dies before the mortgage is paid off, the parent could cancel the debt by a provision in his or her will.

A sale and leaseback arrangement provides a monthly stream of income, but unlike a reverse mortgage, it does not create debt for the homeowner. The arrangement is a way for a child to contribute to the parent's income, but eventually get repaid by the value of the house. The parents who sell their houses free up their capital (the equity in the house), have a higher monthly disposable income, and continue to live in the house at a rent they can afford, free of the costs and trouble of maintaining the property.

The major disadvantage is the time, effort, and expense involved in creating the sale and leaseback. The concept is usually foreign to the parent homeowner as well as to the child who buys the house. Protracted negotiations and discussions may be required before the parties are fully comfortable with the idea. The buyer/child who rents out the house takes on the tax complexities of owning rental property. The increased income to the parents could disqualify them for public benefits such as Supplemental Security Income (SSI) and Medicaid. There is also a risk for the seller that the buyer, the child, might decide to occupy the house or even sell it to a third party, thereby dispossessing the parent.

[c]   House Sharing

One solution to a large, mostly empty and costly house is to house share by living with others, whether family members, friends, or even strangers. This is a particularly good option for an older person who dislikes living alone, or fears illness or injury, but does not want to move. Yet sharing a house can result in either warm companionship or seemingly endless quarrels.

House sharing helps financially because the sharer pays for the right to live in the house, either with rent or a portion of the household expenses, and helps socially because the house sharer provides companionship for the older person. Institutions such as churches or community service organizations promote house sharing and function as "brokers." That is, they bring together older homeowners and non-homeowners who are interested in sharing a house. It is very useful to have such a "broker" to supply structure to the agreement and think to ask important questions. The brokers try to match people who are compatible, based on income, age, education, and interests. They usually provide the parties with a model agreement, containing such items as cost sharing and termination rights that can be modified to meet the parties' particular needs. When a religious group promotes house sharing, it often attempts to bring fellow congregants together.

When considering house sharing, the homeowner and house sharer should discuss how the arrangement might have to change as the older homeowner ages. This can be a difficult conversation because some harsh but unlikely possibilities must be discussed. For example, suppose the homeowner loses the ability to clean the house, cook meals, or drive a car. A house sharing relative may be willing to offer some assistance, but it is unlikely that he or she would be willing to act as a personal attendant.

The parties to house sharing, even if they are close friends or relatives, must also agree on conditions for ending the arrangement. Certainly the homeowner must have the right to terminate unilaterally; the only question should be the amount of notice required — from two weeks to a month is reasonable. The housemate should also be able to terminate and also should be required to give notice, probably an interval equal to that required of the homeowner. Notice by the housemate protects the older homeowner, who might not be safe, if he or she is in ill health, in the event of a sudden departure. The parties also should agree that the homeowner can evict the housemate for cause.

The homeowner must also have adequate insurance to protect both the home and the house sharer in the event of negligence by either the homeowner or house sharer. Local zoning laws must also be considered; renting to a stranger may violate the local housing code.

QUESTIONS

1. Consider what you would do to address some of the typical potential concerns of house sharing, like:

a. How do you determine the honesty of the house sharer?

b. Should there be a formal contractual agreement for a relative?

c. Under what conditions can the homeowner terminate the arrangement and summarily evict the house sharer? Does it make a difference if the sharer is a relative?

d. What rights of occupancy does the sharer have (such as the right to have overnight guests)?

2. Thelma, age 77, invites her niece, Nancy, age 45, to live with her. Thelma asks you if she should name Nancy her agent under a power of attorney. What would you advise? Should she name Nancy her surrogate health care decision maker? Why, or why not?

[d] State Property Tax Relief

States have a variety of property tax relief programs to insulate low-income and elderly homeowners from the financial burden of the residential property tax. The oldest type is the homestead exemption, which reduces the property tax on owner-occupied housing. The exemption may be a fixed dollar or a fixed percentage reduction in the assessed value of the homestead (the primary residence of the taxpayer) or a fixed reduction in the amount of the tax bill. Generally the income of the property owner is not a factor in determining the amount of relief, but it may be used as a criterion for eligibility. Over half the states now offer homestead property tax relief to elderly citizens. While a few states make the program available to renters, a majority offer it only to homeowners.

Other states use a circuit breaker, designed to protect homeowners from property tax "overload." If the property tax bill exceeds a set percentage of the household income, the circuit breaker takes effect and the taxes are frozen at that level. In some states, the homeowner must pay the tax and then apply for a refund from the state.

Some local governments have instituted tax freezes that hold the tax rate constant after the applicant reaches a designated age, usually age 65. Thereafter the participant is excused from any further tax increases on the home. A few states and localities offer deferral of all or part of the tax bill of elderly persons, who meet any income eligibility criteria, until their death or the sale of the house. The taxes mount as a lien on the property, which is collected upon the death of the homeowner or the sale of the house.

[2] ACCESSING AND PROVIDING QUALITY IN-HOME SERVICES

Given the different individual preferences for assistance, the growing number of sources of assistance, and the varied circumstances in which home assistance for the elderly is delivered, the most significant issue is to identify what the older individual needs and to coordinate the delivery of care.

[a] Geriatric Care Managers

Geriatric care managers have become very important participants in arranging access to services for elders at home. The care manager will assess the older person's needs and plan for service delivery in coordination with the client and family. Initially, case managers or care managers were government employees who coordinated the range of services available to elders under the Older Americans Act and other programs. Now, private sector care managers and professional guardians are available to those who want such assistance and are able to pay. Many geriatric case managers are professional social workers, but some are just individuals who understand the needs of the elderly.

[b] Employment of Care Givers: Choices and Employer Requirements

The elderly who hire helpers to come into the home generally are considered employers for the purposes of federal taxes and benefits, and so incur federal and tax reporting obligations. For example, they are required to obtain an Employer Identification Number (EIN) for the purposes of paying federal taxes. The employer must withhold FICA tax of 7.65 percent and file a Form W-2 (Wage and Tax Statement) showing the total compensation, including any in-kind such as free room and board. The employer also must pay unemployment taxes.

If the in-home workers are immigrants, the elder should take care to comply with the Immigration Reform and Control Act of 1986 (8 U.S.C. § 1101). The Act requires that new employers verify their employees' citizenship status and complete an INS Form I-9, which must be retained for the longer of three years or one year longer than employment. On the form, employees provide biographical information under penalty of perjury specifying whether they are United States citizens or aliens authorized to work in the United States. It is prudent for an employer to keep copies of the employee's documents.

Faced with the myriad of reporting requirements, many elderly will decide that it is more sensible to hire in-home assistance through an agency that will be responsible for all filing requirements as well as screening their employees for honesty and reliability. In some cases, the adult children of an elderly individual, who wishes to age in place, will volunteer to pay an agency to provide the degree of assistance needed to keep the parent safe and secure. Sometimes both a geriatric social worker and an in-home agency are hired with the social worker being responsible to monitor the quality of care being provided by the agency.

[c]   Government Assistance to the Elderly in Their Homes

The model of publicly funded, community-based care originated in the 1960s. Because of inadequate funding, the programs fall far short of their original concepts, but the model remains. In 1965, Congress enacted the Older Americans Act (OAA), unique among services programs in that it benefits older persons regardless of income. The programs of the Act are intended to meet the social services needs of older people in the community. The OAA establishes the administrative structure and delivery system which provides many services to the elderly, including assistance with housing, obtaining employment, securing restorative care, and coordinating community services.

Title II of the OAA establishes the Administration on Aging (AOA), in the Department of Health and Human Services, which serves as the chief federal advocate for older persons under the direction of the Commissioner on Aging.

The program of broadest community-based services, Title III of the OAA, sets out services that may be provided to the general elderly population with OAA funding. Fifty-seven state agencies and over 670 Area Agencies on Aging (AAAs) have been established throughout the United States to administer the funds allotted for community-based social services. These services may include meals at nutrition sites, home delivered meals, homemaker services, transportation, counseling and referral, health screenings, job counseling and referral, crime prevention, adult daycare, respite, abuse prevention, and a number of others.

OAA funds may also be used to provide services to assist in obtaining adequate housing and to avoid unnecessary institutionalization. A "minimum percentage" of funding must be allotted for three priority supportive services — access, in-home (which includes homemaker, home health aide, visiting and telephone reassurance, and chore services), and legal services. In addition, services are to be coordinated for persons with Alzheimer's disease and their families, mental illness, disabilities, or a need for community-based long-term care services. If possible all services are to be provided from a multipurpose senior center.

The selection of services for a locality is made by the Area Agency on Aging (AAA) based on existing services and assessed needs. The AAA prepares an area plan for services, which meets the requirements of the OAA, and submits it to the State Agency on Aging. The area plan is incorporated into the state plan, which is forwarded for approval by the AOA.

The Low Income Housing Energy Assistance Program (42 U.S.C. § 8601 *et seq.*) provides block grants to each of the states, the District of Columbia, six U.S. territories, and 114 Indian tribes. The program is not limited to the elderly but over half the benefits are paid to persons age 62 or older. The funds are allocated to low income households, either directly or by payments to vendors of fuel or services, to help pay the costs of home heating, cooling, and weatherization aid.

D.   HOUSING DESIGNED FOR OLDER PERSONS

Despite the attractions of aging in place, many older persons choose to relocate. Some do so upon retirement, but many age in place until their physical or mental condition causes them to move to more appropriate housing. Some moved to sunny climes for the active phase of their retirement and moved back, or near family members, in advanced age. This section discusses housing typically chosen by older people who want easily maintained, secure housing, but otherwise are generally self-sufficient.

[1]   RESTRICTED COMMUNITIES

Some older persons want the homogeneity and security of a community that is closed off from the community and its diversity. For some, the order and rules of a planned community are enough. Others want the enhanced security of a gated community. Still others want a community that excludes all residents under a certain age.

[a]   Planned Unit Developments

Planned communities are popular with many older buyers. There is no single definition of "planned unit developments," or PUDs, for they can occur as cluster or zero-lot line housing (without yards), fee simple detached or attached housing, combined high-rise and low-rise units, or even as a mixed-use development with a variety of elements. What planned unit developments have in common is the strict regulation of design, living units and amenities by strict zoning, covenants, equitable servitudes, and easements.

A planned unit development (PUD) generally features common ownership of recreational facilities, such as a swimming pool or golf course. Sometimes the homeowners' association owns the common areas, with each unit owner's having an easement for the use and enjoyment of these areas. Residents may have limited easement rights over one another's property in order to have access to the facilities and open spaces. Frequently, the streets and entry ways are owned in common and the development is surrounded by a fence or wall, with the main gate manned by a guard and entry strictly limited.

Every homeowner is a member of the homeowners' association, which runs the community. The association board, typically comprised of resident volunteers, creates and enforces rules and regulations designed to preserve the quality of life anticipated by the purchasers. The homeowners' association enforces the rules of the community, including easements and covenants placed on individual lots, and also operates the commonly owned facilities and can assess fees to maintain them.

Planned developments have proved to be very attractive to retirees, and often have an older population regardless of whether the covenants set any age limits on residents. However, as residents age in place or experience different life circumstances, the rules originally considered desirable may create conflict. For example, limits on entry into the community may interfere with the delivery of goods and services required by an aging resident.

[b] Age Restricted Communities

Many older people wish to live in an environment occupied exclusively by older residents and so favor age-restricted housing. To accommodate this segment of the population, housing of various types is available only to the elderly, including apartment buildings, condominiums, mobile home parks, retirement subdivisions, villages, and even entire towns.

Some older persons reject age-restricted housing because it seems artificial and isolating from the vitality of the larger community. They prefer neighbors of various ages and reject the scheduled, organized group life identified with age-restricted communities.

Yet many elderly prefer age-restricted housing. In response, when Congress amended the Federal Fair Housing Act (FHA) to bar discrimination based on "familial status" — allowing no discrimination against families with children under age 18 — it provided exemptions for communities of older persons. The statute provided three acceptable categories of housing for older persons:

1.   Housing provided under any state or federal program "specifically designed and operated to assist elderly persons";

2.   Housing "intended for, and solely occupied by, persons 62 years of age or older";

3.   Housing "intended and operated for occupancy by persons 55 years of age or older and —

   (i)   at least 80 percent of the occupied units are occupied by at least one person who is 55 years of age or older;

   (ii)   the housing facility or community publishes and adheres to policies and procedures that demonstrate the intent required under this subparagraph; and

   (iii) the housing facility or community complies with rules issued by the Secretary for verification of occupancy, which shall —

      (I)   provide for verification by reliable surveys and affidavits; and

      (II)   include examples of the types of policies and procedures relevant to a determination of compliance with the requirement of clause (ii). Such surveys and affidavits shall be admissible in administrative and judicial proceedings for the purposes of such verification." 42 U.S.C. § 3607(b).

Housing that qualifies by virtue of requiring all units to be occupied by residents aged 62 or older cannot permit a couple to live in any unit if one of them is under age 62. The only exception to the 62-or-older rule is employees and their family members who live in the facility and perform substantial duties directly related to its maintenance or management.

The largest age-restricted developments are retirement towns that cater to relatively affluent older persons. They are self-contained small cities or towns that are designed for and occupied exclusively by older residents. Examples include Leisure World in southern California, which has over 20,000 residents, and Sun City in Arizona, which has over 45,000 residents. Such retirement towns contain detached single-family houses and town-houses. They typically feature extensive recreational facilities, stores, banks, restaurants, and religious facilities. The towns are either managed by the developer (or a successor management entity), who may own common areas such as roads or recreational facilities, and interacts with a residential association. A professional staff is responsible for the day-to-day functioning of the town, with oversight by resident committees or by the owner/manager.

Retirement villages are smaller in area, have fewer residents (usually between 1,000 and 5,000), and often have fairly homogenous housing in terms of price and style. Retirement villages are usually located at the edge of urbanized areas because they are not self-sufficient. These villages appeal to older residents who can drive and expect to use and interact with the larger community.

[2] LOW COST HOUSING

[a] Mobile Homes and Manufactured Housing

Mobile homes and manufactured housing traditionally are disfavored and relegated to areas away from costly single-family homes. However, elderly residents are often considered a desirable population group, bringing economic and social stability to where they live. Recognizing that many older people need low cost housing, many municipalities make special provision for housing the elderly. Some planned towns and villages for retirees feature less expensive manufactured housing. As with other planned development, such communities typically are governed by a homeowners association. Some offers various amenities while others aim for the lowest possible cost to the resident.

The term "manufactured housing" refers to any prefabricated house that is manufactured off-site and erected or set-down on-site. Most manufactured housing is anything but mobile. The cost of moving a mobile home may be $5,000 to $15,000. Once sited, therefore, it usually is never moved again. Mobile homes typically cost about one-quarter or one-third the amount of a comparable sized house. For a couple, who sell their house to retire to manufactured housing, the resulting savings can be a substantial amount that can generate more income to be spent on their retirement.

Most owners pay cash because mortgages for such homes have high interest rates reflecting the fact that a mobile home on a leased lot is usually treated as if it is personal property, not real estate. The resident either buys a home and site in the park or, more typically, purchases an on-site home and then leases the lot. The homeowner is responsible for utilities such as water, sewage, and electricity.

Due in part to federal construction and safety standards, manufactured homes are better built, more spacious, stronger, and more fire and wind resistant than in the past. Many are located in age-restricted or "retirement" villages in Florida or California that create attractive though homogeneous environments. In contrast, many mobile homes are individually sited, often in rural areas, which do not have zoning codes that typically prohibit mobile homes in many towns and cities.

[b] Single-Room Occupancy Hotels

Although not well known, single-room occupancy (SRO) hotels house many poor urban elderly. These residential hotels vary in size and degree of services, but most offer at least housekeeping and a lobby with a television. They particularly appeal to older men, though some women do live in them. Those that cater to the elderly often exclude younger renters who might cause disruption.

In a single room, the resident typically gets a small cooking facility, perhaps just a small refrigerator, a sink and a hot plate or microwave. The bath might be down the hall.

Residents often are those who retired to the area many years ago and have sought the simplest and least expensive form of housing as their retirement income diminished with inflation. The SRO and its neighborhood can be rich in services, including government assistance. Typically, an SRO catering to elderly residents may be the site for a weekly blood pressure check by the Visiting Nurse's Association and Meals on Wheels may be delivered daily to some residents.

QUESTION

What is the difference between the urban, single-room occupancy hotels and upscale assisted living communities in which the tenant has a room or studio apartment and takes meals in a common dining room?

E. SUPPORTIVE HOUSING

Supportive housing refers to housing that is accompanied by the provision of personal care services needed because of the frailties or disabilities of the residents. Usually supportive housing does not include health care or nursing services. Supportive housing is offered in a variety of forms and at a range of prices for all but the poorest elderly who must rely on government subsidized housing.

The names of supportive housing — assisted living, board and care homes, personal care homes, and retirement homes — reflect state licensing requirements, marketing strategies, and regional usage, though their purposes are the same: to provide assistance with activities of daily living and watchful oversight. Board and care (used here as a generic label encompassing personal care homes and retirement homes) is the older term and is associated with small boarding homes appealing to moderate or lower income residents. Assisted living is the newer term and has been adopted by larger, more modern facilities that attract middle and upper income residents.

[1] ASSISTED LIVING

"Assisted living" is the fastest growing form of supportive housing. Originally it was a private sector creation, intended to fill a market niche for elderly who need the assurance of available in-unit assistance. For those with sufficient financial income and wealth or long-term care insurance, assisted living has become the housing of choice if forced to leave home. Assisted living, being non-medical residential housing for the aged and disabled, draws upon its predecessor, board and care homes. Several states have different licensing requirements for assisted living and board and care homes.

Assisted living provides supportive housing for older individuals who need daily help. It combines individualized support services with modest health care to help people live as independently as possible. Assisted living facilities also provide recreation, social activities, and meals in common areas. The essence of assisted living is custodial care in the form of assistance with bathing, grooming, and dressing. The facility will almost certainly have 24-hour nursing oversight as well as other licensed staff, such as dieticians. Health care needs are monitored to prevent medical problems that might require care in a hospital or nursing home. In particular, the facility will ensure that the residents take their prescribed medications.

In some states, assisted living facilities are held to higher standards than board and care homes in the ratio of employees to residents, training and education of employees, and the degree of assistance available for residents. Assisted living does not offer nursing care nor is it permitted to house bedbound individuals, but it does provide care for frail elderly and even moderately demented elderly. Increasingly, assisted living is seen as a much less expensive alternative to nursing home care — it costs about half as much — while still providing the kind and degree of care needed by many elderly with physical or mental deficits.

[a] Assisted Living Residents

Approximately 90 percent of individuals who live in assisted-living facilities are single, since married couples with similar needs are usually able to care for each other at home. Because women outlive men, over 70 percent of residents at assisted living are women. The average age of assisted living residents is over 80 with the average length of stay of two-and-a-half years. Nearly all speak English, and most have a higher than average level of education.

About one third have significant hearing impairment or uncorrectable visual impairment. About 30 percent are incontinent. Every day, the average resident takes six prescription drugs. After assistance with medications, the most common need among activities of daily living (ADLs) is help with bathing. Among instrumental activities of daily living, the most common need is help with laundry.

Many residents have chronic impairments, most commonly hypertension and cardiovascular disorders, arthritis, depression, congestive heart failure, and diabetes. A common reason for residing in an assisted living facility is confusion or dementia. About one fourth of all residents are diagnosed with Alzheimer's disease or related disorders. Many assisted living facilities have separate wings or floors to house the more demented residents.

Most state laws prohibit assisted living facilities from admitting individuals who are confined to bed. Such residents usually require a degree of health care that can be provided only in a licensed nursing home and are also unable to help themselves in the event of an emergency that requires leaving the room or building. Some states permit assisted living facilities to continue to house residents who become confined to bed if a physician will certify that these residents are not in need of skilled nursing care. However, the facility must meet state requirements for a level of care that will meet the resident's daily needs and provide adequate protection and assistance in case of an emergency.

[b] How Assisted Living Is Financed

Generally assisted living units charge daily rates ranging from $70 to $150. It is estimated that nearly 90 percent of assisted living costs are paid by the residents or their families. Many residents use the sale proceeds of their houses to pay the cost, because there is only modest government support of assisted living.

In the past, a number of states were granted "waivers" on a limited basis to use federal Medicaid funds to purchase health care services for individuals in their home or in a community-based setting including assisted living facilities. The Patient Protection and Affordable Care Act of 2010 contained provisions designed to encourage more use of home and community-based care and less reliance on nursing homes. The Act permits the states much greater leeway in using federal Medicaid funds to support eligible elderly who reside in the community rather than a nursing home. Whether the Act will actually result in significantly greater state support of publicly funded residency in assisted living facilities remains to be seen. The amount of Medicaid "waiver" dollars used for assisted living has been small in comparison to the amount of Medicaid dollars spent on nursing-home care.

Medicare does not pay for assisted living. However, individuals may qualify for Medicare home health care coverage for physical and occupational therapy that is provided at the assisted living facility. Typically an assisted living facility contracts with a visiting home health care provider who provides physician authorized, Medicare reimbursed therapy for a resident at the assisted living facility.

Long-term care insurance pays benefits for assisted living for some residents. While long-term care insurance is typically thought of as a means to pay for nursing home care, most policies pay for care whether provided in a nursing home or in an assisted living facility. Whether a long-term care policy will pay for assisted living depends upon what triggers the payment of benefits. Generally policies pay for institutional care if the insured person has a cognitive impairment or has two or more deficits in ADLs. Many assisted living residents need help with bathing and dressing — both ADLs — and so qualify for reimbursement under a long-term care insurance policy.

[c]   The Contract of Admission

Residents of assisted living sign a contract of admission with the facility under which they agree to pay a monthly fee. In return the facility agrees to provide room, meals, and specified services. For the most part, such agreements are not subject to government oversight or regulation. Some assisted living facilities also charge an "entrance fee," which can be equivalent to two months' rent and may not be refundable or applicable to the final month of services. There is no standardized contract for assisted living, so the contents, the legality, and the readability of contracts vary greatly from facility to facility. However, the contract will generally contain the following:

— Date of occupancy.

— Identification of specific unit.

— Furnishings, if any, supplied by the facility.

— Resident health requirements on entry. (The contract will usually require that the resident have a physical examination. Facilities require this in order to protect themselves from admitting residents with severe health problems.)

— Unit structural alterations permitted (if any).

— Unit maintenance to be provided. Generally, the facility assumes all maintenance and cleaning of the unit.

— Services. The contract will include a list of the services that the facility will perform for the base monthly rate. The contract may also include a list of additional services that can be purchased on a per-diem or monthly basis.

— Security deposit.

— Monthly occupancy fee. The contract also states under what conditions the fee can be raised and what notification must be given to the resident.

— Residents' Rights. The contract should list the rights of the residents, such as a right to privacy, the right to visitors, and the right to organize a resident's council.

— Liability. The contract will probably attempt to limit the liability of the assisted living facility. The validity of such language depends on the applicable state law.

The contract should contain a clause dealing with termination of residence. Termination may occur because the resident dies, voluntarily leaves, or because the facility evicts the resident because the facility is no longer an appropriate residence for that individual. Residents may be evicted from the facility for reasons of poor health or non-payment of fees. The contract should state the conditions under which the facility may evict a resident, including physical or behavioral reasons.

Some residents leave the facility temporarily for hospitalization. The contract should state how long the resident's room will be reserved and at what cost. For example, suppose the resident enters the hospital and after 40 days is well enough to return to assisted living. Can the resident reserve his room by paying a reduced fee to reflect the lack of services and the lack of food being provided during his hospital stay? This is called a bed hold policy, which is expressly required by nursing home regulations, but in assisted living is usually a matter of contract.

If the facility provides special units for dementia, the contract should state who makes the decision that the resident must move into such a unit. For example, Mary enters the assisted-living facility when she is frail but mentally alert. After living in the facility for a year she begins to suffer dementia. It progresses to the point at which the facility believes she would be better cared for in a dementia unit. Mary, however, does not wish to move. The contract should state how the decision to move Mary will be made.

[d]   Negotiated Risk

A number of ethical issues remain unaddressed or unresolved with regard to assisted living, including the amount and nature of risk the elderly resident can undertake while in the facility's care. The concept builds on the legal rubric that the care provider is not an insurer of the safety of the resident. Rather, the provider has a duty of care to have sound practices that are likely to protect residents from harm through negligence.

Negotiated risk, first implemented in Oregon and Washington, is having an impact on the regulatory language of assisted living across the country. It provides a measure of clarity to counteract apparently boundless fears on the part of providers about a resident's right to sue when injured.

Negotiated risk attempts to permit residents greater autonomy by permitting them to choose their lifestyle while absolving the facility of liability for the resident's choice. For example, a diabetic resident, Rosa, who wishes to eat sweets might sign an agreement stating that she will eat sweets despite the potential risk to her health. In turn, she would agree not to hold the facility liable if the eating of sweets caused her harm. In the absence of such an agreement, the facility might be reluctant to permit Rosa any access to sweets in light of her diabetic condition.

Almost half the states have adopted the concept of negotiated risk in their statutes that regulate assisted living. Usually the statutes refer to the facility adopting a service or care plan that respects the resident's needs and desires. While risk agreements are supposed to be individualized for the particular resident, it seems likely that facilities will resort to standard or formulaic agreements in order to save time and lawyer's fees and to insure that the facility understands its obligations and liabilities under the agreement. The application of assumed risk is illustrated in the following case.

STORM v. NSL ROCKLAND PLACE, LLC
898 A.2d 874 (Del. Super. 2005)

I.

In this opinion, the Court considers whether an assisted living facility may advance the affirmative defense of primary assumption of the risk in response to a resident's claim that the facility provided negligent or reckless care to him. To the

Court's knowledge, the question of whether primary assumption of the risk is a viable defense in the healthcare context has not been decided in Delaware.

A. Paul Storm, Jr. ("Mr. Storm") was a resident of a licensed assisted living facility owned and operated by Defendant, NSL Rockland Place, LLC ("Rockland"). On February 9, 2002, two Rockland employees found Mr. Storm in his room at Rockland lying face-down on the floor. It was presumed that Mr. Storm had fallen while alone in his room. As a result of the fall, Mr. Storm allegedly suffered serious physical injuries.

Plaintiff, JoAnn Storm, Mr. Storm's wife (collectively "the Storms"), filed this action individually and as guardian *ad litem* of Mr. Storm alleging, *inter alia*, that Rockland was negligent, reckless and wanton in the care and services it rendered to Mr. Storm. Rockland answered by denying the allegations of wrongdoing and raising Mr. Storm's primary and secondary assumption of the risk as affirmative defenses.

Arguing that primary assumption of the risk would operate as a complete bar to recovery, Rockland now seeks summary judgment. Rockland contends that Mr. Storm was aware of and expressly consented to the risks involved when residents of an assisted living facility are given appropriate opportunities to exercise independence in their day-to-day living activities. Under such circumstances, Rockland argues that injuries sustained by Mr. Storm in the course of exercising his independence may not be the subject of a claim against the institutional care provider to the extent such injuries fall within the range of foreseeable risks expressly assumed by the resident. For the reasons that follow, the Court finds that Delaware "healthcare providers" may not, as a matter of law, invoke the affirmative defense of primary assumption of the risk in claims brought by patients alleging substandard care. In the healthcare context, key elements of the defense will always be missing. Specifically, the healthcare defendant will rarely be able to establish that the plaintiff knowingly and expressly consented to engage in inherently risky conduct and will never be able to establish that the plaintiff consented to allow the healthcare provider to exercise less than ordinary care during the course of treatment. Moreover, the Court is satisfied that it would be endorsing bad public policy if it were to allow a healthcare provider to escape liability for proven negligence in rendering care on the ground that the patient purportedly consented to the risk of negligent care and consequent injury by agreeing to receive the treatment or healthcare services in the first place. . . .

II.

In January 2002, the Storms approached the intake staff at Rockland to inquire whether Rockland could provide a full-time residence for Mr. Storm where he could receive individualized medical care and twenty-four hour supervision. Prior to admitting Mr. Storm, Rockland arranged for him to receive a medical evaluation so that it could prepare an initial service assessment outlining the assistance that Mr. Storm would require. The preadmission evaluation was performed by Dr. Bean, Mr. Storm's neurologist. Dr. Bean opined that Mr. Storm suffered from multiple sclerosis, alcoholism, hypertension and depression. He noted that Mr. Storm would require assistance with ambulation due to falls and poor judgment.

He also was in need of psychological and drug and alcohol rehabilitation.

With the pre-admission evaluation in hand, Rockland created a Medical Service Agreement which outlined the assistance and services it would provide to Mr. Storm while he resided at Rockland. This agreement was to remain in effect until Rockland performed its own evaluation of Mr. Storm and determined whether Mr. Storm required additional or different services. On January 10, 2002, both Mr. Storm and Rockland executed the Medical Service Agreement. Thereafter, as a final step of establishing residency at Rockland, Mr. Storm and Rockland entered into a Residency Agreement on January 26, 2002.

Mr. Storm was a resident at Rockland from January 26 through February 9, 2002. During his first week, Mr. Storm was able to ambulate with a steady gate while using a cane, eat his meals, refrain from alcohol consumption, and take his prescribed medications. His conduct, however, soon changed for the worse.

On February 1, Mrs. Storm came to Rockland to take her husband out for dinner only to find that Mr. Storm had been drinking alcohol and was intoxicated. She immediately contacted Rockland and directed its staff not to permit Mr. Storm to leave the facility without informing her because he was likely to consume alcohol and then be a danger to himself or others. According to Mrs. Storm, Rockland agreed to pay extra attention to Mr. Storm to ensure that he was in compliance with his treatment plan. In the ensuing days, however, Mr. Storm continuously would leave Rockland's campus and return intoxicated and smelling of alcohol. He also refused to take his prescribed medication and to eat many of his meals. On one occasion, when prompted by Rockland employees to take his medication, Mr. Storm responded: "I'm not in prison — I'll do what I want." According to Mrs. Storm, Rockland did not inform her of her husband's recalcitrance.

On the morning of February 9, Mr. Storm again refused to eat and take his medication and instead told a certified nursing assistant to leave him alone and that he would not be coming to breakfast or lunch. He remained in his room throughout the day. As evening approached, the Rockland staff once again attempted to coax Mr. Storm to leave his room and eat dinner. Mr. Storm did not respond. When two certified nursing assistants were dispatched to check on Mr. Storm, they found him unresponsive lying face-down on the floor. Mr. Storm apparently had fallen while alone in his room. He allegedly sustained an acute subdural hematoma and severe anoxia resulting in irreversible brain damage and permanent physical and neurological impairments and disabilities.

Mrs. Storm subsequently filed a complaint individually and as guardian ad litem of Mr. Storm alleging medical negligence, reckless and wanton conduct, breach of statutory duties, breach of contract, and loss of consortium. Rock-land's answer denied wrongdoing and alleged, *inter alia*, that Mr. Storm's claims were barred by the doctrine of primary assumption of the risk.

III.

Rockland has moved for summary judgment. It contends that Mr. Storm's conduct constitutes primary assumption of the risk and should operate to relieve Rockland from liability. According to Rockland, Mr. Storm was aware of, and consented to, the risks associated with the independent living environment at Rockland. He exercised his independence and was injured as a result of his own conduct. In this regard, Rockland relies primarily upon the exculpatory language contained in the Residency Agreement which provides, in pertinent part:

> [Rockland] is designed to provide residential living in an apartment setting combined with individualized personal assistance and 24 hour supervision. The objective of the assisted living program is to provide the supportive services needed by residents of [Rockland] to manage on their own in their daily lives and to ensure that each resident can exercise a maximum level of independence, control and choice in his or her daily life.

> The Resident acknowledges that these principles of independence, control, and choice will result in a higher quality of life for each resident in the community, recognizes the additional risk that results from the ability of the Resident to make such choices, and agrees to mutually accept and share this risk . . . .

> Resident agrees that [Rockland] shall not be liable to Resident for personal injuries or damage to property, even if resulting from the negligence of [Rockland] or its employees, unless resulting from its gross negligence or willful misconduct. Resident acknowledges that the independence, control and choice afforded within [Rockland] requires that the Resident assume responsibility for any loss, injury or damage resulting from Resident's personal actions and conduct.

As further support of its position, Rockland cites the "Resident Rights" section of the Residency Agreement which afforded Mr. Storm the right to leave and return to Rockland at reasonable times and the right to privacy of self and possessions. According to Rockland, Mr. Storm's execution of the Residency Agreement, coupled with Mr. Storm's clear exercise of his "Resident's Rights," as demonstrated when he exclaimed "I'm not in prison — I'll do what I want" and admonished Rockland staff to "leave [him] alone," all evidence his express acknowledgment and consent of the risks inherent in living at Rockland. Rockland argues that Mr. Storm expressly assumed the risk of injury and is barred, therefore, as a matter of law, from recovery.

. . . .

V.

A. Primary Assumption of the Risk As a Matter of Law

. . . .

When a defendant invokes the affirmative defense of primary assumption of the risk, the Court must evaluate the viability of the defense as part of its duty analysis because primary assumption of the risk "obviates the duty owed by the defendant." Stated differently, a finding by the Court that a plaintiff expressly assumed a risk in a manner that would implicate primary assumption of the risk is tantamount to a finding that the defendant owed no duty to the plaintiff. . . .

. . . . Two common themes appear in each instance where primary assumption of the risk has been deemed to be an appropriate affirmative defense. First, the plaintiff chooses to engage in the activity, not out of necessity but out of a desire to satisfy a personal preference, e.g., to participate or watch others participate in a sporting event. Second, when the plaintiff chooses to engage in the inherently risky activity, he acknowledges that he and others engaging in such activity may not act with "ordinary care." . . .

Of the two themes prevalent in primary assumption of the risk scenarios, the first is rarely extant in the healthcare context and the second never is in play and could not be countenanced in any event. As to the first theme, it is rare that a consumer of healthcare services chooses to be sick or otherwise in need of care. Most people, with the exception of those who have elective or cosmetic surgery, seek out health care because they must. In this case, for example, Mr. Storm went to Rockland for healthcare services because he suffered from, among other conditions, multiple sclerosis and an alcohol addiction that required specialized care. One can safely say that he did not choose to suffer from those conditions and did not choose to be in need of care for them. The element of choice is missing.

As to the second theme, there is virtually no scenario in which a patient can consent to allow a healthcare provider to exercise less than "ordinary care" in the provision of services. Even if given, a patient's consent to allow a healthcare provider to exercise less than ordinary care would be specious when considered against the strict legal, ethical and professional standards that regulate the healthcare profession. Regardless of whether the patient elects to have healthcare or requires it, the patient appropriately expects that the treatment will be rendered in accordance with the applicable standard of care. This is so regardless of how risky or dangerous the procedure or treatment modality might be.

Rockland's attempt to invoke the primary assumption of the risk defense fails because it cannot demonstrate that Mr. Storm chose to be sick or that he consented to allow Rockland to exercise less than ordinary care when it provided healthcare services to him. Even assuming *arguendo* that Mr. Storm was aware of the risks associated with independent living, he accepted these risks only because he was in need of medical care. Moreover, by accepting the risks inherent in the Rockland treatment environment, he did not in any way consent to allow Rockland to exercise less than what the applicable standards of care required of it when providing services. Permitting a primary assumption of the risk defense under these circumstances would simply be unconscionable.

. . . .

Based on the foregoing, the Court is satisfied that Rockland's legal status as a licensed assisted living facility and healthcare provider do not allow it to assert a primary assumption of the risk defense as a means to escape liability for allegedly substandard health care. Rockland's motion for summary judgment is DENIED.

QUESTIONS

Is the assisted-living environment right for frail elders? Perhaps some state laws are insufficient. Consider the comments of "Rooms without Rules," a series in the N.Y. Times:

> If John Anselmo, 82, had entered a nursing facility instead of Senior Quarters, odds are he would not have enjoyed the private room, sumptuous meals and rambling chats with nurses' aides that $3500 a month bought him at the Great Neck, N.Y. residence for the elderly.
>
> But when he went into congestive heart failure late one night in June 1999, Mr. Anselmo . . . might have received speedy attention from a trained nurse. Instead . . . an inexperienced aide — the only staff member on duty at the newly opened 144-bed center, save for the security guard — walked him down a long hallway to a waiting ambulance, the equivalent for someone in his condition of a long, fast run. A few days later, he died.

What went wrong here? Are there resources that should always be available in a place where residents may become acutely ill in the middle of the night?

[2] BOARD AND CARE HOMES

Board and care homes (also known as "retirement" or "personal care" homes) are community-based residences for older adults who need supportive assistance. Board and care homes vary from very small mom-and-pop operations with three or four residents to large, institutional type facilities with 100 or more residents. Regardless of their size, they typically provide room and board, 24-hour-a-day supervision, housekeeping, laundry, some personal care, and other miscellaneous services to the residents.

Board and care homes usually provide fewer amenities and charge less than assisted living facilities, though larger board and care homes are similar. The distinction is more of nomenclature and cost, with most board and care homes being less expensive. In some states the licensing requirements differ, but in others the same laws apply to assisted living and board and care. The larger the board and care home, the more "medicalized" it tends to be, as economies of scale permit more nursing assistance. Conversely, the small board and care may be served only by a husband and wife and lack any trained medical personnel. Some homes specialize in housing the poor elderly. Some will house only physically capable and mentally alert older residents. Others prefer frail, older residents but require them to be mentally alert, while other homes house older residents who have significant cognitive impairments.

The number of residents of such homes nationwide is uncertain given the lack of any consistent definition, although it is estimated that there are probably 50,000 licensed homes across the nation, housing 600,000 or more residents. In addition, there are probably as many, if not more, small unlicensed homes serving a million or more individuals.

Board and care homes are usually paid for by the resident. Private pay board and care homes attract individuals of moderate income. There are also publicly funded board and care homes that rely on Social Security and SSI payments as the source of payment for older dependent adults with limited economic resources. Some states pay a supplement in order to meet the cost of care for residents who receive only SSI or have limited incomes.

Board and care homes are primarily regulated by local and state governments. The federal government does require states to establish, maintain, and enforce standards in institutions or other group living arrangements in which a significant number of SSI recipients live. 42 U.S.C. § 1382e(a). However, the only penalty for violating the act is to reduce the SSI payment to a resident of a facility that fails to meet the state standards and so it is rarely invoked. Regulation has thus devolved to the states. Regulatory attempts are explained in the following material:

> All states attempt to regulate board-and-care homes in some manner or another, though in many cases many board-and-care homes operate outside the law. State regulation tends to come from a variety of sources, including housing departments, insurance departments, departments of health or aging, adult protection units, and even disability laws. The bifurcation of responsibility for oversight of board-and-care homes at the state level is probably in part responsible for the relative lack of enforcement of laws and the tendency to look the other way when there are violations. State regulation tends to be soft because if a board-and-care home were to be shut down, there might be no alternative for the low-income residents. States are well aware that these homes are not optimal environments, but nevertheless they fill a vital role in providing housing and service to a great many older persons who have limited income and few resources.

LAWRENCE A. FROLIK, RESIDENCE OPTIONS FOR OLDER OR DISABLED ADULTS 9-20 (1997).

[3] CONTINUING CARE RETIREMENT COMMUNITIES

Continuing care retirement communities (CCRCs) are supportive housing that guarantee residents lifetime appropriate care in the form of independent living, assisted living, and nursing home care. They are quite popular, but because of their cost, they are overwhelmingly filled with middle and upper-income residents. Over 90 percent of CCRCs are owned by not-for-profit entities, many of which are associated with religious groups.

CCRCs vary greatly in physical appearance. Some are high-rise, some low-rise, some feature apartments and others have individual houses, and some combine garden apartments with high-rise nursing homes. They are located in suburbs, in cities, and even in rural areas. Most have recreational amenities, such as swimming pools and tennis courts, but all have a common dining room and other common areas. They attract individuals who wish to: (1) live in a community with facilities designed for older people, (2) enjoy recreational and social activities with their peer group, (3) know there will be adequate support if they need assistance with daily living, and (4) have on-site nursing care. Most people enter CCRCs in their 70s or 80s, with three-fourths of the residents being women. CCRCs almost always require new residents to be physically and mentally capable of independent living in the facility's separate houses, townhouses, or apartments. As the residents become more frail or in need of more supportive services, the CCRC will provide more assistance in the independent living unit, in separate assisted-care units, or a nursing home. This continuum of care is offered for a monthly fee that in many CCRCs does not change even though the degree of assistance increases. CCRCs accept Medicare reimbursement for home health care and skilled nursing home care. Most CCRCs that offer nursing-home care, however, do not participate in Medicaid as its reimbursement amounts are too low to support the quality of care offered by the facility.

In addition to a monthly occupancy fee, CCRCs charge a high admission fee ($150,000 to $400,000 is common), which is sometimes refundable, usually by a formula that refunds less to the resident the longer he or she resides in the facility. (Residents often finance the admission fee by selling their current residences.) The admission fee helps support the capital costs of the CCRC but, more importantly, it functions as a health care insurance payment as it is used to subsidize medical care for the more sick and frail residents. Upon admission to a CCRC, the resident will be informed as to the amount of the entrance fee that is attributable to medical care; that amount qualifies as a medical deduction for purposes of the federal income tax. The medical prepayment aspect of the CCRC is very popular as it both limits future exposure of the resident to the high costs of assisted living or nursing home care and ensures the resident appropriate care without the need to move to a new facility.

A prospective resident signs an admission contract whereby the CCRC agrees to provide housing, a certain level of activities, and health care support in exchange for the payment of an entrance fee and monthly occupancy fees. The CCRC may also offer additional services, such as ambulance service, on a fee-for-service basis. The substantial admission fee to enter a CCRC gains residents the right to lease a unit and be a tenant or lessee. (A few CCRCs sell the unit to the resident.) The units are generally unfurnished. New residents are encouraged to renovate the units, though the CCRC usually will not reimburse the resident for the cost of the redecoration even if the resident leaves or dies within a short time after moving in.

Residents are charged a monthly occupancy fee that pays for utilities (except phone service), house cleaning, maintenance and repair of the unit, linen service, recreational facilities, organized clubs and entertainment, on-site nursing assistance, and some meals. The fee for most CCRCs includes evening meals served in a restaurant setting. Breakfast and lunch may be available on a per diem payment. CCRCs usually mandate participation in the evening meal to encourage socializing and create a sense of community. Failure to attend dinner may also be a signal to the CCRC to check on the resident in his or her unit to see whether assistance is needed.

Most CCRCs monitor the residents' health and provide appropriate care. On-site nurses visit sick residents, often on a daily basis. Some CCRCs, for no additional charge, provide daily in-unit nurse assistance such as helping residents who need insulin shots, dispensing prescription drugs, and monitoring blood pressure. The health care support offered by CCRCs attracts many residents. Individuals, whose health or physical condition declines, will either be offered more assistance in their unit, be moved to an assisted living unit, or, if necessary, be moved to the facility's nursing home. Transfers within a CCRC are governed by the contract of admission, but the interpretation of that contract can lead to disputes between the resident and the CCRC as to degree of assistance the individual requires. If the ailment is temporary and the person's health improves, he or she can move back to the independent living unit. A more serious decline in health may force the resident to move permanently into a smaller assisted living unit. While traditionally CCRCs offer assisted living in separate quarters, increasingly CCRCs provide some degree of assisted living in the independent living units, although at an increased monthly fee.

The individual's entrance fee may lock in a fixed rate for continuing care, usually less than the market rate for a nursing home. Thus, individuals move into a CCRC, in part, as insurance against the day they may need nursing-home care. In effect the CCRC becomes a form of long-term care insurance. Couples sometimes move into a CCRC to ensure that if one spouse must enter the nursing home, the other spouse will be living nearby. The most attractive feature of a CCRC, however, is its promise of lifetime care. A resident of a CCRC has made his or her last move regardless of his or her physical or medical condition. (A few CCRCs provide nursing home care off-site.) Some CCRCs operated by religious-affiliated entities even promise that residents who exhaust their financial resources and are unable to pay the monthly occupancy fee will not be forced to leave. The CCRC will make-up the shortfall either by drawing on its endowment or from gifts made to the CCRC for that purpose. State law may require a CCRC to exhaust all of the entrance fee and any applicable public benefits before discharging an impoverished resident.

QUESTIONS

1. What are the advantages and disadvantages of a CCRC?

2. Who are most likely to be residents of a CCRC? Is there any reason an individual must change residences in order to enter into a continuing care contract? Could such care be delivered to an elderly person who wants to "age in place"? Must the provider be a corporation, or could a private individual provide such care in return for a lump sum payment or other consideration?

A potential problem with CCRC agreements is the possibility that the prospective resident will pay a substantial entrance fee, move into the facility, and die suddenly and unexpectedly. Or, what if the move was a mistake and the resident leaves, as in the following case? Note the type and extent of services that the CCRC promises to provide.

MORRIS v. DEERFIELD EPISCOPAL RETIREMENT COMMUNITY, INC.
635 S.E.2d 536 (unpublished) (N.C. Ct. App. 2006)

On 22 June 2000, Mr. Morris and his wife entered into a Residence and Services Agreement with Defendant Deerfield Episcopal Retirement Community, Inc. ("Deerfield") for an independent living residence in the retirement community operated by Deerfield. The relevant portion of that written agreement states:

1.C. *Common Areas and Amenities*. Deerfield will provide common areas and amenities for the use and benefit of all residents such as a central dining room, private dining room, library, mail boxes, multipurpose room, lounges, woodworking shop, arts and crafts room, walking areas, exercise areas, and on-site Health Center, and other common areas and amenities described in the Community's current literature.

. . .

1.F.11. *Nursing and Health Care*. Deerfield will provide nursing and health care facilities and services as follows:

a. *Levels of Care*. A Health Center at Deerfield will be provided for the benefit of the residents. The Health Center will have accommodations, equipment, and staffing necessary for skilled nursing care and assisted living care.

Deerfield's literature included a "Questions & Answers" pamphlet containing the following pertinent information:

5. What kind of common areas and amenities will Deerfield's expansion offer?

A community center and wellness center will host most of the common areas and amenities. The community center will include a handsome lobby, a well-appointed formal dining room, private dining room, casual dining café, beverage lounge, outdoor terrace, library and reading room, multi-purpose auditorium, game room, woodworking shop, arts and crafts studio, classroom, computer lab, aerobics room, exercise/weight room, beauty and barber salon, physical therapy, bank, boutique, and country store, and central post office facilities. An indoor swimming pool and croquet court are in the developmental stage.

. . .

12. What residential services are offered at additional cost?

In addition to the standard services provided in the Monthly Fee, Deerfield will provide at an additional cost: . . . dementia day program . . . beyond the standard services.

. . .

17. What are the health care services and what are the accommodations available in Deerfield's new health center?

. . .

Dementia Day Program

A special area for residents with dementia or related conditions will be located within the health center . . . . Special programming will be provided for residents as well as an outdoor garden to allow the residents freedom to enjoy the outdoors in a secured environment. There will be an additional charge for this service.

Per the agreement, the Morrises made an initial payment of $198,365; moved into the apartment in November 2000; and began paying a monthly fee of at least $2,045.

On 21 November 2002, Mr. Morris met with Robert F. Wernet, Jr., Deer-field's President and Chief Executive Officer, and Mary "Dee" Mason, Deer-field's Director of Marketing, regarding the possibility of moving to a cottage in the facility. At that time, Mr. Morris's wife had begun to exhibit signs of dementia, including paranoia, agitation, and short-term memory loss, and Mr. Morris believed the move might help their situation. A cottage became available approximately one month later, but Mr. Morris objected to the additional fee that would be imposed for the move. On 21 December 2002, Mr. Morris notified Deerfield by letter that he was terminating the couple's residency in accordance with the written agreement. In January 2003, the Morrises moved into a larger apartment in Asheville.

On 22 October 2003, Mr. Morris filed his initial complaint in this case, alleging that Deerfield had breached its contract by failing to provide an on-site dementia daycare program for residents. Mr. Morris amended his complaint on 28 June 2004 to include the allegation that Deerfield had engaged in unfair and deceptive trade practices through its representations that an on-site dementia daycare program would be provided. Deerfield moved for summary judgment on both causes of action on 24 August 2005; after a hearing on 6 September, the trial court granted summary judgment to Deerfield on both claims.

Mr. Morris now appeals that ruling, assigning as error that the trial court erred by granting summary judgment in favor of Deerfield on his claims of

(1) breach of contract and (II) unfair and deceptive trade practices.

I.

Mr. Morris first contends the trial court committed reversible error by granting summary judgment on his breach of contract claim, as he presented sufficient evidence to create a genuine issue of material fact as to the claim.

. . . .

The written contract at issue in this case, the Residence and Services Agreement, does not include any direct mention of an onsite dementia daycare program, but it does incorporate by reference Deerfield's "current literature." Dementia daycare is discussed in two places in that literature: (1) in a description of other residential services available at an additional cost; and

(2) in a description of the services available in Deerfield's new Health Center, referred to in the Residence and Services Agreement. However, those references are only to a "dementia day program" that will be provided at additional cost to residents, as well as a "special area for residents with dementia," "[s]pecial programming," and "an outdoor garden."

The record shows that Deerfield, in fact, started an on-site dementia daycare program in February 2001, including a secure garden for residents, dedicated staff, and special programming. Because only a few residents used the facility, Deerfield determined it could not offer the flexibility and diverse programming necessary to best serve residents' needs. Deerfield therefore discontinued its on-site program after several months, deciding instead to form a partnership with a nearby local dementia daycare program that apparently offered service with which residents seemed pleased. The secure garden and other constructed facilities remained in place at Deerfield's continuing care community.

Thus, according to the record, Deerfield did offer a dementia daycare program, first on-site and then as contracted through a local, off-site provider, with special programming for residents with dementia, and did construct and make available a special area and outdoor garden for residents with dementia. Mr. Morris offered no evidence to refute these facts, arguing instead only that he was not aware of the facilities provided and that the contract guaranteed an on-site program. Both the record and the plain language of the contract itself contradict Mr. Morris's claim of breach of contract. Moreover, nothing in the record suggests that such a breach, if it did occur, rose to the level of materiality by "substantially defeat[ing] the purpose of the agreement," given that Mr. Morris himself stated that he did not know that such a daycare center was ever provided, nor did he or his wife ever use either the on-or off-site program prior to terminating their residency, nor did they state its existence as a primary reason for either entering into or terminating the contract.

Thus, no genuine issue of material fact as to this claim was presented to the trial court. Accordingly, we uphold the trial court's grant of summary judgment to Deerfield on the breach of contract claim.

II.

Mr. Morris also argues that the trial court committed reversible error by concluding that Deerfield had not engaged in unfair or deceptive trade practices.

. . . .

Mr. Morris contends that he presented sufficient evidence to create a genuine issue of material fact as to the question of unfair and deceptive trade practices under Chapter 75. To prevail on a claim for unfair and deceptive trade practices, a claimant must demonstrate the existence of three factors: "(1) an unfair or deceptive act or practice, or unfair method of competition, (2) in or affecting commerce, and (3) which proximately caused actual injury to the plaintiff or his business." However, this Court has previously held that "[i]t is well recognized . . . that actions for unfair or deceptive trade practices are distinct from actions for breach of contract, and that a mere breach of contract, even if intentional, is not sufficiently unfair or deceptive to sustain an action under N.C.G.S. § 75-1.1." The plaintiff must therefore show "substantial aggravating circumstances attending the breach to recover under the Act, which allows for treble damages."

. . . . Indeed, he argues no such aggravating circumstances attending the alleged breach of contract in this case, only that Deerfield's representations regarding a dementia daycare program were "deceptive and calculated to induce Plaintiffs to enter into an agreement with Deerfield for the purchase of life care." The record contains no evidence that supports this contention of deliberate deception; moreover, Deerfield made no misrepresentations, as Deerfield subsequently provided to its residents what the written agreement and promotional materials indicated.

In sum, because no genuine issue of material fact exists as to Mr. Morris's claims of breach of contract and unfair and deceptive trade practices, we affirm the summary judgment for Deerfield.

Affirmed.

———————

The greatest risk to residents is that the community will have insufficient funds to operate. Often, the problem arises soon after the CCRC commences operations and before the units are fully occupied. Typically, the developer has projected too brief a time for the units to be occupied by paying residents. Possibly, some residents have developed significant care needs early in their stay. Such a development may create unsustainable costs because the community does not yet have the number of residents required to bear the high health care costs.

The best way to protect a CCRC from financial failure (in addition to sound actuarial projections, typically required by the state) is to have several backers, whose resources greatly exceed the community's expected needs. Such backing often is inferred from promotional materials that feature the community's association with a church or charitable organizations. Any such representation should be investigated to determine whether the large, stable organization in fact backs the community with its resources, rather than just promoting it by lending a name.

[4]   LEGAL CONSTRAINTS ON SUPPORTIVE HOUSING

Most communities have some form of controls on land use and the nature of residents allowed in their neighborhoods. Traditionally, single-family neighborhoods were protected from intrusions by multifamily housing, which was considered undesirable under so-called Euclidian zoning. The definition of the family also was cast in traditional terms of blood or marriage. Commercial uses were segregated from residential uses, and some facilities such as congregate living facilities were more often excluded than welcomed.

[a]   Zoning and Other Restrictions

Developers who wish to open any type of group living such as an assisted living facility or a board and care home must find a location which does not violate local zoning laws. Assisted living facilities are usually large enough to require locating in neighborhoods zoned for apartments. Smaller board and care homes, however, often wish to locate in single-family housing areas by converting what was formerly a single-family house into a group home.

Zoning ordinances, however, typically have restricted occupancy of a single-family unit to the traditional family by defining it in terms of relationship by blood, marriage, or adoption, and permit only a limited number of unrelated persons to occupy a single-unit dwelling. Though such restrictions allegedly control population density, they are primarily intended to promote neighborhood economic homogeneity and traditional living patterns, with an eye to maintaining property values.

The effect is often to ban group homes from neighborhoods in which they would like to locate.

Many cities define family by placing a cap on the number of unrelated people who can live together in a dwelling unit. These restrictive limits found constitutional support in the Supreme Court case of *Belle Terre v. Boraas*, 416 U.S. 1 (1974), which held that a local zoning statute could bar any group of more than three unrelated individuals living together. As a practical matter such a definition would bar most if not all board and care homes.

Other cases have been more supportive of non-related individuals living together. In *Horizon House Developmental Servs., Inc. v. Upper Southampton*, 804 F. Supp. 683 (E.D. Pa. 1992), the court struck down a requirement that group homes be located at least a thousand feet from one another. The court held that this requirement was intended to discriminate against people with disabilities because there was "no rational basis or legitimate government interest" (*id.* at 693) for such discrimination. The court pointed out that the thousand feet distancing sharply limited numbers of people with disabilities who could reside within the township of Upper South Hampton. This, in effect, restricted their rights of mobility and reduced their ability to access community services. The court noted that even if "clustering" of group homes could be a legitimate goal of the township, the thousand-foot distance was overbroad, and therefore illegal.

An interesting case in Puerto Rico involved the attempts of neighbors to bar a group home for frail, older persons. The neighbors argued that the owners of the group home had failed to obtain necessary zoning variances. The state court had supported the neighbors and ordered the facility closed. The federal court, meanwhile, determined that the frail older residents were "handicapped" within the meaning of the Fair Housing Act (42 U.S.C. § 3602(k)) (FHA). The neighbors and the state and local government were therefore found in violation of the FHA in their attempts to deny these older handicapped citizens the right to live in the neighborhood. *Casa Marie, Inc. v. Superior Court of Puerto Rico for Dist. of Arecibo*, 752 F. Supp. 1152 (D.P.R. 1990).

A similar outcome was reached in the case of *United States v. Taylor*, 798 F. Supp. 442 (E.D. Mich. 1992), in which the city attempted to bar a home for older disabled adults claiming that the home would adversely affect automobile traffic. Again, the court found the city to be in violation of FHA and rejected the claim about the automobile traffic particularly in light of the fact that none of the residents owned the car or was even able to drive.

The most significant case is the *City of Edmonds v. Oxford House*, 514 U.S. 725 (1995). The City of Edmonds, Washington, attempted to bar a group home that would house 10 to 12 adults recovering from alcoholism and drug addiction, relying on a zoning provision that barred more than five underage individuals living together in a single-family neighborhood. The parties agreed that the Fair Housing Act prohibits discrimination in housing against, among others, persons with handicaps. However § 3607(b)(1) of the Act entirely exempts from the FHA "any reasonable, local, state, or federal restrictions regarding the maximum number of occupants permitted to occupy a dwelling." The sole question before the Court was whether the zoning provision, which described the family as five or fewer persons, was a maximum occupancy restriction exempt from the FHA under § 3607(b)(1). The Court found that the restriction was not exempt under that section. Because the purpose of the Act is to create broad and inclusive rights for the handicapped to live in the community, the exceptions must be read narrowly. The Court held that because the zoning law created a limit on the number of unrelated persons and not the total number of persons who might live together, the exception was not a "maximum" occupancy restriction. Rather, it was simply a restriction on the number of unrelated people, as opposed to related persons, who might live together. Hence it was not within the exemption and so violated the FHA and was not enforceable.

Another exclusionary technique is to limit the issuance of the special use permit that is required to establish the group home in a residential district. Special use, sometimes known as "conditional use," permits are designed to permit cities to carefully analyze the impact of a different kind of use coming into a community. Though not specifically aimed at group homes, they have been proven very effective at barring group homes. A request for special use permit will almost always require a public hearing at which time neighbors can voice objection to the proposed group home. Given the relative political power of the neighbors who oppose the group home and the powerless elderly group home residents, all too often cities will deny the special use permit. The only recourse at that point is for the group home to sue.

[b]   Construction and Land Use Restrictions

States and localities enforce significant building and construction requirements. Though not necessarily designed to exclude the elderly, the result has been to prohibit innovative or inexpensive housing attractive to the elderly. For example, local building codes often prevent the use of manufactured housing — primarily mobile homes and prefabricated housing — which is desirable for housing the elderly because it is less expensive than site-built housing.

Another alternative, which is often barred by zoning laws, is a small, temporary living unit, known as a "granny flat," placed in the yard of a conventional home to house an elder relative. The family members can live in close proximity and yet still maintain some independence and privacy. A related housing idea is the accessory apartment, a small, complete living unit installed in the excess space in a single-family home so the inhabitants each have their own facilities but live under the same roof. These too are often illegal because of zoning restrictions despite their advantages such as reducing travel costs for care-givers, providing security for frail, older residents, and allowing a degree of protective oversight in the event of accidents and emergency health problems.

Unfortunately, courts have not always been supportive of accessory apartments.

ROWATTI v. GONCHAR
500 A.2d 381 (N.C. 1985)

To summarize, several factors lead us to the conclusion that the addition converted the owners' residence into a two-family or multifamily dwelling and allows both the owners and the occupant of the addition itself to live as more than a single housekeeping unit. First, with its separate kitchen, boiler, bathroom, heating system, and entranceway, the addition can function independently from the original residence. Second, there is the closely-related factor that because of its design and physical appearance, the addition may impair the intent and purpose of the zoning plan for the entire area around Briarwood Lane. Third, the owners themselves contemplate an arrangement that would provide Mrs. Gonchar's mother with the opportunity to live and cook separately from the rest of the family whenever she so desires. Finally, as a matter of judicial review, local boards of adjustment must be accorded great latitude in determining facts that may adversely affect a municipality's entire zoning scheme.

We are sensitive to the fact that at the heart of this case there lies a daughter's concern for an elderly parent. Indeed, this Court has recognized that the older members of our society must deal with a number of special problems, particularly in the area of housing. We would like to think that our concern for the profound social problems associated with increasing life-expectancies and calculating housing costs is at least as great as that of our dissenting colleague. But we do not view this case as presenting the vehicle by which to address those concerns. At oral argument before us, on at least two occasions in response to questions from different members of the Court, counsel specifically and unmistakably eschewed any constitutional attack on the ordinance. No constitutional challenge was made in any of the proceedings below. Moreover, we are not presented with an ordinance that seeks to regulate or restrict the use of land on the basis of the user's age. The Northvale ordinance seeks merely to prohibit a certain type of structure, irrespective of the owners' or occupants' ages, or any other classification. Nor are principles of estoppel applicable here. The Gonchars were on notice at several different phases of the construction that they were proceeding at their own risk. Unfortunately, the risk materialized into an actual violation of the Northvale code that the Board of Adjustment correctly recognized.

When, as in this case, the Court is confronted with an ordinance that contains provisions that are, as the dissenter observes, arguably inconsistent, our obligation is to reconcile those provisions, to read them so as to make sense of them, and then to apply the ordinance in accordance with the intent of the municipality. It is clear to us that the intent of the Northvale ordinance is that when a residential structure is capable of housing two completely independent family units in the kind of lifestyle that, as a matter of fact, characterizes such independent living as defined in the ordinance, the entity is then a multiple dwelling; as such, it is prohibited.

Affirmed.

[In his dissent, JUSTICE STEIN observed:]

What *is* evident from this record is that an addition that was concededly designed for occupancy by the expanded Gonchar family — and no one else — was determined by the Board to have been designed, at least potentially, for more than one family. To this day, no one knows what specific feature of the addition was the proverbial straw that broke the camel's back. An addition constructed to accommodate any family's elderly parent or married child would typically include a bedroom, bathroom, and living area. Separate kitchen facilities obviously afford a measure of added independence, particularly for a parent accustomed to maintaining her own home in her own way. Perhaps the addition without a separate entrance would have passed muster, although the testimony indicated that this entrance was constructed at ground level in order that Mrs. Gonchar's mother could avoid the use of a stairway. The conflict inherent in this case is that the very same design features that accommodated Mrs. Gonchar's mother's desire for both independence and the security of living with relatives were relied upon by the Board for its conclusion that the dwelling was theoretically adaptable to multi-family use.

The dilemma that confronted the Gonchar family in this case is one that confronts many families as life-expectancies increase and housing costs escalate. How does a family accommodate a relative in its home while preserving a reasonable degree of independent living for both the basic family and the invited relative?

A common response will be the construction of an addition to the existing dwelling in order to accommodate the expansion of the family. To the extent that zoning ordinances determine whether or not such additions may be constructed, such ordinances must provide clear standards to guide both applicants and local officials in ascertaining the extent to which a single family dwelling may be altered to provide independent facilities for a family member without converting it into a multiple dwelling.

Since the original Northvale ordinance did not provide any standards, the Gonchars, their architect, the building inspector — and particularly the local board of adjustment — were required to rely solely on subjective criteria to determine whether the proposed addition was permissible. That the Board reached a different conclusion from the Gonchars' and the building inspector's as to the ordinance's meaning hardly justifies the harsh outcome of this litigation, especially since the root of the entire controversy can be traced directly to the lack of specificity in the Northvale ordinance.

QUESTIONS

1.   Do you agree with the majority or the dissent in *Rowatti*?

2.   Is it rational for U.S. zoning laws to almost universally oppose accessory flats in traditional, single-family neighborhoods?

3.   If zoning allowed the installation of an ECHO or accessory unit in the yard of the younger generation of family members for the use of the senior citizen, should it also allow installation in the yard of the senior's residence for occupancy by an adult child? Why, or why not?

4.   Innovative housing for the elderly is often victim of the NIMBY ("Not In My Back Yard") syndrome. Picture a quiet, orderly single-family neighborhood in which you may have lived, and the effect of little, modular living units in the backyards. Just what is the problem with this? If legalized, do you think they would become widespread?

F. SUBSIDIZED HOUSING FOR THE ELDERLY

The national housing policy has, at least in theory, addressed essentially all of the problems posed by the needs of an aging population. In practice, the situation is more complex.

In 1949, Congress adopted a national housing policy calling for a decent home and suitable living environment for every American family. The Federal Government has developed a variety of tools and programs in an effort to achieve this goal. One approach has been to provide housing directly through new construction programs and rental assistance payments aimed at providing adequate and affordable housing for those who could not otherwise afford it.

In 1990, Congress passed the National Affordable Housing Act (NAHA), which represented a new consensus on who should receive housing assistance, whether government should fund new construction or rely on existing housing stock, and how to administer the federal funding. One of the purposes of the Act was to enlarge the supply of supportive housing and services so that the frail elderly, mentally ill, and other vulnerable groups can live in dignity and independence. While the NAHA generally followed earlier statements of national housing policy, it also raised hopes for a new vitality in housing assistance.

Implementation of NAHA can be seen in the Department of Housing and Urban Development (HUD) use of the Section 202 program. In 1998, over half of the funds ($402 million) for Section 202 housing were targeted for use by nonprofit organizations to expand the supply of supportive housing for very low-income older persons. This housing was supposed to be designed to accommodate the special needs of the elderly and to provide a range of services tailored to those needs. Meanwhile on the demand side, HUD stepped up its use of Section 8 rental vouchers for elderly to enable them to afford private housing rents.

The federal government supports a number of programs for making housing affordable to low-income, elderly persons. Some of these programs are known as supply side assistance, which are designed to promote the production of more affordable housing. Typically supply side programs subsidize housing developers or rehabilitators by low-interest loans, loan guarantees, and even cash assistance. In return the operator of the housing must limit the selling price or the rental cost of the subsidized housing. In the most extreme form, the government builds and operates housing which it rents out at below market rates. In contrast, demand side housing assistance programs help the individual to pay subsidized or fair market value housing payments. Subsidies are given to individuals to enable them to afford the market rate of housing.

[1] BASIC ELIGIBILITY

Programs are administered at the federal level by the Department of Housing and Urban Development (HUD). At the local level, most government housing programs are administered by a public agency, usually called the public housing authority or agency (PHA), which is authorized to develop and operate housing and housing subsidy programs for low and very low income families. 42 U.S.C. § 1401 *et seq.* Eligibility for most government subsidized housing depends on income tests. A family qualifies for the "low income" category if adjusted income does not exceed 80 percent of the median for the area in which they live and as "very low income" if their income does not exceed 50 percent of the area median. 42 U.S.C. § 1437; 24 C.F.R. § 813.101 *et seq.* HUD determines the median for each housing authority's area. In rural areas, the Farmers Home Administration (FmHA), which serves as a rural public housing authority, sets the median income.

Total income includes all anticipated income from all sources received by the head of family and spouse for 12 months from the initial determination of eligibility. Income includes Social Security payments, pensions, disability and death benefits, and income from assets, but not casual or sporadic gifts, reimbursements for medical expenses, inheritances, scholarships, or earnings of minor household members. 42 U.S.C. § 1437a(b)(3).

An applicant for housing assistance generally must provide proof of all income and expenses to the public housing authority or Farmers Home Administration. The agency must respond with prompt notification of its decision regarding eligibility. If benefits are denied, the applicant must receive written notification of the reasons. Upon the applicant's request, the agency must also provide review of the determination and the applicant's objections by someone other than the original decision maker. 24 C.F.R. § 813.101.

[2] DEMAND-SIDE GOVERNMENT ASSISTANCE PROGRAMS: SECTION 8 RENT SUBSIDIES

The government provides demand-side assistance by subsidizing housing costs for individuals with income insufficient to pay the market rate. Some demand-side assistance is coupled with supply-side assistance in the form of subsidies to the developer or owner of the housing maintenance costs. Originally referred to as Section 8 housing, in 1998 it was renamed as the Housing Choice Voucher Program (HCVP). The term Section 8, however, remains the more familiar designation.

The Section 8 rent subsidy program provides rent vouchers to qualifying individuals. 42 U.S.C. § 1437(f). Households with income at or below 50 percent of an area's median income are eligible. The program provides four types of assistance:

1. Rental assistance.

2. Project designated rental assistance.

3. Homeowner assistance.

4. Downpayment assistance.

Rental assistance is the most common form of Section 8 assistance. It operates by creating a rental voucher that enables the individual to locate and pay for private sector housing at the fair market rent. Originally the program was structured to stimulate new construction, but over the years it has come to be seen as a demand side solution to housing for the poor. Its goal is to permit the poor to afford private sector housing, thus avoiding being forced to live in public housing. Section 8 vouchers are available to all eligible poor, not just the elderly, though the elderly make up a disproportionate share of Section 8 voucher recipients. The Section 8 voucher system is criticized by some housing advocates because it does not alleviate shortage of decent low-cost housing and may just encourage private landlords to increase rents.

The tenant's right to choose type and location of housing is not significantly affected by participation in the program. A Section 8 subsidy may be used to rent an apartment, a house, a mobile home, or a congregate housing unit, provided the housing meets basic structural and sanitation standards in accord with the law's purpose to provide decent, safe, sanitary dwellings. The only limitation is that the landlord must agree to accept Section 8 vouchers. If the family wishes to move, the agency must issue a new certificate if it has sufficient funds and the tenant qualifies. If the subsidy ends for any reason, the tenant's rights under the lease are unaffected, though he or she must pay the fair market rent.

In theory Section 8 is a pure demand side program in that it offers no direct subsidies to owners which reduce rents from the fair market value. In practice, however, Section 8 subsidies are often linked with particular housing projects and the unit owner may be the state or local government as well as a private individual. This is a practical necessity, in that the public housing authority must locate and inspect a reasonable supply of housing units in order to help applicants locate suitable housing. If a large proportion of a project's units are eligible for Section 8, however, it detracts from the concept of Section 8 as a program which was supposed to disperse disadvantaged persons throughout the community to avoid the problems that arise from concentrating low income housing.

[3] SUPPLY-SIDE GOVERNMENT ASSISTANCE PROGRAMS

The federal government has a number of programs which assist owners and developers, including local governments, to build, refurbish, and maintain units to be rented at costs affordable to low income families.

[a] Public Housing

Public housing is owned and operated by a local public housing authority (PHA), which receives loans from the Department of Housing and Urban Development (HUD) to construct housing for low income persons. The PHA can also borrow money on its own to help finance construction costs. A public housing authority must comply with HUD eligibility requirements in the selection of tenants and with HUD management regulations. It must select tenants who have very low incomes and give preference to the elderly and handicapped.

Public housing (42 U.S.C. § 1437a; 24 C.F.R. § 941 *et seq.*), the oldest program providing housing for the elderly, began in the 1930s to revitalize the construction industry and provide housing for families of unemployed blue collar workers. Today more than 3.5 million people live in 1.4 million public housing units, with almost half of the units occupied by elderly persons.

Elderly people living in public housing frequently have been subject to deplorable living conditions because of crime associated with substance abuse by their younger neighbors. The situation is particularly difficult for the elderly who are physically vulnerable or who realistically cannot move from the housing project. Though the priority standards — lowest income, living in substandard housing, or involuntarily displaced — help to target assistance to the most needy persons, they also assure that very disadvantaged persons are concentrated in a single location. The standards also tend to give priority to families with the greatest social malfunctions. Managers of public housing projects complain that this makes it impossible to maintain acceptable conditions.

In addition to being victimized by crime, the aging in place of public housing tenants is a critical problem. Elderly public housing tenants are more likely than other elderly persons to live alone, and 15 percent of elderly tenant families (about seven percent of all families in public housing) have at least one disabled member. About 30 percent of public housing authorities provide some on-site services for impaired persons but such services are not consistently available nor offered to all residents who need them.

Does Section 8 serve older people as well as public housing? Consider the following commentary on the demand-side, neighborhood diversity program versus the supply-side, dedicated purpose housing project model:

Kevin M. Cremin,
Note: *The Transition to Section 8 Housing: Will the Elderly Be Left Behind?*
18 YALE L. & POL'Y REV. 405 (2000)[*]

During the last twenty years, HUD has increasingly utilized demand-side as opposed to supply-side programs to provide affordable housing. As a result, more Americans now rely on Section 8 rental vouchers for affordable housing than on conventional public housing. This shift in programmatic emphasis has produced a voluminous amount of commentary. Proponents of the complete voucherization of housing subsidies have focused on the economic efficiency and mobility-enhancing qualities of the Section 8 program. Critics are divided as to whether to call for additional spending on auxiliary services to ensure real choice in relocation or to question the effect of subsidized mobility on the vitality of inner-city communities. . . .

One of the key areas of emphasis in this re-evaluation of priorities and preparation for the future is on the inter-relatedness of long-term care and housing policy. Given elderly persons' well documented preference to "age in place" and the considerable cost of nursing home care, there is an overwhelming consensus on the importance of fostering the continued independence of elderly individuals with home-or community-based supportive services. As a result, over the last two decades, HUD has gradually been shifting away from a "brick and mortar" conception of housing assistance to allow more spending on supportive services components. However, the impact of this broadening of the conception of housing assistance has been dulled considerably by two other trends at HUD — budget

---

[*] Copyright © 2000. Reprinted by permission of Yale Law & Policy Review.

cutbacks and a shift in emphasis from supply-to demand-side housing. . . .

One area where the popular conception of public housing and the actual data diverge considerably is the number of low-income elderly people who depend on public housing: most Americans would be surprised to learn that over one-third of the households residing in public housing are headed by an elderly person.

Cremin asks to what extent public housing subsidies under Section 8 can serve the elderly and their families, who are severely burdened by the need to move out of their neighborhoods and are unable to get supportive services when dispersed throughout the community. He recommends so-called "split subsidy" which provides tenants with Section 8 vouchers and also assists developers who create elderly housing under Section 202, as described below.

[b] Section 202 Housing Assistance

The principal public housing program for elderly tenants, Section 202 (12 U.S.C. § 1701q; 24 C.F.R. § 813), was originally enacted as a loan program for developers in the Housing Act of 1959, but was fundamentally changed by the National Affordable Housing Act of 1990 (NAHA). The original Section 202 financed construction and rehabilitation of low-rent apartments for low-income older and disabled persons. The post-NAHA Section 202 program funds construction and rehabilitation of housing exclusively for older persons.

In the past Section 202 loaned funds to private nonprofit sponsors for construction or rehabilitation of rental units. Today Section 202 gives sponsors funds based on the projected capital costs. Project sponsors (as owners or developers often are called) must pass on at least 50 percent of the savings due to the subsidy to their tenants in the form of reduced rents. Tenants must be 62 years of age or older and have "very low incomes," which are defined as less than 50 percent of their area's median income.

Most Section 202 housing consists of apartment houses, which often feature laundry facilities, community rooms, recreational services and special design features for the elderly. Project administrators can include in their project's operating budget the salaries of staff who coordinate supportive services. There are over 3,500 Section 202 projects operating. They are very popular as they provide affordable, safe housing that is usually linked in to supportive services. Waiting lists are very long since the average turnover rate is only about 13 percent annually. Tenants seldom leave, except to move to a nursing home or on account of death.

Consider the following development in government housing for the elderly, using a Massachusetts example of a national phenomenon:

Christine M. Cedrone,
Public Housing for the Elderly in Massachusetts: How Federal and State Disability Laws and Regulations Have Created a Sense of Confinement
8 ELDER L.J. 337, 338–39 (2000)[*]

Because their income is fixed and their housing is limited, elderly individuals have had to put up with increasing problems associated with their housing. The influx of "mixed housing" has increased the level of confinement among this elderly population. In addition, the definition of disability has changed over the years. It now encompasses alcoholics and drug addicts.

Because mixed housing includes the elderly and nonelderly disabled persons, alcoholics and drug addicts can live among the elderly. Therefore, the elderly are concerned for their safety and the issues surrounding nonelderly disabled individuals' addictions. The actions feared include physical attacks and threats. The elderly are not only afraid to leave their apartments, but to complain to local housing officials as well because they feel that they will lose their housing or suffer other consequences from their nonelderly disabled neighbors if they do.

There have been limited support services for the nonelderly disabled living in elderly housing. For example, local housing authorities cannot mandate that those who are suffering from alcohol or drug addiction attend support programs. Nor can LHA's randomly check to make sure that once they are approved for housing, nonelderly disabled residents do not continue the behavior that would have kept them from obtaining the housing in the first place.

Alcohol and drug abusers are typically younger than those currently living in elderly housing. This fact alone has created friction between them. Elderly housing was once a safe haven. It is now a place where the elderly feel threatened by drugs and crime.

People with disabilities and elders have always lived together in public housing. Only the nature of the people with disabilities has changed to include those with mental illness as well as ambulatory and vision disabilities. In response to problems in public housing, government has adopted stringent eviction procedures for any drug offenses. The entire household is evicted should one member be found with drugs or dealing in drugs. Can you envision the disadvantages of such a policy?

Perhaps the only solution is an adequate supply of elderly low income housing with services. For the moment, however, there is no right to such housing and all programs are discretionary. As a result, the need is far from being met.

QUESTIONS

1. If the government provides a loan for construction of low income housing and elderly tenants take up residence, how long should the building continue to serve as low income housing?

2. How would you structure a housing program for the elderly? Would you have age-segregated projects? Would you fund supportive services? Would you serve lower-middle income retirees?

3. Senator Doe proposes to abolish age-segregated public housing for the elderly and, instead, integrate poor elderly into public housing open to all. Do you agree with the Senator's proposal? What are its advantages and disadvantages?

Chapter 9

GUARDIANSHIP

When individuals no longer have the mental capacity to make decisions necessary to manage their property and personal affairs, someone else must make those decisions for them. The law's answer is to have a guardian appointed for the mentally incapacitated individual. Because all adults are presumed to be mentally competent enough to make their own decisions, only a court can appoint a guardian with the authority to make decisions for another person. Guardianship is the device by which a capable person is empowered to make decisions for an impaired person. The substitute decision maker is generally referred to as a guardian and the impaired person a ward or incapacitated person.

There are alternative ways to provide substitute decision makers for the property of incapacitated individuals, such as a durable power of attorney or revocable trusts. These and other voluntary means are discussed in Chapter 10, *Property Management*. Non-judicial methods of providing a substitute decision maker for health care decisions are covered in Chapter 11, *Health Care Decision Making*.

The principal issues in guardianship are the extent to which an individual's right to self-determination must be recognized, and the reasons and procedures for limiting that right. In the United States, the wishes of a substitute decision maker may be imposed on an autonomous, non-criminal adult only after a judicial adjudication of mental incapacity. The key questions are: who is incapacitated, and what are the consequences of being found incapacitated?

Mental incapacity is not the same as "insanity" or "mental illness." "Insanity" is a term applied principally to the mental state of defendants charged with a criminal offense. The term "mental illness" is used in civil commitment statutes to define persons who may be involuntarily committed to mental treatment facilities. Mental incapacity refers to a legal determination that an individual lacks the mental ability to care for his or her person or property. A determination of mental incapacity does not mean that the individual is insane or mentally ill.

A. THE NEED FOR GUARDIANSHIP FOR THE ELDERLY

It is estimated that 80 percent of adults under guardianship are age 60 or over, though this age group represents less than 20 percent of the population, reflecting the high incidence of dementia among the elderly. For example, it is estimated that 40 percent of those age 85 or older have some degree of dementia, with the most frequent, though not the only, cause of dementia being Alzheimer's disease.

G. Webster Ross, Helen Petrovitch & Lon R. White, *Update on Dementia*
20 Generations 4, 22–27 (1996)*

Dementia is a syndrome characterized by acquired impairment in at least three of five neurophysical and behavioral domains — memory, language/ speech, visuospatial ability, cognition (the ability to manipulate previously learned information), and mood/personality (Cummings and Benson, 1992). For a diagnosis, the *Diagnostic and Statistical Manual of Mental Disorders* (American Association Press, 1994) requires that the cognitive deficits be severe enough to cause significant impairment in social or occupational functioning.

The various types of dementia are as follows:

Alzheimer's disease. Standardized clinical criteria have improved the accuracy of diagnosing Alzheimer's disease to around 85 percent. Once dementia has been established, the diagnosis of probable Alzheimer's disease requires that the course of memory impairment be gradually progressive, the onset between the ages of 40 and 90, and there be no disturbance of consciousness and no other systemic disorders known to cause dementia (McKhann et al., 1984). The clinical diagnosis can be confirmed after death by examination of the brain. Brains of patients with Alzheimer's disease are atropic (wasted), reflecting the neuronal and synaptic loss characteristic of the disease.

Cerebrovascular dementia. The diagnosis of cerebrovascular dementia depends on the presence of a dementia syndrome and cerebrovascular disease sufficient to cause the dementia. The classical clinical presentation is one of abrupt onset with a fluctuating or gradual decline in cognitive function. In these cases, the distinction between Alzheimer's and cerebrovascular dementia is not difficult. However, there are cases of the latter that progress slowly. Most patients have a history of stroke or exhibit focal (localized) neurological signs.

Other degenerative forms of dementia, which account for 10 to 15 percent of cases, are caused by changes in the brain due to Parkinson's disease and frontal lobe degeneration. Each cause produces specific cognitive losses and physical effects. Dementia differs from mental retardation, in that it represents a loss of previous abilities, and from delirium, a transient state of mental impairment which may occur in addition to dementia or in healthy persons.

. . . .

Not only are some elderly afflicted with dementia, many are required to make difficult health care decisions. At one time few treatment choices existed and the differences among them were insignificant because none were very effective. Today medical care often offers several alternatives. If the patient is too impaired to choose, someone else must do so. Health care providers traditionally relied on informal consent by the family, but with the possibility for intrafamily disputes over treatment choices and a more litigious society, health care providers now frequently seek a formally approved, legal substitute decisionmaker. Many

---

hospitals and nursing homes routinely attempt to identify surrogate decisionmakers for elderly patients or residents. Obtaining consent from a substitute decisionmaker avoids delay and disputes when the patient's ability to understand and give consent is questionable.

. . . .

Finally, the need for property management is often the cause of guardianship. As more older persons own significant assets or real property there is greater need for substitute decision making. Many elderly are "house rich," owning dwellings with paid-off mortgages that have risen in value since their purchase decades ago. Others have accumulated substantial savings or have inherited significant assets which they have difficulty managing.

B.   THE DEVELOPMENT OF GUARDIANSHIP LAW

In order to understand the current guardianship law, it is useful to consider its origins. The state's responsibility to care for the person and property of a disabled person appears in early English law, which formalized the right and responsibility of a lord to maintain order on his land as described in the following case.

IN THE MATTER OF THE GUARDIANSHIP OF HEDIN
528 N.W.2d 567 (Iowa 1995)

LAVORATO, JUSTICE.

. . . . Incompetency proceedings predate guardianship and involuntary commitment. As early as the first century B.C., Rome had machinery in place to protect the property of the mentally disabled. But there was no corresponding protection for their person.

England and the American colonies followed this approach. Some of the colonies passed legislation to protect the estate of "insane persons" long before they passed any legislation concerning the personal welfare of the mentally disabled.

England did not become concerned with the personal welfare of the mentally disabled until long after the Norman Conquest. In medieval England, the lord of the manor had responsibility for guardianship of the mentally disabled. This responsibility included protecting the property and personal interests of the mentally disabled. The driving force behind development of such a guardianship arose not from any humane concern but from a selfish one: "to prevent the mentally disabled from becoming a public burden or dissipating their assets to the detriment of their heirs."

Initially this guardianship applied to mentally deficient persons only but was later expanded to include mentally ill persons. The responsibility for such persons shifted to the Crown.

The Lord Chancellor exercised the Crown's guardianship through a special commission of the Crown rather than through the general authority of the chancery court. The Lord Chancellor held an inquiry to determine if the mentally disabled person was an "idiot" or a "lunatic." If such a determination was made, the Chancellor appointed a committee for the person and property of the mentally disabled person.

In contrast, in this country, courts of equity — through the common law, statutory, or constitutional provisions — assumed jurisdiction over the person and property of mentally disabled persons in the form of guardianship proceedings. The legal and philosophical basis for such proceedings is the doctrine of parens patriae. This doctrine "obligates the state to care for the vulnerable and the less fortunate."

The concept of guardianship as a helpful state response to the needs of mentally incapacitated individuals (formerly referred as "incompetents") remains part of modern guardianship:

Lawrence A. Frolik,
Plenary Guardianship: An Analysis, a Critique, and a Proposal for Reform
23 ARIZ. L. REV. 599, 611–13 (1981)[*]

The "Therapeutic Model" of guardianship also has its origins in the responsibility of the state, acting under its parens patriae power, to protect orphans and incompetents.

Over time, protection developed into intrusive attempts to "cure" or "reform" the incompetent. The nineteenth century saw the growth of the asylum as the logical end-point of the doctrine of parens patriae; the desire to protect led to a desire to reform, which led to the desire for control, which in turn led to the development of the asylum. The goal of promoting the interests of the ward gradually became juxtaposed with the goal of promoting the interests of the sovereign to "cure" the ward. Thus, orphans were not merely to be sheltered until they reached majority, but were to be raised in a manner designed to mold them into respectful, diligent and moral citizens. Over time, the insane came to be considered "mentally ill," and restrictive chains were replaced by therapy. Similarly, guardianship began to attract advocates of the therapeutic state who saw in its control of the ward the opportunity for the state to assist the ward beyond merely providing protection for his person and property. Therapeutic state advocates began to press for guardianship to be integrated into a total system of the delivery of state services that would assure adequate legal consent even if the ward, because of his incompetency, either could not or would not allow the state to help him.

The view that guardianship provides a vehicle for the delivery of state assistance to the disabled has led proponents of the "Therapeutic Model" to the belief that guardianship should be more widely available. To that end, they advocate a broadening of the definition of those eligible for a guardian to accommodate

---

[*] Copyright © 1981 by the Arizona Board of Regents. Reprinted by permission.

everyone who might benefit from having one. Thus, they would eliminate the traditional requirement that the ward lack mental capacity or that the individual suffer from an identifiable disorder; instead, the need for a guardian, it is felt, should be based solely upon the behavior of the alleged incompetent. Any individual who demonstrates by his behavior that he cannot make or communicate reasonable decisions would be a candidate for a guardian.

The relationship between the state and the disabled adult, however, cannot be the same as that between a parent and a child. The child is presumed to be legally incompetent by the objective fact of age, and the state's power supplements or replaces power which would be held by a parent. While the state's responsibility to provide appropriate care may be similar, the right to determine what should be done differs when the recipient is a disabled adult, because that person is presumed to have the right to self-determination.

C.   FUNDAMENTAL LIBERTIES AND GUARDIANSHIP

Guardianship intrudes on or removes fundamental liberty interests protected by the Constitution of the United States. Persons found to be incapacitated and for whom a guardian is appointed lose control of their personal lives, including the right to choose whether to travel, where to live, and the kind of health care they receive. They also lose the right to manage their property and assets, to contract, to sue, to make gifts, and to engage in other types of financial transactions.

A troubling aspect of guardianship is the stigma of being identified as one who lacks the rights normally accorded to any adult to make independent decisions. The following passage pinpoints the issue:

> At stake in the petition to appoint plaintiff's committee was plaintiff's right to enter into legal relations, to control and dispose of property, to enter into contracts, and to sue and be sued — in short, at stake were all the incidents of being a competent individual which are lost when one is declared to be incompetent. Although the plaintiff requests recovery of money alleged to have been illegally spent by the committee, any right she may have to the money is not the critical interest sought to be protected. The important ones are, rather, those affected by the declaration that she was incompetent to handle her own affairs. The stigma of incompetency, the implication that she has some kind of mental deficiency, with attendant untrustworthiness and irresponsibility, and the consequences to her reputation and her normal human relationships with others in her community involve more than a property right. Unlike the claim in *Bradford Audio Corp. v. Pious*, 392 F.2d 67 (2d Cir. 1968), the adverse impact of the officials' action on her rights of personal liberty would exist regardless of the alleged illegal use of the money. We hold that plaintiff has stated a cause of action under 42 U.S.C. § 1983.

Dale v. Hahn, 440 F.2d 633 (2d Cir. 1971).

Stigma is a mark of disgrace or discredit, or perhaps the ill-defined justification for a variety of negative attitudes and attributions. For the individual, the stigma of being declared mentally incapacitated can be traumatic. Even families of wards often feel that the family has been stigmatized by having a member declared too mentally incapacitated to handle his or her own affairs.

QUESTIONS

1. Do you agree or disagree with the observations about stigma?

2. How can stigma best be minimized or eliminated?

3. Is stigma to the ward's family worthy of our concern? If so, what can be done about it?

NOTE ON THE VOCABULARY OF GUARDIANSHIP

States use a variety of terms. While "guardian" is almost universally used, states also use the term "conservator," often to refer to a guardian of the property. The disabled person may be called a "ward," an "incapacitated person," or a "conservatee." Usually a conservator has authority only to manage property. Louisiana, reflecting its civil law, refers to guardianship as "interdiction."

In the past, statutes used the term "incompetent." Today the term "mentally incapacitated" is preferred. The difference is more than mere nomenclature; it represents different concepts of when it is appropriate to appoint a guardian.

Consider the language of incompetency in Missouri's now repealed statute:

An "incompetent" is any person who is incapable by reason of insanity, mental illness, imbecility, idiocy, senility, habitual drunkenness, excessive use of drugs, or other incapacity, of either managing his property or caring for himself or both.

MO. REV. STAT. § 475.010 (1982).

What effect do you believe such language had on people's attitudes toward wards, and treatment of them?

The reformed Missouri statute reads as follows:

(8) An "incapacitated person" is one who is unable by reason of any physical or mental condition to receive and evaluate information or to communicate decisions to such an extent that he lacks capacity to meet essential requirements for food, clothing, shelter, safety or other care such that serious physical injury, illness, or disease is likely to occur. The term "incapacitated person" as used in this chapter includes the term "partially incapacitated person" unless otherwise specified or apparent from the context.

(13) A "partially incapacitated person" is one who is unable by reason of any physical or mental condition to receive and evaluate information or to communicate decisions to the extent that he lacks capacity to meet, in part,

essential requirements for food, clothing, shelter, safety, or other care without court-ordered assistance.

Mo. Rev. Stat. § 475.010(8), (13).

D.   DUE PROCESS IN GUARDIANSHIP PROCEEDINGS

The law of guardianship traditionally did not perceive adverse interests between the petitioner (often the prospective guardian) and the respondent (the prospective ward). The respondent was perceived as trying to help an incapacitated, vulnerable person. Guardianship proceedings were not considered adversarial. Therefore, complicated legal procedures were considered to be unnecessary, expensive, and a waste of time. In this spirit, in the past guardianship proceedings were largely exempt from due process requirements.

The lack of basic procedural rights in guardianship hearings is illustrated in the following 1980s guardianship hearing described in the St. Petersburg Times series, "Wards of the Court."

> It took two minutes for an 82-year-old woman named Adele to lose her civil rights.
>
> It happened at a court hearing in St. Petersburg last month, but Adele wasn't there. Neither was the man appointed to be her guardian.
>
> Nobody at the hearing talked about any plans for Adele. There was a doctor's report that suggested putting her in the hospital for tests, but that wasn't discussed either.
>
> Adele didn't have a lawyer to represent her. Nor had she met the lawyer who told the judge she needed a guardian.
>
> And, as often happens, the judge declared Adele incompetent and appointed her a guardian without demanding more information.
>
> The court was not informed correctly about the ward's residence, assuming it was a nursing home when she still lived in her unkempt house. Because she was unwilling to answer the court interviewer's questions, she did not have legal counsel in the proceedings. Neither the attorney handling the petition nor the guardian had been to see the ward. Only the attorney and a state social worker attended the two-minute hearing in the judge's chambers.

Good & King, *The Judges: Some Are Thorough, But Others Exercise Little Oversight.*

In the 1980s state legislatures enacted reform statutes intended to protect the rights of such vulnerable people by requiring various procedural protections, such as adequate notice, the presence of the respondent at the guardianship hearing, and, in some states, mandatory counsel for the respondent.

[1] NOTICE

Guardianship begins with the filing of petition that requests that an individual be found mentally incapacitated — as defined under the state statute — and in need of a guardian. Providing adequate notice to the alleged incapacitated person, the respondent, of the petition and the upcoming court hearing presents a number of problems. At a minimum the individual should be given notice of the nature of the proceedings. A respondent, upon being served with a notice of guardianship hearing, is very likely to have cognitive and emotional impediments to understanding the meaning of the notice. Even physical impairments, such as diminished vision, can interfere with understanding what the notice is about. State laws attempt to make the notice as meaningful as possible.

Consider the requirements of the Virginia statute:

A. Upon the filing of the petition, the court shall promptly set a date, time, and location for a hearing. The respondent shall be given reasonable notice of the hearing. The respondent may not waive notice, and a failure to properly notify the respondent shall be jurisdictional.

B. A respondent, whether or not he resides in the Commonwealth, shall be personally served with the notice, a copy of the petition, and a copy of the order appointing a guardian ad litem pursuant to § 37.2-1003. A certification, in the guardian ad litem's report required by subsection B of § 37.2-1003, that the guardian ad litem personally served the respondent with the notice, a copy of the petition, and a copy of the order appointing a guardian ad litem shall constitute valid personal service for purposes of this section.

C. A copy of the notice, together with a copy of the petition, shall be mailed by first class mail by the petitioner at least seven days before the hearing to all adult individuals and to all entities whose names and post office addresses appear in the petition. For good cause shown, the court may waive the advance notice required by this subsection. If the advance notice is waived, the petitioner shall promptly mail by first class mail a copy of the petition and any order entered to those individuals and entities.

D. The notice to the respondent shall include a brief statement in at least 14-point type of the purpose of the proceedings and shall inform the respondent of the right to be represented by counsel pursuant to § 37.2-1006 and to a hearing pursuant to § 37.2-1007. Additionally, the notice shall include the following statement in conspicuous, bold print.

WARNING

AT THE HEARING YOU MAY LOSE MANY OF YOUR RIGHTS. A GUARDIAN MAY BE APPOINTED TO MAKE PERSONAL DECISIONS FOR YOU. A CONSERVATOR MAY BE APPOINTED TO MAKE DECISIONS CONCERNING YOUR PROPERTY AND FINANCES.

THE APPOINTMENT MAY AFFECT CONTROL OF HOW YOU SPEND YOUR MONEY, HOW YOUR PROPERTY IS MANAGED AND CONTROLLED, WHO MAKES YOUR MEDICAL DECISIONS, WHERE YOU LIVE, WHETHER YOU ARE ALLOWED TO VOTE, AND OTHER IMPORTANT RIGHTS.

     E.   The petitioner shall file with the clerk of the circuit court a statement of compliance with subsections B, C and D.

VA. CODE ANN. § 37.2-1004 (2006).

In addition to notice to the respondent, state laws require notice to other interested parties.

For example, the Uniform Probate Code requires notice on the following:

   (1)   the person alleged to be incapacitated and spouse, or if none, adult children, or if none, parents;

   (2)   any person who is serving as guardian or conservator, or who has the care and custody, of the person alleged to be incapacitated;

   (3)   in case no other person is notified under paragraph (1), at least one of the nearest adult relatives, if any can be found; and

   (4)   any other person as directed by the Court.

U.P.C. § 5-304(a).

The National Conference of the Judiciary recommends requiring personal service upon respondent by a court officer in plain clothes trained in dealing with the aged. The Conference recommends that, in addition to the respondent, notice should be given by mail to the spouse, all the next of kin, the person with physical custody of the respondent, the proposed guardian, and any other providers of service. The notice should be in plain language and large type and should indicate the time and place of hearing, the possible adverse results to the respondent (such as loss of rights to drive, vote, marry, etc.) and a list of rights relating to the proceedings (such as the right for court-appointed counsel or guardian ad litem). A copy of the petition for appointment of a guardian, which names the petitioner and the reasons for the request, should be attached.

QUESTIONS

   1. Does the U.P.C. provide meaningful notice to the respondent of the impact the proceedings are likely to have? What measures would you require or eliminate to assure meaningful notice is given?

   2. Surely, it would be less upsetting to an impaired individual living alone to have the "news" of the guardianship proceeding delivered by a known individual who has their interests as a priority. Is notice appropriate and sufficient if it is served on the respondent's court-appointed counsel? What problems are likely to arise in the relationship or in subsequent proceedings?

3.   Florida requires that the petition be read to the alleged incapacitated person. FLA. STAT. § 744.331(1). The New Hampshire statute (N.H. REV. STAT. ANN. § 464-A:5) specifies that notice must be in type which is 10-point boldface with a dark border and contain a statement that the respondent has the right to contest the petition and that a lawyer has been appointed, who will shortly contact the respondent to discuss the case. Which is likely to be more effective? Do any of the requirements which seem inappropriate or ineffective?

4.   The purpose of notice is to allow the respondent to protect his or her interests. The Recommended Judicial Practices would require "at least fourteen days' notice before the hearing unless the court otherwise orders." Is this long enough? If not, how much time should be required? How much delay is likely to be too much?

[2] EXPERT TESTIMONY

To prove incapacity under a typical statute requires medical testimony. However, in some states such testimony can be provided by any physician, without regard to whether he or she was trained to diagnose mental incapacity. In the past the "testimony" was often merely an affidavit prepared by a physician that gave a cursory description of the mental state of the respondent such as "suffers from dementia" and often concluded that the respondent was "mentally incompetent." Today most statutes require that the medical testimony be given by someone with the requisite professional competency to make an assessment of the respondent's mental capability and that the evaluator either testify in person or by deposition.

In order to obtain reliable, objective information, the practice of professional functional assessment has been developed. A functional assessment typically requires observing the individual in a number of representative, common tasks. In emergency intervention, the assessment may only test tasks or abilities which are alleged to create risk of harm. In non-emergency proceedings a detailed instrument may be created that catalogs the person's actual or self-assessed ability in a range of activities necessary for independent living. These activities include bathing and dressing, preparing and eating food, and walking in and near the home. They also include tasks necessary to obtain information or services, such as paying bills, making doctor's appointments, and securing transportation.

Who is qualified to provide this information to the court? A geriatric psychiatrist provides the following description of an ideal assessment.

J. STREIM, M.D., THE ROLE OF THE GERIATRIC PSYCHIATRIST IN EVALUATION OF MENTAL HEALTH PROBLEMS IN ELDERLY PATIENTS (1989)*

The geriatric psychiatrist is often called upon to evaluate a wide range of signs and symptoms that commonly occur in older adults. These include disturbances of mood or emotion, abnormalities in thought process or content, impairment of

---

*   An address to the Training Conference on Mental Health and Aging sponsored by Philadelphia Bar Association Young Lawyers Section, Senior Citizens Judicare Project, and Elderly Law Project of

cognitive function, changes in behavior, and the disability that results from any of these signs or symptoms of illness. There are four basic goals of the psychiatric evaluation. First it is important to determine whether the symptoms are a manifestation of psychiatric disorder, an underlying medical disease, or a normative phenomenon. For example, some changes in cognition like mild forgetfulness can occur as a part of the normal aging process. This must be distinguished from memory deficits that are symptoms of psychiatric disorders or disease.

Once it is determined that a pathological condition exists, the second goal is to discover any treatable or reversible causes for the condition. The geriatric psychiatrist must conduct a thorough medical evaluation, since older patients may have one or more medical conditions with symptoms that mimic psychiatric illness. Conversely, psychiatric symptoms may be a manifestation of an underlying medical disorder. The evaluation must detect the presence of cardiovascular disease, endocrine abnormalities, metabolic disturbances, vitamin deficiency, drugs and toxins, infectious diseases, tumors, immune diseases, trauma, and neurological conditions. Within each of these categories, there are many diseases which can cause or aggravate psychiatric disorders, and some of these are treatable and reversible. The third objective of the psychiatric evaluation is to assess the functional level of the patient and determine the degree of disability caused by disorder or disease. That is, beyond making a diagnosis of a specific disease or disorder, it is important to evaluate how the patient's illness effects his ability to perform the activities of daily living. This is where geriatric evaluation goes beyond traditional medical diagnostics. Fourth, the evaluation helps to ascertain what supports the patient already has and what additional resources the patient requires in order to function in the most optimal way possible.

The conditions most commonly encountered by geriatric psychiatrists in community populations are the mood disorders such as depression and anxiety; the dementias, such as Alzheimer's Disease and multi-infarct dementia; and the primary thought disorders such as schizophrenia and delusional disorders. In the hospital setting, delirium, or acute confusional states are frequently encountered in the context of acute medical illness.

Particular attention should be paid to a history of systemic diseases, head trauma, nutritional compromise, substance abuse, prescription medication use, and exposure to environmental toxins. This is crucial, because all of these factors may be associated with dementia and in many cases may aggravate or even cause the dementia.

The next component of the evaluation is the physical examination. Again, this is conducted to discover treatable causes of the dementia. A mental status examination is performed to assess the patient's mood, affect, thinking, behavior, and various aspects of cognitive function such as attention, concentration, memory, abstract thinking, and judgment. There are many standardized cognitive testing instruments which can be used to rate the patient's cognitive function numerically.

Community Legal Services (Apr. 26, 1989). Reprinted with the permission of Joel E. Streim, MD, Associate Professor, Psychiatry, University of Pennsylvania.

One of the commonly used questionnaires for this purpose is the Folstein Mini Mental State Examination.

The next part of the routine evaluation includes laboratory testing, neuropsychological testing, and brain imaging. Laboratory tests that are routine in the evaluation of dementia include a urinalysis; complete blood counts to screen for anemia, infection, and malignancies; a serologic test for syphilis; vitamin B12 and folate levels; and blood chemistries to detect abnormal liver, kidney, and thyroid function. A CT scan of the head or magnetic resonance imaging (MRI) are also done routinely. These can be useful in visualizing strokes, brain tumors, blood and trauma. Ideally, when resources permit, neuropsychological testing should be done, since this may be useful for distinguishing the types of dementia and the extent of cognitive impairment. The need to do other tests is determined on an individual basis, depending mostly on the findings from the history of the physical examination. These might include a spinal tap to examine the cerebral spinal fluid for signs of infection, bleeding, tumors or immune diseases; an electroencephalogram to detect seizures and abnormalities that may be present with metabolic disturbances or tumors; a toxicology screen looking for drugs or heavy metals; HIV testing when AIDS is suspected; and further serology when Lyme disease is a possibility.

Once the diagnosis is established and the underlying cause is determined, the evaluation turns to a functional assessment. This is because the diagnosis by itself doesn't tell us the extent of disability caused by the illness. For example, some patients with a diagnosis of dementia or depression can be completely independent, and others with the very same diagnosis may require intensive 24-hour care. This is one reason that interdisciplinary evaluation and treatment is particularly important in geriatrics. For example, a functional assessment of a patient with dementia might include evaluation by a speech therapist to determine the extent of language dysfunction in order to know whether it interferes with the patient's ability to communicate. That is, dementia is the diagnosis, language dysfunction is a symptom of it, but inability to communicate is one of the disabilities that determines at what level the patient can function in the world. The occupational therapist may also be helpful with functional assessment, helping us to look at the patient's capacity to perform activities of daily living such as feeding, dressing, grooming, and toileting; and household management abilities such as using the telephone, paying bills, cleaning, using public transportation, and shopping. Once the patient's functional level has been assessed, the next step is to determine which needs are currently being met and which are not. Here social workers can be particularly helpful in discerning any mismatch between needs and resources. This part of the evaluation is critical, because in addition to medical treatment of conditions associated with dementia, the mainstay of management is coordination of needed support services.

In some cases, the evaluators find that adequate support of the patient requires the appointment of a guardian and/or residential care. The geriatric psychiatrist must often make a clinical determination of the patient's capacity to care for himself, to manage his property, or to make decisions in his own behalf. However, legal judgments about the patient's competence or need for a guardianship are made by the courts.

Either by statute or as a practical necessity, medical evidence of mental incapacity is almost always required. For example, Florida requires the following medical evidence:

The examination of the alleged incapacitated person must include a comprehensive examination, a report of which shall be filed by the examining committee as part of its written report. The comprehensive examination report should be an essential element, but not necessarily the only element, used in making a capacity and guardianship decision. The comprehensive examination must include, if indicated:

1. A physical examination;

2. A mental health examination; and

3. A functional assessment.

If any of these three aspects of the examination is not indicated or cannot be accomplished for any reason, the written report must explain the reasons for its omission.

FLA. STAT. § 744.331.

Should the examiners, whether physicians or other professionals, be the patient's usual caregivers? Certainly such familiarity increases the knowledge upon which a sound opinion might be based. However, G.K. Goodenough observes in *The Lack of Objectivity of Physician Evaluations in Geriatric Guardianship Cases*, 14 J. CONTEMP. L. 53 (1988):

The physician may be biased in his statement by previous interactions with the patient and the family. Often, it is the patient's family that wants a guardian appointed. In these cases, it is likely that no one will challenge the guardianship solicitation. This leaves the physician in a position of pleasing everyone by agreeing with the family, or pleasing no one by disagreeing. Even the patient, the subject of the investigation, may offer little resistance in the face of persuasion by multiple family members. If the patient's age exceeds sixty years, there is an "ageism" bias, that somehow senility (i.e., old age) is equivalent to impaired mental capacity. Indeed, the meaning of the word "senile" is often taken to mean forgetful or unclear in thinking, when actually the word means "old" or "associated with aging."

In Florida, the attending or family physician may not be appointed unless good cause is shown.

In addition to medical testimony, family members, friends, and others may also offer testimony regarding the respondent's behavior and decisions. The determination of mental capacity must be based on recent evidence, to assure that an adjudication is made based on the individual's current capabilities. The New Hampshire guardianship statute (N.H. Rev. Stat. Ann. § 464-A:21) requires evidence of occurrences within six months before the filing of the petition, with at least one incident in the 20 days before filing: "Isolated instances of simple negligence or improvidence, lack of resources, or any act, occurrence or statement if that act, occurrence or statement is the product of an informed judgment shall not constitute evidence of the inability to provide for personal needs or to manage property."

QUESTION

If you were defending the alleged incapacitated person what would you want to know about the timing, duration, and location of the interview and the doctor's qualifications? Would you recommend that your client undergo another examination? If so, by whom?

[3] PRESENCE AND PARTICIPATION AT THE HEARING

The respondent's presence at the hearing would seem to be necessary. Yet, in a study of 1,010 guardianship petitions in Los Angeles, conducted by the National Senior Citizens' Law Center, more than 80 percent of the respondents were adjudicated incompetent in their absence. For some, attendance was physically or emotionally impossible. The question, however, is how to determine which ones.

The Recommended Judicial Practices comments:

> Courts have the responsibility to evaluate the circumstances of each case with a view toward balancing avoidance of trauma for the alleged incompetent with preservation of his/her right to be directly involved in a proceeding determinative of fundamental rights. The presence of the proposed ward could be extremely useful to the court in allowing it to judge for itself the level of mental incapacity. If a court appearance would seriously disturb the person, an interview might be arranged in the judge's chambers or some less threatening environment.

Some judges hold the guardianship hearing where the respondent resides.

Presence at the hearing may be waived if it would be detrimental to the respondent. Michigan law (MICH. COMP. LAWS ANN. § 330.1617(4)) requires an affidavit, from a physician or psychologist who has recently examined the respondent, that the respondent's attendance would subject him or her to serious risk of physical or emotional harm. Other statutes provide no guidance regarding the evidence or severity of potential harm to the ward.

Is it sufficient for the court to strictly limit the opportunity for a waiver of appearance or must it take more affirmative steps to assure the respondent's participation? The Recommended Judicial Practices recommends that the court hold a telephone interview if the ward is not mobile. This is convenient for the court, possibly better than no "appearance" at all by the prospective ward, but is it likely to provide information comparable to physical presence at the hearing? In many states the hearing may be held at the respondent's location, such as in a hospital.

QUESTIONS

1. Can you describe a situation in which the presence of the respondent might create a "serious risk of physical or emotional harm?"

2. At the hearing, your client, Linda, is very confused and combative, quite different from her manner on other occasions. You ask for adjournment and a rescheduled hearing. What factors would you argue to persuade the judge that continuing the hearing would be unfair? What would you do before the next hearing to ensure that she behaves more appropriately?

[4] BURDEN AND STANDARD OF PROOF

The burden of proof is on the petitioner, the party claiming that the older person is mentally incapacitated. Most states require "clear and convincing evidence" of the incapacitation, though a few states permit the burden of proof to be met by the preponderance of evidence.

Although the burden of proof rests with the petitioner, the weight of expert testimony supporting the allegations of the petition tend to shift the burden to the respondent to show that he or she does in fact have capacity. Even the filing of the petition can have the effect of introducing doubt about the respondent's mental capacity.

The petitioner must not only prove that the respondent is mentally incapacitated as defined in the state statute, but must also offer proof that the respondent needs a guardian. If the respondent has arranged for his or her property to be managed by placing it in a trust or by appointing an agent under a power of attorney, has appointed a surrogate health care decision maker, and lives, for example, in an assisted living facility that meets all his or her personal needs, the court may find that there is no need for a guardian and so refuse to appoint one. The test for guardianship thus has two parts: proof of mental incapacity as well as proof of the need for the assistance of a guardian.

QUESTIONS

1. What kind of evidence should be permitted to establish mental incapacity? Absent other evidence, should changes in spending habits, lavish expenditures, or gifts to new charities be considered indications of incapacity?

2. What is clear and convincing evidence of mental incapacity? Must all of the expert testimony agree? If they do not, is that enough to dismiss the request for guardianship?

3. Where should the burden of proof lie in a petition for the termination of a guardianship? That is, does the ward have the burden of showing he or she has regained capacity?

[5] REPRESENTATION AND ADVOCACY

Many, but not all, states require that at the guardianship hearing the respondent be represented by either legal counsel or a guardian ad litem. A guardian ad litem is a representative of the court "for the case"; that is, to provide the court with information without commitment to the interests of the parties. If the respondent cannot afford counsel, the state will bear the cost. States that permit the waiver of counsel point to the case of a respondent in a coma as an example of a case where counsel would be superfluous. Yet others maintain that even if the respondent's incapacity is not at issue, there still may be a dispute as to whom to appoint as guardian.

There is dispute regarding the roles to be filled by either the attorney or guardian ad litem. The traditional role of an attorney is one of zealous advocacy, as required by the ethical canons discussed in Chapter 2. The guardian ad litem, in contrast, is the representative of the court empowered to investigate the evidence and present information. In some jurisdictions legal counsel is expected to fill the role of guardian ad litem and not simply advocate the client's wishes. In other states, one of the duties of the guardian ad litem is to determine whether the respondent should be represented by counsel.

There are several reasons for requiring that legal counsel provide zealous advocacy:

> First, if counsel has already concluded that his client needs "help" and that a guardian might be an effective source of the "help" (albeit not the only possible source) then counsel is less likely to challenge expert testimony, either by effective cross-examination or introducing experts with opposing points of view. Second, counsel acting for the "best interest" of his client has no standard by which to judge the quality of his efforts. In any particular case, it would be difficult for anyone (including the counsel) to judge whether the strategy employed by counsel was, in fact, in the best interests of the client. In the extreme instance, it would be almost impossible to claim an attorney was guilty of ineffective assistance of counsel. Third, the best interest test can too easily lead to counsel providing only procedural formality to legitimize the routine approval of guardianship petitions. Presence of counsel does not necessarily mean that the petition for incompetency will be vigorously resisted. True adversarial counsel will result only if the lawyer takes seriously his obligation to "zealously" defend his client. Finally, and perhaps most fundamentally, to allow counsel to act in the "best interest" of the client would allow attorneys to make decisions concerning the mental capacity and well-being of their clients, decisions that attorneys are totally unqualified to decide. Attorneys are not equipped to independently determine the physical and psychological needs of their clients. It is for the court, not counsel, to decide what lawful course of action will serve the best interests of the client.

Frolik, at 634–35, *above*.

Some recommend the appointment of a guardian ad litem who in turn will determine the respondent's interests and advise counsel accordingly. Others oppose this procedure on the grounds that it grants too much power to the guardian ad litem and undercuts the efforts of counsel to provide zealous representation for a client.

QUESTIONS

1.   Do you think a guardian ad litem can fairly investigate and represent the ward's interests? Or should legal counsel also be appointed for the ward? Can you identify any types of cases in which there can be no doubt that there is no need for counsel?

2.   What if counsel advocates a course of action that may place an incapacitated client at risk? Suppose she wants to stay at home, but counsel fears that her habit of using candles might start a fire? Should counsel nevertheless support her plea not to be placed in a nursing home?

NOTE ON GUARDIANSHIP COSTS AND FEES

An individual, who is declared incapacitated and becomes the ward of a guardian, is responsible for the costs of the guardianship, including costs such as expert witness and attorney fees.

Typically the respondent is not required to pay if the proceeding does not result in the appointment of a guardian, on the theory that no individual should have to pay for an unpleasant, unwanted experience that had no beneficial outcome. Instead, the unsuccessful petitioner bears the costs, which discourages some petitioners from instituting questionable guardianship proceeds. Rhode Island specifically waives the petitioner's fee on a finding of "Good Samaritan" guardianship, i.e., when the respondent's property is insufficient to pay for the services of a guardian.

The Texas statute strikes a neutral stance: § 626. Guardianship Fee Book

> The county clerk shall keep a record book styled "Guardianship Fee Book" and shall enter in the guardianship fee book each item of costs that accrue to the officers of the court, with witness fees, if any, showing the:
>
> (1)   party to whom the costs or fees are due;
>
> (2)   date of the accrual of the costs or fees;
>
> (3)   guardianship or party liable for the costs or fees; and
>
> (4)   date on which the costs or fees are paid.

TEX. PROB. CODE § 626.

As for fees for guardians and conservators, in some states, fees are based on a percentage of the total assets. In others, the fees must be reasonable with reference to the work done and the size of the estate. Many courts limit fees to hourly rates that are relatively low in relation to a typical hourly rate for an attorney. Many family or spousal guardians waive the right to collect a fee.

[6]   ONGOING OVERSIGHT BY THE COURTS

A guardian for an older person often serves until the ward's death. The ward, because of mental, physical, and legal disabilities, is typically incapable of overseeing or objecting to the guardian's activities. Consequently, oversight of the guardian is the responsibility of the appointing court. Unless the court oversees the guardian's activities, there is opportunity for personal and financial abuse including self-dealing, making inappropriate gifts, failure to carry out responsibilities and theft.

To protect the ward's person and property, in most states a guardian must file an annual report describing the ward's personal and financial circumstances and account for all income and expenditures in the past year. The Uniform Guardianship and Protective Proceedings Act of 1997 requires a report by the guardian within 60 days of appointment and annual reports thereafter. All states require a final accounting by the guardian at the death of the ward.

If these reports were carefully scrutinized, some blatant abuses could be detected. However, the courts usually lack the resources to scrutinize the reports from guardians to assure that an appropriate arrangement is in place to protect the ward's health, welfare, and safety, and to see that the guardian is not abusing or neglecting the ward or the ward's assets.

E. MEDIATION IN GUARDIANSHIP

The loss of capacity by an older person can precipitate intense family disagreements. For example, the adult children often become so embroiled in arguments about what to do and who should do it that the needs of the older person go unmet. In other cases the older person refuses to admit that he or she needs help and interprets the family efforts to assist as hostile acts.

Susan N. Gary, *Mediation and the Elderly: Using Mediation to Resolve Probate Disputes over Guardianship and Inheritance*
32 WAKE FOREST L. REV. 397 (1997)[*]

[A] type of conflict may develop when two adult children each want to be appointed guardian of their mother or father. The conflict may have roots in differing views of appropriate care for the parent, it may hide concern over protecting an inheritance, or it may simply reflect a long-standing sibling rivalry.

Different opinions about decisions that have been made or that need to be made on behalf of the older adult may also lead to conflict before the appointment of a guardian. Family members may disagree about medical or financial decisions. They may disagree about where the older person should live and what type of living arrangement is appropriate. Although the older person may not be incapacitated, if the person is of somewhat limited capacity, failure to resolve a dispute about any of these issues may result in a guardianship proceeding as a last resort. Mediation may be useful as a means of resolving the dispute and eliminating the need for a guardianship proceeding.

After a court appoints a guardian, disputes may occur if other family members disagree with actions taken by the guardian. The conflict may be over the appropriateness of decisions and quality of care, or it may focus on whether the guardian is breaching his fiduciary duties and misusing the protected person's funds. Although the guardian may be acting under legal authority, family disagreements may escalate into adversarial battles that lead to continued fighting within the family.

While these kind of disputes can be resolved by the court, litigation often only exacerbates the feelings of anger and betrayal. Fortunately, there is an alternative: mediation.

Susan D. Hartman, *Mediation of Disputes Arising in Adult Guardianship Cases*
41–APR Res Gestae 41 (1998)[*]

Mediation, as practiced in our projects, is a voluntary process in which the parties to a dispute, with the assistance of a neutral third-party facilitator, explore their options and attempt to reach agreement. Unlike a judge or arbitrator, the mediator does not make any judgment or even recommend a solution. While it is important that mediators in these cases understand guardianship procedure, the mediator does not provide legal advice to the parties, but will encourage them to get independent legal advice.

Mediation can be used at any stage in a guardianship dispute — before a court petition is filed, before a hearing, or after a guardian has been appointed, for example when someone challenges the need for a continuation of the guardianship or disputes the guardian's action or inaction. In most cases, the mediation process is confidential, and discussions at mediation are not admissible into evidence in a later court hearing. In mediation the parties talk directly with each other, rather than through their attorneys, and have the opportunity to listen to and understand each other's interests and positions.

. . . .

There are, however, some cases in which the respondent cannot take part in mediation because he or she is not able to communicate in any reasonable way or cannot understand the mediation process. If the respondent is an active disputant, but does not understand the mediation process sufficiently to take part, mediation may not be appropriate. . . .

A competent mediator is trained and experienced in ways of balancing power between parties. Through communication and procedural techniques, the mediator can help assure that parties have opportunities both to talk and to listen, and that a less assertive or less verbal party is heard. An additional important balancing tool in these cases is to have a representative for the respondent, usually an attorney, present at the mediation session. The representative can, if necessary, act as an advocate, advisor or negotiator for the respondent.

. . . . Does an agreement reached through mediation have to be approved by the court? Certainly, an agreement to have a guardian appointed must be approved

---

by the court. If a solution other than guardianship is agreed upon, in many states, the petitioner may simply dismiss the petition, and the parties can agree to whatever other solution is satisfactory. In a case in which a guardian has already been appointed, the agreement may take the form of a stipulated proposed order.

Next we inquire about the kinds of issues that are best-resolved in mediation. Almost any contested issue can be mediated, if the parties are able and willing to talk to each other. Often the issue can be mediated, if the parties are able and willing to talk to each other. Often the issues that get discussed in the mediation session are not the same ones raised in court. For example, in one case, in which an objection to an annual accounting had been filed, the financial issues in mediation were quickly resolved; the parties focused on the ward's need for personal privacy and other relatives' desire to have fuller information about how needs were being met.

In another case, the legal issue was whether a power of attorney granted to one child was a valid legal document. In court, the parties would have argued over the competency of the parent at the time the document was signed. In mediation, the parties focused not on the legality of the piece of paper, but on the parent's current needs and who could best meet them. A substantial number of cases involve fears about subsequent inheritance rights. These may involve the respondent's children, a new companion or spouse, or a caretaker.

Sometimes well-meaning family members are so concerned with safety of their older relative that they want to eliminate all risk-taking activity. Many mediated guardianship cases focus on the issues of safety versus autonomy. Adult children, sometimes through guilt over not being able to do as much as they think they should, want to protect their parents. Mediation in these cases sometimes offers the first opportunity for adult children to really listen to their parents' perspective. In one mediated case, the adult children were amazed to learn that their parents recognized and understood the risks in living alone and chose to take those risks and remain independent rather than move to a different, more restrictive setting.

. . . . Considering the variety of issues that could arise, how does a practitioner know when it is appropriate to suggest mediation? An attorney for a potential ward might suggest mediation to his or her client after considering the following questions: Does the client want a day in court to prove that he or she is not incapacitated? Or does the client simply want to be able to avoid restrictions? Does the client want to maintain or reestablish a good relationship with his or her children? Or does the client want them out of his or her life? Is a court hearing, even a successful one, going to be traumatic? A client who wants to keep relationships intact, to avoid a court process, and to communicate needs and wishes to other family members may find mediation to be a good route. . . .

Petitioners' attorneys may also consider mediation. Sometimes mediation can be suggested when it is questionable whether the standard of incapacity necessary for appointment of a guardian is needed, and yet the family has not been able to find other means to meet real needs. If it is fairly certain a guardian will be appointed, limitations on powers granted, means of communication among interested parties, and even who should be the guardian, are issues that a family may be in the best position to decide, even if they have been unable to agree in the past without outside facilitation.

———————

Not all commentators consider mediation to be an appropriate response.

Mary F. Radford, *Is the Use of Mediation Appropriate in Adult Guardianship Cases?*
31 STETSON L. REV. 616, 640–48 (2002)[*]

A. The First Argument: Incompatibility

The first argument against the use of mediation in adult guardianship cases highlights the contrast between the theoretical construct underlying the mediation of legal disputes and that underlying an adult guardianship case. The argument presumes that mediation is designed to resolve disputes in a dyadic situation -that is, to resolve specific disagreements between two parties. An adult guardianship case, on the other hand, is neither a traditional legal dispute nor is it dyadic. The outcome of an adult guardianship case is crucial primarily (and arguably only) to the individual who is the focus of the case. Unlike litigation, in which two or more parties have competing interests at stake, the only individual whose interest is at stake in an adult guardianship case is that adult.

. . . .

The first flaw in this argument is that it restricts too severely the breadth of issues that may arise in an adult guardianship case. Although the core issue in a guardianship case is the protection of the adult's autonomy and welfare, related issues may involve disputes between two parties that resemble traditional dyadic disputes. For example, two siblings may be arguing over which of them should be appointed the guardian of their comatose parent. A mediator can help the siblings explore the "real" reason underlying the dispute (e.g., one sibling is worried that, if appointed guardian, the other sibling will move the adult out-of-state and essentially isolate him or her from the rest of the family).

. . . .

The second flaw is that this argument views mediation in too narrow a way. . . . Mediation offers opportunities not only for dispute resolution, but also for conflict resolution in that it allows the parties to recognize and deal with their incompatibilities and work together productively to manage them.

B. The Second Argument: Lack of Protection

The second argument against the use of mediation in an adult guardianship case is that mediation does not provide the protection of the adult that is the foundation of the formal guardianship system, the proceeding for imposing a guardianship is

———————

[*] Copyright © 2002 Stetson Law Review. Reprinted with permission.

laden with due-process guarantees for the adult respondent. These due-process components "work to ensure that putative wards are fully informed, properly evaluated, zealously defended, that the issues are fully developed and heard, and that an intervention is finely tuned to the needs and preferences of individuals." Mediation, on the other hand, focuses on informal process and agreement among the parties. In a mediation, there is a danger that the family or other participants will not ensure proper representation and evaluation of the adult and will structure a solution that meets only their own needs, or one they deem to be in the adult's best interest rather than one that respects the adult's autonomy.

. . . .

C. The Third Argument: Mediation Is Grounded in Self-Determination

"Self-determination is the fundamental principle of mediation. It requires that the mediation process rely upon the ability of the parties to reach a voluntary, uncoerced agreement." Proponents of the third argument would assert that issues involving an individual with diminishing capacity are not suited to mediation because mediation presumes participation by individuals who are capable of self-determination.

Many adult guardianship cases are not referred to mediation for precisely the reason stated in the self-determination argument, in that the principal player in the case (the adult for whom the guardianship is sought) is not able to participate in the mediation. Furthermore, if the mediator begins an adult guardianship mediation but then determines that a party has become incapable of participating in the mediation, the mediation will terminate. However, the mere fact that an adult has diminished capacity does not automatically mean that he or she does not retain the ability to enter into an agreement or, at the very least, express an opinion and thus participate in a mediation, perhaps with the aid of an attorney or other representative.

The self-determination argument takes a somewhat narrow view of mediation in that it assumes that the only measure of success in a mediation is whether the parties are able to reach agreement. It is true that a mediation often will end with an agreement, which means that all the parties must have the capacity to enter into a legally binding agreement. However, a mediation need not always result in a tangible settlement of issues. Sometimes a mediation will end without the parties reaching any agreement, but the process itself will have been "successful" if it promotes understanding and communication among them and facilitates future interaction. . . .

The self-determination principle presents unique challenges for adult guardianship mediation. The principle encompasses two concepts: 1) each party must be capable of entering into a "voluntary, uncoerced agreement" and 2) it is the parties themselves who reach the agreement rather than having an outsider impose a decision on the parties. Application of the first concept in an adult guardianship case mandates special attention to the adult's capacity and to the vulnerability of the adult to coercion by other parties. Application of the second concept raises questions as to the style of mediation that is most appropriate for an adult guardianship case.

F.   THE DETERMINATION OF INCAPACITY

There is no doubt that some individuals are mentally incapacitated and in need of help. The critical issue is how to accurately identify those who are incapacitated. Attitudes to who is incapacitated have changed. At one time, advanced age alone was frequently thought to be an indicator of incapacity, but in the 1980s, the category of age was deleted from the Uniform Probate Code and from most state statutes.

The Model Guardianship and Conservatorship Act, prepared by the American Bar Association Commission on the Mentally Disabled and the Legal Problems of the Elderly, and section 501 of the Uniform Probate Code permit an individual who cannot communicate to be considered incapacitated and in need of a guardian. As technology progresses, however, very few mentally alert persons who are physically incapacitated are completely unable to communicate. Consider the situation of world-famous physicist Stephen Hawking, whose theory of the origin of the universe demonstrates a critical error in Einstein's theories. Dr. Hawking suffers from a wasting disease which has made it impossible to move more than a few muscles. He communicates decisions using a specially designed electronic system. If he were unable to communicate electronically, he would need a guardian, though the quality of his decision making would be unchanged. Mere physical disability is now rarely sufficient to warrant the appointment of a guardian.

QUESTIONS

1. If Dr. Hawking were not a prominent scientist, it is possible others would prefer to do as they think best for him, rather than consult his wishes. Do you think that, in some matters, his assistants do exactly that? On what authority would they do so?

2. Guardians sometimes are appointed for physically impaired, institutionalized elderly. Is this always because they cannot understand or express decisions, or because it is inconvenient and time-consuming to communicate with them?

[1]   FUNCTIONAL CONCEPTS OF IMPAIRMENT

The respondent can counter evidence of mental incapacity by a showing of functional capability. Because an individual's ability to function is more susceptible than mental status to objective evidence, many guardianship statutes place great emphasis on this aspect of legal capacity. Consider Florida's statute:

> "Incapacitated person" means a person who has been judicially deter-mined to lack the capacity to manage at least some of the property or to meet at least some of the essential health and safety requirement of such person. (a) To "manage property" means to take those actions necessary to obtain, administer, and dispose of real and personal property, intangible property, business property, benefits, and income. (b) To "meet essential

requirements for health or safety" means to take those actions necessary to provide the health care, food, shelter, clothing, personal hygiene, or other care without which serious and imminent physical injury or illness is more likely than not to occur.

FLA. STAT. § 744.102(12).

The question of mental capability is not absent from this statute, but clearly the emphasis has shifted to the question of functional capability. Rather than a diagnosis of mental status, the petitioner will allege that the impaired person is mismanaging funds or failing to attend to matters of practical and physical well being.

The New Hampshire guardianship statute relies solely on functional capacity as a basis for competency determination, stating explicitly that incapacity is a legal, not a medical disability, to be measured only by functional limitations. N.H. REV. STAT. ANN. §§ 464-A:25, 464-A:26.

Statutes, which base intervention only on the individual's functional need, may permit involuntary services to be imposed on competent individuals who live in situations of neglect by idiosyncratic choice. The inescapable conclusion of assessment of need alone is that anyone managing life poorly should have a guardian appointed. This definition threatens to impose "better," i.e., more logical or conventional, decision makers on sane, independent, but eccentric elderly individuals.

Need alone is also a potentially unfair standard because it depends on factors beyond the individual's control and results in different treatment for those with fewer financial resources. The poor are particularly subject to intervention because a modest decline of their mental capabilities puts them at risk of falling below bare subsistence. For example, forgetting to pay the rent may trigger quick eviction and homelessness. A well-to-do elderly mortgage holder, in contrast, has a longer time and ample notice before foreclosure for nonpayment. Frailty and forgetfulness make an individual more vulnerable when the community has a high crime rate. A reasonably cautious or fearful person, who lives in a dangerous neighborhood, may rarely leave home and so lack basic necessities.

A functional determination of mental incapacity might also result from a change in the person's lifestyle. More affluent elderly may be subject to unwarranted intervention if they choose to accept an altered lifestyle in order to maintain independence despite their impairments. For example, a severe arthritic person may choose to live in virtually complete isolation, spending extraordinarily long hours confined to bed or chair, and rarely leave home. The lifestyles of such individuals are inevitably weighed against their well-organized, middle-class past. Their isolation and seemingly single minded intent on the goal of living at home may be interpreted as evidence of mental decline. Once the social service system becomes aware of their circumstances, they may be subject to intervention because society expects them to be cleaner, better fed, better attended, and more social.

Does need alone warrant intervention absent any showing of mental incapacity? The Florida guardianship statute's standard of need is "meeting the essential requirements for health or safety," which means taking those actions necessary to provide the health care, food, shelter, clothing, personal hygiene, or other care without which serious and imminent physical injury or illness is more likely than not to occur. This is a higher standard of mental and functional status than the standard applied in civil commitment for the mentally ill, which requires dangerousness to oneself or others.

Competent "management of property" means taking those actions necessary to obtain, administer, and dispose of real and personal property, intangible property, business property, benefits, and income. An individual who persistently loses his or her money and so lacks the resources for survival is either very foolish or mentally incapacitated. But how do we distinguish bad judgment from mental incapacity?

[2] ASSESSING MENTAL CAPACITY

Some states require more than one professional to assess an individual's mental capacity and need for guardianship assistance. The most frequent allocation of assessment responsibility calls for a medical professional, a mental health professional, and a community health professional to assess how the individual functions in his or her environment.

[a] Medical Assessment

Over 60 physical conditions have been found to produce symptoms similar to dementia, including vitamin deficiencies, depression, and mild strokes. These and many other conditions, unlike Alzheimer's disease, are treatable, and even an individual diagnosed with Alzheimer's disease who has had a period of unusual behavior can benefit from treatment for associated problems that compromise mental function. A thorough geriatric assessment requires a specialist who may need to see the older individual repeatedly and run a series of tests to produce a profile of the impact of physical condition on that individual's mental and emotional functioning.

[b] Psychological Assessment

Two principal tools are used for psychological evaluation: standardized tests and assessment interviews. The earliest and least reliable are unstructured interviews, which have persisted in use in guardianship in some jurisdictions. More structured interviews have been tested for reliability and validity, which makes them far more useful evidence in court. The interviewer should utilize a checklist of items to assure no area is inadvertently omitted and produce a report of findings that can assist the court in determining capacity and structuring of the guardianship.

The interviewer may utilize a standardized test in order to discern the individual's mental status. The categories assessed include general appearance and behavior, mood and affect, perception of self and the world, and thinking, which includes intellectual functioning, memory, attention, concentration, insight, and judgment. The Mini-Mental State Examination (MMSE) (originally published in M.R. Folstein, S. Folstein & P. R. McHugh, *Mini-Mental State Examination: A Practical Method for Grading the Cognitive State of Patients for the Clinician*, 12 J. Psychiatric Res. 189 (1975)) has been used so frequently that its questions have become the source for cartoons and dark humor. Questions typically ask the individual to perform such tasks as counting backward by sevens from one hundred; naming the day of the week, the year, the President of the United States, the individual's age and number of children; and spelling "world" backward. Other tests require the recall of a series of words previously related after a period of distraction. The patterns of memory, rather than any particular lapses, guide the diagnosis.

Memory impairment is often the most apparent symptom of dementia and may be most clear in the inability to remember recent events and information, such as names, telephone numbers, conversations, and directions. An individual with memory impairment may forget to return to a task in progress, such as cooking or washing, leaving the stove on or the water running.

Other impairments might be observed or found in an interview. An individual with impaired abstract thinking will have trouble with new, complex tasks, and may avoid them. A common test asks the person to find similarities and differences in related words. Impaired judgment and impulse control might be observed in the individual's disregard for conventional rules of behavior and social interaction. An individual might neglect his or her personal hygiene (or some particular part of it), speak or joke crudely, or even shoplift without regard for the consequences. Previously cautious people might enter into risky financial arrangements or associations.

[c] Functional Assessment

A functional assessment consists of an inventory of basic activities of daily living (termed ADLs) such as eating, bathing, and dressing; and instrumental activities of daily living (IADLs) such as making appointments, paying bills, and using the telephone. The examiner, who may be a nurse or social worker, interviews and observes the proposed ward to determine the level of capacity. Usually, the assessment also notes the individual's level of social involvement or isolation, and attitudes that may indicate depression. Based on the interview, a professional skilled in the interpretation of functional assessments can then offer an opinion on the individual's ability to manage independently or whether there is a need for guardianship assistance.

[d] The Quality of the Respondent's Decision Making

Guardianships are often sought when others believe that the respondent cannot make rational decisions. An individual who exhibits a pattern of unwise or apparently irrational choices is likely to be considered mentally incapacitated. Yet it is not the quality of decision making but whether the individual *can* make a rational decision that is at issue. Older persons have the right to make "bad" decisions without being considered incapacitated. As stated by one court:

> The section [dealing with incompetency] implies physical or mental defects which interfere with the rational functioning of the mind. If the mind functions rationally but the individual acts in a way commonly designated as eccentric, that is, his acts deviate from the usual principally

because he is less susceptible to public opinion than are many of us, he is not incompetent. He may be foolish in the eyes of many of us, but he is not incompetent. Competency is not measured by one's ability to accumulate and hold the material things of life. Were it so, there would be many of our ministerial [brethren], not to mention some of our learned judicial associates, behind mental bars.

In re Boyer, 636 P.2d 1085 (Utah 1981).

Critical medical choices are often the catalyst for the filing of a guardianship petition, especially if the patient refuses to agree to the recommended course of treatment.

TENNESSEE DEPARTMENT OF HUMAN SERVICES v. NORTHERN
563 S.W.2d 197 (Tenn. Ct. App. 1978)

In the present case, this Court has found the patient to be lucid and apparently of sound mind generally. However, on the subjects of death and amputation of her feet, her comprehension is blocked, blinded or dimmed to the extent that she is incapable of recognizing facts which would be obvious to a person of normal perception.

For example, in the presence of this Court, the patient looked at her feet and refused to recognize the obvious fact that the flesh was dead, black, shriveled, rotting and stinking.

The record also discloses that the patient refuses to consider the eventuality of death which is or ought to be obvious in the face of such dire bodily deterioration.

As described by the doctors and observed by this Court, the patient wants to live and keep her dead feet, too, and refuses to consider the impossibility of such a desire. In order to avoid the unpleasant experience of facing death and/or loss of feet, her mind or emotions have resorted to the device of denying the unpleasant reality so that, to the patient, the unpleasant reality does not exist. This is the "delusion" which renders the patient incapable of making a rational decision as to whether to undergo surgery to save her life or to forego surgery and forfeit her life.

The physicians speak of probabilities of death without amputation as 90 to 95% and the probability of death with surgery as 50-50 (1 in 2). Such probabilities are not facts, but the existence and expression of such opinions are facts which the patient is unwilling or unable to recognize or discuss.

If, as repeatedly stated, this patient could and would give evidence of a comprehension of the facts of her condition and could and would express her unequivocal desire in the face of such comprehended facts, then her decision, however unreasonable to others, would be accepted and honored by the Courts and by her doctors. The difficulty is that she cannot or will not comprehend the facts.

Mrs. Northern's response can be compared with that of Mrs. Candura (*Lane v. Candura*, 376 N.E.2d 1232 (Mass. App. 1978)), who found herself in a very similar situation. In that case, the hospital sought appointment of a guardian because the patient, Mrs. Candura, refused amputation of her foot. The court observed that the respondent had "a high degree of awareness and acuity [w]hen responding to questions concerning the proposed operation. She has made it clear that she does not wish to have the operation even though that decision will in all likelihood lead shortly to her death." *Id.* at 1234–35. It noted also that her train of thought wandered, and that her concept of time was distorted. *Id.* at 1235. The court acknowledged the irrationality of her decision (*id.* at 1234–35) and maintained her right to make a competent, if unwise, choice (*id.* at 1235–36). The *Candura* court stated that an individual must be cognizant of the specific need and purpose for the procedure, though cognizance of other matters may be lacking. The individual must also be aware of the consequences of refusing treatment. If so assistance can be refused, even if the consequences are permanent or likely to result in death.

Researchers have developed an instrument for measuring an individual's ability to make decisions. It is based on findings that show that some considered to lack legal capacity do have significant practical decision-making abilities including: (a) ability to communicate a choice; (b) ability to understand relevant information; (c) ability to appreciate the nature of the situation and its likely consequences; and d) ability to manipulate information rationally. *See* Jessica Wilen Berg, J.D., Paul S. Appelbaum, M.D., & Thomas Grisso, Ph.D., *Constructing Competence: Formulating Standards of Legal Competence to Make Medical Decisions*, 48 Rutgers L. Rev. 345 (1996).

The level of capacity required for an individual to make a valid decision varies. The law provides different levels of mental capacity required to undertake different tasks such as the making of a contract or a will. To validly agree to a contract requires that the individual have a reasonable understanding of what is proposed. In contrast, the capacity needed to execute a valid will is lower; a person for whom a guardian has been appointed may still have sufficient capacity to execute a valid will

What if capacity is a transient state? That is, the person understands and communicates a decision in the morning, but cannot understand it at the end of the day? This is a common pattern with early stage Alzheimer's disease patients. Generally, the law recognizes temporary capacity, so that a will executed during a lucid interval is valid. Capacity can also decline if the individual is hospitalized or suffers from an illness or stroke, and many common long-term medications can lead to decreased mental function.

What significance does this have for persons under the legal disability of guardianship? Are they considered incapacitated for all times and all purposes or should they retain some rights?

QUESTIONS

1.   What is required to be able to withhold consent to assistance, according to the court in *Northern* and *Candura*?

2. Can you reliably distinguish an irrational decision from one that arises from mental incapacity? Are there guidelines for identifying a "good" decision?

3. Is behavior necessarily an indication of incapacity? Was Hamlet mentally incapacitated?

[e]   Vulnerability

Often guardianship is sought because the older person appears to be vulnerable and has assets at risk. Consider the following case of an alert but vulnerable person.

DEFFENBAUGH v. CLAPHAN
893 S.W.2d 350 (Ark. Ct. App. 1995)

ROBBINS, JUDGE.

Appellant, Laura Deffenbaugh, appeals from a decree of the Crawford County Probate Court, which refused to appoint guardians for the persons and the estates of her parents, appellees William Claphan and Lena Mae Claphan. We affirm the portion of the probate court's order denying the appointment of a guardian for Mr. Claphan.

. . . .

Appellant also contends that the probate court erred in not appointing a guardian for her father, Mr. Claphan. She argues that the probate judge found Mr. Claphan was easily influenced and the undisputed evidence shows that Mr. Claphan has been victimized by his grandson, Roger. She argues that Roger's influence, coupled with Mr. Claphan's failure to remember the power of attorney he executed in 1989 or the contents of his will clearly demonstrates that Mr. Claphan is unable to understand his actions and manage his estate and therefore justifies the appointment of a guardian on his behalf.

In support of her contentions, appellant testified that, in 1991, she discovered that thirty-eight blank checks had been stolen from her father and that, over a one-year period, her deceased brother's son, Roger, had written these checks to himself in an amount totaling $20,458.00. She stated that her father had to press criminal charges against Roger in order to collect this money from the bank and that he was able to collect only $9,000.00. She stated that, because of this loss, she had to cosign a note with her father in March 1991 so that he could obtain money to feed his cattle. She also testified that, after a discussion with Roger's family members, her father had revoked a power of attorney he had given her in 1989 and that, in 1993, her parents had deeded their home to Roger and his sister, reserving in themselves a life estate. She stated that she is concerned that Roger may steal from her father as he did before and that she is trying to protect her parents' assets. She also testified that her father's health has gotten progressively worse and that he frequently stumbles and falls. She stated: "He is much more uncooperative with me today than he was a year ago." She also testified that her father cannot look up a telephone number, her mother cannot dial a telephone, and they cannot really provide for themselves.

Dr. Jennings testified that he first saw Mr. Claphan in July 1991 and last saw him in June 1993. Dr. Jennings testified that he had some concern that Mr. Claphan is not adequately able to take care of his wife, that appellees were not able to manage their financial affairs, and that they were getting to the point that they could not manage their health affairs. He admitted, however, that his assessment of Mr. Claphan was based 90% upon the history that was provided to him by appellant and that he could not have formed his opinion regarding Mr. Claphan without appellant's statements.

Appellee William Claphan testified that he is eighty-one and will be eighty-two the first day of the following month. He was able to name the date and the day of the week, his address, when he was married, and the president of the United States. He testified that he has worked on a farm for the past ten years; that he worked at Riverside Furniture prior to that; that he receives $77.00 per month in retirement income; and that he and his wife together receive about $800.00 a month in social security. He stated that, when he discovered that his grandson, Roger, had forged his checks, he discussed the matter with him and that Roger offered to get a loan to repay him. He stated that he did not want to prosecute Roger but that appellant and the bank had insisted on it. He also stated that Roger helps him around the farm, that he did not know how he would manage without Roger's help, and that he pays Roger minimum wages whenever he does help. He also testified that he goes through the canceled checks he receives from the bank.

In reference to the deed to their house, reserving a life estate, that Mr. and Mrs. Claphan had given Roger and Roger's sister, he explained that Roger and Barbara wanted to keep the house in the family; that he knew he and his wife would be able to stay in the house until they died; and that, if he wanted to sell the property, Roger and Barbara would help him convey it. He stated that he understood that Roger and Barbara would have to sign an instrument in order for him to sell the house; however, on examination by the court, he admitted he was not real sure of the purpose of the deed that he signed. He also did not remember that a will he executed in 1989 left everything to appellant; he thought it went to appellant and "the boys." He also testified that he did not remember giving appellant his power of attorney and, when he discovered it a year ago, he had it revoked because Roger and Roger's relatives told him that the power of attorney would allow her to do whatever she wanted with his property. He testified that he did not think he needed a guardian, that he could take care of his own business, and that appellant has tried to boss them around "like we were kids."

Here, there was evidence that Mr. Claphan continues to farm, that he pays his grandson to help him with farming, and that he has watched his checks and checkbooks since his checks were stolen. The burden was on the appellant to prove by clear and convincing evidence that appellee Mr. Claphan was no longer able to handle his affairs, and the court below had the benefit of not only hearing and observing the witnesses, but more importantly, it had the opportunity to hear and observe Mr. Claphan. We therefore cannot say that the court's finding that Mr. Claphan was not mentally incapacitated is clearly erroneous.

. . . .

It is probable that, within the near future, Mr. Claphan may be incapacitated and require the appointment of a guardian for himself; however, the court must act on his capacity at the time of trial. Accordingly, the decree is affirmed as to Mr. Claphan.

QUESTION

Should an individual ever be declared incapacitated for spending or giving away money or assets if his or her remaining assets are sufficient for an ordinary standard of living?

G. TYPES OF GUARDIANSHIPS

Guardianships are typically one of three types:

- Guardianship of the estate
- Guardianship of the person
- Plenary guardianship.

A guardianship of the estate is the result of the court appointing a guardian with authority only over the estate (assets) of the ward. A guardian of the estate has no authority over the person of the ward. A guardian of the estate controls and manages any savings and real property owned by the ward, including a personal residence, collects the income of the ward, and spends the ward's income and savings as needed to support the ward. In short, unless otherwise limited by the appointing court, the guardian of the estate has complete control over the financial affairs of the ward. If the ward owns an estate of considerable value or has significant income, a court may prefer to appoint a bank or trust company as guardian of the estate for fear that an individual might be overwhelmed by the responsibilities or might misuse or abuse the powers that are granted to a guardian of the estate.

A guardian of the person is granted the authority to make decisions concerning the person of the ward. The guardian can decide where the ward resides and makes health care decisions for the ward. Spouses and family members are often appointed guardians of the person because courts believe that they have the ability to do what will be best for the ward. Sometimes a court will appoint a bank as the guardian of a ward's estate and a family member, such as an adult child, as the guardian of the person.

Because of the very personal nature of the decisions made by a guardian of the person, state statutes or appointing courts often place limits on the scope of the guardian's authority. For example, the guardian may not be able to file for divorce for the ward and may even need prior court approval to defend a divorce action. Health care decisions can be made by the guardian, and usually the guardian can refuse or terminate life-sustaining treatment for a ward, though often with limits, such as only if the ward is terminally ill. In some jurisdictions, the guardian will need court approval to move a ward into a nursing home. Another possible limitation on a guardian of the person is when there is also a guardian of the estate. Some decisions about the person of the ward require the expenditure of funds. Unless the guardian of the estate is willing to commit to the expenditure, the guardian of the person will be unable to act. For example, if a guardian of the person decides that it is best for a ward with physical limitations to remain at home, but to do so requires expensive adaptations of the house such as building ramps, the guardian of the estate must agree to pay for the adaptations. If the guardian of the estate refuses to pay for the requested home modifications, the ward may have to move to a new home or to an institution, such as an assisted living facility. Alternatively, the guardian of the person could file a petition with the appointing court, asking it to order the guardian of the estate to pay for the requested modification of the home.

Finally, the court can appoint a plenary guardian with powers over both the estate and person of the ward. This is the most common solution when the ward has only modest assets and a spouse or family member is willing to serve as guardian. A plenary guardian has all the powers of a guardian of the estate and of a guardian of the person, subject to any limitation imposed by the court in the order of appointment.

The division of personal and property powers has some basis in practical reality in that individuals more often lose abstract reasoning and property management abilities while still capable of making health care and other personal decisions. By appointing only a guardian of the property (guardian of the estate), sometimes called a conservator, the ward retains the legal right and responsibility for making important personal decisions.

QUESTIONS

Is the law's division of personal decision making and property matters a historical accident, which should be eliminated? Or, does the personal/property division have a valid basis in the needs of individuals to control their own persons, and of third parties to depend upon financial agreements?

H. THE LEAST RESTRICTIVE ALTERNATIVE AND LIMITED GUARDIANSHIP

The doctrine of the least restrictive alternative requires that the type of assistance provided an impaired individual must be the one which least restricts that person's rights. It was developed in the law of the civil commitment of the mentally ill but is now being advocated by critics of guardianship. They insist that before naming a guardian, the court consider the possible assistance of family, friends, and social and community services as alternative ways of meeting the individual's needs.

Whether, and how, the doctrine of the least restrictive alternative applies to guardianship in most states is unclear. For example, can it be used to avoid placement of the ward in a nursing home? The New Hampshire statute (N.H. REV. STAT. ANN. § 464-A:9) requires a determination that there are no available alternative resources, such as visiting nurses, home care, multipurpose senior centers, powers of attorney, representative payees, or board and care homes, which will meet the respondent's needs and specifies that guardianship is appropriate only if it is the least restrictive alternative.

QUESTIONS

1. Should the least restrictive alternative be applied when a guardian wishes to have a ward admitted to a nursing home?

2. The least restrictive alternative doctrine assumes that all disabled persons would rather live in the community, even though that arrangement typically provides less assistance, less security from accidental harm, and more personal isolation than living in a nursing home. Is this assumption sensible?

3. What is the matter with institutions, aside from their cost, that they should be disapproved as a matter of policy?

Limited guardianship is a means of implementing the least restrictive alternative doctrine. Under limited guardianship, the guardian is granted specific, limited powers. In theory, the power granted to the guardian reflects the specific loss of capacity by the ward. The guardian is authorized to act only in areas in which the ward cannot make competent decisions. The policy has not achieved great success, as very few limited guardianships are actually implemented.

The following case claiming a violation of civil rights is brought by a woman subject to civil commitment whose guardian (termed "committee") authorized certain expenditures. The opinion is an early, landmark discussion illustrating the unity of personal rights and property decision making, with implications for limited guardianship and the use of the least restrictive alternative.

IN RE BOYER
636 P.2d 1085 (Utah 1981)

[T]he appellant argues that the statutory provision specifying the powers of the guardian is unconstitutionally overbroad because the full scope of powers which may be, and in this case were, conferred on a guardian are not necessary in specific cases. In this case the least restrictive alternative is closely allied with the more general overbreadth issue,[1] and, therefore, we address both together. Appellant specifically contends that the State must adopt the alternative least restrictive of the alleged incompetent's liberty and that the Utah procedure sweeps too broadly in permitting a guardian to be invested with wide-ranging powers over the personal decision of one who has no need of complete supervision, although there may be a

---

[1] In *Grayned v. City of Rockford*, 408 U.S. 104, 114, 92 S. Ct. 2294, 2302, 33 L. Ed. 2d 222 (1972), the Court stated: "A clear and precise enactment may nevertheless be 'overbroad' if in its reach it prohibits constitutionally protected conduct." [Footnote omitted.] In *Shelton v. Tucker*, 364 U.S. 479, 488, 81 S. Ct. 247, 252, 5 L. Ed. 2d 231 (1960), the Court stated:

> In a series of decisions this Court has held that, even though the governmental purpose be legitimate and substantial, that purpose cannot be pursued by means that broadly stifle fundamental personal liberties when the end can be more narrowly achieved. The breadth of legislative abridgement must be viewed in the light of less drastic means for achieving the same basic purpose. [Footnotes omitted.]

need for assistance in handling specific aspects of his or her personal affairs.

A legitimate state purpose cannot be accomplished by means that broadly "stifle fundamental personal liberties when the end can be more narrowly achieved." The means adopted must be narrowly tailored to achieve the basic statutory purpose.

The least restrictive alternative standard has been applied in involuntary commitment proceedings. In *Welsch v. Likins*, 373 F. Supp. 487, 502 (D. Minn. 1974), the Court required state officials to make "good faith attempts to place [involuntarily committed] persons in settings that will be suitable and appropriate to their mental and physical conditions while least restrictive of their liberties."

Although the restrictions on, and deprivation of, personal freedom by appointment of a guardian are less in extent and in intrusiveness than by involuntary commitment, nevertheless, the loss of freedom may be substantial. Accordingly, a court in appointing a guardian must consider the interest of the ward in retaining as broad a power of self-determination as is consistent with the reason for appointing a guardian of the person.

The nature and extent of the powers to be conferred on a guardian is for the court to decide. Section 75-5-312(1) provides: "A guardian of an incapacitated person has the same powers, rights, and duties respecting his ward that a parent has respecting his unemancipated minor child . . . except as modified by order of the court. . . ." Although the powers conferred upon a guardian may be very broad, the court is authorized to tailor the powers of a guardian to the specific needs of the ward. In appointing a guardian, the court should state with particularity the powers granted, unless the full scope of the statutory authorization is warranted. The process should be individualized and based upon careful consideration of the particular need for supervision.

To enable the court to fashion an appropriate remedy, the parties should submit evidence ". . . showing the proposed ward's inability to think or act for himself as to matters concerning his personal health, safety, and general welfare. . . ." *Fazio v. Fazio*, 375 Mass. 394, 403, 378 N.E.2d 951 (1978). Based on this evidence, findings of fact should be made to support the powers conferred on the guardian, and those powers should be as clearly defined as the circumstances permit. So construed, the guardianship statute is not unconstitutionally overbroad.

QUESTION

According to the *Boyer* court, it is sufficient protection for Boyer's interests that the court has the authority to modify the broad powers usually conferred on the guardian to the specific needs of the ward. Do you agree? If not, why not?

Studies suggest that neither the petitioners nor the courts have embraced the philosophy of limited guardianship.

Lawrence A. Frolik, *Guardianship Reform: When the Best Is the Enemy of the Good*
9 STANFORD L. & POL'Y REV. 347, 354 (1998)[*]

To date, limited guardianship has not been a success. Though touted as perhaps the most significant of all reforms, it has been used very little. Plenary guardianship continues to be used despite the statutory alternative of limited guardianship. . . . It seems that as long as the law permits plenary guardianship, courts will prefer to use it. But not all guardianships are so clearly candidates for plenary guardianship. Surely, there exist some individuals who, though in need of a guardian, still have the ability to handle some of their affairs. In these cases, the failure to use limited guardianship may reflect the belief that despite the plenary guardianship, the guardian will permit the ward to control his or her life to the greatest extent possible. For example, a guardian might give the ward small amounts of spending money for discretionary spending. More likely, judges may not use limited guardianship because they do not understand its value nor do they appreciate the gain to the ward in limiting the power of the guardian. Rather, judges know all too well the financial costs of additional court appearances as guardians with insufficient authority to deal with the needs of their wards ask the courts to expand the limits of the guardianships. Here, as with the value of mandatory counsel, the reformers have not yet convinced the judges of the value of limited guardianship. Now that limited guardianship exists as an option, the concept must be "sold" to the judges. Until the judiciary shares the reformers' zeal for limited guardianship, it will never be more than an empty, little-used statutory right.

Even without formal limited guardianship, wards retain some rights.

FLA. STAT. § 744.3215 provides the following list of rights retained by the ward:

§ *744.3215 Rights of persons determined incapacitated.* —

(1) A person who has been determined to be incapacitated retains the right:

(a) To have an annual review of the guardianship report and plan.

(b) To have continuing review of the need for restriction of his rights.

(c) To be restored to capacity at the earliest possible time.

(d) To be treated humanely, with dignity and respect, and to be protected against abuse and neglect.

(e) To have a qualified guardian.

(f) To remain as independent as possible, including having his preference as to place and standard of living honored, either as he expressed or demonstrated his preference prior to the

---

determination of his incapacity or as he currently expresses his preference, insofar as such request is reasonable.

(g) To be properly educated.

(h) To receive prudent financial management for his property and to be informed how his property is being managed, if he has lost the right to manage property.

(i) To receive necessary services and rehabilitation.

(j) To be free from discrimination because of his incapacity.

(k) To have access to the courts.

(l) To counsel.

(m) To receive visitors and communicate with others.

(n) To notice of all proceedings related to determination of capacity and guardianship, unless the court finds the incapacitated person lacks the ability to comprehend the notice.

. . . .

(3) Rights that may be removed from a person through a petition to determine capacity and which may be delegated to the guardian include the right:

(a) To contract.

(b) To sue and be sued.

(c) To apply for government benefits.

(d) To manage property or to make any gift or disposition of property.

(e) To determine his residence.

(f) To consent to medical treatment.

(g) To make decisions about his social environment or other social aspects of his life.

I. REPRESENTATIVE PAYEE FOR GOVERNMENT BENEFITS

One alternative to limited guardianship is the use of a representative payee, an individual appointed by a government agency to receive federal income benefit funds, such as Social Security, on someone else's behalf, when the recipient is unable to manage the funds personally. Under federal law, five government agencies offer an arrangement called representative or substitute payeeship, the two largest being the Social Security Administration and the Veterans' Administration.

Typically the agency is informed of the beneficiary's need for a representative payee by some interested third party, such as a friend, relative, or nursing home, or the beneficiary may request a representative payee. The agency determines whether the beneficiary is incapable of managing the benefit payments by examining court determinations, medical evidence, and any other evidence pertinent to the question of whether the beneficiary's interests would be served by the appointment of a representative payee. There is no hearing. If the agency decides that a payee is necessary, it will notify the beneficiary, who has opportunity to object.

In selecting a representative payee, agencies use a priority list based on the relationship between the parties and who has custody of the beneficiary. The list includes, in typical priority order, (1) a legal guardian, spouse, or other relative with custody or a "strong concern" for the beneficiary; (2) a custodial friend with the same concern; (3) a custodial institution; and (4) other persons who are willing to serve.

The representative payee receives the benefit checks on behalf of the beneficiary and is obliged to use the funds for the beneficiary's current maintenance, including food, shelter, and medical care. Anything left over can be spent for the maintenance of dependents. The payee is required to submit an annual report and may be called upon by the agency at any time to show how the funds are being spent. If funds are misspent or overpaid by the agency, the payee is personally liable for repayment.

Many question whether the practice has sufficient safeguards to prevent fraud or misuse of the benefits. The Social Security Administration routinely appoints payees without a face-to-face interview, based on very little evidence of need. Sometimes creditors of the ward are appointed. A few have taken unreasonable fees for their services.

QUESTIONS

1. Is representative payeeship a reasonable and useful nonjudicial form of limited guardianship?

2. Should the representative payee program provide more due process and greater oversight?

J. VOLUNTARY GUARDIANSHIP AND GUARDIANSHIP DIVERSION

Voluntary assistance is a less restrictive alternative than any type of involuntary assistance because the stigma associated with incompetency is absent. The individual may also have the opportunity to choose among types of assistance and the manner of delivery. Voluntary services are therefore to be preferred. However, the legal status of voluntary guardianship — in which the court appoints a guardian upon petition of the individual who becomes the ward — has gone from little use to none. Courts have never been clear on the rights and powers of the voluntary ward vis-à-vis the guardian, and advance directives provide a sound alternative.

Substitution of voluntary services for guardianship services is called guardianship diversion. In the course of a guardianship proceeding, the court secures from the parties an agreement to meet the respondent's needs; the agreement may include the type and frequency of any services necessary for the ward's well-being.

Guardianship diversion remains a seldom-tested concept, in part because it raises serious ethical questions about the prospective ward's willingness to accept services. Once some authority has intervened and recommended assistance, it is difficult to assure that the services are not the result of coercion. In succumbing to the pressure of the court proceedings, the elderly impaired person is essentially compelled to accept unsought services.

K. SCOPE OF THE GUARDIAN'S AUTHORITY

Guardians may exercise any powers given by the court so long as they act in good faith as a fiduciary of the ward. With regard to financial affairs, the guardian and fiduciary is most often held to deal with the ward's assets as one would deal with the assets of another, i.e., more conservatively than one might deal with one's own. When the guardian makes decisions about the person of the ward, the guardian is held by state statutes to either a best interests standard (deciding for the ward in a way that best promotes health, safety, and financial security) or a substituted judgment standard (deciding for the ward as the ward would most likely have decided). A number of statutes, regardless of whether they require best interests or the substituted judgment standard, also require the guardian to consult the ward as to his or her preferences regarding living arrangements and caregivers and to follow the ward's wishes if feasible.

Depending on state law, the guardian can base choices on one of two standards: the best interests of the ward or substituted judgment. The best interests standard tries to promote the ward's health, safety, and security. The decision maker concentrates on tangible factors, such as physical and financial risks, harm or pain, and benefits. The standard advocates rational outcomes, such as acting like a reasonable person would.

Substituted judgment charges the guardian to reach the decision the incapacitated person would make if he or she were able to choose. The phrase might initially be misleading since no other person's choice is substituted for the ward's; rather, the guardian's decision is a substitute in the sense that it attempts to duplicate a hypothetical decision by the ward.

The "Substituted Judgment Model" of guardianship takes its name from the legal doctrine that states that the court can substitute its judgment and to act for an incompetent in all matters "touching on the well-being" of the incompetent. The doctrine is first recorded in 1816, in the English case of *Ex parte Whitbread*, in which the court authorized expenditures from the estate of an incompetent in order to provide for his needy relatives. The court justified the payments because it was believed to be what Whitbread would have done, because it would be beneficial to him to do so and avoid the prospect of his impoverished relatives begging others for support — a disgrace to Whitbread himself.

In the American case *In re Willoughby* in 1844, the court developed the substituted judgment model to more closely resemble its use today. The court held that it had the power to deal with the estate of an incompetent "as it supposes the lunatic himself would have acted if he had been of sound mind." Thus the court refused to approve gifts from the estate of an incompetent to his stepdaughter asserting that Willoughby, if restored to competence, would have rejected her claim to benefit from his property. The evidence of Willoughby's likely action was that, prior to his incompetency, he had refused to provide the claimant with support.

Two principles were established: First, the assets of the ward may be used for the benefit of someone other than the ward, so conservation of the estate is subject to other considerations. Also the ward's asset must be allocated according to evidence of the ward's intent, i.e., what the ward would probably do if he or she were capable.

Lawrence A. Frolik, *Plenary Guardianship: An Analysis, a Critique, and a Proposal for Reform*, 23 Ariz. L. Rev. 599, 620 (1981).

Often courts are not clear as to which doctrine they are enforcing.

IN RE MEDWORTH
562 N.W.2d 522 (Minn. Ct. App. 1997)

[The court was reviewing the decision of the guardian to place the ward, his mother, in an assisted living arrangement.]

After a careful reading of the record, we conclude that although the trial court properly found an assisted-living arrangement would suffice to provide needed medical services for Medworth, there remains insufficient evidence to show relocation was in Medworth's best interests or essential to provide for her care, or that the decision was made in consideration of her overall welfare. The record demonstrates: (1) with the exception of the congregate-living apartment in Amery, Wisconsin, the conservator failed to consider seriously any additional housing alternatives for Medworth; (2) the trial court entertained no evidence as to the cost of making Medworth's home safer; (3) the conservator made only one telephone call to explore possible in-home care arrangements; (4) two doctors testified that with the provision of proper support services, Medworth is capable of living at home; and (5) the social worker assigned to Medworth's case testified that while Medworth required 24-hour care, proper care could be provided either in her home or in a retirement center. The record also shows that Medworth is deeply attached to the home she has lived in for many years and has repeatedly expressed her preference to remain there.

Although the trial court properly determined Medworth required 24-hour medical services, there is no evidence in the record that moving Medworth from her home to an out-of-state congregate-living apartment was analyzed in consideration of her best interests or general welfare or is necessary to provide Medworth with care.

Reversed.

In practice the best interest standard and substituted judgment doctrine nearly always reach the same conclusion because a person usually wants what is in his or her objective best interests. It is only when the ward's desires depart from the conventional interests in security, health, and life that the application of substituted judgment is at issue.

QUESTIONS

1. Is the substituted judgment doctrine always sufficient guidance for decision making? Can a guardian freely effect decisions based on substituted judgment that expose the ward to risk of harm?

2. In order to determine the correct substituted judgment, what evidence is sufficient to clearly establish the ward's desires? Can it be inferred from the lifestyle of the ward?

[1] FINANCIAL DUTIES AND PROPERTY MANAGEMENT

State guardianship statutes have a lengthy list of property powers that may be exercised either independently or with court approval. Typically a guardian or conservator can invest the funds of the ward; collect, hold, and dispose of assets; continue or participate in operation of a business; handle banking transactions; make alterations and repairs to real estate; enter into leases; engage in securities transactions; pay the ward's expenses and debts; settle or contest legal claims; pay taxes; expend funds for the support of the ward's dependents; and employ others to assist in the administration of the ward's estate.

A guardian must also adequately support the ward. In *Anthony v. National Bank of Commerce*, 468 So. 2d 41 (Miss. 1985), for example, the guardian of the person of the colorful personality, Alex H. Anthony, petitioned for a review of the annual statement submitted by National Bank of Commerce as conservator of Anthony's estate.

The court related:

> On May 19, 1982, Grover Anthony, daughter of Alex H. Anthony, filed a petition to appoint conservator of her father. At that time, Alex Anthony was near ninety-five (95) years of age. . . . Alex Anthony obviously was a shrewd businessman. He accumulated an estate consisting of approximately one hundred fifty thousand dollars ($150,000) in cash and numerous parcels of real property for which no valuation or appraisal had been made, but which produced approximately twelve hundred dollars ($1,200) per month in rental income.
>
> NBC, the conservator, was ordered by the court to pay various expenses and to pay the sum of $500.00 per month to David Van Every, a local attorney, for the purpose of meeting Anthony's daily living expenses. The annual accounting shows at the beginning the following disbursements to Alex Anthony:

July 21, 1982 $5.00; August 2, 1982 $5.00;

September 27, 1982 $15.02; September 28, 1982 $8.25;

October 4, 1982 $30.00; November 23, 1982 $150.00;

January 28, 1983 $16.00; February 23, 1983 $100.00;

March 17, 1983 $100.00; March 18, 1983 $10.00;

April 5, 1983 $100.00; April 19, 1983 $105.00;

April 29, 1983 $100.00; May 4, 1983 $100.00;

May 17, 1983 $100.00

It is almost incredible that a 95-year-old man, who has accumulated wealth estimated at three hundred thousand dollars ($300,000), has no duty to support anyone, and, at the most, has only a few years to live, be required to exist in such a meager and niggardly fashion.

[The court ordered removal of the bank as conservator.]

The traditional bifurcation of guardianship between guardians of property and guardians of the person fails to take into account the circumstances of the elderly, for whom control of property translates into control of their personal lives. For example, the ability to hire a companion may be the alternative to entering a nursing home. Within a family unit, the elderly person's ability to spend has a direct relationship to his or her status and well-being. Indeed, it may establish, maintain, or destroy the individual's role within the family unit. As with no other group, the property interests of the elderly are critical to their fundamental personal interests.

Consider the following observations.

Alison Barnes, *The Liberty and Property of Elders: Guardianship and Will Contests as the Same Claim*
11 ELDER L.J. 1, 27 (2003)[*]

[O]lder wards frequently have significant property, the management of which is important not only to heirs but also in assuring quality of life for the ward throughout old age. The property is not more important than civil or human rights, surely, but instead is a means by which to deliver quality long-term care selected from the options the community offers. In keeping with this view, it seems most reasonable that the principal opposition to guardianship reforms in every state is the bar's section of real property, probate and trust lawyers. For these attorneys, their clients' interests are best served by professional management of the assets, often with cooperation and assistance from family members. Limited guardianship complicates the ability of attorney and family to manage the property by raising questions in the minds of third parties to management transactions, because the extent of the guardian's authority is not the familiar plenary power.

To the extent that guardianship acts to disadvantage family members in their relationships with their elderly relative, it is likely to be seldom used. The reforms place unwanted burdens on the family members of elderly wards in a number of ways, beginning with the basis in the rights of the elderly individual to testamentary freedom. The perspective and rhetoric of individual legal rights is particularly unsuited to the relationship between these participants in guardianship, a relationship that exists to provide care over time, giving and receiving based on trust, duty, need and, ideally, love. The values system of such long term caregiving has been termed an "ethics of accommodation."

It appears that guardianship reform is particularly ill-suited to the circumstances and relationships of most elderly wards. Rather, it is directed toward subgroups with distinct legal rights issues. Recognizing this, why has no further reform in the law been proposed? Why do most states continue to address guardianship for younger disabled wards and elderly wards under the same statute? And advocates stump without result for active monitoring over the course of the guardian/ward relationship?

QUESTIONS

1. Do you think that family guardianship that provides control of an elder's property can be essentially an effort to prematurely determine the outcome of a will contest, i.e., to be sure the elder does not transfer assets to one other than the younger family members?

2. Should the guardian attempt to preserve the estate of the ward for the benefit of the heirs of the ward?

3. What should the conservator's duty be when the assets are insufficient to adequately maintain the ward?

4. Some state statutes require a guardian to file a plan for services, usually annually, which describes the ward's needs and the arrangements intended to meet them. This provides a basis for the court's review. Should it also create a case for liability for negligent care?

Financial planning for some older persons may involve giving away assets to minimize taxes and probate costs or the guardian may want to make gifts from the ward's assets because the ward's loved ones are in need. Courts are divided on the extent of a guardian's powers for such purposes. Some courts require a showing of dire need before authorizing a significant transfer of assets, even if the transfer anticipates the disposition of the assets by will or intestacy. The justification is that the ward might come to need the assets for his or her care (or even upon the unlikely event of a return to competency). Also, the transfer might not be justified if the recipient is not in dire need or did not have a close relationship with the ward. Finally, the guardian might be altering the ultimate disposition of the ward's property, i.e., not following the disposition pattern of the ward's will. These variations all raise questions about whether the ward would have made the contemplated gift. All jurisdictions now permit the possibility of such gifts by relying on either substituted judgment, the use of a best interests tests, or a combination of the two.

[2] SPECIFIC POWERS REQUIRING COURT ORDER

Some powers are considered too sweeping or subject to conflict of interests for a guardian to exercise without explicit, ad hoc authorization by the court. In many states the guardian cannot place the ward in long-term nursing home care or a mental institution; authorize electroconvulsive therapy, psychosurgery, or experimental medical treatment; or allow participation of the ward as a research subject. Such decisions require court review to determine whether action would be in the best interest of the ward.

Many guardians are acquainted with their wards and so are confident as to what health care decisions to make for the ward because they have some idea as to how the ward might have responded to the choice faced by the guardian. How should a guardian proceed, however, if the guardian never knew the ward and is unable to learn anything about the ward's attitudes, beliefs, or values? In particular, when is it appropriate for a guardian to terminate life-sustaining treatment? Consider how the court approached that issue in the following case.

PEOPLE EX REL. YEAGER
93 P.3d 589 (Colo. App. 2004)

In this involuntary guardianship proceeding, Leo M. Yeager, an incapacitated person who died during the pendency of this appeal, through his attorney, appealed the order holding that Yeager's guardian, the Morgan County Department of Human Services (MCDHS), is a person for purposes of § 15-18.6-101 *et seq.*, C.R.S. 2003 (article 18.6), and authorizing MCDHS to execute a "do not resuscitate" (DNR) order on Yeager's behalf. We affirm.

The parties stipulated to the relevant facts. Yeager, born June 6, 1924, was without any known relatives, friends, or acquaintances and suffered from numerous medical and mental health conditions. In February 1998, the trial court appointed a visitor and a guardian ad litem (GAL) for Yeager. The following month, it determined Yeager to be legally incapacitated and appointed MCDHS to be his guardian. The order required MCDHS to involve the trial court in any extraordinary medical actions, including "no CORE [no cardiopulmonary resuscitation] or no CODE orders."

In January 2002, MCDHS filed a motion for a DNR order with respect to Yeager. The court appointed independent counsel for Yeager. Counsel, together with the parties, stipulated that Yeager suffered from advanced dementia, congestive heart failure, chronic obstructive pulmonary disease, and anemia. At hearings in August 2002 and March 2003, Yeager, his attorney, the GAL, and MCDHS representatives were all present.

The only witness at the March 2003 hearing was Yeager's personal physician. He testified as to Yeager's medical prognosis both with and without cardiopulmonary resuscitation (CPR). In addition, the trial court admitted a letter by the physician outlining his reasons for supporting the execution of a DNR order and a medical journal article discussing the ethics of CPR.

According to the physician, the likelihood of resuscitating Yeager would be approximately one out of a hundred. Even if resuscitation were successful, it was highly likely that he would be worse off after resuscitation. Resuscitation would likely cause injuries such as rib fractures and pneumothorax. His prognosis would worsen, his existing medical conditions would be exacerbated, and his life expectancy would be minimal. Yeager's physician concluded that attempting resuscitation would be futile, cruel, and unethical.

Following the March 2003 hearing, the court found by clear and convincing evidence that Yeager lacked sufficient understanding or capacity to communicate responsible decisions concerning his person or to make financial or medical decisions. The court noted the physician's observations that Yeager's condition continued to deteriorate, that he had severe dementia, and that CPR was contraindicated. It found that Yeager presently had severe dementia, Alzheimer's, chronic obstructive pulmonary disease, hypothyroidism, osteoar-thritis, valvular heart disease, pulmonary hypertension, stenosis, and gastroe-sophagial reflux disease. The court modified the original order appointing MCDHS as guardian to allow MCDHS "unlimited authority to approve and consent to medical decisions for Mr. Yeager, including but not limited to authority to enter DNR directives and orders on behalf of Mr. Yeager." That modified order is the subject of this appeal.

. . . .

Yeager's attorney contends that the trial court erred by substituting its judgment for that of an incapacitated person to allow the execution of the DNR order when no evidence existed to rebut the statutory presumption of consent to resuscitation found in § 15-18.6-104(3). We disagree.

First, we are not persuaded by the assertion that the presumption of § 15-18.6-104(3) applies here. That subsection states: "In the absence of a CPR directive, a person's consent to CPR shall be presumed."

Thus, the presumption arises only in the absence of a CPR directive. Here, the trial court authorized MCDHS to enter a DNR order. Therefore, if the trial court acted within the scope of its authority in doing so, the presumption is inapplicable.

We also disagree that the trial court erred by substituting its judgment for that of Yeager in the absence of clear and convincing evidence of Yeager's actual wishes.

A clear and convincing standard of proof applies to the decision to authorize a DNR order under these circumstances.

"All adult persons have a fundamental right to make their own medical treatment decisions, including decisions regarding medical treatment and artificial nourishment and hydration." Section 15-18.5-101(1)(a), C.R.S. 2003. A clear and convincing standard of proof is required in cases where a fundamental right is concerned.

In § 15-18.6-102, the General Assembly specifically permits other authorized persons to execute CPR directives for incapacitated persons.

Here, MCDHS presented expert evidence to support its motion to authorize a

DNR order at the March 2003 hearing. Yeager presented no evidence to rebut the motion. After specifically considering the absence of evidence as to Yeager's wishes, the trial court found that the original guardianship order should be modified to allow MCDHS unlimited authority to consent to and approve medical decisions for Yeager, including entering a DNR order.

In light of the evidence presented and in the absence of an existing medical directive or any evidence of Yeager's wishes, we conclude that the trial court did not err. Thus, MCDHS was authorized to execute the DNR order, and the statutory presumption was not applicable.

QUESTIONS

1.   Why does the state statute presume "a person's consent to CPR"?

2.   Why should the law presume anything about an incapacitated person's wishes?

3.   Is the court's decision to approval a DNR order the equivalent of presuming that the ward would have preferred that outcome? Or is it an admission that when the desire of the ward is unknowable, some other value must decide the case? If so, what other value is that?

4.   In this case, does a DNR order serve the best interests of the ward or society?

L.   WHO SHOULD SERVE AS GUARDIAN?

Very frequently, the individual who initiates the guardianship petition requests that he or she be named guardian. The court need not appoint that person if it believes that someone else would be preferable.

[1]   PRIORITY OF APPOINTMENT

Courts are guided in their choice by state guardianship statutes which typically include preference of priority for who should be appointed guardian. Though the statutes favor the appointment of family members, the court is free to appoint any competent person twenty-one years of age or older may be appointed guardian of an incapacitated person.

Subject to a determination by the court of who is in best interest of the incapacitated person, priority for appointment as guardian is typically:

(a)   The person nominated as guardian by the incapacitated person either in a durable power of attorney or an advance health care directive;

(b)   The spouse of the incapacitated person;

(c)   An adult child of the incapacitated person;

(d)   A parent of the incapacitated person; or

(e)   An adult with whom the incapacitated person has resided immediately before the filing of the petition;

If there is more than one person with equal priority, the court will select the one it considers most qualified. *See, e.g.,* Colo. Rev. Stat. § 15-14-310.

Florida's statute approaches the matter somewhat differently:

Considerations in appointment of guardian.

(1)   . . . [t]he court may appoint any person who is fit and proper and qualified to act as guardian, whether related to the ward or not.

(2)   The court shall give preference to the appointment of a person who:

(a)   Is related by blood or marriage to the ward;

(b)   Has educational, professional, or business experience relevant to the nature of the services sought to be provided;

(c)   Has the capacity to manage the financial resources involved; or

(d)   Has the ability to meet the requirements of the law and the unique needs of the individual case.

(3)   The court shall also:

(a)   Consider the wishes expressed by the incapacitated person as to who shall be appointed guardian; and

. . .

(c)   Consider any person designated as guardian in any will in which the incapacitated person is a beneficiary.

Fla. Stat. § 744.312.

Alaska Stat. § 13.26.113(g) (1985) includes, as the first choice, "[the nominee of] the incapacitated person, if at the time of the nomination the incapacitated person had the capacity to make a reasonably intelligent choice" and adds to the list "a relative or friend who has demonstrated a sincere, longstanding interest in the welfare of the incapacitated person."

Conflicts among children as to what is best for an incapacitated parent often end up before the court in the form of a dispute as to who should be named guardian. The guiding principle for the court is what is best for the incapacitated person.

IN RE HOLLOWAY
555 S.E.2d 228 (Ga. Ct. App. 2001)

Beverly Harris and Harriett Taylor instituted this proceeding for appointment of themselves as guardians for the person and property of their mentally incapacitated 86-year-old mother, Mamie Bell Holloway, a widow. Holloway's sons intervened and sought appointment of themselves or others as guardians. Finding none of the children qualified to act as guardian, the Superior Court of Crisp County appointed certain third parties as guardians under O.C.G.A. § 29-5-2. The daughters appeal. They contend that the trial court erroneously relied on O.C.G.A. § 29-4-8 and *Kelley v. Kelley*, and they challenge the court's determination that they are not qualified to act as guardians. We find no ground for reversal and affirm.

Evidence introduced at the hearing below showed that Holloway's support needs were being adequately met through Social Security benefits and interest earned on $320,000 invested in bank certificates of deposit (CDs) when one of her sons obtained power of attorney from her, redeemed the CDs, transferred the proceeds to an irrevocable trust, named himself as trustee, and put the money in a stock brokerage account. Her daughters later removed Holloway from her home in Cordele to Macon without informing her sons. As a result, she was reported missing, and law enforcement authorities undertook a frantic search for her. The daughters filed a petition in the Probate Court of Bibb County for invalidation of the trust and appointment of themselves as guardians for the person and property of their mother. The guardianship proceeding was later transferred to Crisp County because it is Holloway's legal residence, and she was placed in a nursing home there. In the nursing home, she fell and broke her hip. Because of her children's inability to agree on whether she should receive medical treatment in Cordele or Macon, an emergency guardian had to be appointed to consent to immediate surgery.

O.C.G.A. § 29-5-2 sets forth statutory preferences to be considered by a court in selecting guardians for incapacitated adults. Unless disqualified, spouses and adult children are preferred over all other persons except for individuals who have been formally nominated by the ward prior to the ward's becoming incapacitated. Although the statutory preferences must be considered by the court in selecting a guardian, the court may pass over a person having preference and appoint a person having lower preference or no preference "for good cause shown." In determining whether to depart from the statutory preferences, the court shall consider "all relevant factors, including the ability of the person to perform the duties of a guardian . . . and the period of time which has elapsed since any person was nominated by the prospective ward or another."

. . . .

In the order appealed, the court ruled "that none of Mrs. Holloway's children is qualified to act as her guardian because each has in some way recently acted in such a way as to call into question whether his or her judgment as to Mrs. Holloway's best interests would be clouded by or influenced by his or her disdain for or mistrust of one or more siblings." The court found that although the daughters seemingly have the financial acumen and medical knowledge to serve as guardians, their actions in surreptitiously taking their mother from Cordele to Macon, and in refusing to consent to their mother's surgery in Cordele even though she was in excruciating pain, raise questions as to their objectivity in deciding guardianship issues. The court also noted that it is unlikely that any of the children could make an objective evaluation as to whether establishment of the trust was in Holloway's best interests and that, in all probability, if any of the children were appointed guardian of Holloway's person or property, further litigation would be the likely result. As strongly urged by Holloway's court-appointed attorney, the court therefore appointed the Crisp County Department of Family & Children

Services (DFACS) Director as guardian of Holloway's person and the Crisp County Guardian as guardian of her property. In its order, the court, citing *Kelley* and O.C.G.A. § 29-4-8, also noted that it would be adverse to Holloway and her estate to appoint any of her children as guardian.

The evidence supports a determination that "good cause" has been shown for not appointing any of Holloway's children as guardian of her person or property. Therefore, O.C.G.A. § 29-5-2 authorized the court to refuse to appoint her children as guardians and to appoint the DFACS director and county guardian instead. . . .

[2] PUBLIC AND PROFESSIONAL GUARDIANS

In some cases no family member or friend is willing or capable of acting as guardian. A guardian's duties are numerous and demanding. The commitment entails dealing with the ward's housing, finances, medical decisions, long-term care issues, and legal problems as well as daily personal care and the filing of court-required reports. As a result a growing number of paid professional guardians provide guardianship services or give advice to private guardians. Compensation for professional guardians may be paid from the estate of the ward or by the state.

To provide assistance for individuals for whom no guardian is available, a number of states have created an office of public guardian, an agency or public official whose primary purpose is to act as guardians. The role of public guardian may be filled by an officer of the court, an employee of the department of social services, or an official of local government. Often the state will make a contract with a private, nonprofit agency to act as a guardian.

The merits of public guardianship have engendered a vigorous debate. Supporters contend that there are many individuals who need a public guardian because they lack family or friends to serve as guardians or their estates are too small to interest a bank. Detractors fear that public guardianship will lead to the overuse of guardianship and the intrusion of the state into the lives of its citizens. Still worse, they claim, the system will become bureaucratized and overburdened so that individual wards will receive little or no personal attention.

Regardless of the merits of these arguments, public guardianship does raise critical issues. First, the system must guard against the public guardian resorting to institutionalization of the ward. An overburdened guardian can limit the workload by placing the ward in a nursing home or other institution where all the ward's needs for care and supervision are reliably met. Nursing home placement may also be cost effective for the guardian (if not for society) since visiting a number of wards who all live in the same facility may be cost efficient.

Some fear that a public guardian might lead to excessive use of guardianship; the office of the public guardian may become bureaucratized, with the primary goal its own survival and growth. What better way to promote the need for itself than by instituting more guardianships? To prevent this some suggest that the public guardian should not be allowed to petition for guardianship. Even if the public guardian cannot initiate guardianships, however, the existence of the public guardian may encourage social service agencies to bring guardianship proceedings since it will facilitate dealing with uncooperative clients.

Finally, the public guardian may have a conflict of interest in the provision of services to the ward. Here the structural independence of the public guardian is paramount. If the public guardian is merely a branch of the social services agency, it may be under orders to minimize the provision of services to its ward or at least minimize its demand for the services from other branches of the social service agency. To avoid this, the public guardian must be an independent agency whose role is to protect and promote the interests of the ward regardless of the cost to other governmental agencies. Realistically, public guardians are typically understaffed and may lack sufficient resources to aggressively pursue the interests of their wards.

Private sector professional guardians are often the choice for many elderly with financial means but who have no family nearby or willing to serve. Consider whether the appointment of a professional guardian may be better for the ward in some circumstances.

Alison Barnes, *The Virtues of Corporate and Professional Guardians*
31 Stetson L. Rev. 942, 958 (2002)[*]

A Little Knowledge About Practicing Guardians

Four categories of persons or entities having no prior relationship with the ward might provide guardianship services: professionals in private practice, corporations for profit or non-profit, and public guardians. Each brings somewhat different strengths and motivations to guardianship service delivery. The duties of volunteers, which might be utilized by any guardianship agency or practice, are also considered. The following section is presents some survey information and commentary regarding the most significant issues in choice of a guardian.

In 1998, the National Guardianship Association conducted a Survey of Private Professional Guardians. Professional and corporate guardians profess intense interest in the nature and practices of other entities providing similar services. The literature is quite sparse. Most recent data can be derived from a 1998 survey that asked for voluntary self-reporting.

Members who responded are categorized in four groups: private, for profit organizations (39); private, non-profit organizations (59); public organizations (41); and, solo practitioners (38). It is unknown how representative the responders are of the proportion of like entities in the NGA membership, or the larger group of non-member corporate and professional guardians. Also, the categories sometimes fail to capture the complexity of the funding and services of an entity. For example, many non-profit organizations provide substantial services under contract with the state, making them in significant part public guardians. "Solo" practitioners may not practice alone, but rather have various other workers to deliver guardianship services, and may be lawyers or non-lawyer guardians. Thus, generalities are merely indications of the compelling business and motivations and values of the participants.

The survey nevertheless provides a wealth of information about guardianship providers. With regard to services provided, for example, the most common primary service was personal guardianship. It appears that either the designated guardian might be the individual professional guardian, or might be the corporate entity. The profile of services by for-profit corporations differs from other providers in that the second most prevalent service by for-profits was care management; for others the second service was characterized as social services. The implied (but not defined) distinction appears to be between private and public services programs. For-profits listed their third service as the financial service representative payee. For all but for-profit providers, the fourth most frequently provided service was adult protective services. Durable power of attorney services figured next in prevalence.

Typically, guardianship entities made no selection among clients of different types, though services providers such as social workers often have training targeted to the emotional and social needs of specific groups. Nevertheless, most organizations indicated willingness to serve persons with developmental disabilities, mental illness, brain injury, advanced age, veterans, children and persons with dual diagnoses (of mental retardation and mental illness.) In all cases, the great majority of wards are adults.

Most organizations are very small. Most for-profits (24 of 39) had one to five employees. Though not for profits are larger, 24 of 59 had one to five employees. Ten had as many as twenty employees. Many public entities are small (13 of 41 having one through five employees) but the largest entities had over 200 employees. Most likely, the viable scale represents at least one of two possible differences: A concentrated urban population; or, more likely, a public entity authorized to provide services to paying clients.

. . . .

The professional health care provider model requires professional self-regulation. . . . Commentary on professionalism for physicians provides an enlightening analogy, commitment among members to high standards of quality, and de-emphasis on economic issues. If guardianship is to provide the protection of professionalism for wards, it must develop and implement similar components of regulation and hold guardians accountable.

Professionalization entails significant shifts in social and economic power to the members of the profession. The establishment of a profession awards to those qualified to join a monopoly, or at the least a dominant role, in delivering the types of services included in the licensing or certification. The practitioners are removed from, or distinguished within, the marketplace of competition. Such a step reduces the number of available providers and can cause an increase in the fees for services. In order to justify a monopoly, therefore, the public must be in need of protection from unethical providers.

The public needs protection when the recipients of services cannot effectively monitor the quality and appropriateness of services, or knowledgeably compare prices. In health care, for example, a patient often cannot tell whether the physician's treatments are valuable in treating the patient's sickness. Thus, traditional health care providers are deemed to be professionals, requiring long and rigorous education, their market protected from quacks by state licensing laws, and regulated by those with similar education and licensing.

The model contrasted with professionalism is commercialism, which calls for competition among providers for a portion of market share, and thus a greater emphasis also on financial interests. For most goods and services, the market is the most desirable way to determine price and assure quality. In addition to its quick response to supply and demand changes that might be unrecognized by regulators, commercialism implies recognition of alternative providers of better or less costly services, and emphasis on the professional's duty to the client or patient.

In the *Matter of Guardianship of Esther L.K.*, Wis. Ct. App. No 00-2960-FT, P32 409, March 8, 2001, the court chose a professional guardian over a daughter petitioning for guardianship of her mother. The trial court appointed Lutheran Guardian Services (LGS) when the administrator of Esther L.K.'s nursing home sought an order for protective placement. Esther's daughter, Patricia, petitioned to be appointed guardian. Patricia had not seen her mother for two years prior to the nursing home admission and was omitted from the list of those allowed access to information from the home. There was evidence that Patricia, who had differences with the nursing home, would move her mother to one near her home in another state. On Patricia's appeal, the Court of Appeals reversed and remanded, stating that the prospect of Patricia's decision to move her mother could not be used to disqualify her as guardian. On remand, the trial court again appointed LGS, stating that Patricia's actions showed "a propensity to ignore the wishes of a loved one to serve her own self-interest." On the daughter's second appeal, the Court of Appeals ruled that the trial court had property exercised its discretion in choosing the guardian, noting that the record supported a finding that Esther would have opposed Patricia's appointment, and the appointment of the corporate guardian was in Esther's best interests.

QUESTION

If guardianship is to be considered a profession, who should be eligible to join? What kind of training or credentials should be required? What ethical standards should guide members? See 31 STETSON L. REV. 996 (2002) for the Standards of Practice of the National Guardianship Association.

M. TERMINATION OF GUARDIANSHIP

A guardianship can be terminated if the ward regains capacity. Usually the termination is initiated by filing a petition or letter by the ward or a third party in the court that created the guardianship. Although most statutes do not specify the information the court requires, any request for termination should state the changes in the ward's abilities and circumstances that demonstrate capacity. A change in medical or psychiatric status should be confirmed by a statement from a qualified physician. Most statutes require notice to interested parties, including the guardian. In some states, termination of a guardianship is an informal matter. Unless the guardian objects, the court may, upon a review of the evidence and without a hearing order, terminate the guardianship. In other states, termination of guardianship requires a formal hearing. In all states the powers of a guardian terminate upon the death of the ward.

IN RE HARRIS
480 So. 2d 1131 (Miss. 1985)

This is an appeal from a decree of the Chancery Court of Benton County removing the appellant, Matthew Harris, from the office of conservator of the estate of his aunt, Susie Alice Harris.

Susie Alice Harris (known as "Miss Susie") is an elderly woman believed to be about ninety years of age, who lives alone at her home in rural Benton County. She never married and has neither children nor living siblings. On September 3, 1982, her nephew Matthew Harris and three of his brothers filed a petition in the Chancery Court of Benton County. Harris lives in Memphis, as do his brothers (except for one who lives in Millington, TN). The petition alleged that Miss Susie was incapable of managing her estate by reason of advanced age and mental weakness.

Soon afterwards, trouble began. Miss Susie complained to visitors and county officials that Matthew Harris seldom visited her, that her bills were remaining unpaid and that she had little money. Visitors also reported that Miss Susie had little food in the house, that the house and yard were generally in a run-down condition, and that the house was infested with mice. On October 13, 1983, a petition was filed in the Chancery Court of Benton County by Jackie Tatum and Bonnie King, a nurse employed by the Benton County Board of Health. It enumerated the complaints mentioned above, and also charged that Harris had failed to file his inventory as required, and his attorney Lee Calvin Buckley had refused to talk with the petitioners about the needs of Miss Susie. The petition prayed that Matthew Harris be removed as conservator and Bonnie King be appointed in his stead. Harris answered, contending that the petitioners lacked standing and insisting that he had diligently attempted to perform his duties, and that his shortcomings were due to the opposition of Miss Susie and others who had not been in favor of his appointment.

The cause was heard on January 5, 1984. The chancellor issued an opinion finding it in the best interest of Miss Susie to have Matthew Harris removed as conservator. Bonnie King was appointed to succeed him. (On appeal, the court affirmed.)

QUESTION

Who should have standing to petition for a guardian's removal or replacement? Why?

Guardianship terminates upon the death of the ward. The guardian has no authority over the person or property of a deceased ward, but the guardian will be required to make a final accounting of the property of the ward. This accounting will be turned over to the personal representative of the estate of the ward. The death of a guardian does not terminate the guardianship. The court will appoint a successor guardian. If the guardian is unable to carry on as a guardian for reasons of health or because of the loss of mental capacity, the guardian should petition the court to be relieved and ask for the appointment of a successor guardian. If the guardian wishes to resign as guardian, perhaps because the guardian no longer feels up to the duties or because the guardian has moved and is no longer physically near the ward, the guardian must petition the court to be relieved as guardian. Until the court accepts the petition and appoints a new guardian, the original guardian is still responsible to act as the guardian of the ward.

Chapter 10

PROPERTY MANAGEMENT

Many elderly individuals wish to plan ahead for the management of their assets and affairs in the event they become too impaired to competently manage things by themselves. Often they hope to avoid ever being the subject of a guardianship, which they may perceive as a failure to properly plan. Fortunately, alternatives exist that, when appropriately used, can minimize or even eliminate the need for a guardian. None of the alternatives, however, provides the degree of court supervision that an involuntary guardianship does, and so they do create a greater risk of error and exploitation by the substitute decision maker. Attorneys who advise older clients must be careful that the use of alternatives to guardianship provide the assistance the client needs while minimizing unnecessary risk.

A variety of federal and state statutes provide means to assist individuals to avoid or minimize the need for guardianship. For example, under the Social Security Act, individuals can appoint a representative payee to manage their benefits. (Representative payees are discussed in Chapter 9, *Guardianship*.) State statutes permit the use of a revocable or living trust, a popular method of providing asset management for individuals with decreased mental capacity. Guardianship also can be avoided by the use of state laws that authorize living wills and advance health care directives that permit an individual to record instructions regarding the use of life-sustaining treatment or permit the appointment of a surrogate health care decision maker. These powers, and the limits of their usefulness, are considered in Chapter 11, *Health Care Decision Making*.

This chapter examines the most commonly utilized methods for assisting older people with the management of their property and financial affairs, including durable powers of attorney, joint ownership of property and bank accounts, and the use of trusts.

A. POWER OF ATTORNEY

The power of attorney, which can provide a substitute decision maker for all types of property decisions, is the primary nonjudicial method of property management for an incapacitated person. A power of attorney is a written authorization for one individual, referred to as an agent or attorney-in-fact, to act on behalf of another individual, the principal, for the purposes stated in the document. Under the common law of agency, powers of attorney terminated upon the mental incapacity of the principal. Current state laws, however, permit a power to continue to be valid, i.e., "durable," even if the principal becomes mentally incapacitated. In order to be recognized as a durable power of attorney, the authorizing document must be prepared and executed according to the formalities specified in the applicable state statute. Most states have similar requirements, and a durable power executed in one state may be readily accepted in another state. A few states specifically recognize as valid any power executed according to the law of the state in which it was signed, but generally individuals who change their state residence should create a new power of attorney that conforms to the law of their new residence. Under the law of most states, to be valid a power of attorney must be in writing, signed by the principal, witnessed, and dated. Some states require notarization. To be "durable," in some states the power must specifically state that the power is durable and the right of the agent to act is not affected by the mental incapacity of the principal. In other states, all powers of attorney are considered durable and need not so state. The death of the principal, of course, terminates the power and the agent's right to act for the principal. Some states require the agent (the attorney-in-fact) to sign the power of attorney and acknowledge the responsibilities of acting as an agent under a power of attorney.

Powers of attorney are simple to create and can be tailored to individual needs and circumstances. Many state statutes detail what powers can be delegated to the agent, but generally they permit the principal to grant the agent all rights to manage the property of the principal and to spend income and principal in whatever manner the principal might have. The principal can delegate whatever power the principal believes to be appropriate or necessary, including a general power to make all decisions the principal could make.

The breadth of the power is also a potential disadvantage, since it allows for abuse or misuse by a dishonest or inept agent. The law holds the agent to the standards of trustworthiness and good faith action required in a fiduciary relationship, much like a guardian. Principals who believe that their agent has abused his or her powers or acted negligently can revoke the power and sue the agent for restitution. Because a principal who lacks mental capacity may not be capable of objecting to the acts of the agent, some state statutes permit the principal's legal representative (successor agent or guardian), a family member, or any other interested person to petition the court to require the agent to give an accounting. Anecdotal evidence suggests that some agents do abuse their authority by making gifts of the principal's property to themselves, by ill-advised investments and self-dealing, or by failing to adequately provide for the well-being of the principal. In the great majority of cases, however, the relationship works well and serves the best interests of the principal. As a result, powers of attorney are very popular and widely used.

[1]   CAPACITY TO CREATE A POWER OF ATTORNEY

Individuals can execute a valid power of attorney only if they have sufficient mental capacity to delegate power to an agent. Generally the capacity required for executing a power of attorney is similar to that needed to enter into a contract: the ability to understand the nature of the document and the significance of signing it. There is no formal determination at the time of the execution of the power as to the mental competency of the principal, so lawsuits concerning the capacity of the principal at the time of the signing of the power are rare. Usually the issue arises only if someone later objects to the right of the agent to act by challenging the validity of the power.

In the following case, the agent appointed under a revoked power of attorney seeks to set aside the revocation and the appointment of a different agent under a new durable power of attorney.

THAMES v. DANIELS
544 S.E.2d 854 (S.C. Ct. App. 2001)

JUDGE STILWELL.

Doris W. Verdery brought this action seeking to set aside a power of attorney and a revocation of an earlier power of attorney, both executed by her mother, Doris W. Thames. Verdery alleges that on December 16, 1996, the date both documents were executed, Thames lacked mental capacity. The probate court dismissed Verdery's action, holding Thames was mentally competent when she executed the power of attorney in favor of Betty Jane Daniels and revoked the former power of attorney which appointed Verdery her attorney in fact. The circuit court affirmed. Verdery appeals, and we affirm.

BACKGROUND

Thames, who was in her late eighties at the time of trial, has been married to Harry A. Thames (Mr. Thames) since 1969. Verdery and Daniels are her daughters from a previous marriage, and Daniels' husband, C. Covert Daniels, is her son-in-law.

Thames had been living with her husband, but in the latter part of 1995 she began living at Verdery's home in Orangeburg. During March of 1996, Verdery attempted to have a guardian and a conservator appointed for her mother, apparently on the ground that her mother suffered from dementia and was mentally incompetent. After reviewing the medical evidence, the probate court declined Verdery's request, concluding Thames was mentally competent.

In May of 1996, Thames, while still living with Verdery, executed a durable power of attorney in Verdery's favor. In the summer of that year, Mr. Thames brought a family court action seeking visitation with or custody of his wife. Under a consent order in that case, Thames remained in Verdery's home, but other family members, including her husband, were granted limited visitation. The order also prohibited family members from discussing or transacting business during these visits. The court later held Mr. Thames in contempt after he, Daniels, and Daniels' son, during a visit with Thames, took her to a bank where she withdrew money and refused to return her to Verdery's home. The family court's order included the following statements regarding Thames' competency:

> The Defendant, Doris O. [sic] Thames, is not competent to manage her affairs. Dr. Vann Beth Shuler expressed her medical opinion that Defendant Thames was not competent. The Court further finds from Defendant Thames' testimony that she is not competent and has very little memory.

It appears that Defendant Thames is not competent and constantly gives contradictory statements.

Mr. Thames later brought an action in probate court to have a guardian appointed for Thames, alleging she was an "incapacitated person." The court appointed him guardian, noting that the parties' counsel stipulated that she was incapacitated. In its order, the probate court discussed in detail the difference between a guardian and a conservator. The court did not appoint a conservator.

Less than one month later, Thames executed the documents which are the subject of this lawsuit. In addition to asking that the documents be set aside, Verdery asked the court to recognize her as the attorney in fact for Thames, enjoin Daniels and her husband from interfering with Verdery's management of Thames' business affairs, order Daniels and her husband to make an accounting to Verdery regarding transfers of Thames' real and personal property, and award Verdery attorney's fees and costs.

DISCUSSION

While Verdery raises several grounds for appeal, her arguments essentially boil down to two main issues: (1) what is the applicable standard of review for an appellate court in an action to set aside a power of attorney and a revocation of a power of attorney for lack of mental capacity; and (2) based on the appropriate standard of review, did the circuit court err in affirming the probate court's finding that Thames was competent to execute the challenged documents on December 16, 1996?

I. Standard of Review

Verdery first argues the circuit court erred in concluding this was an action at law and thus applied the wrong standard of review. We agree.

The standard of review applicable to cases originating in the probate court is controlled by whether the underlying cause of action is at law or in equity. . . .

. . . .

A durable power of attorney allows a person, the principal, to designate another as his or her attorney in fact to act on the principal's behalf as provided in the document even if the principal becomes mentally incompetent.

. . . .

With a durable power of attorney, a principal creates an agency in another that continues despite the principal's later physical disability or mental incompetency. . . . Moreover, in order for the principal to create the agency relationship in the first instance, the principal must have the mental capacity to contract. . . . Therefore, in order to execute or revoke a valid power of attorney, the principal must possess contractual capacity.

South Carolina has defined contractual capacity as a person's ability to understand, at the time the contract is executed, the nature of the contract and its effect. . . .

Other jurisdictions addressing this issue have found contractual capacity is required to execute a power of attorney. . . .

Because a person must possess contractual capacity to execute or revoke a valid power of attorney, we believe a cause of action to set aside such a document is more closely akin to an action to set aside a contract, deed, or petition than it is to a will contest. Additionally, the reasoning of courts from other jurisdictions analogizing powers of attorney to contracts lends persuasive influence to this conclusion. . . . Therefore, we hold that an action to set aside a power of attorney and an instrument revoking a power of attorney on the ground of a lack of mental capacity sounds in equity.

II. Thames' Competency

Although Verdery poses some twenty-two issues on appeal, they all hinge on the question of Thames' mental capacity as of December 16, 1996.

Having carefully reviewed the record, we find ample evidence to support the probate court's finding that Thames possessed the requisite mental capacity to execute the challenged instruments on the date in question. Where a transaction is challenged on the ground of mental incompetency, the individual's competency on the date of that transaction must be determined. Furthermore, the party alleging incompetence bears the burden of proving incapacity at the time of the transaction by a preponderance of the evidence. We agree with the circuit court and the probate court that Verdery failed to meet her burden.

At trial, Verdery relied primarily on the probate court's order appointing Thames' husband her guardian as evidence of her lack of mental capacity on the date in question. Verdery's reliance on this order is misplaced. In that action, counsel for the parties stipulated Thames was incapacitated and in need of a guardian. The probate court, however, discussed the difference between a guardianship and a conservatorship, including the respective duties of each. Because the court appointed a guardian for Thames and not a conservator, the court's reference to her as incapacitated can only be seen as an adjudication of her physical condition. We do not view the probate court's order in this action as an adjudication of Thames' mental capacity.

. . . . An adjudication of incompetency is merely prima facie evidence of that fact. . . . A prior adjudication of an individual's incompetence does not conclusively bind the trial court in another action where the person's competency is directly at issue. . . .

In addition to the probate court and family court orders, Verdery offered the testimony of Dr. Vann Beth Meyers Shuler, who examined Thames upon a prior probate judge's request and found her mentally incompetent to make decisions regarding her welfare or finances. Doctor Shuler reported Thames' mental deficiencies were permanent, thus supporting Verdery's claim that Thames lacked capacity to execute the challenged documents. However, Dr. Shuler also testified Thames had been incompetent since the first time she saw her in February 1996.

This testimony, if found to be credible, is in direct conflict with the finding of the probate court in March 1996 that Thames was mentally competent and would also invalidate the May 1996 power of attorney in Verdery's favor that Verdery now seeks to enforce. Verdery subpoenaed Thames to testify, but the trial court quashed the subpoena after hearing testimony from Thames' personal physician that the stress of testifying would be hazardous to Thames' physical health.

Finally, Verdery herself testified that her mother lacked mental capacity to revoke the earlier power of attorney and to issue a new one on December 16, 1996. She also testified Daniels knew her mother lacked mental capacity to execute such instruments.

In contrast to Verdery's offer of proof, Daniels and her husband produced five witnesses who testified to Thames' mental capacity in December of 1996. Rebecca Bryant, a certified nursing assistant, and Dorothy Josey, a registered psychiatric nurse, visited Thames in her home in December 1996 to care for and examine her. Bryant testified that around Christmas of 1996, she saw Thames five times a week in visits lasting forty-five minutes to an hour. Bryant recalled Thames' mental state was "good" for her age when she saw her. Josey testified Thames was oriented to person, place, and time during her December 19 and 20, 1996 visits. Likewise, when Josey saw Thames on December 23 and 25, 1996, Thames was "cooperative and talkative" in addition to being oriented to time, place and person. Doctor Lea B. Givens, Thames' personal physician, saw Thames on December 12, 1996, and approximately thirteen other times between September 1993 and August 1997. While Dr. Givens said he had not conducted a detailed mental exam of Thames, he testified that each time he saw her, Thames was pleasant, answered his questions, and was oriented to time and place.

The other two witnesses, Angela Hester and Daniels, were present on December 16, 1996, when Thames revoked her prior power of attorney and executed a new one. Hester, a legal assistant at the law firm where Thames executed the challenged instruments, signed the documents as a witness. She specifically recalled explaining the documents to Thames and, when asked, Thames told Hester she understood. Daniels testified she went with her mother to the attorney's office and Thames "knew exactly what she was doing" when she signed the disputed documents on December 16, 1996.

Thus, under either a legal or equitable standard of review, we find the evidence contained in the record fully supports the probate court's finding that Thames possessed the requisite mental capacity to execute the documents in question on December 16, 1996.

. . . .

For the reasons discussed, the order of the circuit court affirming the order of the probate court is

AFFIRMED.

QUESTIONS

1. Why is the standard of capacity required to execute a power of attorney higher than that needed to execute a valid will?

2. Why was the probate court's determination that Mrs. Thames required a guardian not conclusive as to whether she had the capacity to execute a valid power of attorney?

3. Mrs. Thames' physician, Dr. Givens, testified that though he had never conducted a detailed mental exam of her, each time he saw her, she was "pleasant, answered his questions, and was oriented to time and space." If you represented her daughter who was challenging the new power of attorney, how would you have challenged the testimony of Dr. Givens?

[2] FORMALITIES OF EXECUTION

State statutes govern the formalities required to create a power of attorney. Generally the power must be in writing and include language showing the principal's intent to create an agency that will not terminate with the onset of incapacity. Note the Colorado requirements:

> COLO. REV. STAT. § 15-14-501: When Power of Attorney Is Not Affected by Disability
>
> (1) Whenever a principal designates another his attorney-in-fact or agent by a power of attorney in writing and the writing contains the words "This power of attorney shall not be affected by disability of the principal." or "This power of attorney shall become effective upon the disability of the principal." or similar words showing the intent of the principal that the authority conferred shall be exercisable notwithstanding his disability, the authority of the attorney-in-fact or agent is exercisable by him as provided in the power on behalf of the principal notwithstanding later disability or incapacity of the principal at law or later uncertainty as to whether the principal is dead or alive.

In recognition that the principal's usual reason for creating a power of attorney is to provide for the management of his or her assets in the event of mental incapacity, many state statutes make all powers of attorney durable and so do not require any special language to make them durable. *E.g.*, ME. REV. STAT. ANN. tit. 18-A § 5-901. A careful drafter, however, will always specifically state that the power is durable to insure that the agent's power to act will not be questioned by third parties.

The formalities of execution vary. In South Carolina, a durable power must be executed and witnessed in the same manner as a will and the power must be recorded in the same manner as a deed. S.C. CODE ANN. § 62-5-501. Pennsylvania requires the agent to sign the power attesting to understanding among other things that he or she will exercise the powers for the benefit of the principal, keep accurate records, and "exercise reasonable caution and prudence." 20 PA. CONS. STAT. ANN. § 5601. Regardless of the state statutory requirements, as a precautionary matter, the drafter should insure that the power of attorney is signed, dated, has two witnesses, and is notarized. This will insure that it meets the requirement of all states, and that it can be used to transfer real property. Many drafters also have the agent sign the document, both as a means of informing the agent of the existence of the power and as a means of authenticating the agent's signature for third parties. Multiple copies of the power are usually signed. The agent often needs an original signed copy when dealing with third parties, but, some banks or stockbrokers insist upon retaining an original signed copy. A signed copy may also need to be filed with the register of deeds if the power permits the agent to sell real estate owned by the principal.

Generally, any person of legal majority may serve as agent, regardless of place of residence. Most powers, however, name an agent who lives near the principal as it may be difficult for an individual who lives far away to carry out the duties required of an agent. Successor agents should be named in case the original agent resigns, becomes unable to perform or dies. Typically, married persons name their spouses as their agent, with a child named as successor agent. Although it is permissible to name joint agents, it is not considered advisable because both agents will have to agree to any action under the power. It is possible to name joint agents who have the power to permit only one agent to act, but third parties may be reluctant to respond to the request of only one agent.

Usually agents serve without compensation, though they can reimburse themselves for reasonable expenses. Some state statutes specifically permit "reasonable compensation" of the agent. Mo. Stat. § 404.725. Agents can also "hire" themselves to perform duties for the principal. For example, the agent might pay herself for caregiving services provided to the principal. Unless provided for by state law or in the power of attorney, the agent, however, should not expect payment for carrying out her duties. Of course, any time the agent accepts compensation from the assets of the principal the opportunity exists for misappropriation or abuse. Agents must be very careful to document any payments to themselves in case they are ever challenged about the appropriateness of the compensation or expense reimbursement.

QUESTIONS

In drafting a power of attorney for Maud, age 67, who is unmarried and has no children and wishes to appoint her long-time friend and neighbor, Dinah, age 69, as attorney-in-fact, would you include:

    a. A provision appointing a successor agent if Dinah is unable to act as Maud's agent?

    b. A requirement that Dinah complete an annual accounting of expenditures and income? To whom should the accounting be submitted?

    c. A requirement that Dinah have a co-signer if the transaction involves more than a specified amount of money?

    d. Permit Dinah to make gifts? Up to a specified limit? Only to charities? To herself?

[3] REVOCATION

A power of attorney, being a form of agency, may be revoked by a competent principal at any time by notifying the agent. A number of states have added requirements intended to assure that the attorney-in-fact and third parties will know if the power has been revoked. For example, N.C. Gen. Stat. § 32A-13 provides:

> (b) Every power of attorney executed pursuant to the provisions of this Article which has not been registered in an office of the register of deeds in this State shall be revoked by:
>
> (1) The death of the principal;
>
> (2) Any method provided in the power of attorney;
>
> (3) Being burnt, torn, canceled, obliterated, or destroyed with the intent and for the purpose of revoking it, by the principal himself or by another person in his presence and by his direction, while the principal is not incapacitated or mentally incompetent; or
>
> (4) A subsequent written revocatory document executed and acknowledged in the manner provided herein for the execution of durable powers of attorney by the principal while not incapacitated or mentally incompetent and delivered to the attorney-in-fact in person or to his last known address by certified or registered mail, return receipt requested.

Generally, a power is still effective if the attorney-in-fact is unaware it has been revoked. Until the agent has knowledge of the revocation, his or her acts on behalf of the principal are legally binding on the principal. Some state statutes exonerate third parities from liability if they in good faith accept the agent's apparent authority to act on behalf of the principal even if the power had been terminated by the principal.

QUESTION

Tara executed a durable power of attorney that, in the event of her mental incapacity, named her sister, Althea, as her agent. Tara had a stroke and was taken to the hospital where she remained for four weeks. Althea employed the power of attorney to sell Tara's car to a friend, Brad. When Tara left the hospital she asked about her car. Althea explained that she had sold it and used the proceeds to help pay Tara's considerable medical expenses. Tara protested, saying that since she was never mentally incapacitated, Althea had no right to use the power of attorney. Althea explained that Tara was very ill and in no state to make decisions. When Tara tried to reclaim the car from Brad, he refused. Does Tara have any legal remedy against Brad? Against Althea?

IN RE GUARDIANSHIP OF HOLLENGA
852 N.E.2d 933 (Ind. Ct. App. 2006)

BAILEY, JUDGE.

Appellant-Respondent Dorothy C. Hollenga ("Hollenga") and Appellant-Intervenor Daniel J. Cook ("Cook") appeal the trial court's orders granting Gene Stephen Harris ("Harris"), Greg Stewart ("Stewart"), and Janet Becker's ("Becker") (collectively "the Estate Guardians") petition to set aside Hollenga's power of attorney naming Cook as her attorney in fact. Hollenga also appeals the trial court's order authorizing the Estate Guardians to sell some of her real estate. We reverse and remand.

Issue

Hollenga and Cook frame the issue on appeal as whether the trial court erred by revoking Hollenga's durable power of attorney naming Cook as her attorney in fact; however, we conclude that the relevant issue is whether the trial court abused its discretion by naming the Estate Guardians as the guardians over Hollenga's estate, instead of Cook, who was Hollenga's nominated guardian in her power of attorney, when the trial court had already issued an order denying the Estate Guardians' petition to set aside Hollenga's power of attorney.

Facts and Procedural History

I. Background

Hollenga, who was born on January 28, 1920, is a reclusive, childless widow with an estate totaling approximately $900,000.00. Cook is a disabled former LPN. In 1998, Cook began living in a rental property, which was owned by Hollenga and located across the street from Hollenga's house. Cook helped Hollenga by mowing her yard, remodeling and maintaining her properties, and staying with her when she was sick and had requested him to come.

In late 2002, Cook helped Hollenga discover that she was being taken advantage of by her financial advisor, whom Hollenga had named her attorney in fact via the execution of a power of attorney, and Hollenga credited Cook with saving her from further financial loss. Hollenga lost approximately $70,000.00 as a result of her former financial advisor's actions. In December 2002 and May 2003, Hollenga recovered some of her funds that the financial advisor had transferred and purchased three annuities, all of which named Cook as her beneficiary. In January 2004, Hollenga purchased a fourth annuity and named Cook as a beneficiary.

On August 5, 2003, Hollenga's neighbor, Harris, and two of his friends from his church, Stewart and Becker, (collectively, "the Estate Guardians"), filed a petition for appointment of a guardianship over Hollenga's estate. That same day, the trial court appointed Robert S. Laszynski as the guardian ad litem ("the GAL").

On October 2, 2003, Hollenga, who was opposed to the guardianship petition, executed a durable power of attorney naming Cook as her attorney in fact and becoming effective "upon the determination by [her] treating physician that [she is] incompetent or incapacitated to such an extent as to affect [her] ability to govern [her] affairs[.]" Attorney Edward Kennedy ("Kennedy"), who prepared the power of attorney for Hollenga, explained each paragraph of the power of attorney and discussed reasons why she wanted Cook to be her attorney in fact. Kennedy testified that he believed that Hollenga was competent to sign the document. On October 13, 2003, Hollenga went back to Kennedy's office and executed a living will and a will, which left everything to Cook.

On October 23, 2003, the GAL interviewed Hollenga and filed a report with the trial court on November 7, 2003. On November 12, 2003, the Estate Guardians filed a petition to set aside Hollenga's power of attorney ("First Petition to Set Aside Power of Attorney"). In the petition, the Estate Guardians alleged that the GAL's report "substantiated the position" that Hollenga was "not capable of making sound financial decisions" and, further, that "it would be in the best interest of [Hollenga] to set aside the Power of Attorney until a final determination is made by the Court with regard to [Hollenga's] competence."

The trial court issued an order denying the Estate Guardians' First Petition to Set Aside Power of Attorney.

Thereafter, the Estate Guardians petitioned the trial court to appoint a temporary guardian over Hollenga's estate, and the trial court held a hearing on the petition on December 16, 2003. The trial court, upon finding that there was "no evidence that there is any likelihood of abuse" and "no evidence that there is in fact an emergency[,]" denied the Estate Guardians' petition for a temporary guardianship.

In February 2004, the trial court held a hearing on the Estate Guardians' original petition for the appointment of a guardianship over Hollenga's estate. On March 1, 2004, the trial court issued an order finding that Hollenga was "incapable of handling her property because of confusion about her financial affairs, her inability to manage, protect, and care for her property, and her susceptibility to undue influence." Thus, the trial court granted the petition for guardianship and appointed the Estate Guardians as co-guardians over Hollenga's estate ("Order Establishing the Estate Guardianship").

Following the establishment of the guardianship over Hollenga's estate, Hollenga's niece, Carol Griffin, and great-niece, Elizabeth Chavez, (collectively, "the Nieces") filed a petition for guardianship over Hollenga's person.

On May 23, 2005, Hollenga fell at her home and was hospitalized. On May 26, 2005, Hollenga's doctor determined that she was incapacitated; thus, her power of attorney became effective. On June 15, 2005, the Estate Guardians filed another petition to set aside Hollenga's power of attorney ("Second Petition to Set Aside Power of Attorney"), alleging that she was incompetent and under undue influence at the time she executed it.

On July 8, 2005, the trial court held a status conference, during which the Estate Guardians and the GAL expressed their concern that Cook as the attorney in fact "could make off with ten, fifteen, [or] twenty thousand dollars" of Hollenga's money and asked the trial court to take action on their Second Petition to Set Aside Power of Attorney. The trial court ruled that it was going to enter an "injunction type order" or temporary order "trumping the code" that would specifically preclude the Estate Guardians from making any disbursements to Cook until the court held a hearing on the matter. Thereafter, the trial court issued an order ("Order Disregarding Power of Attorney"), which provided that the Estate Guardians "are to disregard a certain Durable Power of Attorney executed by [Hollenga] on October 2, 2003 appointing Daniel J. Cook as [Hollenga's] Attorney of Fact until further Order of the Court."

Following the trial court's issuance of its Order Revoking Hollenga's Power of Attorney and Order to Sell Real Estate, Cook filed a motion to intervene. The trial court granted the Estate Guardians' Second Petition to Set Aside Power of Attorney; authorized the Estate Guardians to change the beneficiary on four annuities from Cook's name to Hollenga's estate; found that Cook was not fit to serve as guardian over Hollenga's person; and appointed the Nieces as guardians over Hollenga's person. Cook now appeals that order.

Discussion and Decision

The issue is whether the trial court abused it discretion by naming the Estate Guardians as the guardians over Hollenga's estate, instead of Cook, who was Hollenga's nominated guardian in her power of attorney, when the trial court had already issued an order denying the Estate Guardians' petition to set aside Hollenga's power of attorney.

In this appeal, the parties' arguments focus on the trial court's orders revoking Hollenga's power of attorney and whether Cook was entitled to notice of any challenge to Hollenga's power of attorney. However, prior to the time the trial court issued those orders revoking Hollenga's power of attorney, it had already denied the Estate Guardians' First Petition to Set Aside Power of Attorney and subsequently issued its Order Establishing the Estate Guardianship in which it established the guardianship over Hollenga's estate and named the Estate Guardians as co-guardians over the estate. Because the trial court's actions — naming the Estate Guardians as co-guardians over the estate and failing to name Cook as guardian when a durable power of attorney existed naming Cook as Hollenga's nomination for guardian — were contrary to Indiana Code Section 30-5-3-4, we address the trial court's Order Establishing the Estate Guardianship.

In a guardianship proceeding, the appointment of a guardian is guided by statute. Specifically, Indiana Code Section 29-3-5-3 provides that the trial court "shall appoint a guardian" if the trial court finds that: "(1) the individual for whom the guardian is sought is an incapacitated person or a minor; and (2) the appointment of a guardian is necessary as a means of providing care and supervision of the physical person or property of the incapacitated person or minor[.]" The trial court's discretion in appointing a guardian, however, is somewhat limited by Indiana Code Section 29-3-5-4 and Indiana Code Section 29-3-5-5. Indiana Code Section 29-3-5-5 sets forth the order of people that are entitled to consideration as guardian and lists "[a] person designated in a durable power of attorney" as the first person to be considered when appointing a guardian. Indiana

Code Section 29-3-5-4 provides, in part, that "[t]he court shall appoint as guardian a qualified person or persons most suitable and willing to serve, having due regard to . . . [a]ny request made by a person alleged to be an incapacitated person, *including designations in a durable power of attorney under IC 30-5-3-4(a).*" (emphasis added). Indiana Code Section 30-5-3-4 provides, "A principal may nominate a guardian for consideration by the court if protective proceedings for the principal's person or estate are commenced. The court *shall* make an appointment in accordance with the principal's most recent nomination in a power of attorney except for good cause or disqualification." Ind. Code § 30-5-3-4(a) (emphasis added). Thus, pursuant to these statutes, a person designated in a durable power of attorney is entitled to primary consideration as the person to be appointed as guardian and *shall* be appointed guardian unless good cause or disqualification is shown.

Here, after the Estate Guardians filed their petition for appointment of a guardianship over Hollenga's estate and prior to the establishment of the guardianship, Hollenga executed a power of attorney, which named Cook as her attorney in fact. At the time the trial court granted the petition to establish an estate guardianship, Hollenga's power of attorney was in existence and had not been revoked. Therefore, pursuant to Indiana Code Section 30-5-3-4(a), the trial court, upon establishing the guardianship over Hollenga's estate, was required to appoint Cook, who was Hollenga's most recent nomination in a power of attorney, as Hollenga's guardian, unless there was a showing of "good cause or disqualification." The trial court, however, appointed the Estate Guardians as co-guardians and did not make a finding that good cause had been shown or that Cook was disqualified. Because the trial court's actions were contrary to statute, we reverse the trial court's Order Establishing the Estate Guardianship.

Therefore, we remand with instructions to: (1) have the Estate Guardians file an accounting and inventory for Hollenga's estate; (2) remove the Estate Guardians as guardians over Hollenga's estate; and (3) appoint Cook as guardian over Hollenga's estate and person unless within thirty days there is a challenge as to "good cause or disqualification" of Cook pursuant to Indiana Code Section 30-5-3-4(a) and a subsequent determination of such by the trial court. We note that if a challenge to Cook's qualifications to serve as guardian is forthcoming, then the trial court should make that determination by conducting a hearing that complies with due process by providing notice and an opportunity to be heard to Cook to defend his power as attorney in fact.

Conclusion

For the foregoing reasons, we reverse the trial court's order appointing the Estate Guardians as the co-guardians over Hollenga's estate and remand to the trial court with instructions as described above.

Reversed and remanded.

QUESTIONS

1. Hollenga signed her power of attorney on October 13, 2003. The court-appointed guardian ad litem interviewed Hollenga on October 23, 2003. If you represented Hollenga, how would you exploit the different dates?

2. Why was guardianship for Hollenga sought? Is this case about protecting her from Cook? Why did her neighbor, Harris, and two of his friends file the petition to be appointed guardians of Hollenga's estate?

3. Why does Indiana law give priority for appointment as guardian to the person designated in the durable power of attorney?

If a guardian is appointed for an individual who had previously executed a valid power of attorney, the question arises whether the power of attorney remains valid. The answer depends upon state law. South Carolina provides:

> The appointment of an attorney-in-fact under this section does not prevent a person or his representative from applying to the court and having a guardian or conservator appointed. Unless the power of attorney provides otherwise, appointment of a guardian terminates all or part of the power of attorney that relates to matters within the scope of the guardianship, and appointment of a conservator terminates all or part of the power of attorney that relates to matters within the scope of the conservatorship.

S.C. CODE ANN. § 62-5-501(B).

Connecticut's statute terminates a power of attorney if a conservator of the principal's estate is appointed and requires that the attorney-in-fact provide an accounting to the conservator, rather than to the principal. CONN. GEN. STAT. § 45a-562. In Maine, the agent's authority continues unless it is limited, suspended, or terminated by the court. ME. REV. STAT. ANN. tit. 18 § 5-908(b).

QUESTIONS

Why does the South Carolina statute terminate the power of the agent upon the appointment of a guardian? Why does the Maine statute not do so unless the court specifically does so? Which is the better rule?

Conversely, under some guardianship statutes the existence of an attorney-in-fact may prevent the appointment of a guardian. If the statute conditions appointment on a finding that the prospective ward is incapable of caring for himself or his property and needs a guardian in order to meet his basic needs or protect property from dissipation, and if the attorney-in-fact has the power to meet those needs, the appointment of a guardian may be unnecessary.

[4]   DETERMINING INCAPACITY: "SPRINGING" POWERS

Unless otherwise stated, a power of attorney becomes effective when it is executed, with the result that the principal and agent are capable of exercising the authorized powers simultaneously. This may be contrary to the intent of the principal and potentially confusing to third parties if the power is intended for use only during periods of incapacity. To forestall the agent from acting under the power, the principal can retain possession of the power (and all signed copies), since no third party should permit someone without a signed power of attorney to assert a valid agency. If the principal becomes incapacitated, the agent will take possession of the document and begin to act in accordance with its powers. For example, Arthur names his daughter, Alice, as his agent. One day, Arthur has a stroke and is taken to the hospital. Alice, who knows of the power, finds it in Arthur's files and uses it to deposit his pension check, pay his bills, and arrange for the maintenance of his house. Later, when Arthur recovers, Alice returns the signed copy of the power of attorney to him since he is capable of handling his affairs.

Some persons do not feel comfortable signing a power of attorney that takes effect immediately. They prefer to use a "springing power of attorney." Most state statutes allow the power of attorney to become effective upon the incapacity of the principal, i.e., to "spring" into being upon the fulfillment of this conditional event. While the use of springing powers eliminates the problems of overlapping authority of a competent principal and the agent, it raises another: the question of when the principal is to be considered incapacitated. The power should describe who determines if the principal is incapacitated. For example, the power might require a finding by a physician that the principal is incapacitated before the power "springs" into being. However, if the determination is too time-consuming or too expensive, much of the benefit of the power of attorney over guardianship would be lost.

Moreover, determination of mental incapacity is not an all-or-nothing proposition. Because many individuals suffer a gradual decline of mental ability, it may be difficult to determine just when they should no longer be permitted to handle their own affairs. Other individuals experience fluctuations in their mental capacity so that they may be quite capable in the morning but incapacitated by afternoon. Consequently, a springing power must contain some standard or procedure to determine when the principal is sufficiently incapacitated. The drafter of the springing power of attorney should consider carefully, in consultation with the client, how to establish the simplest means to make a reliable determination that will avoid disputes or costly litigation as to when the agent can act under the power of attorney. Because the principal may regain capacity, the document should also provide a triggering mechanism to terminate the agent's power, short of revocation of the power by the principal. Because of the potential problems raised by triggering the power of attorney, most attorneys recommend that the principal not use a springing power of attorney except under special circumstances.

QUESTIONS

1.   Other than the use of a springing power of attorney, what practical methods could you employ to delay the beginning of the agent's authority until the beginning of incapacity?

2.   Should family members be notified if the agent intends to activate a springing power? Should interested parties have the right to ask for judicial review of the appropriateness of the action?

3.   Suppose you are the attorney for Juliet who has signed a power of attorney that names her niece, Mary, as her agent. Juliet has left all signed copies of the power with you to release if she needs an agent to handle her financial affairs. One day, Mary calls you up and tells you that Juliet's accountant called Mary and told her that he needs Mary to sign Juliet's federal income tax return because he thinks that Juliet seems very confused and forgetful and does not understand what the document is. Should you release the power to Mary? If not, what should you do?

[5] SCOPE AND USE OF THE POWER

A general power of attorney authorizes the holder to undertake the broadest range of transactions on behalf of the principal. For example, S.C. CODE ANN. § 62-5-501(A) provides:

> The authority of the attorney in fact to act on behalf of the principal must be set forth in the power and may relate to any act, power, duty, right, or obligation which the principal has or may acquire relating to the principal or any matter, transaction, or property, including the power to consent or withhold consent on behalf of the principal to health care.

Other states provide a specific list that can be delegated to the agent. In Pennsylvania, the following powers may be included in the power of attorney:

(1) To make limited gifts.

(2) To create a trust for my benefit.

(3) To make additions to an existing trust for my benefit.

(4) To claim an elective share of the estate of my deceased spouse.

(5) To disclaim any interest in property.

(6) To renounce fiduciary positions.

(7) To withdraw and receive the income or corpus of a trust.

(8) To authorize my admission to a medical, nursing, residential or similar facility and to enter into agreements for my care.

(9) To authorize medical and surgical procedures.

(10) To engage in real property transactions.

(11) To engage in tangible personal property transactions.

(12) To engage in stock, bond and other securities transactions.

(13) To engage in commodity and option transactions.

(14) To engage in banking and financial transactions.

(15) To borrow money.

(16) To enter safe deposit boxes.

(17) To engage in insurance transactions.

(18) To engage in retirement plan transactions.

(19) To handle interests in estates and trusts.

(20) To pursue claims and litigation.

(21) To receive government benefits.

(22) To pursue tax matters.

(23) To make an anatomical gift of all or part of my body.

. . . .

20 PA. CONS. STAT. § 5602

If the power of attorney is created with a particular transaction in mind, it is prudent to specify the scope of powers necessary to complete it since some types of powers are presumed to be omitted unless they are specified.

QUESTIONS

1. Are there any powers listed in the Pennsylvania statute that you would hesitate to include in a power of attorney?

2. Are there any types of powers that should not be granted to the agent under any condition? Would your answer depend on the relationship of the agent to the principal?

3. If a state statute neither lists particular powers that can be exercised under a general power of attorney nor forbids exercise of any power, what specific powers would you list in the form you are preparing for standard use in your office?

Frequently, the principal merely uses a standard form of a power of attorney that authorizes very broad powers. The need for the principal to take care to delegate the proper powers to the agent is demonstrated by the following case.

IN RE ESTATE OF KURRELMEYER
895 A.2d 207 (Vt. 2006)

JUDGE BURGESS.

Martina Kurrelmeyer appeals an order of the Chittenden Superior Court declaring void, as a matter of law, the revocable inter vivos trust she created under her husband's durable power of attorney prior to his death. Mr. Kurrelmeyer's surviving children claimed the power of attorney did not grant authority to create a trust and that transfer of Mr. Kurrelmeyer's property to the trust constituted unauthorized self-dealing and a breach of Martina Kurrelmeyer's fiduciary duty as her husband's agent. We reverse the superior court's determination that the trust is void as a matter of law, and remand for further proceedings to determine whether Martina Kurrelmeyer's actions breached her fiduciary duty of loyalty as her husband's agent.

The undisputed facts are summarized as follows. In 1996, Louis Kurrelmeyer executed two durable general powers of attorney to appoint his wife, Martina Kurrelmeyer, and his daughter, Nancy Kurrelmeyer, as attorneys-in-fact. Louis Kurrelmeyer was competent at the time he executed the powers of attorney. In December of 2000, Martina, pursuant to her powers under the durable power of attorney, executed a document establishing the "Louis H. Kurrelmeyer Living Trust," with herself and Nancy as co-trustees. Days after she created the trust, Martina transferred certain real estate owned by her husband, the "Clearwater" property, to herself and Nancy as co-trustees of the trust. At the time of the creation of the living trust and the transfer of the Clearwater property, Louis Kurrelmeyer was no longer competent. Mr. Kurrelmeyer died testate a year later, and Martina was appointed executrix of his estate.

Louis Kurrelmeyer's last will and testament, executed in 1980, contained a specific provision for the Clearwater property. Under the will, Martina would take a life estate in the property, with responsibility for taxes and upkeep, and upon her death the property would pass to Mr. Kurrelmeyer's surviving children as joint tenants with rights of survivorship. In contrast, the terms of the trust provide Martina additional rights with regard to the property. Under the terms of the trust, Martina may occupy the home as long as she wishes and the trust is permitted to pay the expenses on the property should she fail to do so. The trustees would be required, however, on Martina's unilateral request, to sell the home, with the sale proceeds to be used either to purchase another home for Martina or, alternatively, to be added to the trust principal. Additionally, the trust provides that all income from the trust property would be paid to Martina, as well as so much of the principal as the trustees deem necessary and proper for her support. Upon Martina's death, the trust principal would be distributed to Louis's children, if they survived him, with any deceased child's share to be distributed to that child's descendants or held in trust until such descendants reached the age of twenty-five. The trust requires that there be at least one other trustee serving so long as Martina is serving as a co-trustee, and the co-trustees must act by mutual agreement.

During the probate administration of Louis Kurrelmeyer's estate, his son, Louis Kurrelmeyer Jr., objected to the exclusion of the Clearwater property from the inventory completed by Martina Kurrelmeyer. Claiming that Martina exceeded her authority in creating the trust, Louis Jr. asked the probate court to set aside the trust and include the Clearwater property in the probate estate to be distributed in accordance with Mr. Kurrelmeyer's will. The probate court upheld the trust, and the children appealed to the superior court.

Martina Kurrelmeyer moved for summary judgment, arguing the creation of the trust and transfer of the Clearwater property to the trust were authorized under the broad authority granted to her by the durable power of attorney. The children moved for a judgment in their favor, arguing that the power of attorney did not authorize creation of a revocable trust, that the transfer of the Clearwater property to the trust was a breach of Martina's fiduciary duty because it constituted self-dealing, and that the transfer violated the gift-giving proscription of the power of attorney.

The superior court reversed the probate court's order. Granting summary judgment for the children, the superior court concluded that the power of attorney did not authorize Martina to create a trust. The court found the power of attorney ambiguous on the trust issue, and narrowly construed the language to authorize only maintenance of, and additions to, trusts already existing when the power of attorney came into being. The superior court also opined that, because the appointment of Martina as attorney-in-fact did not authorize her to make a will on behalf of the principal, she was without authority to convey his property in trust in a manner that would "alter" his existing will. . . .

. . . .

I.

We first address Martina's claim that the trial court erred in concluding as a matter of law that the power of attorney did not authorize her to create a trust on Louis Kurrelmeyer's behalf. We disagree with the superior court's characterization of the power of attorney as ambiguous, and find that the express language of the power of attorney authorized the attorney-in-fact to create a trust. . . . Accordingly, we will not apply a rule of narrow construction to particular words and phrases used in the power of attorney, but will examine the express terms and the context of the instrument as a whole to give effect to the principal's intent.

To determine whether the power of attorney authorized Martina to create a trust, we look to Mr. Kurrelmeyer's "written authorization," entitled "Durable General Power of Attorney." As its title suggests, this power of attorney is indeed "general" and quite broad. The power of attorney was to survive, and be unaffected by, the principal's subsequent disability or incompetence. It authorizes Martina, as attorney-in-fact, to act in the principal's name "in any way which I myself could do, if I were personally present, with respect to the following matters to the extent that I am permitted by law to act through an agent." Among the delineated powers, the first subsection authorizes the agent "[t]o add all of my assets deemed appropriate by my said attorney to any trust of which I am the Donor" by transferring in trust a variety of types of property, including stocks, bonds, bank accounts, real estate, and "other assets or property of any kind" owned by the principal. The subsection immediately following provides:

> In *addition*, I authorize my said attorney to: (i) *execute and deliver any assignments, stock powers, deeds or trust instruments*; (ii) sign my name to any instrument pertaining to or required in connection with the transfer of my property; (iii) give full receipts and discharges; (iv) re-register the title to stock certificates, bonds, notes, bills and other securities; (v) change the name on bank, brokerage and commodity accounts; (vi) withdraw any or all

funds standing in my name in any bank; (vii) endorse and deliver any checks, drafts, certificates of deposit, notes or other instruments for the payment of money payable or belonging to me; (viii) change life insurance beneficiaries . . . (ix) elect lump sum or optional settlements of life insurance . . . and annuity proceeds and proceeds from a qualified plan or an individual retirement account; (x) convey any real estate, interest in real estate, any mortgages and notes or any beneficial interest in real estate which I may own or have any interest in; and (xi) record deeds of conveyance in the appropriate land records.

(Emphasis supplied.) The text continues, authorizing the attorney-in-fact to examine and obtain copies of the principal's will. The attorney is authorized to "make gifts to members of my family (other than himself or herself) whom my said attorney has reason to believe I would have wished to benefit, but my said attorney shall not give any more than $10,000.00 per year to any one donee." Among other powers, the attorney-in-fact is also granted unrestricted access to, and an unrestricted right to remove, the contents from "any and all warehouses, safe deposit boxes, drawers, and vaults" owned in the principal's name alone and in common with others. The attorney-in-fact is authorized to disclaim interests in property on behalf of the principal, to convey title to his motor vehicles, to "convey any and all real estate owned by [the principal] to any person or entity," and, finally, the attorney-in-fact is authorized

> [t]o do and perform all and every act and thing whatsoever necessary to be done in the premises, as fully to all intents and purposes as I might or could do if personally present, with full power of substitution and revocation, hereby ratifying and confirming all that my said attorney may do pursuant to this power.

We conclude that the express terms of the power of attorney unambiguously grant the attorney-in-fact the authority to create a trust and to add assets to a trust to accomplish estate planning objectives. The first subsection, empowering the attorney to add any and all assets to a trust of which he is the donor, does refer to a trust already in existence, but does not suggest lack of authority to create a new trust when considered together with the second subsection — granting the power "to execute and deliver . . . trust instruments" expressly in *addition* to adding assets to existing trusts. . . . Given the express language granting the authority to execute trust instruments, particularly in the context of the breadth of the attorney's other express powers, including, ultimately, her authority to fully substitute herself for the principal to do all things "whatsoever necessary . . . to all intents and purposes" as the principal "might or could do if personally present," we find that the agent's authority under this power of attorney includes the authority to create a trust on the principal's behalf.

II.

Alternatively, the children argue that, even if the principal intended to authorize the attorney-in-fact to create a trust, the power to create a trust is personal to the settlor and nondelegable as a matter of law. We agree that certain acts may require personal performance as a matter of public policy, statutory law, or under the terms of an agreement. . . . We do not agree, however, that delegation of authority to create a trust through a durable general power of attorney to serve the interests of the principal violates public policy as a matter of law, even when a trust's dispositive terms may serve a function similar to that of a will.

. . . .

We find unpersuasive and inapposite the cases cited by the children in support of their position that the power to create a trust is nondelegable. The courts in those cases found that the powers of attorney did not expressly authorize the agent to create a trust, which, as we hold above in Section I, is not the case with this power of attorney. . . .

For the same reason that trusts can be beneficial to an estate, we are not persuaded on the current record that this trust is necessarily an invalid usurpation of the principal's last will and testament. The trial court was concerned that, by conveying Clearwater to the trust, Martina did "indirectly what she [could] not do directly," that is, alter the will by depriving the children of their expected inheritance of Clearwater's appreciation. When the principal expressly granted his attorney-in-fact the power to convey realty from his estate, he must have anticipated that the terms of his will might be so altered. It is not clear, then, why conveyance of Clearwater to a trust would be a per se impermissible alteration of the will, when the power of attorney expressly authorized Martina to convey any real estate outright to others. Therefore, these additional arguments do not persuade us that the trust must be rendered void as a matter of public policy.

III.

The question of whether Martina's actions breached her fiduciary duties remains. Even though we conclude that Martina had authority from her principal to create a trust on his behalf, her authority to act under that power was not limitless. A fiduciary duty of loyalty is implied in every agency as a matter of law. . . . The attorney-in-fact was prohibited from making gifts to herself by the express language of the power of attorney and was also prohibited from using the agency for her own benefit or the benefit of others except as authorized.

The children complained below that Martina's conveyance of the Clearwater property to the trust provided no benefit to Louis Kurrelmeyer, served no apparent tax or estate planning purpose, and was prohibited by the gifting provision of the power of attorney as well as by Martina's fiduciary duty of loyalty to her principal. Martina argued, in response, that the trust and conveyance were justified by generally recognized and prudent tax and estate planning objectives, that the conveyance of Clearwater to the trust could not, as a matter of law, constitute a gift prohibited by the power of attorney, and that the co-trustee approval requirement was a safeguard against any self-dealing.

. . . . Despite recitations in their cross-motions for summary judgment, the parties do not appear to agree upon facts material either to Martina's contention that the dispositive terms of the trust and the conveyance of the Clearwater property were justified as prudent estate planning or to the children's contentions that the terms of the trust and the transfer of property were unauthorized self-dealing.

Therefore, we remand the case to the superior court for further proceedings to consider whether there was a breach of a fiduciary duty on the part of Martina Kurrelmeyer, as agent, in light of all the relevant circumstances at the time the trust was executed.

---

[a]   Gifts by the Agent

Among the powers that can be granted to an agent under a power of attorney is the power to make gifts. In some states the power to make gifts is implicitly granted, but in most states the power of attorney must explicitly grant the agent the authority to make gifts. There are several reasons why a principal might include the power to make gifts. The principal may want the agent to make gifts in order to continue a pattern of estate depletion that is intended to minimize or avoid federal estate taxes or state death taxes. Some principals want the agent to be able to assist relatives of the principal, such as a grandchild who needs financial assistance in order to attend college. Finally, the principal may want the agent to make gifts as part of a plan designed to create Medicaid eligibility for the principal. Regardless of the reason for granting a power to make gifts, the principal must decide whether the agent can make the gifts alone or must seek the approval of another party, whether the agent can make gifts to him or herself or to his or her immediate family, and whether to place any limits on the amount of the gift.

Even if the agent can make gifts, the propriety of any gifts by the agent is subject to a fiduciary standard because of the agency relationship between the attorney-in-fact and the principal. As a fiduciary, the agent is bound by common law principles including a duty of loyalty and the obligation to act exclusively in the best interests of the principal. The state statute that grants authority for a power of attorney may list additional or more specific duties of the agent.

Granting the agent a power to make gifts creates the risk the agent may misuse or abuse the power.

MOWRER v. EDDIE
979 P.2d 156 (Mont. 1999)

JUDGE WARNER.

Clara Mowrer was born September 13, 1894. She lived in Kansas until August of 1995, when she was brought to Montana by her niece, Peggy Eddie, and her niece's husband, Maurice Eddie. She has remained in Montana and now lives at a care facility in Kalispell.

Mowrer fell and broke her hip in June of 1995. She was hospitalized for about two months. The day before she was released from the hospital, Peggy Eddie arrived in Kansas. Maurice Eddie arrived in Kansas shortly thereafter. Mowrer was released from the hospital in late July 1995 and returned home. The Eddies stayed with her in her home.

On August 5, 1995, Mowrer executed a durable power of attorney to the Eddies at her attorney's office in Kansas. That same day, several of Mower's bank accounts were closed, and the funds transferred to the Eddies. Other assets, including cash and certificates of deposit, were also transferred to the Eddies.

The Eddies brought Mowrer to Montana in late August of 1995. Before the end of that year, $594,715.00 of Mowrer's assets had been transferred to Peggy and Maurice Eddie by means of the power of attorney and upon Mowrer's signature. In addition, in September of 1995, Maurice Eddie received cashier's checks in the amount of $99,950.00, from certificates of deposit that had been owned by Mowrer.

In the fall of 1995, the Eddies took stock certificates with a value in excess of $300,000.00 from Mowrer's safety deposit box in Kansas, brought them to Montana, and made arrangements with a broker for the transfer of such stock to themselves on the death of Mowrer.

In October of 1995, Maurice Eddie consulted attorney James Johnson, a partner of Gary Christiansen, concerning Mowrer making a new will and filing a gift tax return. Near the end of this meeting Johnson and Maurice Eddie also discussed a possible estate plan for the Eddies. An appointment was made to return to Johnson's office with Mowrer. That appointment was not kept. Later, the Eddies took Mowrer to an attorney in Kalispell who had previously represented them and their family. This attorney prepared, and Mowrer signed, a new will that left all of her property to the Eddies. This new will excluded her other nieces, nephews, long-time friends, and charitable organizations to which she had bequeathed property in prior wills.

The Eddies used their power of attorney to spend Mowrer's money on living expenses and to acquire land, remodel their home, travel, and make gifts to their son and grandson. They also spent some of Mowrer's funds that are not accounted for.

During 1995, 1996 and until February, 1997, Mowrer lived with the Eddies. She then moved to the BeeHive care facility in Kalispell, where she still lives. On May 16, 1997, Mowrer revoked the power of attorney to the Eddies. Her counsel, Gary Christiansen, wrote the Eddies a letter demanding an accounting.

On June 19, 1997, Eddies filed a petition to be appointed guardians and conservators of Mowrer. She responded by resisting the appointment of either a guardian or conservator, and counterclaimed for an accounting. Substantial discovery was undertaken. The trial took seven different days between December 22, 1997, and March 10, 1998. On July 27, 1998, the District Court entered its Findings of Fact, Conclusions of Law and Judgment. The court found that Mowrer was competent, did not need a guardian or conservator, had not made gifts to the Eddies and that the transfers to the Eddies had been the result of duress and undue influence. The court ordered the Eddies to repay $807,582.44 to Mowrer, and imposed a trust on certain real property owned by Eddies to secure the judgment. Eddies' motion for new trial was denied September 22, 1998, and they appeal from such denial.

[The Supreme Court upheld the findings of the lower court that reversed the transfers to the Eddies as being obtained by fraud, undue influence and abuse of the power of attorney.]

QUESTION

If the principal wishes to permit the agent to make gifts, would you advise limiting the power to make gifts in any way? If so, how?

[b] Safe Deposit Box Access

The right of the agent to enter the principal's safe deposit box has proved to be a thorny problem in many states. Sometimes the original power of attorney document is kept in the grantor's safe deposit box. If the agent does not also have an original of the document which explicitly authorizes entry, the bank cannot authorize access to the contents of the box. Even holders of an original, duly executed power have been refused admission by banking institutions seeking to protect their own interests and those of their box holders. This suggests that the principal should not keep the power of attorney in a safe deposit box, but rather in a file or location accessible by the agent.

[c] Other Issues

The principal drawback to the use of a power of attorney is the difficulty of getting third parties to accept the agent's authority to act. Unless required by statute, third parties are usually under no obligation to recognize the authority of the agent. Banks, insurance companies, and stockbrokers very often require the use of their own power of attorney forms and refuse to recognize the validity of any other form. In addition, many third parties, particularly insurance companies, are reluctant to accept a power of attorney which is several years old since the passage of time leaves room for doubt about its current validity.

Faced with the reluctance of third parties to honor a power of attorney, several states have enacted statutes that impose penalties on those who refuse to deal with an agent acting under a valid power of attorney. For example, the Florida statute provides:

> In any judicial action under this section, including, but not limited to, the unreasonable refusal of a third party to allow an attorney in fact to act pursuant to the power, and challenges to the proper exercise of authority by the attorney in fact, the prevailing party is entitled to damages and costs, including reasonable attorney's fees.

FLA. STAT. ANN. § 709.08(11).

QUESTIONS

1. Will the Florida statute offer much help if the local bank manager refuses to let the agent access the bank account of the principal? What would you advise the agent to do?

2. How can you avoid the problems of "staleness," i.e., having the power of attorney rejected because it is considered too old to be reliable? What language would you add to a document to help assure that a durable power created several years ago will be accepted?

The agent's role as a fiduciary requires acting in good faith, intending to bring no harm to the principal, and avoiding acting out of self-interest. Traditionally, however, there is little oversight to ensure that those duties are fulfilled. In response to complaints about abusive or negligent agents, a number of states have enacted statutes that require periodic accountings. For example, North Carolina's statute provides:

§ 32A-11. File with clerk, records, inventories, accounts, fees, and commissions.

(a) Within 30 days after registration of the power of attorney as provided in G.S. 32A-9(b), the attorney-in-fact shall file with the clerk of superior court in the county of such registration a copy of the power of attorney. Every attorney-in-fact acting under a power of attorney under this Article subsequent to the principal's incapacity or mental incompetence shall keep full and accurate records of all transactions in which he acts as agent of the principal and of all property of the principal in his hands and the disposition thereof.

(b) Any provision in the power of attorney waiving or requiring the rendering of inventories and accounts shall govern, and a power of attorney that waives the requirement to file inventories and accounts need not be filed with the clerk of superior court. Otherwise, subsequent to the principal's incapacity or mental incompetence, the attorney-in-fact shall file in the office of the clerk of the superior court of the county in which the power of attorney is filed, inventories of the property of the principal in his hands and annual and final accounts of the receipt and disposition of property of the principal and of other transactions in behalf of the principal. . . . If the powers of an attorney-in-fact shall terminate for any reason whatever, he, or his executors or administrators, shall have the right to have a judicial settlement of a final account by any procedure available to executors, administrators or guardians.

QUESTION

1. The provisions of the North Carolina statute require accountings to the clerk and provide for fees for services of the attorney-in-fact. How does a power of attorney under this statute differ from accounting requirements under a plenary guardianship?

2. If the principal does not reside in a state, like North Carolina, that requires an accounting, what should be done to monitor an agent's actions to insure that she has acted honestly, in good faith and competently?

B. JOINT OWNERSHIP

Many older persons use various types of joint ownership arrangements to help them manage their assets, particularly real property and bank or brokerage accounts. While popular, joint ownership often creates significant legal problems, either because the legal rights of the parties are ambiguous or because the parties did not understand the legal consequences of their acts. Still, in many cases the use of joint ownership is an effective means of providing property management for an incapacitated person.

The most common form of joint ownership is the tenancy in common, which creates ownership interests in property in two or more individuals. When property is held jointly but the nature of the interest is not specified, many state statutes create a presumption that the owners are tenants in common who own equal shares. Most tenancies in common, however, are created by a deed or testamentary will in which the proportional ownership interests are specifically stated. None of the owners have a right of survivorship to the others (i.e., to inherit another's share upon the owner's death). Rather, the deceased individual's share is passed by will or intestate succession. Any tenant who is a common owner can sell his or her interest in the property without permission of the other owners so there is no need for an order of partition. In reality, finding a buyer for a partial interest in commonly held real estate is difficult and so sales to third parties are uncommon. The tenants in common may hold unequal shares with their degree of ownership specified in the document. While real property is sometimes held in unequal share, bank accounts are typically owned in proportion to the number of account holders.

The other common form of multiple ownership is a joint tenancy with right of survivorship. Normally it is created by a written instrument providing each owner (there may be two or more) with equal ownership interests and a right of survivorship. That is, when one joint owner dies, the other(s) inherit the deceased owner's interest. The jointly owned property is not part of the probate estate and its disposition is not controlled by the decedent's will. It automatically passes to the surviving owners. A creditor of a joint tenant has no rights to collect against the joint property after the death of the joint tenant, since the tenant's rights in the property were extinguished at death. During their lives, joint tenants can sever the joint tenancy and defeat the survivorship interest of the other owners by selling or giving away their ownership interest. The new owners become tenants in common with the previous owners. For example, Adam and Carl are joint owners with right of survivorship of Greenacre. Adam sells his half interest to his niece, Norma. The result is a tenancy in common between Carl and Norma.

Husbands and wives often own property jointly with the right of survivorship. (In some states, joint ownership by spouses is known as a tenancy by the entirety, a form of ownership that cannot be dissolved unless agreed to by both parties.) Typically, spousal bank accounts and brokerage accounts are held as joint tenants, which allows either of them to manage the accounts should the other become mentally or physically incapacitated. So long as there is complete trust between the spouses, this arrangement is an ideal informal solution to managing the assets. If the property is owned jointly with right of survivorship, on the death of one of the spouses the survivor takes ownership and possession of the property with no need to wait for probate.

An older client without a spouse is sometimes tempted to place property into joint ownership with a child or other trusted relative or friend. Unfortunately, the documents used to create joint bank accounts are often confusing as to respective ownership rights of the account holders. Frequently, the older person who opens the account does not intend to grant ownership rights to the other person whose name is on the account. Often they only want to create joint ownership of bank accounts or certificates of deposit to create a "convenience" account, which will permit the younger co-owner to manage the money for the benefit of the older person, e.g., deposit funds and withdraw money to pay bills. Although the use of such an account is understandable, it can lead to several problems. For example, can the donee (the person other than the older person who funded the account) take out money for his or her benefit? Can the creditors of the donee reach the account? Upon the death of the older person, does the survivor inherit the account or do the funds in the account (all or half) belong to the estate of the deceased account holder? These questions of ownership, coupled with danger that the joint tenant may abscond with the funds, cause many attorneys to advise against the use of joint accounts with anyone other than a spouse.

Despite the misgivings of attorneys, joint bank accounts are very popular as informal means of creating a form of proxy money management. A joint account is quick to create, inexpensive to maintain, and straightforward to manage, particularly with the direct deposit of benefit and pension checks. The convenience, however, must be weighed against the risk of the joint owner withdrawing the funds for his own benefit.

KITCHEN v. GUARISCO
811 So. 2d 112 (La. Ct. App. 2002)

JUDGE MURRAY.

This suit was commenced by Caroline Werling Kitchen in her capacity as administratrix of the successions of Sophie Cunningham widow of/and Alvin Louis Werling. Although Mr. Werling died on August 8, 1982, his succession was not opened until after Mrs. Werling died in August 1994. During their marriage, Mr. and Mrs. Werling had three children: one son (who is not a party to this dispute) and two daughters, Ms. Guarisco (the defendant) and Ms. Kitchen (the plaintiff-succession administratrix).

On February 9, 1990, Mrs. Werling and Ms. Guarisco opened four identical certificates of deposit at Whitney National Bank. Each certificate was in the amount of $1,000.00 and was issued in the names of Mrs. Werling and Ms. Guarisco. On July 1, 1994, Mrs. Werling and Ms. Guarisco opened another certificate of deposit at the Whitney in the amount of $4,536.18 and in the names of Mrs. Werling "or" Ms. Guarisco.

During this same period, Mrs. Werling and Ms. Guarisco also opened a checking account together at the Whitney in the names of Mrs. Werling "or" Ms. Guarisco.

This balance in this account on June 30, 1993, was established at trial to be $5,824.52. Mrs. Werling also had a personal checking account at First National Bank of Commerce ("FNBC") that was solely in her name. On both August 4 and 5, 1994, Mrs. Werling wrote a check from that account payable to Ms. Guarisco in the amounts of $2,000.00 and $1,500.00, respectively. On each check, Mrs. Werling noted the purpose to be for bills.

On August 7, 1994, Mrs. Werling died. Shortly thereafter, Ms. Kitchen became administratrix of the successions of both her parents, Mr. and Mrs. Werling. In that capacity, she learned that on February 24, 1995, her sister, Ms. Guarisco, cashed in the five certificates of deposit and the checking account at the Whitney Bank that had been opened in the names of both Ms. Guarisco and Mrs. Werling. After unsuccessfully requesting that Ms. Guarisco return the funds she withdrew from those accounts to the estate, Ms. Kitchen, in her capacity as administratrix, commenced this suit.

Following a trial on the merits, the trial court found the accounts in question belonged to the decedent, Mrs. Werling, and that the proceeds of the accounts were properly included in the gross patrimony of the decedent's estate. The trial court thus rendered judgment against the defendant in the amount of $26,335.35, plus legal interest and costs. The trial court further ordered that plaintiff, as succession representative, could deduct from any succession proceeds owed to defendant any sums due plaintiff as a result of this judgment. From that judgment, Ms. Guarisco appeals.

This case presents solely a factual issue of ownership of funds withdrawn from various bank accounts. . . .

Defendant argues that the trial court erred in finding plaintiff's hearsay testimony regarding the source of the funds in the accounts credible. Defendant further argues that as the party seeking to establish ownership of the funds, plaintiff had the burden of proof and that plaintiff failed to meet that burden. We disagree.

As the trial court noted in its written reasons, plaintiff established at trial that the Whitney Bank accounts in question shared the following features: (i) the accounts were all in the names of Sophie C. Werling and Vivian W. Guarisco; (ii) the accounts all listed the decedent's name as the lead name; (iii) the accounts all bore the decedent's Social Security number as the federal tax identification number; (iv) all the 1099 statements on the accounts were sent to decedent's home address; (v) the decedent reported all the interest income on the accounts on her tax returns; and (vi) the accounts all listed as the owner/contact address decedent's home address. Based on these factors, the trial court determined that the "decedent consistently treated these accounts as her own from the time the accounts were opened until her death." We agree, and we add that plaintiff's establishment of these factors sufficed to shift the burden to defendant.

In finding defendant failed to offer any evidence that the money belonged to her, the trial court stressed defendant's failure to offer any explanation as to the source of the funds used to establish the accounts. At trial, defendant simply testified that the money in the account was her money. When asked why she opened these accounts with the decedent, defendant responded:

> I was a single parent, and I had no one to take care of my daughter if anything happened to me. And, my mother did not feel comfortable getting into a legal situation with all kinds of documentation. And, at the same time my mother was not well. I was taking care of her as best I could. And, it was just easier for us to place this money and take the money I had, place it into an account with both our names on it. . . . It was set up so that [my mother] would have access to something if something happened to me. I had no one to take over any of my things or to manage my daughter. And, my daughter was still in college at that time. So, that's why we set up the accounts and that's why my name was on them. And, it was my money originally. . . ."

The trial court contrasted defendant's testimony, which it found "vague" and "self serving," with plaintiff's testimony, which it found "detailed" and "credible." Particularly, the trial court noted that plaintiff testified the decedent told her the money in the account was hers and that the source of the money was two-fold: (1) from Mrs. Werling's predeceased husband, and (2) from Ms. Werling's severance package from D.H. Holmes, where she was a long-time employee. As to the latter, plaintiff indicated that her mother received stock and had converted some of the stock. The trial court thus held that the funds in the accounts belonged to the decedent's estate. We hold that factual finding was reasonable and thus not manifestly erroneous.

Bank accounts with more than one name listed as "owner" often create confusion as to the rights of the various parties.

Some jurisdictions attempt to distinguish joint accounts from "convenience type" accounts that the depositor did not intend to create rights of ownership in the other named joint account holder.

New Jersey grants the Commissioner of Banking authority to prescribe, by rule or regulation, the form and content of deposit contracts to assure that each contract bears out the intentions of the persons named on the account. Other jurisdictions have "conclusive evidence" so that the creation of an account in the form set out in the statute serves as conclusive evidence that a right of survivorship was created.

The creation of joint accounts can lead to an allegation of constructive fraud.

FORBIS v. NEAL
649 S.E.2d 382 (N.C. 2007)

Martin, Justice.

This case arises from a dispute over the assets of Bonnie Sustare Newell (Newell) and her sister Augusta Lee Sustare (Sustare). LaMarr Garland Forbis, Newell and Sustare's niece, brought a fraud action on behalf of her aunts' estates against Beverly Lee Neal (defendant), her first cousin and the nephew of Newell and Sustare. The trial court granted summary judgment for defendant, and the Court of Appeals affirmed. We affirm in part, reverse in part, and remand with instructions.

During the 1990s, Newell and Sustare resided in an assisted living facility in Matthews, North Carolina. Sustare had spent her working years as a hair stylist, and Newell had worked at various jobs in insurance and real estate. When they entered the assisted living facility, neither sister had been a member of the workforce for approximately twenty years. Their nephew, defendant, was a licensed real estate broker who held a bachelor's degree from the University of Georgia and a Masters of Business Administration degree from the University of Utah.

On 5 November 1991, both sisters executed powers of attorney designating defendant as their attorney-in-fact. The powers of attorney authorized defendant to act for each sister with respect to real and personal property transactions, banking, taxes, and similar transactions. Neither power of attorney, however, authorized defendant to make gifts of the sisters' assets to himself or anyone else.

In December 1995, Newell and Sustare executed wills, leaving most of their respective estates to each other by means of residuary clauses. Secondary residual provisions, which were designed to activate upon the death of the last surviving sister (as between Newell and Sustare), left any remaining assets to various nephews and nieces, including defendant and Forbis.

On 19 June 1996, Newell personally executed two signature cards with Branch Banking and Trust (BB & T). The first card, which she alone signed, created a payable-on-death account (the POD account) and designated defendant as the beneficiary. The other card, which both Newell and defendant signed, created a joint account with right of survivorship (the ROS account). At the time, BB & T accepted the signature cards as authentic and established the corresponding accounts.

On 26 June 1998, defendant and Newell set up a joint Paine Webber account with right of survivorship. In his capacity as attorney-in-fact, defendant signed the Paine Webber account application on Newell's behalf, listing her as the primary account holder and himself as a joint account holder. The Paine Webber account application does not bear any signature purporting to belong to Newell. Defendant stated during the course of discovery that Newell "opted to create the Paine Webber account because it ha[d] a significantly better rate of return than she could receive at BB & T, there was no penalty for early withdrawal, and it facilitated the incremental sale of her . . . stock, if needed." Over the course of several years, defendant sold tracts of Newell's real property and deposited funds into the Paine Webber account.

Defendant also established a second system of accounts for managing Sustare's assets. Although Sustare's system of accounts was similar to Newell's system, it is undisputed that Sustare signed all the relevant documents.

Newell died on 19 December 1999, just before her ninety-first birthday. Her death certificate listed "Dementia of [the] Alzheimer's type" as an underlying cause of death. Upon Newell's death, defendant received $70,000.00 as the sole beneficiary of the POD account. He also became the sole account holder of the Paine Webber account, which contained stock and other assets valued at $175,204.00, and the ROS account, worth $1,963.73. In total, defendant received $247,167.73 in cash and stock as a result of Newell's death, all of which passed to him outside of her will.

On 14 February 2000, defendant and Forbis qualified as co-executors of the Newell estate. They filed an inventory of the estate on 8 May 2000. After various personal items, cash, and other specific bequests were distributed in accordance with Newell's will, Sustare received, through the residuary clause, cash in the amount of $5,828.70, a promissory note valued at $165,000.00, and real property interests. A final accounting of the Newell estate was filed on 15 February 2001, and the estate was closed.

After her sister's death, Sustare lived alone at the assisted living facility, and her own funds eventually ran short. At that time, Sustare and other family members requested that defendant provide assistance to help ease Sustare's financial difficulties. Defendant refused.

By March 2001, Sustare had cancelled all the accounts she held jointly with defendant or which listed defendant as a beneficiary. By October 2002, she had also revoked the power of attorney that named defendant as her attorney-in-fact and appointed Forbis as her new attorney-in-fact. On 17 December 2002 Forbis reopened Newell's estate, and the Clerk of Superior Court re-issued letters testamentary, reinstating Forbis and defendant as co-executors.

Forbis, on behalf of the Newell estate, and Sustare (collectively, plaintiffs) instituted the present action against defendant on 18 December 2002, alleging fraud and related claims. Following discovery, all parties filed motions for summary judgment. After a hearing, the trial court entered an order granting defendant's motion for summary judgment and denying plaintiffs' motion for summary judgment.

. . . .

. . . . Although the original complaint alleged various causes of action including fraud, undue influence, and breach of fiduciary duty, plaintiffs did not brief the undue influence and breach of fiduciary duty claims before this Court and thereby abandoned them. *See* N.C. R. App. P. 28(b)(6) ("Assignments of error not set out in the appellant's brief, or in support of which no reason or argument is stated or authority cited, will be taken as abandoned."). Accordingly, our analysis narrows to whether summary judgment was proper on plaintiffs' fraud claims.

Fraud may be actual or constructive. While actual fraud "has no all-embracing definition," the following essential elements of actual fraud are well established: "(1) False representation or concealment of a material fact, (2) reasonably calculated to deceive, (3) made with intent to deceive, (4) which does in fact deceive, (5) resulting in damage to the injured party." *Ragsdale v. Kennedy*, 286 N.C. 130, 138, 209 S.E.2d 494, 500 (1974). Additionally, any reliance on the allegedly false representations must be reasonable. The reasonableness of a party's reliance is a question for the jury, unless the facts are so clear that they support only one conclusion.

As to the Paine Webber account, defendant stated that he and Newell created the account because it had a better rate of return than a regular bank account, it carried no penalties for early withdrawal, and it enabled Newell to liquidate her stock incrementally. Defendant's right of survivorship in Newell's Paine Webber account, however, was not necessary to accomplish these stated goals. Moreover, Newell did not sign the Paine Webber account application, and defendant's power of attorney did not confer upon him the authority to make gifts of Newell's assets, including joint ownership of an account, to himself or anyone else. Despite the limitations on his power of attorney, defendant purported to sign the Paine Webber account application on Newell's behalf giving every appearance that he was carrying out her wishes. He then sold real estate titled exclusively in Newell's name and deposited the proceeds into the Paine Webber account. Through this process, he became joint owner of a significant portion of Newell's assets.

Whether this series of transactions accorded with Newell's wishes is a question of fact which must be decided by a jury. Genuine issues of material fact exist as to whether defendant's signature on the Paine Webber application was a "false representation or concealment of a material fact," *Ragsdale*, 286 N.C. at 138, 209 S.E.2d at 500, namely, the "material fact" that his power of attorney did not actually authorize him to open this joint account with right of survivorship on Newell's behalf. It follows that similar issues exist as to the other elements of actual fraud: Whether defendant's signature was "reasonably calculated to deceive" and "made with intent to deceive"; whether it did "in fact deceive," *id.*; and whether reliance upon it was reasonable. Plaintiffs have also forecasted sufficient evidence to survive summary judgment as to damages, since Newell's will reveals that Sustare would have received the contents of the Paine Webber account through the residuary clause in the event that the account had passed as part of the Newell estate. Accordingly, the Court of Appeals erred by affirming the trial court's grant of summary judgment as to the actual fraud claim on the Paine Webber account.

As to the POD and ROS accounts, the trial court properly granted summary judgment in favor of defendant on the actual fraud claim. Unlike the Paine Webber account application, Newell signed the BB & T signature cards for these two accounts. Put simply, plaintiffs did not forecast any evidence to indicate that defendant forged the signatures or caused them to be forged. In the absence of such evidence, there is no false representation or concealment of a material fact to support a claim that defendant engaged in actual fraud in setting up the two accounts. Moreover, without any forecast of an evidentiary link between defendant and the alleged forgeries, plaintiffs have not adequately forecasted evidence of defendant's mental state, such as whether the alleged forgery was reasonably calculated to deceive or made with intent to deceive. For these reasons, no genuine issue of material fact exists on the issue of whether defendant committed actual fraud in setting up the POD and ROS accounts. Accordingly, summary judgment in defendant's favor was proper as to the actual fraud claims in connection with the POD and ROS accounts.

Although summary judgment on the actual fraud claim was appropriate for the POD and ROS accounts and inappropriate for the Paine Webber account, it remains for us to evaluate the propriety of summary judgment on the constructive fraud claim as to all three bank accounts. "A claim of constructive fraud does not require the same rigorous adherence to elements as actual fraud." Rather, this cause of action "arises where a confidential or fiduciary relationship exists," which has " 'led up to and surrounded the consummation of the transaction in which defendant is alleged to have taken advantage of his position of trust to the hurt of plaintiff.' " Thus, "[c]onstructive fraud differs from actual fraud in that 'it is based on a confidential relationship rather than a specific misrepresentation.' " Another difference is that intent to deceive is not an element of constructive fraud.

When, as here, the superior party obtains a possible benefit through the alleged abuse of the confidential or fiduciary relationship, the aggrieved party is entitled to a presumption that constructive fraud occurred. . . . Once the presumption arises, the alleged fiduciary "may rebut the presumption by showing, for example, that the confidence reposed in him was not abused."

. . . .

Here, it is undisputed that defendant and Newell were in a fiduciary relationship created by the power of attorney vested in defendant. Plaintiffs forecasted evidence that all three bank accounts were established at defendant's initiative. They also forecasted evidence that the Newell estate, Sustare, and later the Sustare estate were damaged by the fact that a large portion of Newell's assets passed to defendant outside her will.

In opposition to plaintiffs' forecast of evidence, defendant filed a six-page affidavit in which he claimed that Newell had full knowledge of all his financial activities on her behalf and that she understood defendant would receive the contents of the three accounts upon her death.

This forecasted evidence raised genuine issues of material fact as to whether defendant committed constructive fraud in relation to the three accounts. Unlike in *Watts*, a genuine issue of material fact exists as to whether defendant's fiduciary relationship with Newell "led up to and surrounded the consummation" of the transactions that effectively transferred most of her assets to him. This issue must be decided by a jury.

. . . .

After a careful review of the record, we conclude plaintiffs demonstrated that genuine issues of material fact exist as to whether defendant perpetrated a constructive fraud in setting up and maintaining Newell's Paine Webber, ROS, and POD accounts. The Court of Appeals therefore erred in affirming the trial court's grant of summary judgment on these claims.

We conclude summary judgment was properly granted for defendant with respect to actual fraud on the ROS and POD accounts. Defendant was not entitled to summary judgment, however, as to the actual fraud claim on the Paine Webber account. Moreover, summary judgment was improper as to plaintiffs' constructive fraud claims on all three accounts.

We therefore remand to the Court of Appeals for further remand to the trial court with instructions to proceed on the following issues: (1) the claim of actual fraud as to the Paine Webber account, and (2) the claims of constructive fraud as to the Paine Webber, ROS, and POD accounts.

AFFIRMED IN PART; REVERSED IN PART AND REMANDED.

QUESTIONS

1. Margie, age 77, executes a power of attorney naming her son, Stan, her attorney-in-fact. She also has a joint bank account with her daughter, Doris, which she uses to deposit her monthly social security check to pay expenses. Margie becomes mentally incapacitated. Can Doris pay Margie's bills from the joint bank account?

2. Carlos, age 71 and a widower, moves in with Angelina, age 68, who is divorced. They open a joint checking account with right of survivorship at Big Bank & Trust (BBT). Each has their Social Security check directly deposited into the account. The account is used exclusively to pay the expenses of their joint household. Each as separate investment accounts that have no survivorship interests. Five years later, Carlos has a stroke and is in a coma. The next day Angelina draws out $40,000 from the account. Carlos then dies. Carlos' son, Jose, his sole heir, asks the probate court to order Angelina to return the $40,000. Should the court order her to return the funds to the account?

3. James, age 76, lives alone in his house, which he owns jointly with his daughter, Dot. He creates a durable power of attorney naming his son, Jake, as his agent. James becomes mentally incapacitated and moves into a nursing home. Jake wants to sell the house to his friend, Frank. Dot wants to keep it and rent it to her friend, Faith. Who will prevail?

4. State law governing powers of attorney and joint accounts can sometimes conflict. Suppose the state law governing joint bank accounts presumes donative intent by the party who supplied the funds. The removal of funds from the account by the non-contributor joint account owner is therefore permissible. Suppose the same state's law of powers of attorney presumes that any withdrawals from a bank account by an agent for the agent's benefit are fraudulent as to the principal. Suppose Susan, age 80, opens a joint bank account with her 55-year-old daughter, Dana. Susan deposits $200,000 in the account. The next year, Susan appoints Dana as her agent under a power of attorney with full authority to handle all of Susan's financial affairs. Susan becomes very demented and mentally incapacitated. Dana withdraws $190,000 from the joint account and deposits in an account in her name. Susan dies. Her will leaves her estate in equal shares to Dana and Walt, her other child. Walt sues Dana demanding the return of the $190,000 claiming her removal of the funds was fraudulent. Dana replies that she removed the funds as a joint owner, not as an agent. What result? *See Russ v. Russ*, 734 N.W.2d 874 (Wis. 2007).

A similar device to a convenience account is the Totten trust, a bank account opened and funded by one person who holds the funds "in trust for" another person. A Totten trust (from *In re Totten*, 179 N.Y. 112, 71 N.E. 748 (1904)) creates a trust revocable by the grantor until death. If not revoked, the trust assets automatically vest in the beneficiary at the death of the creator. The basic Totten trust allows an elderly grantor to continue to use her own funds without making them available to the beneficiary and to avoid having the account subjected to probate upon her death. Similar to the Totten trust are pay on death (POD) accounts. For example, Sam opens an account and names Peter as a joint owner. Sam retains the bank book, and does not expect Peter to have any rights in the funds until Sam's death, at which time Peter is to come into sole possession of the account. A POD account is valid only if permitted by state law. Otherwise, it fails as not meeting the requirements of the statute of wills.

C.   REVOCABLE TRUSTS

Revocable trusts have become a common way of avoiding probate and for providing management of assets in the case of mental incapacity. Popularized as "living trusts," they are perceived of as a low-cost way of passing on assets after death without the use of a will or the need to have the property pass through what is assumed to be an expensive probate system. When used with a power of attorney, they also promise to reduce or eliminate the need for guardianship.

A trust is a fiduciary relationship in which the person who has title to the property, the trustee, holds it for the benefit of another, the beneficiary. The creator of a trust is called the settlor (in federal income tax terminology, the grantor), and the assets of the trust are referred to as the corpus or principal. The trustee has a legal interest and the beneficiary has a beneficial interest in the trust assets. The trust instrument sets forth the terms of the trust, which, given the nature of a trust, can be almost as varied as the imagination of the settlor. A trust created by a declaration or deed of trust during the settlor's life is an inter vivos or living trust. If the settlor creates the trust by will it is a testamentary trust, which does not come into existence until the death of the settlor. Trusts are almost always in writing. If they contain real property, the Statute of Frauds requires that they be written. Once created, a trust is irrevocable unless the settlor reserves the right to revoke or amend it.

A trust requires a settlor, a trustee, and a beneficiary, though the settlor can act as trustee and may even be the beneficiary of the trust. Any competent adult can establish a trust, and any person or institution can be the beneficiary of a trust. Many trusts have more than one beneficiary, and frequently trusts have successor beneficiaries in the event of the death of the original beneficiary.

A trust may have one or more trustees, but if there are more than one, the trust instrument must provide whether all must act in unison or if a majority of the trustees can act. Individuals and corporations (generally banks) may act as trustees. The beneficiary can be named as trustee or as a co-trustee with an independent (non-beneficiary) trustee. No trust will be allowed to fail because of a lack of trustee. If the named trustee should fail (die, become incapacitated, or resign), the appropriate court will appoint a successor trustee. Alternatively, the trust instrument can (and should) provide successor trustees.

Inter vivos revocable trusts are often created to avoid probate and to provide lifetime management of the settlor's assets in the event that the settlor becomes incapacitated. At the death of the settlor, the provisions of the trust document determine what happens to the trust corpus. The assets of the trust are not governed by the decedent's will. Some settlors provide that the trust will continue for the benefit of another beneficiary such as a spouse or child, while other settlors terminate the trust at their death and distribute the assets. The avoidance of probate is a popular goal, particularly among lay persons. Some lawyers are less enthusiastic, claiming that the cost savings are largely illusory. Other lawyers advocate the use of revocable trusts that are funded with the bulk of the settlor's assets as a more desirable way to pass on the estate than by a will.

The assets of the revocable trust are not part of the decedent's probate estate since the decedent does not own the assets. This is true even if the settlor is the trustee since the ownership is by virtue of being a trustee, not as the individual who transferred the assets into the trust. At the settlor/trustee's death, a successor trustee named in the trust continues to manage the trust or terminates the trust and distributes the assets as provided in the trust instrument. Many revocable trusts are created by couples, who each create their own trust but name their spouse as a co-trustee. When one spouse dies the surviving spouse continues as trustee and often is joined by a child or a bank as successor trustee.

Increasingly, revocable trusts are used to provide lifetime management of the settlor's property should he or she become incapacitated. The trust instrument will provide that if the settlor becomes incapacitated he or she will no longer serve as trustee. Either the co-trustee will take command of the assets or a successor trustee will take control. Upon the incapacity of the settlor, the other trustee(s) will be able to manage the assets and support the settlor by distributions from the trust.

The following is a narrative example of how a living trust might operate: A married couple, Nora and Nick each created a revocable living trust and transferred their assets to their respective trusts. They owned their house as joint tenants with right of survivorship and so did not place the house in either trust. When Nora and Nick transferred their assets to their trust, they, in effect, inventoried what they owned and created an updated list of their assets. As a result they dissolved their joint ownership of some stocks and combined some certificates of deposit in order to invest in larger certificates of deposit that paid a higher interest rate. They also found that their stock investments consisted of a small number of shares of many different stocks. They sold off some stock and created a more rational portfolio. Each named the other as co-trustee with their adult daughter, Dora, named as successor co-trustee for both trusts along with The First Bank of Erehwon. If she ever became trustee, Dora was given the right to remove the Bank and replace it with another corporate co-trustee. (This is done to insure that Dora, and not the Bank, would be in control.)

After a few years Nick died, leaving the assets in his trust to Nora's trust. She then sold the house, rented an apartment, and placed the proceeds of the house sale into her trust. A few years later, Nora, unhappy with Dora's behavior (she suspected alcohol abuse), amended her trust to remove Dora as successor co-trustee and named the Bank as sole successor trustee. Later, Nora, suffering from dementia, moved into an assisted living facility. After a few months she became too mentally incapacitated to handle her affairs. The assisted living facility notified the Bank of Nora's failing mental abilities. As a result the Bank sent a representative to interview Nora, who concluded that Nora was mentally incompetent. The Bank assumed the duties of trustee of Nora'a trust. Although Nora was mentally incapacitated, there was no need for a guardian since she was living safely in the assisted living facility and her financial affairs were managed by the Bank, which invested trust assets and paid Nora's support and upkeep. Before Nora moved into the assisted living facility she had signed an advance health care directive naming Dora as her surrogate medical care decision maker. When Nora became terminally ill, Dora, in consultation with the attending physician, decided to terminate life sustaining treatment for Nora. After Nora died, the Bank turned over the trust assets to the personal representative of Nora's estate, Dora, who was also the sole heir. The filing of the federal estate tax return for Nora's estate was relatively simple since everything she owned for federal estate tax purposes was held by her trust.

A living trust does not save income taxes or estate taxes. Because the settlor, by virtue of the power of revocation, at all times controls the trust assets, the settlor is treated as if he or she owned the trust assets outright. For federal income taxes the trust is ignored and the settlor is treated as the recipient of all trust income, whether distributed or not. Similarly, at the death of the settlor the trust assets are considered part of the settlor's taxable estate. I.R.C. § 2036.

The powers and duties of trustees are determined by law and by the provisions of the trust instrument. If the trust fails to address a particular point, state trust law governs. Most trust law arose gradually over the years through the common law. As a result the trustee's duties and responsibilities are well defined even if the trust instrument is silent. However, the trust can specifically address what the trustee can and cannot do, thereby overriding prevailing state law. The trustee has the powers conferred by the trust and any other powers permitted by state law to carry out the intent of the creator of the trust, unless those powers are specifically barred by the trust.

No one can be forced to serve as a trustee, but once the trusteeship has been accepted the trustee is under a fiduciary duty to administer the trust. The trustee can resign only with permission of the court or all of the beneficiaries, or as provided by the terms of the trust. The fundamental duty of a trustee is the duty of loyalty. The trustee has a fiduciary relationship to the beneficiaries and must administer the trust in their best interests. The trustee must never allow his or her own interests to interfere with the duty of loyalty. The trustee cannot delegate away his or her responsibility. Certainly the trustee may hire assistance: an accountant, an investment advisor, and so forth, but the trustee remains responsible for the operation of the trust. The trustee must also exercise the care and skill reasonable for a person of ordinary prudence. Professional corporate trustees may be held to an even higher standard.

Trustees who fail in their obligations are answerable to the court that has jurisdiction over the trust, usually the local probate court. The beneficiary has the power to sue the trustee for failing to uphold his or her duties. Even beneficiaries with only a future or contingent interest may sue. No other parties, except co-trustees, have standing to sue to enforce the provisions of the trust.

The existence of a trust to manage the property of the settlor may forestall the need for a guardian. The combination of a living trust and a power of attorney for property should be sufficient to permit the trustee and the agent (who may be the same person) to manage the incapacitated person's property. The individual will also need an advance directive that appoints a surrogate health care decision maker. If all three documents exist there is little justification for the appointment of a guardian.

While a power of attorney does provide a means of property management for an incapacitated individual, many lawyers prefer a revocable trust because an agent may find it difficult to have his or her authority accepted. Over the life of the trust, banks and stockbrokers will have become accustomed to the incapacitated settlor's assets being managed in a trust and so normally have little difficulty in accepting the authority of the remaining or successor trustee. This is in sharp contrast to the difficulties many agents have in obtaining cooperation from banks and other financial institutions.

While in theory a settlor could place all of his or her assets in a revocable trust, in practice personal property, a personal checking account, and perhaps the family home are often not included in the trust. A power of attorney should be created to manage these assets, and because these assets will pass through probate a will should be executed to govern their post-death distribution.

Inter vivos revocable trusts have a few disadvantages. First, there is a cost for the creation of the trust and for transferring of the assets to the trust. There is also the need to open bank and brokerage accounts in the name of the trustee. The trustee must maintain records of trust income and distributions, but if the trust assets consist mostly of investments such as stocks and bonds, the recordkeeping is not too much trouble.

QUESTION

Your client, Alma, age 83 and a widow, has two surviving children, Beth, age 63, and Bob, age 60, and a grandchild, Gina, age 35, of Alma's deceased son, Gary. Alma wants to create a living trust to hold her assets worth $450,000. Alma lives in Seattle. Beth, a housewife, lives in Miami. Bob lives in Seattle and recently was divorced for the second time. He has just filed for bankruptcy after the failure of his restaurant. Gina, who lives in Seattle, is a criminal defense lawyer. Alma asks who you would advise to act as her successor trustee? What if Gina was a painter who was poor enough to qualify for food stamps?

Chapter 11

HEALTH CARE DECISION MAKING

Due to declining physical vigor, longer involvement with acute conditions, and increased susceptibility to chronic conditions, the elderly as a group are disproportionate consumers of health care. It is estimated that over one-third of all personal health care costs are spent on those age 65 and older. The extraordinary demand for health care by the elderly raises two primary issues. One, "Who will pay the costs?," is examined in Chapter 5. The other, "Who decides what kind of medical care is appropriate for an elderly individual?," is the focus of this chapter, which examines how health care decisions are made by or on behalf of the elderly patient.

In theory, patients control their medical treatment, choosing what kind of treatment they do or do not want. If the patient does not want a particular medical treatment, the patient can usually prevent it. If the patient wants particular medical care and can pay for it, the patient will usually prevail. The exception is some rationed health care, such as organ transplants, for which patients must wait their turn because of the limited availability. Sometimes medical personnel may be reluctant to provide care if it is considered medically inappropriate. If the physician believes that the care the patient requests is futile, the physician may refuse to provide the treatment.

A. THE DOCTRINE OF INFORMED CONSENT

In most circumstances, patients' desires prevail because the doctrine of informed consent grants patients control of their medical care. The goal of informed consent is patient autonomy or self-determination. Personal autonomy rests upon bodily integrity, which, in turn, is an essential component of personal liberty. If you do not control your body, you are not free. To be autonomous, individuals must be able to control their bodies by controlling their medical care through the right to consent to or refuse treatment.

To make choices, however, requires information, since decisions cannot be made in a vacuum. Merely having the right to decide is meaningless unless the patient has sufficient information to understand the consequences of the decision and the possible alternatives. The doctrine of informed consent thus requires that the patient be provided with sufficient information to be able to give meaningful (informed) consent to proposed medical care.

The foundation for informed consent is a 1914 case in which a patient was operated upon without her consent. In determining whether she had a cause of action against the hospital in which the operation was performed, Judge Cardozo wrote:

In the case at hand, the wrong complained of is not merely negligence. It is trespass. Every human being of adult years and sound mind has a right to determine what shall be done with his own body; and a surgeon who performs an operation without his patient's consent commits an assault, for which he is liable in damages.

Schloendorff v. Soc'y of N.Y. Hospital, 105 N.E. 92, 93 (N.Y. 1914).

Informed consent remains as necessary today as it was in 1914. Subsequent cases, such as the one below, have explained the nature of the information which must be provided in order for the patient's decision to be an informed one.

SCOTT v. BRADFORD
606 P.2d 554 (Okla. 1979)

DOOLIN, JUSTICE.

This appeal is taken by plaintiffs in trial below, from a judgment in favor of defendant rendered on a jury verdict in a medical malpractice action.

Mrs. Scott's physician advised her she had several fibroid tumors on her uterus. He referred her to defendant surgeon. Defendant admitted her to the hospital where she signed a routine consent form prior to defendant's performing a hysterectomy. After surgery, Mrs. Scott experienced problems with incontinence. She visited another physician who discovered she had a vesico-vaginal fistula which permitted urine to leak from her bladder into the vagina. This physician referred her to a urologist who, after three surgeries, succeeded in correcting her problems.

Mrs. Scott, joined by her husband, filed the present action alleging medical malpractice, claiming defendant failed to advise her of the risks involved or of available alternatives to surgery. She further maintained had she been properly informed she would have refused the surgery.

The case was submitted to the jury with instructions to which plaintiffs objected. The jury found for defendant and plaintiffs appeal.

Anglo-American law starts with the premise of thoroughgoing self-determination, each man considered to be his own master. This law does not permit a physician to substitute his judgment for that of the patient by any form of artifice. The doctrine of informed consent arises out of this premise.

Consent to medical treatment, to be effective, should stem from an understanding decision based on adequate information about the treatment, the available alternatives, and the collateral risks. This requirement, labeled "informed consent," is, legally speaking, as essential as a physician's care and skill in the *performance* of the therapy. The doctrine imposes a duty on a physician or surgeon to inform a patient of his options and their attendant risks. If a physician breaches this duty, patient's consent is defective, and physician is responsible for the consequences.

If treatment is completely unauthorized and performed without any consent at all, there has been a battery. However, if the physician obtains a patient's consent but has breached his duty to inform, the patient has a cause of action sounding in negligence for failure to inform the patient of his options, regardless of the due care exercised at treatment, assuming there is injury.

More recently, in perhaps one of the most influential informed consent decisions, *Canterbury v. Spence*, 464 F.2d 772 (D.C. Cir. 1972), *cert. den.* 409 U.S. 1064, the doctrine received perdurable impetus. Judge Robinson observed that suits charging failure by a physician adequately to disclose risks and alternatives of proposed treatment were not innovative in American law. He emphasized the fundamental concept in American jurisprudence that every human being of adult years and sound mind has a right to determine what shall be done with his own body. True consent to what happens to one's self is the informed exercise of a choice. This entails an opportunity to evaluate knowledgeably the options available and the risks attendant upon each. It is the prerogative of every patient to chart his own course and determine which direction he will take.

The decision in *Canterbury* recognized the tendency of some jurisdictions to turn this duty on whether it is the custom of physicians practicing in the community to make the particular disclosure to the patient. That court rejected this standard and held the standard measuring performance of the duty of disclosure is conduct which is reasonable under the circumstances: "[We cannot] ignore the fact that to bind disclosure obligations to medical usage is to arrogate the decision on revelation to the physician alone." We agree. A patient's right to make up his mind whether to undergo treatment should not be delegated to the local medical group. What is reasonable disclosure in one instance may not be reasonable in another. We decline to adopt a standard based on the professional standard. We, therefore, hold the scope of a physician's communications must be measured by his patient's need to know enough to enable him to make an intelligent choice. In other words, full disclosure of all *material risks* incident to treatment must be made. There is no bright line separating the material from the immaterial; it is a question of fact. A risk is material if it would be likely to affect patient's decision. When non-disclosure of a particular risk is open to debate, the issue is for the finder of facts.

. . . . To the extent the plaintiff, given an adequate disclosure, would have declined the proposed treatment, and a reasonable person in similar circumstances would have consented, a patient's right of self-determination is *irrevocably lost.* This basic right to know and decide is the reason for the full-disclosure rule. Accordingly, we decline to jeopardize this right by the imposition of the "reasonable man" standard.

If a plaintiff testifies he would have continued with the proposed treatment had he been adequately informed, the trial is over under either the subjective or objective approach. If he testifies he would not, then the causation problem must be resolved by examining the credibility of plaintiff's testimony. The jury must be instructed that it must find plaintiff would have refused the treatment if he is to prevail.

Although it might be said this approach places a physician at the mercy of a patient's hindsight, a careful practitioner can always protect himself by insuring that he has adequately informed each patient he treats. If he does not breach this duty, a causation problem will not arise.

The final element of this cause of action is that of injury. The risk must actually materialize and plaintiff must have been injured as a result of submitting to the treatment. Absent occurrence of the undisclosed risk, a physician's failure to reveal its possibility is not actionable.

In summary, in a medical malpractice action a patient suing under the theory of informed consent must allege and prove:

1) defendant physician failed to inform him adequately of a material risk before securing his consent to the proposed treatment;

2) if he had been informed of the risks he would not have consented to the treatment;

3) the adverse consequences that were not made known did in fact occur and he was injured as a result of submitting to the treatment.

As a defense, a physician may plead and prove plaintiff knew of the risks, full disclosure would be detrimental to patient's best interests or that an emergency existed requiring prompt treatment and patient was in no condition to decide for himself.

Affirmed.

[The court continued with a description of the standard to be used in determining whether the lack of informed consent constituted an actionable tort.]

An Illinois court provided a forceful statement as to the right of a competent adult to refuse medical treatment even if that should result in death.

FICKE v. EVANGELICAL HEALTH SYSTEMS
674 N.E.2d 888, 889 (Ill. App. Ct. 1996)

CERDA, J., filed opinion concurring in part and dissenting in part.

As a general principle of Illinois law, competent adults have the right to refuse any type of medical care, including life-sustaining treatment. The right to refuse medical care has been recognized under constitutional right-to-privacy principles and is deeply ingrained in common law principles of individual autonomy, self-determination, and informed consent. See *Union Pacific Ry. Co. v. Botsford*, 141 U.S. 250, 251 (1891) ("No right is held more sacred, or is more carefully guarded, by the common law, than the right of every individual to the possession and control of his own person, free from all restraint or interference of others, unless by clear and unquestionable authority of law").

[1]   THE EMERGENCY CARE EXCEPTION

The need for informed consent is not absolute. There are exceptions. Chief among them is the emergency exception, which applies when the patient is incapable of giving consent or receiving information and the time necessary to obtain consent would place the patient in immediate danger, or "makes it impractical to secure such consent." *Dunham v. Wright*, 423 F.2d 940, 941 (3d Cir. 1970). It is commonly said that the patient's consent is "implied" in an emergency because it is presumed that, if able, any particular patient would consent under the circumstances.

As described by one court, the elements necessary to invoke the emergency care exception:

> Thus, there are four essential elements required to establish that the common-law emergency exception applies: (1) there was a medical emergency; (2) treatment was required in order to protect the patient's health; (3) it was impossible or impractical to obtain consent from either the patient or someone authorized to consent for the patient; and (4) there was no reason to believe that the patient would decline the treatment, given the opportunity to consent.

Moriarity v. Rockford Health Sys. (In re Estate of Allen), 365 Ill. App. 3d 378 (2006).

It is the urgency of the need for care that defines the emergency exception. "It would indeed be most unusual for a doctor, with his patient who had just been bitten by a venomous snake, to calmly sit down and first fully discuss the various available methods of treating snakebite and the possible consequences, while the venom was being pumped through the patient's body." *Crouch v. Most*, 432 P.2d 250, 254 (N.M. 1967).

[2]   THERAPEUTIC PRIVILEGE EXCEPTION

Informed consent also is not necessary if the physician invokes "therapeutic privilege," based on the belief that the disclosure of information would so upset the patient that he or she would be unable to make a rational decision. The physician is freed from the requirement of informed consent in order to promote the primary duty to do what is beneficial for the patient. Several states have codified the concept. In the past therapeutic privilege was invoked to justify not telling a patient of a fatal diagnosis. Given current mores and attitudes toward death, reliance upon the privilege is in decline.

[3]   PATIENT WAIVER

Patients may also waive their right to informed consent. To give a valid waiver, the patient must know what rights are being given up, but the physician is not required to tell patients that they have a right to information. After all, informed consent is not a *Miranda* type warning. The patient can waive both the right to information ("Don't tell me anything more.") and the right to decide ("You decide what should be done. You know best."). Patient waiver recognizes patient autonomy, while allowing the patient to defer to the professionalism of the physician.

Some critics of the doctrine of informed consent are dubious about the ability of patients to understand the difficult choices presented to them. The language of medicine may be particularly foreign to the average person.

> Indeed, some empirical studies purport to have demonstrated this by showing that the lay public often does not know the meaning of common medical terms, or by showing that, following an encounter with a physician, patients are unable to report what the physician said about their illness and treatment. Neither type of study establishes the fact that patients cannot understand. The first merely finds that they do not currently know the right definitions of some terms; the second, which usually fails to discover what the physician actually did say, rests its conclusion on an assumption that information was provided that was subsequently not understood. In the Commission's own survey, physicians were asked: "What percentage of your patients would you say are able to understand most aspects of their treatment and condition if reasonable time and effort are devoted to explanation?" Overall, 48% of physicians reported that 90–100% of their patients could understand and an additional 34% said that 70–89% could understand.

President's Commission for the Study of Ethical Problems in Medicine and Biomedical and Behavioral Research, Making Health Care Decisions, Vol. 1, 57–60 (Oct. 1982).

The doctrine of informed consent is not suspended even if the patient is incapacitated and unable to grant consent. Instead, it must be obtained from a surrogate, most often a family member or a judicially appointed guardian. The key issue is whether the patient lacks the capacity to provide or withhold consent. Incapacity issues are discussed below in part C.

[4] INFORMED CONSENT: MYTH OR REALITY?

Scholars of several disciplines — philosophers, theologians, lawyers, and bioethicists — support the value of patient autonomy and the need for informed consent. Case law and state statutes similarly support the doctrine of informed consent. Yet, while the concept of a fully informed patient working with his or her physician to decide the appropriate medical treatment is appealing, it may not reflect the reality of the patient-physician relationship. Many commentators argue that often physicians are unwilling to share decision-making authority with their patients. For many physicians informed consent means little more than a requirement to give a minimum description of the proposed course of treatment and the need to obtain the patient's signature on a consent form. They perceive little value in involving the patient in choosing among treatment alternatives. Physicians who fail to see much value in patient involvement are likely to make only halfhearted attempts to involve the patient. As a result the patient, fearful of appearing ignorant and believing that the physician "knows best," may simply tell the physician to decide or agree with whatever is recommended.

A lack of openness and sharing of decisional responsibility by physicians may be a serious problem with older patients. Physicians, like many of us, may subconsciously (or even consciously particularly) believe that an older patient, particularly a very old patient, lacks the capacity to understand treatment decisions and options. The elderly patient may appear more passive and less "consumer-like" than younger patients. The physician may mistakenly interpret the elderly patient's politeness and respect for authority as deference to the physician's right to control the treatment decisions.

The elderly patient's physical condition may also contribute to a lack of involvement in decision making. A loss of hearing, diminished short-term memory, or clouded vision may make it difficult for elderly patients to assimilate information. Rather than ask the physician to slow down or repeat the information, the elderly client may defer to the physician's professional judgment. Of course, every time an elderly patient withdraws from involvement in a treatment decision he or she contributes to the physician's suspicion that informed consent is merely a legal fiction, not a practical reality. Consequently, the physician, who is pressed for time, may attempt less enthusiastically to obtain meaningful informed consent from the next elderly patient. The patient, in turn, sensing the physician's lack of interest in the patient's opinion, may find it easier to let the physician decide things, thereby reinforcing a cycle of retreat from informed consent and patient decision making.

The probability of death may also interfere with the goal of informed consent. If the diagnosis reveals a terminal illness or condition, the physician may find it difficult to be open with the patient. The physician may fear that the patient needs an optimistic prognosis, not a gloomy discussion of the risks and possible shortcomings of the probable treatment. Hoping to keep up the patient's spirits, the physician may downplay the worst aspects of the illness and focus on the hope (however slight) of recovery. Better to hide the truth and "give the patient a few more happy months" than to tell the patient the truth when nothing can be done. The failure of physicians to reveal the likelihood of a patient's impending death is probably in decline, as the doctrine of informed consent is more widely honored. Other cultures may view the disclosure differently. Reportedly in Japan, for example, physicians routinely withhold a prognosis of death, particularly from cancer patients. Apparently this is acceptable to their patients.

QUESTIONS

1.   Should a physician always tell a patient about a terminal condition? Why?

2.   Is it possible to tell the patient too much? What is the danger if a patient is told too much?

3.   Can the physician's own fear of death interfere with open discussions with the patient?

4.   Do diminished senses of hearing or vision justify a failure to fully inform a patient?

5. Is hope a component of human recovery that should be protected by nondisclosure?

B.   THE RIGHT OF A COMPETENT PATIENT TO DIE

Although all people must die, it does not follow that individuals have a right to choose to die. The state has an interest in their continued existence, arising from its responsibility to protect health, safety, and welfare. Do these state interests outweigh an individual's decision not to live? Although no state has a law against suicide, courts and commentators routinely assert that the state may rightfully prohibit and attempt to prevent suicide. The refusal to accept medical care or the request that it be discontinued, however, is perceived as something other than suicide. Even if the denial of medical treatment results in death, the individual is only expressing his or her right to bodily integrity and autonomy — rights which the state should protect.

[1]   THE COMMON-LAW RIGHT TO DIE

The state has several reasons to desire to protect the lives of its citizens. The most often quoted expression of those state interests appeared in a 1977 Massachusetts case.

SUPERINTENDENT OF BELCHERTOWN STATE SCHOOL v. SAIKEWICZ
370 N.E.2d 417 (Mass. 1977)

. . . . Recent decisions involving the difficult question of the right of an individual to refuse medical intervention or treatment [indicate] that a relatively concise statement of countervailing State interests may be made. As distilled from the cases, the State has claimed interest in: (1) the preservation of life; (2) the protection of the interests of innocent third parties; (3) the prevention of suicide; and (4) maintaining the ethical integrity of the medical profession.

It is clear that the most significant of the asserted State interests is that of the preservation of human life. Recognition of such an interest, however, does not necessarily resolve the problem where the affliction or disease clearly indicates that life will soon, and inevitably, be extinguished. The interest of the State in prolonging a life must be reconciled with the interest of an individual to reject the traumatic cost of that prolongation. There is a substantial distinction in the State's insistence that human life be saved where the affliction is curable, as opposed to the State interest where, as here, the issue is not whether but when, for how long, and at what cost to the individual that life may be briefly extended.

A second interest of considerable magnitude, which the State may have some interest in asserting, is that of protecting third parties, particularly minor children, from the emotional and financial damage which may occur as a result of the decision of a competent adult to refuse life-saving or life-prolonging treatment.

The last State interest requiring discussion is that of the maintenance of the ethical integrity of the medical profession as well as allowing hospitals the full opportunity to care for people under their control. Prevailing medical ethical practice does not, without exception, demand that all efforts toward life prolongation be made in all circumstances. Rather, as indicated in *Quinlan*, the prevailing ethical practice seems to be to recognize that the dying are more often in need of comfort than treatment. Recognition of the right to refuse necessary treatment in appropriate circumstances is consistent with existing medical mores; such a doctrine does not threaten either the integrity of the medical profession, the proper role of hospitals in caring for such patients or the State's interest in protecting the same. It is not necessary to deny a right of self-determination to a patient in order to recognize the interests of doctors, hospitals, and medical personnel in attendance on the patient. Also, if the doctrines of informed consent and right of privacy have as their foundations the right to bodily integrity, *see Union Pac. Ry. v. Botsford*, 141 U.S. 250 (1891), and control of one's own fate, then those rights are superior to the institutional considerations.

QUESTION

In a footnote, the *Saikewicz* court said that the state's interest in preventing suicide required little discussion. Do you agree? Suicide is not a crime in any state, although assisting a suicide is criminal behavior in many (but not all) states.

While the courts give lip service to competing state interests, the outcome of the cases indicates a judicial deference to the right of the individual. "Although courts routinely invoke these state interests, the case law teaches that the balance has already been struck for competent patients." 73 Md. Op. Att'y Gen. 253, 266 (Op. No. 88-046, Oct. 17, 1988). It is almost inconceivable that a court would override the decision of a competent, terminally ill patient to be allowed to die rather than to continue medical treatment. The state's interest in the preservation of life is overwhelmed by the sanctity of individual choice and self-determination.

A competent patient's request to terminate or refuse life-sustaining medical treatment does not constitute suicide. If, as a result of a choice not to be treated, the individual dies, death is a result of the medical condition and not because of a deliberate, affirmative act by the patient. Death comes as a natural result of a disease, not because of a self-inflicted injury.

In *Satz v. Perlmutter*, 362 So. 2d 160 (Fla. Dist. Ct. App. 1978), Abe Perlmutter, age 73, suffered from amyotrophic lateral sclerosis (Lou Gehrig's disease) and was virtually unable to move. He could breathe only with the aid of a mechanical respirator, but he was mentally alert and could speak with difficulty. His doctors predicted that he would soon die. Though he was aware that removal of the respirator would result in death within one hour, he nevertheless requested its removal. The court approved his request and discussed why the removal of the respirator would not be contrary to the state's interest in the prevention of suicide:

Prevention of Suicide

As to suicide, the facts here unarguably reveal that Mr. Perlmutter would die, but for the respirator. The disconnecting of it, far from causing his unnatural death by means of a "death producing agent" in fact will merely result in his death, if at all, from natural causes. The testimony of Mr. Perlmutter . . . is that he really wants to live, but do so, God and Mother Nature willing, under his own power. This basic wish to live, plus the fact that he did not self-induce his horrible affliction, precludes his further refusal of treatment being classed as attempted suicide.

Moreover we find no requirement in the law that a competent, but otherwise morally sick, patient undergo the surgery or treatment which constitutes the only hope for temporary prolongation of his life. This being so, we see little difference between a cancer ridden patient who declines surgery, or chemotherapy, necessary for his temporary survival and the hopeless predicament which tragically afflicts Abe Perlmutter. It is true that the latter appears more drastic because affirmatively, a mechanical device must be disconnected, as distinct from mere inaction. Notwithstanding, the principle is the same, for in both instances the hapless, but mentally competent, victim is choosing not to avail himself of one of the expensive marvels of modern medical science.

Id. at 162–63.

QUESTION

Is it possible, in *Perlmutter*, that the patient's age influenced the court's decision? What if he were 30 years old?

The right of a competent adult to refuse medical treatment, even if the result is death, appears well-established by case law. Of course, in many instances, when a competent patient refuses medical care, the case is resolved by the parties rather than the courts. The patient either is allowed to die or is persuaded to accept life-saving treatment. The few cases that the courts hear result either from conflict between the parties (the patient wants to die, while the family or physicians want to treat) or fear of liability if the physicians or hospital allow the patient to die.

[2] THE CONSTITUTIONAL RIGHT TO DIE

The right to refuse treatment also has constitutional grounds. "The right to refuse medical treatment is basic and fundamental. It is recognized as a part of the right of privacy protected by both the state and federal constitutions." *Bouvia v. Superior Court*, 225 Cal. Rptr. 297 (Cal. Ct. App. 1986).

The Supreme Court, in *Griswold v. Connecticut*, 381 U.S. 479 (1965), held that the right of privacy is protected by the Federal Constitution. Because bodily integrity is fundamental to personal privacy, the right to refuse medical treatment may be a constitutionally protected right. The New Jersey Supreme Court addressed that issue in *In re Quinlan*, 355 A.2d 647 (N.J. 1976):

> Although the Constitution does not explicitly mention a right of privacy, Supreme Court decisions have recognized that a right of personal privacy exists and that certain areas of privacy are guaranteed under the Constitution. *Eisenstadt v. Baird*, 405 U.S. 438 (1972); *Stanley v. Georgia*, 394 U.S. 557 (1969). The Court has interdicted judicial intrusion into many aspects of personal decision, sometimes basing this restraint upon the conception of a limitation of judicial interest and responsibility, such as with regard to contraception and its relationship to family life and decision. *Griswold v. Connecticut*, 381 U.S. 479 (1965).

> The Court in *Griswold* found the unwritten constitutional right of privacy to exist in the penumbra of specific guarantees of the Bill of Rights "formed by emanations from those guarantees that help give them life and substance." 381 U.S. at 484. Presumably this right is broad enough to encompass a patient's decision to decline medical treatment under certain circumstances, in much the same way as it is broad enough to encompass a woman's decision to terminate pregnancy under certain conditions. *Roe v. Wade*, 410 U.S. 113, 153 (1973).

Many state constitutions specifically protect the right of privacy. For example, ARIZ. CONST. art. 2, § 8, "Right to Privacy," provides that "No person shall be disturbed in his private affairs, or his home invaded, without authority of law." This has been interpreted by the Arizona Supreme Court to mean that the Arizona Constitution "provides for a right to refuse medical treatment." *Rasmussen v. Fleming*, 741 P.2d 674 (Ariz. 1987). The Florida Supreme Court held that article I, section 23 of the Florida Constitution provides explicit privacy protections which include the right to choose or refuse medical treatment. *In re Guardianship of Browning*, 568 So. 2d 4 (Fla. 1990). The Washington Supreme Court held that an adult "who is incurably and terminally ill has a constitutional right of privacy that encompasses the right to refuse treatment that serves only to prolong the dying process." The Court cited article 1, section 7 of the Washington Constitution. *In re Welfare of Colyer*, 660 P.2d 738, 742 (Wash. 1983).

A few states have codified the need for informed consent. The Florida statute, for example, reads as follows: ·

§ 766.103. Florida Medical Consent Law

(1) This section shall be known and cited as the "Florida Medical Consent Law."

. . . .

(3) No recovery shall be allowed in any court in this state against any physician licensed under chapter 458, osteopath licensed under chapter 459, chiropractor licensed under chapter 460, podiatrist licensed under chapter 461, or dentist licensed under chapter 466 in an action brought for treating, examining, or operating on a patient without his informed consent when:

(a) 1. The action of the physician, osteopath, chiropractor, podiatrist, or dentist in obtaining the consent of the patient or another person authorized to give consent for the patient was in accordance with an accepted standard of medical practice among members of the medical profession with similar training and experience in the same or similar medical community; and

2. A reasonable individual, from the information provided by the physician, osteopath, chiropractor, podiatrist, or dentist, under the circumstances, would have a general understanding of the procedure, the medically acceptable alternative procedures or treatments, and the substantial risks and hazards inherent in the proposed treatment or procedures, which are recognized among other physicians, osteopaths, chiropractors, podiatrists, or dentists in the same or similar community who perform similar treatment or procedures. . . .

The Supreme Court, in *Cruzan v. Director, Missouri Dep't of Health*, 497 U.S. 261 (1990), came close to stating that a competent patient has a constitutionally protected right to refuse treatment, even if that refusal results in death.

CRUZAN v. DIRECTOR, MISSOURI DEPARTMENT OF HEALTH
497 U.S. 261 (1990)

CHIEF JUSTICE REHNQUIST.

As these cases demonstrate, the common-law doctrine of informed consent is viewed as generally encompassing the right of a competent individual to refuse medical treatment. Beyond that, these decisions demonstrate both similarity and diversity in their approach to decision of what all agree is a perplexing question with unusually strong moral and ethical overtones. State courts have available to them for decision a number of sources — state constitutions, statutes, and common law — which are not available to us. In this Court, the question is simply and starkly whether the United States Constitution prohibits Missouri from choosing the rule of decision which it did. This is the first case in which we have been squarely presented with the issue of whether the United States Constitution grants what is in common parlance referred to as a "right to die."

The Fourteenth Amendment provides that no State shall "deprive any person of life, liberty, or property, without due process of law." The principle that a competent person has a constitutionally protected liberty interest in refusing unwanted medical treatment may be inferred from our prior decisions.

Just this Term, in the course of holding that a State's procedures for administering antipsychotic medication to prisoners were sufficient to satisfy due process concerns, we recognized that prisoners possess "a significant liberty interest in avoiding the unwanted administration of antipsychotic drugs under the Due Process Clause of the Fourteenth Amendment." *Washington v. Harper*, 494

U.S. 210, 221–222.

But determining that a person has a "liberty interest" under the Due Process Clause does not end the inquiry; "whether respondent's constitutional rights have been violated must be determined by balancing his liberty interests against the relevant state interests." *Youngberg v. Romeo*, 457 U.S. 307, 321.

Petitioners insist that under the general holdings of our cases, the forced administration of life-sustaining medical treatment, and even of artificially-delivered food and water essential to life, would implicate a competent person's liberty interest. Although we think the logic of the cases discussed above would embrace such a liberty interest, the dramatic consequences involved in refusal of such treatment would inform the inquiry as to whether the deprivation of that interest is constitutionally permissible. But for purposes of this case, we assume that the United States Constitution would grant a competent person a constitutionally protected right to refuse lifesaving hydration and nutrition.

C. THE MENTALLY INCAPACITATED PATIENT AND INFORMED CONSENT

A patient who is unable to make a reasonable decision because of mental incapacity cannot give informed consent to medical treatment decisions. The determination of who is mentally incapacitated is therefore critical. In particular, what level of competence is required for a patient to give or withhold informed consent, and how is it determined whether the patient has the requisite competence?

[1] DOES THE PATIENT HAVE THE REQUISITE MENTAL CAPACITY?

Although some patients, such as an unconscious or severely demented patient, obviously lack the mental capacity to give informed consent, often the patient's degree of mental capacity is not clear. Even individuals with reduced or impaired capacity possess the ability to communicate and perhaps to formulate a response that is consistent with their values and desires. The question is whether they understand enough to meaningfully participate in their health care decisions.

QUESTIONS

1. Is a determination that an individual lacks the capacity to make health care decisions, in effect, a decision that the individual's physical well-being is more important than the individual's right to self-determination?

2. Lee, age 79, lost Lacy, his wife of 55 years, last year when she died of cancer. Now Lee has been diagnosed with lung cancer. Lee had a tumor removed but his doctor says he must also undergo chemotherapy. Though his doctor gives Lee only a 10% chance of surviving for a year without chemotherapy and a 30% chance of survival for at least five years if he undergoes it, Lee refuses to undergo chemotherapy. He notes that his wife underwent chemotherapy that was very

debilitating and still died of cancer. He has also repeatedly said, "Why bother. Those drugs didn't help Lacy. I might as well join her. I'm ready to die." At other times he seems confused and keeps asking, "Why do I need those drugs? I'm fine." The doctor suspects that Lee is suffering early stage dementia as well as suffering from clinical depression because of the death of Lacy and his lung cancer. The doctor suggests that a guardianship be sought for Lee so that the guardian can consent to the chemotherapy. Do you agree?

Even if the patient exhibits symptoms of dementia, the treating physician must make the attempt to communicate with the patient as underscored by the following case.

PAYNE v. MARION GENERAL HOSPITAL
549 N.E.2d 1043 (Ind. Ct. App. 1990)

JUDGE BUCHANAN.

Case Summary

Counter-plaintiff-appellant, the Estate of Cloyd Payne, (Estate) appeals from the entry of summary judgment in favor of the counter-defendants-appellees Miles W. Donaldson, M.D. (Dr. Donaldson), Marion General Hospital, Inc. (Hospital) and Marion Family Practice, Inc. (Practice), claiming the trial court erred when it determined there was no genuine issue of material fact.

We reverse in part and affirm in part.

Facts

The facts most favorable to the non-moving party (the Estate) reveal that Cloyd Payne (Payne) was admitted to the Hospital on June 6, 1983. Payne was suffering from a variety of maladies, including malnutrition, uremia, hypertensive cardiovascular disease, chronic obstructive lung disease, nonunion of a previously fractured left humerus, and congenital levoscoliosis of the lumbar spine. Payne was a 65-year-old alcoholic who had allowed his condition to deteriorate to the point he required hospitalization.

Throughout his stay in the Hospital, Payne was subjected to various tests, which confirmed the admitting diagnosis of malnutrition and uremia. By June 10 his condition was deteriorating. He ate poorly and his respirations became labored. On the morning of June 11, Dr. Donaldson examined Payne but made no modifications in Payne's treatment. Payne ate poorly and was visited by family. At approximately 7:00 p.m., Payne's condition worsened as his temperature rose and his respirations became more frequent and labored. Payne appeared to be awake and alert.

At approximately 9:25 p.m., Payne became congested and mucus was aspirated from his lungs. Shortly thereafter, the nurses attempted to reach Payne's nephew, but were unable to contact him. The nurses did contact Payne's sister and she arrived at the Hospital a short time later. The nurses also contacted Dr. Donaldson and related Payne's condition. Dr. Donaldson then ordered some minor adjustments in Payne's treatment.

After observing Payne for several minutes, his sister informed the nurse she did not want Payne resuscitated if he began to die. The nurse contacted Dr. Donaldson and informed him of Payne's condition and of his sister's request. After consulting with the nurse and talking to Payne's sister, Dr. Donaldson then authorized the entry of a "no code" on Payne's chart, after verifying his order with another nurse pursuant to the Hospital's policy. A "no code" is a designation on a patient's chart that no cardiopulmonary resuscitation is to be given in the event the patient begins to expire. The "no code" was entered by the nurse attending Payne, and no efforts to give Payne cardio-pulmonary resuscitation were attempted.

Supportive care was continued, including the suctioning of mucus from Payne's lungs. Occasionally, Payne was awake and alert, and he made eye contact with the nurses attending him. Payne was conscious and capable of communicating with the nurses until moments before his death. His condition continued to worsen, and at 12:55 a.m. on June 12, 1983, Payne died, and no cardiopulmonary resuscitation was attempted.

Dr. Donaldson later sued the Estate for compensation, and the Estate counterclaimed, alleging Dr. Donaldson committed malpractice when he issued the "no code." The counterclaim averred that Dr. Donaldson was acting as an agent of the Practice, and joined the Practice as a party. The counterclaim also included a claim of negligence against the Hospital for failing to provide the proper procedural safeguards when doctors issue "no codes." Dr. Donaldson, the Practice and the Hospital moved for summary judgment and introduced the medical review panel's opinion, issued in accordance with the requirements of the medical malpractice law, which determined the defendants were not negligent. The motions were granted and summary judgment was entered in favor of Dr. Donaldson, the Practice and the Hospital.

Issues

1. Whether the trial court erred when it entered summary judgment in favor of Dr. Donaldson and the Practice?

2. Whether the trial court erred when it entered summary judgment in favor of the Hospital?

Decision

Issue One

Did the trial court err when it determined there was no issue of material fact and that Dr. Donaldson and the Practice were entitled to judgment as a matter of law?

Parties' Contentions

The Estate claims that genuine issues of material fact exist as to whether Payne was competent and terminally ill, and therefore summary judgment was inappropriate. Dr. Donaldson and the Practice respond that the Estate's failure to produce any expert opinion in support of its claim is fatal and therefore summary judgment was correctly granted.

Conclusion

The trial court erred when it entered summary judgment in favor of Dr. Donaldson and the Practice.

Our focus is different. The Estate's claim is that Payne was competent at the time the "no code" was issued and that Dr. Donaldson failed to obtain Payne's informed consent before he issued the "no code." The Estate appeals from the grant of a motion for summary judgment in favor of Dr. Donaldson and the Practice.

In Indiana, the tort of medical malpractice has the same elements of other negligence torts. The elements are: (1) a duty on the part of the defendant in relation to the plaintiff; (2) a failure on the part of the defendant to conform his conduct to the requisite standard of care required by the relationship; and (3) an injury to the plaintiff resulting from that failure. *Burke, supra.*

The duty owed to Payne by Dr. Donaldson is well established as a matter of law. A physician has the duty to make reasonable disclosure of material facts relevant to the care of a patient.

Dr. Donaldson's first response is that Payne was an incompetent, terminally ill patient, and therefore he owed Payne no duty to obtain his consent for the entering of the "no code," and that his sister's consent was sufficient. *Appellee's Brief* at 27.

Whether Payne was competent and terminally ill, however, are questions of fact. An examination of the record reveals that genuine issues of fact exist as to whether Payne was competent and terminally ill, precluding the entry of summary judgment in favor of Dr. Donaldson and the Practice.

There is evidence in the depositions of the nurses who attended Payne during the last day of his life from which a jury could conclude Payne was conscious, alert, and able to communicate when the "no code" was entered, and that he remained competent until shortly before his death.

Shirley Lyons, a licensed practical nurse who attended Payne in the morning and early afternoon on the day of his death, testified as follows:

Q   Did you have occasion during his confinement to speak with him at all?

A   Yes.

Q   What would the nature of your speech have been?

A   As to how he felt and what I could do for him to assist him.

Q   Do you recall whether or not he was capable of verbal response?

A   Yes.

Q   I assume that means you can recall, will you tell me whether or not he was verbal in his responses?

A   I did not have a lengthy conversation with him.

Q   But he did speak to you?

A   Yes.

Q   Did he speak in words or phrases that you could understand?

A   Yes.

Q   Did his answers appear to be responsive to your questions?

A   Yes.

Q   Did he appear capable of communicating meaningful thoughts to you?

A   Meaning what?

Q   Did he give you the information that you sought in your questions?

A   Yes.

Record at 158–62.

Edna Cardwell, a registered nurse who received Dr. Donaldson's order issuing the "no code," attended Payne during the afternoon and evening on the day he died. She testified:

Q   Do you have any reason to suspect that on the 11th of June, 1983, Mr. Payne was unable to speak?

A   Well, it would be the same as he would respond to conversation. If you would talk to him he would look at you and appeared to understand but he verbally did not respond to me.

Q   Do you have any reason to suspect that he was not capable of responding verbally?

A   How do you mean not capable?

Q   Not physically able to speak words?

A   He was quite short of breath but I would not say that he wasn't capable.

Q   I believe in your prior answer you indicated that on the 11th of June, 1983, he appeared to understand what was being said to him, is that what you said?

A   Yes. Because he looked up at you, when you would speak to him he would look at you. He did not respond to me but you would know that he could hear you.

Record at 194–96 (emphasis supplied).

Bonnie Jean Cunningham, a licensed practical nurse who attended Payne during the last hours of his life, testified:

Q   Do you have reason to believe that he was aware of your presence?

A   Yes.

Q   Do you have reason to believe that he was aware of his condition and surroundings and where he was?

A   In my mind I thought so.

Q   In your mind was he oriented as to time and place?

A   I doubt that he was oriented as to the time.

Q   In your impression did he know that he was at Marion General Hospital?

A   I would think so.

Q   And that you were nurses on the staff?

A   Yes.

Q   And that you were treating him for a medical condition of some sort?

A   Yes.

Q   In situations where patients are weak physically or for one reason or another unable to communicate in words, do members of your profession devise ways of communicating and answering the questions with the movement of a body part?

A   I think eye contact has a lot to do with it.

. . . .

Q   In your opinion was this method of communication possible with Mr. Payne during the hours of 11:00 p.m. on the 11th to shortly before he died?

A   Yes.

Q   Do you feel that he would have had the capacity to hear and understand what you were saying to him?

A   Yes, part of the time.

Q   Do you feel that he would have had the ability to process that information and give you a response?

A   I don't know about a verbal response.

Q   How about eye contact or whatever? [A] His eye contact — yes. He looked into your eyes a lot.

Record at 270–76 (emphasis supplied).

This evidence unmistakably establishes a genuine issue of fact exists as to whether Payne was competent when the "no code" was issued. Therefore, viewing the evidence in the light most favorable to the nonmovant, we must conclude Payne was competent when Dr. Donaldson issued the "no code." *See Kreegar, supra.*

Because the evidence could support a conclusion that Payne was competent and not terminally ill at the time the "no code" was issued, we cannot accept Dr. Donaldson's and the Practice's claim that no duty to obtain his consent was owed to Payne.

We believe that this is a situation within the realm of the ordinary laymen's comprehension. No disclosure whatsoever was made. Further, the evidence establishes that Dr. Donaldson made *no* effort to determine if Payne was competent. The "no code" was issued over the phone and Dr. Donaldson had not seen Payne for several hours when he issued the "no code." *Record* at 105. If a jury concludes that Payne was competent at the time the "no code" was issued, it could conclude that the fact Dr. Donaldson made *no* effort to obtain Payne's consent and that he made *no* effort to determine whether Payne was competent was a breach of his duty to obtain Payne's consent.

Whether Payne was damaged by Dr. Donaldson's failure to obtain his informed consent is a question of fact for the jury to determine. The record demonstrates that, had the "no code" not been issued, efforts to resuscitate Payne would have been undertaken, including cardiopulmonary resuscitation. *Record* at 106. Even Dr. Donaldson and the Practice admit that resuscitation efforts offer *some* chance for the patient to keep body and soul together. *Appellee's Brief* at 30. As a jury could conclude Payne was not terminally ill, it could determine some damage was sustained due to Dr. Donaldson's failure to obtain Payne's informed consent, and therefore summary judgment was inappropriate.

To recapitulate, genuine issues of material fact exist as to whether Payne was competent and as to whether he was terminally ill when Dr. Donaldson issued the "no code." Because of the existence of these issues, the trial court erred by granting summary judgment in favor of Dr. Donaldson and the Practice.

The trial court's judgment as to Dr. Donaldson and the Practice is reversed, and in all other respects affirmed.

QUESTIONS

1. How would you determine whether someone lacks capacity to make a particular health care decision?

2. What if the physician makes a good faith mistake and believes that the patient does have decision-making capacity? If the patient refuses to consent, should the physician be liable for withholding treatment or, if the patient consents, for providing treatment?

3. Does the family or anyone else have a duty to disclose information that leads them to believe the patient lacks medical decision-making capacity?

Although the standard for determining incapacity is a legal one, the law necessarily looks to the medical profession for guidance. Unfortunately there is no bright line that defines the limit of mental capacity. As in law, mental incapacity for medical purposes is situational and definitional.

Kevin R. Wolff, Note, *Determining Patient Competency*
24 Ga. L. Rev. 733, 744–49 (1990)*

B. Medical Tests for Competency

Competency in the medical field does not refer to a judicial determination but, rather, to a medical evaluation of a patient's mental capabilities. Clinicians also refer to this concept as "capacity." Clinicians have identified five traditional approaches to evaluating capacity in the informed consent context: (1) evidencing a choice; (2) reasonable outcome of choice; (3) rational reasons for choice; (4) ability to understand; and (5) actual understanding. Each approach balances patient autonomy against social goals in a different way. Although judges inherently use a specific competency test, their opinions rarely document which test was used, or what factors about the patient led to the patient's passing or failing the test.

1. Evidencing a Choice.

The first and least stringent test is "evidencing a choice." If a patient can make a choice — any choice — that decision serves to prove sufficiently his competency. This test values highly the patient's autonomy in the decision making process and is, therefore, the least paternalistic: only the presence of a decision of some sort by the patient is required, without any evaluation by others of the quality of that decision. By focusing on purely behavioral evidence, the test is also very reliable.

"Evidencing a choice" does not, however, function well for screening competency in refusal of medical treatment cases. All consents or refusals constitute a choice; therefore, under this rationale only nondecisions are incompetent choices.

2. Reasonable Outcome of Choice.

The "reasonable outcome of choice" test requires that an evaluator agree the patient has made the "right" or "responsible" decision. This test emphasizes social goals by favoring the state interests in the preservation of life and the integrity of the medical profession.

"Reasonable outcome of choice" does not value highly patient autonomy, though, because the opinion of the outside observer unconditionally trumps the patient's decision if the parties merely disagree about the outcome of that decision. Given the medical profession's predisposition for sustaining life, the patient is likely to be adjudged incompetent whenever he chooses to refuse treatment. This result occurred in *United States v. Charters*, where a psychiatric patient's refusal of antipsychotic drugs, which prescribed to make him competent to stand trial, was a basis of his adjudged incompetency to refuse the medication.

---

3. Rational Reasons for Choice.

This third test does not look at the outcome of the decision; instead, this test evaluates the quality of the decision making. It asks whether the choice was based on rational reasons. Psychiatrists are most comfortable with this "rational" test because of their expertise in assessing irrationality. The traditional irrationality test is an evaluation of the patient's ability to manipulate data and reach a conclusion based on hypothetical situations.

Despite psychiatric expertise in this area, an obvious problem with this test is distinguishing between a rational and an irrational decision. This test necessarily includes a subjective evaluation by the evaluating psychiatrist; however, this subjectivity only impinges on patient autonomy if the psychiatrist does not allow for the possibility that idiosyncratic responses might still result from rational decision making. One commentator suggests calling this the "recognizable reasons test" to account for reasons that support the patient' decision but with which the evaluator disagrees.

A second problem with this test is proving a causal link between the irrational decision and the patient's incompetence. The irrational decision can result from phobia, panic or depression, but these conditions do not necessarily indicate incompetence. The causation problem should not eliminate this test, however, because it still identifies incompetent decisions although the reason for the incompetence might remain obscured. One proposed solution is to limit the responses that constitute failures under this test to those premised on known falsities or nonsequitors.

4. Ability to Understand.

This test requires an evaluation of the patient's ability to understand the risks, benefits, and alternatives of treatment. The traditional method of testing begins when patients are given information necessary to make an informed decision. They are later asked for their decision and the information they considered relevant in making their decision. This test is consistent with standards of informed consent that allow the patient to make treatment decisions only when those decisions are informed, voluntary and competent.

A limitation of this test is that the patient may understand the risks but not the benefits. Furthermore, the test does not specify how sophisticated the understanding must be, a value decision in and of itself. Also, the test's reliability is questionable because the test does not rely on observable behavioral elements but rather on inferential mental processes. Finally, one can criticize the test as placing too much influence on the patient's ability to memorize and recall the information given to him, a factor which may obscure the later impact this information may have.

5. Actual Understanding.

The fifth test requires that the patient actually understand the costs, benefits, and alternatives of treatment and be able to apply these to his current situation.

This shares, with the "ability to understand" test, the practical problems of determining the nature of understanding. The subjectivity problem is more pronounced, however, because the emphasis is not on the patient's *ability* to understand but on whether the patient *actually* understands. This requirement theoretically makes validation more difficult.

———

Determination of a lack of mental incapacity by physicians in clinical settings is commonplace. Typically the physician concludes that the patient lacks mental capacity and so turns to the family and involves them in the decision-making process. Only in unusual cases do the courts become involved. Disagreements among family members as to the proper course of treatment may cause someone to resort to the courts or some may claim that the patient still has capacity and his or her decisions should be respected. More commonly, all the parties agree that the patient lacks mental capacity, but disagree as to who should make health care decisions for the patient or what is the proper decision, particularly in cases of end-of-life treatment.

[2] INCAPACITATED OR JUST ECCENTRIC?

Individuals who have capacity have the right to make idiosyncratic or even "wrong" decisions. Capacity does not mean making the wisest choice; rather, it means having the capability to choose rationally. As long as individuals have the ability to make decisions that promote their own values and preferences they would appear to have sufficient capacity to make their own medical decisions. The fact that they do not act to promote their self-interest as we would understand it does not mean that they are incapacitated.

While mental capacity is supposed to be determined with reference to the individual's ability to process information and communicate, rather than the "correctness" of the decisions, in reality courts often adopt a behavior-based approach. The individual's behavior is thought to create compelling evidence of mental capacity since it is one of only two sources of evidence, the other being the opinions of expert witnesses. The results of psychological or cognitive tests can also be used but they must be interpreted or validated by experts. In the end the court must determine capacity based upon the individual's behavior and expert testimony.

If the individual's behavior is bizarre or inexplicable, courts may find it difficult to reject the "objective" behavioral evidence of mental incapacity. It is not easy for a judge to conclude that individuals who act in a self-destructive or irrational manner have the mental ability to care for themselves. That is, the judge would have to decide that such individuals understand reality and comprehend the available choices but choose to act in a way likely to bring harm to themselves. Naturally, when faced with that choice many judges will conclude that the individual lacks capacity.

The testimony of witnesses can itself be tainted by paternalistic or protective instincts which may color their judgment. Because of an excess of concern for the elderly person, family members might be too eager to conclude that the individual is mentally incapable of making rational health care decisions. Physicians may interpret rejection of their suggestions as evidence of incapacity in the belief that the patient who is unwilling to follow generally approved medical treatment procedures must be incompetent.

In some cases, the patient's religious beliefs cause them to reject the advice of the treating physician. A Jehovah's Witness, for example, may reject a blood transfusion even though it may mean her death. Today, courts almost always uphold a patients' right to follow the dictates of their conscience even if that means refusing life saving medical treatment.

IN RE MILTON
505 N.E.2d 255 (Ohio 1987)

JUSTICE WRIGHT.

There is a dichotomy between modern medicine which is scientific and based upon provable theories and religion which is *inherently* mystical, intangible and a matter of individual faith. Yet, the Ohio and United States Constitutions mandate that when the dictates of modern medicine and religious beliefs collide, the conflict be resolved by leaving the medical treatment decision to the individual.

While there may be a variety of opinions as to the efficacy of spiritual healing through faith, the courts below acknowledged that it is a form of religious belief and practice. We recognize that extending constitutional protection to a belief in spiritual healing and other religiously motivated refusals to accept medical treatment can be very troubling to those who do not share these beliefs, since, in cases such as this one, the patient may die as a result of refusing the recommended treatment. . . .

Appellant has expressed a long-standing belief in spiritual healing, and great weight must be given to her statement of her personal beliefs. We cannot evaluate the "correctness" or propriety of appellant's belief. Absent the most exigent circumstances, courts should never be a party to branding a citizen's religious views as baseless on the grounds that they are non-traditional, unorthodox or at war with what the state or others perceive as reality.

The testimony of Dr. Green supports our conclusion that appellant's belief in spiritual healing stands on its own, without regard to any delusion. We can probe no further. Appellant's religious freedom to believe and act according to the dictates of her belief in spiritual healing prevents a court from ordering treatment against her will that would violate her religious beliefs. Thus, we hold that the state may not compel a legally competent adult to submit to medical treatment which would violate that individual's religious beliefs even though the treatment is arguably life-extending. Therefore, the probate court's determination was erroneous and the judgment of the court of appeals upholding it is reversed.

D. SURROGATE DECISION MAKING FOR THE MENTALLY INCAPACITATED PATIENT: ADVANCE HEALTH CARE DIRECTIVES

Patients who are incapacitated and unable to give informed consent are still protected by the doctrine since consent must be obtained from a proxy decision maker before treatment is provided. Absent an emergency, medical personnel must obtain consent before providing care. If the patient lacks capacity to consent, the formal solution is to require that a guardianship petition be filed requesting that the court find the patient to be mentally incapacitated and appoint a guardian of the person. The guardian may then provide consent on behalf of the ward. Far more common, however, are informal arrangements in which the spouse or family members provide consent without judicial appointment of a guardian. As long as family members are in agreement and consent to generally acceptable medical procedures, such an informal arrangement is usually effective.

Another formal solution is for the patient, prior to the onset of the incapacity, to appoint a proxy or surrogate (the two words are often used interchangeably) to make decisions in his or her stead in the case of mental incapacity. If the patient is concerned with being kept alive when there is no hope of recovery, the patient may wish to create a living will or empower a proxy decision maker to terminate life-sustaining treatment.

Advance health care directives either state a person's wishes and instructions regarding future medical treatment in the event of incapacity or appoint someone to act as a surrogate decision maker. Some do both. The choice between the two depends upon what the applicable state law permits and whether the declarant (the maker of the advance directive) prefers to try to control the future or is content with naming a proxy decision maker.

A living will is an attempt to anticipatorily control the medical decision-making process and is usually (though need not be exclusively) directed at life-sustaining treatment. A durable power of attorney for health care names a surrogate or proxy decision maker in the event that the creator of the power should become incapacitated. Other forms of advance directives include creating a non-binding statement of health care desires and oral directives to spouses, family, or friends.

Advance directives can and do take many forms, formal and informal, written and oral. Whatever their form, they give the individual some control over future health care decisions in the event of incapacity. By making provision for prospective health care decisions the individual promotes autonomy and self-determination since the individual's values can be honored only if the individual makes them known prior to the onset of incapacity. In the absence of any advance directive (even the most informal oral statements), medical decisions for an incapacitated individual necessarily will be based upon generalized or commonly assumed values or upon the values held by the surrogate decision maker. In either case the patient's hopes, wishes, and values may go unfulfilled.

State statutes authorize a variety of different advance directives. Living wills were the first legalized form of advance health care directive. Today most attorneys recommend also creating an advance directive that appoints a surrogate decision maker and not rely solely on a living will.

[1] LIVING WILLS

The use of the term "living will" (apparently coined by Luis Kutner in *Due Process of Euthanasia: The Living Will, A Proposal*, 44 IND. L.J. 539 (1969)) is unfortunate since it confuses medical decision making with a testamentary instrument, i.e., a will. A better term would be natural death instructions. Just as a competent patient can terminate medical treatment, so should an incapacitated patient. Living wills were conceived as a way for a mentally incapacitated individual to terminate medical care when the prognosis was hopeless and to permit a dignified death. A living will provides instructions from the patient as to future end-of-life medical care.

Every state statutorily recognizes some version of a living will. Though the statutes vary, all permit the declarant to terminate life-sustaining treatment in case of a terminal illness or a permanent unconscious state. Many statutes also permit a living will to be used to give instructions on what kind of treatment the declarant might prefer.

A living will can be a custom created document, but most are based on a form, perhaps one provided, or sometimes required, by the state statute. Living will forms abound on the internet, some of which were created by bar associations, by medical organizations, and by those concerned with the rights of terminally ill individuals.

A living will becomes operative only if the declarant loses the mental capacity necessary to give informed consent, that is, lose the ability to make health care decisions. By the time a living will takes effect, the declarant will not be mentally capable of assisting in interpreting the intent of the document.

[a] Terminally Ill Requirement

In reality, living wills often fail to be of much practical use because it is impossible to know in advance what medical conditions will arise. General statements to the effect that the individual does not want to be treated under vaguely identified medical conditions frequently fail to offer sufficient guidance. The physician and family are often unsure of what the declarant would have wanted if faced by a particular medical condition. Suppose, for example, that the living will states that treatment should be terminated if the declarant is terminally ill. The declarant is diagnosed with inoperable cancer with death expected in four to six months. The declarant comes down with pneumonia, which if not treated is likely to result in the death of the declarant. Should the pneumonia be treated with antibiotics because it is not a terminal condition or does the underlying terminal condition dictate that the pneumonia not be treated?

A diagnosis of terminal illness means that the patient's condition is irreversible or incurable. The phrase is used when the patient is expected to die relatively soon despite medical treatment. Of course, before a patient is identified as being terminally ill the attending physician must be convinced that the patient's condition is hopeless. Given the ability of modern medicine to provide some slim reed of hope for most patients, a diagnosis of terminal illness is not announced lightly.

Legally even an incurable patient may not be considered terminal unless the prospect of death is imminent, but how soon is "soon"? (Some time limit must be set; otherwise, everyone could be considered "terminal.") Case law and statutes provide some guidance. The New Jersey Supreme Court held a patient to be terminal if death is expected within a year. *See In re Conroy*, 486 A.2d 1209, 1231 (1985). Medicare hospice care for the terminally ill requires a diagnosis of a life expectancy of six months or less. Courts generally look for the imminent probability of death from some identifiable condition or illness — the closer death approaches, the easier it is to predict.

The uncertainty as to who is "terminal" and the movement away from its use is reflected by the absence of the term in the Uniform Health Care Decisions Act, which merely grants the incapacitated patient the right to appoint an agent the right to make a decision about "any care, treatment, service, or procedure to maintain, diagnose, or otherwise affect an individual's physical or mental condition." (Section 1, Definitions, (6) Health Care.) The term "terminal" is being supplanted in some instances by the term "end-stage condition," which is thought to encompass a greater variety of conditions and because it focuses on the outcomes of treatment rather than whether the patient is dying soon. For example, Florida law defines "end-stage condition" as "an irreversible condition that is caused by injury, disease, or illness which has resulted in progressively severe and permanent deterioration, and, which, to a reasonable degree of medical probability, treatment of the condition would be ineffective." FLA. STAT. ANN. § 765.101(4).

Some statutes permit the living will to take effect if medical treatment only serves to postpone the moment of dying. Virginia's Health Care Decisions Act states:

> "Life-prolonging procedure" means any medical procedure, treatment or intervention which (I) utilizes mechanical or other artificial means to sustain, restore or supplant a spontaneous vital function, or is otherwise of such a nature as to afford a patient no reasonable expectation of recovery from a terminal condition and (ii) when applied to a patient in a terminal condition, would serve only to prolong the dying process. The term includes hydration and nutrition. However, nothing in this act shall prohibit the administration of medication or the performance of any medical procedure deemed necessary to provide comfort care or to alleviate pain.

VA. CODE ANN. § 54.1-2982.

QUESTIONS

1.   What should the term "terminally ill" mean? Can you think of a better term? Would the term "death is imminent" be more helpful?

2.   If you had only six months to live, would you want to terminate medical treatment except for pain suppressors? If you were competent? Incompetent? What if you had 30 days to live? One week?

3. John, age 67, was in an auto accident in which he suffered severe traumatic chest injury. He was rushed to the hospital and placed on a ventilator, without which he would have died. John's wife, Joan, produced his living will, in which he expressed a refusal of life-sustaining treatment. She therefore asked that the ventilator be removed. John's sister, Rachel, claims that the living will does not apply because John will survive the injuries so long as he is on the ventilator. Therefore, he is not terminal. Is Rachel correct?

To predict death, of course, it is necessary to define what is meant by the term. Contrary to popular belief, death is a definitional term, not the description of a fixed reality. As one philosopher stated it: "The declaration of death is clearly an event, just as the heart attack is an event, but it is not a biological event. It is an action, based on a decision of significance, and is therefore an event that has social, moral, and metaphysical roots and implications." K. Gervais, Redefining Death 3 (Yale 1986).

The identification of death has changed over time. The traditional legal definition of death was the cessation of circulation and respiration, known as a systemic definition of death. Today it is understood that even though circulation and respiration cease, all biological activity does not, because nonintegrated organic functioning can continue even though integrated organic functioning has ended. For example, the heart may beat on though the brain is dead. Moreover, because of the respirator or mechanical ventilator, a patient's respiration can be maintained almost indefinitely. As long as respiration continues, so does circulation. Hence, though permanently unconscious, having suffered irreparable brain damage, and kept alive only by mechanical devices, under the traditional definition of death the patient would be considered alive.

Around 1960 the concept of brain death emerged to describe a condition of irreversible coma and loss of the capacity to breathe independently when the patient had suffered massive, irreversible brain damage. Today every state statutorily incorporates brain death along with the traditional systemic definition of death.

The Uniform Definition of Death Act (UDDA) defines brain death as the "irreversible cessation of all functions of the entire brain, including the brain stem." UDDA, 12 U.L.A. 292. While the death of the upper brain leaves the patient permanently in a noncognitive state — unconscious, unthinking, and unaware — the death of the brain stem terminates the involuntary or vegetative functioning of respiration (and therefore of circulation). A Harvard Medical School Committee Report recommended that death (brain death) be declared when a patient exhibits "(a) unresponsiveness to normally painful stimuli; (b) absence of spontaneous movements or breathing; and (c) absence of reflexes." Ad Hoc Committee of the Harvard Medical School to Examine the Definition of Brain Death, *Definition of Irreversible Coma*, 205 J. Am. Med. Ass'n 337 (1968). A flat electroencephalogram (EEG) reading or lack of blood flow to the brain confirms the existence of brain death. If the criteria are properly used, brain death can be diagnosed with almost absolute certainty.

The requirement that the patient be terminal rules out the applicability of living wills to those patients who are permanently unconscious, i.e., in a persistent vegetative state (PVS). Because persistent vegetative state patients who are given life-sustaining treatment may live for years, they are not terminally ill. Fortunately, some statutes do make living wills applicable to persistent vegetative state patients by defining a terminal condition to include the condition of permanent vegetative state. Other states permit a living will to be invoked for a qualified patient and define that term to include patients who are either terminal or in a persistent vegetative state.

Many older persons fear living with severe dementia or Alzheimer's disease. If dementia becomes severe enough, the person lacks an awareness of their surroundings, loses control of bodily functions, and must be kept alive first by hand feeding and eventually by the use of a feeding tube. For some, the prospect of being alive in a state of severe dementia is intolerable. They would prefer to be permitted to die by an intervening illness, such as pneumonia. Unfortunately severe dementia does not mean that death is near nor is the individual in a persistent vegetative state. Most state living will statutes, therefore, do not specifically grant them the right to refuse treatment through the use of a living will. Despite this apparent limitation of living wills, many individuals will insert a clause in their living will which in the event of severe dementia will call for a termination of treatment just as if the individual were in a terminal condition. Most commentators believe that a living will may request termination of treatment under conditions not described in the state statute. For example, the living will might contain language such as:

> If I suffer from irreversible brain disease or brain damage with no hope of significant recovery, I want my health care providers to treat such condition as if I were terminally ill and treat any intervening life-threatening illness accordingly.

[b] Foregoing Nutrition and Hydration

A controversial issue concerning living wills is whether the patient can authorize the foregoing of artificial nutrition and hydration. Patients who are unconscious, delirious, or in the advanced stages of dementia and who are unable to take food by mouth require a feeding tube because intravenous feeding cannot supply enough nutrients to maintain life. Absent any other medical condition a patient can be kept alive indefinitely on a feeding tube. If the feeding tube is removed the patient will die.

Artificial feeding by a tube is considered to be a form of medical treatment. The American Medical Association (AMA) has stated that "artificially or technologically supplied . . . nutrition and hydration" is a medical procedure in the same way that the use of a respirator is a medical treatment. AMA Council on Ethical and Judicial Affairs, Op. 2.18 (1986). Virtually every case has held that artificial nutrition and hydration are a form of medical treatment and can be terminated without invoking laws against assisted suicide or homicide. As stated in an opinion issued by the Maryland Attorney General, "Every appellate court that has addressed the issue has held that there is no difference as a matter of law between artificially administered sustenance and other forms of life-sustaining treatment." 73 Md. Op.

Att'y Gen. 253, 270–71 (Op. No. 88-046, Oct. 17, 1988).

When faced with the issue of whether prior statements by an individual can permit the discontinuance of tube feeding, the Maine Supreme Court stated:

> Gardner's decision to live without artificial life-sustaining procedures would not constitute suicide since the grievous injuries resulting in his present condition were not self-inflicted. He in no sense has decided to kill himself. Gardner did not suffer his injuries by intentionally placing himself in such a position that his continued biological existence would depend upon the provision of life-sustaining procedures. Accident has brought him to that state. Following his mishap Gardner is simply exercising his right to control the course of his medical care. Because of the unfortunate condition into which his 1985 accident put him, his refusal of all artificial feeding will be followed by death. Yet this coupling of his treatment decision and his ultimate death should not mask the obvious point that the cause of his death will be not his refusal of care but rather his accident and his resulting medical condition, including his inability to ingest food and water. . . . Forcing upon him the life-sustaining procedures he has decided to refuse would only prolong the ultimate moment of his death. His decision not receive such procedures, far from constituting suicide, is a choice to allow to take its course the natural dying process set in motion by his physiological inability to chew or swallow.

In re Gardner, 534 A.2d 947 (Me. 1987).

The right of an individual to terminate artificial nutrition or hydration by a directive in a living will may be protected by common law or under the state constitution. The Missouri State Supreme Court, however, held that the evidentiary requirements of the Missouri living will statute had to be met even if the patient had not signed a living will. That statute required clear and convincing evidence of the intent of the incompetent before the surrogate could terminate life sustaining treatment such as nutrition and hydration. *Cruzan v. Harmon*, 760 S.W.2d 408, 425 (Mo. 1988), *aff'd*, *Cruzan v. Director, Missouri Dep't of Health*, 497 U.S. 261 (1990).

QUESTIONS

1. Do you agree that artificial nutrition and hydration are forms of medical procedures?

2. If you think of artificial nutrition and hydration is not a medical procedure, should an incapacitated patient be allowed to require their cessation as part of a living will?

When first enacted, many living will statutes did not permit the declarant to refuse the termination of artificial nutrition or hydration. However, in light of case law supporting the proposition that artificial nutrition and hydration are merely a form of medical treatment, state living will statutes have been revised to permit the declarant to refuse artificial nutrition and hydration.

Beyond tube feeding is the issue of whether individuals should be able to use a living will to refuse feeding by hand in the event they have severe enough dementia so that they no longer understand how to feed themselves. When that occurs, the caregiver (often the nursing home) must resort to hand feeding. Some individuals do not want to be kept alive by hand feeding because the procedure depends upon placing food in the patient's mouth and inducing the gag reflex to cause swallowing. Rather than endure this, some would prefer death or a "natural" death as it is sometimes referred to. The living will that refuses hand feeding is also likely to insist that the individual not be hydrated (given water by mouth or by an IV). The lack of nutrition and hydration are likely to cause death within 7 to 14 days. The living will would permit alleviation of thirst by procedures such as a glycerin swipe, but not by the provision of water that would only prolong the process of dying. While refusal of hand feeding in a living will is legal, it is less clear whether third parties will enforce it. Permitting a patient to die in such a manner may be too troubling for family members to endure.

[c] Formalities of Execution, Revocation, and Validity in Other States

Most statutes provide that only a competent adult can execute a living will, which must be in writing and signed by the declarant. The statutes typically require two witnesses and some require notarization as well. Almost all preclude anyone with a conflict of interest from acting as a witness, which may include spouses, close relatives, potential heirs of the declarant's estate, the declarant's physician, an employee of the health care facility in which the declarant is a patient, and, in a few cases, a fellow patient. These prohibitions are an attempt to ensure that the witnesses are disinterested observers with nothing to gain from the declarant's death. If the declarant is in a nursing home stricter provisions may apply, such as mandating that the declaration be notarized.

Many state living will statutes contain a model form of a directive, the use of which in most states is optional though a few states require the declarant to use the statutory form. Optional forms are preferable because they allow the creation of a document that better expresses the desires of the declarant. Still, the mere existence of a form is likely to result in its being used even if the needs of the declarant might better be served by a different document. Some declarants will not consult an attorney and will merely fill out the statutory form. Even attorneys may use the form from habit rather than undertaking an adequate inquiry as to the particular needs of the client.

Living will forms, both state sanctioned and those created privately, have been criticized for being poorly designed, confusing, internally inconsistent, and too reliant upon technical language. When patients complete such forms without adequate counseling, there is a risk that the form will not accurately portray the patient's attitude toward the use of life-sustaining medical care.

Living wills generally are valid until revoked by the declarant, and they can be revoked at any time. Revocation can occur by physical destruction of the document, written revocation, and verbal revocation. The revocation becomes effective upon notification of the physician. Most statutes also permit verbal revocation of the most casual kind. For example, suppose the declarant, Helen, has fallen unconscious and is taken to the hospital. In the ambulance she stirs awake and murmurs that although she has a living will she wants to live "no matter what." She then lapses back into unconsciousness. Her statement would be taken as a valid revocation of her living will. The apparent statutory goal is to err on the side of treatment for declarants who might have changed their minds. If there is more than one directive then the directions in the most recent document will govern.

Living wills can also be superseded by later statements. Imagine, for example, a hospital patient who discusses his treatment with a physician without mentioning the living will that he signed a year before. After the patient has become incapacitated the living will turns up and conflicts with the statements by the patient to the physician. Which instructions should the physician follow? In such circumstances the most recent instructions govern. Even in the absence of an explicit statute, the most recent attitude of the patient would appear to govern since a living will is created expressly to provide evidence of the declarant's attitude towards life-sustaining treatment. If the declarant's contemporaneous views are known they should prevail since the goal is to know and act upon the patient's current views

QUESTIONS

1. How long should a living will remain valid? Should living wills remain valid until revoked, or should they automatically terminate? Why? If so, when?

2. Does it make sense to allow revocation by the declarant without any formalities? A testamentary will, in contrast, cannot be verbally revoked. Why should a carefully considered advance directive be revocable in a moment of panic or fear?

3. Some statutes allow a revocation by a declarant who has been declared legally incompetent. Why and under what conditions should a mentally incapacitated individual be allowed to revoke a living will?

4. Are there any conditions that should cause the automatic revocation of a living will? Should marriage, for example?

5. Assume that an incapacitated patient executed a living will over 20 years ago. Since that time medical technology has undergone significant changes. Should a direction that in effect says "pull the plug" still be honored? If not, why not?

If an individual executes a valid living will in state A, but later is hospitalized in state B, is the living will valid? Testamentary wills are generally recognized as valid in any state if valid in the state where they were signed. Most state statutes treat living wills similarly. They provide that a living will is enforceable if valid in the state where it was executed or in the state where it is to be enforced. Of course, even if the living will is not valid it provides strong proof of the patient's attitude about life-sustaining treatment, which can be used to guide the actions of a proxy decision maker.

[d] Notification and Liability

A declaration becomes operative when its existence is communicated to the attending physician. The physician is not under a duty to inquire as to the existence of a living will, though some physicians routinely inquire of patients whether they have executed an advance health care directive. The responsibility to notify the physician rests with the declarant. In practice, relatives or spouses often will present a copy of the living will to the attending physician or hospital. Many state statutes require that a copy of any living will be placed in the patient's medical record. Since December 1991 the federal Patient Self-Determination Act (1990 Omnibus Budget Reconciliation Act, Pub. L. No. 101-508) has required all hospitals participating in the Medicare or Medicaid programs to advise patients upon admission of their rights under state law to refuse medical treatment. Presumably, while providing such information the hospital will inquire whether the patient has executed an advance health care directive. Some hospitals now routinely provide advance directive forms to their patients.

All statutes provide immunity for the health care personnel who follow the directions of a living will. The physician or other health care provider is not subject to criminal or civil liability if he or she acts in accord with reasonable medical standards. If the attending physician cannot or will not abide by the directive, state laws require that the patient be transferred to a physician who will effectuate the patient's advance directive. A few states provide criminal penalties for failure to do so.

[2] APPOINTMENT OF A SURROGATE DECISION MAKER

[a] Appointment by the Patient

Living wills are not the only form of an advance health care directive. Individuals can also execute an advance directive that appoints a surrogate health care decision maker, sometimes referred to as a proxy or agent, to make health care decisions if the individual becomes mentally incapacitated. The individual who executes an advance health care directive is referred to as the "declarant." The appointment of a surrogate provides a means for medical decisions even if the declarant had not contemplated or provided for the particular situation that arose. Because of the greater flexibility provided by the naming of a surrogate, attorneys increasingly advise clients to appoint one. Some advocate combining a living will with an advance health directive that names a surrogate decision maker. However, if not done with care, the combination can lead to confusion as to whether the surrogate must follow the language of the living will or is to use his or her own judgment to make the best decision under the circumstances.

The purpose of appointing a surrogate is to preserve the autonomy of declarants by permitting them to identify who is to make medical decisions for them. The surrogate provides the physician someone with whom to consult about treatment decisions. Absent a surrogate, the physician may be faced with dealing with family members who are unable to reach a consensus as to the appropriate treatment for the incapacitated patient. Together, the surrogate and the physician determine the course of medical care for the incapacitated patient, including termination of life sustaining treatment.

To assist the surrogate (sometimes referred to as an agent or proxy) in making decisions, the declarant may include precatory or mandatory instructions in the directive such as no tube feeding. A declarant should discuss his or her attitude about end-of-life care with the surrogate in order to provide the surrogate with an understanding and appreciation of the declarant's values and concerns about medical treatment, personal dignity, and what other conditions death might be preferable to continued care. Making end-of-life decisions for another person is a difficult task. Surrogates need the assurance that what they are doing comports with the wishes of the patient. If the surrogate is confident of doing what the declarant would have wanted, the surrogate is more likely to make hard decisions and not later suffer a sense of guilt or recrimination about having made a choice that resulted in the death of the declarant.

In some instances, the selection of who should be named as surrogate decision maker can be problematic. Someone selected today may be inappropriate, unavailable, or unwilling to act when needed, which may be years hence. The spouse is the most common choice, but who should serve as the successor agent if the spouse is not available? If a child is selected, will other children feel slighted? What if the surrogate lives far away? Particularly for the very old, there may be a dearth of appropriate individuals to name as a surrogate decision maker. Still, the appointment of a surrogate is usually preferred even if the individual named is not ideal.

[b] Appointment by State Statute

Many states have enacted surrogate decision-making statutes to provide for the appointment of a surrogate if the patient has not done so. The statutes provide that if the patient is mentally incapacitated, as determined by the treating physician, and has not appointed a surrogate decision maker, the statute automatically appoints a surrogate. The statutes provide a list of surrogates, beginning with the spouse, then the adult children and so forth. The surrogate takes on the right to make decisions without any resort to the court. The individual with priority to be the surrogate may decline taking on that responsibility and pass the right on to the next individual in line. For example, if a spouse chooses not to act as a surrogate or cannot because of physical or mental loss of capacity, the adult children would become the surrogate. Anyone can petition the court to intervene and name a surrogate other than the individual designated by the statute. Suppose the patient is not married and has no children with the result that a first cousin is the statutorily identified surrogate. The unmarried partner of the patient could petition the court and ask that she be appointed surrogate in light of her relationship to the patient. The court has the responsibility to appoint who can best serve as the surrogate.

[c] Surrogate Decision-Making Standards

The surrogate decision maker's authority to act becomes effective when the principal suffers a loss of mental capacity. When appointed by the patient or by a state statute, the surrogate must act in the best interests of the patient; surrogates are not permitted to do whatever they think is best. The surrogate is expected to act according to any instructions given in the instrument. If there are none or if they do not address the situation, the surrogate is expected to make decisions in light of the principal's personal values, oral or written statements, or other evidence of what the patient would have wanted. Doing what the patient would have done is known as the substituted judgment doctrine. According to that doctrine, the surrogate, as the agent of the patient, attempts to do what the patient wanted or would have wanted.

Absent actual knowledge of what the patient would want, the surrogate is expected to infer what the patient would have wanted based on the patient's statements and conduct. In the absence of specific inference evidence, courts have permitted surrogates to look to the lifestyle and values of the patient as guides to what the patient would have wanted. The surrogate should consider the patient's prior statements about and reactions to medical issues, and all the facets of the patient's personality that the surrogate is familiar with — with particular reference to his or her relevant philosophical, theological, and ethical values — in order to extrapolate what course of medical treatment the patient would choose.

The substituted judgment doctrine extends to the termination of life sustaining treatment. Every day across America scores of surrogates, families, and physicians conclude that it is futile to continue medical treatment for an incapacitated patient. Reluctantly, they decide to terminate treatment and allow nature to run its course, with death the inevitable conclusion. Often they do so without the aid of a written advance directive or without any certainty as to what the patient would have wanted. They terminate treatment because they think that it is the right thing to do and because they hope that it is what the patient would have wanted. As long as the family, the attending physician, and the hospital agree, no resort to a court is necessary. *In re Jobes*, 529 A.2d 434, 450 (N.J. 1987).

If the surrogate has no information as to what the individual would have decided and so no basis to invoke substituted judgment, the surrogate should act in the best interests of the individual. In some cases, discontinuing treatment and allowing the individual to die may be acting in his or her best interests.

The current state of surrogate decision making at the end of life for incapacitated patients is summarized in the following case.

WOODS v. COMMONWEALTH OF KENTUCKY
142 S.W.3d 24 (Ky. 2004)

JUSTICE COOPER.

This appeal challenges the constitutionality of KRS 311.631, a provision of the Kentucky Living Will Directive Act, insofar as it permits a judicially-appointed guardian or other designated surrogate to authorize the withholding or withdrawal of artificial life-prolonging treatment from a ward or patient who is either in a persistent vegetative state or permanently unconscious. If the statute is constitutional, the issue becomes how to implement it.

Matthew Woods was born on November 24, 1941; he died during the course of these proceedings on June 2, 1996. His intelligence quotient (I.Q.) was between 70 and 71 and, by judicial appointment, various state agencies had managed his affairs since May 12, 1970. On January 28, 1991, pursuant to a jury's verdict that he was partially disabled, KRS 387.570; KRS 387.580, the Fayette District Court appointed an agent of the Cabinet for Human Resources ("CHR") as Woods's limited guardian with authority to make certain decisions for him, including consent to medical procedures. Woods lived in a state-approved group home, attended church, had a girlfriend, participated regularly in day-treatment programs, and was able to travel across town by bus to visit friends. He was treated for asthma by doctors at the University of Kentucky Medical Center.

On April 18, 1995, Woods suffered cardiopulmonary arrest while being transported by a friend to the Medical Center for treatment of a severe asthma attack. His friend detoured to the nearest hospital, St. Joseph Hospital, where medical personnel resuscitated Woods and connected him to a mechanical ventilator. Efforts to further revive him failed and he never regained consciousness. An electroencephalogram (EEG) examination revealed severe global encephalopathy, which his doctors agreed was caused by hypoxia, i.e., oxygen deprivation that occurred between the cardiopulmonary arrest and the resuscitation. His treating physician, Dr. Jeremiah Suhl, and a consulting neurologist, Dr. William C. Robertson, agreed that Woods had suffered total and irreversible cessation of all normal brain functions. He responded to neither voice nor pain stimuli. He was unable to breathe or swallow. A tracheos-tomy was performed to permanently attach a mechanical ventilator that pumped oxygen into his lungs. At first, nutrition and hydration were provided through nasal feeding tubes. Later, a gastrostomy was performed so that nutrition and hydration could be mechanically pumped directly into his small intestines. Nevertheless, Woods was not dead as defined in KRS 446.400 because short bursts of electrical activity still emanated from his brain stem. . . . He remained in a state of permanent unconsciousness, a condition more severe than a persistent vegetative state, in mors interruptus, suspended by "merger of body and machine" in a Limbo somewhere between cognizant life and legal death.

Dr. Suhl estimated that Woods's biological functions could be maintained for one to two years on ventilation, and possibly up to ten years, but that if the ventilator were removed, death would occur in less than forty-eight hours. Drs. Suhl and Robertson both recommended withdrawing artificial ventilation so that the mechanically interrupted natural process of dying could conclude. They did not recommend withdrawal of the artificially administered nutrition and hydration until after death occurred. . . .

On September 21, 1995, the district court entered an opinion and order holding that KRS 311.631 authorizes a judicially-appointed guardian of an adult patient who lacks decisional capacity and has not made an "advance directive," to make health care decisions on behalf of the patient, including withdrawal of artificial life-support systems, without obtaining advance judicial approval, so long as the guardian acts in good faith and in the best interest of the patient.

The guardian ad litem appealed to the Fayette Circuit Court, asserting that

KRS 311.631 is unconstitutional or, if constitutional, the judicially-appointed guardian must prove by clear and convincing evidence that withdrawing artificial life support is in the patient's best interests; and that the statute violates public policy and modern ethical standards. . . .

. . . .

We do not write on a clean slate. Since the Supreme Court of New Jersey's seminal decision in *In re Quinlan*, 70 N.J. 10, 355 A.2d 647 (N.J. 1976), many state courts, including this Court, as well as the United States Supreme Court, *Cruzan*, have addressed various issues relating to the right of a terminally ill patient to refuse unwanted life-prolonging treatment. . . .

I. COMMON LAW BACKGROUND.

Woods's guardian ad litem does not question the right of a competent person to forego medical treatment by either refusal or withdrawal. . . . That right derives from the common law rights of self-determination and informed consent; *see also Cruzan*, 497 U.S. at 270 ("The logical corollary of the doctrine of informed consent is that the patient generally possesses the right not to consent, that is, to refuse treatment."); and in the liberty interest protected by the Fourteenth Amendment to the United States Constitution ("nor shall any State deprive any person of life, liberty, or property, without due process of law"), *id.* at 278 ("The principle that a competent person has a constitutionally protected liberty interest in refusing unwanted medical treatment may be inferred from our prior decisions.")

. . . . However, this right is not absolute. The individual's liberty interest must be balanced against relevant state interests. *Cruzan*, 497 U.S. at 279. Courts and commentators have identified four state interests that may limit a person's right to refuse medical treatment: (1) preserving life; (2) preventing suicide; (3) safeguarding the integrity of the medical profession; and (4) protecting innocent third parties. . . .

It is also universally accepted that the state may not deprive citizens of their constitutional rights solely because they do not possess the decisional capacity to personally exercise them. . . . Courts have identified three methods by which to determine whether an incompetent's right to refuse or terminate artificial life-support systems should be exercised:

(1) Previously expressed desires.

The explicit wishes of an incompetent patient regarding extraordinary life-prolonging treatment should be respected if expressed, while competent. *See Cruzan*, 497 U.S. at 289–90. Wishes expressed in a written document, i.e., a living will, provide the clearest evidence of a person's desires. However, unequivocal oral statements also carry great weight.

(2) Substituted judgment.

If the incompetent's own unequivocal wishes are unknown, some courts have permitted a guardian or designated surrogate, or if none, a family member or close associate, to make a substituted judgment as to what the incompetent would have decided had he or she been competent.

. . . .

This inquiry is a subjective one in which "the court . . . must . . . act upon the same motives and considerations as would have moved [the patient]." . . . (factors include "[1] the patient's expressed preferences; [2] the patient's religious convictions and their relation to refusal of treatment; [3] the impact on the patient's family; [4] the probability of adverse side effects; and [5] the prognosis with and without treatment").

. . . . The incompetent's attitudes should be considered even if contrary to convention. "The right of self-determination, both for competents and incompetents, is understood to include the right to refuse treatment even when such refusal would be neither in one's best interest, nor in agreement with what most rational or reasonable persons would elect to do in similar circumstances." Allen E. Buchanan, *The Limits of Proxy Decisionmaking for Incompetents*, 29 UCLA L. Rev. 386, 389–90 (1981).

(3) Best interest.

Where no reliable evidence of the patient's intent exists, precluding substitution of the incompetent's judgment, courts have permitted the surrogate to base the decision on an objective inquiry into the incompetent patient's best interest. The decision is not based on the surrogate's view of quality of life, but " 'the value that the continuation of life has for the patient, . . .' not 'the value that others find in the continuation of the patient's life' " *Rasmus-sen*, 741 P.2d at 689. . . . Courts have established various criteria to consider in determining whether it is in the best interest of a patient who is permanently unconscious or in a persistent vegetative state to remove artificial life-prolonging treatment.

Evidence about the patient's present level of physical, sensory, emotional, and cognitive functioning; the degree of physical pain resulting from the medical condition, treatment, and termination of the treatment, respectively; the degree of humiliation, dependence, and loss of dignity probably resulting from the condition and treatment; the life expectancy and prognosis for recovery with and without treatment; the various treatment options; and the risks, side effects, and benefits of each of those options.

In re Rosebush, 491 N.W.2d 633, 640 (Mich. Ct. App. 1992).

. . . .

IV. 1994 LEGISLATION.

. . . .

Although not specifically stated in KRS 311.631(3), the legislative intent in enacting the statute obviously was to authorize a surrogate acting in good faith to direct the withholding or withdrawal of life-prolonging treatment from an "adult patient" lacking decisional capacity who has not executed an advance directive pertaining to that decision if doing so would be in the patient's best interest. . . .

V. CONSTITUTIONAL ISSUES.

We find no constitutional infirmity per se in the Kentucky Living Will Directive Act. It specifically avoids violating the inalienable right to life because it does not "condone, authorize, or approve mercy killing or euthanasia," or "permit any affirmative or deliberate act to end life other than to permit the natural process of dying." KRS 311.639. The statute recognizes a distinction between an affirmative intent to kill and a passive decision to allow a natural death to occur in accordance with a patient's constitutional liberty interest and common law right of self-determination. A corollary to any determination that withdrawal of artificial life-prolonging treatment is in the patient's best interest is that the patient's liberty interest to be free of treatment outweighs any interest the patient may have in maintaining a biological existence. Absent KRS 311.631, there is no way for a person like Woods, who had not made an advance directive, either oral or written, to exercise his constitutional liberty interest. Thus, the statute, by permitting a third party to authorize the termination of life-sustaining treatment, does not violate Woods's constitutional rights but instead provides a mechanism for balancing two competing rights.

. . . .

As noted in Part I of this opinion, the patient's right to self-determination must also be balanced against relevant state interests, *Cruzan*, 497 U.S. at 279, usually regarded as "[1] preserving life; [2] preventing suicide; [3] safeguarding the integrity of the medical profession; and [4] protecting innocent third parties." Of the four state interests, the strongest is the Commonwealth's interest in preserving the lives of its citizens. However, "the State's interests Contra weakens and the individual's [interest] grows as the degree of bodily invasion increases and the prognosis dims. Ultimately there comes a point at which the individual's rights overcome the State interest." *Quinlan*, 355 A.2d at 664. . . . There was no suicide issue in this case. Nor was the integrity of the medical profession at stake. All of the medical doctors involved in this case agreed that Woods's condition was irreversible and that artificial life-prolonging treatment should be withdrawn for humane reasons. The American Medical Association authorizes withdrawal of life-prolonging treatment from persons who are permanently unconscious or in a persistent vegetative state. Finally, there were no third parties to protect. Woods was unmarried and childless. There is no evidence that either his brother or his niece depended on him for monetary or emotional sustenance. In fact, CHR had difficulty even locating them so as to elicit their input into the decision-making process. We conclude that Woods's constitutional right of self-determination far outweighed any interests the Commonwealth may have had in his continued biological existence.

VI. CLEAR AND CONVINCING EVIDENCE.

. . . .

A consensus has arisen among state courts that the withholding or withdrawal of artificial life-prolonging treatment is authorized only upon a finding of clear and convincing evidence that the incompetent ward or patient is permanently unconscious or in a persistent vegetative state and that the ward or patient would choose to withhold or withdraw the life-prolonging treatment if able to do so or that it Would be in the best interest of the ward or patient to withhold or withdraw the treatment. . . .

We join the majority for the reason that "when evidence of a person's wishes or physical or mental condition is equivocal, it is best to err, if at all, in favor of preserving life." . . .

IX. JUDICIAL OVERSIGHT.

Of the approximately 2 million people who die each year, 80% die in hospitals and long-term care institutions, and perhaps 70% of those after a decision to forgo life-sustaining treatment has been made.

Cruzan, 497 U.S. at 302–03 (BRENNAN, J., dissenting).

Thus, it would be logistically impossible to require court approval of every decision to withhold or withdraw life-prolonging treatment. Furthermore, "judicial intervention into private decision-making of this sort is expensive and intrusive." It is both impossibly cumbersome and "a gratuitous encroachment upon the medical profession's field of competence." Thus, unless the interested parties disagree, resort to the courts is unwarranted. . . .

Nor is it necessary to obtain the appointment of a guardian where there is no disagreement with respect to the appropriate treatment. "If all parties, the immediate family, the treating physicians and the prognosis committee [if there is one], agree as to the course of treatment, a guardian is not necessary."

X. CONCLUSION.

To summarize, when an incompetent patient has not executed a valid living will or designated a health care surrogate, KRS 311.631 permits a surrogate, designated in order of priority, to make health care decisions on the patient's behalf, including the withholding or withdrawal of life-prolonging treatment from a patient who is permanently unconscious or in a persistent vegetative state, or when inevitable death is expected by reasonable medical judgment within a few days. The statute requires that such decisions be made in good faith and in the best interest of the patient. In that regard, the statute is not unconstitutional and does not contravene public policy or modern ethical standards. If there is no guardian and the physicians, family, and ethics committee (if there is one) all agree with the surrogate's decision, there is no need to appoint a guardian. If the surrogate, as here, is a judicially-appointed guardian, and the physicians, family and ethics committee agree with the guardian's decision, there is no need to seek court approval or the appointment of a guardian ad litem; and that is true whether the guardian is a member of the patient's family or an institution or, as here, a governmental entity. If there is a disagreement, however, resort may be had to the courts; and, if so, the burden will be upon those seeking to withhold or withdraw life support from the patient to prove by clear and convincing evidence that the patient is permanently unconscious or in a persistent vegetative state, or that death is imminent, and that it would be in the best interest of the patient to withhold or withdraw life-prolonging treatment.

————————

In *Woods*, the court states that if there is no credible evidence of what the patient would have wanted and so no way to invoke substituted judgment, the surrogate should act in the best interests of the patient. Known as the best interests test, it is an objective test that looks to factors other than the patient's wishes, which presumably are unknown. The best interests test has not found much support in the context of termination of life support — at least in judicial opinions. Some courts have rejected it on the basis that termination of treatment that leads to death cannot be in an individual's best interest. Commentators suggest, however, that the best interests test is often used by surrogates without resort to courts. At times, it is combined with some knowledge of what the patient might have wanted to reach the conclusion that, indeed, the patient is best served by terminating treatment even though death is the result.

[d] Do Not Resuscitate Orders

A living will or advance health care directive are not always effective. If the individual is in a hospital and even though the patient is terminally ill, the hospital will attempt to resuscitate him in the event of a cardiac or respiratory arrest. To prevent that intervention, a physician, with the consent of the patient, can write a "do not resuscitate" order or DNR in the patient's chart. A DNR is usually subject to a state statute and may vary, including ordering no code (no intervention) and slow-code, which results in slower response time. Consent to a DNR is not a global renunciation of treatment, but rather a request that particular interventions not be initiated.

If the patient is at home or in hospice and suffers a cardiac or respiratory arrest, someone may call the local emergency medical service — EMS. By law the EMS must intervene and attempt to stabilize the patient and take her to a hospital. Many terminally ill patients do not want the EMS to attempt to save their lives. As a result, states have enacted laws or regulation that permit out-of-hospital DNR orders that must be obeyed by EMS personnel. The order is a separate document that may have to be printed on a particular color of paper — the idea being to have a document that is easily identified and understood by EMS personnel. The document will be signed by the patient's physician and possibly the patient. State law may permit the issuance of such a DNR only if the patient is suffering from a terminal condition. The state law may require the document to be kept in a particular location so that EMS personnel can find it. Many states require the patient to wear a medallion or bracelet that alerts the EMS that the patient has a no-code out-of-hospital DNR. Once notified of the DNR, and if it complies with the state statute, the EMS is supposed to honor the directive. The patient, however, can orally override the DNR and ask for resuscitation.

QUESTIONS

1. Should there be a rebuttable assumption in favor of life? Unless the patient gave some previous indication, should treatment be continued, regardless of what a reasonable person might have wanted?

2. Even if we have a clear expression of the patient's views about treatment, how can we be sure that those views express what the patient would express today? Are we sure that the statements of a vigorous 70-year-old woman are still held by her when she is 90, suffering from multiple organ failure?

3. Explain the difference between substituted judgment and a best interests standard? When would they produce different outcomes?

4. If a patient was "completely unable to interact with her environment," and the probability that she would return to a cognitive sapient state was "virtually nonexistent," would this necessarily mean that her best interests would be served by allowing her to die? If not, why not?

5. What kind of interests or values are worthy of consideration? Emotional? Philosophical? Religious? Financial?

[3] THE FUTURE

The "right-to-die" issue is likely to be resolved state by state in the coming years, through case law and statutory enactments. Whether there will be any uniform resolution is doubtful, though four emerging categories of questions can be discerned:

1. Does a competent patient have an unqualified right to order discontinuation of life-sustaining treatment? The law permits termination of life-sustaining treatment by competent adults. The future arguments will likely center on who is competent. It is unclear, for example, whether a patient with a history of clinical depression can terminate treatment if the result could be death. The future will also hold compelling debates over the right of a terminal patient to have access to the means to commit suicide, rather than passively awaiting death.

2. Will a properly executed advance directive determine the course of care? Here, the question will be whether the state's statutory requirements have been met. If so, the living will or the health care power of attorney will be honored. If not, the effect of such a document is less clear. Questions also remain regarding the patient's oral statements made subsequent to the written directive, and whether health care providers can be compelled to obey. Can the appropriateness of a designated surrogate be challenged in court?

3. When there is no evidence of the incapacitated patient's views concerning life-sustaining treatment, can a guardian or other surrogate order termination of treatment? If so, under what standard and under what conditions? Must the court give prior approval? If the family is divided as to what to do, whose wishes control, and why?

Although public attitudes about these issues are still in flux, it appears that the public increasingly favors the right to terminate life-sustaining treatment. A correlative issue is whether, when the spouse, family, or guardian wishes treatment to continue, the physician may overrule them and discontinue treatment on the basis that continuation would be futile. The issue has already arisen when the patient was in a persistent vegetative state.

In 1991, the Hennepin County Court of Minnesota rejected the advice of the physicians of a severely brain damaged woman that she be taken off her respirator over the objections of her husband. The court held that the 87-year-old woman, who had been in a persistent vegetative state for over a year, must continue to be treated. The doctors had asked that an independent conservator be appointed to decide the woman's fate, hoping that the conservator would agree that she should be taken off life-support systems. Her husband objected, arguing that he and his wife had a high regard for the sanctity of human life and that her care should be continued. The court rejected the physicians' argument that the woman's case was hopeless and that a respirator was not meant for prolonging life in such a case. The court concluded that the husband was in the best position to understand and act upon his wife's moral beliefs. The cost of medical care was not an issue because it was fully paid by the family's insurance policy.

E. EUTHANASIA AND PHYSICIAN-ASSISTED SUICIDE

Beyond the right to terminate life-sustaining treatment lie questions regarding euthanasia, which is the taking of measures to end a consensual patient's life. Some commentators use the term euthanasia to refer both to active measures, such as giving the patient a lethal dose of medicine, and to passive acts, such as termination of treatment. The latter is sometimes called passive euthanasia. Most observers, however, reserve the term euthanasia for active assistance to a patient who wishes to die. Merely terminating life-sustaining treatment generally is not thought of as euthanasia. The difference is between allowing a person to die and killing that person, albeit at his or her request. If the physician turns off a respirator, the resulting death arises from the underlying condition that prevents the patient from breathing. On the other hand, a physician who injects a patient with a substance that kills the patient is guilty of euthanasia or homicide, because the physician, not the underlying condition, is the cause of death.

> The *Medical Dictionary for Lawyers* defines euthanasia as "[a]n act or practice, which is advocated by many, of putting persons to death painlessly who are suffering from incurable and malignant diseases, as an act of mercy." While most commentators suggest that euthanasia is motivated by kindness and a desire to end the intense suffering of another, not all individuals view euthanasia in such a positive manner. For example, some commentators think euthanasia is a euphemism for murder, while others object to euthanasia because it is contrary to the Hippocratic Oath, or because it violates their religious and moral beliefs.

> Involuntary euthanasia occurs when an individual, other than the patient, decides to discontinue treatment or to terminate an incompetent or a competent unconsenting person's life. In contrast, voluntary euthanasia occurs when the patient himself decides to terminate treatment or to end his life. Thus, involuntary euthanasia and voluntary euthanasia differ in

that the former occurs without the patient's consent, while the latter occurs with the patient's consent.

It is the nature of the third party's actions that distinguishes active euthanasia from passive euthanasia. With active euthanasia, a physician administers treatment which induces a painless death, while with passive euthanasia, the physician withdraws or withholds treatment or nourishment. Thus, involuntary and voluntary euthanasia may either be active or passive.

Note, *Euthanasia: Is It Murder or Mercy Killing?*, 12 LOY. L.A. INT'L & COMP. L.J. 821, 822–24 (1990).*

Today, the term euthanasia is giving way to "assisted suicide" or "physician assisted suicide," though the terms are not synonymous. Euthanasia refers to a mercy killing at the request of the patient. For example, at the request of a patient a physician gives the patient a lethal injection. Physician assisted suicide refers to the case where the patient commits suicide but relies on the assistance of the physician. For example, at the patient's request, the physician supplies the patient with a lethal number of pills, but the patient acting alone takes the pills and thereby dies. The term is also applied to situations where the physician, at the patient's request, administers the cause of death, such as a lethal injection.

Tom L. Beauchamp, *The Justification of Physician-Assisted Suicide*
29 IND. L. REV. 1173 (1996)**

The primary justification advanced in both law and morals for requirements that competent informed refusals be honored is the right of self-determination. The principle of self-determination in recent legal literature is the functional equivalent of the moral principle of respect for autonomy. A major concern of the law is to prescribe the precise duties that devolve upon physicians in order that rights of autonomy be protected. In the last two decades it has become clear that a valid refusal of treatment obligates the physician to forgo treatment, even if it is a refusal of hydration and nutrition or a life-support system that will result in death. Whenever valid refusals occur, it is never a moral offense to comply with the refusal, and how the death occurs from the refusal is irrelevant.

By not categorizing the withholding or the withdrawing of a validly refused medical treatment as "killing," we have signaled our acceptance of the physician's nontreatment even when treatment is medically indicated. Had we judged withholding and withdrawing treatment morally unacceptable when competent persons refuse treatment, we would have categorized such conduct by physicians as killing (perhaps mercy killing, but still killing). Similarly, had we found moral grounds not to accept refusals by competent persons, we might have chosen not to

---

categorize such conduct as forgoing life-sustaining treatment, and instead have categorized it as suicide.

In some cases, patients in a close relationship with a physician both decline a possible treatment and request an accelerated death in order to lessen pain or suffering. In these cases, the refusal and the request are combined as parts of a single plan. If the physician agrees with the plan, assisted suicide or active euthanasia grows out of the close patient-physician relationship established by the two parties.

When patients make reasonable requests for assistance in dying, physicians cannot escape responsibility for their decisions by refraining from helping their patients die. Physicians who reject requests by patients cannot magically relocate responsibility by transferring it to the patient's disease. The only relevant matter is whether the physician has an adequate justification for the chosen course of action. Physicians have a responsibility to act in the best interests of their patients, and they cannot, without adequate justification, avoid what a patient believes to be in his or her best interests. It is undisputed, physicians often reject courses of action requested by patients and have good reasons for doing so. The question is whether the physician, who conscientiously believes that the patient's request for assistance in dying is justified and assumes responsibility for assistance, acts in a morally justifiable manner in complying with the request even when it is not legally justifiable.

The person who attempts suicide, the person who seeks active euthanasia, and the person who forgoes life-sustaining treatment to end life are identically situated except that they may select different means to end their lives.

Medicine and law now seem to say to many patients, "If you were on life-sustaining treatment, you could withdraw the treatment and we could let you die. Because you are not, we can only give you palliative care until you die a natural death." This position condemns the patient to live out a life he or she does not want — a form of cruelty that violates the patient's rights and prevents discretionary discharge of the fiduciary duties of the physician. This is not to claim that physicians face large numbers of desperately ill patients. Pain management has made circumstances at least bearable for many of today's patients, reducing the need for physician-assisted suicide and euthanasia and increasing the need for adequate facilities, training, and hospice programs. Nonetheless, the available medical literature indicates that some patients cannot be satisfactorily relieved, and, even if they could, questions would remain about the autonomy rights of patients to pursue their own plans in life and about the fact that many patients are more concerned about suffering and indignity than about pain.

[1] JUDICIAL RESPONSE

Despite the beliefs of many that physician-assisted suicide should be legalized, it remains illegal in all states except Oregon, whose voters approved it by referendum. (Discussed below.) The constitutionality of the state laws criminalizing assisted suicide was considered by the U.S. Supreme Court, which upheld the rights of states to bar assisted suicide even if performed by physicians.

WASHINGTON v. GLUCKSBERG
521 U.S. 702 (1997)

JUDGES: REHNQUIST, C.J., delivered the opinion of the Court, in which O' CONNOR, SCALIA, KENNEDY, and THOMAS, JJ., joined. O'CONNOR, J., filed a concurring opinion, in which GINSBURG and BREYER, JJ., joined in part. STEVENS, J., SOUTER, J., GINSBURG, J., and BREYER, J., filed opinions concurring in the judgment.

OPINION: CHIEF JUSTICE REHNQUIST delivered the opinion of the Court.

The question presented in this case is whether Washington's prohibition against "causing" or "aiding" a suicide offends the Fourteenth Amendment to the United States Constitution. We hold that it does not.

It has always been a crime to assist a suicide in the State of Washington. In 1854, Washington's first Territorial Legislature outlawed "assisting another in the commission of self-murder." Today, Washington law provides: "A person is guilty of promoting a suicide attempt when he knowingly causes or aids another person to attempt suicide." Wash. Rev. Code 9A.36.060(1) (1994). "Promoting a suicide attempt" is a felony, punishable by up to five years' imprisonment and up to a $10,000 fine.

Petitioners in this case are the State of Washington and its Attorney General. Respondents Harold Glucksberg, M.D., Abigail Halperin, M.D., Thomas A. Preston, M.D., and Peter Shalit, M.D., are physicians who practice in Washington. These doctors occasionally treat terminally ill, suffering patients, and declare that they would assist these patients in ending their lives if not for Washington's assisted-suicide ban. In January 1994, respondents, along with three gravely ill, pseudonymous plaintiffs who have since died and Compassion in Dying, a nonprofit organization that counsels people considering physician-assisted suicide, sued in the United States District Court, seeking a declaration that Wash Rev. Code 9A.36.060(1) (1994) is, on its face, unconstitutional. *Compassion in Dying v. Washington*, 850 F. Supp. 1454, 1459 (WD Wash. 1994).

The plaintiffs asserted "the existence of a liberty interest protected by the Fourteenth Amendment which extends to a personal choice by a mentally competent, terminally ill adult to commit physician-assisted suicide." *Id.*, at 1459. Relying primarily on *Planned Parenthood v. Casey*, 505 U.S. 833 (1992), and *Cruzan v. Director, Missouri Dept. of Health*, 497 U.S. 261 (1990), the District Court agreed, 850 F. Supp., at 1459–1462, and concluded that Washington's assisted-suicide ban is unconstitutional because it "places an undue burden on the exercise of [that] constitutionally protected liberty interest." *Id.*, at 1465. The District Court also decided that the Washington statute violated the Equal Protection Clause's requirement that " 'all persons similarly situated . . . be treated alike.' " *Id.*, at 1466 (quoting *Cleburne v. Cleburne Living Center, Inc.*, 473 U.S. 432, 439 (1985)).

A panel of the Court of Appeals for the Ninth Circuit reversed, emphasizing that "in the two hundred and five years of our existence no constitutional right to aid in killing oneself has ever been asserted and upheld by a court of final jurisdiction."

Compassion in Dying v. Washington, 49 F.3d 586, 591 (1995). The Ninth Circuit reheard the case en banc, reversed the panel's decision, and affirmed the District Court. *Compassion in Dying v. Washington,* 79 F.3d 790, 798 (1996). Like the District Court, the en banc Court of Appeals emphasized our *Casey* and *Cruzan* decisions. 79 F.3d, at 813–816. The court also discussed what it described as "historical" and "current societal attitudes" toward suicide and assisted suicide, *id.,* at 806–812, and concluded that "the Constitution encompasses a due process liberty interest in controlling the time and manner of one's death — that there is, in short, a constitutionally-recognized 'right to die.'" *Id.,* at 816. After "weighing and then balancing" this interest against Washington's various interests, the court held that the State's assisted-suicide ban was unconstitutional "as applied to terminally ill competent adults who wish to hasten their deaths with medication prescribed by their physicians." *Id.,* at 836, 837 n.6. The court did not reach the District Court's equal-protection holding. *Id.,* at 838. We granted certiorari, 519 U.S. (1996), and now reverse.

I

We begin, as we do in all due-process cases, by examining our Nation's history, legal traditions, and practices. In almost every State — indeed, in almost every western democracy — it is a crime to assist a suicide. The States' assisted-suicide bans are not innovations. Rather, they are longstanding expressions of the States' commitment to the protection and preservation of all human life. More specifically, for over 700 years, the Anglo-American common-law tradition has punished or otherwise disapproved of both suicide and assisting suicide. The earliest American statute explicitly to outlaw assisting suicide was enacted in New York in 1828.

Though deeply rooted, the States' assisted-suicide bans have in recent years been reexamined and, generally, reaffirmed. Because of advances in medicine and technology, Americans today are increasingly likely to die in institutions, from chronic illnesses. President's Comm'n for the Study of Ethical Problems in Medicine and Biomedical and Behavioral Research, Deciding to Forego Life-Sustaining Treatment 16–18 (1983). Public concern and democratic action are therefore sharply focused on how best to protect dignity and independence at the end of life, with the result that there have been many significant changes in state laws and in the attitudes these laws reflect. Many States, for example, now permit "living wills," surrogate health-care decision making, and the withdrawal or refusal of life-sustaining medical treatment. At the same time, however, voters and legislators continue for the most part to reaffirm their States' prohibitions on assisting suicide.

California voters rejected an assisted-suicide initiative similar to Washington's in 1993. On the other hand, in 1994, voters in Oregon enacted, also through ballot initiative, that State's "Death With Dignity Act," which legalized physician-assisted suicide for competent, terminally ill adults. Since the Oregon vote, many proposals to legalize assisted-suicide have been and continue to be introduced in the States' legislatures, but none has been enacted. And just last year, Iowa and Rhode Island joined the overwhelming majority of States explicitly prohibiting assisted suicide.

Thus, the States are currently engaged in serious, thoughtful examinations of physician-assisted suicide and other similar issues.

II

Our established method of substantive-due-process analysis has two primary features: First, we have regularly observed that the Due Process Clause specially protects those fundamental rights and liberties which are, objectively, "deeply rooted in this Nation's history and tradition," *id.*, at 503 (plurality opinion); *Snyder v. Massachusetts*, 291 U.S. 97, 105 (1934) ("so rooted in the traditions and conscience of our people as to be ranked as fundamental"), and "implicit in the concept of ordered liberty," such that "neither liberty nor justice would exist if they were sacrificed," *Palko v. Connecticut*, 302 U.S. 319, 325, 326 (1937). Second, we have required in substantive-due-process cases a "careful description" of the asserted fundamental liberty interest. *Flores, supra*, at 302; *Collins, supra*, at 125; *Cruzan, supra*, at 277–278. Our Nation's history, legal traditions, and practices thus provide the crucial "guideposts for responsible decisionmaking," *Collins, supra*, at 125, that direct and restrain our exposition of the Due Process Clause. As we stated recently in *Flores*, the Fourteenth Amendment "forbids the government to infringe . . . 'fundamental' liberty interests at all, no matter what process is provided, unless the infringement is narrowly tailored to serve a compelling state interest." 507 U.S. at 302.

Turning to the claim at issue here, the Court of Appeals stated that "properly analyzed, the first issue to be resolved is whether there is a liberty interest in determining the time and manner of one's death," 79 F.3d, at 801, or, in other words, "is there a right to die?," *id.*, at 799. Similarly, respondents assert a "liberty to choose how to die" and a right to "control of one's final days," Brief for Respondents 7, and describe the asserted liberty as "the right to choose a humane, dignified death," *id.*, at 15, and "the liberty to shape death," *id.*, at 18. Thus, the question before us is whether the "liberty" specially protected by the Due Process Clause includes a right to commit suicide which itself includes a right to assistance in doing so.

We now inquire whether this asserted right has any place in our Nation's traditions. Here . . . we are confronted with a consistent and almost universal tradition that has long rejected the asserted right, and continues explicitly to reject it today, even for terminally ill, mentally competent adults. To hold for respondents, we would have to reverse centuries of legal doctrine and practice, and strike down the considered policy choice of almost every State.

Respondents contend, however, that the liberty interest they assert is consistent with this Court's substantive-due-process line of cases, if not with this Nation's history and practice. According to respondents, our liberty jurisprudence, and the broad, individualistic principles it reflects, protects the "liberty of competent, terminally ill adults to make end-of-life decisions free of undue government interference." Brief for Respondents 10. The question presented in this case, however, is whether the protections of the Due Process Clause include a right to commit suicide with another's assistance.

Respondents contend that in *Cruzan* we "acknowledged that competent, dying persons have the right to direct the removal of life-sustaining medical treatment and thus hasten death," Brief for Respondents 23, and that "the constitutional principle behind recognizing the patient's liberty to direct the withdrawal of artificial life support applies at least as strongly to the choice to hasten impending death by consuming lethal medication," *id.*, at 26. Similarly, the Court of Appeals concluded that "Cruzan, by recognizing a liberty interest that includes the refusal of artificial provision of life-sustaining food and water, necessarily recognized a liberty interest in hastening one's own death." 79 F.3d, at 816.

The right assumed in *Cruzan*, however, was not simply deduced from abstract concepts of personal autonomy. Given the common-law rule that forced medication was a battery, and the long legal tradition protecting the decision to refuse unwanted medical treatment, our assumption was entirely consistent with this Nation's history and constitutional traditions. The decision to commit suicide with the assistance of another may be just as personal and profound as the decision to refuse unwanted medical treatment, but it has never enjoyed similar legal protection. Indeed, the two acts are widely and reasonably regarded as quite distinct.

The history of the law's treatment of assisted suicide in this country has been and continues to be one of the rejection of nearly all efforts to permit it. That being the case, our decisions lead us to conclude that the asserted "right" to assistance in committing suicide is not a fundamental liberty interest protected by the Due Process Clause. The Constitution also requires, however, that Washington's assisted-suicide ban be rationally related to legitimate government interests. See *Heller v. Doe*, 509 U.S. 312, 319–320 (1993); *Flores*, 507 U.S. at 305. This requirement is unquestionably met here. As the court below recognized, 79 F.3d, at 816–817, Washington's assisted-suicide ban implicates a number of state interests.

First, Washington has an "unqualified interest in the preservation of human life." *Cruzan*, 497 U.S. at 282. The State's prohibition on assisted suicide, like all homicide laws, both reflects and advances its commitment to this interest.

Those who attempt suicide — terminally ill or not — often suffer from depression or other mental disorders. . . . Research indicates, however, that many people who request physician-assisted suicide withdraw that request if their depression and pain are treated. H. Hendin, Seduced by Death: Doctors, Patients and the Dutch Cure 24–25 (1997) (suicidal, terminally ill patients "usually respond well to treatment for depressive illness and pain medication and are then grateful to be alive"); New York Task Force 177–178. The New York Task Force, however, expressed its concern that, because depression is difficult to diagnose, physicians and medical professionals often fail to respond adequately to seriously ill patients' needs. *Id.*, at 175. Thus, legal physician-assisted suicide could make it more difficult for the State to protect depressed or mentally ill persons, or those who are suffering from untreated pain, from suicidal impulses.

The State also has an interest in protecting the integrity and ethics of the medical profession. The American Medical Association, like many other medical and physicians' groups, has concluded that "physician-assisted suicide is fundamentally incompatible with the physician's role as healer." American Medical Association, Code of Ethics at 2.211 (1994).

Next, the State has an interest in protecting vulnerable groups — including the poor, the elderly, and disabled persons — from abuse, neglect, and mistakes. If physician-assisted suicide were permitted, many might resort to it to spare their families the substantial financial burden of end-of-life healthcare costs.

The State's interest here goes beyond protecting the vulnerable from coercion; it extends to protecting disabled and terminally ill people from prejudice, negative and inaccurate stereotypes, and "societal indifference." 49 F.3d, at 592. The State's assisted-suicide ban reflects and reinforces its policy that the lives of terminally ill, disabled, and elderly people must be no less valued than the lives of the young and healthy, and that a seriously disabled person's suicidal impulses should be interpreted and treated the same way as anyone else's.

Finally, the State may fear that permitting assisted suicide will start it down the path to voluntary and perhaps even involuntary euthanasia. The Court of Appeals' decision, and its expansive reasoning, provide ample support for the State's concerns. The court noted, for example, that the "decision of a duly appointed surrogate decisionmaker is for all legal purposes the decision of the patient himself," 79 F.3d, at 832, that "in some instances, the patient may be unable to self-administer the drugs and . . . administration by the physician . . . may be the only way the patient may be able to receive them," *id.*, at 831; and that not only physicians, but also family members and loved ones, will inevitably participate in assisting suicide. *Id.*, at 838. Thus, it turns out that what is couched as a limited right to "physician-assisted suicide" is likely, in effect, a much broader license, which could prove extremely difficult to police and contain. Washington's ban on assisting suicide prevents such erosion.

. . . .

Throughout the Nation, Americans are engaged in an earnest and profound debate about the morality, legality, and practicality of physician-assisted suicide. Our holding permits this debate to continue, as it should in a democratic society. The decision of the en banc Court of Appeals is reversed, and the case is remanded for further proceedings consistent with this opinion.

It is so ordered.

Commentators have advanced yet additional reasons to be wary of assisted suicide.

Robert J. Burt, *Rationality and Injustice in Physician-Assisted Suicide*
19 W. New Eng. L. Rev. 353 (1997)*

Let me articulate one speculation about the possible harm that would fall on many patients with life-threatening illnesses if physician-assisted suicide were to be legally approved, notwithstanding the persistence of irrational confusions between physicians and patients. If numerous physicians have resisted

---

acknowledging their patients' wishes for death because of some deep subjective conviction that this acknowledgment would compromise the physicians' own struggles against feared death — if, we might say, the physicians' empathic identification with their patients spilled into an over-identification with them — then the physicians who now understand themselves to be participating in their patients' deaths (whether by acquiescing in their treatment refusals or by engaging in some more active assistance) must somehow accommodate their prior over-identifications with patients. One possible route is to relent in their prior resistance to patients' deaths by denying any empathic identification with them — by, we might say, an under-identification with patients, by a heightened aversion to the possibility of death that finds expression as a too-quick support for the patients' hastened death and disappearance in order to deny the force of the persistent underlying belief that the patients' death threatens the physicians' personal integrity.

There are already many identifiably powerful social pressures that are conspiring toward this speeded end: financial pressures from the new organizational structure of health care services into managed care settings that reward nontreatment of patients, the socially marginalized and devalued status of many dying people such as the impoverished elderly in nursing homes and AIDS-infected drug abusers; and the heightened public fears about the dying process that have made Jack Kevorkian a folk hero, in the media and before successive criminal juries, notwithstanding his obvious flouting of legal constraints and his bizarre personal characteristics. The "conscience of the medical profession" has often been invoked as a claimed counterweight to these social forces pressing toward hastened deaths of patients; but this counterweight disappears if physicians can persuade themselves that morality demands acquiescence in their patients' expressed wishes for death, no matter how tentative, ambivalent, or premature those expressed wishes might be. What a happy conjunction, then, if "doing good" for one's patients — doing the socially approved act of hastening the patient's death — also "felt good" to the physician who, by this hastening, could avoid any anxiety-provoking acknowledgment of the personal threat embodied in the patient's death.

The conjunctive impact of these psychological forces with other social pressures toward hastening the death of vulnerable patients would create considerable problems not only for the proper implementation of legally recognized physician-assisted suicide but also for patients' legal rights to refuse treatment.

Marshall B. Kapp, *"Old Folks on the Slippery Slope": Elderly Patients and Physician Assisted Suicide*
35 DUQ. L. REV. 443 (1996)*

The current controversy in the United States over the morality and constitutionality of state statutes that prohibit physicians from assisting patients to commit suicide entails a variety of difficult ethical and legal issues. In policy terms, the debate has tended to focus on whether legislatures can erect sufficiently stringent yet workable safeguards within state statutes authorizing physician-assisted suicide to protect against serious ethical abuses of this patient/physician prerogative. . . .

Most of the arguments on both sides of this discussion have been crafted in generic terms. While a persuasive case against recognition of a constitutional right to physician-assisted suicide generally can be mounted, as analyzed in the particular context of elderly individuals, the anxieties of the slippery slope skeptics appear especially compelling. These are anxieties evidently shared by a substantial portion of the elderly population, since public opinion polls consistently show lower support for legalization of physician-assisted suicide among older citizens than among younger citizens. The primary reasons for these well-founded worries are briefly outlined below.

I. PARTICULAR RISKS FOR THE ELDERLY

A. Decision Making Capacity

. . . .

As even proponents of physician-assisted suicide have acknowledged, a capable decisionmaker is an especially indispensable prerequisite in a physician-assisted suicide situation, as the costs of error are so great and irremediable. Notably, there are at least a couple of grounds for suspecting that a suicidal individual's capacity may be particularly problematic in cases of purported requests for physician-assisted suicide by older persons.

First, the prevalence of dementia increases dramatically in older patients. While the presence of dementia (a diagnostic category) by itself, particularly in its early stages, does not necessarily equate with decisional incapacity (a functional concept), in its more severe stages, dementia ordinarily does substantially interfere with an individual's ability to engage in a rational decisionmaking process with respect to important and complicated matters.

B. Voluntariness

In health care decision making generally, and certainly in the context of physician-assisted suicide, only voluntary patient requests made without duress, undue influence or coercion have any plausible claim to legal and ethical legitimacy. Several factors may significantly and perhaps inherently impinge on the voluntariness of purported requests for physician-assisted suicide made by elderly patients.

First, the United States is currently a fundamentally ageist society in which older individuals are often made to feel that they are of little or vastly reduced worth. Despite the tremendous (arguably even disproportionate) public financial resources devoted to the health care and income support of the elderly mainly for political reasons, the continual social message to which the elderly are exposed is a theme that glorifies youth and vitality while devaluing the present contributions of the aged. The upshot of this psychological atmosphere is a potential endangerment of older individuals' freedom of choice. . . .

. . . .

. . . . Notably, the impact of an ageist society is evidenced already in the disproportionately high rate of suicide attempts and completions among the elderly in the United States. By contrast, the suicide rate of the elderly in societies which hold and communicate more respect for the aged is a much rarer event.

A second ground for suspicion about the voluntariness of an older individual's purported request for physician-assisted suicide arises from the role of an individual's family in this decision. While normally, families of older patients are an integral, positive force in supporting and assisting the effectuation of the patient's autonomous decision making, this is not always the case. The psychological, physical and financial burdens on family members of very sick and frail individuals, especially those with chronic conditions requiring extensive, ongoing provision of care in the home, are great and can affect the patient's exercise of autonomy in many different ways. With respect to the present analysis, even the most sincere and well-intentioned families in such circumstances may end up, consciously or not, subtly or more directly pressuring the older patient to relieve the family's burden by selecting the physician-assisted suicide option. . . .

[2]　STATUTORY RESPONSE

In 1994, Oregon voters approved by referendum the Oregon Death with Dignity Act (Measure 16), OR. REV. STAT. §§ 127.800–.897, which legalized procedures for physician-assisted suicide. Initially held up by court challenges, the proposal was reaffirmed by referendum in 1997 and was put into practice in 1998. The first reported suicide using the assisted-suicide statute took place in March of 1998. In 2008, Washington voters approved the Washington Death with Dignity Act, which is quite similar to the Oregon law.

By the end of 2004 in Oregon, 208 individuals had used it to gain access to lethal medication. Thirty-seven did so in 2004. In 2004, forty physicians prescribed 60 lethal doses of medication, but 13 of those died from their illness and the remainder were still alive at the end of the year. According to the prescribing physicians, patients request lethal medication because of their decreased ability to participate in activities that made life enjoyable, the loss of personal autonomy, and the loss of dignity.

The essential elements of the Oregon Act are described in the following article.

Edward R. Grant & Paul B. Linton, *Relief or Reproach?: Euthanasia Rights in the Wake of Measure 16*
74 OR. L. REV. 449 (1995)[*]

B. Who Does Measure 16 Really Protect?

Measure 16 exempts a health-care provider from criminal or civil liability for assisting in a suicide so long as the provider has complied in good faith with the statutory conditions for such assistance. The prospective suicide must: (1) be an adult, legal resident of the state, suffering from a terminal illness; (2) have made two oral requests not less than 15 days apart to receive a dose of medication sufficient to take her own life; and (3) have executed a written request for such medication in the presence of two witnesses, at least one of whom is not a relative. The attending physician must: (1) confirm the diagnosis of terminal illness; (2) determine that the patient is mentally competent and that the request is voluntary; (3) inform the patient of the diagnosis, her medical prognosis, the risk of the lethal medication, the results of ingesting the lethal medication, the availability of "feasible alternatives" to suicide, and the patient's right to rescind the request for lethal medication; (4) refer the patient to another physician to confirm the terminal diagnosis, the patient's mental competence, and the voluntary nature of the decision; (5) refer the patient for counseling if the physician believes that the patient may be suffering from a psychiatric disorder or depression causing impaired judgment; and (6) verify immediately prior to writing the prescription for lethal medication that the patient is making an informed decision. Measure 16 imposes no conditions on how lethal medication is to be administered. Presumably, the patient may take the dose in the hospital or at home. Measure 16 disclaims any intent to legalize mercy killing, active euthanasia, or, somewhat remarkably, suicide itself.

Once this is understood, it becomes clear that Measure 16 is not a means to protect the rights of patients — who, after all, cannot now be prosecuted for planning their own suicides — but a vehicle for providing immunity to doctors who participate in assisted suicide. The extent of that immunity is remarkable: "No person shall be subject to civil or criminal liability or professional disciplinary action for participating in good faith compliance with this Act." "Good faith compliance" is not defined. But it is clearly a more subjective and less stringent standard than those customarily employed in medical malpractice litigation.

Measure 16 does contain liability provisions. Forgery of a request for lethal medication with the intent of causing the patient's death is a Class A felony, as is coercion or undue influence of a patient to request such medication. There are also clauses preserving "further liability for civil damages" and criminal liability for actions "inconsistent with the provisions of the Act." It will be difficult to make out a claim of civil liability, however, as long as the standard for immunity is good faith, as opposed to actual, compliance with the provisions of Measure 16. On the other hand, an actual compliance standard could ground Measure 16. Fewer physicians might be willing to take the risk that they may be found not to have actually

---

[*] Copyright © 1995 by Oregon Law Review. Reprinted with permission.

complied with all of the procedural safeguards set forth in the Act.

Even as written, however, Measure 16 could present a formidable task to physicians. First, the law could be read to require a welter of factual and quasi-legal determinations that lie, at best, on the outer boundaries of medical judgment. For example, in addition to diagnosing terminal illness, both the primary and the referring physician are responsible for determining whether the patient is competent and has made the request for lethal medication voluntarily. There is no definition of competency in the Act, and no reference to any existing legal standard on the subject. Determining whether the patient has acted voluntarily could require an open-ended inquiry into family relationships, conversations, and other factors that may be influencing the patient's statements. An "actual compliance" standard might stop most physicians at this point. Under the "good faith" standard, however, a physician would be able to accept at face value a patient's statement that "I want to die," and presume, in the absence of apparent evidence to the contrary, that the patient is both competent and acting voluntarily.

Second, in the interest of preserving the privacy of the patient's decision, a physician is exposed to the reactions of relatives who have not been informed in advance of the patient's suicide. Section 3.05 requires the physician to ask the patient to notify the next of kin of her intent to commit suicide, but provides that if the patient is unwilling or unable to do so, the suicide may go forward.

[3] THE NETHERLANDS EXPERIENCE

Stephen G. Potts,
Looking for the Exit Door
25 HOUS. L. REV. 493, 495–96, 504–08 (1988)[*]

The country that has come closest to legalizing euthanasia is Holland. In a celebrated 1973 court case in which a doctor was accused of killing her own mother, the presiding judge surprised observers by suggesting guidelines within which acts of mercy killing might be appropriate. Public support for euthanasia, already strong, was further bolstered and medical resistance to it diminished, so that thousands of patients now die at the hands of their doctors. The Dutch Criminal Code still prohibits the practice and provides for a maximum punishment of twelve years, but there has been a divergence of case and statutory law, so that doctors who do it are rarely punished. In general, doctors so charged who have acted at the patient's express request, after consultation with colleagues and relatives, have been found guilty, but discharged on grounds of "medical necessity." A small number of less conscientious doctors who acted in what they thought was the patient's best interests, but without consent or consultation, have been convicted and imprisoned for as long as eight years.

Julia Belian, *Deference to Doctors in Dutch Euthanasia Law*
10 EMORY INT'L L. REV. 256 (1996)[*]

Dutch physicians are not attempting to force their belief in euthanasia into the common weal. As many as eighty percent of all Dutch people already accept the practice. Judges and legislators who have followed the doctors' lead in crafting euthanasia law seem to have done so out of a sincere desire to find the best answer to the dilemma posed by suffering patients. Certainly, judges have often looked outside the court system for expert opinions to help them make reasonable and fair judgments. In the case of Dutch euthanasia law, however, the courts have not merely brought in outside advice to fashion solutions in a few hard cases. Rather, doctors themselves have worked out a set of guidelines that prospectively adjudicate one of the most difficult questions any decision-maker must face: When is it right and proper to end the life of another human being?

By handing this difficult decision over to a body of competent, professional scientists, the Dutch statute creates an illusion that euthanasia decisions will be scientifically grounded. In reality, physicians appear to use the same subjective criteria any other person might use: their personal convictions about what makes a life worth living and their subjective judgment that a patient's condition has slipped below that line. One might ask if this is worth worrying about at all. Perhaps euthanasia decisions cannot be made from a strictly medical point of view; perhaps doctors are acting reasonably when they allow their moral sensibilities to affect their decision-making. If these propositions are true, however, it would indicate that decisions regarding euthanasia are not scientific questions at all. "Questions that are forever open . . . are the domain of philosophy and religion, not of science. . . . The language of could, possible, may, might and maybe . . . is not the language of science."[233] If questions regarding the appropriate use of euthanasia are not scientific questions, then those who seek answers to the euthanasia problem must look to some source other than science and medicine to try to answer them. The courts and the legislature may provide that source, but they cannot even begin the task until they recognize the true nature of the questions.

In 2002, the Netherlands became the first country to legalize euthanasia. Significantly, the Dutch law makes no specific mention of whether the patient need be terminally ill. The enactment of legalization was the culmination of almost 30 years of growing approval of mercy killings in the Netherlands. The new law removes the possibility of doctors being prosecuted for euthanasia, which previously carried a maximum 12-year sentence. Under the new law, patients will be required to make persistent, well-considered, and voluntary requests to their doctor with whom they must have a relationship. The patient's suffering must be assessed as being unbearable and without the prospect of improvement. Every feasible treatment must be exhausted before the doctor can recommend euthanasia and seek a second opinion from an independent physician. Finally, an independent commission must review the physicians' decision.

---

[233] Peter W. Huber, GALILEO'S REVENGE: JUNK SCIENCE IN THE COURTROOM 210.

QUESTIONS

1. Is there any difference between a positive act that causes death and terminating (or withholding) treatment to cause death? Practically speaking, the result is the same. Some argue that acts and omissions are psychologically different. Would you agree? Should the difference matter in law?

2. If the patient is in a terminal condition, would it be morally wrong to hasten the inevitable? Why, or why not? Is it wrong if the patient requests the means to die, such as pills, but the patient alone undertakes the act that causes death? If the patient requests to be killed by a lethal injection?

3. Assuming assisted suicide were legal, should it be limited only to terminal patients?

4. Imagine that you are 67 years old and have been diagnosed as having Alzheimer's disease. If your physician offered to assist your death in a painless manner before you became mentally incompetent, would you accept the offer? What if she offered to kill you after you became incompetent?

5. If it were legal, would you assist another to commit suicide? If you were a physician? If he or she were terminally ill? Ill, but not terminally ill? Deeply, chronically depressed about life? Fearful of old age? Competent? Incompetent?

Chapter 12

ELDER ABUSE, NEGLECT, AND CRIME

A. INTRODUCTION

In the past 30 years, Americans discovered domestic violence, abuse, and neglect. While the public was aware that some parents beat their children, some husbands abuse their wives, and some children take advantage of elderly parents, few realized the extent of domestic violence. We have learned, however, and now we all are aware of child abuse, spousal abuse, and elder abuse.

Domestic violence is sustained physical or psychological assaults by one member of a household upon another. A spouse, usually a husband, may berate and insult the other spouse, beat her, or threaten to kill her. Society's response includes services to help the abused spouse live more safely, criminal sanctions against the abuser, and tort actions that require the abuser to pay compensation to the abused. Similarly, parents abuse their children. Parental beating and abuse of children has led to mandatory reporting of suspected abuse, monitoring of abusive households by state agencies, and the strengthening of penalties for abusers, including removal of abused children from the care of their abusers.

Public awareness of elder abuse and neglect came more slowly. In the 1970s, a number of studies in Britain and the United States identified elder abuse as a significant problem. As a result, by 1986 all states had legislation establishing a reporting and response system for abuse of persons without regard to age.

The extent of elder abuse is not accurately known. Best estimates are that each year between one million and one-and-one-half million elderly are abused or severely neglected. The lack of information as to the numbers of abused and neglected elderly arises from the lack of a national collection of data and the variance in the definition of elder abuse and neglect. Many claim that the rate of incidence is greatly under-reported. Some allege that for every reported incident, there are five unreported incidents of abuse or neglect.

B. DEFINING ABUSE AND NEGLECT

The frequency of abuse and neglect, the degree of under reporting, and the causes and cures all depend upon what behaviors fall within the definitions of these terms. Every state has enacted laws, termed adult protective services statutes, that define elder abuse and neglect. However, the definitions vary. Neglect is generally defined as when a caregiver fails to provide care and services necessary for the adequate health and welfare of a dependent adult. Abuse includes financial, physical, sexual, and mental abuse as well as forced isolation.

Audrey S. Garfield, Note, *Elder Abuse and the States' Adult Protective Services Response: Time for a Change in California*
42 HASTINGS L.J. 861 (1991)*

The definitions of what constitutes elder abuse vary widely. Typically the broad categories include physical, psychological, fiduciary, and sexual abuse or exploitation as well as neglect; the definitions of each type of abuse vary within these respective categories.

All states . . . include physical harm in their definitions of abuse. States may distinguish, however, between instances of willful infliction of physical abuse and negligent infliction or failure to prevent the physical abuse. A more limited number of states consider infliction of mental anguish or psychological injury a form of abuse. Among those that do, some definitions only include those cases that require medical attention; others do not specify such a requirement. As one commentator noted, psychological abuse is common and its omission in many state statutes is unfortunate. He notes, however, that failure to include psychological abuse may be attributed to a number of factors. These include problems in defining the term, investigating the abuse, and providing the necessary services, as well as the difficulty of taking into consideration differing individual levels of tolerance for psychological abuse. A few states recognize unreasonable confinement as a form of potential elder abuse; even fewer define abuse as including intimidation. A number of states also include sexual abuse either within the general abuse definition or consider it as a separate category of abusive behavior.

Almost all states include neglect in their [adult protective services] laws. Neglect typically is defined as the failure to provide or deprivation of basic needs such as clothing, food, shelter, supervision, and care for physical and mental health. Some states merely have a negligence level of culpability for actionable neglect; others require willfulness.

Exploitation also is a common element in these provisions. It usually is defined as the illegal or improper use of a vulnerable or incapacitated elder, his resources, or property for the exploiter's or another's monetary profit or personal advantage. At least one state defines exploitation more restrictively as a caretaker's improper use of funds that have been paid by the government to an adult or his caretaker. This definition has been criticized as too narrow because it fails to protect the elder's personal resources from exploitation.

Varying definitions of abuse, neglect, and exploitation unfortunately hinder an accurate determination of the true extent of the problem. As one author noted, "[A]cceptance of a definition should be followed by research to accurately quantify the extent of the problem. Agreement on definition is essential in order to compare various research studies and to fashion responses."[80] More importantly, overbroad definitions may lead to implementation of relief programs that are more intrusive

---

    * Copyright © 1991 by University of California, Hastings College of the Law. Reprinted from HASTINGS LAW JOURNAL Vol. 42, No. 3, pp. 872–874 with permission.

    [80] Faulkner, *Mandating the Reporting of Suspected Cases of Elder Abuse: An Inappropriate, Ineffective and Ageist Response to the Abuse of Older Adults*, 16 FAM. L.Q. 69, 71 (1982).

than necessary and that may unconstitutionally invade the elder's independence.

A congressional report presents elder abuse in graphic terms.

Elder Abuse: A Decade of Shame and Inaction
(Report of the Subcommittee on Health and Long-term Care of the House Select Committee on Aging, No. 101-752, 101st Cong., 2d Sess., Apr. 1990, at 1, 3–5, 11, 14, 17, 18, 23, 24, 26)

Physical Abuse and Neglect

Physical abuse is violent conduct which results in bodily harm or mental distress. It can include assault — putting the elderly in fear of violence — at one end of the spectrum, all the way to murder and mayhem at the other end. . . . Passive abuse is known as neglect, and behaviors in this category include the withholding of medication, medical treatment, food and personal care necessary for the well-being of the elderly person.

Financial Abuse

Financial abuse involves the theft or conversion of money or anything of value belonging to the elderly by their relatives or caretakers. Sometimes, this theft or misappropriation is accomplished by force — even at gunpoint. In other cases, it is accomplished by stealth through deceit, misrepresentation and fraud. In most instances, the taking of the elderly person's property happens swiftly, but in a few instances involving undue influence in the writing of wills, greedy family members have been willing to wait months or even years to acquire the property of a loved one.

Psychological Abuse

In addition to being abused financially and physically, the elderly can also suffer emotional or psychological abuse at the hands of their relatives or other caregivers. In its mildest form, psychological abuse includes simple name calling and verbal assaults. In its severer forms, it is a protracted and systematic effort to dehumanize the elderly, sometimes with the goal of driving a person to insanity or suicide. The most common weapon used in this kind of warfare is the threat of nursing home placement.

Sexual Abuse

Sexual abuse of the elderly by their caregivers is a gruesome subject. It needs no further explanation.

[Note: Eight years later, the NCEA is more enlightening: Sexual abuse is defined as nonconsensual contact of any kind with an elderly person. Sexual contact with any person incapable of giving consent is also considered sexual abuse. It includes but is not limited to unwanted touching, all types of sexual assault or battery, such as rape, sodomy, coerced nudity, and sexually explicit photography.]

Violation of Rights

The "violation of rights" . . . includes being forced out of one's dwelling or being forced into another setting against the older person's will. It also includes the violation of the right to move freely, with no physical restraints, the right to receive adequate and appropriate medical treatment, the right to have a clean and safe living environment, the right to privacy, the right to freedom from verbal abuse and the right to complain and seek redress of grievances, among others.

[The Committee reported the following among many detailed instances of abuse:]

In New Jersey, a 70-year-old woman was beaten by her 32-year-old son, who did not contribute to the household expenses and whom she suspected of abusing alcohol and drugs. She said she was terrified of his unprovoked attacks and that he had broken her glasses and once attacked her in bed while she was sleeping. A social worker saw her badly bruised left breast, the result of the son punching her.

In Iowa, a 67-year-old woman with AIDS (from a blood transfusion) and diabetes suffered bruises to her face, shoulder, arm, hand and hip. Doctors noted that the bruises were not the sort of discolorations which can accompany AIDS but rather the result of trauma. The doctors disputed a home aide's explanation that the patient had fallen in her bed, theorizing instead that the aide turned her too vigorously in the bed, thus slamming her into the bed's side rails. The bruises on her face probably resulted from the aide forcing her to take medication.

A home health aide in New Hampshire was startled to find her client, an elderly woman, in urine and feces-soiled clothing. The woman had suffered severe weight loss, too. The woman's husband, her caregiver, had failed to contact his wife's physician as he had promised the aide he would, although his wife was weak and malnourished and had to be hospitalized.

A 72-year-old North Dakota man was financially exploited by his 28-year-old grandson. The elderly man and his wife took the grandson in and raised him, but the young man has a history of drug and alcohol use and has been arrested several times. The young man makes threats and so the client gives him about $1,000 a month, although he admits that the sum is far too generous, considering the work the grandson does on the farm. He has also given the grandson undisclosed gifts of automobiles and cash.

A 65-year-old California woman had an unruly son who was discharged from the Army and came to live with her. He confiscated her benefit checks and threw away her medications for arthritis and pain. He demanded sexual gratification from her on repeated occasions and kept her in submission by threatening to throw her out in the street if she made his practices known.

In North Dakota, an elderly woman lives in an upstairs apartment in her son's home. She says the son uses her as a slave to do household chores. The son and grandchildren take her money without asking and insult her mental capacity and continually use profanity when talking to her.

———————

Based on a 1994 study, The National Center on Elder Abuse (NCEA) reported the following breakdown in categories of domestic maltreatment:

Neglect	58.5%
Physical Abuse	15.7%
Financial/Material Exploitation	12.3%
Emotional Abuse/Neglect	7.3%
Sexual Abuse	0.5%
Other	5.1%

Little is known about the effects of abuse on mortality. However, a study at Cornell reported that, after adjusting for such variables as chronic disease, functional status, and social networks, elders who are abused or exploited are three times as likely to die within the follow-up period. *See* M.S. Lachs et al., *The Mortality of Elder Mistreatment*, 280 JAMA 428 (1998).

QUESTION

A finding of elder abuse depends upon how we choose to label the abuser's behavior. For example, every Friday night after work and a few drinks, Steve comes home and berates his 85-year-old mother for living with him and threatens to move her into a boarding house. The reality is that Steve has yelled at his mother, complained about her living with him, and threatened to evict her. But how should we label his behavior? Is he abusive? Is he a whiner? Is he justified in feeling put upon? Is he someone who should stop drinking? Is he inconsiderate? Is he a poor example of a son? Is he the victim of a parasitical mother?

C. WHO ARE THE VICTIMS OF ELDER ABUSE?

The NCEA reports the demographics of elderly abuse victims: the median age (based on a 1994 study) is 76.5 years. The race and ethnicity of abuse victims is in rough proportion to the population, with 65 percent being white, 21 percent black, and 10 percent Hispanic. The proportion of men and women are also very roughly in proportion to the older population, with about 60 percent of victims being female and 40 percent male. The typical victim is a very elderly woman, primarily because women more often survive to a state of dependency in old age.

Though virtually anyone might suffer abuse in some circumstances, many abuse victims share similar characteristics. The most likely victims are women age 75 or older who are dependent on the abuser for care and protection. The greater the victim's financial dependency the more probable that physical or psychological abuse will occur. Likewise, the older the individual the greater the probability of abuse, most likely because of greater dependency and a lesser ability to resist. If the victim is a problem drinker, he or she is more likely to be abused. One factor is low self-esteem, which can cause the victim to internalize the blame for the abuse and not to object to or report it. Finally, provocative behavior can lead to abuse. Some elderly persons are overly demanding of caregivers, ungrateful for care or assistance, and generally unpleasant to interact with. Such behavior can aggravate a stressed and burdened caregiver far beyond the burdens of caregiving. Anger or frustration in the caregiver can erupt into abuse.

While admitting that some abused elderly are difficult individuals, we must be careful not to blame the victim. Being unpleasant or uncooperative cannot justify retaliatory abuse or neglect. Although we may be more sympathetic to an abuser, that cannot excuse the abuse. But the existence of an abusive victim does suggest that at least some abuse and neglect represents a pathological relationship between the victim and the abuser in which both parties are caught in a web of provocation and response. "[I]t is not always possible to separate the victims from the perpetrators. The meshing of personalities combined with a long history of intimate interaction often obliterates clear-cut distinctions between the abused and the abuser — victim or perpetrator." *See* S. STEINMETZ, DUTY BOUND: ELDER ABUSE & FAMILY CARE 602 (1988).

QUESTIONS

1.   How does the inappropriate behavior of an elderly person affect the scope of the caregiver's reasonable responses to the behavior?

2.   Does the abusive or provocative victim profile help explain the failure of many victims to report abuse?

D.   WHO ABUSES OLDER PEOPLE AND WHY?

Most elderly abuse and neglect is caused by caregivers, typically family members such as spouses or adult children, or nursing home employees. In part this is because elderly abuse and neglect are usually defined as *repeated* physical assault or neglect or ongoing psychological abuse. One-time incidents such as a mugging, a phony home repair scheme, or a theft from the home are certainly crimes and are certainly abusive of the elderly but they are not usually thought of as "elder abuse." That term is reserved mainly for transgressions by those in a position of power and trust over the elderly victim. Elder abuse occurs when the abuser violates a duty of care or a fiduciary responsibility to the victim.

The reasons that individuals abuse or neglect the elderly are probably as varied as the number of abusers. Yet there are some useful generalizations. Abuse is an exercise of power and control over the victim. Sometimes the abuser has lost control he or she would rather have; sometimes abuse is an exercise of evil intent.

Hedwig Reichle, seventy-four years old at the time of Pruett's sentencing, was a German immigrant who met Pruett in the early seventies. Pruett and Reichle became friends, and Pruett invited Reichle to move into her home and work as a housekeeper in exchange for room and board. It appears that the relationship was congenial for the first few years. Reichle testified that, in 1976, Pruett began to slap her on occasion, and by 1982 had progressed to striking her on a daily basis with a hammer, feet or hands about her head and shoulders. In addition, Reichle testified that Pruett forced her to work many hours cleaning the house and doing yard work. Reichle testified to a consistent course of substantial physical abuse culminating on November 28, 1983, when Reichle wandered away from the Pruett residence to a local Qwik Stop convenience market where her injuries were observed and she was referred to the Brother Francis Shelter. At the Brother Francis Shelter, a nurse listed her injuries to be bruises on her lips, right arm, elbow and legs. She had multiple cuts on her right arm and a cut on her cheek; she had bumps on her lips and the back of her head. A physician's exam showed that Reichle had multiple scars on her arms, a chronic dislocation of the right shoulder, an old fracture of the nose, a cauliflowered left earlobe, multiple contusions on her body, and several broken and missing teeth. Pruett's neighbors testified to seeing Pruett strike, push and kick Reichle while both were in the yard outside Pruett's house.

Pruett v. State, 742 P.2d 257 (Alaska Ct. App. 1987).

QUESTIONS

1. An understanding of the causes of abuse and neglect are critical to any solution for the problem. If the abuser is reacting to stress or is overwhelmed by the responsibility of being a caregiver, what does that suggest about prevention of abuse and neglect? What if the problem is in the personality of the abuser?

2. If the abuser is financially dependent upon the victim, what does that suggest about prevention of abuse?

3. If part of the solution to institutional abuse is better pay and better training for employees, who is going to pay the costs?

[1] DOMESTIC CAREGIVERS

Experts in the field have identified the conditions under which abuse is most likely to occur. In domestic settings the major precipitating factor is family stress. The financial and emotional pressure of caring for a frail, dependent elderly individual's daily needs can create an intolerable burden and transform some caregivers into abusers. When family financial and emotional resources are strained, the burden of care can give rise to despair, anger, or resentment. The strain of caring may cause emotional fault lines to open, exposing weaknesses in the family structure or emotional and psychiatric problems of the caregiver. Low family income means few resources to deal with the elderly person's needs or provide the caregiver with respite, distraction, or compensating satisfactions. The caregiver has little hope that things will improve. The need to care for an elderly parent or relative may interfere with an employment prospect. A new job or overtime work may have to be rejected and a long commute may be impossible because of the need to return home to care for the relative.

Elder abuse also may be a form of retaliation or revenge. Many of those who abuse the elderly were themselves victims of abuse as children. They literally learned violence as "normal" behavior. Only one in 400 children reared nonviolently later attacks his parents; however, one out of two abused children will. Moreover, abusers seem to share abusive personality traits or character disorders. They may suffer from arrested development and have failed to mature beyond the stage of adolescent rebellion. In such instances the abuse of the parent can be seen as a demonstration of revolt and emancipation.

Abusers often have alcohol or drug problems and a significant proportion of abuse occurs when the abuser is drunk or on drugs. Other abusers suffer some level of mental illness, the symptoms of which can be triggered by the stress of caregiving.

Though it may seem counterintuitive, the caregiver who is financially dependent on the victim has a greater likelihood of becoming an abuser. Abusers are significantly more dependent than nonabusers on the elderly victim for financial assistance, housing, household repair, and transportation. Apparently dependence on an elderly person creates hostility that may be expressed by abuse or neglect. Anecdotal evidence suggests that employees hired by older people for in-home housekeeping or personal care may abuse their employers in part because of dependency and resentment.

Abuse by family caregivers can be seen as a form of control. All caregivers need some degree of control, and abuse may be considered as control by unacceptable means. Caregivers who abuse may desire control either to make their job easier (the victim will obey the caregiver) or may obtain psychological pleasure from controlling and tormenting the victim. Abusers yell at the older person, psychologically abuse them, physically threaten them, and deny medical treatment as means of asserting control. Psychological abuse includes threats and ignoring the elderly person. The elderly victim may be threatened with no access to the television, getting put in a nursing home, or having a hearing aid or a walker taken away.

Claims of abuse and neglect invoke both common-law issues of battery, assault, and negligence, and also violations of state statutes designed to protect the elderly.

ESTATE OF KAYLE
2006 Cal. App. Unpub. LEXIS 10578 (Nov. 22, 2006)

Stewart Kayle, conservator of the persons and estates of his parents Jerry P. Kayle and Celia S. Kayle, appeals judgment dismissing his action after demurrers were sustained to his Second Amended Complaint and Third Amended Complaint against attorney William Remery and others for negligence, elder abuse under the Elder Abuse Act, kidnapping, intentional infliction of emotional distress, and legal malpractice arising out of the care of the conservatees at a residential facility. We affirm in part and reverse in part.

FACTUAL BACKGROUND AND PROCEDURAL HISTORY

1. *Background Facts.*

The Kayles suffer from dementia. On June 28, 2002, Stewart Kayle was appointed the Kayles' temporary conservator; on August 26, 2002, he became their permanent conservator. In addition to dementia, the Kayles suffered from other physical ailments such that they were unable to manage their finances or take care of their physical needs, or to resist fraud and undue influence. Remery had acted as the Kayles' attorney prior to their conservatorship.

The Kayles were placed at Woodland Park Retirement Hotel (Woodland Park), and resided there during 2002 and 2003. During the relevant time periods, Jerry Kayle was being treated by Robert Neshkes, M.D., of the West Los Angeles Veterans Administration Hospital. Plaintiff alleged that defendant Woodland Park, which was run by defendant Longwood Management Corporation (Longwood), and members of Woodland Park's staff (defendants Susan Weisbarth, an employee and agent of Longwood, and Donna Lee Hogg, a licensed vocational nurse employed at Woodland Park), who were the Kayles' care custodians, failed to adequately care for the Kayles by, among other things, failing to adequately monitor the Kayles' health, failing to follow medication orders, failing to arrange for emergency care when necessary, and failing to advise Kayle of the condition of his parents. While in Woodland Park's care, Celia Kayle suffered a stroke and severe cellulitis; Jerry Kayle fell and hit his head, requiring hospitalization at Stewart Kayle's instigation after Woodland Park personnel failed to act. Furthermore, the conduct of Woodland Park, Longwood, and Woodland Park's employees resulted in the disruption of Dr. Neshke's treatment program for Jerry Kayle.

Plaintiff alleged that in June 2003, he attempted to terminate Jerry Kayle's contract with Woodland Park and move him elsewhere. On July 27, 2003, plaintiff moved Jerry Kayle to Laramie Manor, where he resided until he was hospitalized at the West Los Angeles VA Hospital on August 9, 2003. Plaintiff claimed that defendants Woodland Park, Longwood, Weisbarth and Hogg removed Jerry Kayle from treatment at the VA Hospital in West Los Angeles on August 11, 2003, without plaintiff's permission and re-admitted him to Woodland Park; failed to report to plaintiff concerning Jerry Kayle's condition and withheld information concerning his condition; failed to notify his doctor about his condition; and failed to make Jerry Kayle's medical information available to his doctor at Stewart Kayle's written request. Plaintiff alleged that defendants, including Remery, engaged in this conduct with the knowledge that Jerry Kayle was legally incompetent, and engaged in conduct designed to harass and intimidate Jerry Kayle so that he would remain at Woodland Park, including making statements to Jerry Kayle that plaintiff was going to harm and abuse him. These acts were done in defiance of plaintiff's position as conservator, and caused the conservatees emotional and physical distress and discomfort.

. . . .

DISCUSSION

Plaintiff argues that: the allegations of conspiracy are sufficient to hold Remery liable for the underlying tortious acts committed by the other defendants; Remery may be held directly liable for elder abuse, false imprisonment, and kidnapping; the allegations sufficiently allege negligence, legal malpractice, and intentional infliction of emotional distress; and Remery had a duty of care to warn of legal problems even though they were outside the scope of his legal representation of Jerry Kayle.

. . . .

II. PLAINTIFF'S CONSPIRACY ALLEGATIONS ARE SUFFICIENT TO IMPOSE VICARIOUS LIABILTY UPON REMERY FOR PLAINTIFF'S ELDER ABUSE AND KIDNAPPING CLAIMS.

Conspiracy is not an independent tort; it is a method of imposing liability on co-tortfeasors for vicarious commission of an underlying tort. . . .

Although there are no allegations that Remery directly participated in the alleged kidnapping or elder abuse (neglect, isolation, and physical abuse), these allegations of conspiracy are sufficient to impose liability on Remery for the conduct of the custodial care defendants for such acts. Plaintiff has alleged the agreement and intent to further its purpose by committing wrongful acts.

III. PLAINTIFF'S CLAIMS OF DIRECT LIABILITY FOR ELDER ABUSE (NEGLECT, PHYSICAL ABUSE, AND FALSE IMPRISONMENT) AGAINST REMERY FAIL.

Claims under the Elder Abuse Act are statutory, and as such must be pled with specificity. Section 15601.07 defines " '[a]buse of an elder or a dependent adult' " as either of the following: "(a) Physical abuse, neglect, financial abuse, abandonment, isolation, abduction, or other treatment with resulting physical harm or pain or mental suffering," or "(b) The deprivation by a care custodian of goods or services that are necessary to avoid physical harm or mental suffering." Under the Elder Abuse Act, section 15610.17, care custodians are defined as ". . . persons providing care or services for elders or dependent adults, including members of the support staff and maintenance staff. . . ."

1. *Neglect.* The Elder Abuse Act defines "neglect" as either of the following: "(1) The negligent failure of any person having the care or custody of an elder or a dependent adult to exercise that degree of care that a reasonable person in a like position would exercise," or "(2) The negligent failure of an elder or dependent adult to exercise that degree of self care that a reasonable person in a like position would exercise." (§ 15610.57.) Plaintiff makes no allegations that Remery had the care or custody of either of the conservatees, and this claim therefore fails.

2. *Physical Abuse.* The Elder Abuse Act defines "physical abuse" to include battery, as defined in Section 242 of the Penal Code. (§ 15610.63.) Penal Code section 242 defines battery as "any willful and unlawful use of force or violence upon the person of another." There is no allegation that Remery actually participated in the acts alleged to have constituted a battery, namely the allegedly unconsented medical procedures upon Jerry Kayle.

3. *Isolation.* Finally, the Elder Abuse Act at section 15610.43 provides that "(a) 'Isolation' means any of the following: . . . [¶] (3) False imprisonment, as defined in Section 236 of the Penal Code. . . ." Penal Code section 236 defines "false imprisonment" as "the unlawful violation of the personal liberty of another." The personal liberty of the victim is violated where the victim is compelled to remain where he or she does not wish to remain, or to go where he or she does not wish to

go; the offense may be committed by acts or by words, or both, and by merely operating upon the will of the individual or by personal violence, or both.

Plaintiff alleges that Remery participated in making threats to Jerry Kayle with the intent to induce Jerry Kayle to remain at Woodland Park. However, plaintiff, not Jerry Kayle, had the authority as conservator to determine where the conservatees resided. (Prob. Code, § 2351.) Plaintiff has not alleged how Remery's statements prevented plaintiff from moving Kayle, nor has plaintiff alleged that Remery actually prevented plaintiff from moving the incompetent Jerry Kayle from Woodland Park for over three months. Without such allegations, the claim fails.

. . . .

VI. PLAINTIFF CANNOT ESTABLISH NON-PROFESSIONAL NEGLIGENCE LIABILITY SOLELY BASED UPON THE ATTORNEY-CLIENT RELATIONSHIP.

Plaintiff's negligence claim alleged that Remery, as the Kayles' attorney, had a duty "to protect them from health and safety hazards (to the extent that such protection is within the scope of a lawyer's duties when the lawyer is providing services in like circumstances), including but not limited to the duty to refrain from knowingly putting the lawyer's mentally impaired client into the path of harm (or into circumstances where the probability of serious and substantial harm is high), and to protect the client from hazards presented by predatory individuals who would sometimes contact the Conservatees for the purpose of extracting funds from them and/or otherwise harming or abusing the Conservatees."

Plaintiff's claim of generalized negligence based upon Remery's attorney-client relationship fails for lack of duty. None of the claims alleged in the negligence claim are premised upon duties arising from the attorney-client relationship, and plaintiff has not alleged that Remery undertook any affirmative duties. There is no generalized duty to affirmatively act on behalf of another person. Because plaintiff's claims of duty are based on Remery's failure to control the conduct of third persons, no negligence claim can be stated.

DISPOSITION

The judgment of the superior court is affirmed in part and reversed in part. Plaintiff's claims for elder abuse and kidnapping against Remery based upon a conspiracy theory are reinstated.

QUESTIONS

1. In *Estate of Kayle*, the court held there was duty and so negligence. What kind of relationship between parties is required to create legal duty?

2. Are threats a form of abuse? Should they be considered abuse in the same way that physical aggression is abuse?

3.   Why is it abusive to ignore an elderly person? Does it matter how long you ignore the individual or what he or she wants?

4.   If an individual abused by their spouse were younger, we would classify the behavior as spousal abuse. Younger victims of spousal abuse may later show up statistically as victims of elder abuse. Of course, some abuse of an elderly spouse does not begin until the victim is older and perhaps *because* the victim is older. Is there any reason to classify some abuse of older spouses as spousal abuse rather than elder abuse? Does it matter?

5.   Marriage creates unique duties and dependencies. Can you explain how this might contribute to elder abuse? Why might the aging of a marriage partner precipitate abuse?

[2] INSTITUTIONAL CAREGIVERS

Institutional abuse, such as in a nursing home, is correlated with too few staff, low wages, and inadequate training. Abuse is often a means of gaining control of the institution's residents, particularly for an overworked staff who may tie down residents or physically threaten them to impose control. A shortage of staff may also lead to neglect as it is physically impossible for the overworked staff to meet all of the needs of the residents. The very low wages paid by some institutions may attract only those employees whom no one else would hire. Past records of criminality by a potential employee may be ignored when there are no alternative candidates. Additionally, poorly paid employees may be more tempted to steal from their patients or may be hostile to them simply because they are so poorly paid. Lack of training may leave the staff with few legitimate methods for dealing with elderly patients, so they resort to abuse.

The most frequent type of abuse committed by nursing home staff is physical restraint beyond that which is legitimately needed to control the patient. Staff also hit, slap, push, grab, shove, or pinch patients. To control behavior the staff members deny food or take away privileges. Psychological abuse is common. Patients are yelled at in anger, insulted, threatened, sworn at, and placed in isolation.

In one study, 40 percent of nursing home workers surveyed admitted committing at least one abusive act in the past year and 10 percent admitted committing a physically abusive act. *See also* Karl Pillemer & David W. Moore, *Abuse of Patients in Nursing Homes*, 29 GERONTOLOGIST 314 (1989).

The following facts from a 1984 North Carolina case illustrate the abuse and neglect of a 100-year-old resident of a nursing home:

> However, after Mrs. Cranfill lost control of her bowel and bladder functions and could no longer visit the bathroom by herself, plaintiff began to find Mrs. Cranfill sitting or lying in her own waste. There came a time when plaintiff would visit WSCC three times daily, usually around meal time so that she could feed Mrs. Cranfill who was virtually unable to feed herself in an orderly manner. Plaintiff testified that she continuously found Mrs. Cranfill soiled with her own wastes and opined that Mrs. Cranfill had

been so soiled for a considerable period of time. She complained to defendant's nurses and nurse's aides about this problem. At times, the WSCC staff kept Mrs. Cranfill, her linens, and her room clean and responded to plaintiff's complaints. However, in plaintiff's mind, these satisfactory times were few and far between. Her testimony referred to unsanitary and uncomfortable room conditions and to a WSCC staff that was rude and unreasonably forceful to Mrs. Cranfill and unresponsive to plaintiff's requests.

On one visit in March 1981, plaintiff found Mrs. Cranfill in a dreadful state. She had severe bruises about her eye, mouth, hands, and wrists. Photographs taken the following day, depict the severity of Mrs. Cranfill's condition. Plaintiff's Trial Exhibits Nos. 1-4. Like plaintiff, the Court finds the pain and agony illustrated by the photographs extremely difficult to put into words.

Plaintiff had previously complained about the cold temperature in Mrs. Cranfill's room and on this day found the window open letting in outside wintry air. A nurse's aide explained that she had opened the window to allow the odor to escape. Apparently the nurse's aide knew nothing about Mrs. Cranfill's physical condition. Upon inquiry from plaintiff about Mrs. Cranfill's bruises, a nurse on duty stated she did not know what plaintiff was talking about. Plaintiff complained to William H. Beilfuss, then Administrator of WSCC. Beilfuss searched in vain for an accident report and told plaintiff he would investigate the matter. Plaintiff never received an accident report and stated that Beilfuss had no adequate explanation for the circumstances.

Makas v. Hillhaven, Inc., 589 F. Supp. 736 (M.D.N.C. 1984).

E.   SELF-NEGLECT

The concept of self-neglect — that is, an older person who fails to meet his or her basic needs for food, shelter, clothing, or health care — provides a legal battlefield between the principle of individual autonomy and the power of the state to provide for a citizen's health and safety. Ten states have a separate category of "self-neglect" as a basis for intervention; 21 subsume self-neglect in the broader category of "neglect."

Note how Illinois defines self-neglect to including hoarding.

(i-5) "Self-neglect" means a condition that is the result of an eligible adult's inability, due to physical or mental impairments, or both, or a diminished capacity, to perform essential self-care tasks that substantially threaten his or her own health, including: providing essential food, clothing, shelter, and health care; and obtaining goods and services necessary to maintain physical health, mental health, emotional well-being, and general safety. The term includes compulsive hoarding, which is characterized by the acquisition and retention of large quantities of items and materials that produce an extensively cluttered living space, which significantly impairs the performance of essential self-care tasks or otherwise substantially threatens life or safety.

302 Ill. Comp. Stat. 20/2

Consider the following self-neglect case:

DAVIS v. CUYAHOGA COUNTY ADULT PROTECTIVE SERVICES
2000 Ohio App. LEXIS 4754 (Oct. 12, 2000)

On May 10, 1999, Michael Debs, a health inspector with the City of Cleveland's Department of Health, went to appellant's home in the company of Cleveland Police officers and Christina Rakowsky, a social worker for the Cuyahoga County Department of Human Services, Adult Protective Services Division. Numerous complaints and referrals were made since 1976 about appellant and the condition of her home. Alice Gilliland, appellant's sister, purchased the house in 1991 for the purpose of providing appellant with a place to live. Rakowsky first met appellant in 1996 after she received a self-neglect referral regarding appellant. Appellant refused any services and did not permit Rakowsky or anyone else to enter her house. Rakowsky went back to the home over the years in response to other referrals but met with the same response from appellant.

Debbs, the health inspector, also had been to the residence a number of times over the previous two to three years. No one would respond to his knocks on the door or to the notes Debbs left in the mailbox or under the door. Cleveland Police Officer Riley was familiar with appellant and her home. In the spring of 1999, Officer Riley observed appellant in the middle of the street, yelling at two neighborhood children. Officer Riley approached to see if he could be of assistance. He noted appellant had open sores on her face and arms. Appellant appeared to be disheveled and had not bathed for some time. Appellant refused to tell Officer Riley her name or any other information. Instead, she walked toward her house. Officer Riley stood between appellant and her residence to ask when appellant last had medical attention. Appellant responded it was none of his business and entered her home. Officer Riley saw the house contained garbage which was piled up inside and noticed a rancid smell coming from the house. Officer Riley contacted his superior and appellant was transported to the hospital for treatment.

Appellant also had refused an offer from the housing director of the Westown Community Development Corporation to assist her in maintaining the exterior of the property.

Finally, the City of Cleveland obtained a warrant to allow the Environmental Health Department to enter the residence. Upon the arrival of Inspector Debbs, Officer Riley, and Rakowsky, appellant appeared from a neighbor's home and refused to permit them to enter her house at first. She did open the door after Inspector Debbs explained they had a search warrant. Inside, Inspector Debbs noted that clothing, unopened cans of food, opened cans of cat food, and refuse were strewn about the premises. Cat and dog feces were present. The electricity did not work and twenty-six kerosene cans were found in the house. Ten to twelve of the kerosene cans were full and surrounded by garbage. One dog and twelve to fifteen cats were living there. The premises were infested with insects including fleas and cockroaches. Evidence of the presence of rodents was observed. The police transported appellant to St. Vincent's Charity Hospital where she was admitted into the psychiatric ward. Debbs returned the following day, using a protective suit he had borrowed from the air pollution department to enter the house.

The Department of Public Health issued an order to abate nuisance. The order declared the conditions present in the house were a threat to the immediate health and safety of the occupant. The order stated the house was uninhabitable in its present condition. Appellant received a copy of this order but made no attempt to arrange for the property to be cleaned. Gilliland did hire a cleaning crew. Three people spent ten days cleaning the house and clearing it of debris. All three wore protective clothing while working at the house.

On June 3, 1999, probate court issued an emergency protective services order. On July 21, 1999, an application for the appointment of a guardian was filed in probate court. The application alleged appellant to be incompetent by reason of mental impairment.

Probate court held a hearing on the application. In addition to hearing the testimony of several witnesses, including Rakowsky, Debbs, Officer Riley, and appellant, the court also admitted into evidence the depositions of Dr. Goldman and Dr. Wilkes. Dr. Goldman examined appellant while she was staying at a nursing home. Dr. Goldman found appellant to be extremely agitated, hostile, reserved, suspicious, guarded, and delusional. He considered appellant's judgment and insight to be very disturbed and felt there was a high probability she suffered from an Alzheimer's type of dementia. Dr. Goldman believed appellant required a guardian.

Dr. Wilkes became involved in appellant's care upon her admission to the psychiatric unit at St. Vincent Hospital. Dr. Wilkes found appellant's manner to be very intense. She was in denial about her problems. Dr. Wilkes opined appellant suffered from mild dementia but diagnosed her primary problem as a severe obsessive compulsive personality disorder which would cause appellant to hoard possessions. Dr. Wilkes concluded appellant needed a guardian because he did not believe she was capable of conducting her business affairs by herself. His opinion was that appellant was not mentally competent.

Probate court granted the application for an appointment of a guardian of appellant's person. The court concluded appellant suffered from dementia and severe obsessive compulsive disorder. Her ability to care for herself or her property was impaired because of a mental illness. Probate court declared appellant to be incompetent as defined under R.C. 2111.01(D).

In her first assignment of error, appellant contends probate court abused its discretion by finding she suffered from a mental impairment severe enough to make her incapable of caring for herself or her property. Appellant asserts the evidence about the condition of her residence was not enough to justify a finding of incompetency and was against the manifest weight of the evidence.

Under R.C. 2111.01(D) an "incompetent" person is defined, *inter alia*, to mean:

Any person who is so mentally impaired as a result of a mental or physical illness . . . that he is incapable of taking proper care of himself or his property. . . .

R.C. 2111.02(A) permits the probate court to appoint a guardian of the person, of the estate, or of both for an incompetent person. R.C. 2111.02(C) sets forth the procedure to be followed. Probate court is required to conduct a hearing before a guardian may be appointed for an alleged incompetent. The burden of proving incompetency is by clear and convincing evidence. The court is to consider evidence of a less restrictive alternative if it is introduced at the hearing and may deny a guardianship if it finds that a less restrictive alternative exists. Probate court must find a person is mentally impaired before it can conclude he or she is incompetent.

Probate court enjoys broad discretion in matters involving the appointment of a guardian. In matters relating to guardianships, probate court must act in the best interests of the incompetent. Even so, when an alleged incompetent objects to the appointment of a guardian, the probate court must be extremely cautious in proceeding. Appellant asserts the findings of probate court were against the manifest weight of the evidence. In determining whether a judgment is against the manifest weight of the evidence, an appellate court must be guided by the presumption that the findings of fact made below were correct. This is because the trier of fact observes the witnesses and their demeanor, gestures, and voice inflections, making the fact finder the best judge of credibility. Judgments supported by some competent, credible evidence going to all the essential elements will not be reversed by a reviewing court as being against the manifest weight of the evidence.

Appellant first argues the trial court abused its discretion by appointing a guardian based upon the condition of her home. Appellant ignores the overwhelming evidence submitted below regarding the deplorable conditions of her residence. Refuse was strewn throughout the home. Animal feces, rodents, insect infestations, opened cat food, and clothing were among some of the items found within the home. Three men spent ten full days cleaning and removing debris from the house. People donned protective suits before entering. The electricity did not work and appellant used kerosene in the house. Full and empty containers of kerosene were nestled in among the garbage, creating a fire hazard. Appellant remained in denial about the horrendous condition of the home. She claimed a neighbor boy helped clean and constantly stated the house was not that bad.

Evidence admitted at the hearing supported probate court's determination that appellant could not care for herself. Appellant argues there was testimony indicating she sought medical care, bathed, conducted financial transactions, and cooked. She did not appear malnourished. Appellant contends this evidence demonstrates her competency to care for herself. However, testimony admitted below also demonstrated appellant had open sores on her face and arms at one point. Because of her severe obsessive compulsive personality disorder, appellant hoarded possessions and animals. She exhibited these traits while staying with friends and at the hospital. This disorder directly led to the terrible conditions in which appellant resided before her removal by the police. Probate court had ample evidence before it indicating that the deplorable state of appellant's home showed she required a guardian to help safeguard her person.

Appellant maintains the evidence adduced at the hearing showed her ability to conduct her daily affairs such as shopping, cooking, cleaning, bathing, and seeking medical attention. Appellant apparently ignores any evidence to the contrary when making this argument. Appellant obviously could not care for her home. The electricity was not repaired and appellant utilized kerosene, creating a fire hazard. Appellant stated several times that she did not like living in the home but there was very little prospect she could obtain suitable housing on her own. Officer Riley observed appellant with open sores on her face and arms. He described her appearance as disheveled and dirty. All of this evidence strongly shows appellant was not capable of managing her daily affairs and had become a danger to herself.

Appellant's first assignment of error is overruled.

[The second appeals issue, failure to consider a less restrictive alternative than guardianship, also was overruled.]

Judgment affirmed.

QUESTIONS

1.   Does self-neglect legitimately warrant intervention?

2.   If so, was it appropriate to intervene in the case above?

3.   To what extent is self-neglect about the well-being of the individual, and to what extent about the community?

Self-neglect is not always considered an appropriate reason for intervention.

FLORIDA DEPARTMENT OF CHILDREN AND FAMILY SERVICES v. McKIM
869 So. 2d 760 (Fla. 2004)

PER CURIAM.

The Florida Department of Children and Family Services (Department) appeals from a final judgment denying its request for adult protective services for the appellee, Jo Lynn McKim. The Department asserts that the trial court erred as a matter of law in determining that it had no statutory authority to order protective services under section 415.1051(1), Florida Statutes, of the Adult Protective Services Act, even though the court found by clear and convincing evidence that appellee lacks capacity to consent to protective services and is a vulnerable adult in need of services. We affirm.

Pursuant to section 415.1051(1), Florida Statutes, the Department filed a petition for an order authorizing adult protective services for the appellee, alleging . . . that the appellee had difficulty walking; she required assistance for dressing, bathing, grooming, and toileting; she had a history of hospitalization, alcohol abuse, falling and being unable to get up, weakness, failure to eat, dehydration, incontinence, skin breakdown, and confusion; and she suffered from a potassium deficiency and hypothyroidism, requiring several prescription medications which she was unwilling or unable to manage as prescribed. The petition also stated that the appellee was found in her home covered in feces, and that she had not eaten or taken liquids for multiple days, resulting in her hospitalization. The petition alleged that the appellee lacked capacity to consent to the provision of protective services based on the following facts: the respondent had been diagnosed with cognitive impairment, specifically related to memory, which prevents her from making informed decisions regarding her care; the respondent has impaired attention and concentration, an inability to give a history due to memory impairments, and impaired insight and judgment.

At the hearing on the petition, the Department presented evidence to support the allegations made in the petition through the testimony of witnesses, including the appellee's father, her physician, and the social worker from the hospital. The medical testimony and that of the social worker established that the appellee required 24/7 care, and it would not be safe for her to return to her home.

The trial court found by clear and convincing evidence

> [The appellee] lacks the capacity to consent to protective services and meets the statutory definition of a "vulnerable adult in need of services" as defined in § 415.102(27), Fla. Stat., because of self neglect.

Nevertheless, the court found as a matter of law that it did not have authority to order protective services in the form of involuntary placement in a licensed facility because the statutory definition of "neglect" requires that "neglect" have occurred at the hand of a caregiver, and there was insufficient evidence of caregiver neglect.

The Department urges us to consider overall statutory intent and allow it to provide adult protective services for appellee, a party clearly in need of such services. While the Department's view in this case may be supported by sound public policy consideration, we are constrained as the trial judge was by the unambiguous language of the statute: adult protective services may only be provided to a non-consenting adult if such adult is subject to abuse, exploitation, or neglect of another person.

[W]here a department's construction of a statute is inconsistent with clear statutory language it must be rejected, notwithstanding how laudable the goals of that department. Section 415.1051, Florida Statutes, authorizes the court to order protective services for a vulnerable adult who is being "abused, neglected, or exploited." As the trial judge held, section 415.1051 applies exclusively to a vulnerable adult who is being mistreated by another person. This limitation is clear from the statutory definitions of abuse, neglect, and exploitation. "Abuse" is defined as *"any willful act or threatened act by a caregiver* that causes or is likely to cause significant impairment to a vulnerable adult's physical, mental, or emotional health." Likewise, "neglect" is defined as *"the failure or omission on the part of the caregiver* to provide the care, supervision, and services necessary to maintain the physical and mental health of the vulnerable adult.

The Department argues that the first two sentences of section 415.102(15), define neglect as an omission or failure by a caregiver, but concludes that the statute is ambiguous, because the third sentence of the definition does not use the term "caregiver." The problem with this analysis is that the third sentence necessarily refers to the first two. It cannot be read in isolation as if it created a new and different kind of neglect. When the Legislature said in the third sentence that neglect is "repeated conduct or a single incident of carelessness," it was merely defining the *kind* of omission that can be regarded as neglect. This sentence does not change the subject entirely by introducing for the first time the concept of self-neglect.

The Department also relies on the fact that the definition of "vulnerable adult in need of services" in section 415.102(27), is broad enough to include self-neglect. The phrase "vulnerable adult in need of services," however, is used in another part of the statute, which deals exclusively with services provided with the consent of the adult. This phrase is used only in section 415.105, which states:

> (1) PROTECTIVE SERVICES WITH CONSENT. — If the department determines through its investigation that a vulnerable adult demonstrates a need for protective services or protective supervision, the department shall immediately provide, or arrange for the provision of, protective services or protective supervision, including in-home services, *provided that the vulnerable adult consents. A vulnerable adult in need of services* as defined in s. 415.102 shall be referred to the community care for disabled adult's program, or to the community care for the elderly program administered by the Department of Elder Affairs.

§ 415.105(1), Fla. Stat. (emphasis added). This section is the only part of Chapter 415 that uses the phrase "vulnerable adult in need of services."

Section 415.1051, Florida Statutes, which is at issue in this case, does not employ the phrase "vulnerable adult in need of services." Rather, it uses the phrase "vulnerable adult," which is defined separately in the statute. Unlike the definition of "vulnerable adult in need of services," the definition of "vulnerable adult" does not include the concept of self-neglect. We therefore affirm.

QUESTIONS

1. Can you explain the distinction between the above cases on their facts?

2. What reasons might a state have for categorically declining to provide services to persons who are incapable of caring for themselves but do not or cannot ask for assistance?

3. Is self-neglect merely a personal choice of how to live? When do such decisions rise to the level that the state has an interest in intervention?

4. Does it matter that the older individual has always lived in an unkempt, poorly heated house? Does it make any difference to a determination of self-neglect if acute medical needs are new with the onset of old age?

5. At some point the denial and hardship of self neglect may be a symptom of mental illness or incapacity. If so, why shouldn't the mental health laws apply? If an individual is not a danger to herself or others (the mental health law standard),

should the state anti-abuse and neglect statute justify state interference in the person's life?

F.   ADULT PROTECTIVE SERVICES SYSTEMS

Federal hearings beginning in 1981 dramatically publicized the problem of elder abuse by showing that the traditional remedies provided by the law — criminal prosecution and tort litigation — were ill-suited responses to elder abuse. In the 1980s, in response to the promise of federal financial support, states created abuse response service networks, called adult protective service systems. Significant federal funding never followed, however, and the states have tried to fulfill their obligation to the "health, safety, and welfare" of older people as best they can.

[1]   PROCEDURES

Every state has enacted some form of adult protective services to prevent abuse and neglect of vulnerable persons and to provide supportive services either in the home of the vulnerable person, or, if necessary, to remove the vulnerable person from the care of abusers to a new, probably permanent, home. Some state protective services statutes are limited to the elderly. In other states, elder abuse is addressed in the domestic violence act or the protective services act applies to any vulnerable adult. Adult protective services vary from state to state, but most include procedures for investigation and voluntary and involuntary interventions, and many require mandatory reporting of suspected abuse by specified professionals. Protective services are initiated either by a request from an abused or neglected older person or a report by a third party who suspects abuse or neglect. The alleged victim must consent to intervention unless the state seeks a determination of mental incapacity. The state may provide services without consent of the alleged victim if there is a need to prevent imminent harm to the individual's health or safety.

The following excerpt from a student note, *Elder Abuse in California*, 42 HASTINGS L.J. 861 (1990-91),* clarifies the possibilities for investigation and intervention:

> All state statutes provide for some type of initial investigation after a report of alleged abuse is received. The laws vary with respect to which agency has responsibility for conducting this investigation. The majority of statutes name the state human services, social services, or welfare department as the entity with primary responsibility. A number of statutes assign this responsibility to the local welfare agency or law enforcement agency. Depending on the type of suspected harm, many statutes provide for certain reports to be referred to a specific agency for investigation. For example, law enforcement agencies or the district attorney's office often are referred cases involving suspected violations of the state's penal code or danger of imminent grave bodily harm. Jurisdiction over abuse investiga-

---

* Copyright © 1991 by University of California, Hastings College of the Law. Reprinted from HASTINGS LAW JOURNAL Vol. 42, No. 3, pp. 892–893, 897, with permission.

tions sometimes is determined by the type of locale where the suspected abuse is alleged to have occurred. The fact that the reported abuse took place in a long-term care facility, for example, often will dictate the agency responsible for the investigation. Some states assign investigatory responsibility to whichever agency receives the initial report of abuse. Other states fail to address clearly who ultimately is responsible for the investigation. In most states more than one agency has jurisdiction to conduct an investigation and cooperation between or among these entities is encouraged or mandated to ensure efficient and appropriate handling of cases.

The time frame within which an investigation must be initiated also varies. The specific time limits delineated in the statutes range from within twenty-four hours of receiving the report to ten days thereafter. Many states do not establish a specific time frame, requiring an investigation to begin "promptly."

. . . .

Once an investigation is completed or the elder requests assistance, provision of protective services may be recommended for the elder. Adult Protective Services statutes typically contain at least some provisions that are aimed at providing services to needy adults. These services are designed to assist elders in whatever way they require, while also permitting the elder to continue residing in the community.

The services component generally includes some combination of health, social, psychological, medical, and legal assistance. These services are not intended to function as random aids administered by unrelated agencies. Rather, the goal is to render coordinated services and assistance through a caseworker, usually a social worker, who can assess the individual's needs and combine the various programs and community resources to meet those needs. The services offered vary and often include visiting nurses, clinical services, special transportation, and hot home-delivered meals. These services are intended, among other things, to alleviate or prevent harm resulting from elder abuse. The availability of services depends on the funding allocated by the state to assist abused elders.

To avoid excessive or unnecessary intervention into the lives of older persons, careful investigation of reported abuse or neglect is crucial. At a minimum, no intervention should occur without consideration of the relevant medical, psychological, social, and financial factors. The investigation should weigh the immediate and long-term risk to the elderly individual against the loss of privacy and autonomy.

[2] CONSENT TO PROTECTIVE SERVICES

The issue of consent by the elderly person arises both when the investigation begins and when there is a determination that services are needed. Generally, statutes authorize, or simply assume, that state protective services workers will investigate an abuse report without any recognition of the right of individuals to be free of state inquiry into their private lives. A few states permit the elderly individual to terminate the investigation by refusing to consent or withdrawing consent, but even in those states the investigation can continue under court order by the use of a search warrant. Sometimes whether the older person would consent cannot be determined because the investigator is refused access by the caregiver and possible abuser. In many states the investigator may be accompanied by a police officer, but right to enter must be authorized by a warrant based upon probable cause or a specific court order that permits entry over the objections of the caregiver.

Most states permit the provision of services only if the elderly individual consents. Services may include regular visits by a nurse or social worker, meals-on-wheels, transportation to a clinic or a senior citizen center, and the linking up of the elderly victim with volunteers. If the older person refuses or withdraws consent, the services cannot be continued. Services can generally be provided over the objections of the caregiver if the elderly individual consents.

The goal of the protective services is to secure the freedom and safety of elderly victims but to do so in a way that is least intrusive upon their autonomy. The intervention should be for as short a period of time as possible and should be the minimum action needed to stop the abuse. While safety is important, it should not be considered superior to the need for freedom and independence. The service provider must balance these sometimes competing values. While most lawyers might argue that the provider should err on the side of freedom and independence, social workers or others faced with an actual case of abuse may find the need for safety to be more compelling.

If the elderly individual refuses to consent or lacks capacity to consent, should services be provided? The provision of services without the consent of the elderly individual is controversial. If the elderly individual is competent and still refuses services, it is difficult to justify "rescuing" the elderly individual. Presumably, a competent adult has the right to bear abuse or neglect if he or she so chooses. The issue, of course, is whether such an individual is in fact competent and is making a reasoned (though not reasonable) choice. If the elderly individual is mentally incapacitated, a guardian must be appointed who can then decide whether to consent on behalf of the abused, incapacitated person to the proposed services.

The difficulty arises in the determination of incapacity. Too often incapacity is equated with an older individual making what appear to be unwise decisions. If an abused individual refuses services, the providing agency is likely to conclude that he or she is incapacitated. Why else would the services be refused? The obvious solution is the appointment of a guardian who can consent to what is needed to stop the abuse and remove the victim from harm's way. Many statutes include no meaningful definition of incapacity leaving open the likelihood of benevolently intended but unprincipled judgments and actions by emergency services workers. The statutes rely on their judgment that a person is "unable" to "accept services" or even unwilling to consent to services. The vagueness of these terms, and potential for misuse, is particularly significant since protective intervention can be a "fast track" to guardianship, institutionalization, or both.

[3] NONCONSENSUAL AND EMERGENCY INTERVENTION

Two procedures are used to impose involuntary services on abuse victims in the nonemergency setting. The majority of states use the traditional guardianship or conservatorship mechanisms that already exist within their probate codes. Others have established a special procedure within their adult protective services laws that operates independently of the guardianship or conservatorship sections of the probate code. For the most part these procedures function in the same manner as guardianships and conservatorships. Most proceedings result in an order by the court designating an individual, organization, or agency to act as the functional equivalent of a guardian or conservator.

An exception to the rule that involuntary services may be provided only after formal guardianship or guardianship-like proceedings is the provision of short-term emergency services. Emergency provisions in adult protective services laws constitute an exception to the rule that services only may be provided with the elder's consent, although some state Adult Protective Services laws exclusively apply to elderly who are in the equivalent of an emergency situation. The New York Adult Protective Services laws, for example, only apply to "endangered adults," those individuals who are in a condition or situation that poses an imminent risk of death or serious physical harm and who lack the capacity to comprehend the consequences of remaining in the situation. Emergencies typically are defined as circumstances that "present a substantial risk of death or immediate and serious physical harm" to the elder. Some states define an emergency to include a situation that poses a risk of death or immediate and serious physical harm to the elder or to others. A few states do not limit emergencies to circumstances that pose a risk of imminent danger to physical health but also include danger to mental health. It is highly questionable whether danger to mental health is a legitimate criteria for emergency intervention.

Once a police officer or a representative of the responsible social services agency has determined that an emergency exists and that the individual cannot consent, most statutes allow the officer or representative to take the individual into emergency protective custody and remove him from the dangerous circumstances. In addition a few statutes specify that the individual should be transported to the appropriate medical or protective services facility. The Florida statute also contains a specific provision regarding emergency authorization of medical treatment. Once an older person has been taken into emergency custody, most statutes stipulate that a petition for an emergency order authorizing emergency services be filed with the court.

Typically the petition must be filed within 24 to 72 hours after the initial intervention.

If the older person is thought to be incapacitated, the protective service provider may seek the appointment of a guardian, something that may not be welcomed by the elderly individual, who may resent the loss of personal freedom and autonomy. The imposition of a guardianship may seem worse to the older individual than enduring the abuse and neglect. But if legally incapacitated, the older person's opinion is largely irrelevant and the imposition of a guardian is legally justified.

Some states permit the delivery of nonconsensual services without the need to find the elderly individual incapacitated and in need of a guardian. The protective services agency can bring a court proceeding in which the elderly individual is found to be in need of services. The court can appoint the agency as the functional equivalent of a guardian of the elderly individual to "consent" to the provision of services which the agency will then provide. The fig leaf of "consent" has been preserved without allowing it to interfere with the agency doing what it believes best — a textbook example of a legal fiction that makes perfect sense to a lawyer and none at all to the public.

If the system seems a bit out of focus it is in part because the statutes are often a poor match for the reality of elderly abuse. Because of financial constraints the provisions for investigation seldom are used. Instead intervention occurs only when the situation is an emergency because of threats to the older persons' health and safety. As a result, elderly individuals often live with continual abuse and self-neglect without any response from adult protective services. While in theory the system exists to minimize abuse and neglect, in practice it rarely intervenes until there has been significant harm.

QUESTIONS

1.   If the victim refuses to assist investigation, what should be done? Even if the victim does not consent, are there societal reasons for continuing the investigation?

2.   Is it appropriate for society to override the objections of the abused victim and insist upon the delivery of services? Are there some circumstances that provide a more compelling justification for nonconsensual services than others?

3.   Is the refusal of assistance by an abuse victim per se evidence of a lack of mental capacity? If not, what is? Can elderly abuse victims be said to voluntarily refuse services or assistance even if they live in fear of their abuser?

4.   If the abuser is the spouse, does it mean that state intervention is more justified? Less justified? Irrelevant to the decision?

5.   If an emergency exists, why is no consent needed for the delivery of services? How would you define an emergency?

[4]   MANDATORY REPORTING

In many states certain professionals, such as health care providers, must report suspicion of elder abuse, following the model of child abuse statutes. Those in favor of mandatory reporting stress that often the victim is incapable of reporting the abuse. The image is one of an isolated, dependent elderly person who is either physically or psychologically unable to seek help. Such victims may deny the existence of the mistreatment because of feelings of guilt, shame, and self-blame. Others fail to report abuse and neglect because they are physically isolated, fear retaliation, or fear the loss of the abusive caregiver.

Mandatory reporting is controversial, however, because it represents a paternalistic stance with regard to the elderly that is inappropriate for adults who are capable of reporting abuse and asking for assistance. It necessarily implies unwanted investigations and the possibility of unwanted services.

As a case-finding tool, it is questionable that mandatory reporting will locate a significant number of cases not already known to service providers. Beyond that, we are presently unable to serve those cases we already know about except by institutionalizing the older person.

While not assisting in the solution of the problem, mandatory reporting may, in fact, increase the potential for abuse by further infantilising the elder adult's position in society. Mandatory reporting legislation based on age rather than condition will decrease the decision-making authority of older persons and further erode their position in society, as well as reduce their ability to control their own lives. The ability to refuse assistance, even in the form of an investigation, is as important to self-image as the ability to seek and secure the assistance. Mandatory reporting for cases of suspected elder abuse, while reenforcing the view that older persons, as a group, need protection, will also act to discourage many from seeking help, thus, making the stereotype of helplessness a self-fulfilling prophecy.

Faulkner, *Mandating the Reporting of Suspected Cases of Elder Abuse: An Inappropriate, Ineffective and Ageist Response to the Abuse of Older Adults*, 16 FAM. L.Q. 69, 86–70 (1982).

A number of studies have observed that elders are reluctant to report abuse and accept help, which may be true in some instances. However, other researchers paint a different picture. In 95 percent of the cases analyzed, the elderly victim had approached social services for help, help which apparently was not forthcoming. Unlike other abused dependents, abused elders did seek help but were unsuccessful in finding it. If further research establishes that abused elders are capable of and are seeking protection which is not forthcoming, the solution may be voluntary prevention and treatment services, not mandatory reporting statutes which may trigger an unwelcome intrusion into the lives of elder abuse victims who do not want to be protected.

Even well developed services will not reach the most egregious abuse cases in which the victim is isolated and severely mistreated. In order to "discover" these individuals, it would be necessary to tolerate widespread violations of the fourth amendment, the "specter of elder abuse squads raiding homes to detect evidence of mistreatment."

The effectiveness of mandatory reporting clearly remains in doubt. One national study reported by the NCEA estimates that only one in fourteen incidents of elder abuse is reported, suggesting that mandatory reporting would at the least identify more cases for possible intervention.

An employer may object to an employee reporting suspected abuse even though the employee is mandated to do so. In a 2004 case, a Nebraska nursing home fired a nursing assistant who reported that a resident had been injured as a result of using improper procedures when moving the resident from a wheelchair to her bed.

The employer claimed that it had the right to terminate the employee because she was an at-will employee who could be discharged for any lawful reason, and nothing in the state's adult protective services act limited the right of an employer to discharge an employee. On appeal, the Nebraska Supreme Court held when the law imposes a duty on employees to prevent abuse of residents, and the employee fulfills that duty by reporting abuse, it would be against public policy to permit an employer to retaliate by firing the employee. The Court noted that an employee should not be faced with choosing between reporting abuse and being fired or failing to report abuse and being prosecuted for that failure. *Wendeln v. Beatrice Manor, Inc.*, 712 N.W.2d 226 (Neb. 2006).

QUESTIONS

1. Do you think mandatory reporting and investigation is warranted even if there are relatively few cases to report?

2. Mandatory reporting requirements are based on the assumption that professionals will not report elder abuse when they suspect it. Do you think this is true of physicians? If so, why? What about social workers? Community health nurses?

3. Does the problem of false or erroneous reporting outweigh the difficulties that might be caused by the reports? What are the problems if the report is wrong and the investigation is unwarranted?

4. Should there be penalties for failure to report suspected elder abuse? Would you seek criminal penalties (with criminal standards of proof) or are civil penalties sufficient?

[5] CONFIDENTIALITY OF ABUSE REPORT RECORDS

The issue of confidentiality arises at many points in the process of protective intervention. The reporter of the abuse, the victim, and the alleged perpetrator each has an interest in limiting access to the information in the initial report. One of the most compelling reasons offered for confidentiality is to encourage hesitant reporters. Confidentiality or anonymity protects reporters and encourages reporting by those who otherwise might be hesitant for fear of retaliation or discovery by the alleged abuser or abused.

Concerns for privacy and encouraging reporters must be weighed against the need for information among those who investigate or prosecute elderly abuse and neglect. To assure reliable access to abuse information a number of states have established central registries of abuse reports. While the report is on file only specified persons have access to it, including the victim, certain agencies involved in the investigation such as local law enforcement and administrative agencies, the court, and (in some states) bona fide and approved researchers. Records of abuse investigations may be misleading and unfair to those named in them either because they are too dated to be relevant to current circumstances or they were never substantiated. Therefore states typically provide for expungement of records either automatically if the record is categorized as unsubstantiated or upon request of the alleged victim.

[6] CIVIL CONSTRAINTS AND CRIMINAL PENALTIES FOR ABUSERS

The purpose of the Adult Protective Services statutes is to help identify incidents of abuse and provide a procedure for intervention and a system of services for victims. Penalties for the abusers are omitted from many Adult Protective Services statutes, which rely on other criminal and civil law to provide a remedy for victims in the form of court orders of protection and assistance.

Some states are beginning to appreciate that many elderly who are abused hesitate to seek assistance in part because of the formal, forbidding nature of courts and judges. At least one California court has come up with an innovative judicial response that has made a difference.

A report in the *California Bar Journal* described how Alameda County Superior Court Judge Julie Conger was able to draw out an elderly woman's story of abuse by her son. The woman, supported by the court's elder abuse case manager and a Spanish interpreter, told the court that she needed to get free from her son.

The hearing took place during the weekly special elder abuse court session held in an Oakland courtroom. The special court was created three years ago because abuse victims were often unable to appear in court since they could not or would not wait through the day as the court proceeded through its schedule. Many found waiting in a crowded courtroom too stressful or were physically unable to wait for their opportunity to be heard. The special elder abuse sessions ensured the abused elderly that their cases would be heard in a timely manner.

At first, very few elderly took advantage of the special sessions, but after a few months as many as 15 abuse victims came seeking protective orders and other relief. Their complaints ranged from having their life savings stolen, to enduring neglect, to having to lock themselves in their rooms to avoid physical attacks by a drug abusing relative.

To encourage the reporting of abuse, the petitioners get help filling out forms and deciding what relief to ask for. The assistance of the court provided to geriatric abuse case managers is considered key to effective intervention. When an elder cannot come to the courthouse, the judge goes to the petitioner or holds a hearing by telephone, as requested by the elder. *See* Kristina Horton Flaherty, *Abused Seniors Turn to Alameda Court for Help*, CAL. B.J., Oct. 2004, at 1.

Emergency intervention can lead to criminal charges being brought against an abuser.

LAW v. STATE
292 S.W.3d 277 (Ark. 2009)

JUSTICE WILLS.

On March 14, 2005, emergency medical personnel were called to a residence at 4701 Elmwood in Little Rock. Once there, the emergency workers found eighty-six-year-old Geneva Law, covered in bruises and bedsores, with rodent feces on the bedroom floor and ants and cockroaches crawling on the floor, on the bed, and on Geneva. Geneva died in the hospital about a month later. Her son, appellant Warren Law, and her daughter, Mary Law, were both charged on September 11, 2005, with abuse of an adult pursuant to Ark. Code Ann. § 5-28-103 (Repl. 1997).

. . . .

In his first point on appeal, Warren contends that the evidence was insufficient to convict him of abusing an adult. A motion to dismiss in a bench trial is identical to a motion for a directed verdict in a jury trial in that it is a challenge to the sufficiency of the evidence. . . .

As mentioned above, Warren was charged with abuse of an adult in violation of Ark.Code Ann. § 5-28-103. That statute provides that it is "unlawful for any person or caregiver to abuse, neglect, or exploit any person subject to protection under the provisions of this chapter." Ark. Code Ann. § 5-28-103(a) (Repl. 1997). Although the judgment and commitment order does not specify the particular subsection under which Warren was convicted, the order does state that he was convicted of a Class D felony, and the court commented that this was a case of "extreme neglect." Therefore, we conclude that Warren was convicted under Ark. Code Ann. § 5-28-103(c)(1) (Repl. 1997), which provides as follows:

> (c)(1) Any person or caregiver who neglects an endangered or impaired adult in violation of the provisions of this chapter, causing serious physical injury or substantial risk of death, shall be guilty of a Class D felony and shall be punished as provided by law.

At the time of the offense, Ark.Code Ann. § 5-28-101 (Supp. 2003) provided the following definitions for the relevant portions of the statute:

> (3) "Caregiver" means a related or unrelated person . . . that has the responsibility for the protection, care, or custody of an endangered or impaired adult as a result of assuming the responsibility voluntarily, by contract, through employment, or by order of the court;

> . . . .

> (5) "Endangered adult" means:

> (A) An adult eighteen (18) years of age or older who is found to be in a situation or condition which poses an imminent risk of death or serious bodily harm to that person and who demonstrates a lack of capacity to comprehend the nature and consequences of remaining in that situation or condition;

. . . .

(8)(A) "Impaired adult" means a person eighteen (18) years of age or older who, as a result of mental or physical impairment, is unable to protect himself or herself from abuse, sexual abuse, neglect, or exploitation, and as a consequence thereof is endangered;

. . . .

(10) "Neglect" means acts or omissions by an endangered adult; for example, self-neglect or intentional acts or omissions by a caregiver responsible for the care and supervision of an endangered or impaired adult constituting:

(A) Negligently failing to provide necessary treatment, rehabilitation, care, food, clothing, shelter, supervision, or medical services to an endangered or impaired adult;

(B) Negligently failing to report health problems or changes in health problems or changes in the health condition of an endangered or impaired adult to the appropriate medical personnel; or

(C) Negligently failing to carry out a prescribed treatment plan[.]

Thus, to convict Warren of abuse of an adult, the State was required to prove that: 1) Geneva was an endangered or impaired adult; 2) Warren was a caregiver responsible for her protection, care, or custody; 3) he neglected her; and 4) such neglect caused serious physical injury or risk of death. Warren does not challenge the fourth of these elements. Instead, he contends that the State failed to prove that Geneva was endangered or impaired, that he was her caregiver, and that he neglected her.

The first of these elements is whether Geneva was an endangered or impaired adult. As proof on this issue, the State's first witness at trial, Donna Brady, introduced a report from the Adult Protective Services Division of the Department of Health and Human Services. According to Brady, the report indicated that Geneva came to the attention of Adult Protective Services (APS) in April of 2001. At that time, Geneva was living with her sister in Searcy because the home in Little Rock where she had been living with her daughter had been condemned as unsanitary and unsafe. Brady testified that a relative called APS to report that the sister could no longer care for Geneva. The case worker's report from April of 2001 indicated that Geneva was "confused to [the] point [that she] has to be cued to bathe." The report described her as "very confused" and, although ambulatory, she was incapable of meeting her activities of daily living. The report also noted that she was "very confused and could not provide information without relying on her sister."

Because Geneva's sister could no longer care for her, and her own home had been condemned as "unfit for human habitation," APS contacted Warren, who eventually picked Geneva up and took her to live with him and Mary. On April 18, 2001, the APS case worker confirmed with Geneva's sister that Geneva was unable to care for herself. Further, Mary testified at trial that, four years later, Geneva was still unable to care for herself and had undergone "a rapid deterioration."

Clearly, the State proved that Geneva was an impaired or endangered adult. A frail, confused, elderly woman who was incapable of meeting her own activities of daily living would certainly have been unable to protect herself from abuse or neglect, thus meeting the definition of "impaired." . . . And as will be discussed more fully below, Geneva's situation most assuredly put her at imminent risk of death or serious bodily harm. Accordingly, the State proved that Geneva was an "endangered or impaired adult."

As to the second element of the offense, Warren asserts that the State failed to prove that he was Geneva's caregiver. As discussed above, a "caregiver" under section 5-28-101(3) is "a related or unrelated person . . . that has the responsibility for the protection, care, or custody of an endangered or impaired adult as a result of assuming the responsibility voluntarily, by contract, through employment, or by order of the court." Ark. Code Ann. § 5-28-101(3) (Supp. 2003). Warren argues that the State failed to prove that he voluntarily assumed the responsibility of protecting or caring for Geneva.

At the outset, we note that "caregiver," as defined in section 5-28-101(3), is one who "has the responsibility for the protection, care, *or* custody" of an endangered adult. (Emphasis added.) The use of the disjunctive "or" indicates that the State need only prove that an individual has the responsibility for one of these aspects before he or she may be deemed a "caregiver." Because the State introduced proof that Warren agreed to pick Geneva up from her sister's house in Searcy and bring her home to live under his roof, there was clearly substantial evidence that Warren voluntarily assumed responsibility for Geneva's custody.

. . . .

. . . . [W]hile Warren may have acted grudgingly and belatedly, the evidence introduced below supports the trial court's finding that he acted voluntarily and thus was Geneva's "caregiver" under section 5-28-101(3) and was responsible for her "care and supervision" under section 5-28-101(10). Despite his protests that he only took Geneva in when APS told him he "had to," he nonetheless took her in, instead of telling APS to take his mother into the custody of the Department of Human Services or place her in a nursing home. The case summary report from APS states that APS contacted Warren and he indicated that "he would be coming to pick [Geneva] up on [April 18, 2001] to live with him in Little Rock." That it took a few days to locate Warren does not refute or negate the fact that he ultimately took his mother into his home where, according to the report, she could "receive full time supervision."

. . . . [A]lthough Warren apparently preferred to have his sister attend to Geneva's day-to-day needs, it was nonetheless his decision to personally pick up his endangered and impaired mother and bring her to live under his roof. This decision thereafter effectively denied Geneva any further services from APS, as the case summary report reflected that there was "[n]o further APS needed at this time."

Having brought her into his home under these conditions, Warren voluntarily assumed the responsibility for the protection, care, or custody of an endangered and impaired adult, making him a "caregiver" under section 5-28-101(3), and he was responsible for the care and supervision of that person for purposes of the definition of "neglect" under section 5-28-101(10). Therefore, we conclude that there was substantial evidence showing that Warren was Geneva's caregiver and that he was a caregiver as that word is used in the definition of neglect.

This leads us to the balance of Warren's third sub-point, wherein he argues that the State failed to prove that he neglected Geneva. . . .

Warren's argument on the first portion of the "neglect" inquiry focuses on his claim that he owed no legal duty to Geneva. He notes that the statute requires an intentional act or omission, and he contends that, in order to demonstrate such an act or omission, the State had to prove that he owed a legal duty to act. However, by proving that Warren was Geneva's caregiver under section 5-28-101(3), as well as a person responsible for her care and supervision under section 5-28-101(10), as discussed above, the State proved that Warren did, in fact, have a legal duty to act.

. . . .

This court has noted that negligent conduct is distinguished from reckless conduct primarily in that it does not involve the conscious disregard of a perceived risk. In order to be held to have acted negligently, it is not necessary that the actor be fully aware of a perceived risk and recklessly disregard it. It requires only a finding that under the circumstances he should have been aware of it and his failure to perceive it was a gross deviation from the care a reasonable, prudent person would exercise under those circumstances. The facts introduced at trial satisfy this requirement.

Angela Bain, a paramedic with Metropolitan Emergency Medical Services (MEMS), testified that she responded to a non-emergency call at 4701 Elmwood in Little Rock on March 14, 2005. As she walked around to the back of the home, she was met with a strong odor that "smelled like rotting flesh." Upon entering the house, she found Geneva, whom she described as having "all kinds of bruises of varying age on her" and in an environment that "was not . . . appropriate . . . for anyone to be in." Bain stated that there were rodent feces on the floor and ants and cockroaches crawling on the bed and on Geneva. Geneva was lying on a mattress that appeared to be soaked with urine and feces with a deflated plastic mattress, a plastic garbage bag, and soaked newspapers underneath her.

Sergeant Cristie Phillips of the Little Rock Police Department testified that when she got to the scene, Geneva had already been transported to the hospital by medical personnel, but she could "immediately smell just an overwhelming stench of feces. It smelled like rotting flesh." Phillips also went to the hospital to take photographs of Geneva, whom Phillips said was "black and blue all over." One of Geneva's ears was completely swollen shut, and she had bruises all over her face. She also had "crater-sized" bedsores that "you could have stuck your fist in." Phillips noted that at the time she arrived in the emergency room, there were still ants crawling on Geneva, and nurses were "picking the ants off her skin."

Kimberly Finklestein, a crime scene specialist with the Little Rock Police Department, testified that the house was in "disarray" and was "extremely, extremely filthy." She saw what appeared to be animal feces on the floor of Geneva's room, as well as the rest of the house. The mattress of Geneva's bed was soaked and stained with urine and mold, as was the carpet underneath the bed. There were ants and roaches "just crawling everywhere." When Finklestein went to the hospital to see Geneva, she said that she knew she was approaching Geneva's room because, as she was walking down the hallway, she could smell the same stench she had smelled in the house. On redirect examination, Finklestein testified that there was no part of Warren's house where one could not smell "that smell."

Little Rock Code Enforcement Supervisor Sheila Reynolds testified that she was asked to go the Elmwood residence by police. After confirming in the property records that the house belonged to Warren, Reynolds went to the residence some four and a half hours after Geneva had been taken to the hospital. She stated that when she got to the door, there was "such a strong odor that we had to turn around and go back to our vehicle and get some Vick's and put across our nose so we could go in." She described the smell as being a "very strong urine smell" and a "rotted-flesh type smell."

Reynolds described the house, stating that there was a "lot of stuff piled on the floor." In Geneva's room, there were "feathers and rat droppings, possibly rabbit droppings" on the floor by her bed, and the bed appeared to be stained with bodily fluids. Ants were crawling on the comforter, and there was "trash and stuff in the closet, kind of like maybe an animal had lived in there." The remainder of the house was "unsanitary" and "filthy," and the bathtub was black with mold and mildew. There was nothing between Geneva's room and the rest of the house that would have sealed her area off, other than a bedroom door.

The State also called Lynn Espejo, the clinic administrator for Geneva's former doctor, Dr. Scott Brown. Espejo testified that Geneva had not been in to see the doctor since January of 2001. At that time, Geneva weighed 162 pounds and was classified as "obese." She noted that there had been calls from the pharmacy to refill Geneva's blood-pressure medication, but she said that in 2004, Dr. Brown refused to confirm her prescription until she came back in to see him.

Dr. Moses Ejiofor was the emergency room physician on call the day that Geneva was brought to the hospital. He said that she "looked like bone" and was very weak, disheveled, unkempt, and malnourished. Dr. Ejiofor also described the smell of rotting flesh, which he determined was coming, at least in part, from a large wound on her back through which he could see the outline of her spine. Geneva had other large ulcers on her pelvis, a large blood clot in her left ear, and bruises all over her body; further, the bruises were not all consistent with her having fallen. Her bedsores were necrotic and black and appeared to have been there for some time. Dr. Ejiofor said that he knew Geneva was in pain and he could hear her moaning, but she was so weak that she could not even flinch away from him. In addition to her other injuries, Geneva also had a fluid build-up or bleeding inside her brain, which was consistent with trauma. Cultures of her eyes revealed the presence of three different bacteria, and "approximately eight to nine organisms" were cultured from the ulcers.

Plainly, the above testimony constituted substantial evidence that Warren should have been aware of the risk to Geneva, and his failure to perceive the risk posed to his mother was a gross deviation from the care a reasonable, prudent person would exercise under those circumstances. Numerous witnesses testified to the filth in the house and the overwhelming stench of rotting flesh that permeated the environment. It is inconceivable that these conditions went unnoticed, and it is equally inconceivable that these conditions arose overnight. By allowing the squalor to proliferate unchecked, and by either failing or refusing to remedy the circumstances, it is plain that Warren, as caregiver, negligently failed to "provide necessary treatment, . . . care, . . . shelter, [or] supervision" for Geneva, an endangered or impaired adult. In short, the evidence demonstrated that Warren was guilty of neglecting Geneva.

. . . .

Affirmed.

G. FINANCIAL ABUSE

Financial abuse of older people comes in many types, perpetrated by strangers and close family members. In every instance, the task is to identify the abusive acts, categorize them as fraud, theft, negligent conversion, or other legally defined conduct, and correct the problem by restoring funds to the elder. This task may be simple enough when the elder and the abuser are strangers. Because relationships are complex, the most difficult elder financial abuse to respond to is abuse by close family members. Consider the following hypothetical and discussion:

Carolyn L. Dessin,
Financial Abuse of the Elderly
36 Idaho L. Rev. 203, 204–09 (2000)[*]

Although a recent national study of elder abuse indicates that financial abuse is somewhat less prevalent than physical abuse, there is still much cause for concern. Financial abuse can be as devastating to the quality of life of an individual as physical abuse. The likelihood that an elder person's income is relatively fixed may make it extremely difficult to recover from a financial loss. Additionally, the difficulty of detecting financial abuse suggests that it may actually be more widespread than physical abuse.

The fact that approximately seventy percent of all funds deposited in financial institutions are controlled by persons age sixty-five and older makes senior citizens prime targets for those desiring to take financial advantage of someone. Additionally, seniors may be isolated due to their lack of mobility. As one conservator put it, "[i]t just seems like when times get tough, old people are easy money."

Virtually everyone who has considered the issue of financial abuse of the elderly sees reason for concern. Tom Zlaket, Chief Justice of the Arizona Supreme Court, stated that there have been enough instances of financial abuse to merit concern, even though the practice is not widespread. The practice, however, does appear to be spreading as indicated in Massachusetts, where almost one-half of the cases of elder abuse serious enough to require reporting to district attorneys involved financial exploitation. The purpose of this article is to discuss the types of financial

---

abuse and to examine various possible means of alleviating such abuse.

Financial abuse of the elderly has been defined in a number of different ways. At its heart, it is the improper use of an elder's assets. This definition is, of course, overly simplistic without some reasoned interpretation of "improper." In attempts to flesh out the idea of impropriety, some states have defined exploitation to require benefit to a person other than the victim. A state might also require either disadvantage to the victim or advantage to one other than the victim. The distinction may be an important one. A jurisdiction that requires benefit to someone other than the victim would not be criminalizing the wasting of the victim's assets.

Forms of activity that might be characterized as abusive run the gamut from intentional criminal acts to negligent mishandling of assets. This breadth of activity adds to the difficulty of crafting a prevention of and solution for financial abuse. Accordingly, it is not surprising that legislative measures for dealing with financial abuse can often be criticized as "piecemeal."

The range of potentially abusive activity can be broken down into four main categories: (1) theft, (2) fraud, (3) intentional breach of duty by a fiduciary or caregiver, and (4) negligence. Although there is some overlap between the categories, they provide a useful framework for examining the issue.

Some abuse is simply the outright theft of assets. Thus, traditional crimes including robbery and burglary could be characterized as financial abuse. This is probably the area with which the law enforcement community feels the most comfortable because there is no question that theft is an "improper" use of another's funds.

A second type of abuse occurs through fraud and scams. Within this category there is a broad range of activity. Acts that obtain money by fraudulent means are clearly "improper." There is, however, a level of activity that does not rise to the level of fraudulent that could be characterized as a "scam." The dictionary defines "scam" as "to cheat or swindle, as in a confidence game." The primary difference, then, between fraud and scam is that the information given in a scam transaction is true, though perhaps misleading. Senior citizens seem particularly vulnerable targets to these attacks, either because diminished capacity may impair the ability to rationally evaluate proposed courses of action or because the difficulties of living on a fixed income may enhance one's willingness to try a "get-rich-quick" scheme.

Although the activity is neither a fraud nor a scam, the activity of the hard-selling salesman might be appropriately added to this category. The element of overreaching inherent in a scam is present in some hard-sell transactions as well. Many believe that older Americans are targeted by unscrupulous salespeople, including unscrupulous telemarketers, because older people are perceived as having significant disposable income or as being particularly susceptible to certain selling techniques. A salesman who pushes an unneeded and overpriced product on an elderly buyer is arguably "improperly" using the elder's assets.

A third type of abuse is intentional misuse of an elder's assets by a fiduciary or caregiver. There is clearly an overlap between this and the first category, as these transactions include theft and embezzlement. There may also be overlap with the second category if fraud or overreaching are involved in the acquisition of the victim's assets. Thus, this category is the most amorphous because its parameters are defined by the relationship of the abuser and the victim rather than by the type of conduct involved. The fiduciary relationship may arise from a variety of contexts. In the most traditional relationship, the fiduciary is a trustee who owes a duty to the trust beneficiary. Similarly, the guardian of the estate owes a fiduciary duty to his ward. Third, an agent acting under a power of attorney is a fiduciary with respect to the principal. The duty exists regardless of whether the power is durable or non-durable. These three fiduciary relationships constitute the most likely breeding ground for financial abuse because the trustee holds legal title to the potential victim's assets, the agent has power to act with respect to the potential victim's assets, and the guardian has either title or power, depending on the state.

A fourth type of abuse occurs when someone negligently mishandles a senior's assets. This is perhaps the most difficult category to deal with because the abuser is not intentionally misusing funds. Thus, the question is whether such misuse should be addressed under criminal statutes at all since the required mens rea is lacking.

The following example aids in distinguishing the categories and in seeing the potential overlap. The example is also helpful in appreciating the difficulty of deciding whether conduct is abusive. Consider Mae, an eighty-six year-old woman who has recently moved into an assisted living community. Her assets consist of a home worth $50,000 and cash and marketable securities worth $100,000. Her only son, Jim, is her agent under a durable power of attorney. Jim moves into Mae's house and lives there rent-free. He pays all expenses associated with the house from Mae's cash. In addition, he transfers $3,000 each month from Mae's bank account to his own account.

This brief fact pattern suggests the possibility of all four categories of abuse. The act that seems most likely to be outright theft is the transfer of $3,000 each month. Yet, perhaps Jim is paying his mother's assisted living bill with his credit card, leaving his mother's funds in her interest-bearing account until the credit card bill comes due, and making the transfer in time to pay the bill. Rather than financial abuse, the act may be sound financial treatment of Mae's assets.

Jim's move into the house and rent-free/expense-free life there could be viewed in several ways. It could be outright theft of assets. Alternatively, if Mae allowed the arrangement because Jim falsely told her that the house could not be profitably sold or rented because of a bad market for such real estate, then he might be committing the type of fraudulent abuse that falls into the second category. Another possibility is that Jim simply decided, as agent under the durable power, not to sell the house and to move in. This arguably could be abuse of either the third or fourth type depending on whether Jim's conduct was intentional or negligent. If he is acting under the durable power of attorney, then he owes a fiduciary duty to Mae. Obviously, if he intentionally misappropriates Mae's assets, he has breached his fiduciary duty to her. Even if, however, he has merely unintentionally failed to act as a reasonably prudent fiduciary, he still could be liable for breach of fiduciary duty.

On the other hand, it is possible that none of Jim's acts with respect to Mae's house are abusive. It is entirely plausible that Mae wanted Jim to live in her home in the event that she could not. Perhaps the prospect of abandoning her home was particularly troubling to Mae, and the idea of a family member living there comforted her. She may simply have welcomed the opportunity to provide a home for her son. Perhaps real estate market conditions suggested that the best course of action was for Jim to move in to preserve the home for a future sale at a larger profit than could be currently obtained. Perhaps Jim plans to renovate the home in exchange for the right to live there rent-free.

The following cases demonstrate the family disputes that may arise when one member "uses" assets of a senior.

IN RE THE ESTATE OF GASPARAC v. MAE SCHUNK
655 N.W.2d 546 (Wis. Ct. App. 2002)

Unpublished Opinion

JUDGE VERGERONT.

The estate of Mary Gasparac appeals summary judgment dismissing its claims of conversion and breach of fiduciary duty against Mae Schunk, Gasparac's daughter. We conclude that the trial court correctly decided that the breach of fiduciary duty claim was barred by the statute of limitation, and we therefore affirm the dismissal of that claim. With respect to the conversion claim, we conclude the trial court correctly decided that the statute of limitation barred that claim insofar as it arose prior to October 4, 1994. However, we also conclude that Schunk did not make a prima facie showing of a defense to that claim and, accordingly, she was not entitled to summary judgment. We therefore reverse the dismissal of the conversion claim and remand for a trial on that claim insofar as it arose on or after October 4, 1994.

Gasparac resided with her daughter, Mae Schunk, and Schunk's husband at their home in Minnesota from 1987 until her death on September 12, 1996. Gasparac was eighty-six years old at the time of her death. She executed her will on February 21, 1988, naming Schunk as her personal representative, and on March 4, 1989, she executed a durable power of attorney designating Schunk as her attorney-in-fact.

Upon her mother's death, Schunk filed an application for informal administration, and letters were issued by the Clark County Probate Court appointing her as personal representative. She filed an inventory listing her mother's net value of property as $17,665.80. On September 9, 1997, Schunk's sister, Katherine Ratkovich, and her brother, Jack Gasparac, demanded a formal proceeding, and Schunk stipulated to convert the matter to a formal probate proceeding.

On July 20, 1998, Schunk's siblings moved for Schunk's removal as personal representative. They alleged that she had converted assets of their mother while their mother was alive. During proceedings on that motion, the court appointed a special master to investigate the allegations against Schunk. The special master's report concluded that between August 1, 1987 and December 12, 1996, Schunk received at least $181,473.88 from her mother's funds, spent $23,536.45 for her mother's benefit, and provided her mother with room and board for 113 months. The report also concluded that documents filed by Schunk in Dakota County, Minnesota, which allowed Gasparac to receive aid, were materially inaccurate. The report concluded that Schunk must either resign or be removed as personal representative of her mother's estate. Schunk subsequently resigned as personal representative. The court accepted the special master's report, but stayed Schunk's siblings' motion for "adoption and judgment" of the report because Schunk had requested a jury trial on the conversion claim the estate intended to file against her.

On October 9, 2000, the estate filed a complaint against Schunk that alleged she had intentionally transferred her mother's funds exceeding $181,000 to herself or to third parties, wrongfully converting these funds and thereby breaching her fiduciary duty to her mother. Schunk moved for summary judgment on the grounds that the statute of limitation had expired for the claim of breach of fiduciary duty, that any claim for conversion arising prior to October 4, 1994, was time-barred, and that under the power of attorney all of Schunk's actions regarding her mother's financial affairs had been ratified. In support of the motion, Schunk filed an affidavit averring that no court had ever judged Gasparac incompetent nor had any proceedings been instituted to have her declared incompetent. In paragraph 7, Schunk's affidavit stated that, based on her personal knowledge and experience, Gasparac "approved and/or ratified all financial matters that [Schunk] handled on her behalf." In response, the estate moved to strike paragraph 7 on the ground that under the dead man's statute Schunk was incompetent to testify as to any transaction or communication with her mother. The estate also opposed summary judgment and submitted the affidavit of Schunk's brother, which averred that in a telephone conversation in February 1997 Schunk had told him that she had taken money from their mother, and on March 1, 1997, Schunk provided him with an incomplete and inconsistent accounting of their mother's finances.

In reply, Schunk submitted the affidavits of her husband, William Schunk, and of Mary Preston, Gasparac's home health aide from the spring of 1991 until Gasparac's death. William's affidavit averred that Gasparac lived with him and Schunk from August 1, 1987, until the time of her death on December 12, 1996, and, based on his personal knowledge and experience, Gasparac "on numerous occasions approved the financial matters that Mae Schunk handled on her behalf." Preston's affidavit averred that based on her personal knowledge and experience, Gasparac "had on numerous occasions, stated to your affiant that she was satisfied with and approved all financial matters that Mae Schunk had been doing on her behalf." At the hearing on the motion for summary judgment, Schunk did not dispute that her testimony was barred under the dead man's statute, but she contended that William's was not.

The trial court granted Schunk's motion for summary judgment on both the breach of fiduciary duty and the conversion claims and dismissed both claims. The court determined that the breach of fiduciary duty was discovered in March 1997, and any claim filed after March of 1999 was barred by the statute of limitation. With respect to the conversion claim, the court concluded that the six-year statute of limitation applied, and therefore any conversion alleged to have occurred prior to October 4, 1994, was time barred. The court concluded that Preston's affidavit was not subject to the dead man's statute and neither was William's affidavit. However, the court stated, even if it were to disregard William's affidavit, based on Preston's affidavit there was no dispute that Gasparac expressed her approval and therefore ratified Schunk's acts. The court reasoned that it was undisputed that Gasparac had knowledge of the power of attorney and chose to delegate management of her affairs to Schunk; Gasparac was competent at all times prior to her death; she never withdrew the authority given to Schunk, which she could have done if she did not like something Schunk was doing; and there was nothing in the record to establish that Schunk was hiding anything from Gasparac. The court therefore concluded that Schunk was entitled to judgment as a matter of law that Gasparac had either authorized all of her actions regarding her financial affairs or, if she had not authorized them, she had ratified them. Although the court did not expressly state in its written decision that Schunk's affidavit was inadmissible under the dead man's statute, the court did state in its oral decision that her affidavit was excluded under the dead man's statute.

. . . .

[The court reviews the standard of review of summary judgment, de novo, and whether the defendant established a prima facie defense to the claim. We review the grant or denial of a summary judgment de novo, and we apply the same standard as does the trial court. If so, the court will determine whether there is a genuine issue of material fact that defeats the motion for summary judgment and entitles the plaintiff to a trial.]

Accordingly we conclude, as did the trial court, that the claim for breach of fiduciary duty is barred by Wis. Stat. § 893.57, and the claim for conversion is limited under Wis. Stat. § 893.51(1) to acts occurring on or after October 4, 1994.

Schunk's Submissions

Schunk frames her defense to the conversion claim in terms of the doctrine of ratification, while the estate argues it does not apply because Schunk had the authority to act for Gasparac under the power of attorney. Ratification is "the affirmance by a person of a prior act which did not bind him, but which was done or professedly done on his account, whereby the act, as to some or all persons is given effect as if originally authorized by him." However, the power of attorney did not give Schunk the authority to dispose of Gasparac's assets for Schunk's own purposes. Therefore, if Gasparac did not consent to Schunk's use of her funds for the benefit of Schunk or third parties, then Schunk converted those funds; conversely, if Gasparac consented to the use of her funds for the benefit of Schunk or third parties, either before or after Schunk used Gasparac's funds for those purposes, then there was no conversion. We see no reason why the doctrine of ratification does not properly describe the legal effect of any approval by Gasparac of Schunk's use of her funds which were not authorized by the power of attorney.

NOTE: The elements of tortious conversion are: (1) intentionally controlling or taking property belonging to another, (2) doing so without the owner's consent, and (3) those acts resulting in serious interference with the rights of the owner to possess the property

However, the real dispute between the parties is whether the affidavits submitted by Schunk meet the requirements for summary judgment submissions and whether they show that Gasparac did consent to Schunk's use of her funds for Schunk's own benefit or the benefit of third parties, either before or after Schunk used the funds for those purposes. We turn to these issues now.

We next consider Preston's affidavit. We need not decide whether the court properly ruled that her testimony of Gasparac's statements came within exceptions to the rule against hearsay, because we conclude that, even if it did, Preston's testimony does not establish a prima facie defense to the conversion claim. Preston's affidavit does not indicate what Gasparac knew about Schunk's use of her funds for Schunk's own benefit or the benefit of third parties; it does not indicate that she knew anything at all of that use of her funds. Therefore, Gasparac's statements to Preston "on numerous occasions" that she "was satisfied with and approved all financial matters that Mae Schunk had been doing on her behalf" is not evidence that she approved of Schunk's use of her funds for Schunk's own benefit or the benefit of third parties. Logic dictates that Gasparac could not approve of Schunk's use of Gasparac's funds for Schunk's own benefit or the benefit of third parties unless Gasparac knew that it had occurred or was occurring, and there is nothing in Preston's affidavit indicating that Gasparac had such knowledge. While express knowledge of the voidable act is not required, there must be evidence from which such knowledge may be inferred. Preston's affidavit presents no evidence from which such knowledge may be inferred.

The same is true of William's affidavit. He avers that "Gasparac on numerous occasions approved the financial matters that Mae Schunk handled on her behalf," but does not indicate what those financial matters were. In particular, he does not state that Gasparac knew Schunk was using her funds for Schunk's own benefit or the benefit of third parties, nor does he present evidence from which that knowledge might be inferred. Therefore, even if Schunk is correct that William's testimony is not barred by the dead man's statute, an issue we do not decide, his affidavit does not establish a prima facie defense to the conversion claim.

Since Schunk's submissions do not establish a prima facie defense to the conversion claim, she is not entitled to summary judgment on that claim. Accordingly the trial court erred in granting her summary judgment. We therefore reverse and remand to the trial court for a trial on the conversion claim insofar as it arose on or after October 4, 1994.

Some accusations of abuse or exploitation only arise after the death of the elderly victim.

IN RE ESTATE OF OSTROWSKI v. LEA
655 N.W.2d 546 (Wis. Ct. App. 2002)

Unpublished Opinion

PER CURIAM.

Lorraine Kostuch, acting as personal representative for the estate of her mother, Irene Ostrowski, appeals related judgments and an order granting Ostrowski's grandson, Robert Lea, Jr., specific performance on a land contract, awarding Lea immediate possession of the family farm and ordering the Estate to pay a portion of Lea's attorney fees as a sanction for having maintained several frivolous defenses to Lea's claims against the Estate. We affirm in all respects.

Following Ostrowski's death in 2000, Lea presented a claim to her estate asserting that he and his grandmother had previously entered into an agreement to transfer certain farm equipment and to execute a land contract wherein Ostrowski would sell her 160 acre farm to Lea. Lea attached to his claim a copy of an agreement signed by Ostrowski and Lea in 1995. The agreement provided that once Lea had paid Ostrowski $32,000 at the rate of $500 per month, the parties would enter into a land contract applying the $32,000 to the total purchase price of $160,000. Under the agreement, the parties were to divide the real estate taxes on the property until execution of the land contract. Under the land contract, Ostrowski would maintain a "life lease," and payments on the purchase price were to continue at the rate of $500 per month, without interest.

Kostuch, in her capacity as personal representative, objected to Lea's claim for specific performance of the land contract. Kostuch challenged the authenticity of the agreement on the grounds that Lea had not offered the original document, that there were no witnesses other than Lea and Ostrowski, that the signatures were dated several months after the agreement itself and that many of the objectionable terms were not on the signature page. She further argued that, even if genuine, the agreement was unenforceable because certain formalities the statute of frauds required had been omitted, the terms of the agreement were not sufficiently definite, there was a lack of consideration and Ostrowski's declining competence had allowed Lea to exert undue influence over her.

After a three-day hearing, the circuit court found "overwhelming" evidence that Ostrowski had signed the agreement, had taken a copy of it to her accountant, and had been accepting monthly payments of $500 from Lea over the course of the preceding five years in accordance with the agreement. The court determined that there was no undue influence, based on the testimony of a number of witnesses, including Ostrowski's doctor and a local bank president. They said that Ostrowski was strong-willed, independent, and still mentally sharp in her later years, and that she had expressed a desire to keep the farm in the family. The court concluded that offer, acceptance and consideration had been established and that Wisconsin law did not require the written agreement to have been witnessed by third parties, acknowledged, delivered, or recorded, in order to be valid and enforceable. In addition, citing its inherent power to fashion equitable relief and its concern that animosity among the parties would continue once they left the courtroom, the court ordered the Estate to turn over possession of the farm immediately and directed the parties to sign a State Bar Form 11 in specific performance of the agreement to execute a land contract.

Lea moved for attorney's fees. The court acknowledged that the Estate had a right to investigate the validity of Lea's claim. However, it may be inferred from the court's comments that it concluded that the Estate should have quickly discovered that it lacked any reasonable basis in fact to contest that Ostrowski was mentally competent, had signed the agreement and had delivered it to Lea for photocopying. Accordingly, the Estate should have known that it had no reasonable basis in fact or law to argue that the agreement was invalid for lack of witnesses, notarization and recording. The court found that the Estate had used its "deep pocket" to contest what it should have recognized as a legitimate claim, for the improper purpose of "trying to frustrate a claimant," thus forcing Lea to run up "outrageous" attorney's fees in excess of $40,000. Consequently, the court ordered the Estate to contribute $25,000 toward Lea's attorney fees.

The Estate's contentions on appeal are that: (1) the agreement lacked sufficiently definite terms to be enforceable; (2) the form land contract the court directed the parties to sign included terms that were not part of the agreement; and (3) the positions taken by the Estate before the circuit court were not frivolous.

Wisconsin Stat. § 706.02 (1999-2000) provides, among other things, that a contract to convey land must identify the parties; the land to be conveyed; the interest to be conveyed; and "any material term, condition, reservation, exception or contingency upon which the interest is to arise, continue or be extinguished, limited or encumbered." The Estate concedes that Lea and Ostrowski's agreement identified the parties, the land to be conveyed, the purchase price and the fact that payments were to be made in monthly installments without interest. It argues that the agreement should nonetheless be unenforceable because it does not indicate whether prepayment is acceptable, whether there is a default interest rate, who should insure the property, whether the land contract could be assigned, and how the life lease was to work. The Estate has not, however, pointed to any precedents in which the absence of similar details was deemed fatal, and we are not persuaded that the listed details were essential to the terms of the contract.

[The court reviewed the terms of the land contract.] The Estate contends that the circuit court exceeded its authority by requiring it to execute Form 11 because none of the foregoing provisions or other standard clauses used in the land contract were specified in the agreement.

Specific performance, however, is an equitable remedy resting in the discretion of the court. In addition, the personal representative of an estate is subject to the probate court's supervision. Here, the parties would have been free to use a standard land contract form utilizing typical clauses to fulfill their agreement had Ostrowski not died shortly before Lea had finished paying the initial $32,000 triggering the obligation to enter into a land contract. The circuit court determined that additional guidance on what it deemed non-essential terms for the land contract was appropriate and necessary to effectuate the intent of the parties, given the personal representative's continuing hostility towards Lea's claim. We are satisfied that the circuit court's direction that the personal representative sign a standard land contract incorporating the specified provisions of the agreement did not alter the essential terms of the parties' agreement, and was within the court's equitable and supervisory powers.

[The court reviewed other defenses raised by the estate.]

Finally, the Estate maintains that none of its defense positions were frivolous. It argues that its evidentiary objections to Lea's attempts to authenticate the agreement were reasonably well-founded in law and that its handwriting expert's opinion that Ostrowski had not signed and dated the document provided a reasonable factual basis for the challenge. However, the record shows that the Estate had the original of the agreement whose authenticity it was challenging within its possession the entire time it was denying Lea's claim. The Estate's contention that it was not required to produce the agreement until a formal discovery request had been made is disingenuous at best, because it ignores the Estate's obligation to make a reasonable inquiry into the facts before making factual assertions to the circuit court. In addition, the Estate had no factual basis to dispute that Lea had been making monthly payments of $500 to Ostrowski with checks bearing notations "farm payment" since shortly after the date on the signature page of the agreement. The personal representative knew that Ostrowski had given a copy of the agreement to her own accountant for use in tax preparation and that the accountant recognized Ostrowski's signature. Given the totality of the facts within the Estate's knowledge, we have no difficulty affirming the circuit court's conclusion that the Estate's challenge to the authenticity of the agreement was frivolous.

Similarly, while the Estate sets forth an accurate summary of the law applicable to undue influence and competency determinations, it fails to acknowledge its lack of a reasonable factual basis to challenge Ostrowski's competency. The Estate claims that certain statements and actions Ostrowski took after the agreement was signed could be interpreted as showing that she had some confusion over the legal effect of the agreement. However, in addition to the observations of various family members, acquaintances and the personal representative herself that Ostrowski was competent to handle her day-to-day affairs, the Estate was also aware nearly a month before the hearing that Ostrowski's doctor was of the opinion that Ostrowski had been mentally competent. Furthermore, with regard to the undue influence claim, the Estate had no factual basis to challenge Lea's assertions that Ostrowski herself had set the price per acre for selling her farm to her grandson, based on the price that she had received for other property she had sold previously through an independent auction, and that Ostrowski had commented to others that she was glad the farm was staying in the family. We concur with the circuit court's assessment that it could not reasonably be questioned, based on all the evidence available, that Ostrowski had freely and competently entered into the agreement.

In sum, we see no basis to reverse the circuit court's decisions in this matter.

By the Court. — Judgments and order affirmed.

Financial abuse can be prevented or discouraged by such means as direct deposit of checks and automatic transfers or debits to cover typical expenses. Utility companies frequently have arrangements that allow the individual to prepay to avoid problems with check writing, and businesses may offer third-party notice service, by which the business sends a copy of any overdue or cancellation notices to a family member or friend.

If the financial abuse arises from authority given by the elder to the abuser, it should be revoked. Unfortunately, so long as the original authorization document is in the hands of the former agent, he or she can continue to try to use the document. It is possible, but difficult, to notify all third parties who have dealt with the agent as agent. A more drastic measure is to close accounts on which the agent has access and then name a new agent. If a representative payee for Social Security benefits is abusing an elder's funds, the SSA should be notified to remove that representative payee.

The recovery of lost funds has been a most difficult part of financial abuse. The victim must sue to recover the lost property, usually under common-law theories of trover and conversion or for replevin. If the abuser still has the property, the court can impose a constructive trust to preserve the property until it can be returned to the victim. If the abuser was acting as an agent, the victim can sue under the common law of fiduciaries to recover the value of the property and for any other damages.

Why don't elders often seek relief for financial abuse? Dessin, cited above, provides some reasons:

1. The victim may be afraid that his life will actually change for the worse if the abuser stops because the abuser is providing needed care along with the abuse.

2. The victim may be embarrassed to admit that a loved one or even a trusted friend or employee is abusing him or her.

3. The victim may be reluctant to "turn in" a family member, friend, or employee, perhaps because the victim feels some responsibility for the abuser's actions.

4. The victim may be afraid of the abuser.

5. The victim may not know where to turn for help.

6. The victim may feel that some level of abuse is "normal."

7. The victim may be too impaired to realize or to report the abuse.

Id. at 211–12.

H. OLDER PERSONS AND THE CRIMINAL JUSTICE SYSTEM

The rising numbers of older people in many roles in society raises the issues of aging and crime — of the aged as crime victims, as criminals, and as prisoners. The special case of the elderly with regard to crime turns on their vulnerability, or perceived vulnerability; and the limited time and health in a lifetime.

[1] THE ELDERLY AS TARGETS OF CRIME

The elderly are perceived as being particularly vulnerable to crime due to characteristics such as diminished physical vigor and strength and social isolation. Older women are thought to be especially vulnerable because they are less likely to resist a theft or violent crime. Perpetrators of fraud may view the elderly as less likely to perceive the deception and more easily confused. Surely the isolation or loneliness of some in old age creates greater susceptibility to "friendly" overtures, thus allowing the criminal to promote the fraud.

The true picture is quite different. Persons over age 65 are the least likely group to be criminally victimized. In fact, those age 65 or older have the lowest rate of victimization of any age group of the U.S. population age 12 and older. Though the rate of crime against the elderly may be relatively low, the fear of crime is naturally very high among older persons. In a number of respects, crimes committed against the elderly are often more serious than crimes against younger people. Elderly violent crime victims are less likely to try to defend themselves and more likely to be injured. Older men are more often victims of crime than older women, particularly violent crimes, but women are more frequently the victims of personal larceny — most likely because they are seen as easier targets. Older African-Americans have higher victimization rates than whites, particularly for violent crimes. Except for household larceny, elderly persons with lower family incomes have higher victimization rates.

QUESTIONS

1.   How do you explain the difference in the perception of the victimization of older persons and the reality?

2.   Is the problem crimes against the elderly or is it elderly fear of crime?

3.   Is crime against older persons primarily a problem for the criminal justice system or the social services system?

———————

Older people are often the target of criminal fraud, including con games, health insurance fraud, and home repair or consumer fraud. The type and extent of fraud is limited only by the ingenuity of the criminal mind. Old frauds such as the "Bank Examiner Swindle" continue to be used. The victim is approached by the criminal, who presents himself as a bank examiner. He explains that the bank believes that a certain teller is suspected of stealing. He asks the elderly bank customer to help uncover the criminal by withdrawing a large sum of money. After the money is withdrawn, the customer watches as the bills are "marked" by the con artist. The customer is told to deposit the money with the suspected bank teller who will steal part of the deposit. The marked bills in the hands of the teller will reveal the crime. The customer is given back the bills. The examiner stays outside the bank to watch. Of course, the "bills" given back to the customer are not money. That remains with the con artist, who flees with the money while the elderly customer attempts to deposit the "bills."

Many elderly are victimized by door-to-door sales, either because they are not assertive enough to resist the seller or because they like the apparent convenience. Others fall victim to direct mail schemes. A writer to Ann Landers complained that her 97-year-old mother, who was mentally alert and handled her own affairs, was repeatedly induced into buying unneeded products (magazines, light bulbs, etc.) in hopes of winning a "sweepstakes prize." Other elderly give and give again to mail-order charitable requests, unaware that most of what they give is used for "administrative" costs while very little goes to the charity.

Fraudulent telemarketing schemes victimize thousands of elderly every year. They are sold nonexistent or shoddy products, worthless land, overpriced resort homes, and unnecessary insurance by phone. They enter bogus "sweepstakes" contests. They are induced to give to fraudulent "charities." Even if the charity is legitimate, almost all of what they give goes to the solicitor. They are also pressured to buy tickets to support what sounds like a worthwhile event when in fact the event does not exist.

The con artist preys on the isolation and loneliness of the victim and may also exploit a failing memory that would rule out a series of purchases far beyond the victim's budget. Older women, who may be lonely and welcome a change in their routine, are more likely to open their door to another woman and offer sympathy for the "plight" of the scammer who spins a tale of woe. Women are particularly successful in defrauding the elderly since they generally are perceived to be less threatening. Some con artists target home-owning widows who may lack knowledge about home repairs. The victim is told that the "repair" man just happened to notice the state of her roof as he drove by her house. The victim is told that failure to repair the roof could cause serious water damage to the house. As it happens, the repairman has a little spare time and could repair the roof right now. The deal is struck, the "repairs" made, the check accepted and immediately cashed and the victim may never be the wiser.

Older men are often approached on the streets by young women criminals. Flattered by the attention of a younger woman, or wanting to be polite and helpful, the victim falls prey to a fraud or con game. Once the victim realizes that he has been taken, he may be too embarrassed to report it. It is bad enough to be defrauded, but why compound the shame by reporting it to the police?

Many elderly people are victims of investment swindles which require the victim to put up money for work opportunities or property purported to be likely to increase in value. The variety of scams includes fake franchise distributorship; investment in coins, gems, and stocks; and sale of land that is worthless or nonexistent. Land sales schemes are thought to cost the elderly over $10 million a year. Work-at-home schemes abound. The most common offerings involve envelope stuffing or the making of a product. The promoter falsely alleges there is a market for such a product or that the promoter will buy the product. Variations include worm farms, sew-at-home schemes, plant growing franchises, and chinchilla breeding enterprises.

In addition to formal con games and theft by fraud, the elderly also are frequently victimized by consumer frauds that deliver inferior or useless goods and services. These include the "black-top driveway specialists" who coat driveways with very cheap material that washes off during the first rain, or "furnace repairmen" who find "leaks" that must be repaired immediately at high cost when, in reality, the heating equipment is fine. Other variations include "dance instructors" who sell courses which extend beyond the purchaser's life expectancy or far beyond the purchaser's physical capacity to complete. Health and safety are ripe areas for consumer fraud. Some older people buy "youth restoring beauty aids," defective hearing aids, fake personal alarm systems, and fake arthritis cures.

Insurance fraud and deceit abounds. The elderly, who face escalating health care costs and decreasing Medicare coverage, are easily victimized. They buy health care policies that do little but duplicate the available Medicare coverage. Nursing home cost insurance is purchased that is later found to cover almost none of the actual costs because of deductibles and exclusions.

QUESTIONS

1. Are there characteristics typical of older people that make it more likely they will be victims of fraud than younger persons? Less likely?

2. What can be done to minimize fraud against the elderly?

3. How can we resolve the tension between home repair frauds and the desire of the elderly to remain in their own homes? Is fraudulent home repair just a risk that the elderly home owner must bear?

[2] "VULNERABLE VICTIM" SENTENCING STANDARDS

The federal government and a minority of states provide for enhancement of penalties for criminal offenses if the victim was vulnerable because of age or physical or mental disability. The penalties, calculated under standardized sentencing guidelines, typically call for longer sentences. An alternative is to deem the crime itself to be more severe because the victim was older and more vulnerable. For example, a criminal who mugged an elderly person in the street might be charged with aggravated or first degree battery rather than simple robbery. If the defendant has had prior convictions for crimes against vulnerable victims, the penalties might be still more severe.

Federal law demonstrates the practice of considering the characteristics of the victim in the sentencing calculations:

§ 3A1.1. Hate Crime Motivation or Vulnerable Victim

(a) If the finder of fact at trial or, in the case of a plea of guilty or nolo contendere, the court at sentencing determines beyond a reasonable doubt that the defendant intentionally selected any victim or any property as the object of the offense of conviction because of the actual or perceived race, color, religion, national origin, ethnicity, gender, disability, or sexual orientation of any person, increase by 3 levels.

(b) If the defendant knew or should have known that a victim of the offense was a vulnerable victim increase by 2 levels.

18 U.S.C. § 3A1.1

The following cases illustrate both the application of the federal enhanced penalties statute and examples of the varieties of financial abuse and exploitation of the elderly.

UNITED STATES v. FELDMAN
83 F.3d 9 (1st Cir. 1996)

SELYA, CIRCUIT JUDGE.

Defendant-appellant Jonathan Feldman pleaded guilty to a twelve-count indictment charging him with fraud and interstate transportation of stolen property. Using the version of the guidelines that was in effect on that date . . . the court computed the guideline sentencing range (GSR) at 30-37 months and imposed a 33-month incarcerative sentence. Feldman now challenges the court's determination of the GSR and, ultimately, the sentence imposed. We affirm.

I. OVERVIEW

The defendant worked for Norman and Eleanor Rabb as a home attendant from May to October of 1993, assisting them with their personal care. The Rabbs were octogenarians. In addition, Mr. Rabb was in failing health and afflicted by a deteriorating mental condition. The couple could not handle their personal finances and a long-time retainer, herself seventy-eight years old, wrote checks to pay their household expenses.

During the course of his employment, the defendant became privy to the Rabbs' finances. Having obtained Mr. Rabb's social security number and the account numbers for a Fidelity Investments trust account and a Bank of Boston checking account, he set out to defraud the Rabbs upon leaving their employ. His modus operandi involved siphoning funds from both the trust and checking accounts by impersonating Mr. Rabb, forging negotiable instruments, and similar artifices. To cover his tracks, he submitted to the postal service change of address forms directing that all the Rabbs' business mail be forwarded to the address of his own dwelling. The defendant then retained the mail that would have revealed his skulduggery (such as the monthly trust account statements) and forwarded the remainder to the Rabbs to quell any suspicions. All told, the defendant pilfered

$139,972.00 from the trust account and $59,423.68 from the checking account before his shenanigans were discovered.

B. Vulnerable Victims.

Feldman's second assignment of error calumnizes the district court's imposition of a two-level upward adjustment attributable to the Rabbs' status as vulnerable victims.[5]

1. Generic Traits. The defendant's first sally — which contends that the sentencing court applied the wrong legal standard because it based the enhancement on the Rabbs' membership in a generic class of elderly persons rather than on some individualized vulnerability that they might have possessed — need not occupy us for long. We are in general agreement with the defendant's premise: in determining the propriety of an upward adjustment for vulnerability, the sentencing court's sights must be trained on the victim's individual characteristics. Thus, in order to warrant a finding of unusual vulnerability, there must be some evidence, above and beyond mere membership in a large class, that the victim possessed a special weakness that the defendant exploited.

Contrary to the defendant's importuning, the record reflects that the district court apprehended and applied the standard enunciated above. This conclusion is buttressed in two separate ways. First, at the sentencing hearing Judge Gorton explicitly found (a) that "the defendant knew that the victim, Norman Rabb, was elderly and that his mental faculties were failing" (emphasis supplied), and (b) that the defendant proceeded to exploit this condition. Second, the judge expressly adopted the factual findings contained in the PSI Report — a document that made clear, inter alia, that Mr. Rabb was physically debilitated and that the Rabbs were unable to handle their personal finances. We have accepted such findings as long as the purport and intent of the sentencing court is clear.

To say more would be supererogatory. The record simply does not bear out the claim that the sentencing court applied the enhancement only because the Rabbs were octogenarians or shared certain generic aspects of a class of elderly persons.

2. Targeting. The defendant also contends that the sentencing court erred in applying section 3A1.1 because the government did not show that he targeted the Rabbs due to their particular vulnerability to the planned fraud. The defendant maintains that, unless we are prepared to disregard Rowe's interpretation of the "target" language, the government must demonstrate that the offender selected his victims because of some "special susceptibility." Rowe, 999 F.2d at 17.

Applying Rowe generously, i.e., assuming arguendo, favorably to Feldman, that targeting was an essential element of the government's proof, the defendant's argument founders. Rowe merely requires that a special susceptibility have been a factor in the offender's process of selecting his prey. . . . This means that the

---

[5] The guidelines provide for a two-level upward adjustment when an offender "knew or should have known that a victim of the offense was unusually vulnerable due to age, physical or mental condition, or that a victim was otherwise particularly susceptible to the criminal conduct." U.S.S.G. § 3A1.1 (Nov. 1994).

government did not need to prove here that the defendant set out to defraud elderly, infirm people, and targeted the Rabbs because they fit the bill. It also means that the government did not need to prove that the Rabbs' infirmities were the sole reason that the defendant zeroed in on them. Even under the Rowe regime, expansively construed, the government had to show only that the defendant selected the Rabbs as his victims in part because they were elderly and infirm.

The record in this case contains more than enough evidence to justify a finding that the defendant targeted the Rabbs because of their vulnerability. After all, he entered the Rabbs' employ only because of their infirmity and, in his capacity as a home care assistant, he gained copious knowledge of their afflictions. Knowing of their diminished capacity, he obtained information necessary to carry out his plot. Given these and other facts, we believe that the record establishes a nexus between victims' susceptibility and victimizer's criminality adequate to establish targeting. . . . Thus, the district court's finding that the defendant targeted his victims on account of their age and infirmity warrants our approbation.

We need go no further. Here, the defendant selected his victims because he had been their personal caretaker and had discovered their vulnerabilities at first hand. The victims were elderly, in failing health, and no longer in control of their finances. The defendant enacted his scheme with full knowledge that these vulnerabilities would make his crime easier to accomplish. Consequently, the district court did not clearly err in determining that the Rabbs were vulnerable victims within the scope of U.S.S.G. § 3A1.1, and that the defendant had targeted them on that basis.

Affirmed.

UNITED STATES v. CHARLES LOWELL KENTZ
251 F.3d 835 (9th Cir. 2001)

RYMER, CIRCUIT JUDGE.

Charles Kentz, who was convicted on twenty-one counts of telemarketing fraud in violation of 18 U.S.C. §§ 1341, 2326 and 3147, challenges his sentence primarily on the ground that he was not given adequate notice in the pretrial release order that committing a new offense while released could lead not only to a new prosecution (which in fact happened), but also to an enhanced sentence under § 3147, which also happened. The district court held that specific notice in the release order was not required and that the notice actually given, of serious consequences for violating the conditions of release, was sufficient. We agree, and now join the majority of other circuits in holding that failure to give specific notice in the pretrial release order of the increased penalty in § 3147 (and USSG § 2J1.7) for being convicted of an offense committed while on release does not preclude the sentencing judge from imposing it. As no other issues require reversal, we affirm.

Kentz ran telemarketing schemes in which he would call elderly victims and falsely tell them that they had won a large cash prize, but to redeem it they must send a check in advance for taxes or fees. When a victim was reluctant, Kentz would threaten suit, a collection action by the IRS, or forfeiture of social security payments. The first of his schemes was Associated Publishers, which he operated with Robert Walters. It took in over $500,000 before Kentz started Moon Bay Periodicals (by himself) in October 1998. Kentz was arrested December 18, 1998 and posted bond the same day. The written release order set out a number of conditions of release, including that Kentz was forbidden from any form of telemarketing activities. He was also ordered not to commit any federal, state or local crime during the period of release. By signing the order, Kentz acknowledged that he understood that "violation of any of the general and/or additional conditions of release as given on the face of the bond may result in a revocation of release, an order of detention, and a new prosecution for an additional offense which could result in a term of imprisonment and/or fine."

Nevertheless, Kentz continued to engage in the telemarketing business (and to commit fraud) while on pretrial release. He worked through Moon Bay Periodicals and a new enterprise called Long Beach Discount. He called at least two victims in February 1999, including one whom he had defrauded in 1998, and received a check in February and another in March. Moon Bay and Long Beach produced $30,000. Altogether the three schemes involved more than 300 victims. A First Superseding Indictment was returned June 15, 1999, charging Kentz with twenty-four counts of mail fraud in violation of 18 U.S.C. § 1341 (later redacted to eliminate three counts), and enhanced penalties pursuant to § 2326 because the mail fraud was committed in connection with telemarketing as well as pursuant to § 3147 because two of the counts involved offenses committed while he was on pretrial release. After a jury trial, Kentz was convicted on all twenty-one counts. He was sentenced to a term of 150 months on each of the mail fraud counts, a 10-month consecutive sentence pursuant to § 3147, and three years of supervised release. n2 Kentz was also ordered to pay $587,053.23 in restitution.

In calculating the sentence, the district court started from a base offense level of 6 for fraud, added 10 levels for the amount of loss, 2 for more than minimal planning, 2 for committing a fraud offense in connection with telemarketing, 3 for committing offenses on pretrial release, 2 for using a minor to make calls, 2 because of vulnerable victims, and 2 for a large number of vulnerable victims. In addition, the court found that this case was outside the heartland of fraud cases and that Kentz's conduct was unusually cruel or degrading and extremely harassing. For this, the court departed upward two levels. Given a criminal history category III, this resulted in a guideline range of 135-168 months.

. . . . Kentz further seeks reversal due to the two-level upward adjustment applied for a large number of vulnerable victims pursuant to USSG § 3A1.1(b)(2). He first contends that the government failed to show by a preponderance that there were 300 vulnerable victims. However, it is too late to question the number because the PSR found that Kentz defrauded over 300 mostly elderly victims and he never objected. Given the age of the victims who testified and evidence that it was the elderly whom Kentz targeted, and no evidence to the contrary, the finding is not plainly erroneous.

Assuming there were 300, Kentz maintains that this number of victims is not sufficient to trigger the adjustment. He notes that the guidelines do not define what a "large number" is, nor have we. Nonetheless, we have no difficulty concluding that the district court had discretion to find that 300 was large enough. We agree with Kentz that telemarketing is a mass marketing technique designed to reach a lot of people, but this does not mean that "large number of vulnerable victims" for purposes of § 3A1.1 should be construed as "larger than the average telemarketing fraud," as Kentz would have us do. It is true that some fraudulent telemarketing schemes involve thousands of victims, while others involve fewer. But here, the district court found that 300 vulnerable victims was a large number, and nothing in the record indicates that this is not a "large" number either in absolute terms or by comparison with other frauds where vulnerable victims are impacted.

Finally, Kentz asserts that imposing the adjustment was double counting in light of the other adjustments that were imposed. However, double counting is not impermissible when it accounts for more than one type of harm. Enhancing for the amount of monetary loss, degree of planning, mass marketing, victimizing vulnerable victims during telemarketing, and impacting a large number of vulnerable victims, as the court did here, accounts for different aspects of the harm that Kentz's conduct caused. Further, "there is nothing wrong with 'double counting' when it is necessary to make the defendant's sentence reflect the full extent of the wrongfulness of his conduct." As the Sentencing Commission has explained, the increased penalty for a large number of vulnerable victims was designed to implement Congressional intent to increase penalties for fraudulent schemes, including telemarketing schemes having a large number of victims over the age of 55. . . .

UNITED STATES v. RUMSAVICH
313 F.3d 407 (7th Cir. 2002)

COFFEY, CIRCUIT JUDGE.

Peter J. Rumsavich was charged and found guilty of five counts of mail fraud and two counts of perjury. The district court sentenced Rumsavich to 75 months in prison followed by a 3-year term of supervised release and ordered the sentences and subsequent periods of supervision be served concurrently with each other, as well as ordering restitution totaling $571,700 to the victims and payment of a special assessment of $550. We affirm.

I.

Beginning in the summer of 1979, Peter Rumsavich embarked upon the first of his numerous failed business ventures that tended to be funded by a selected group of naively trusting investors both in the city and suburbs of Chicago, Ill. Rumsavich incorporated three businesses — D'Martine Financial, D'Martine Food, G.P. Services, and Goo-Cheese Pizza — none of which was profitable for more than a short period of time. In May 1988, when Rumsavich was faced with the imminent collapse of the Goo-Cheese Pizza and D'Martine Financial enterprises, he sought to raise cash with the selling of $750,000 of so-called "D'Martine Food Services,

Inc. Zero Coupon Corporate Bonds."

Rumsavich devoted extensive time and energy to making contact with thousands of individuals, and thereafter proceeded to identify and persuade certain unknowledgeable investors to purchase these bonds. He began by mailing more than 150,000 brochures and postcards to a targeted selection of people in neighborhoods known as being inhabited with an unusually large number of senior citizens with fixed incomes. The brochures invited the recipients to attend "financial seminars" conducted by Rumsavich at libraries and hotels in the nearby suburbs of Chicago. The brochures recited that Rumsavich was a former vice president for the investment firm of Dean Witter with impressive credentials as a "registry financial planner," a "certified financial planner," and a "registered financial planner." These claims were false: the position of a "registered financial planner" does not exist within the investment banking industry, Rumsavich never was a certified financial planner, and Rumsavich's only experience with managing portfolios was acquired during several years at Dean Witter where he was employed as a low-level office manager rather than a vice president of the company as represented.

However, according to the record, a large number of people, acting in reliance upon Rumsavich's misrepresentations, attended his seminars and listened (with dreams and hopes) to his promises of helping them take advantage of the supposedly low-risk, high-yield investment opportunities he represented to them. He presented each of the attendees with carefully crafted questionnaires designed to elicit specific information about their experience and knowledge of investing, their levels of income and wealth, and their financial histories. After collecting the completed questionnaires during his opening contact session with this select group of people, Rumsavich next engaged in a process of "cherry picking," weeding out and focusing only on those individuals whom he described as "suitable" investors and inviting them to his private office for one-on-one meetings where he promoted the D'Martine Food Services zero-coupon bond.

The record reflects that during these meetings, Rumsavich conducted himself like "a pitchman at a county fair," advising his soon-to-be victims that the bonds would pay an inflated annual interest rate of 12 percent, mature in six years, and repay each investor two-fold upon maturity. Just as Rumsavich had made misleading statements in his earlier brochures about his investment experience, so did he mislead investors during his individual meetings about the nature of the bonds. Rumsavich claimed, for example, that D'Martine Food was an Illinois corporation when, in fact, D'Martine has never been incorporated in any state. Rumsavich also referred to the bonds as "zero-coupon bonds" despite the fact that they resembled interest-bearing bonds in the sense that they were sold at face value rather than at a discount rate. Rumsavich further misled investors when talking to senior citizens and stating that "he would invest in something with security" and that his bonds in the food services industry were "a sure thing" with "no risk involved."

Rumsavich's "no-fail" bond-selling statements were clever but at the same time somewhat misleading, for at no time did he ever disclose, much less even infer that his prior track record when acting as the manager of pizza restaurants was miserable and/or that his D'Martine enterprise had been plagued with financial troubles and significant debt since its incorporation. In addition, Rumsavich never did make known that the proceeds from the bond sales were being used mainly to pay off his debts to Goo-Cheese Pizza and D'Martine Financial, in addition to his paying himself and his wife substantial salaries, despite the fact that she was neither an employee nor a member of the board of directors of D'Martine Food Services. He also found it to his benefit to use his client-investors' funds to help pay off his personal debts as well as the creditors of his failed limited partnership, G.P. Services.

. . . .

[J]udge Hibbler adopted the recommendation in the presentence report and imposed a 2-level sentencing enhancement, reasoning that Rumsavich "knew or should have known that many of the people who ultimately purchased the bonds were vulnerable victims because of their advanced age, their need to get solid retirement planning advice, and their overwhelming unsophistication in financial matters." U.S.S.G. § 3A1.1(b)(1). The judge also enhanced Rum-savich's sentence with a second 2-level enhancement after finding that he had abused a position of private trust as a financial planner by misleading his customers and using their money for improper purposes. Thus, after applying the relevant guideline limits for "vulnerable victim" and "abuse of trust" enhancements, the judge sentenced Rumsavich to a total of 75 months' imprisonment for committing five acts of mail fraud and two acts of perjury.

II.

. . . .

At the sentencing hearing, and after reviewing the record, the trial judge noted that the majority of Rumsavich's client-victims were elderly persons who lacked the necessary knowledge, experience, training, or personal judgment required to make intelligent investment decisions with respect to their retirement. Additionally, a number of them were widows who were dependent in the past on their former husbands for financial planning and advice. The district judge concluded that a vulnerable victim enhancement was appropriate, finding that Rumsavich deliberately and methodically used a series of targeted mailings, presentations, and one-on-one meetings as a means of discovering and capitalizing upon his researched knowledge about the victims' ages, severe physical or emotional difficulties, widowhood, pronounced need for investment advice, limited incomes, and/or demonstrated lack of understanding about financial matters. As the district judge noted, "It was clear that [Rumsavich] did, in fact, target these particular individuals, knew of their particular financial situation, [and] used that information in such a manner as to approach them with certain opportunities that he knew they would be more likely to accept because of the lack of security that they now had with their particular investments."

. . . .

[T]here is no question that at least one victim, Ms. Gladys Paine, qualifies as a "vulnerable victim" within the meaning intended by the Guidelines.

By sending out the brochures to those residing in areas with a disproportionate number of elderly people, Rumsavich piqued Paine's attention, lured her to one of his seminars, and preyed upon her fears of bankruptcy with the presentation of pamphlets titled, "The Cruel Cost of Long-Term Care," "Long-Term Health Care and Poverty: Price of Nursing Care Is Poverty, Survey Says," and "A Retiree's Biggest Poverty Trap: Nursing Homes." Rumsavich convinced Paine to fill out a selected number of questionnaires in an attempt to gain a wealth of information focusing on the question of whether she had appreciable cash reserves and, if so, what amount could be invested without necessitating the securing of a loan or sale of other assets. From these questionnaires, Rumsavich learned that Paine had retired, having resigned from her position as a nursing home administrator in 1987, and had recently suffered the loss of her husband. Next he determined that Paine was, in his words, a "suitable" target for his investment scheme, and he telephoned Paine and invited her to meet with him for a second, personal, one-on-one interview at a sprawling office complex in Rolling Meadows, Ill., which he held out to be the office of his so-called "financial planning agency."

During their tete-a-tete, Paine confirmed that she was "not very knowledgeable" in financial affairs and that her now-deceased husband had managed the family's entire investment portfolio. Rumsavich gained Paine's confidence by misrepresenting the nature of his investment scheme and convincing Paine he was concerned about her financial well-being. He further promised Paine that he would offer her financial security and mischievously recommended that she purchase an $18,000 bond at a price that coincided exactly with the amount of money she had received from her husband's insurance policy upon his death. At this time, Rumsavich obviously knew that his food-service industry bonds were risky investments, to say the least, for none of his retail pizza businesses ever turned a profit and each one was bordering on bankruptcy as early as February 1988. Nevertheless, following their first meeting in June 1988, Rumsavich relieved Paine of her retirement nest egg and all of the monies he could get his hands on. Rumsavich pulled off this feat by lulling Paine into a false sense of security with the alleged mailing of the previously referred-to fraudulent, pre-printed 1099 tax forms which indicated that her investments were earning taxable income in the form of accrued interest. . . .

. . . . We agree with the court's decision to enhance Rumsavich's sentence because he deliberately, systematically, and purposefully targeted Paine and a number of other widowed, aged, unsophisticated and unwary investors as victims in his high-risk business ventures and then proceeded to systematically and deliberately defraud them. . . . It was only towards this group of people — those financially inexperienced elderly people who needed Rum-savich's help and were particularly likely to rely upon his advice to their detriment — that Rumsavich targeted his fraudulent investment schemes.

We are convinced that an unscrupulous person like this — who methodically schemes and plans to separate out those elderly and inexperienced investors in dire need of prudent investment planning and thereafter proceeds to cheat them out of their life savings — is eligible for a "vulnerable victim" enhancement . . . . We agree with the trial judge's determination that Rumsavich's victims were vulnerable because they had "a lower than average ability to protect themselves" against his fraudulent investment programs, due to a combination of their age, severe physical or emotional difficulties, widowhood, pronounced need for sound and truthful investment advice, limited incomes, and frequently combined with a demonstrated lack of knowledge and understanding of financial ventures. . . .

The trial court acted within its discretionary boundaries when enhancing Peter J. Rumsavich's sentences based upon a clear and convincing finding that he deliberately abused a position of trust and cruelly inflicted harm upon at least one vulnerable victim . . . the judgment of the district court is AFFIRMED.

Some state statutes increase the severity of the crime itself when the victim is elderly.

ABRAMS v. DELAWARE
689 A.2d 1185 (Del. 1997)

Per Curiam.

In this appeal involving an eighty-year-old victim, we hold that a statute classifying theft as a felony when the victim is sixty years of age or older and theft as a misdemeanor when the victim is less than sixty years of age does not violate the Equal Protection Clause of the 14th Amendment to the United States Constitution. We further hold that the Superior Court did not abuse its discretion when it denied the defendant's request to admit testimony about the victim's prior use of a gun in an incident unrelated to the case before the Superior Court.

Facts

Troy E. Abrams was convicted of felony theft for snatching a wallet containing $350.00 out of the hands of octogenarian victim George Terry. On September 4, 1995, Abrams, Terry's neighbor, knocked on Terry's door and asked for fourteen dollars. Terry went to retrieve his wallet which contained $350.00. When Terry produced the wallet, Abrams snatched the wallet out of Terry's hand and ran away. On September 6, 1995, Terry reported the theft at the Camden, Delaware, police station.

During the ensuing jury trial, counsel for Abrams presented testimony, including a cross-examination of Terry himself, to show that Terry was forgetful and that he often misplaced items, later calling them stolen, only to have them turn up again. Additionally, Abrams' counsel wanted to present testimony that Terry owned a gun and had, on a previous occasion unrelated to the current trial, fired the gun at "imaginary" intruders. The Superior Court denied counsel's request to present this testimony due to its potential for confusing or misleading the jury.

Because of Terry's age, Abrams was convicted of a felony instead of a misdemeanor pursuant to 11 Del.C. § 841(c)(2).[1] Abrams appeals his conviction to

---

[1] § 841. Theft; class G felony; class A misdemeanor; restitution. (a) A person is guilty of theft when

this Court based on equal protection grounds and because he believes the Superior Court abused its discretion when it did not allow him to admit testimony concerning Terry's prior use of a gun.

Age-Based Distinctions and Equal Protection

Abrams argues that 11 Del.C. § 8418 ("section 841") violates the 14th Amendment to the U.S. Constitution because it classifies theft of less than $1,000.00 as a misdemeanor, unless the victim is 60 years old or older, in which case the theft is a felony. He contends that the statute treats him differently from similarly situated offenders based on an arbitrary and unreasonable distinction, viz., the age of his victim.

According to Abrams, it is not proper to assume that most or even many persons over 60 are vulnerable or that they have decreasing physical or mental ability. He therefore submits that the proper way to account for the age of the victim in a statute such as section 841 is through consideration of the victim's age as an aggravating factor on a case-by-case basis. Abrams relies on an incorrect analysis of the rational basis standard of judicial scrutiny to arrive at his conclusions. Therefore, his contention is without merit.

Distinctions based on age involve neither a suspect class nor a fundamental right. Therefore this Court reviews age-based distinctions using rational basis scrutiny. Under rational basis review, if the age-based distinction in the statutory provision is neither irrational nor arbitrary, the provision will stand.

The facts of the case sub judice present a prime example of the type of harm the legislature sought to redress by visiting harsher penalties upon those who prey on the elderly: a forgetful, absentminded man in his eighties, living alone, has his wallet snatched by the son of a neighbor. Because protecting the elderly is neither an arbitrary nor irrational basis upon which to make an age-based distinction under section 841, this provision does not violate the Equal Protection Clause.

Moreover, Abrams argues incorrectly that the statute treats him differently from similarly situated offenders. Section 841 subjects all offenders whose victims are above a certain age to the same felony classification. Age-based classifications are made in other provisions of the code in a similar manner. For example, 11 Del.C. § 773(2) subjects all offenders whose victims are below a certain age to the same felony classification. Again, since the age-based distinction in each provision bears a rational relationship to a legitimate state interest, and since all individuals who commit offenses governed by these provisions are treated in the same manner, these provisions do not violate the Equal Protection Clause.

---

the person takes, exercises control over or obtains property of another person intending to deprive that person of it or appropriate it. . . . (c)(1) Except where a victim is 60 years of age or older, theft is a class A misdemeanor unless the value of the property received, retained or disposed of is $1,000 or greater, in which case it is a class G felony.

> (2) Where a victim is 60 years of age or older, theft is a class G felony unless the value of the property received, retained or disposed of is $1,000 or greater, in which case it is a class F felony.

11 Del.C. §§ 841(a), (c).

We hold that Abrams' contention that section 841 violates the Equal Protection Clause of the 14th Amendment is without merit. . . .

Accordingly, the judgment of the Superior Court is *Affirmed*.

[3] ELDERLY CRIMINALS

In the past 20 years researchers have "discovered" elderly criminals as a worthwhile subject for study. Though the rate of arrest and imprisonment decreases with age, a growing number of crimes are committed by older people, many of whom have no prior criminal record. In addition, prisons hold more older people as younger prisoners age in place.

The elderly who commit crimes can be divided into three categories: the aging recidivist offender, the relapsing aged offender, and the elderly first offender. The aging recidivist is a professional criminal or an inveterate psychopath. As they age, recidivists may change the form of their criminal activity; for example, a former burglar may become a fence. A relapsed aged offender is someone who had a criminal record as a young person, went straight, and then, in old age, again commits crimes. The elderly first offender with no prior criminal record appears to take up crime in old age

Why previously law-abiding citizens should turn to crime and why some may return to crime after decades is unclear. Some crime may be due to reduced circumstances; for instance, poverty may induce theft. There is some evidence that larceny by the elderly increases toward the end of the month as pensions and Social Security checks run out. Some elderly persons express the justification for shoplifting (the most common elderly crime) as merely getting what is due them. Feeling unwanted, unappreciated, and under-pensioned, some feel justified in stealing what they want, or at least their necessities. Some crime by the elderly may be due to the onset of dementia, although this is disputed. The claim of mental incapacity may merely be an attractive defense if one is caught.

Whether the rate of crimes by elderly people is increasing substantially is not clear.

William E. Adams, Jr., *The Incarceration of Older Criminals: Balancing Safety, Cost, and Humanitarian Concerns*
19 Nova L. Rev. 465, 467, 471 (1995)[*]

It is difficult to draw precise conclusions about the extent of elderly crime by reviewing the academic research. The studies often fail to use the same definitional categories, which can cause results to at first appear contradictory. The first interpretational problem arises with the definition of "elderly." Social scientists who have researched older persons and their criminal behavior have failed to come to a uniform agreement on what age constitutes "old." This reflects a similar confusion in the law and in American society in general. Social Security retirement benefits, for example, begin at age sixty-five, or sixty-two if one takes "early"

---

retirement. On the other hand, the Older Americans Act provides benefits for persons aged sixty and over. The National Institute of Corrections chooses the even younger age of fifty as the age which defines the older criminal.

In addition to the age discrepancies in the studies, there are also differences in the crimes reviewed. Furthermore, the percentage increases can sometimes be misleading because the absolute numbers of elder arrests in previous decades were so small. Even though there does appear to be an increased number of older persons in the criminal justice system, there are reasons to be skeptical that this constitutes a rising elderly crime wave . . . recent studies indicate that the ratio of younger persons to older persons violating the law has not changed, and that the proportion of crime committed by older persons is still quite low. However, other studies seem to indicate that elderly crime is increasing at a significant rate. While some may take solace in the statistics of proportion, the problem of elderly crime, measured in real numbers, is growing.

There is . . . disagreement as to whether the factors predicting illegal behavior are the same at all ages. The consensus seems to be that crimes such as fraud, embezzlement, and theft are the crimes for which the elderly are most often arrested. A distinct increase in the number of shoplifting arrests of elderly persons has also been noted. Many of these involve first-time offenders; one study of elderly inmates in Florida found that a majority of the elderly inmates in the sample had either one or no prior arrests. Although older persons are most likely to be arrested for alcohol-related offenses, at least one study has found that when asked to self-report on illegal activity, residents of retirement communities, age sixty and older, reported illegal gambling as the offense in which they most often engaged.

In addition, the statistics reflect that older persons do commit some violent crimes. For example, approximately 5% of homicide arrestees are fifty-five and older. Although this percentage is less than the proportion of elderly in the population, it nevertheless demonstrates that stereotypes of the harmless elderly person are not completely accurate. While disagreement over the causes of criminal behavior by the elderly continues, it is agreed that violent crime by older persons tends to be against those who are related to or are acquaintances of the perpetrator. These are usually the people who are present to suffer the effects of the elderly criminal's drinking habit.

Alcohol abuse and, consequentially, unstable social relationships are frequently found among older offenders. Studies have identified a nexus between these conditions and criminal behavior among the elderly, as with other age groups. One national study of prisoners over age fifty found that 59% had previously been convicted of a violent crime in which alcohol use was connected. The study also indicated that older offenders who committed violent crimes were likely to be unmarried males, nonwhite, with lower incomes and fewer dependents. The older criminal was found to have a history of part-time employment and unemployment. This combination of joblessness, lack of family ties, and alcohol abuse increases the likelihood of criminal behavior, even more so than in younger drinkers.

The factor most predictive of violent behavior, however, is past offenses. Aggravated assault is the violent offense most often committed by persons over age sixty-five. Murder ranks second. The increased attention being given to the types of crimes more frequently committed by older offenders, such as shoplifting, alcohol-related offenses, and family violence, will likely result in even more older persons being sentenced to prison. The impact of this growing problem on states like Florida, which has a disproportionate share of the elderly population, will be felt even more severely.

QUESTIONS

1. Is crime by the elderly a social issue arising from lack of adequate financial and psychological support or a crime-and-punishment problem? Would you be willing to support an administrative intervention process for anyone arrested for the first time after, say, age 65? What else would you want to know?

2. What is the proper punishment for the elderly criminal who has not had an arrest for decades? If a person age 30 would receive a sentence of five years of incarceration, is there any reason to change that sentence for the person age 70? What would you want to know about the crime? About the individual?

3. What would you consider to be mitigating circumstances for older criminals? Mrs. Jones was widowed three years ago after 50 years of marriage, and lives on modest Social Security benefits. She has barely enough income to pay the taxes on her house. She is arrested for shoplifting a bottle of vitamins. Would you consider these mitigating circumstances? If not, would you change your mind if Ms. Jones was widowed six months ago? If so, would you change your mind if Ms. Jones also took an expensive compact disk?

[4] REDUCED SENTENCES DUE TO AGE AND PHYSICAL CONDITION

Another aspect of sentencing guidelines is the possibility of reduced sentences for criminals who are old or ill.

UNITED STATES v. BROOKE
308 F.3d 17 (D.C. Cir. 2002)

In this appeal, defendant Juan Brooke challenges the sentence he received after pleading guilty to a drug conspiracy charge. At sentencing, the district court denied Brooke's request to depart downward from the applicable United States Sentencing Guidelines range based on his age and physical condition. Because the district court properly understood the guidelines and its authority to depart, and did not make clearly erroneous factual findings, we affirm the court's decision not to grant the defendant a departure.

On April 6, 2000, officers of the Metropolitan Police Department searched Brooke's apartment pursuant to a search warrant. Upon entering the apartment, the officers found Brooke in the bedroom, sitting on the bed. In his pants pocket was a bag containing seventy individually-wrapped packets of cocaine base, totaling 8.8 grams of the drug. On the bed next to Brooke were three large plastic bags containing a total of 63 grams of cocaine base. . . .

Brooke's conviction, at the age of 82, was his third since coming to the United States in 1980. In 1989, at the age of 70, he was convicted in federal district court of possession with intent to distribute cocaine base. After serving 60 months in prison, Brooke was placed on supervised release. In 1997, at the age of 78 and while on supervised release for the 1989 conviction, Brooke was convicted in District of Columbia Superior Court on cocaine-related charges. After serving six months in prison, he was released on probation. Brooke was still on probation at the time of the April 6, 2000 arrest that led to the sentence that is the subject of the current appeal.

For a person with Brooke's criminal history, and with credit for acceptance of responsibility, the amount of drugs found on his person and on his bed would normally have generated a guideline sentencing range of 121-151 months. In this case, however, the government's agreement to charge Brooke with conspiracy under rather than with the substantive offense of distribution under dictated a guideline sentence of only 60 months, the statutory maximum for violations of § 371.

After his plea, Brooke filed a sentencing memorandum with the district court, seeking a downward departure from his guideline sentence based on his age and physical condition. Brooke's memorandum stated that he was 82 years old, and that he had the following "serious physical infirmities": (1) a "markedly swollen right knee" with "obvious joint effusions, and tenderness and flexion of knee of only 6 degrees with some pain"; (2) "stiffness in his hands and difficulty holding objects"; (3) prior evaluations for "chest pains"; and (4) "respiratory problems and arthritis." Although the district judge told Brooke that "I recognize I have discretion" to grant the requested departure, he declined to do so and sentenced the defendant to 60 months' imprisonment.

. . . .

Our standard for reviewing a district court's refusal to depart downward from an applicable guideline range is by now well settled. We may review such a decision only to determine whether the sentence was imposed "in violation of law" or "as a result of an incorrect application of the sentencing guidelines." . . .

. . . .

Brooke contends that the district court erred by failing to grant him a departure under policy statements contained in two sections of the Sentencing Commission's GUIDELINES MANUAL, § 5H1.1 and § 5H1.4. . . . We find to the contrary: The district court correctly understood the guidelines, expressly recognized its discretion to depart, and made no clear factual errors.

The first section cited by the defendant is § 5H1.1, which is entitled "Age" and provides:

> Age (including youth) is not ordinarily relevant in determining whether a sentence should be outside the applicable guideline range. Age may be a reason to impose a sentence below the applicable guideline range when the defendant is elderly and infirm and where a form of punishment such as home confinement might be equally efficient as and less costly than

incarceration. Physical condition, which may be related to age, is addressed at § 5H1.4. . . .

. . . .

There was, of course, no question that the 82-year-old defendant was "elderly." Nor did the court dispute that the defendant was "infirm." To the contrary, the court stated that "I have gone through the medical records which you have attached, as I've said, as to his age and his disabilities, and I think his disabilities are there." Further, the court accepted all of Brooke's specific representations regarding his disabilities.

. . . .

Nor did the court hold that these medical infirmities were insufficient to permit a departure under § 5H1.1. Rather, the problem the court discerned was with the third element of § 5H1.1: that an alternative "form of punishment such as home confinement . . . be equally efficient as . . . incarceration." The court concluded that home confinement would not be effective in restraining the defendant's criminal conduct because Brooke had a history of drug dealing in his home: "In your apartment, at least on two separate occasions, you've been arrested and convicted of dealing drugs. . . ."

Brooke also contends that the district court erred in declining to depart under § 5H1.4, which applies to departures based on "Physical Condition" and states in relevant part:

> Physical condition or appearance, including physique, is not ordinarily relevant in determining whether a sentence should be outside the applicable guideline range. However, an extraordinary physical impairment may be a reason to impose a sentence below the guideline range; e.g., in the case of a seriously infirm defendant, home detention may be as efficient as, and less costly than, imprisonment.

U.S.S.G. § 5H1.4 (emphasis added). As with § 5H1.1, the court read the section verbatim at the sentencing hearing and explained why it did not regard the section as warranting departure. This time, however, the court concluded that Brooke's impairment was insufficient to qualify under the section. Unlike § 5H1.1, § 5H1.4 requires not just "infirmity" but "extraordinary physical impairment," and while the court did not dispute the underlying facts of Brooke's medical condition, it did not regard them as reflecting an extraordinary impairment. . . .

The court's express consideration of additional grounds for departure belies the claim that it thought itself constrained by the two guideline sections. For example, exploring a potential ground for departure not mentioned in § 5H1.4, the court suggested that "perhaps" it could "depart where there is serious physical impairment[] that can be exacerbated by incarceration and cannot be adequately treated by the Federal Bureau of Prisons," In the end, the court declined to depart on that ground because it concluded that the Bureau of Prisons could adequately treat Brooke's maladies "at least . . . as well as any other place can," a factual finding that is not contradicted by anything in the record.

. . . .

The district court went on to consider . . . whether the defendant's advanced age alone warranted a departure, concluding that "in this case, I do not see age as a reason alone." This was so, the court explained, because the defendant's age did not appear to serve as a deterrent to his continuing criminal conduct: "Even though you're elderly, it's evident that you were a drug dealer and that's what you decided to do when you were 70 years old and have kept it up." The district court did not misunderstand the sentencing guidelines or its authority to depart from the applicable guideline range. Nor did it clearly err in finding the facts relevant to a potential departure. . . . Accordingly, the judgment of the district court is

Affirmed.

QUESTIONS

1. Would you favor a reduced sentence for a healthy individual who is age 70? Age 80? Is there an age at which there is no purpose in incarcerating the individual?

2. Aaron, age 73, shot and killed his wife during a drunken argument between them. The sentencing guidelines call for 15 years, which exceeds his life expectancy. It is therefore a life sentence. Is a 15-year sentence fair? Is it necessary that society give him the same sentence as a 30-year-old? Would you like to use the option, found in sentencing guidelines in a number of states, of a downward departure based on age alone? Would you consider sentencing Aaron to time served plus probation if permitted by the guidelines?

[5] ELDERLY PRISONERS

The number of older prison inmates is increasing in part due to current sentencing practices, which mandate fixed determinate terms without parole. Whether it is wise to incarcerate so many elderly prisoners is subject to debate. Alterntives do exist.

Patricia S. Corwin, Comment, *Senioritis: Why Elderly Federal Inmates Are Literally Dying to Get Out of Prison*
17 J. CONTEMP. HEALTH L. & POL'Y 687, 693 (2001)[*]

The number of elderly inmates in the federal prison system is on the rise. In 1998, 13,673 inmates over fifty years of age entered the federal prison system. By 2005, the Federal Bureau of Prisons (BOP) predicts that this population of elderly inmates will increase by sixteen percent. This population can be broken down into two categories: Elderly criminals and criminals who will become elderly during

---

their sentence. Both categories of inmates have a remarkably low recidivism rate; ninety-nine percent are never convicted of another crime upon release.

The average annual cost of confining an elderly prisoner is $69,000. This is more than three times the cost expended to incarcerate younger inmates, and more than twice the average annual cost for a full service nursing home. One reason for this cost is exemplified by a study of 1,051 federal elderly inmates which found that each inmate averaged twenty-four medical encounters a year. In the year 2000, the national cost for housing and caring for the elderly reached over $2.8 billion.

The disparity in caring for elderly prisoners is attributable to their unique and costly health problems. The most adverse effect of medical needs for elderly prisoners is the collateral cost associated with obtaining medical treatment. Although governments may have to pay for elder inmates' medical needs regardless of whether they are incarcerated, transactional costs of providing health care in the prison system compound state and federal expenditures.

States are making significant progress by dealing with their elderly prison population in a variety of ways. Conversely, the federal government offers no special programs, policies or treatment for reducing the costs of caring for elderly prisoners. Despite the need to alleviate many of the problems associated with elderly inmates, the federal government has made little movement towards mitigating these problems. Factors such as the federal sentencing guidelines, the abolition of parole, truth-in-sentencing statutes, mandatory minimums and the growing number of baby boomers entering their fifth decade, all account for the increase in the number of elderly prisoners in the federal system.

. . . .

States are dealing with their elderly prisoner populations in a variety of ways. However, few jurisdictions have specific written policies addressing aged or infirm inmates. Only a few states–Alaska, Florida, Illinois, Michigan, Mississippi and South Carolina–make policy decisions based solely on age. Minnesota, New Jersey, Rhode Island, Alaska, Mississippi and South Carolina use age unofficially as a means for making policy decisions. For example, Minnesota and New Jersey provide elderly inmates with separate geriatric units; Rhode Island gives inmates aged sixty-five and over special attention. Alaska occasionally provides modified sentencing for elderly inmates beset with disease. In Mississippi, inmates over fifty years of age are housed in geriatric units if their security classification permits. In South Carolina, inmates may retire from work at age sixty-five.

Despite the relatively small number of states that have an inmate age-based policy, the majority of states have some kind of elder inmate response. Several states offer compassionate leave for those who are terminally ill or who are not capable of physically functioning within the correctional system. Usually, an inmate must have received a prognosis of from one year to six months or less to live and must meet specific criteria with regard to custody classification and medial requirements in order to qualify for compassionate leave. When compassionate leave is impossible due to the nature of the crime or lack of available alternatives, resourceful states have begun building comprehensive facilities to accommodate elderly inmates. In Washington, Ahtanum View is a 120 inmate minimum-security facility, which tailors its programs to the needs of elderly inmates. The state cuts costs by incarcerating all elderly inmates in one facility. Texas is developing a comprehensive system of facilities to provide a complete range of care. Texas currently operates a sixty-bed geriatric center. Finally, some states attempt to eliminate the number of elderly prisoners in their system during sentencing. Nine states' statutes provide that the defendant's age at the time a crime is committed can be a mitigating factor for sentencing.

Nadine Curran, Note, *Blue Hairs in the Bighouse: The Rise in the Elderly Inmate Population, Its Effects on the Overcrowding Dilemma, and Solutions to Correct It*
27 N.E. J. ON CRIM. & CIV. CON. 225, 240 (2000)[*]

Although age is a common factor among elderly inmates, geriatric prisoners have traits that lend them to more specific categorization. Using the typology of two different studies, elderly inmates are broken down into four classifications: 1) the first-time older offender; 2) the chronic offender; 3) the prison recidivist and 4) the inmate who has grown old in prison. "The [first category] 'older offenders,' constituting 41 percent of those studied, were serving their first prison term, having committed their crimes after reaching the age of 55." The chronic offender is a "younger short-term offender" who has been "incarcerated before reaching the age of 55." The recidivist is a career criminal or one who lapses back into a life of crime. The inmate who grows old in prison, or "old-timers," have been incarcerated "at least 20 years in prison, thus growing old while incarcerated." These classifications assist in the management and placement of the elderly prisoner.

B. Reasons for the Increase in the Elderly Prison Population

1. Elderly Crime Wave: Fact vs. Fiction

"Inmates over the age of 50 will comprise 33 percent of the total prison population by the year 2010." One reason for this increase is the increase in elderly persons committing crimes. This is contrary to the common belief that the majority of elderly inmates are individuals who committed crimes in their early years and are serving life sentences. The Bureau of Justice Statistics reports that in reality, "twenty-five percent [of elderly inmates] have been in prison for less than a year and 68 percent for less than five years . . . Only one percent of geriatric prisoners have been incarcerated for 30 years or more."

Compared to younger inmates, the elderly are surprisingly more likely to be imprisoned for violent crimes. Allen J. Beck, Chief of Correction Statistics for the Bureau of Justice Statistics, reports that "of all prisoners 55 and older, . . . two thirds are serving time for a violent crime: 25 percent for murder or manslaughter and 27 percent for rape or sexual assault." In further support of the elderly crime wave theory, David Shichor, a well-known author and researcher of elderly offenders, reports that "elderly arrests for index crimes increased by 256 percent between 1964-79, while the rate of increase for all other age groups was 177 percent."

Reasons given for violent acts committed by the elderly are the same as those that explain criminal behavior by nonelderly offenders: economic status, surroundings, drugs and alcohol. Some factors, however, are clearly associated with common mental and physical reactions to the aging process. "Chronic brain syndrome in the aged may be associated with loss of inhibitions resulting in illegal sexual behavior such as exhibitionism and in rigidity, quarrelsomeness, and aggression." Feelings of depression, worthlessness, and boredom commonly associated with retirement may compound the elderly's aggression. Feelings of violence or the propensity to commit non-violent crimes may be the result of economic hardships. These economic hardships are often the result of increasing medical costs and the desire to maintain social status. The loss of a spouse or confinement to a nursing home may also be an exacerbating factor. Violent acts by elderly offenders are often committed against people the offender knows well, such as a family member or close friend.

Susan Lundstrom, *Dying to Get Out: A Study on the Necessity, Importance, and Effectiveness of Prison Early Release Programs for Elderly Inmates Suffering from HIV Disease and Other Terminal-Centered Illnesses*
9 BYU J. Pub. L. 155 (1994)*

A large share of geriatric costs can be reduced and even reclaimed through decreases in fixed security costs. "Personnel [costs] will often amount to nearly fifty percent of the operating costs of a correctional facility." A marked decrease in these costs, however, can be realized by assigning some inmates to specialized geriatric units. Inmates suitable for reassignment to such institutions would include the non-violent, who comprise the vast majority of elderly prisoners, and other older or terminally ill prisoners. These geriatric units may be located in segregated wings of prison housing, in under-utilized hospital facilities, or in hospitals located on military bases listed for government closure. An added benefit to this proposed housing structure is the freeing of cells in the main part of the prison for the more dangerous, and usually younger, inmates.

A model for such a specialized facility exists at the McCain Correctional Hospital in McCain, North Carolina. The approximately 350-bed facility was converted from a tuberculosis hospital into a correctional hospital. Placing older inmates in a facility such as McCain serves several purposes: (1) protection of elderly inmates from victimization by younger prisoners; (2) reduction in security costs; (3) concentration of a multi-discipline health care plan targeted for the elderly; (4) establishment of open cells in medium and maximum security units for use by higher risk, younger inmates; and (5) creation of an environment wherein

---

inmates may socially interact more appropriately and possibly improve both physically and emotionally.

. . . .

Another possible solution to prison overcrowding is electronic home detention programs. An average of $65 a day is spent by most states on the housing costs for one inmate. The use of electronic detention devices (ED), commonly called electronic "bracelets," can reduce this daily cost by $57. . . .

The ED program has been determined to be cost-efficient in Illinois and other states. Additionally, Illinois has refined its program to decrease the daily costs, and rarely are inmates monitored by the bracelet for longer than nine months. Electronic detention is an effective alternative to incarceration because (1) technical improvements have reduced the amount of human control needed; (2) equipment costs are lowered; and (3) an escalating number of inmates are participating. Furthermore, inmates who are capable of working must obtain employment and pay a percentage of their earnings to reimburse the state for their housing costs.

. . . .

. . . . Application of the ED system to the correctional overcrowding problem, and especially the inclusion of elderly inmates convicted of violent crimes in the selection process, will definitely reduce the prison inmate population immediately.

Because of elderly inmates' low recidivism rates, an ED program could be designed to increase their chances of selection for parole and medical or compassionate release. They could be committed to their pre-incarceration homes within the individually specified confines of the ED and monitored for a designated time frame.

However, some elderly inmates have lost all ties to their families and remain without housing arrangements. This makes it difficult for them to get parole because the nation's current parole system generally requires an inmate to have definitive housing before his or her release. "[A]bout 50% of ED candidates who pass the statutory requirement and are initially approved for the ED program are ultimately denied participation because they have no place to go for their detention." Group homes for these offenders, especially those who are in good health, are a good resource and would contribute to reduction of prison costs. Halfway houses, managed by the correctional system or private enterprises, can effectively provide temporary residences for released inmates. In these homes, releases must comply with household duties, residence rules, and seek employment. Under these housing conditions, the elderly inmates could easily be monitored by their electronic bracelets. The costs to a correctional system to maintain group homes "would likely be higher per offender than conventional ED but would still be considerably less than conventional prison incarceration."

QUESTION

Harry, age 70, has served 20 years of a life sentence imposed for a robbery that resulted in felony murder of a store clerk. For the last 10 years he has been a model prisoner. He has inoperable lung cancer, which is currently in remission. Maintaining him in prison costs $45,000 a year, a cost that is likely to rise. Would you release Harry from prison? Where would you place him? Would your answer be the same if Harry was in prison for the rape and murder of a 20-year-old girl?

TABLE OF CASES

[References are to pages]

[References are to pages]

[References are to pages]

INDEX

[References are to sections.]

[References are to sections.]

[References are to sections.]

[References are to sections.]

[References are to sections.]

[References are to sections.]

[References are to sections.]